NEGRO AND WHITE CHILDREN

A Psychological Study in the Rural South

SOCIAL PSYCHOLOGY

A series of monographs, treatises, and texts

Edited by

Leon Festinger   and   Stanley Schachter

NEGRO AND WHITE CHILDREN

A Psychological Study in the Rural South

E. EARL BAUGHMAN
and W. GRANT DAHLSTROM
DEPARTMENT OF PSYCHOLOGY
UNIVERSITY OF NORTH CAROLINA
CHAPEL HILL, NORTH CAROLINA

ACADEMIC PRESS New York and London   1968

ACADEMIC PRESS, INC.
111 Fifth Avenue, New York, New York 10003

United Kingdom Edition published by
ACADEMIC PRESS, INC. (LONDON) LTD.
Berkeley Square House, London W.1

LIBRARY OF CONGRESS CATALOG CARD NUMBER: 68-14651

Second Printing, 1969

PRINTED IN THE UNITED STATES OF AMERICA

To Carol C. Bowie, Rosemary F. Funderburg, Musia G. Lakin, Sophie S. Martin, Barbara S. Nixon, and Anne M. Spitznagel, who so willingly carried out the field work upon which this book is based. Their competence, persistence, sensitivity, and sense of commitment never failed to earn our respect.

FOREWORD

As recently as 1938, the late President Franklin D. Roosevelt could accurately describe the South as the nation's number one economic problem. He referred in particular to the corrosive poverty of the rural South. Thirty years later, economic deprivation as a national issue has surfaced again. But this time "wars," or at least skirmishes, are waged against poverty with the urban slum replacing the mill village and farm as the primary target for change. Lean and desperate living in the squalor of New York City's cold-water tenements is now the popular focus rather than the impecunious existence of Millfield, North Carolina.

Psychological research has reflected this shift of attention from the rural to the urban scene. While there was brisk interest in the rural South among behavioral scientists in the 1930's, in the 1960's the incomparably more extensive resources of behavioral science in this realm have centered on the urban poor. From Frank Riessman's *The Culturally Deprived Child* to the *Life* magazine coverage of Martin Deutsch's research on learning disabilities of ghetto youth in New York, psychological studies on the urban slum child have attracted special attention. Indeed, massive federal efforts throughout the nation such as Project Headstart owe their political existence to this arousal of public interest.

The underlying demographic reasons for this shift of focus are clear. In the 1930's both white and Negro Southerners were predominantly rural. Today well over half of both groups are urban. Moreover, both whites and Negroes have been leaving the South in search of better opportunities. This is particularly true of Negroes, roughly three million of whom have migrated from the South since Roosevelt spoke in 1938. And they have migrated to the largest cities of the North and West. Thus, metropolitan New York now has more Negroes than *any* southern state, metropolitan Chicago more than the state of Mississippi, and metropolitan Philadelphia more than the states of Arkansas and Kentucky combined. Within the South, too, Negroes have left the farm and the hamlet for the city, usually for the principal centers such as Atlanta, Houston, Memphis, and New Orleans. Little wonder the exploding urban ghetto has seized the headlines and the country's concern. Nevertheless, one out of every five Negro Americans is still a rural Southerner. And this fact of American race relations is generally overlooked, even though many of the city's race and poverty problems can be directly traced in part to the continuing stream of migrants who are often literally starved off the land.

Meanwhile, back in Millfield, life goes on and economic prospects remain bleak. Many white families are poor and Negro families even poorer. Though new federal programs—including the research reported in these pages—reach Millfield, national growth has largely passed it by. And the plain truth is that the special characteristics and depth of its problems have invoked scant professional or public concern. Millfield, and the thousands of hamlets like it, have been lost from sight.

This work is significant because it attempts to right the balance in our national and psychological perspective on deprivation. *Negro and White Children* presents precisely what its title states—a psychological study in depth of children in the rural South. It encompasses a broad view of the individual—intellectual, social, motivational, and temperamental factors are considered; and its measures cover the sweep of the best in present-day psychological instrumentation. Professors Baughman and Dahlstrom have managed to provide at once both breadth and depth in their portrayal of the children of Millfield.

It would be comforting if the authors could report that restricted experience and economic deprivation have not retarded and damaged Millfield's children. Not surprisingly, however, such is not the case. In general, the data are not encouraging, for the effects of cultural isolation, racial discrimination, and continuous poverty are almost always ugly and depressing. But this bleak picture adds to the importance of this work. Adequate remedy, we should never forget, requires accurate diagnosis.

The authors courageously present their results and specify the implications to the limits of what is known in psychology today. The word "courageous" is appropriate, because in the politically and racially turbulent times in which we live many of the research findings reported in this book are subject to distortion, misuse, and heated charges. As the authors themselves make clear in their Preface, vulgar claims of racial superiority and inferiority are irrelevant. Those who would twist these data to fit their preconceived racist dogmas and others who would denounce these data as "racist" both obscure the central issue at stake: What *are* the psychological conditions of children, Negro and white, who remain in a typical rural southern hamlet, and what intelligent and meaningful interventions can be devised and executed to improve these conditions?

Like any extensive study, *Negro and White Children* is necessarily technical in parts and often raises more questions than it manages to answer. Nevertheless, this work should prove valuable to a variety of interested readers. Thus, those with special concerns in personality and intellectual development, personality, rural problems, economic deprivation, comparative research, the South as a region, and multivariate studies will all find much of unique substance. And readers interested in effective remedial education programs will find Chapters 8 and 9 especially revealing.

As a race relations specialist, I welcome this book, in addition, as a contribution to this particular field. Thus, a number of its findings fit convincingly with studies performed in radically different American social settings—for example, the indications of the special developmental problems faced by Negro boys and the distinct verbal deficits of Negro children of both sexes. Other findings fill in critical gaps in our knowledge—for instance, the approximate intellectual level of the Negro children of Millfield. This general level falls above those noted by investigators for Negro children in the rural areas of the deep South, somewhat below those in the urban South, and further below those of the urban North—a rank order corresponding directly with the continuum of deprivation and discrimination. Still other findings prove an intriguing surprise—for example, the insignificance of the father absence variable for intellectual functioning. All of these racial findings, it should be noted, derive from and reflect a community context of formal patterns of racial segregation.

The final chapter, "Narrowing the Gap," is of unusual interest to those concerned with effective intervention in the lives of disadvantaged children. Not content with merely "presenting the facts," authors Baughman and Dahlstrom make clear the action implications of their results as they view them. Their forceful calls for preschool education programs reaching beyond that of the Project Headstart model, public school teaching as a twelve-month profession, more male teachers, curriculum specialists, school psychologists and guidance specialists, the racial integration of schools, the expanded use of available facilities, the development of Saturday, summer, and television educational efforts, and local incentives for student achievement constitute a significant package of psychological interventions not only for the Millfields of the South but for public schools throughout the nation. And the authors venture a further social intervention. The Millfields of our land need socially concerned industries to remain viable; and the writers suggest governmental inducements to encourage the private sector to locate manufacturing plants in such smaller communities and to serve as centers for health, educational, and recreational services. Their basic point is critical: The needs of Millfield's children range far beyond formal schooling and require a general restructuring and upgrading of the area's resources for human welfare. The serious situation documented by the study's results commend these recommendations as necessary steps for a better future for America's Millfields.

In short, this work is an important contribution to psychological understanding in a range of realms. It deserves the reader's most careful and thoughtful study.

THOMAS F. PETTIGREW

Harvard University
Cambridge, Massachusetts

PREFACE

The 1960 census confirmed what most observers already knew, that the United States in the mid-century was becoming more and more an urban society. And, during the same years, even the nonreader among us would have been hard pressed to escape recognition of the fact that this was also a period when the Negro minority began to assert itself seriously in its quest for full citizenship. Together, these forces have combined to create for our society unique and challenging problems of the utmost importance.

The pervasive difficulties of our sprawling urban areas are too well known to need delineation here. The sometimes brutalizing impact of their slums upon the human spirit is all too obvious to the person who looks and cares. Nor can one deny that it is the nonwhite citizen who is most likely to be deeply and perhaps irremediably wounded by these conditions, a fact that Kenneth B. Clark has spelled out in sharp detail in his recent *Dark Ghetto*. Not so obvious is the fact that the poor white citizen is also injured by these adverse conditions; indeed, even the affluent white person is crippled in the sense that he relinquishes a portion of his own humanity if he attends only to his personal comforts and avoids any involvement in alleviating the social ills around him.

The problems of the urban areas, then, are obvious even if the solutions are not. Not so apparent, though, are the problems of our rural areas, especially in large sections of the South. As bad as conditions in the cities may be for the poorly educated and economically deprived individual, he still seems to see more hope for his future there than in the still, quiet countryside. And, though his illusions may quickly be shattered once he has experienced the city first-hand, he nevertheless finds it difficult to return to the country. Psychologically it is not easy to go home, for he also knows that there is no self-fulfillment there.

In a sense, then, the thesis can be defended that the burgeoning ghettos of this nation are symptoms, symptoms of the impoverishment and inadequacy of rural life in some sections of the United States. And, while there is great need for innovative efforts whose goal is to relieve the misery of the ghettos, it is also apparent that more comprehensive programs extending beyond the ghettos are needed if basic solutions to social problems are to be achieved. To rehabilitate tens of thousands— in itself an extremely difficult task—will not provide a solution to our problems if even more thousands are at the same time continuing to pour into the ghettos. Rehabilitation in the city, in our view, needs to be combined with meaningful, concurrent efforts in the countryside which, in the long run, could alter the nature of the problems pushed upon the urban centers.

The research reported in this book grew out of the belief that the impoverished in the rural areas no less than those in the city deserve our most serious attention. And, since the child is clearly father to the man, we decided to concentrate our efforts upon the children growing up in what we believe is a reasonably typical area of the rural South. What can modern psychological science tell us about such individuals? What are their intellective, social, and motivational characteristics? Also, viewing the children developmentally, how do these attributes change as they grow older? Furthermore, are there characteristics of their families which relate to and possibly determine to some extent the children's traits and the course of their development?

There is by now a vast literature available pertaining to the Negro. It is, however, an imbalanced literature with a heavy emphasis on prejudice and its measurement, on segregation and its impact, and on debates about the causes of racial differences in intelligence. Also, attempts have been made to comprehend such matters as crime and delinquency. Relatively neglected, though, is the basic question of personality: What are the personal qualities of individuals being reared in a segregated society? The neglect in this domain is so striking that Thomas F. Pettigrew entitled a lead article in a recent issue of *The Journal of Social Issues*, "Negro American Personality: Why Isn't More Known?" If we turn our attention to the white Southerner, moreover, we soon discover that even less effort has been directed toward studying his personal attributes, either separately or in comparison with his Negro neighbor.

Although we have a major interest in the Negro American, it is, we believe, potentially misleading to consider him separate from his white neighbor, even though this is what has been done in a large majority of the studies that have been reported. From the outset of our efforts, therefore, we directed equal attention to the white children being reared in the same geographical area as the Negro children. And, throughout the years of our work, we simultaneously studied white and Negro children in precisely the same way, using identical techniques and procedures with children of both races. It is our conviction that the understanding of both Negro and white children is enhanced by such a comparative treatment. The reader will, of course, be able to form his own judgment with respect to the validity of this belief.

In a limited sense, what we mean by personality is defined by the substantive chapters that follow. It is a broad definition, one that includes intellective as well as nonintellective behavioral attributes of the individual. There are, of course, students of personality who define their subject matter more strictly, emphasizing nonintellective qualities exclusively. To eliminate intellective dimensions, however, is, in our judgment, both artificial and undesirable if one's objective is to comprehend the behavioral repertoire of a person. His intellective talents determine, in part, his responses to his environment, and must be addressed along with his motivational, social, and temperamental characteristics if he is to be understood. In the same way, clearly, it would be artificial to address oneself to the intellective structure of a person without attending also to his other personal qualities.

In studying personality, it is clear that there is no royal road to the truth; i.e., there is no one technique or methodology which if applied guarantees to reveal to us the essence of a person. Our work, consequently, proceeded on the assumption that we would advance understanding with greater certainty if we studied our subjects from a variety of positions using an array of techniques rather than limiting ourselves to a single mode of attack. Thus, the data to be reported have been generated by the use of interviews, intelligence tests, personality tests (both projective and objective), direct observations combined with ratings, and sociometric choices. In using such diverse techniques, we have also embraced another principle, namely that objectivity should always be sought and that careful quantification of the data is an important step in enhancing objectivity. Furthermore, we have endeavored to report these quantified data comprehensively so that the reader will be able not only to consider our interpretive statements but also to form his own.

The fact that we were committed to multiple techniques, objectivity, and quantification suggests, we believe, that we did see a serious deficiency in the literature that is available on the Negro American. A great deal of this literature is highly subjective and personal, as reflected, for example, in the in-depth case studies of Kardiner and Ovesey or the essays of James Baldwin.[1] We suspect, moreover, that many individuals familiar with writings like these view them not as sources of ideas or as starting points for more definitive inquiries but rather as near final delineations of the problems involved. We cannot agree. With even the highest fidelity of reporting, case studies reveal only a few, sometimes quite unrepresentative, instances of personality processes. Furthermore, the account that is in reality almost purely autobiographical cannot be accepted without question as a generalized representation of what is true for the author's fellowmen. Such documents are extremely valuable as sources of hypotheses to be subjected to scientific scrutiny, as means for arousing new converts to action, and as ways to highlight new problems and areas of concern. There are real dangers, however, in basing social diagnoses or prescriptions upon such reports, lacking as they are in proper scope, representative sampling, measurement, and many other scientific safeguards. It is our hope, then, that the research reported here will contribute to the slowly accumulating basic data required for objective understanding and for the effective planning of remedial programs.

In presenting these data we are only partially prepared for what we fear may be a questioning of our motives with respect to racial matters. We live in the South and this book is about Southerners, but who can write objectively about them? Is this only the latest effort to prove the inherent inferiority of the Negro American, a thesis that so many Southerners have been defending now for generations? Or is it at the opposite pole, another in a series of emotional attacks upon a way of life that has long characterized a particular section of our country? We believe that it is neither of these, yet we suspect that both judgments will be made by various persons. Let us, therefore, make a few personal statements about our own convictions with respect to race so that the reader will be informed in this regard as he considers the chapters that follow.

All behavior of the type that we will be describing must be conceptualized as the resultant of the interaction of biological and environmental factors; i.e., the processes of neither domain act in isolation to produce this behavior. Thus, for example, a portion of the variance in scores on intelligence tests must be attributed to innate factors—but only a portion. Environmental factors also contribute to this variance. Scientifically, then, the problem becomes one of determining the portion

[1] *Notes of a native son.* Boston: Beacon, 1955. *The fire next time.* New York: Dial, 1963.

of the total variance attributable to factors in each domain rather than seeking a complete explanation in one domain or the other.

Reshaping the nature–nurture question this way is helpful, yet it does not lead to immediate answers to the age-old questions which continue to plague us. Our investigative techniques simply are not powerful enough as yet to permit us to partial out the portions of the variance attributable to heredity and environment, at least with respect to such behaviors as those which we label intelligent acts, motivational processes, and so on. As a result, no one can prove that one race is innately inferior to another. Nor can it be proved that there are not racial differences in some behaviors attributable at least in part to genetic factors.

What has been proved beyond a shadow of a doubt, however, is that the kinds of behaviors which we have studied are influenced by environmental conditions. Scores on an intelligence test, for instance, are not static, determined once and for all by the genes which one happened to inherit. The same conclusion holds for our aspirations, our moral sensitivities, and those other qualities which go together to define our unique humanity. The context in which we live does make a difference with respect to such attributes.

Because biology is not unimportant, man as a product *might* be improved by carefully planned eugenic studies, just as the farmer improves his herds by the use of such methods. We see no indication, however, that man is about to adopt such procedures for his own kind. It is necessary, therefore, to concentrate upon the environment in this regard, to see how modifications therein can be developed in order to enhance the realization of the potentials that are within us. Obviously, it would be a mistake to underestimate the difficulties inherent in such an undertaking. Many strong and influential voices within our society seem to assert that we have created the perfect society, that to change any of its forms is potentially disastrous. Commitment to the status quo should not be underestimated as an important force in contemporary society.

Regardless of the difficulty of the task, however, we feel that changes in the forms of some of our social institutions are long overdue, and that this need is nowhere more apparent than in the rural South. Change for change's sake, though, would be foolhardy; in the long run it might be not only extremely wasteful but also destructive. Despite the voices which urge "action now" and express complete intolerance for studies and plans, careful plans based upon factual knowledge are critical. Moreover, we need data which will permit us, after the innovations have been introduced, to assess the actual changes that these innovations have brought about. Without such careful planning, initial enthusiasm may very well be followed by discouragement and retrogression, not to mention a waste of material resources that are always insufficient in the absolute sense.

We believe, then, that there is no scientific way to prove racial inferiority, superiority, or a one-to-one equality. With respect to the behaviors that are peculiarly human, we are beginning to discover how the environment affects them. Contrary to the impressions held by many, however, no comprehensive and objective mapping of the intellective, social, motivational, and temperamental similarities and differences between Negro and white children growing up in the rural South has yet been provided. And, because the differences that do exist (especially those deemed undesirable) may very well be attributable in significant degree to modifiable aspects of the social order in which they are created, we need to know about these differences with as much precision and objectivity as possible if we are to maximize the likelihood that planned innovations will result in less behavioral inequality. It is the purpose of this book, then, to contribute to the development of such a comparative behavioral map, and to make recommendations for action programs based upon our findings. In this way we hope to make our contribution to the achievement of a social order in which the question of race becomes truly only an academic question.

We have called the area in which we worked *Millfield* to suggest the fact that the people there are very much dependent upon the mills and fields for their livelihoods. In presenting our data and interpretations, we have nourished the hope that they might prove to be of value to educators, laymen, and other concerned individuals who may not have pursued advanced study in the behavioral sciences. Also, of course, we believe that our findings should be of interest to professionally trained people in many disciplines. Obviously, others will have to judge how successfully our presentation meets such broad objectives.

Finally, let us make one suggestion to the reader who may want to read selectively among the substantive chapters. First, we would advise that he begin by reading Chapters 1 and 2. These chapters will provide him with a brief description of the research area and its people, as well as an overview of the various research procedures that were used. Then, at the conclusion of Chapter 2, he will find the plan of the book described in such a way as to make subsequent reading more meaningful.

E. EARL BAUGHMAN
W. GRANT DAHLSTROM

Chapel Hill, North Carolina
April, 1968

ACKNOWLEDGMENTS

Literally hundreds of individuals contributed in a variety of ways to the completion of this study. We are grateful to them even though each person's contribution cannot be recognized explicitly. Also, we are very much aware of the fact that the recognition accorded individuals here is an insufficient expression of our indebtedness to them.

The primary financial support for this work was provided by the National Institute of Mental Health (Research Grant Number MH-04944). We alone, however, are responsible for the presentation of the data and for the interpretations drawn. In addition, financial support was provided by the Research Council of the University of North Carolina at Chapel Hill. The National Institute of Mental Health also provided Professor Baughman with a one-year fellowship which contributed materially to the completion of the study. In a similar manner, the Kenan Fund of the University of North Carolina at Chapel Hill supported Dr. Dahlstrom during one semester in order that he might devote his full energies to this project.

A study of this magnitude would have been impossible without the continuing support of the local school personnel. We are deeply indebted to the Orange County Board of Education and to its superintendent, G. Paul Carr, for providing such support. It should be a matter of record that there was never any interference with our efforts and that we were permitted to proceed according to our best judgment. No school official has attempted to influence in any way the contents that are to be found between these covers. We only hope that the quality of the product that has emerged is commensurate with such trust. Furthermore, at a day-to-day operational level, the cooperation extended by the pupils, their families, their teachers, and their principals was magnificent. These people gave much and asked little or nothing in return.

We have dedicated this book to our six field workers who collected most of the data. We want to emphasize that these individuals cannot and should not be held accountable for the interpretations that are made; the responsibility for these rests with us. At various times, Dorothy Cansler, Jane Church, Jean E. LaCrosse, and Eva Ray also contributed to this effort. Major responsibilities with respect to organizing and analyzing the data were assumed by Isabel Zimmerman, Beverly Russell, Gerda Fillenbaum, and Joyce Wolf. Assistance with statistical and computational problems was provided by Lyle Jones, R. Darrell Bock, Henri Barik, Steve Zyzanski, Angell Beza, and Jo Maready.

The personnel and facilities of a number of units of the University of North Carolina at Chapel Hill made important contributions to this work, specifically, the Communication Center, the Computation Center, the Duplicating Department, the Institute for Research in Social Science, the Photographic Laboratory, the Photographic Service of the Louis R. Wilson Library, the Psychometric Laboratory, and the Statistics Laboratory of the School of Public Health. A number of outside organizations also contributed: the Community Church Kindergarten, Chapel Hill, North Carolina; the IBM Department of the Hospital Saving Association, Chapel Hill, North Carolina; the Public Health Statistics Section of the North Carolina State Board of Health, Raleigh, North Carolina; the Survey Research Center at the University of Michigan, Ann Arbor, Michigan; and Stanford University, Stanford, California. The latter institution, through the sponsorship of Eleanor Maccoby, provided library resources and working facilities for Professor Baughman during his fellowship year.

Halbert and Nancy Robinson supervised the use of the Stanford-Binet Intelligence Scale. Jeanne Hudson drew the figures while Erie Cocolas and Elizabeth McGowan typed the final copy of the manuscript. Preliminary versions of the manuscript were typed by Ruth Adams and Leona Dahlstrom. Leona Dahlstrom also contributed to the preparation of the Index. Additional secretarial and clerical assistance was provided by Blanche Critcher, Loyce Longino, and Barbara Baughman. From time to time and in vital ways, Eugene Long, John Thibaut, and David Galinsky provided counsel and support. In this regard, we would be remiss if we did not note that from the beginning of our negotiations Academic Press has extended to us the type of assistance which all authors hope to receive from their publisher. Furthermore, as co-editors of this series, Leon Festinger and Stanley Schachter offered every encouragement and assistance.

Finally, let us note the contributions made by Ann Mingione, Thomas Pettigrew, and Patricia Waller. Ann Mingione, a graduate student at the time, initiated a research study which stimulated us to undertake this investigation. Thomas Pettigrew, a foremost authority on the Negro American, encouraged and supported our work from its inception. Patricia Waller, in a manner that was particularly helpful, reviewed the entire manuscript and made many helpful suggestions before it was cast into its final form.

Several individuals and publishers have very kindly granted us permission to reproduce portions of their material in the chapters indicated: Wallace A. Kennedy, Maud A. Merrill, Houghton Mifflin Co., and The Society for Research in Child Development (Chapter 3); Jane C. Church (Chapter 7); and John C. Ball, Robert H. Harrison, Starke R. Hathaway, *Rural Sociology*, the University of Kentucky Press, and the University of Minnesota Press (Chapter 11).

CONTENTS

Chapter 9. A Pilot Project to Accelerate the Intellective Development of Four-Year-Old Negro and White Children

Part IV: Personal Attributes

Part V: Personal Perspectives

Part VI: Integration and Recommendations

NEGRO AND WHITE CHILDREN

A Psychological Study in the Rural South

Part I

SETTING AND METHODS

Chapter 1

LIFE IN MILLFIELD

There were several reasons why Millfield was selected as the site for studying Southern rural children. Most important, preliminary appraisals of the area indicated that the way of life there was rather typical of that which might be found in many parts of the rural South. Also, there was the practical consideration that it was within reasonable commuting distance from the university setting where most of the staff members would be living during the years of the study. Finally, there was the fact that key personnel in the school system of Millfield had cooperated well with us in a small preliminary study, suggesting that we might be able to secure their continuing support which would be essential if a much larger project were to be successful.

Millfield covers approximately 150 square miles of gently rolling land in the central or Piedmont area of North Carolina. Perhaps it is fair to say that it creates no very strong impressions of any sort as one drives through it. There are many wooded areas and countless small plowed fields but nowhere the seemingly endless cultivated expanses that the observer may see, for example, in the farming areas of the Middle West. Scattered about the countryside are clusters of homes where a few families, frequently related, are living in close proximity to one another, but there are also large numbers of homes so isolated that there are no neighbors within sighting distance. And, although several hundred people do live close together along one of the highways, there is no incorporated town within the area. On both its southeastern and southwestern corners, however, there are small towns, each containing about 2000 inhabitants. These two communities are heavily dependent upon mill economies.

One of these towns was founded before the American Revolution and takes great pride in its historical past.

SOCIOECONOMIC CONDITIONS

The people in Millfield have a lot of elbow room, and, from every indication, most of them prefer to keep it that way. In the formal sense of vertical social structure, moreover, very little appears to exist; there are few individuals with clear-cut status or prestige. The community is not organized as such, although at several points within the area the people have developed local identities. To a considerable extent, although not exclusively, these foci have developed around families, schools, and churches.

The people in Millfield depend upon two major resources for their livelihoods, the land and the mills. A variety of crops are grown on the land, but for generations tobacco has been the principal money crop. In recent years, dairying has increased and greater efforts have been directed toward the diversification of crops, but the quantity and quality of the tobacco crop continues to be a critical factor in the economy of the area. Many families, however, have turned away from the land to the mills for the money that they must have. One of these mills, a small hosiery plant, is located in the area, but most of them are not. Some are situated in the two towns referred to earlier, others in more distant communities. In the main, these plants turn out textile, furniture, and tobacco products.

In today's jargon, many of Millfield's families would be described as culturally deprived.[1] However, it would be a mistake to conclude that the people themselves commonly view their condition this way. We were informed of this fact early in our work, being told that many of the people had a great deal of pride, were fiercely independent, and looked up to no man. Obviously, such a characterization could not apply to each of Millfield's residents, yet staff members encountered this posture frequently enough to make them recognize the validity of the description that had been given. In short, these tend not to be people to approach as part of a poverty program or as part of any effort which would appear to them to be based upon assumptions about their inferiorities.

[1] There are some prosperous and well-educated people living in Millfield, a fact which is reflected in the homes they maintain, in the material possessions which are theirs, and in the education they provide for their children. Proportionately, however, such individuals are not very numerous.

At the same time, as one gains their confidence, it is easy to discover that they do recognize a number of basic insufficiencies in their own lives and in their prospects for the future. Expressions to this effect come out most readily and nondefensively when it is their children who are the focus of the conversation. They want their children to have better lives than they are experiencing, and they tend not to want them to earn their livelihoods or live in the conditions that hold for them. And, like parents everywhere, they see education as the key to a better life for their children.

The social class characteristics and economic conditions of Millfield are defined more precisely by three types of data which were collected from the parents of children in the study: family income, parental education, and parental occupation. In the following paragraphs, each of these domains will be examined separately.

Family Income

Except for the family income data, all data presented in this chapter were secured by means of a questionnaire sent to the parents of each child enrolled in any of Millfield's four schools during the 1961–62 academic year (see Chapter 2 and Appendix C). Questions about income were not included in this questionnaire because we were informed that many individuals—especially those in the white community—were very sensitive about this matter and we feared alienating them at the very outset of our work. Instead, we decided to seek information pertaining to income when the mothers of kindergarten-age children were interviewed during the 1962–63 and 1963–64 school years (see Chapter 15 and Appendix A). Even in the interview context, the interviewer was given the option of not asking about income if she felt that the respondent would resent the inquiry or consider it an invasion of privacy. A decision *not* to inquire was made for 21 of the 110 white mothers who were interviewed, whereas such an inquiry was made of each of the 90 Negro mothers. The data secured by this means have been tabulated in Table 1.1.

These data confirm the expectation that there is a marked disparity in family incomes between members of the Negro and white communities. More than one-half of the Negro mothers reported total family incomes of less than $2500, a level so low that they certainly must be considered as being impoverished. There are also white families with comparably low cash incomes, but they number less than 20% of those for whom inquiry was pressed. Even this incidence, of course, is, in absolute terms, enough to merit serious concern.

At the same time, it is encouraging to find a reasonably high incidence

TABLE 1.1

Frequency Distribution of Total Income Reported by Mothers
of Kindergarten-Age Children (1962–63 and 1963–64)

Family earnings (all sources)	Racial group	
	White families	Negro families
$5000 or more	40	7
2500–5000	33	34
1500–2500	9	27
1000–1500	4	14
500–1000	2	8
Less than 500	1	0
Unknown	21	0
Totals	110	90

(45%) of white families who have total incomes that exceed $5000 a year. In many instances this relative affluence has been brought about by the fact that the wife—or some other member of the household—has either a part- or full-time job in addition to the husband.

Parents of kindergarten-age children may not be precisely representative of the larger community as far as income is concerned. Nevertheless, our experiences in the community with a much broader range of families over a period of several years convince us that these data do not in fact seriously distort the picture of the economic resources available to the people living in Millfield.

Parental Education

The formal education of most of the parents has been limited, as can readily be seen by examining Table 1.2. Thus, approximately 25% of the white parents (or parent-substitutes) whose educational histories are known have completed or gone beyond high school; for Negro parents, the comparable figure is about 10%. On the other hand, 63% of the Negro parents have not gone beyond the eighth grade; for white parents this figure is still a high 42%.

Analysis of variance indicates that the four parent groups do differ in education at a highly significant level.[2] Furthermore, t-tests show that white mothers have had more formal education than Negro mothers; white fathers have exceeded Negro fathers; white mothers have sur-

---

[2] Throughout this book, highly significant is used to describe a statistical finding significant at the 0.001 level of confidence. In addition, very significant is used to indicate the 0.01 level, and significant is used for the 0.05 level of confidence.

passed white fathers; and Negro mothers have gone beyond Negro fathers. For each of these comparisons, either a highly significant or a very significant difference is found. White fathers, however, do not differ significantly from Negro mothers. Despite the generally low educational level prevailing in Millfield, there are 13 white college graduates and 8 Negro college graduates who are parents of children in the study; we shall refer to them again in the next section when we discuss the occupations of fathers and mothers.

Parental Occupation

Almost 1 out of 2 Negro fathers or father-substitutes in Millfield is a farmer, which compares with a rate slightly above 1 out of 4 for the white fathers or father-substitutes (see Table 1.3). When tested by chi-square, this difference is found to be highly significant. The non-farmers of both races hold many different types of jobs, skilled and unskilled. Among them, however, some type of factory job—textile, furniture, or tobacco—is most common. Work of this sort is highly desired, and, generally speaking, the white man has been more successful than the Negro man in securing it. Also, when both have been employed, the better job within the mill customarily has gone to the white man.

Sustained unemployment is uncommon for the fathers of either race,

TABLE 1.2

Frequencies and Percentages of Parents and Parent-Substitutes of Each Race
Who Completed Various Levels of School (1961–62)

	Racial group							
	White families				Negro families			
	Fathers		Mothers		Fathers		Mothers	
Level of education	N	%	N	%	N	%	N	%
College graduate	11	3.7	2	0.7	3	0.9	5	1.5
Part college	6	2.0	12	4.0	1	0.3	1	0.3
High school graduate	40	13.4	64	21.4	13	4.0	32	9.9
Part high school	73	24.4	103	34.5	54	16.7	97	29.9
Elementary school or less	130	43.5	93	31.1	199	61.4	158	48.8
Unknown	39	13.0	25	8.4	54	16.7	31	9.6
Totals	299	100.0	299	100.1	324	100.0	324	100.0
Means*	8.7		9.5		6.8		8.3	

* Based upon the exact number of years of education for each parent for whom this information was available.

TABLE 1.3

Frequencies and Percentages of Various Occupations of Fathers
and Father-Substitutes of Each Race (1961–62)

| | Racial group | | | |
| | White families | | Negro families | |
Occupation	N	%	N	%
Farmer	82	27.4	154	47.5
Mill and factory	79	26.4	39	12.0
Other nonfarm work	100	33.4	73	22.5
Unemployed/disabled	6	2.0	9	2.8
Unknown	32	10.7	49	15.1
Totals	299	99.9	324	99.9

but this statement obscures the fact that work for many is seasonal and irregular. The net result, as noted earlier, is a low annual income for many of the families.

The occupations of those relatively few fathers who have graduated from college may be of special interest to the reader. Among the 11 white college graduates, 3 are ministers, 1 is a teacher, 1 is a farmer, 1 is in government service, 1 is an engineer, and 4 are engaged in some type of business activity. Among the 3 Negro college graduates, 1 is a teacher, 1 is an engineer, and 1 is a sheriff's deputy.

With respect to the mothers, we find that approximately one-third of them are known to be gainfully employed; there is no significant racial difference in this regard. However, the work patterns of Negro and white mothers differ markedly. Thus, almost 7 out of 8 white mothers who work do so on a full-time basis (30 hours or more per week), whereas only slightly more than 1 out of 2 working Negro mothers has full-time employment (see Table 1.4).

This racial difference in work pattern is further accentuated when the nature of the jobs is examined. Forty-four Negro mothers, for example, are engaged in domestic work (18 full-time), as against a single white mother. In contrast, 60 white mothers work in a mill or factory (56 full-time), but only 4 Negro mothers are so employed (2 full-time). Furthermore, 21 Negro mothers do laundry work (19 full-time) compared with a lone white mother. Finally, 19 white mothers report employment that can be classified as clerical or business, whereas only 1 Negro mother is so occupied. In short, then, although Negro and white mothers have about equal *rates* of employment in Millfield (disregarding number of hours worked), there is very little overlap in the *kind* of work that they do.

FAMILY BACKGROUND AND STRUCTURE

The people living in Millfield tend to come from large families deeply rooted there, or at least in the immediately adjacent areas. Thus, the vast majority of the families are not only North Carolina families but central North Carolina families; seldom does one encounter an inhabitant who has been born in another state. The population of the area has remained basically stationary for many years now, although in some of the farming areas it has decreased a bit, owing to the ever-increasing difficulty of turning a profit out of a small farm. In talking with both the children and their parents, it does not take long to discover that very few of them see any future in the land as far as farming is concerned. Millfield is not an area, then, that is attracting migrants from distant locales; rather, it is an area supplying migrants, for the children, as they mature, feel that they must move if there is to be a future for them. What are some of the more salient characteristics of these Millfield families?

Parental Birthplace

The statement that most of the inhabitants of Millfield are central North Carolinians by birth is supported by the data given in Table 1.5. Thus, over 60% of the white parents (or parent-substitutes) and more than 70% of the Negro parents (or parent-substitutes) were born in one

TABLE 1.4

Frequencies and Percentages of Mothers of Each Race
Engaged in Work outside Home (1961–62)

	Racial group			
	White families		Negro families	
Employed outside home	N	%	N	%
Full-time (≥30 hr/wk)	85	28.4	59	18.2
Part-time (<30 hr/wk)	12	4.0	45	13.9
None	182	60.9	177	54.6
Unknown	20	6.7	43	13.3
Totals	299	100.0	324	100.0

TABLE 1.5

Numbers and Percentages of Various Locations of the Birthplaces
of Parents or Parent-Substitutes (1961–62)

	Racial group							
	White				Negro			
	Fathers		Mothers		Fathers		Mothers	
Location	N	%	N	%	N	%	N	%
Nuclear counties*	186	62.2	187	62.5	238	73.5	263	81.2
Outside nuclear counties	63	21.1	73	24.4	30	9.3	26	8.0
Outside North Carolina	(23)	(7.7)	(19)	(6.4)	(9)	(2.8)	(8)	(2.5)
Outside the South	(7)	(2.3)	(6)	(2.0)	(1)	(0.3)	(2)	(0.6)
Unknown	50	16.7	39	13.0	56	17.3	35	10.8
Totals	299	100.0	299	99.9	324	100.1	324	100.0

* Four counties that meet close to a single point on the periphery of the research area, which is located in one quadrant of one of the four counties.

of four counties (called nuclear counties) that meet at about a common point on the northwest corner of Millfield. Of those not born in this area, the large majority were born elsewhere in North Carolina; less than 8% of the white parents and less than 3% of the Negro parents (whose birthplaces are known to us) were born outside the state. Furthermore, less than 3% of the white parents and less than 1% of the Negro parents were born outside the South.

Chi-square analyses of these data reveal that more white parents than Negro parents were born outside the four nuclear counties (at a highly significant level). The mobility patterns of the Negro parents, therefore, appear to have been even more restricted than those of the white parents. There is no significant difference, however, between Negro mothers and fathers or between white mothers and fathers in this regard.

Natural Parents and Parent-Substitutes

One important feature of family structure is how many Millfield children are living with their natural parents rather than with parent-substitutes. Data relevant to this question have been tabulated in Table 1.6. Chi-square analyses of these data support the following conclusions:

1. When a child is living with some substitute for one of his natural parents, the absent parent is more likely to be his father than his mother.

2. White children are more likely than Negro children to be living

with their natural mothers; they are also more likely to be living with their natural fathers.

3. Negro children have a parent-substitute more often than white children; this is true for both mothers and fathers.

4. Both Negro and white children are more likely to be without either a father or a father-substitute than without either a mother or a mother-substitute.

Most striking, perhaps, is the fact that more than 25% of the Negro families are without their natural fathers and more than 13% are without any father-figure. In contrast, 10% of the white families are without their natural fathers, while only 4% have no father-figure at all. Overall, step-fathers are much more common than stepmothers among these children: 26 (10 white) versus 3 (1 white), respectively. Even more grandparents than stepparents are serving as parent-substitutes: 21 grandmothers (4 white) and 17 grandfathers (4 white) have this role. In addition, especially among the Negro people, aunts and uncles rather frequently

TABLE 1.6

Frequencies and Percentages of Natural Parents or Parent-Substitutes in the Homes of White and Negro School Children (1961–62)*

	Racial group			
	White families		Negro families	
Parental figures	N	%	N	%
Fathers				
Natural	250	83.1	227	68.8
Substitute†	18	6.0	45	13.6
None in home‡	12	4.0	44	13.3
Not known	21	7.0	14	4.2
Totals	301	100.1	330	99.9
Mothers				
Natural	273	91.3	282	85.2
Substitute†	9	3.0	38	11.5
None in home‡	1	0.3	6	1.8
Not known	16	5.4	5	1.5
Totals	299	100.0	331	100.0

* In some instances, a family contained an adult who was the natural parent of some of the children but a stepparent for others. Both roles have been tabulated in this table; therefore, the totals do not always agree precisely with those reported in Table 1.4.

† Usually a stepparent or a relative.

‡ Includes deaths: white fathers—6; Negro fathers—10; Negro mothers—4.

TABLE 1.7

Numbers and Percentages of Each Type of Family Organization (1961–62)

	Racial group			
	White families		Negro families	
Family type	N	$\%$	N	$\%$
Contained	230	76.9	195	60.2
Extended	49	16.4	112	34.6
Uncertain	20	6.7	17	5.3
Totals	299	100.0	324	100.1

serve in this capacity. Ten aunts (1 white) and 12 uncles (1 white) were so identified in the families of these children.

Family Type

As the data just cited suggest, many of Millfield's homes contain persons other than parents (or stepparents) and their children. To describe this facet of family life more precisely, each of these families was classified as either "contained" or "extended," if available information permitted such classification.[3] A contained family was defined as one in which the children were living with their natural parents, or with one natural parent and one parent-substitute—for example, a stepfather. Half-siblings might or might not be present in such families; however, more distantly related or unrelated children living in the home, such as cousins, resulted in the classification of the family as extended. Also, if grandparents, aunts, uncles, or other related or unrelated adults were living in the home, the family was classified as extended. In short, contained refers to what is commonly regarded as the typical American family (with some stretching of the boundaries), whereas extended refers to a larger family grouping. As Table 1.7 indicates, there are more than twice as many Negro extended families in Millfield as there are white extended families. When this difference is tested by chi-square, it is found to be highly significant.

The frequencies with which various types of individuals were found in the extended families have been tabulated in Table 1.8. As indicated there, grandmothers are found most often as the extra person in the Negro families. Next come grandfathers, aunts, uncles, and cousins, all

[3] In later discussions, "nonextended" is sometimes used as a synonym for "contained."

about equally often. Other related children and adults are less common, yet more frequent than unrelated persons, either adults or children. The general pattern in this regard is quite similar for the white families; perhaps the most notable departure rests in the fact that cousins and other related children are to be found relatively less often in the white homes than in the Negro homes, compared to the relative incidence of grandparents, aunts, and uncles in the homes of the two races.

The data summarized in Tables 1.7 and 1.8 suggest that Millfield families do an important job of caring for their own; this may be true for more than one out of three Negro families and for one out of six white families. In some instances, however, living together is not strictly a matter of caring for a less fortunate member (or members) of the family; instead, it represents a pooling of resources under a single roof so that the extended family can manage on very limited resources.

Number of Children in the Homes

Almost all Millfield school-age children share their homes with other children, usually, of course, with their natural siblings. As indicated in Table 1.9, for example, among the 1961–62 population only about 15% of the white children and 9% of the Negro children lived in homes without other children. Large families are especially common among the Negro people; on the average, there are almost exactly 50% more children in the Negro homes than in the white homes (see Table 1.9).

TABLE 1.8

Numbers and Percentages of the Families of Each Race
Containing Various Persons (1961–62)*

| | Racial group | | | |
| | White families | | Negro families | |
Person	N	%	N	%
Grandmother	29	10.4	41	13.4
Grandfather	12	4.3	27	8.8
Aunt	9	3.2	24	7.8
Uncle	7	2.5	25	8.1
Other related adult	4	1.4	6	2.0
Cousin	4	1.4	24	7.8
Other related child	3	1.1	19	6.2
Unrelated person	1	0.4	6	2.0

* The table entries are in terms of the presence of a particular type of person in a family. Thus, a family with two grandmothers is not distinguished from a family with only one grandmother present.

TABLE 1.9

Frequencies and Percentages of Given Numbers of Children
in the Homes of Each Race (1961–62)

Number of children in home*	Racial group			
	White families		Negro families	
	N	%	N	%
1	46	15.4	28	8.6
2	73	24.4	45	13.9
3	57	19.1	48	14.8
4	46	15.4	50	15.4
5	26	8.7	33	10.2
6	15	5.0	34	10.5
7	8	2.7	23	7.1
8	2	0.7	22	6.8
9	1	0.3	10	3.1
10			5	1.5
11			4	1.2
12			2	0.6
13			2	0.6
Unknown	25	8.4	18	5.6
Means	3.09		4.58	
Totals	299	100.1	324	99.9

* Any person (full sib, half-sib, or nonsib) under the age of 18 and residing in the home
was counted.

THE SCHOOL STRUCTURE AND CHILD POPULATION

It was our plan to focus research efforts upon children of elementary
school age (grades one through eight). There were more than 1200
children in Millfield's elementary grades during the 1961–62 school
year when our study began, but these children represented only 623
families, 299 white and 324 Negro (see Tables 1.2, 1.3, 1.4, 1.5, 1.7,
and 1.9).

A Segregated School System

Millfield has four schools. In 1961, one of these was an all-white school
with twelve grades and an annual enrollment of approximately 325
students. A second was an all-white school with eight grades and an
enrollment of about 300 pupils. Then there were two all-Negro schools,
each with eight grades and enrollments of approximately 300 and 500

students. In the fall of 1963, however, each of the white schools was changed to an elementary school with six grades only, and both the junior high school children and the high school pupils were transferred to schools in the county seat, one of the two small towns just outside of Millfield noted earlier. There have been no comparable changes in the organization of the two Negro schools, so they continue to be eight-grade elementary schools.

Although the changes in the white schools were effected by the county school board in the interest of providing an improved education for the children at consolidated schools, and although the parents of the children in general support the need for better education, the consolidation did not take place without argument; indeed, some bitterness developed. This was particularly true in the district that had its own small high school. The athletic teams and the social life which had developed around this school added a meaningful dimension to the lives of the people in the district, and, understandably, they could not accept this loss easily.

During the years of the study the schools of Millfield remained racially segregated. This segregation, of course, reflected the pattern of life that had characterized the region for all its history, and the 1954 decision of the Supreme Court had no immediate effect upon this way of doing things.[4] The fact that the majority of the population in the area is Negro made no appreciable difference in this regard, for the Negro people were not well organized and few of their number gave evidence of militancy or leadership as far as desegregation was concerned. Moreover, there has been a resurgence of Klan activity within the area during recent years. With respect to the schools, another fact should be noted, since it is possible that it also contributed to the slowness of the Negro people in pushing for change. Both of the Negro schools had been constructed much more recently than either of the white schools and, in the physical sense, were superior structures to the latter. Going to a Negro school in Millfield certainly did not mean going into a comparatively unattractive building.[5]

---

[4] Some integration of the schools did get under way during the 1965–66 academic year. One white child was enrolled in one of the Negro schools then, and one Negro child was enrolled in one of the white schools. More than one dozen Negro children attended the second white school, but no white child was enrolled in the second Negro school.

[5] The reader should realize that the conditions just described are by no means unique as far as the state of North Carolina is concerned. In many sections of the state there had been belated efforts to construct separate but equal schools, at least in the physical sense, before the 1954 Supreme Court decision.

TABLE 1.10

Numbers of Children in Each Racial, Sex, and Age Group (1961–62)*

		Racial group					
		White			Negro		
Age group	Age range (in months)	Boys	Girls	Total	Boys	Girls	Total
1	79–90	26	25	51	40	39	79
2	91–102	33	38	71	55	48	103
3	103–114	24	24	48	51	53	104
4	115–126	28	31	59	39	50	89
5	127–138	29	29	58	49	42	91
6	139–150	26	30	56	50	37	87
7	151–162	36	37	73	44	49	93
8	163–174	38	26	64	54	42	96
Totals		240	240	480	382	360	742

* Ages of subjects were computed as of May 1, 1962.

The Child Population

The school population in Millfield is almost precisely equivalent to the child population during the elementary years. No significant bias is introduced, therefore, by referring to the school population as the child population, if the reader keeps in mind the fact that preschool children are not included.

At each year level there are usually between 50 and 75 white children and between 75 and 100 Negro children living in Millfield. The actual distribution of the children who entered the study during its first year in terms of race, sex, and age is shown in Table 1.10. The children's ages were computed as of May 1, 1962; this date was chosen, since it was quite close to the time when the staff administered achievement tests, collected teachers' ratings, and secured other types of group data. Although some children were studied who were more than 14½ years of age, they have not been included in this report.

It may be of interest to note here that about one child out of five was retarded in his school work during 1961–62. To determine this rate, a child was called retarded if his grade placement was one or more years behind where his chronological age indicated that he should be. As is apparent by inspection of Table 1.11—where these data are recorded—the retardation rates were almost identical for Negro and white children; for each race, however, appreciably more boys than girls were lagging behind.

TABLE 1.11

Numbers and Percentages of Children Retarded in School
in Each Sex and Racial Group (1961–62)

| | Racial group | | | |
| | White pupils | | Negro pupils | |
Sex group	N	$\%$	N	$\%$
Boys	64	26.7	99	25.9
Girls	41	17.1	54	15.0
Means		21.9		20.6
Totals	105		153	

In the fall of 1962 two experimental kindergartens were established in the Millfield schools, one Negro and the other white (see Chapter 8). Beginning at this time, the study was expanded to include children of kindergarten age. Since there were kindergartens at only two schools, staff members had to search for those children not attending kindergarten (but of the appropriate age) and examine them in their homes. This procedure was repeated for the 1963–64 and the 1964–65 school years. The best estimate that can be made is that during each of the above three years studies were initiated with approximately two-thirds of the children whose ages were between 58.5 and 70.5 months as of

TABLE 1.12

Numbers of Kindergarten-Age Children of Each Race and Sex Examined Each Year

	Racial group							
	White				Negro			
	Boys		Girls		Boys		Girls	
Year	K*	Non-K	K	Non-K	K	Non-K	K	Non-K
1962–63	16	11	10	13	9	10	17	16
1963–64	14	8	14	15	7	10	15	13
1964–65	15	14	9	14	14	14	16	11
Totals	45	33	33	42	30	34	48	40

* K = Children attending kindergarten; Non-K = children not attending.

October 15 of the school year then under way.[6] The exact numbers of children who were in these kindergarten-age groups each year are given in Table 1.12. When this total ($N = 305$) is added to the one in Table 1.10 ($N = 1222$), a grand total of 1527 children is obtained.

CONCLUDING COMMENTS

Like so many of the rural areas in this country, Millfield appears to be moving away from dependence upon the land. Farming remains critically important, however, while the availability of nonfarm jobs has not developed rapidly enough to provide for the needs of the people. Providing work for an expanding population appears to be out of the question for the moment; consequently, the youth of the area must seek their futures elsewhere. The adults, most of whom have limited educations and little experience in any other cultural setting, have few choices open to them. The lot of the Negro is especially hard in this regard, for, even though the white man may know poverty, the colored man knows it better.

With respect to its social structure, Millfield has been, is, and is likely to continue for some time to be essentially a segregated society. That its adult Negro citizens want an end to discrimination, injustice, and unequal opportunity is unquestionably true. That they are likely to push effectively for these rights is less certain, nor is it clear that, if they were assured of truly separate but equal facilities and opportunities in all domains, an overwhelming majority would in fact want full integration. In all likelihood, however, the upcoming generations will be much more assertive and less open to "separate but equal" compromises. There cannot be any doubt, though, but that most of the white population is committed to a segregated way of life.

We did not go to Millfield, however, to study segregation or desegregation, racial prejudice, or other racial issues. Rather, we wanted to determine and understand the social, motivational, and intellective characteristics of children being reared in such a setting. Now that we have sketched a general picture of the area, we shall turn our attention in Chapter 2 to a description of the procedures we used to generate the data which are reported and interpreted in the remaining chapters of the book.

[6] To begin kindergarten in September, the child had to be at least five years of age on or before October 15 of his entering year. This meant, then, that he would be eligible to enter the first grade in September of the following year.

Chapter 2

PROCEDURES USED TO
STUDY MILLFIELD'S CHILDREN

The objective in this chapter is to provide the reader with an overview of the procedures used to gather data, as well as a sketch of how these data are presented in the remainder of the book. Greater detail, when appropriate, will be given in succeeding substantive chapters. All the procedures used will be described here, even though it will not be possible in later chapters to present or interpret all the data that were collected.

The techniques used to collect data may be classified under five major headings: (1) intellective tests; (2) personality tests; (3) interviews; (4) questionnaires; and (5) ratings. Before taking up these various procedures, however, a few general points should be made about the examiners and the assessment sites.

EXAMINERS

Tests, interviews, and ratings were always carried out by a staff member who was a woman of the same race as the subject, with one exception (see below under *Ability Tests, Individually Administered;* also, see Chapter 3). These examiners were professionally trained at or beyond the M.A. level in either psychology or social work.[1]

[1] During 1961–62 we were assisted for a short time by one white, part-time examiner who did not have training at the M.A. level. She had had considerable testing experience, however, and she was able to administer the individual projective

19

In all, four Negro and six white examiners gathered data during the four years of the study. The bulk of the data, however, was secured by the six women (three Negro) to whom this book has been dedicated. At any given time, the field staff typically was composed of two Negro women each working five days per week and three white women each working about three days per week. When the work load demanded it, this basic staff was expanded temporarily.

ASSESSMENT SITES

Most of the data were collected in the schools by staff members working either directly with the children or through their teachers. In certain phases of the work, however, staff members visited homes either to interview mothers or to work with kindergarten-age children. In one follow-up study (see Chapter 7), staff members traveled to various locales in North Carolina to reexamine children who had moved from Millfield.

In general, the Negro schools in Millfield provided better working conditions for staff members than did the white schools. Negro school children were always tested or observed in their own schools, either in a private room or in their classroom, depending on whether an individual or group session was needed. Occasionally, additional observations were made in the lunchrooms or on the playgrounds. Some white children were also assessed in their schools; others, however, were taken to one of two nearby small frame houses that had been rented to serve as headquarters for the project. When a junior high school for white children was established in a neighboring town at the beginning of the 1963–64 academic year, white staff members traveled there to carry out their work with the seventh- and eighth-grade pupils who now attended that school. Although the school facilities were by no means ideal for this kind of research, they were adequate. Privacy, when essential, was maintained, and the overall excellent cooperation extended by teachers and school officials more than compensated for any limitations in the available physical facilities.

Mothers of kindergarten-age children were interviewed in two sessions (see Chapter 15). As a matter of policy, one of these sessions was always held in the home of the child. Sometimes, however, the other session was held either in the school or, for the white children, in the

---

test (see below) and assist in the group testing. All the examiners had been trained in psychology, except for one Negro staff member whose specialty was social work. One of the Negro staff members, Carol C. Bowie, had earned the Ph.D. degree.

project headquarters. In addition, the kindergarten-age children were assessed at approximately the same time that the mothers were being interviewed. Those children actually attending a kindergarten were evaluated in the school setting, while those not attending were assessed in their own homes.

Some of this work in the homes was carried out under difficult conditions. The poverty of some of the homes was extreme; physical resources were quite limited, and often considerable improvisation was necessary. Field staff members quickly became adept, however, at making do with available facilities. Here, too, as in the schools, the cooperation extended by most of the families tended to offset any physical limitations.

INTELLECTIVE TESTS

Three types of intellective tests are used frequently in school settings: individual tests of mental ability; group tests of mental ability; and group academic achievement tests. A test of each of these types was used as part of the effort to evaluate the intellective resources of Millfield's children.

Ability Tests, Individually Administered

When an individual's intellective power is being considered, both educators and psychologists tend to place more confidence in the results of an individually administered intelligence test than in results derived in any other way. For example, neither school grades nor group intelligence tests are considered to be as valid for children as an individually administered intelligence test, especially when administered by a competent examiner. Current research generally is based on either the Wechsler Intelligence Scale for Children (WISC) or the Stanford-Binet Intelligence Scale (S-B); either of these two tests would have been suitable for the Millfield study. The choice of the 1960 revision of the Stanford-Binet (Form L-M) was made because two experts were available at the University of North Carolina to guide the staff in the administration and scoring of this revision.

Giving and scoring an individual intelligence test is, of course, quite time-consuming; nevertheless, a total of 1006 children (542 Negro) were tested with the S-B during the 1961–62 school year. With only a few exceptions, all the children at both of the white schools and at one of the Negro schools were tested. At the second and largest Negro school, however, slightly less than 60% of the children could be tested because of time and staff restrictions. In this Negro school, all the first-grade children were tested, while at the older age levels, children were selected randomly for the S-B assessment.

In addition, 78 of the 1006 children were tested twice on the S-B during 1961–62; the second examination took place after a three-to-six month interval. All these children—31 of whom were Negro—were retested by a white examiner, the purpose being to secure some estimate of how an examiner's race may influence a Negro child's performance on an individually administered ability test. The results of this inquiry are described in Chapter 3. Unfortunately, rapport with Millfield at that time was not sufficiently secure that we could risk conducting a similar study of a Negro examiner's effect on the intellective performance of white children.

The S-B was also used in succeeding years of the project to study intellective change in the children. Thus, in Chapter 6 an investigation is described in which Negro children who were tested with the S-B during 1961–62 while they were in the first grade were retested approximately three years later. Similarly, in Chapter 7 a study is described in which white children who were tested as sixth-grade students in 1961–62 were retested after an interval of about three years. In Chapter 8, data are presented which bear on the question of how kindergarten training affects intellective development; one of the criterion measures for the latter is the S-B test. In this last study, kindergarten-age children (about half of whom actually were attending kindergartens) were tested twice with the S-B during the same academic year, first in the fall and again in the spring. All three of these inquiries were, of course, short-term longitudinal studies in which the S-B provided one measure of intellective change.

Ability Tests, Group-Administered

Many paper-and-pencil tests are available which may be administered to children in groups for the purpose of assessing their intellective talents. The popularity of these tests in many school settings is based largely upon the fact that it is feasible, ordinarily, to administer them in a single session to as many children as the teachers or administrators deem advisable. Group ability tests, however, do sometimes provide useful information that is not generated by the individual test. If time and resources permit, both types of tests should be used to evaluate school-age children.

For this project, the Thurstone Primary Mental Abilities Test (PMA) was selected for use as the group test. This selection was based largely on the fact that the scales in the PMA, more than those in most similar tests, are designed to evaluate separate components of intelligence. Moreover, a new revision of the test was being readied for general use at about the time the Millfield study was getting underway.[2] In addition to scores for several components of intelligence (described in Chapter 3), it should be noted that the PMA provides a total quotient score—based upon a child's performance on all the subtests—which is conceptually similar to the S-B IQ.

The PMA was administered to all the children in the late spring of 1962. Despite absences among the children, 1079 (642 Negro) full test protocols were secured. Usually two testing periods were used on different days to minimize fatigue. In addition, to ensure close attention to the task, two and sometimes three proctors were used for each testing session. The test was given to the children in their own classrooms.

The PMA was also administered to kindergarten-age children in 1962–63, 1963–64, and 1964–65. Like the S-B, the PMA was given twice to these children, first in the fall and again in the spring. The test was always administered individually to these youngsters, however, rather than in a group setting described above for the older children. Data growing out of this testing and retesting of kindergarten children are reported in Chapter 8, along with the S-B data, where the effects of kindergarten training are analyzed.

Academic Achievement Tests, Group-Administered

Increasingly, the argument is heard that ability tests are really achievement tests, that they do not measure innate ability. Although there is some merit in this argument, it is frequently overstated, perhaps in an effort to correct the comparable overstatements of those who, for many years, acted as if the IQ were a fixed and immutable fact of nature.

The traditional ability and academic achievement tests have been constructed in quite different ways. Perhaps of greatest importance is the fact that, in general, the builders of ability tests have attempted to avoid constructing their instruments so that they would bear any direct relationship to the content of the subject matter that was being learned in school. In contrast, the traditional academic achievement test has been developed so that it would bear a direct relationship to the subject matter covered in the typical classroom. For this reason, and also because of other considerations, the judgment was made that the picture of the intellectual competence of Millfield's children would be incomplete if a standard academic achievement test were not used along with individual and group ability tests.

The Stanford Achievement Test (SAT), Form M (1955), was selected

[2] We are indebted to Dr. Thelma G. Thurstone and Science Research Associates, Inc., for giving us early access to the 1962 revision of the PMA. Also, Dr. Thurstone was very helpful when questions arose with respect to the test's administration, scoring, and standardization.

for use in the study. Depending upon a child's grade placement, the Primary Battery, the Elementary Battery, the Intermediate Battery Partial, or the Advanced Battery Partial was administered to a child. Each of these forms provides an index of a child's capacity to understand the meanings of words and paragraphs of prose, to spell, to reason arithmetically, and to do arithmetic computations. In addition, except for grades one and two, a measure is provided of a child's competence in language.

The SAT was given to all the children in the spring of 1962; a total of 1155 (700 Negro) complete test protocols was secured. As was true for the PMA, children were tested in their classrooms. Two or three proctors were present, and testing was spread over at least two, and sometimes, three sessions.

PERSONALITY TESTS

While there are a large number of personality tests to consider for any assessment study, many of them have been constructed for adults and have little or no usefulness for children.[3] It is, indeed, difficult to find any consensus among psychologists or educators with respect to the question of which personality tests do provide valuable information in the assessment of children.

Personality tests have been classified in a variety of ways; one of the most widely accepted systems simply distinguishes between objective and projective tests.[4] Although we know of no definitive data in this regard, it is our general impression that in the assessment of children projective methods have been used more commonly than objective methods. Since we were not limited to the use of one personality test, however, one of each type was employed.

[3] The use of the term "personality" here is in a context that suggests the separation of intellective and personality attributes. We are following a common practice in this regard even though, as emphasized in the Preface, we consider intellective processes to be just one aspect of the larger personality domain.

[4] In a projective test, a subject is usually given a series of stimuli (for example, inkblots or pictures of people in a variety of situations) to which he responds by telling what they look like to him, or by making up a story based on the stimuli. Ordinarily, he is given great latitude in deciding how to formulate his responses, the assumption being that he will then project into his responses important aspects of his personality structure and its processes. In the objective test, in contrast, there is usually considerable restriction upon the subject's responses. For example, he reads a series of items and decides whether each one is true or false with reference to himself. The objective test format lends itself to the development of normative tables which are likely to play a more important role in the interpretive process than are similar tables for the projective test.

A Projective Test: The Carolina Picture Series (CPS)

The CPS is an outgrowth of one of the most commonly used projective tests, the Thematic Apperception Test (TAT), developed by Morgan and Murray (1935). In this test, the subject is given a series of pictures —sometimes as many as 20—and is asked to make up a story about each picture. These stories are then analyzed with reference to how the narrator perceives his world, how he perceives himself, his needs, his wishes, his fears, and so on.

Some of the TAT pictures could have been selected for use in the Millfield study. These are pictures of identifiably white people, however, and, even though a Negro version has been created (see Thompson, 1949), serious doubt has been cast upon its suitability as an equivalent test (see, for instance, Korchin et al., 1950). The decision was made, therefore, to use instead a series of 12 pictures (see Figures 12.1 and 12.2) that had been developed for Mingione's earlier study of achievement motivation among some of Millfield's children (see Mingione, 1965). The CPS had two basic advantages as far as the current research was concerned: (1) The pictures were line drawings in which the figures depicted were deliberately made ambiguous as far as their racial identities were concerned; and (2) the scenes had been specially drawn to provide settings with which all the children in Millfield were likely to be familiar. It promised, therefore, to be a test that would be equally applicable to Negro and white children.

The CPS was administered in two testing sessions separated by a two-week interval; Set A (the first six pictures) always preceded Set B (the last six pictures). Children were tested individually, with the examiner writing down the stories told by each child; in this way, any limitations in response arising from differences in writing skill and legibility were avoided.

Because two individual sessions were necessary for administration of the CPS, it was, like the S-B intelligence test, a time-consuming procedure. We decided, therefore, to test a sample of children which would permit evaluation of age, sex, and racial effects upon the variables scored from the CPS. This was done by randomly selecting 15 boys and 15 girls, each of whom was within six months of one of four age levels— 7, 9, 11, and 13 years—from each of Millfield's four schools. In all, 480 children were tested: 30 Negro boys, 30 Negro girls, 30 white boys, and 30 white girls at each of the four age levels. A large majority of the children were tested in the late spring of 1962. A smaller number, however, were tested during the first semester of the 1962–63 school year. It should be noted, too, that, if a child drawn for the CPS testing had not already been evaluated on the S-B, the latter test was administered to him so that a measure of the intellective ability of each CPS subject would be available.

Although the use of the CPS was guided by a major concern with achievement motivation, the stories elicited from the children did lend themselves to the evaluation of many additional variables. The findings relevant to achievement motivation are presented in Chapter 12, and those pertaining to the additional variables are given in Chapter 13.

An Objective Test: The Minnesota Multiphasic Personality Inventory (MMPI)

There is not, in our judgment, a broad-gauged, objective personality test that is suitable for use over the age range included in this study. It was decided, therefore, to limit this phase of the inquiry to the older children—more specifically, to eighth-grade children. For children of this age level, it seemed feasible to consider using the Minnesota Multiphasic Personality Inventory (MMPI), which is probably the most widely used and highly regarded objective test of personality. Special modifications, however, were made in the administration of the test (see below) to compensate for the known intellective deficiencies of many of the children.

The MMPI consists of 566 statements printed either consecutively in booklet form or as separate items on small cards. The subject reads each item and decides whether it is true or false as far as he is concerned.[5] Typical items, for example, are "I am often afraid of the dark" and "I like parties and socials." When the subject has completed the test, the examiner scores it, making use of a number of scales available to him. One scale, for instance, gives a measure of how masculine or feminine the respondent's interests are.

Although the MMPI is used most frequently with adults, it has been used successfully with children as young as 13 to 14 years (see Hathaway and Monachesi, 1963). It was clear, however, that a large number of Millfield's children were not only below average in intellective ability but also below their grade level in reading ability. Therefore, it was decided to limit the administration of the MMPI to eighth-grade children and also to modify the way in which it was administered. Accordingly, a tape recording was made with each of the MMPI items read from the booklet form, with a suitable pause separating each item. This tape was played, then, to the children in their classroom groups, and they recorded their answers on the answer sheet provided. The entire

---

[5] Provision is also made for subjects to give a "Cannot say" response, but they are encouraged to keep these to a minimum.

test was administered in one session of approximately two hours; at least two proctors were always present. The MMPI was given in the above fashion during the springs of 1963 and 1964 to all the eighth-grade children, a total of 265 (145 Negro).

INTERVIEWS

Tests are essential for the careful measurement of intellective talents, and they are often very helpful in the assessment of a number of non-intellective, personal attributes. There are many aspects of an individual's life, however, for which tests either are not available or will not suffice. For investigating some of these matters, the interview has been and continues to be an essential tool.

Oftentimes interviewers do not have a systematic plan of inquiry when they conduct interviews. Their questions and probes are dependent upon whatever happens to develop in the situation as it moves along. While there are advantages in such a flexible approach, there are also serious drawbacks, especially when specific research objectives are to be reached. The flexible interview, for example, does not assure one that the same topics will be covered with each interviewee. Moreover, even if they are covered, they may be handled in quite different ways so that comparability from subject to subject is lost. An adequate quantitative analysis of the resulting data may become difficult or even impossible under these circumstances. The best way to guard against such problems is to make use of a structured interview in which the interviewer asks a series of predetermined questions in a fixed order. Two such interview schedules were constructed for use in the project.

The usual interview, being only a two-person situation, is, like individual testing, a time-consuming procedure. Practically, this meant that we could study only a limited number of individuals in this way. A decision was made, therefore, to interview only two groups, the mothers of kindergarten-age children and eighth-grade pupils. (The interview schedules developed for these two groups may be found in Appendices A and B.) Data generated by these interviews are presented and interpreted in Chapters 15 and 16. In the paragraphs that follow, a brief sketch of each of these interview studies will be given.

Mother Interviews

There were four major reasons for interviewing mothers of kindergarten-age children. First, these interviews permitted us to gather a great deal of information regarding the behavioral development of the children during their first five years, as recalled and reported by their mothers. Second, through the interviews it was possible to inquire about the child-training practices and attitudes of Millfield's parents. Third, the interviews permitted an exploration of the family backgrounds of the children, the education of the parents, certain aspects of the husband–wife relationship, and so on. Finally, the occasion of the interview gave staff members an opportunity to observe the home conditions under which the children were being reared.

Each woman interviewed was the mother of a kindergarten-age child. She was interviewed twice, once during the fall semester and again during the spring semester of a given academic year. The interview schedules were, of course, different for the two occasions. They were of comparable length, however, each session usually taking more than one hour but less than two to complete. In all, during 1962–63 and 1963–64, 200 mothers (90 Negro) were interviewed on two occasions. Of this total, 109 were mothers of children who were *not* attending kindergarten.

Child Interviews

Interviewing a substantial number of children at several age levels would have been desirable; however, the project's resources did not permit such an undertaking. A decision was made, therefore, to limit these interviews to eighth-grade children, the oldest ones in the study. It was felt that the older children could provide more meaningful answers to some of the questions than could the younger children. In addition, there was the consideration that the eighth-grade children were being evaluated by means of an objective personality test, and it was felt that expanding knowledge about this group was likely to be more profitable than scattering the effort on another age level. Furthermore, the completion of the eighth grade marks a critical turning-point in the lives of many of these children; interviewing the children during this period might be particularly helpful in developing an understanding of what growing up in Millfield had meant to them.

The child interviews were conducted in single sessions which took between one and two hours. The structured questions were designed to secure both factual and attitudinal data and covered a wide variety of topics. Thus, questions were asked about the subject's family structure; his house and its resources; family finances; his parents' behavior; his peer-group relationships and activities; recreation patterns; television habits; his thoughts about marriage and family; participation in church activities; educational accomplishments and goals; any current jobs as well as occupational plans; his views of Millfield as a community; and, finally, his perception of himself (see Appendix B).

The child interviews could not be initiated until the 1963–64 school year. During this year, 136 eighth-grade children (78 Negro) were interviewed. All interviews were conducted in the school buildings; children were excused from their classes to participate.

QUESTIONNAIRES

The questionnaire is frequently an efficient method for collecting information. While the impersonal nature of its distribution may sometimes be limiting, in other respects it may actually be advantageous. The questionnaire method was used twice in the Millfield study—first to gather information about the families and later to obtain data relevant to the kindergarten program. Copies of the two questionnaires may be found in Appendices C and D.

Family Questionnaire

This questionnaire was developed early in the study to provide the staff with data on family structure and life in Millfield. From this questionnaire came most of the data presented in Chapter 1.

In the spring of 1962, the questionnaire was sent home to each family that had one or more children enrolled at that time in one of Millfield's four schools. A note accompanied the questionnaire, explaining why it was important to fill out and return the form. The cooperation extended in response to this request greatly exceeded the staff's expectations. In one school, *every* child returned his questionnaire; in the other three schools, as least 93% of the children returned theirs. Some forms, of course, were incompletely filled out or had some ambiguity; nevertheless, the questionnaires did provide a great deal of information relevant to Millfield's families.

Kindergarten Questionnaire

This questionnaire was designed to obtain information about the family structure and life of the children who had participated in the kindergarten program, as well as to secure an opinion from the parents of the influence that the program had had on their children. Data generated by the kindergarten questionnaire have been used in the study which is reported in Chapter 8.

The kindergarten questionnaire was sent in the spring of 1965 to the homes of all those children who had been in either of the two kindergartens during their three years of operation. It was completed and returned by 92% of the white parents and by 97% of the Negro parents who were still living in Millfield at the time of its circulation. No effort was made to contact the 13 families (5 Negro) who had moved out of Millfield after their children had been enrolled in the kindergartens.

RATINGS

Many of the observations that are made of behavior lie outside the relatively formal context that is found (in different ways, of course) in tests, interviews, and questionnaires. To develop a well-rounded picture of an individual, or of a group of individuals, it is clearly necessary to make use of as many of these informal observations as is feasible. At the same time, for research purposes, it is desirable that these observations be reduced to some form which makes quantitative analysis possible. It is in this regard that rating scales are particularly helpful; such scales were used on several occasions in the Millfield study in the ways described below.

Teachers' Ratings

Teachers are in an unusually good position to learn about the more salient and enduring traits of the children under their charge. This is particularly true if the teachers formulate their judgments at the end of the school year, after they have worked with the children for approximately 180 days, or more than 1200 hours. Such data were collected from Millfield's teachers; their analysis and interpretation can be found in Chapter 10.

The teachers recorded their judgments by filling out a rating sheet, one for each child in their classes. This sheet contained 22 graphic rating scales, each divided into seven equal segments. The two extreme positions of each scale were labeled with a descriptive word or phrase. For example, the first scale was anchored by the word "hyperactive" at one end and by the phrase "unusually inactive" at the other. By checking at any point along this scale, the teacher was able to record her judgment about the child with respect to the particular trait represented by the scale.

These rating scales covered most of the important social, motivational, and intellective behaviors that elementary school children might be expected to exhibit in school settings. There is, obviously, no assurance that certain equally important traits were not overlooked. The 22 traits as represented by the graphic scales are shown in Appendix E.

Each teacher in each of the four schools used these scales to rate each of her pupils in the late spring of 1962. In the late spring of 1963, all kindergarten and eighth-grade children as well as the seventh-grade children in one white school were rated. In the late spring of 1964, all children in all four schools were rated again.[6] Finally, it should be noted that the teachers were always told in advance that they would be paid for the time that they would have to devote to making these ratings. Cooperation by the teachers was excellent.

Peer Choices

A very different type of procedure was used to obtain a limited evaluation of each child by the other pupils in his classroom. This procedure resulted in an evaluation of how well each child was liked by his peer group. When applied to a child, it yields what can be called his popularity index. In a very broad sense, this index may be regarded as a type of rating secured by the child from his peer group.

These sociometric indices of the children were secured by having them participate with their classmates in a specially designed game. The format of this game required each child, on three successive trials, to choose individuals from other teams to join his team. By noting and recording the frequency with which each child was selected, data were secured which provided the basis for computing his popularity index. This entire procedure is described in greater detail in Chapter 14, where the results of the analyses of the data and their interpretations are also given. This sociometric procedure was used only once, in the spring of 1962. All children in each of the four schools participated, except for those children who were absent on the day when their room was scheduled.[7]

In addition to the teacher and peer ratings, two other sets of ratings were secured. However, they have not been used directly in the work reported in this volume and will not be described in detail. One of these sets was generated by the staff members who administered the S-B and CPS tests to the children. After each of these tests had been given to a child, he was rated on 17 graphic rating scales (see Appendix F) by the examiner; 11 of the scales were identical with those used by the teachers (compare Appendices E and F). These data helped determine

---

[6] At this time, seventh- and eighth-grade white children were attending the newly established junior high school (see Chapter 1). A child's day in this school was split about equally between two teachers. Each of these teachers made independent ratings for each of the children.

[7] This sociometric device worked well, as the discussion in Chapter 14 indicates. We regret, however, that we did not also use a broader peer-nominating technique in order to have each child evaluated by his classmates on a number of salient behavioral variables. Pupils, like teachers, are in a very advantageous position to make such behavioral observations and, by suitable means, can report them in ratings, choices, or judgments of their classmates.

when a particular individual test administration was invalidated by poor cooperation or low motivation. Otherwise, these data have not been analyzed. The second supplementary rating effort was much more complicated. It involved various pairs of staff members sitting as observers in first-grade classrooms for extended periods of time. Each of these observers made independent behavioral ratings of each child; also, each observer wrote a clinical description of each child. Space is not available to present these data adequately, however, it should be recognized that these reports have undoubtedly influenced our views of the young children in Millfield.

PLAN OF THE BOOK

In Part I, we have attempted to provide the reader with some understanding of what Millfield is like and an overview of the techniques and procedures used in the study. Greater detail on both points will be found throughout the book. Since some readers may wish to read selectively among the chapters that follow, a brief description of how the remainder of the book is organized will be presented here in an attempt to guide such persons to those sections most relevant to their interests.

The bulk of the book (Parts II, III, IV, and V) is devoted to the description and analysis of data generated by the use of the procedures which have been described in this chapter. In these 14 chapters, every effort has been made to report the findings as fairly and as objectively as possible. When interpretations rather than findings in the more narrow sense are presented, the reader should have little difficulty in identifying them as such. In the final part of the book (Part VI), in contrast, we have exercised greater freedom. Thus, in Chapter 17 an attempt has been made to interrelate and interpret some of the more important findings. Then, in Chapter 18 we present an array of recommendations and suggestions for special interventions that might enhance the development of individuals living either in Millfield or the many communities which are like it.

Part II contains three chapters which focus upon differences in measured intellective proficiency between the two racial groups, as manifested separately by boys and girls over the elementary school years. In Chapter 3, data from administration of the S-B are presented first, followed by the findings from the PMA. In Chapter 4, attention shifts to an evaluation of how well the children in Millfield master basic school skills and subjects, as measured by the SAT. In addition to analyzing differences in academic achievement appearing between white and Negro boys and girls over the range of elementary school age, the data are examined to determine whether the children perform academically at a level commensurate with their measured abilities. In Chapter 5, then, these same intellective variables are related to background characteristics of each of these children and their families (parental education, parental occupation, features of the sibships, and so on). Throughout Part II, the data are presented by using a cross-sectional approach.

Part III, containing four chapters, also focuses upon intellective processes. In contrast to Part II, however, the approach in Part III may be described as short-term longitudinal. Thus, Chapter 6 is concerned with the question of whether there is a general decline or an increase in intellective ability among the Negro children during their first three years in elementary school. In addition, personality and family factors are examined to see which ones may relate significantly to the various intellective growth paths followed by these Negro children. Chapter 7 addresses itself to similar problems, but the subjects are white and at an older age level (early adolescence). Both Chapters 6 and 7 are noninterventional; that is, naturally occurring processes are measured and described without any effort having been made to alter the course of development. Chapters 8 and 9, in contrast, are based on interventional efforts. Thus, Chapter 8 measures the effects that kindergarten training has upon the intellective skills of both Negro and white children living in Millfield. Since control groups were used during each of the three years of this study, these data permit a sound estimate of how much intellective change might be anticipated by the addition of such training to the regular school curriculum. Finally, Chapter 9 describes an exploratory study undertaken to determine the feasibility of a home-visiting program for four-year-old rural children which has as its focus the intellective development of these children. In contrast to the preceding three chapters in this section, this concluding one is essentially qualitative rather than quantitative; that is, resources did not permit us to undertake measurement procedures for the purpose of determining changes in intellective skills which might be attributed to the home program. Nevertheless, the experience gained in this endeavor was invaluable in suggesting how such a program might be developed constructively.

The five chapters in Part IV shift away from the intellective domain to the broader area of behavioral characteristics usually designated by the general term personality. Temperamental and emotional attributes, adjustmental reaction patterns, and selected motivational traits are all covered by one or another of the methods of personality study employed. Chapter 10 summarizes the perceptions by classroom teachers of their pupils over a wide variety of different behavioral attributes that they observe during their contacts with them. Some of these ratings describe relatively limited reactions of the children to experiences within the classroom setting, but many of these scales permit the teacher to summarize her knowledge of her pupils in a wide variety of settings and situations. In Chapter 11, data provided by the children themselves are reported, summarizing their self-descriptions on a personality inventory (the MMPI). As noted earlier in the chapter, the requirements of this instrument restricted its administration to the eighth-grade classes. However, children at four age levels (7, 9, 11, and 13) provided projective test data (the CPS) for analysis. The stories that these children told were analyzed for achievement motivation by two rather different scoring systems, and the results are presented in Chapter 12 so that racial, sex, and age comparisons can be readily observed. A large number of additional personality and motivational characteristics were assessed from these CPS stories, and the findings are presented in Chapter 13, again in such a way as to facilitate racial, sex, and age comparisons. The last chapter in this part, Chapter 14, summarizes the results of a study of sociometric preferences carried out among children in each of the schoolrooms in Millfield. These data have been related to a number of other background characteristics of the children to determine the correlates of social acceptance and popularity in this community.

Finally, Part V contains two chapters, each based upon data derived from interviews. The material in Chapter 15 pertains specifically to the circumstances surrounding the children in Millfield as they are about to enter the regular school system. Some of these children were already involved in school-like programs carried out in kindergartens established in the schools that they were scheduled to enter the following year; the rest of the children were still at home with no direct knowledge of the school environment. Interviews were carried out with the mothers of these children (both kindergarten and nonkindergarten), and the data have been analyzed and reported to give as accurate a picture as possible of the Southern rural child and his life at this stage of his development. Chapter 16, then, presents the material obtained from interviews with eighth-grade children. Thus the focus in this chapter is on the final phase of elementary school development, just before the children move on to senior high school (or drop out) and more adult demands and responsibilities. The content covered in these interviews was wide-ranging; it attempted to cover not only the way the children view themselves, but how they look upon many components of life in Millfield and the future prospects that they see for themselves.

Part II

INTELLIGENCE AND
ACADEMIC ACHIEVEMENT

Chapter 3

ABILITY DIFFERENCES BETWEEN
RACIAL, SEX, AND AGE GROUPS

Traditional intelligence tests that use a single, composite score to characterize a given child's scholastic potential are under severe criticism from many sides. Although many skills and aptitudes enter into school success, traditional scales of intelligence provide little basis for separate assessment of each of them. The scores from such scales are based on only one particular combination of these various component skills. They are also seen as tied to particular teaching methods. Traditional teaching approaches are said to be based largely upon verbal transmission of classroom material. Therefore, the traditional ability scales are heavily dependent upon verbal comprehension and are suitable predictors for traditional curricula and prosaic instructional techniques only. Similarly, there are claims that the usual school programs and goals are closely geared to middle-class standards and values, so that traditional intellective instruments, constructed to predict success in such schools, are necessarily biased in favor of children from middle-class families. The use of these tests, it is further contended, may even serve as a basis for exclusion of children who come from less favored ones. The research literature on individual differences in scholastic abilities among children from various age levels, from each sex group, and from different racial groups is largely based upon these traditional psychological instruments.

One of these traditional instruments, the Stanford-Binet Intelligence Scale (Form L-M), was used to furnish some of the data for the study reported in this chapter. The findings from this instrument provide a direct link to the large literature on racial, sex, and age differences. At

37

the same time, one of the newest analytical batteries in the intellective area, the Thurstone Primary Mental Abilities Test, was also used on the same groups. Several separate scores are generated by this battery, not merely one composite score, although a composite quotient is also included. Verbal proficiency is reflected in the battery, but it is only one of several measures provided on each child. Moreover, the analytical battery arises from basic psychological studies of the nature of human intelligence, not just the school-bound world of the classroom and the educational process. It is also contended that class or caste biases do not obtrude so heavily into the factor analytic scales as they do in empirically derived scales via external criteria of socially defined success and failure. Potentially, this analytic battery can meet several (but certainly not all) of the objections raised against the traditional intelligence tests.

THE STANFORD-BINET INTELLIGENCE SCALE
(1960 REVISION)

Administration and Scoring

The Stanford-Binet (S-B) is made up of a series of separate tasks which the examiner presents individually to each child in a prescribed order. The response to each task is recorded and scored in accordance with standards and models in the test manual. The tasks are grouped into age levels in order of increasing difficulty; the examiner proceeds no higher after all tasks at a given level have been failed (called the child's *ceiling age*). Similarly, the examiner does not give any easier tasks once a child has passed all tasks at any given level (called his *basal age*).

Each child's performance on these tasks yields a score expressed in months of mental age credit. When this score is divided by the score he is expected to earn at his particular chronological age, a second score is obtained, his intelligence quotient (IQ).[1] If his actual score is the

[1] The usual formula for the IQ is: $IQ = MA/CA \times 100$, in which MA is the mental age in months, CA is the chronological age in months, and multiplying the ratio by 100 gives a quotient free of decimals. It should be noted, however, that neither of the instruments used in this study, the S-B (Form L-M) or the PMA, uses this formula in the computation of the quotient values. Instead, each score is determined from tabled values of deviation scores that are based upon the amount of difference from the average value for that age, weighted by the standard deviation for that same age. When properly scaled, such deviation scores can be interpreted in the same way as traditional IQ values.

same as his expected score, his IQ is 100. Thus, IQ's above 100 indicate increasingly superior performances, while those below 100 reflect inferior performance for that age level. Research on the S-B shows that about one-half of American school-age children earn an IQ that falls within 10 points of the expected value—that is, between 90 and 110 (see Terman and Merrill, 1937).

Invalid Test Records

Although the examining procedures for the S-B were generally very dependable,[2] a small number of these testing sessions were judged inadequate or unacceptable. The most frequent basis for discarding the results of a particular testing session was an inconclusive determination of a basal or ceiling age. As described above, during the course of each test administration, the examiner has to decide when to cease testing. If some mistake in initial scoring is discovered later when each test booklet is carefully reviewed, the change in scoring can mean that the examiner has made an incorrect decision about discontinuing testing. When such errors were discovered, the examiner arranged to see the child again for further testing. In a few instances, however, completion of the examination was not possible, and the record had to be eliminated from subsequent analyses.

Similarly, any serious lack of interest or cooperation on the part of the child being tested was also a basis for eliminating S-B test records. While most of the children seemed to find the testing experience a welcome and enjoyable respite from classroom routines, a few appeared to be so anxious, so uninterested, or so uncooperative that their S-B performances were judged unacceptable samples of their actual proficiencies. These records, numbering less than 1% of the total sample, were not included in the analyses reported below. Only those test scores generated by cooperative children who were fully and fairly examined over the appropriate range of the scale were used. In all, there were 1006 such children between 6½ and 14½ years of age who were tested on the S-B during the 1961–62 school year.

Race of Examiner

As described in Chapter 2, Negro examiners always evaluated Negro children; white examiners always tested white children. The relevance of this precaution is suggested by a small study carried out in 1961–62

[2] In a special study by Jean Eder LaCrosse, for example, 78 children (31 Negro) were retested on the S-B after an interval of about five months. She found a correlation of .94 between the initial scores and those received on reexamination. This study is discussed in greater detail later in this chapter.

by one of the project's white staff examiners, Jean Eder LaCrosse. LaCrosse selected 78 children for reexamination on the S-B. These children were of both sexes and reasonably representative of the age range covered in the larger study. Sixteen of the children were ones that she herself had tested initially; in addition, there were four other groups, each with 14 to 17 children. Two of these groups had been tested originally by one or the other of two Negro examiners, and two had been tested originally by two other white examiners. LaCrosse retested these children after approximately five months, without reviewing either her own original test protocols or those administered by the other four examiners.

Analyses of these data revealed that the mean scores of the children in the three white groups were higher on reexamination, while those of each of the two Negro groups were lower. For all the white children, the mean gain was 1.5 IQ points. The mean loss for all the Negro children was of identical magnitude, 1.5 IQ points. Only 39% of the Negro children actually showed a gain in IQ on retesting, whereas 62% of the white children increased their scores, a difference that is statistically significant (see Table 3.1).[3] Gains of the sort shown by the white children are usually attributed to greater familiarity with the test procedures and materials (a practice effect). The mean losses shown by the Negro children are inconsistent with such practice effects. Perhaps their greater familiarity with the test procedures on this second testing was not sufficient to offset the impact of being examined by a white woman.

Distributions of IQ Scores

Figure 3.1 provides a summary of S-B IQ scores earned by Millfield's white and Negro children in comparison with scores earned by two other samples of children, one white, the other Negro. In this figure, curve B

---

[3] LaCrosse would have had a more definitive study if a Negro examiner had also retested both Negro and white children. When Negro kindergarten children were retested by a Negro examiner in another study (see Chapter 8), they gained, on the average, 1.1 IQ points from fall to spring. The Negro control children, however, lost, on the average, .2 of an IQ point. Negro children in the primary grades were also retested by a Negro examiner (see Chapter 6) after a much longer interval (about three years); these children dropped, on the average, .6 of an IQ point at the second testing. The drop by LaCrosse's Negro children, then, while not large, did exceed the changes obtained in either of these studies in which all the testing was done by Negro examiners. It is also true, however, that in both of the studies just referred to, Negro children retested by Negro examiners did not gain as much as did the white children retested by a white examiner in LaCrosse's study. There are, clearly, a number of problems in this area that need more extended investigation.

TABLE 3.1

Frequency of Change in Measured S-B IQ Value
on Retesting by White Examiner (1961–62)*

| Race of children | Direction of change | | Totals |
	Lower/same	Higher	
White	18	29	47
Negro	19	12	31
Totals	37	41	78

$$\chi^2 = 3.96$$
$$(p < .05)$$

* Based upon an unpublished M.A. thesis by Jean Eder LaCrosse.

represents the scores obtained by Millfield's white children, and curve C
represents the scores achieved by Millfield's Negro children. Curve A is
based on the scores of 1419 students, representative of white American
school children, ages six through twelve, as reported by Terman and
Merrill (1937).[4] Curve D is based upon a recent study of 1630 Negro

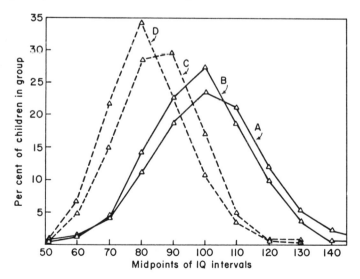

Fig. 3.1: Percentages of children from four research groups who earned various
IQ scores. A = USA white children ($N = 1419$) (Terman and Merrill, 1937).
B = Millfield white children ($N = 464$). C = Millfield Negro children ($N = 542$).
D = Southeast USA Negro children ($N = 1630$) (Kennedy *et al.*, 1961).

[4] The Terman and Merrill data are based upon Form L of the S-B; comparable
data for Form L-M are not available.

school children in five southeastern states (Kennedy *et al.*, 1961). Since there were unequal numbers of children in these four groups, the curves in Figure 3.1 are based upon the percentages of children in their respective groups earning scores at a particular IQ level. (This way of graphing the data equates the area under the curve for each group and makes the curves more directly comparable for visual inspection.)

Intraracial Differences in IQ Scores

It is clear in the data presented in Figure 3.1 that the distribution of scores from Millfield's white children is very similar to the distribution from the national sample of white children. Curve B is displaced slightly to the left of curve A, however, indicating that lower IQ scores are more frequent in the Millfield group. The mean IQ for the white children in Millfield is 97.8 (see Table 3.2), a little over two points below the expected value of 100.

It is also clear that the distribution of scores for the Negro children in Millfield is similar to that obtained by Kennedy *et al.* when they tested 1630 Negro children in Alabama, Florida, Georgia, South Carolina, and Tennessee with the same revision of the S-B. Note, however, that curve C is displaced to the right of curve D, indicating that Millfield's Negro children more often earned higher scores than did those in Kennedy's sample. The mean IQ for Millfield's Negro children is 84.6; in contrast, the mean for Kennedy's group is 81.4. Thus, the data suggest that the Negro children in Millfield may be somewhat more able than those living in some of the other Southeastern states.

TABLE 3.2

S-B IQ Means and Standard Deviations for Several Millfield Groups (1961–62)
and for Two Kennedy Groups

Group	N	S-B IQ Mean	S.D.
Millfield			
White boys	230	97.9	14.8
White girls	234	97.7	14.0
Combined	464	97.8	14.4
Negro boys	270	83.7	12.9
Negro girls	272	85.5	13.1
Combined	542	84.6	13.0
Kennedy*			
Negro boys and girls	1800	80.7	12.5
Negro boys and girls	1630	81.4	12.3

* Based on Kennedy *et al.*, 1961.

It should be noted that Kennedy *et al.* used white male examiners. We must question whether these men were able to get the best performance possible from Negro school children. Although we know of no published studies of the influence of sex of the examiner on S-B scores of Negro children, it is true that most young school children are more accustomed to working with women than with men. It may be, therefore, that the true difference between the S-B proficiencies of Kennedy's sample and of the one from Millfield is less than is suggested by curves C and D in Figure 3.1 or by the data in Table 3.2.

Note should also be taken of the fact that curve D is based upon only 1630 of the 1800 children tested in the Kennedy study. Their staff drew children from the first six grades of the schools they visited; as a result, they included some children who were older than their grade placement would suggest, but they did not seek out comparable children of those ages who were already beyond grade six. Therefore, the total data these investigators reported are more descriptive of existing grade populations in these southeastern Negro schools than they are of the abilities of Negro children at the ages sampled (see Schaefer, 1965). Accordingly, only the scores of children ages six through eleven were used to plot curve D, thus providing a distribution that is more likely to be representative of the children in this age span. As the data in Table 3.2 indicate, however, the mean IQ for this revised distribution deviates by less than one point from the value reported for the entire sample of 1800 children (81.4 vs. 80.7, respectively).

Racial Differences in IQ Scores

It is clear from curves B and C in Figure 3.1, as well as from the data in Table 3.2, that the mean IQ of the Negro children in Millfield falls markedly below that of the white children. As one would anticipate from examination of these data, analysis of variance indicates that this racial difference is highly significant. In terms of this measure of intellective ability, therefore, it is clear that Negro children in Millfield suffer in comparison with white children.

Furthermore, the data indicate that the variation in the scores of the Negro children is less than that of the white children. Thus, the standard deviations in Table 3.2 are smaller for the Negro groups, and, in Figure 3.1, curve C is more peaked than curve B. The national sample of white children shows greater variability than either of the Millfield groups. (When the latter are combined in a single sample, a standard deviation of 15.2 is obtained, which approaches more closely the value of 16.2 reported for the national group.)

Although the white children in Millfield exceed the Negro children on the average by approximately 13 S-B IQ points, it is important to point out that the two distributions of scores overlap to a considerable degree. This means, of course, that there were many Negro children who scored as high or higher than many white children. Consequently, from knowledge of a child's IQ alone it is impossible to predict his race with any certainty. An exception to this rule would be children with IQ's of 130 or above; no Negro child earned an IQ higher than 129. But only four white children in Millfield (less than 1% of the white sample) reached that level. At the lower end of the distribution, both Negro and white children earned IQ's in the 50 to 59 range.

It is apparent from curves B and C that the white and Negro schools contain many children whose ability levels are so limited that they are in need of special programs. From detailed comparisons of these distributions, for example, it can be shown that 9.7% of the white children and 34.9% of the Negro children have IQ's below 80. Below an IQ of 85 fall 17.9% of the white children and 49.1% of the Negro children.

Sex Differences in IQ Scores

There were almost identical numbers of boys and girls in both the Negro and white groups tested in Millfield (see Table 3.2). Since the IQ differences between the white and Negro children were large, the data from boys and girls will be considered separately for the two races.

When the IQ scores earned by white boys and white girls were plotted, the two curves were very similar. As shown in Table 3.2, the means and standard deviations for these two groups are almost identical. The boys are slightly more variable than the girls, primarily because more of them fall at the lower end of the scale. Thus, 8 white boys but only 4 white girls scored below an IQ of 70. At the upper end of the scale, in contrast, there were equal numbers of boys and girls (for example, 16 boys and 16 girls had IQ's beyond 120). Among the white children, therefore, it seems quite safe to conclude that there are no meaningful sex differences in S-B IQ's.

The distributions of scores for Negro boys and Negro girls taken separately are also very similar. The curve for the Negro girls, however, is displaced slightly toward the upper end of the scale in comparison with the curve for the boys. This displacement is also reflected in the mean values reported in Table 3.2; the mean IQ score for Negro girls is 1.8 points higher than that for Negro boys. More girls than boys have IQ's above 110 (5 vs. 2, respectively), whereas a few more boys than girls have IQ's below 70 (38 vs. 32). Furthermore, as indicated in the table, the scores of the Negro girls are slightly more variable than those of the boys. These differences in means and standard deviations are so small, however, that they have no practical implications. To the extent that S-B IQ does indicate potentiality for scholastic performance, then, there is little difference between the boys and girls of either race in Millfield.[5]

Age Differences in IQ Scores

For this purpose, the scores from the children were grouped—separately for each race and sex—according to their chronological ages. Here, as elsewhere in the book, age groups were formed so that each child was within six months of the age used to designate his group. (Children called age nine range from eight and one-half to nine and one-half years of age.) Mean IQ scores for each of the 32 age groups formed in this way are plotted in Figure 3.2. As one would anticipate from the data

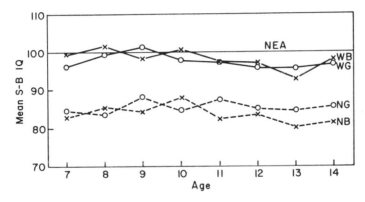

Fig. 3.2: Mean S-B IQ scores for each sex of each race at eight age levels (1961–62). WB = white boys. WG = white girls. NB = Negro boys. NG = Negro girls. NEA = normal expectation for age.

already reported, there are large differences between the mean scores of the two races at each of the eight age levels. There is also the expected tendency for the mean scores of girls to exceed those of boys to a greater degree among the Negro children than among the white children.

Analysis of variance of these data revealed a highly significant age effect, the mean IQ values decreasing with increasing age. This decrease in ability at older ages is found, however, for only three groups: white boys, white girls, and Negro boys; older Negro girls do *not* perform less adequately on the S-B than younger ones. Moreover, inspection of Figure 3.2 indicates clearly that, for the other three groups, the decre-

[5] Neither sex nor any of the interactions involving sex was significant in the analyses of variance.

ments appear in the last half of the age span sampled. Children beyond age ten perform less well on the S-B than children below age ten. The mean IQ's of the white children are either close to or actually above 100 between the ages of seven and ten, but none of the older groups scored this high. The curve for the Negro boys shows variations over the seven to ten age range, but the values for these boys are higher than those for the older groups.

The implications of these age-related findings are quite important. Reports in the research literature (see Pettigrew, 1964a) suggest that Negro children typically develop intellectively rather normally until they approach puberty, at which time they are supposed to begin to drop back. The data just presented, however, indicate that whatever age changes are present are not characteristic of Negro children alone; actually, the lower performances in the older groups are more clear-cut among the white children than among the Negro children. Furthermore, it is the Negro girls who show consistency in measured ability beyond the mid-range of elementary school age.

Vocabulary Raw Scores

Many of the S-B tasks presented to the very young child are non-verbal. He is asked to respond by working with objects or doing something rather than by talking. As the age level increases, however, the tasks become more verbal, and the child's ability to use language effectively becomes a more critical determinant of his success on the test (Jones, 1949). From about the age of six, a child's knowledge of words is measured directly on the S-B by asking him to define orally a series of increasingly difficult words. The performance of the children on this vocabulary test can be treated separately as a subscale of verbal proficiency. There are two reasons for doing this. First, as already noted above, performance on many of the tasks, especially those at the higher levels, is partially dependent upon language proficiency.[6] It is therefore important to see to what extent these children, both white and Negro, are handicapped in their knowledge of what words mean. Second, it is often emphasized that Negro children are at a particular disadvantage because they are not taught the same basic vocabulary as are white children. It becomes essential to determine the extent to which such a difference in vocabulary exists between Millfield's white and Negro children.

Mean vocabulary raw scores were computed separately for each

[6] There is a high correlation (.77) between S-B vocabulary scores and S-B IQ scores when the correlation is computed over all the Millfield children.

racial and sex group at each of the eight age levels; these mean values have been plotted in Figure 3.3. This figure also contains a plot of the scores expected at each age level according to the scoring standards given in the manual for the 1960 revision of the S-B.

According to the graphs in Figure 3.3, the white children are able to define correctly the requisite number of words at ages seven through ten, but at the older ages they are deficient. The Negro children are very much below standards in word knowledge all along the age range sampled, with the deficiency being more pronounced at the upper age levels. Analysis of variance confirmed these racial, age, and sex differences.[7]

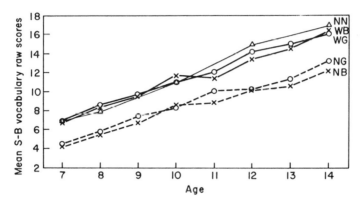

Fig. 3.3: Mean S-B vocabulary raw scores for each sex of each race at eight age levels (1961–62); also, S-B national norm values. WB = white boys. WG = white girls. NB = Negro boys. NG = Negro girls. NN = national norms.

These differences are similar to those already shown for the IQ data plotted in Figure 3.2. It should be noted, however, that additional analyses of the vocabulary scores indicated that the differences found here between Negro and white children were greater than the levels of separation which could have been expected from knowledge of the general performance of these groups on the S-B test as a whole. This latter finding indicates that the Negro children are particularly handicapped in verbal skills. Additional evidence on the verbal components

[7] Since the vocabulary score is a relatively short and potentially undependable measure taken out of context of the S-B battery, the retest reliability of this score was examined in the data reported earlier on the reexamination of 78 of the original research subjects carried out by Jean Eder LaCrosse. The vocabulary level was found to be stable over the five-month interval, shifting only a fraction of a unit from one session to the next. The rank order of ability on the two occasions was also very stable; a correlation of .92 was obtained on the total group of children.

of their intellective behavior will be presented in the next section, where the PMA data are considered, and in Chapter 4, when the academic achievements of the children are analyzed.

THURSTONE'S PRIMARY MENTAL ABILITIES TEST
(1962 REVISION)

Administration and Scoring

The items of the PMA are printed in test booklets that are given to each child to work on at his desk. At the lowest two levels (see below), the child responds to each item by marking directly in the test booklet. At the upper two levels, in contrast, the child records his answers on a separate answer sheet, making machine scoring possible. All the records were hand-scored, however; routine checks were made to ensure accuracy both in the application of the scoring stencils and in the clerical steps necessary for obtaining the various quotient scores described below.

The PMA was administered to each entire class in its regular classroom, always with at least two proctors present (including the chief examiner). Since the PMA requires sustained attention and steady work (sometimes against the clock), every effort was made to reduce boredom or fatigue. The test was spread over two, and sometimes three, sessions, and the examiners took care in their proctoring to make certain that no child lost points because he failed to apply himself consistently to these tests.

Each of the subtests was scored separately; quotients for each scale were provided by appropriate normative tables in the test manuals, given separately for each age level. In addition, the separate raw scores on these subtests were added and converted to a Total Quotient by referring to an additional table in the manual.

Test Levels

The PMA test has been prepared in five forms to provide tasks appropriate to different age levels: K–1, 2–4, 4–6, 6–9, and 9–12. These identifying symbols stand for the grade level (K for kindergarten, 1 for first grade, and so on) for which the particular test booklet should be best suited in terms of the difficulty of the test items, the developmental maturity of the typical pupils enrolled in those grades, and the availability of normative standards for the chronological ages of children most likely to be examined in these grades. (Of the five levels, only the first four were appropriate for the Millfield study.)

In the preliminary forms which were made available to the project prior to their formal publication,[8] level K–1 was originally called K–2. Accordingly, selections of forms for use with the classes in Millfield were made as if a full array of overlapping forms were available. In the light of the S-B data already on hand, the decision was made to employ the *easier* PMA test form at each of the overlapping levels: grades two, four, and six. For example, Form 2–4, rather than Form 4–6, was used with fourth-grade classes. In this way the staff hoped to minimize the number of instances in which a child would be asked to attempt a series of tasks in which even the easiest items would be too difficult for him. This decision, of course, introduced the risk that an occasional child would not be able to show all that he could do on some tasks because he had run out of items before the time was up. Checking of the test booklets, however, showed that this was not in fact a problem; completion of the final items on any of the scales was extremely rare.

The Abilities Measured

Not all the mental abilities are represented in each of the test forms described above, although some tasks appear at all age levels. Thus, scores measuring a child's mastery of word meanings, his facility in using numbers, and his capacity to see spatial relationships are provided in each form. Scores reflecting his speed or quickness in perceptual tasks, however, are available only in K–1, 2–4, and 4–6, while his ability to reason about relationships among symbols such as letters, words, or numbers is assessed only in 4–6 and 6–9. In addition, each form provides a summary or composite score which is based upon the scores from all the subtests contained in that particular form. The test manual claims that this total score "provides a reliable estimate of intelligence, comparable to scores on such tests as the Stanford-Binet . . ." (Thurstone and Thurstone, 1962, p. 4).

Total Quotients

The means and standard deviations of the PMA Total Quotients were computed for each racial and sex group separately (see Table 3.3); these distributions have been plotted in Figure 3.4. The scores for the white children fall only two or three points below the corresponding mean values of the S-B test, but the Negro children score appreciably lower on these PMA national norms than they do on the S-B scale. As can be seen, the PMA distributions for the two racial groupings overlap

---

[8] We are indebted to Dr. Thelma G. Thurstone and Science Research Associates for permission to use this PMA test battery prior to its formal publication. The norms and scores are based on the subsequent published manuals.

TABLE 3.3

PMA Total Quotient Means and Standard Deviations for Each
Group of Millfield Children (1961–62)

| Group | N | PMA total quotients | |
		Mean	S.D.
White boys	212	94.7	15.0
White girls	225	94.4	13.5
Combined	437	94.6	14.2
Negro boys	322	75.5	14.4
Negro girls	320	79.3	13.4
Combined	642	77.4	14.1

less and show more skew than those for the S-B. The range of variation
that each of these subgroups produced on the PMA Total Quotient
scores is quite comparable to the dispersion found among their S-B IQ
values.

The Total Quotient scores from each of these four subgroups were
tabulated separately by age level, and analyses of variance were carried
out on them. The mean values have been plotted in Figure 3.5 for eight
age levels for white and Negro boys and girls. At all age levels the Total
Quotient scores of the Negro children average much lower than those
of the white children. These differences range from a minimum of about
15 points to a maximum of approximately 25 points over the age span
sampled. The very large differences at age seven, however, may reflect in
part an artifact of group testing. The children at this age level were in
grade one at the time of testing, and many more of the Negro children

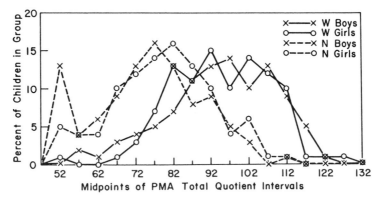

Fig. 3.4: Percentages of children from four subgroups who earned various PMA
Total Quotient scores.

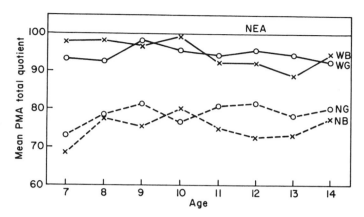

Fig. 3.5: Mean PMA Total Quotient scores for each sex of each race at eight age levels (1961–62). WB = white boys. WG = white girls. NB = Negro boys. NG = Negro girls. NEA = normal expectation for age.

than the white children were not yet adept at using a test booklet and pencil, or in working within time limits (see discussion of the Perceptual Speed Quotients below).

The analysis of variance also pointed up a stable overall sex difference. It is clear from the plots shown in Figure 3.5 that this sex effect reflects differences found primarily in the scores of the Negro children. The mean scores of the Negro girls exceed those of the Negro boys at seven of the eight age levels, whereas the white boys and girls are equally divided in this regard. As noted above, Negro girls also tended to surpass the boys on the S-B, while the white boys and girls were more nearly equal (see Table 3.2; also, Figure 3.2). It is interesting to note that the superiority of the girls is particularly pronounced at the older age levels —at and beyond age eleven. The age trends in these Total Quotients are in fact very similar to those already reported for S-B IQ scores. The scores of the white children, especially those of the boys, are lower beyond age ten. The performance of the Negro boys beyond age ten also tends to be lower than that of the younger boys, but this is not true of the Negro girls.

Verbal Meaning Quotients

Success on this subtest depends primarily upon a child's ability to demonstrate his understanding of words. It is similar, then, to the vocabulary section of the S-B described earlier. There is, however, a crucial difference. On the S-B the child must define words orally, showing that he knows their meanings by recall, without additional prompts. In contrast, on the PMA the child selects either one picture from a

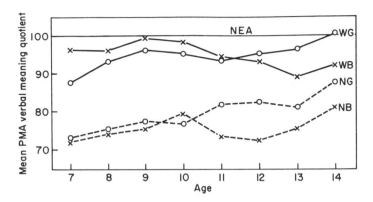

Fig. 3.6: Mean PMA Verbal Meaning quotients for each sex of each race at eight age levels (1961–62). WB = white boys. WG = white girls. NB = Negro boys. NG = Negro girls. NEA = normal expectation for age.

group of pictures or one word from a group of words to indicate his understanding of what has either been read to him by the examiner or what, at the older age levels, he has himself read in the test booklet. These items, therefore, do not actually require the child to use spontaneous speech in the way that the S-B does but rather to recognize a correct answer from the array provided.

The average quotient scores found on this subtest for the 32 groups are shown graphically in Figure 3.6. There is a highly significant racial difference in favor of the white children. Furthermore, there is a significant sex difference, with girls scoring better than boys. The analyses also show a significant age effect, attributable to the fact that the older children are superior to the younger children.

In this important component of academic ability, the Negro–white gap is appreciably smaller at the older age levels (eleven to fourteen) than at the younger age levels (seven to ten). The large differences at the younger age levels is consistent with the fact that the Negro children come from homes that are especially impoverished in training for verbal skills (see Chapters 5 and 9). The fact that these differences are smaller at the older age levels suggests that formal schooling and wider life experiences may help to offset initial handicaps in verbal ability.

The differences at the various age levels reveal that the older Negro girls are much less retarded in verbal skills than the older Negro boys. While the Negro boys perform better at the older age levels, they are not a great deal more able than the younger boys. The older Negro girls, however, do much better than the younger Negro girls. Older white girls also show superiority over younger white girls. In contrast, older white boys are less capable than younger white boys on this verbal measure.

No generalization holds very well about these sex differences in verbal ability; it is necessary to specify the age level being considered. Thus, for white children at the lower age levels, the boys are superior to the girls, but at the upper age levels, the girls are markedly ahead of the boys. For the Negro children, there are some similarities to the pattern of scores for the white children, but there are also differences. At the upper age levels, the Negro girls, like their white counterparts, are clearly superior to the boys, but at the lower age levels the girls also tend to perform more adequately, although the differences here are small and probably of little practical import (see also Yates, 1967).

Perceptual Speed Quotients

On this subtest, a child is presented with rows containing either four or five drawings; the child must find two that are identical and either mark them out or tally them by number on the answer sheet. To do this successfully requires sustained attention, visual searching, and care in noting the slight differences that are presented in these sketches. Moreover, the child must work within short time limits; the examiner tells him that he must work quickly and that he will have to stop when the time has run out. The perceptual speed subtest is included only in Forms K–1, 2–4, and 4–6; therefore, scores for this ability are not available for children more than twelve years of age. Mean quotient scores earned by the resulting 24 groups have been plotted in Figure 3.7. These data also were studied by an analysis of variance.

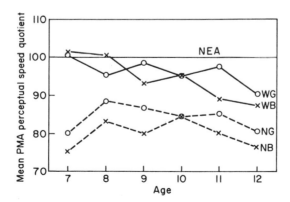

Fig. 3.7: Mean PMA Perceptual Speed quotients for each sex of each race at six age levels (1961–62). WB = white boys. WG = white girls. NB = Negro boys. NG = Negro girls. NEA = normal expectation for age.

The white children achieve significantly higher scores than the Negro children on this subtest, too. It should be noted, however, that, except at age seven, the Negro–white gap is smaller than that found on the Verbal Meaning subtest (compare Figures 3.6 and 3.7). With respect to sex differences, Negro girls clearly out-perform Negro boys, but there are no consistent differences in performance between white girls and white boys. Each of the four racial–sex groups, however, shows a similar significant age change: average scores tend to become lower as the children grow older. One possible source of these age differences may be some tendency for children being reared in this subculture to resist being hurried more than do children growing up in other sections of the country. Unfortunately, there are few other measures anywhere in the evaluation battery on these children in which working against time is heavily weighted. It is difficult, therefore, to explore this implication in the perceptual speed test data.

Any interpretation of the age shifts requires that special note be taken of the results for Negro children at age seven. We are fortunate to have available for this purpose a set of observations recorded by two Negro project staff members who made independent behavioral notes on these children daily in their classrooms for several weeks (see Chapter 2). Their notes were examined to try to identify possible reasons for these low scores on the PMA Perceptual Speed scale. These observers noted that only about one-third of the children were ready and able to cope with the normal demands of a first-grade classroom; the remaining two-thirds were judged not to be ready for first-grade tasks. Such children were likely to perform poorly on tasks and demands that were novel, had narrowly specified instructions, or required them to work fast. Corresponding observations on white first-graders did not reveal very many children who lacked this kind of readiness. For the Millfield children, Negro as well as white, the PMA battery was their first encounter with a timed test. Since many more of the Negro than of the white children were not able to cope effectively with this novel time demand, the points plotted at age seven in Figure 3.7 for the Negro children probably should be considered apart from the remainder of their curves.

Number Facility Quotients

Each form of the PMA asks the child to solve verbally stated number problems which, of course, become increasingly difficult at the older age levels. Usually, however, the Number Facility subtest also involves some further evidence of quantitative skill, such as speed and accuracy in simple arithmetic, number facts, quantitative relationships, or comple-

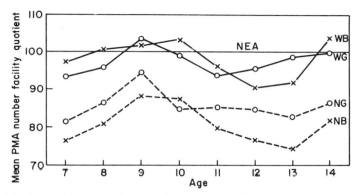

Fig. 3.8: Mean PMA Number Facility quotients for each sex of each race at eight age levels (1961–62). WB = white boys. WG = white girls. NB = Negro boys. NG = Negro girls. NEA = normal expectation for age.

tion of number series. No other component measure in the PMA test varies as widely as Number Facility from one test level to another in the different kinds of tasks represented. The mean quotient score from each of the 32 groups on the Number Facility subtest has been plotted in Figure 3.8. These data also were analyzed by analysis of variance.

On this ability too, there is a very significant racial difference in favor of the white children. As with perceptual speed, there is a significant sex difference among the Negro children (girls higher than boys) but not among the white children. Moreover, it should be noted that this sex difference among the Negro children is more pronounced at the older age levels. Since the problems presented to the older children are stated predominantly in words, requiring reading with comprehension before the number work can proceed, the clear superiority in Number Facility of the Negro girls over boys at these ages may be in part a reflection of their greater facility in reading and verbal comprehension. Obviously, however, this reading bias would not account for the sex differences at all age levels. At ages seven and eight, for example, the examiner always reads aloud the test items. Verbal comprehension but not reading mastery is needed at these lower age levels.

The shifts in this ability over age are large but less systematic than those for some of the other abilities. That is, there are shifts in mean scores from one age group to another, but they do not show any regularity. Since the test items are as heterogeneous as indicated above from one test form to another, it is difficult to formulate an interpretation of these variations.

Another point should be noted about these Number Facility scores. In general, these scores, for both Negro and white children, tend to be

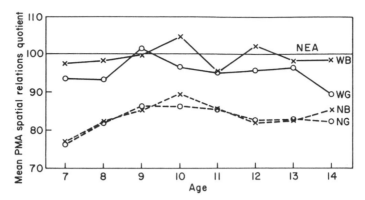

Fig. 3.9: Mean PMA Spatial Relations quotients for each sex of each race at eight age levels (1961–62). WB = white boys. WG = white girls. NB = Negro boys. NG = Negro girls. NEA = normal expectation for age.

higher than those earned on the Verbal Meaning subtest. This superiority in Number Facility is especially pronounced among the younger Negro children, but it is certainly not limited to them. Thus, 5 out of the 16 white age groups scored at or above the national norms on the Number Facility subtest, while only one group even reached this level on the Verbal Meaning subtest. When compared with a national sample, then, Millfield's children perform better on number ability tests than on verbal ability tests.

Spatial Relations Quotients

On this subtest the child must demonstrate his ability to visualize relationships among a variety of geometric forms. In K–1, 2–4, and 4–6, he is given items where he has to select one of the several shapes presented that will complete a figure to form a perfect square. In addition (in K–1 only), the child is given other items on which he must sketch in lines on an incomplete drawing to make it look just like a model printed beside it. In 6–9 this scale includes a series of rather complex geometric figures which have been rotated into a variety of positions. The task for the child on each of these items is to identify all the figures which, if they were turned around, would turn out to be identical in form. Mean scores for the 32 groups on the Spatial Relations subtest are plotted graphically in Figure 3.9.

The performance of the white children on this subtest again surpasses that of the Negro children. The results of the sex comparisons, however, differ from those found on other PMA subtests. This is the only subtest on which the white boys clearly do better than the white girls and on which the Negro girls do not surpass the Negro boys. The results for

Millfield's white children are in keeping with a large research literature that indicates that boys generally perform better on such problems. While the Negro boys do not exceed the Negro girls, their relative performance is better on this subtest than on any of the others in the battery.

Reasoning Quotients

In Form 4–6 a child is asked to solve two different types of problems. First, he is presented with groups of figures, and he must determine which *one* figure does not belong in each group. Second, he must make a similar judgment about groups of words instead of figures. Comparable word groups are used in Form 6–9, along with two new types of items. In one of the latter, a child is given various series of letters and, for each, he must determine the letter that should come next in the sequence. In a similar manner, he is also given various number series to be completed. The mean scores earned by the 16 groups at or above age eleven have been plotted in Figure 3.10.

On this scale, too, the white children's scores were significantly higher than those of the Negro children. Moreover, although only a few age levels are covered by this subtest, the Negro–white gap is larger for the older children than for the younger ones. Both older white boys and white girls tend to do better than younger white children, while the Negro girls perform at about the same level at all ages. Younger Negro boys do relatively better than older ones. These age differences, however, must be accepted with some caution, since they did not prove to be very stable statistically. It is clear, on the other hand, that there are stable sex differences for this measured ability, with girls exceeding boys quite consistently. Furthermore, there seems to be a tendency for this

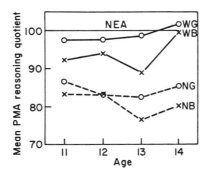

Fig. 3.10: Mean PMA Reasoning quotients for each sex of each race at four age levels (1961–62). WB = white boys. WG = white girls. NB = Negro boys. NG = Negro girls. NEA = normal expectation for age.

sex difference to be somewhat greater among the white children than among the Negro children.

CONCLUDING COMMENTS

The findings presented in this chapter reflect many of the advantages to be gained by using an analytical intellective device like the PMA in conjunction with a global instrument such as the S-B. In evaluating these racial, sex, and age effects, the many similarities between the S-B and the PMA data are obvious, but many important differences are also highlighted. Findings from the several subtests of the PMA show how misleading some of the findings in the literature on racial differences are when they are based solely upon global or composite intellective measures. The average performance of the Negro children was much lower than that of the white children on each of the tests and subtests; however, the size of this gap was dependent upon the particular measures used as well as on the sex and ages of the children being examined. At the lower age levels, for example, Negro children of both sexes fell markedly below white children of both sexes on verbal comprehension, as measured by the PMA, but at ages 13 and 14 the gap was found to be significantly narrower. This was especially true for the Negro girls, whose performance at these older age levels fell very close to that of the white boys. White girls, however, showed a decided superiority over white boys and both of the Negro groups. Older Negro boys were further behind their white age peers than were the Negro girls. On the other hand, the racial gap for some abilities (for instance, number ability) remained quite uniform over the age span tested. Little recognition of the actual complexities in the distribution of intellective abilities revealed here appears in the psychological research literature on the Negro American (see Pettigrew, 1964a).

If the assumption is made (as put forth in the PMA manual) that the S-B IQ and the PMA Total Quotient are comparable, then the differences in the present results between the mean scores from these two instruments on white and Negro boys and girls must be a reflection of the relative appropriateness of these two tests for these children. On the total white samples, the average S-B and PMA quotients are within about three points of each other: S-B, 97.8 and PMA, 94.6. The variabilities of the two sets of scores are also quite comparable (S.D. = 14.4 and S.D. = 14.2). The Negro children scored much higher on the S-B (84.6) than they did on the PMA (77.4), while the variation was narrower on the S-B (S.D. = 13.0) than on the PMA (S.D. = 14.1). As was noted earlier, the S-B permitted the test examiners to monitor the performance of each child better than they were able to do when giving the PMA battery; undoubtedly fewer invalid records escaped their detection in the S-B results. Motivation was also probably more sustained on the S-B than on the PMA. If such sources of invalidity are more frequently encountered in the Negro samples, then the S-B values would be expected to show more departures from the PMA values in their score distributions than in the values obtained from white children. If this interpretation is a reasonable one, the composite scores from the S-B are more representative of overall school potential than the composite scores from the PMA in characterizing the abilities of these Negro children.

There is a second consideration, however, that is unfortunately confounded with form of test administration. That is, the relative contribution of each of various component abilities to these composite quotients, IQ or Total Quotients, shifts from age to age (see Yates, 1967). It would help our understanding of some of these matters if we had primary ability scales that were also individually administered and monitored. The common format of group administration of the PMA in a single booklet may also contribute to the substantial positive intercorrelations found among the component scales. Lacking adequate independent tests, however, the present data are probably the best that can be obtained. They strongly suggest that the shift in component abilities over various levels of both the S-B and the PMA markedly affects the kinds of comparisons being made between racial samples by the summary IQ's or Total Quotients.

As far as sex differences are concerned, the findings are quite dissimilar for the two racial groups. For the Negro children, the performance of the girls was consistently superior to that of the boys, except on the spatial relations items. Furthermore, this sex difference among the Negro children was greater at the older ages than at the younger ages. For the white children, in contrast, there was greater overall equivalence in the performance levels of boys and girls. There were sex differentials on some of the subtests among the white children, but the girls were not consistently superior to the boys.

Age differences present a rather complicated picture. There was little support for the view that basic intellective performances of Negro children undergo a general decline during the elementary school years in comparison to white children. Global intellective indices, the IQ and Total Quotient, were lower at the upper age levels for all children in these samples *except the Negro girls*. The subtests of the PMA, however, make it clear that, while performance does show the general age pattern in some ability domains, in others the relationship with age level is reversed. Furthermore, it is necessary to specify the race and sex of the group when discussing age differences. As an example, on the PMA Verbal Meaning subtest, older white boys scored relatively below younger boys, while all the remaining groups of older children were superior to their younger counterparts.

These data also show considerable inconsistency between the S-B and PMA data with respect to the age differences in the verbal capacities of the children. For example, the S-B Vocabulary scores indicate a relatively lower performance at the older age levels for each of the four groups, whereas the PMA Verbal Meaning subtest shows superior scores at the upper age levels, except for the white boys. One likely explanation for this disparity lies in the different modes of performance required in the two tests. Thus, the S-B requires the children to express their thoughts orally, while the PMA does not. Oral expression appears to be particularly difficult for many of these children; consequently their verbal comprehension may appear to be less adequate than it really is, if the assessment is made only by means of oral tasks. This implies that the PMA verbal scores may be more dependable indices of the verbal potentials of these children than the S-B vocabulary scores.

Chapter 4

ACADEMIC ACHIEVEMENT DIFFERENCES
BETWEEN RACIAL, SEX, AGE, AND ABILITY GROUPS

A well-constructed academic achievement test, properly administered, can provide objective indices of a child's performance in a number of subject-matter areas. At the elementary school level, for instance, these tests usually measure mastery of such tool subjects as reading performance, skill in arithmetic, spelling capacity, and use of the English language. Some tests assess performance in substantive areas as well. The scores earned by a particular child on this type of test provide a basis for comparing his academic achievements with those of other children in his classroom, his age peers in his school, or elsewhere in the school system; also his work can be compared to the performance of the larger group of children who comprise the norms for the particular test. Moreover, these comparisons can be made relatively free of the intrusion of many of the factors other than achievement which inevitably influence the assignment of most grades.

In spite of the many advantages for research on educational problems derived from objective achievement tests, criticisms are being raised against the use of these devices to evaluate school progress. Objections to these tests in part are a reflection of doubts about all psychological instruments (ability, achievement, and personality tests alike) and in part derive specifically from this approach to measuring school accomplishments. It should be noted, however, that some of the criticisms now raised against testing are more properly directed against the way tests are used in some school systems, rather than against the test instrument itself. Not infrequently, for example, testers talk about their results in such a way as to create the impression that they have totally covered what is important about achievement in the schoolroom. The creators of the respected achievement tests make no such claims, however, and there is indeed no test or group of tests that is truly comprehensive in this respect. Most teachers, for instance, consider it important to teach their children ethical standards, yet there is no adequate test for measuring children's learning in this regard. The same point holds true for creativity. Most teachers believe that creative talents in their children can and should be nurtured and cultivated; they want their pupils to develop to their fullest. Standard academic achievement tests do not measure these creative sparks, nor are there serious claims that they do.[1]

The achievement test scores to be presented in this chapter can be viewed as measures of the minimal skills that any elementary school strives to teach. It should be noted that, in any use of such achievement test scores in comparative studies of this kind, the groups to be compared on their test performances should have had comparable learning opportunities on the material covered by the test. It would be meaningless, for example, to compare the spelling performances of two groups if one group had been taught to spell but the other group had not. The achievement battery used in Millfield covered only basic school skills, skills that were taught throughout the elementary school period in each of our four schools. The curriculum was very similar from school to school, showing few innovations or departures from the standard program. Furthermore, the schools operated under the same board of education, the same superintendent of schools, and the same curriculum supervisor. These facts are noted simply to suggest that, in the formal sense, the children in Millfield were being taught within the frameworks of very similar school programs. This is not to deny, however, that each school had established its own pattern, a result that seems to be almost inevitable in any school system. Nevertheless, within the schoolrooms the similarities rather than the differences in what was being taught must be emphasized.[2]

[1] Unfortunately, some individuals interested in creativity sound as though they believe that teaching children basic skills somehow cripples their creative potential. There is, of course, no evidence that being taught to read, to spell, to calculate, and so on actually has such detrimental results. That achievement should be developed in these skill areas is unquestionable; the question, really, is the way that such development should be stimulated and guided, not whether it should be fostered.

[2] We recognize that teaching skill was not necessarily equal either within or between races, but we have no measure of differential competence in this area. It is also obvious that out-of-classroom experiences can contribute to the development of the skills being measured here and that both within-race and between-race differences are known to exist in this regard.

THE STANFORD ACHIEVEMENT TEST (THIRD REVISION)

Reasons for Selecting the SAT

A number of achievement tests are available which would have been suitable for this study. Several factors influenced the ultimate decision to use the third revision of the Stanford Achievement Test (SAT).

First, achievement tests were eliminated from consideration if there was any likelihood that a significant number of the children might have had prior experience with them. Although the schools did not have resources for conducting full or regular testing programs, they were able to administer an occasional achievement battery. For these evaluations, school personnel ordinarily used either the Metropolitan Achievement Battery or the California Achievement Tests; consequently, these instruments were not considered.

In addition to equal familiarity to the children, several other attributes were desired in the test battery: (1) It should be a well-established instrument, one that had been used continuously for a number of years so that adequate norms were available and there was sufficient information about its reliability and validity; (2) the content of the test should focus upon the basic skills that were being emphasized in Millfield's schools; (3) the test should have several levels, constructed so that they would be sensitive to the entire elementary grade range that was being studied; (4) these several levels should be comparable with respect to the skills measured so that, for example, the reading achievement of the children at any age could be evaluated on the same basic scale; (5) the basic mechanics of its administration should be reasonably simple so that children would not be penalized for lack of adaptability to strange or unusual test procedures. Among the test batteries available, based on the critical evaluations made of them by experts in the field, the SAT best met the above criteria.

Levels, Content, and Norms

The SAT was published originally in 1923; it is periodically revised to ensure that its content and norms are appropriate for today's children and school programs. Each revision is published in several comparable forms so that testing with alternate forms is possible. In addition, each of the forms has several levels, scaled appropriately for the various grades. All the academic achievement testing in the Millfield study was based on Form M of the third revision of the SAT, published in 1955.[3]

---

[3] After the testing reported here had been completed, a fourth revision of the SAT was published (in 1964).

To cover the age and grade range of the children, four levels of Form M were used: Primary (grades 1–2); Elementary (grades 3–4); Intermediate Partial (grades 5–6); and Advanced Partial (grades 7–8).

Each of the above levels of the SAT contains five subtests designed to evaluate the competence of the child in the following areas: (1) understanding paragraph meanings; (2) understanding word meanings; (3) spelling; (4) reasoning arithmetically; and (5) computing. In addition, each level, except the Primary, has a language subtest designed to measure competence in the use of English. Brief descriptions of each of these subtests will be given below together with the findings.

The norms for the SAT were established after a nationwide testing program conducted in 1952. Over 460,000 children were examined in schools from every part of the country, from communities of every size, and from school systems of every sort "exclusive of pupils in segregated Negro systems" (Kelley et al., 1953). Thirty-eight states were represented among the 363 school systems participating in the program; North Carolina contributed normative data as part of the Southern region. In the final composite norms derived from this broad testing program, the scores of 104,000 school children were represented. These children were in 340 school systems, 58 of which were in the South.

It should be noted that these norms for Form M were established about ten years before the SAT was administered in Millfield. If the performance level of American school children has changed significantly during this ten-year period, comparisons of the Millfield children against the national norms will be somewhat in error. In actuality, our comparisons involve a contrasting of Millfield children as they performed in 1962 against a national sample as the latter performed in 1952. This problem is irrelevant, of course, in the racial, sex, and age comparisons *within* the Millfield group; all these children were tested within a few weeks of one another.

Administration and Scoring

The SAT was administered to the children in their regular classrooms. To prevent fatigue, the test manual indicates the number of separate test sessions that should be used at each grade level; these suggestions were followed as closely as was feasible. In addition to the chief examiner, at least one and sometimes two proctors were always present for each testing session. Although there are time limits for each subtest (except for Spelling at the Primary and Elementary levels), the limits are generous for these tasks.

As one would expect, a few children appeared to be either unable or unwilling to participate in this testing program. When an examiner or proctor identified such a child, his test record was eliminated from the study. However, less than 1% of the records had to be discarded for any reason.

A special problem was created by some children who were absent from school on the days that particular subtests were administered to their rooms. When this occurred, the examiners made every effort to test the child on these subtests in special testing sessions after he had returned to school. For a small number of children, however, such makeup sessions were impossible to arrange, and they also were dropped from the study. Thus, the data to be presented are based only upon children who completed the full test battery; there were 1155 such children examined in the late spring of 1962.

One of the virtues of the SAT is that, after a child's score on a subtest (or the total test) has been determined, various tables of norms are available so that this raw score can be converted to the particular index that is of most interest to the examiner. For instance, a child's score may be compared to that secured by all children of his grade level; to only those children of his grade level who are in the grade which they should be in, according to their chronological ages; to all children of his chronological age, irrespective of the grade they are in; and so on. Six such converted scores were computed for each pupil, but only one, the Total-Age Equivalent, was used in the analyses of the data which are reported below. This score indicates, in effect, the age level at which the child performed on the test. For example, if a 14-year-old child's accuracy in spelling words was comparable to the average score earned by all 12-year-old children in the normative sample, his Total-Age Equivalent score would be 12–0 years, or 144 months. The Total-Age Equivalent score of a 10-year-old child would also be 144 months if, indeed, he achieved the same raw score on spelling as the 14-year-old child. Using these Total-Age Equivalent scores, it is a simple matter to plot the mean scores for children (grouped by age) to show whether they are ahead, behind, or where they should be with respect to their chronological ages.

RESULTS

Correlations between Subtests

Positive correlations between scores on the several subtests of the SAT are certainly to be expected; that is, a child who does well on one subtest is also likely to do well on another, whereas a child who performs poorly on one subtest is likely to perform poorly on another. However, since intercorrelations among the subtests are not included in the test manual, we could not judge how separate and distinct each achievement area is from the others. It seemed worthwhile, therefore, to determine these interrelationships more precisely using the Millfild data.

Because the Language subtest is not part of the Primary battery, two different age groupings were employed in calculating product-moment correlation coefficients between the subtests: below age 11, and age 11 or older. The data from both white and Negro children of both sexes were combined in the calculations; in all, there were 478 children in the younger group and 480 in the older.[4] The intercorrelation coefficients for each of the two groups have been recorded in Table 4.1.

As had been anticipated, these coefficients are significant in size, ranging from a moderately low .38 to a relatively high .75, excluding correlations with the Battery Median (see below). This pattern suggests a general academic proficiency which tends to cut across the various subtests in the battery. The values are not so high, however, that they rule out individual specific accomplishments being measured by the subtests in the battery. It would seem appropriate, therefore, to employ an index of overall performance, like the Battery Median, in addition to the indices specific to each of the several tasks; this will be done in the following sections.

Before proceeding to these analyses, attention should be drawn to

TABLE 4.1

Product-Moment Correlations among SAT Scores*

	Stanford Achievement Test component scales						
Scales	PM	WM	Sp	Lg	AR	AC	BM
Paragraph Meaning		64	54	48	45	38	72
Word Meaning	75		68	49	47	45	79
Spelling	64	73		54	53	55	81
Language	—	—	—		46	48	72
Arithmetic Reasoning	62	65	63	—		72	76
Arithmetic Computation	49	53	61	—	67		74
Battery Median	83	88	85	—	80	71	

* Correlations have been computed separately for children below age eleven (below the diagonal; $N = 478$) and for those age eleven or above (above the diagonal; $N = 480$). Decimals have been omitted.

[4] These groups were subsamples of the children at these age levels who also had full intellective test scores (S-B, PMA) available in their research files. No detectable bias operated in the exclusion of the two hundred or so children with missing test data.

the fact that the coefficients in Table 4.1 tend to be larger for the younger children than for the older ones. Furthermore, the subtests tend to correlate more highly with the Battery Median for the younger children than for the older children. These findings suggest that school achievement is less clearly differentiated among the younger children; that is, those who do well in one subject also do well in most others. Among the older children, although a similar pattern exists, it is less marked. Consequently, an older child's performance level is more likely to be dependent upon the particular subtest than is true for a younger child.

Battery Medians

A composite score, called the Battery Median, was computed for each child to represent his overall performance on the SAT. This score is the midpoint in the distribution of scores that the child earned on the several subtests; half of his subtest scores were higher than his Battery Median, and half were lower. (Since all scores in the battery show a strong correlation with the Battery Median score [see Table 4.1], there is good evidence that the latter does represent general performance level quite well.) The mean Battery Median scores for the 32 subgroups have been plotted in Figure 4.1. In addition, these scores were subjected to an analysis of variance.[5]

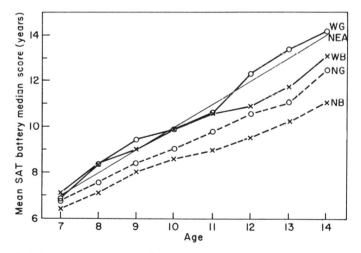

Fig. 4.1: Mean SAT Battery Median scores for each sex of each race at eight age levels (1961–62). WB = white boys. WG = white girls. NB = Negro boys. NG = Negro girls. NEA = normal expectation for age.

[5] The scores on each of the subtests were also subjected to analyses of variance; references to this fact will not be made in the sections that follow.

When the differences between white and Negro boys and girls are examined, it is clear that only the white girls meet national normative standards at all age levels. Young white boys are approximately equal to the girls, but older boys fall below the girls of comparable age. The Negro children fall below national white standards at every age level; the deficiency for both sexes is greater at the older than at the younger age levels. It is also clear that there is a sharp sex difference among the Negro children, not only at the older age levels (as with the white children) but at the younger age levels as well. Negro girls consistently outperform the boys in these classroom subjects.

Paragraph Meaning (PM)

This is the first subtest that the child confronts, whatever his age level. The format of the PM items is the same at every age level, although they become more difficult, of course, at the older ages. Each item is a paragraph with one, two, or three blanks somewhere in the component sentences. For each blank, the child is given four words, one of which is to be inserted to help complete the meaning of the paragraph. His task, then, is to select the correct word to go into each blank. The child must grasp the meaning of the paragraph in order to select the word (or words) that makes most sense in context. As the authors indicate on page three in the test manual: "Special efforts have been made . . . to make certain that the level of vocabulary is such that the test does not become one of word knowledge rather

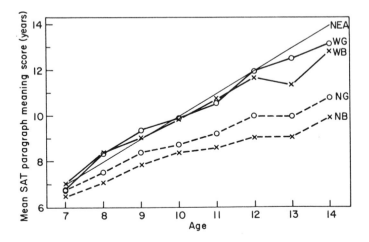

Fig. 4.2: Mean SAT Paragraph Meaning scores for each sex of each race at eight age levels (1961–62). WB = white boys. WG = white girls. NB = Negro boys. NG = Negro girls. NEA = normal expectation for age.

than of comprehension of connected discourse." The mean score earned by each of the 32 groups on the PM scale is plotted in Figure 4.2.

The pattern of the results is very similar to that described above for Battery Median scores, yet there are some divergencies which should be noted. First, although the white girls are able to read at the level expected at most ages studied, they fall below the national norms at ages 13 and 14. The white boys' performance is below that of the white girls at the upper age levels. The mean scores of the Negro children show that the girls are superior to the boys at each age level. The scores of both Negro boys and girls, however, *drop off more sharply with advancing age than is true for their total scores on the battery* (compare, for example, the curves for the Negro children in Figures 4.1 and 4.2). By age 14, the white girls are slightly less than one full year behind where they should be in reading and comprehending this type of material, while the white boys are slightly more than a year below standard. The Negro girls, at age 14, are more than three years below expectations, while Negro boys are deficient by more than four years. This means that, in grade eight, the Negro children's average reading comprehension, by national standards, is comparable to that of children in grades four and five.

Word Meaning (WM)

The second subtest that a child encounters in the SAT is Word Meaning (WM). Although similar in format to Paragraph Meaning, the emphasis in this subtest is upon knowledge of separate words, rather than comprehension of connected discourse. The authors describe the items in this way: "In addition to items measuring knowledge of synonyms, of simple definitions, and of ready associations, there are included items designed to measure higher-level comprehension of the concepts represented by words, and fullness of understanding of terms. For example, Item 3 in Form J of the Intermediate Battery reads

> Mary Smith and John Doe are cousins if they have the same
> grandmother   mother   sister   daughter

Here, obviously, is a way of testing for knowledge of the relation between 'cousin' and 'grandmother' that requires a higher order of understanding than would simple definition of either term." (Kelley *et al.*, 1953, p. 3.)

The format of this subtest is the same for each of the four test levels. The items are incomplete sentences, similar to the one quoted above. The child must select one word to complete the sentence correctly from the four which are given. Mean WM scores earned by each of the 32 subgroups have been plotted in Figure 4.3.

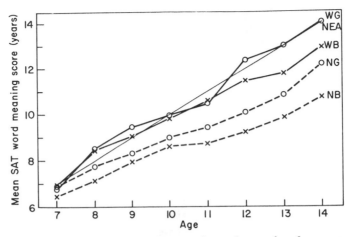

Fig. 4.3: Mean SAT Word Meaning scores for each sex of each race at eight age levels (1961–62). WB = white boys. WG = white girls. NB = Negro boys. NG = Negro girls. NEA = normal expectation for age.

It is clear that the white children do significantly better on WM than do the Negro children, and that this gap is larger at the upper age levels. Also, the Negro girls are again superior to the boys at every age level, while among the white children the girls are superior to the boys only at the upper three age levels.

Overall, of course, the pattern of results just described is very similar to that found on the PM scale. There are two differences worthy of note, however, between the results for the WM items and those for the PM items, both occurring at the upper ages. First, the white girls' mastery of word meanings matches well that of the national sample even at ages 13 and 14. Second, even though the remaining three groups fall below national norms more at the older ages than at the younger levels, this deficiency at the older ages is not as extreme as it was for the PM items. Therefore, the low scores earned by these older children on PM are not attributable entirely to an underlying lack of word knowledge. Since their knowledge of words goes somewhat beyond their capacity to understand connected discourse, the deficiency reflected in the PM scores must come in part from difficulties in grasping meanings from relationships among words.

Spelling (Sp)

A child's competence in spelling is measured by the third subtest in the battery. Unlike the two previously discussed subtests, the format at the upper levels of this one does differ somewhat from the mode at the lower levels. In the Primary and Elementary tests, the examiner pronounces a word, reads a sentence containing the word, then pronounces it again. The child either writes or prints this word in his test booklet. For the Intermediate and Advanced tests, however, a conventional multiple-choice format is used. Each item consists of a sentence or a phrase in which one word is spelled in three different ways; the child must decide if one of these three spellings is correct. Mean scores earned by each of the 32 subgroups for Spelling are plotted in Figure 4.4.

The results shown in Figure 4.4 differ markedly from those reported for the subtests considered above. The white girls still show the strongest performance; however, they score not just at the expected level but consistently above it. Moreover, at the upper age levels, the Negro girls are better than the white boys in spelling proficiency. This pattern is a distinct reversal of the relative performances of these groups as they are found at the younger age levels. Also, at each age, the Negro girls perform very close to the expected level for their age. The Negro boys continue to bring up the rear at each age level, yet it should be noted that they do relatively better at the older age levels on this subtest than they do on either Paragraph Meaning or Word Meaning scales.

Success in spelling obviously depends upon an individual's capacity for verbal memory; these data indicate that many of Millfield's children are strong in this regard. Achievement in spelling will not occur, however, unless a child is also willing to devote himself to the task; in short, even with good capacity for rote memory, he must be motivated if he

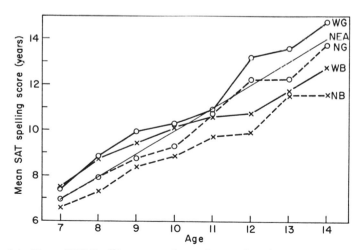

Fig. 4.4: Mean SAT Spelling scores for each sex of each race at eight age levels (1961–62). WB = white boys. WG = white girls. NB = Negro boys. NG = Negro girls. NEA = normal expectation for age.

is to succeed. Thus, these data from the Spelling subscale suggest, we believe, that Millfield girls, both Negro and white, expend effort to do well. This also seems to have been true of the younger white boys, but not equally so for the older white boys. That is, the comparatively poor performance of the older white boys probably reflects more a problem in motivation than in capacity. It may also be that motivational factors account for the increasing gap between Negro boys and girls as they grow older.

There is, we believe, another implication that can be drawn from these data. Since each of the four groups has a relatively high perform-ance level on this subtest (when compared to the group's performance on other subtests), the various findings reported in this section of the book cannot be dismissed by an easy explanation such as testing arti-facts or general lack of motivation to take tests. A general deficit in motivation to try on tests like these should result in a pattern of results for Spelling which is highly similar to the pattern of results on the other subtests; clearly this does not occur.

Language (Lg)

The fourth subtest in the battery, Language, is not included at the Primary level, since in most schools the formal aspects of English grammar and composition are not emphasized in the first two grades. The same test format is used at the Elementary and Intermediate levels, but some changes are introduced at the Advanced level. In the authors' words, "The Language Test consists of exercises in capitalization,

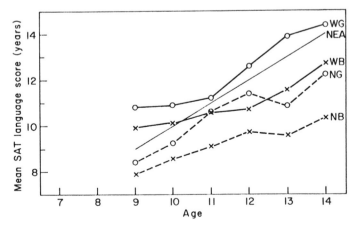

Fig. 4.5: Mean SAT Language scores for each sex of each race at six age levels (1961–62). WB = white boys. WG = white girls. NB = Negro boys. NG = Negro girls. NEA = normal expectation for age.

punctuation, sentence sense, and language usage, with a few additional items of grammar in the Advanced Battery. The exercises in capitalization, punctuation, and sentence sense are presented in connected discourse. . . . In all items a correct and an incorrect, or much less acceptable, usage are presented as options." (Kelley *et al.*, 1953, p. 4.) Mean scores earned by the 24 subgroups on this subtest are shown graphically in Figure 4.5.

The white girls again come up with a very strong performance; indeed, their mean score at each age level is above the national norms. Furthermore, the Negro boys do very poorly; their mean scores are well below expected values at all age levels, and the deficiency is largest at the upper ages so that, at age 14, they perform more than three years below where they should. Of considerable interest is the fact that the Language scores of the white boys and Negro girls are not significantly different from age 11 on. However, this is not because the Negro girls perform better at these age levels than at younger ones; rather, it is because the performance of the older white boys is much below that of the younger white boys.

Arithmetic Reasoning (AR)

The last two subtests in the SAT focus upon how adequately the child has learned to handle quantitative relationships. The first of these, Arithmetic Reasoning, is described by its authors as follows: "The Arithmetic Reasoning Test is divided into two parts. Part I measures reasoning with problems taken from life experiences. The general reading vocabulary has been kept much below the problem-solving level being measured. Computation difficulty has been controlled so that it is only a minor factor. . . . Part II tests two essential components of the ability to reason in arithmetic; namely, the informational background of pupils and their understanding of the number system" (Kelley *et al.*, 1953, p. 4).

Part I of AR contains story problems in a form familiar to almost all school children; at the Primary level, the examiner reads these problems to the children, but at the other levels the children themselves read them. Part II contains a variety of questions and problems about fractions, decimals, Roman numerals, measurement of time, formulas, and so on. The mean score earned by each of the 32 groups on these items has been plotted in Figure 4.6.

The white girls did not depart significantly from the expected level at any point along the age range. This is true for the white boys only at the younger age levels. At the older age levels, the white boys again fall behind the girls, this time by about one year, on the average. The

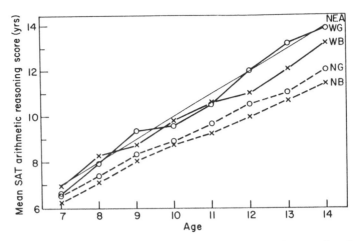

Fig. 4.6: Mean SAT Arithmetic Reasoning scores for each sex of each race at eight age levels (1961–62). WB = white boys. WG = white girls. NB = Negro boys. NG = Negro girls. NEA = normal expectation for age.

mean scores for the Negro children are consistently below those for the white children, and this gap is larger at the upper ages. Although the Negro girls consistently score above the Negro boys, there is no significant variation in the size of this differential over the age range studied.

The pattern just described for AR scores is, by now, a familiar one; however, the spread in the mean scores of the four groups at each of the age levels (particularly at the older ages) tends to be smaller on this subtest than on the scales previously considered. There is not, then, as large an absolute difference between the achievement levels on arithmetic reasoning of white and Negro children in Millfield as there is between their verbal accomplishments.

Arithmetic Computation (AC)

This second subtest in the quantitative domain—and the last subtest in the battery—covers what is probably one of the least controversial areas of school mastery: competence in handling the mechanics of arithmetic operations. Few people debate the need for knowledge of this sort; it is fundamental to a broad variety of human negotiations.

The format used for this subtest at the lower two levels is different from that used at the upper two levels. At the Primary and Elementary levels, children work problems in addition, subtraction, multiplication, and division, recording their answers on the test booklets. A multiple-choice format, however, is used with the separate answer sheet at the Intermediate and Advanced levels. At these upper levels the children must work, in addition to the types of problems noted above, problems that involve decimals, percentages, averages, fractions, the use of formulas, and so on. Mean scores earned by the 32 subgroups on these items are shown graphically in Figure 4.7.

The pattern of results for Arithmetic Computation is essentially the same as that already described for Arithmetic Reasoning. White girls score close to the expected level at each age, whereas only white boys below age 12 do as well as the girls. Furthermore, the mean scores of the white boys are never much higher than those of the Negro girls at any age level. The Negro boys consistently score lower than any of the other groups, yet the gap between their performance and that of the Negro girls does not change significantly over the age span. Finally, as with Arithmetic Reasoning scores, there is less variation among the scores of the four groups on this subtest than on the several verbal subtests.

IQ and Academic Achievement

In Chapter 3, the Negro and white children were found to differ significantly in ability, as measured by the S-B. This difference was appreciable; similar differences in achievement were anticipated. How many of the detailed findings presented so far in this chapter could have been predicted from the IQ data alone? Given the racial difference in measured ability, what is the relationship between ability and achievement in each of the several areas of schoolwork? These questions will be

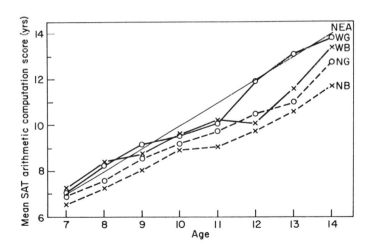

Fig. 4.7: Mean SAT Arithmetic Computation scores for each sex of each race at eight age levels (1961–62). WB = white boys. WG = white girls. NB = Negro boys. NG = Negro girls. NEA = normal expectation for age.

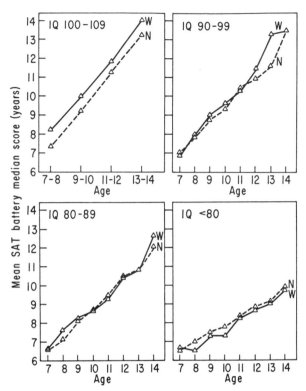

Fig. 4.8: Mean SAT Battery Median scores for white (W) and Negro (N) children at four IQ levels and various age levels (1961–62).

taken up next. More precisely, the following question is to be investigated: When Negro and white children are equated for ability level (as measured by the S-B), are there significant differences in their academic achievements (as measured by the SAT)?

The children who had been measured on both the S-B and the SAT during 1961–62 were divided into four groups according to their IQ scores: below 80, 80–89, 90–99, and 100–109.[6] Separate groups were formed for Negro and white children, but not for the two sexes, since only small sex differences had been found in the IQ data (see Chapter 3).[7] Each subgroup was then separated into eight age levels (7–14), except for children in the 100–109 IQ group. The latter were divided into

[6] Children with IQ's higher than 109 were not included, since the number of Negro children at this level was insufficient for a comparative study.

[7] Also, to have made a division based upon sex would have resulted in smaller groups than was desirable for the analyses that were made. The subgroups would have been as small as seven or eight children per cell.

four age levels, 7–8, 9–10, 11–12, and 13–14, in order to have the Negro
groups sufficiently large to provide stable means for the SAT scores.
After the above groups had been formed, their mean scores were com-
puted on the SAT measures: Battery Median, Paragraph Meaning, Word
Meaning, Spelling, Language, Arithmetic Reasoning, and Arithmetic
Computation. These means were plotted graphically, as is shown in
Figure 4.8 for the Battery Median scores.[8]

Plots of each subtest for the Negro and white children in the 100–109
IQ group are shown in Figure 4.9. Inspection of Figure 4.9 makes one
conclusion immediately obvious: the bright Negro children are not
achieving as well as the white children of comparable ability. This
differential in achievement level holds for each skill area as well as for
overall performance (see Figure 4.8 for the plot of the latter). In these
several plots, there is only one instance (at age 11–12 on the Spelling
subtest) in which the mean achievement score of the bright Negro
children is greater than that of the white children.

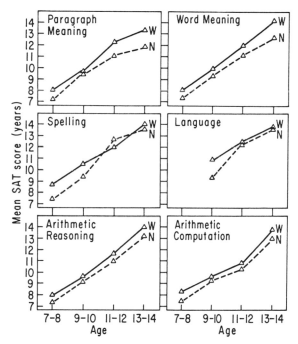

Fig. 4.9: Mean scores on six SAT subtests for white (W) and Negro (N) children
at four age levels and with IQ's between 100 and 109 (inclusive).

[8] Figures presenting comparable plots for each of the subtests are not included
here.

Figure 4.8 indicates, however, that a reverse relationship exists at the opposite end of the ability continuum. That is, Negro children whose IQ's are below 80 have total achievement scores somewhat higher than scores of white children of comparable ability. The gap is not as large as the one noted at the upper end of the ability continuum, but it does favor the Negro children consistently after age seven. Examination of the mean scores of these children on all six subtests makes it clear that most of the gap in the below-80 group plotted in Figure 4.8 results from superior performance by the Negro children on Spelling and Arithmetic Reasoning; there is no consistent racial difference in performance on the remaining subtests.

In terms of overall academic achievement, as reflected in Battery Median scores, there is no consistent racial difference for the two middle ability groups (see Figure 4.8). The same conclusion is indicated when the plots of the other subtest scores for these two middle ability groups are examined, with one exception. On Paragraph Meaning, white children at each age level in each of these ability groups score higher than the Negro children.

These findings lead to the clear conclusion that the relatively bright Negro children are underachieving in their schoolwork. This lack of full achievement for the more able Negro students may stem from the teaching efforts in their classrooms, which probably are geared to modal children with considerably lower ability levels. Such an interpretation would also be consistent with the differential in performance in favor of the Negro children at the lowest ability levels. That is, it is possible that teachers of the white children are addressing their efforts to a higher general ability level so that their slow children are not reached as effectively as are slow children in the Negro classrooms. If this explanation is correct, a situation exists which penalizes the relatively bright Negro child while giving some advantage to the dull Negro child. Among the white students, in contrast, the slower child may be the one who is penalized, comparatively speaking.

COMPARISONS WITH S-B AND PMA DATA

The general findings on the SAT resemble, of course, the findings from the intellective tests reported in Chapter 3. Since intelligence scales were designed to help teachers anticipate ultimate levels of school achievement to be expected from particular pupils, there should be a strong relationship between any good measure of capacity and a dependable measure of achievement, providing there also exist the other requisites to the development of scholastic potential: meaningful interest in learning on the part of the pupils and effective teaching on the part of the school. In the literature, the relationships reported between ability and achievement indices vary widely, from little or no parallel between potential and realization, to close correspondence between these two sets of scores. What are these relationships for Millfield's children?

Total Scores

Three composite or global measures of ability and achievement have been used in the analyses: S-B IQ values, PMA Total Quotients, and SAT Battery Medians (plotted in Figures 3.2, 3.5, and 4.1, respectively). According to the S-B data, the Negro–white gap in IQ remains essentially the same over the ages 7–14 years, although, since older Negro girls perform as well as the younger Negro girls, the differential is a little less at the upper ages. The same trends are found in the Total Quotients earned by these children on the PMA (discounting age 7 data, as noted before). The older children (white and Negro) are a little closer together on this scale than the younger ones, largely because older white children do not perform quite as well as the younger groups do. On the SAT, however, the racial gap is larger at the advanced age levels. This trend is due entirely to the strong performance of older white girls; it is clear that the gap between the white boys and the Negro children on overall achievement is about the same over the entire age range.

As far as sex differences are concerned, neither the S-B nor the PMA indicates a consistent difference in ability among the white children. On the SAT, however, at ages 12 and beyond there is a very meaningful difference in favor of the girls. The pattern among the Negro children is quite different; no consistent sex difference in ability is found below age 11, but beginning with this age the girls are consistently superior to the boys on both the S-B and the PMA. At every age level the Negro girls do better than the boys on the achievement tests, too.

Verbal Subtests

Four different scores in the three batteries reflect primarily verbal proficiency: S-B vocabulary scores, PMA Verbal Meaning Quotients, and SAT Paragraph Meaning and Word Meaning scores (see Figures 3.3, 3.6, 4.2, and 4.3). Each of these subtests used a different task to sample verbal understanding; it is important to keep this fact in mind when considering the results.

The PMA uses two methods to evaluate Verbal Meaning skill. The first of these (used in levels K–1, 2–4, and for one-half of the subtest in 4–6) is probably the simplest procedure used in the four subtests. In this task, the examiner pronounces a word and the child marks one picture in a group of four which best represents that word. On the second part of this subtest at 4–6 (and all of Verbal Meaning at 6–9), more depends upon the reading accuracy of the child. On these items he is given a stimulus word, and he selects, from a group of four words, one that means about the same thing as the stimulus word.

When the children in Millfield are required to find pictures to represent a word, the data show that the Negro children at beginning school age fall far behind the white children. On this PMA scale of essential word comprehension, however, the two groups are closer at ages 13 and 14, when the measure reflects word-to-word relationships. It is also clear that the girls, both Negro and white, do not consistently surpass the boys until the word-to-word format is introduced into the test. In other words, the racial differences are smaller but sex differences are larger on this sort of task.

The performance expected from the child on the S-B Vocabulary test is entirely oral (although he holds a printed card with the word list, the examiner also pronounces each word for him). In some ways, this task is more demanding than the word-picture matching on the PMA, since no clues to a word's meaning are given the child; however, for some children at the older ages it may be easier than the word-to-word matching, since it does not require them to read. In any event, the basic trends in the S-B data are similar to those in the PMA data with respect to both racial and sex differences. At age 7 the white children define correctly about 60% more words on the average than do the Negro children, while at ages 13 and 14 this difference is approximately 35%. Also, as in the PMA data, from age 11 on, the performance of the girls is superior to that of the boys.

The SAT data on both the Paragraph Meaning and Word Meaning scales stand in considerable contrast to those just cited. While both of these subtests sample reading skill, Paragraph Meaning requires comprehension of longer connected discourse. The tasks in the Word Meaning scale require a child to read and understand a complete sentence before he can make a correct response, but the Paragraph Meaning scale requires putting two or more sentences together. On both of these subtests the separation between white and Negro children is larger at the upper age levels than at the lower. The sex difference among the Negro children is rather consistent at all ages in favor of the girls, but this gap does not appear among the white children below age 12.

Quantitative Subtests

Three measures in these batteries involve arithmetic symbols, numerical relationships, and mathematical skills: Number Facility in the PMA, and Arithmetic Reasoning and Computation in the SAT (see Figures 3.8, 4.6, and 4.7).

As noted earlier, the PMA Number Facility subtest contains a very heterogeneous collection of items. Many items are similar to those found in the two SAT arithmetic subtests, but others involve very different tasks as well. The great similarity in the findings for the SAT Arithmetic Reasoning and Arithmetic Computation subtests may be a justification for viewing this as a single intellective domain, as the authors of the PMA have done.

The PMA results indicate that the racial differences in quantitative thinking at ages 13 and 14 are almost identical in size to those found at ages 7 and 8, although there is less separation at the intermediate years. Both the AR and AC scores, in contrast, indicate greater differences between the racial groups at the older age levels. The variation in racial differences over this age range is smaller on the quantitative scales than on the verbal ones.

CONCLUDING COMMENTS

Among white and Negro boys and girls in Millfield, only the white girls consistently measure up to national norms on a variety of academic achievement scales. The performance of the younger white boys is comparably strong, but beyond age 11 they drop below both national norms and the girls in Millfield. Since it is at about this age that boys become more resistant to school, less conforming, and less willing to apply themselves, the decrement in their achievement relative to ability probably reflects a motivational problem.

The work of the Negro boys is consistently poor, a fact that is apparent at even the younger age levels. Although the Negro girls also achieve below normative expectations—except in Spelling—they achieve at a significantly higher level than the boys in each area that was measured. On Spelling, when their measured ability level is taken into account, the Negro girls perform in an outstanding way. The fact that their scores on Spelling are so high, especially in comparison with their scores on tests like Paragraph Meaning, suggests that an emphasis upon rote memory may be characteristic of their classrooms. The data clearly indicate, furthermore, that the Negro girls are utilizing opportunities in the classroom much more effectively than are the Negro boys.

In general, the racial gap in achievement increases with advancing age, although the differences are not the same in each achievement area. It is also true that the sex difference is larger at the older age levels, although this increased separation is more sharply defined among the white children than among the Negro children. This sex difference is particularly clear among the older white children because, at age 11 and beyond, the performance of the boys is relatively inferior to that of the younger boys.

Although the ability and achievement measures are related, the data relating IQ to achievement suggest that the S-B and SAT are not measuring identical behavioral repertoires; also, that understanding of the intellective domain is enhanced when these two types of measuring instruments are used jointly. Thus, there is evidence that the more able Negro children are not achieving up to their potential, while the dull Negro children are doing somewhat better than their white counterparts. These findings suggest that the teachers of the Negro children, surrounded as they are by large numbers of children with below average ability, may be failing to meet the needs of their more able students. The teachers of the white children in Millfield, in contrast, may be similarly failing to meet the needs of their least able pupils.

Chapter 5

THE RELATIONSHIP OF SELECTED FAMILY
VARIABLES TO ABILITY AND ACADEMIC ACHIEVEMENT

As described in Chapter 2, information about the family and home background of each child was sought by means of a special questionnaire (see Appendix C) and through school files and cumulative record forms. The relationships among various aspects of the child's intellective performance and features of his background were examined systematically and the findings will be reported in this chapter. Specifically, the following variables were analyzed as they relate to scores from the Stanford-Binet Intelligence Scale, the Primary Mental Abilities battery, and the Stanford Achievement Test: (1) the geographical origin of the children's parents; (2) the educational level of the children's parents; (3) parental employment; (4) possessions and services available in the home; (5) lack of a father in the home; (6) the presence of individuals other than members of the basic family living in the home; (7) size of sibship; and, (8) ordinal position of the child.

Before proceeding, it must be understood that causality, in any direct sense, cannot be imputed to the variables that were analyzed. For example, the fact that the number of a child's brothers and sisters may relate to his IQ cannot be interpreted as meaning that size of sibship operates directly as a determinant of IQ level; indeed, it is quite possible for a whole pattern of such relationships to be generated by some other single, powerful variable. Empirical study of the nature of such relationships, however, provides some basis for making inferences about the nature of the processes that may be operating to determine

83

the dependent measures which are the focus of interest—in this instance, intellective test performances.

An additional cautionary note should be sounded about the data reported in this chapter. These variables are, clearly, limited in sensitivity and scope, only in a very rudimentary way describing how families differ one from another. They scarcely begin to reflect the many subtle, yet critically important, dynamic processes that operate within each family. These processes are extremely difficult to appraise even in a single family; the task becomes overwhelming when large numbers of families are involved. However, additional explorations into other family life processes were also attempted in Millfield; the results of these efforts are reported in Chapters 15 and 16.

SELECTION OF DATA TO BE REPORTED

Each of the above family variables was analyzed to determine how it relates to the following scores: S-B IQ, S-B MA, S-B Vocabulary, PMA Total Quotient, PMA subtest scores, SAT Battery Median, and SAT subtest scores. In addition to multivariate methods of analysis of variance, these data were plotted in graphs to depict the relationships between each of the family variables and the many scores provided by the intellective tests. Since the number of these graphs was excessive, only one figure for each family variable will be included. In these figures each family variable is related to S-B IQ levels by showing the average IQ's of white and Negro boys and girls, grouped on the basis of their common family characteristic. To construct these plots, adjacent age levels (for example, seven and eight) have had to be combined to get statistically stable groupings. These graphs provide focal points for the following discussion of each family variable; but other analyses which cannot be reported in comparable detail will often be cited also.

GEOGRAPHICAL ORIGIN OF PARENTS

It has already been shown in Chapter 1 that most of the parents in this study were born and reared either in Millfield proper or in the immediately adjacent area. However, since a number of parents were born outside this nuclear area (four counties almost touching at a common point on the northwest corner of Millfield), it was possible to study how the origin of a child's parents related to his intellective perform-

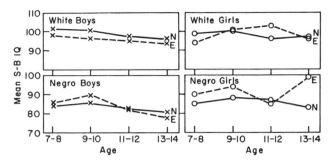

Fig. 5.1: Mean S-B IQ scores for children of each sex of each race at four age levels whose fathers were born either in the nuclear area (N) or elsewhere (E).

ance. Data relevant to this problem will be presented separately for fathers and mothers.

Fathers

For this analysis, the children whose fathers were born in the nuclear area were compared with those whose fathers were born elsewhere. The mean S-B IQ scores earned by each of the four groups at the four age levels have been plotted in Figure 5.1, separated according to father's origin.

These data indicate that white boys whose fathers were born outside the nuclear counties score somewhat lower on the S-B test than their peers whose fathers are from the nuclear area. However, this difference is not statistically significant; also, it is not found in the data for the white girls. The differential among the Negro girls is opposite to that among the white boys: Negro girls whose fathers were born outside this locality earn higher S-B IQ's than those girls whose fathers were born in the immediately surrounding area. This difference is statistically significant, yet it is not present in the data for the Negro boys.

When the S-B Vocabulary data were analyzed, the pattern of results for the white children was not discriminably different from that just described for the IQ scores. The trend in the Negro data was also like that found for the IQ scores, except that the difference between the two groups of Negro girls was less marked.

The PMA data, for both white boys and white girls, failed to show consistent relationships between father's place of birth and child's scores; this was true for the various subtest scores as well as for the Total Quotients. The Negro data, however, revealed rather consistent and sizable differences on these various scales. Moreover, the difference was as sharply defined for the boys as it was for the girls; for both sexes, the scores earned by children whose fathers were not born in the nuclear area tended to be higher.

The mean SAT scores (Battery Medians, as well as subtest scores) among the white boys consistently favored those boys whose fathers were born in the Millfield area. Furthermore, there was a definite tendency in this direction among the white girls, although it was less pronounced than among the boys. In contrast, the SAT scores of the Negro girls with fathers from outside this area were consistently superior to those of the girls with nuclear fathers; however, no appreciable difference could be noted in the scores of the two groups of Negro boys.

In summary, these data indicate that there is a modest relationship between father's place of birth and intellective performance of the child. Among the white children, this relationship is found more consistently for the boys than for the girls; also, the superiority is exhibited by children whose fathers were born in the nuclear area. Among the Negro children, a contrasting pattern emerges: the relationship is found more consistently for the girls than for the boys, and the superior performance is found among children whose fathers came to Millfield later in their lives. There is, then, a suggestion that white families migrating into Millfield may be slightly less able, on the average, than those whose origins are in this area, whereas the reverse is true among the Negro families. It is not clear, however, why these ability and achievement differences appear more strongly in a different sex group within each race.

Mothers

Intellective differences relating to the birthplaces of the mothers were analyzed in a manner similar to that reported above for the fathers. The mean S-B IQ scores earned by the various groups of children have been plotted in Figure 5.2.

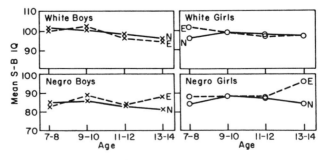

Fig. 5.2: Mean S-B IQ scores for children of each sex of each race at four age levels whose mothers were born either in the nuclear area (N) or elsewhere (E).

Inspection of this figure indicates that the mother's birthplacé shows only a slight relationship to the child's IQ; clearly, the relationships plotted here are less clear-cut than those found in the comparable data for the fathers. The largest differences occur among the Negro children and favor children with mothers born outside the nuclear area. When the data for the S-B Vocabulary scores are analyzed, a pattern very similar to that depicted in Figure 5.2 is obtained. However, the magnitude of the differences between the groups is even smaller.

The PMA data indicate a similar differential significance for mother's birthplace in the two racial groups, a conclusion that is valid for both Total Quotients and subtest scores. Thus, among the white children, with one notable exception,[1] there is no consistent difference between the scores of either boys or girls which can be related to mother's origin. Among the Negro children of both sexes, however, the scores of children with mothers born outside the nuclear area are rather consistently higher than those who have nuclear mothers. This differential is particularly pronounced in scores from the Verbal Meaning subtest of the PMA.

With respect to the SAT data, the differences are small and somewhat inconsistent from one subtest to another. This inconsistency is less pronounced among the Negro children, however, where both boys and girls who have nonnuclear mothers tend to earn the higher scores.

In summary, the data indicate that mother's birthplace is less definitely related to the child's intellective performance than father's birthplace. Also, as a variable, the origin of a child's mother has greater significance among the Negro children than among the white children. In general, Negro children with nonnuclear mothers tend to show stronger intellective performances than children with nuclear mothers.

EDUCATION OF PARENTS

Fathers

Fathers' education was broken down into two levels for statistical analyses: fathers who had completed at least part of a high school curriculum are contrasted with those who did not go beyond elementary school. The mean S-B IQ scores earned by the children of each of these two groups of fathers are shown graphically in Figure 5.3.

Children's performance on this intellective scale is related in an impressive degree to the educational histories of their fathers. The separa-

---

[1] For reasons that we do not understand, the children of mothers born outside this area scored consistently higher on the Spatial Relations subtest; this was true for the children of both races and both sexes.

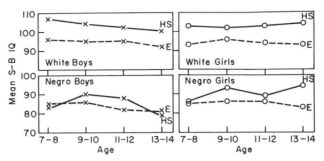

Fig. 5.3: Mean S-B IQ scores for children of each sex of each race at four age levels whose fathers either completed at least part of a high school curriculum (HS) or did not go beyond elementary school (E).

tion between the means is consistent across all four age levels among the white children, at times reaching as much as 12 IQ points. Among the Negro children at ages seven and eight, however, the level of the father's education is unrelated to the child's test performance. At later age levels the expected relationship appears, particularly in the scores of the girls, but the separation is not as large nor as consistent for the Negro children as it is for the white children.

The S-B Vocabulary scores for the white children of both sexes also were consistently higher among the children whose fathers have better educational backgrounds. Among the Negro girls the identical relationship held, although the size of the difference between the two groups tended to be less than that which was characteristic of the white children. A similar relationship was not found among the Negro boys, however; for all age levels the Vocabulary scores for the two groups of Negro boys were almost exactly the same.

The scores on the various PMA scales provided results comparable to those described above for S-B IQ scores. Thus, among the white children, for both boys and girls, the two groups were always separated, often by a large gap. The two groups of Negro girls were also consistently separated, although by a smaller amount than was typical for the white children. Among the Negro boys, however, the data were less consistent and showed only a tendency in the expected direction. On the SAT measures, the separation between children with the two types of fathers was just as consistent and stable as that described for the PMA scores; the separation among the Negro boys was even somewhat clearer.

The father's educational history is, then, very meaningfully related to his child's intellective performance. This relationship holds equally for both sexes among the white children, but it is more clear-cut in the Negro girls than in the Negro boys.

Mothers

The mothers in Millfield are generally better educated than the fathers are. Since the range of the mothers' schooling permitted a finer breakdown of educational levels for statistical analysis than was true for the fathers, as many as four different levels of education were used in the preliminary analyses. However, to facilitate direct comparisons between the analyses for parental schooling, the measured intellective performances of the children are reported in terms of the same two educational levels that were used to summarize data for the fathers: elementary school versus some part of high school (or beyond).

Mean S-B IQ scores earned by each of the groups have been plotted in Figure 5.4. This graph makes it clear that the S-B IQ scores of the white children are separated on the basis of their mothers' educational level in the same manner that was found to be true with respect to their fathers' education. Thus, those white children whose mothers have completed at least some high school work have a mean IQ at or above the national average. In contrast, children whose mothers stopped attending school before entering high school typically perform well below national norms, falling anywhere from 3 to 13 points below the level expected for their age. It is also noteworthy that the differences tend to be more clear-cut among the older groups of children. In the corresponding plots for the Negro children, there is only a slight and statistically insignificant separation between the two groups of children.[2] Nor is there any indication of a significant relationship between mothers' educational level and

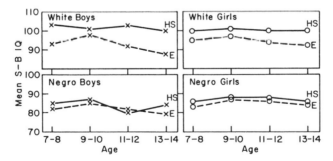

Fig. 5.4: Mean S-B IQ scores for children of each sex of each race at four age levels whose mothers either completed at least part of a high school curriculum (HS) or did not go beyond elementary school (E).

[2] A separation comparable to that shown by the white children does not appear in the plots of S-B IQ levels of the Negro children unless the group of mothers who completed high school (and perhaps had some additional work in college) is identified; only then is a significant difference found.

S-B Vocabulary scores, although there is such a relationship among the white children.

Essentially the same pattern as described above was discernible in the Total Quotients and the various component scores of the PMA battery. The mean scores of white children whose mothers have completed at least some high school work were significantly higher than those of their age and sex peers whose mothers did not go beyond elementary school.[3] In addition, as on the S-B, the mean scores of the children with the better-educated mothers tended to fall at or beyond the national norms for the PMA. These relationships were particularly clear in the data for the white boys. Within the plots for the Negro youngsters, on the other hand, performance on the PMA did not appear to reflect maternal educational levels. The means from the groupings of Negro girls tended to show a little more consistency than the corresponding plots for the boys, but the difference at any one age level seldom exceeded three quotient points. At the lowest age level (7–8), too, there was a consistent reversal for the two sexes: boys with better-educated mothers scored below their counterparts whose mothers stopped at the elementary level, while Negro girls showed the expected positive relationship with mothers' schooling on all components of the PMA battery.

The pattern present in the SAT data was highly similar to the one in the PMA data. The differences in the scores of the white children, when grouped by maternal education, were clear and dependable, although they appeared more strikingly in the boys' data than in those for the girls. The two subtests most clearly related to maternal education were Word Meaning and Paragraph Meaning, measures of reading achievement and mastery. Among the younger white children (ages 7–8), those with the better-educated mothers had an advantage on these subtests of almost a half-year over their age and sex peers who have more poorly educated mothers. This separation generally increased over the ages sampled; at ages 13–14 it measured nearly two years. The children showed almost as large a difference in spelling proficiency as they did on the reading measures when divided on the basis of maternal education. On the arithmetic scales (AR and AC), however, only the boys showed important separations when grouped in this way. Finally, in the data for the Negro children, no systematic differences could be discerned in the average performances of either the Negro boys or the Negro girls.

Mothers' education is, then, definitely related to intellective performance among the white children. Among the Negro children, this rela-

---

[3] There was one exception, at ages 11–12 and 13–14, on the Spatial Relations subtest. The mean scores of these two groups were almost identical at these ages on this measure.

tionship is much less evident. In general, father's education must be considered a more potent predictive variable than mother's education as far as the child's intellective performance is concerned.

Fathers and Mothers as Sets

Thus far, the educational histories of Millfield's mothers and fathers have been treated as separate, independently acting variables. Obviously, however, parents interact as pairs in complex ways to influence each child's development. Equally clear is the fact that the two parents may have highly similar or quite different educational backgrounds. Since data were available on parents with a wide range of educational attainment patterns, it was possible to consider the parents as forming combinations of various educational backgrounds; we shall now examine the significance of these sets as they relate to their children's S-B IQ scores.

For the purposes of this analysis, the children of each racial group were selected from two age levels: young (7–10 years) and old (11–14 years), with equal numbers of boys and girls in each group. The sets of parents for these four groups of children were separated in turn into four groups: (1) low-low (mothers with eight or less years of education and fathers with comparably low educational backgrounds); (2) high-high (mothers with at least part of a high school education and fathers with comparably high educational backgrounds); (3) low-high (mothers with eight or less years of education and fathers with at least part of a high school education); and (4) high-low (mothers with at least part of a high school education and fathers who did not go beyond elementary school). The S-B IQ data for the children were analyzed to see how these scores related to the several sets of parental educational backgrounds. Plots representing the mean S-B IQ score of each group are shown in Figure 5.5.

These data show the general finding already discussed—namely, that

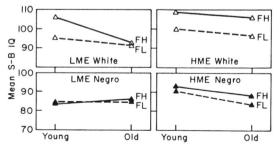

Fig. 5.5: Mean S-B IQ scores for children of each race at two age levels (young, old). Scores are plotted separately for two levels of maternal education (LME = low maternal education, HME = high maternal education) and two levels of paternal education (FL = father low, FH = father high).

the measured IQ of the children is significantly related to the educational level of both mother and father. The overall pattern, however, is quite complex. Particularly important is the pattern in the plots for the Negro children: if the mother has only elementary education, her children, on the average, score low on this intelligence scale, regardless of the educational level of the father or the age of the child. Negro mothers who have an education beyond the elementary level, however, have children whose intellective performance varies directly with the educational level of their fathers. The corresponding plots of the data for the white children indicate that a low mother's educational level is not a conditional factor in the same way, except in the scores from the older group. From these plots of data from the white families, it also appears that father's educational level is more predictive than mother's as far as the intellective standing of their offspring is concerned. In three of the four subgroups of white children whose fathers had at least part of a high school education, the average IQ value exceeds 105. However, the fourth group, composed of older children whose fathers had at least some high school work but whose mothers went no higher than the elementary level, performs on the average closer to 90 on the S-B IQ scale.

In summary, all four factors considered in plotting these data (race, age, maternal education, and paternal education) are relevant; the relationship of each to measured IQ depends in important degrees upon the other three. Furthermore, the special significance of low education in Negro mothers in relation to the measured intellective capabilities in their offspring appears clearly only in this complex analysis of the data.

EMPLOYMENT OF PARENTS

This section takes up the relationship of parental employment patterns to the intellective performances of the children. For fathers, the focus will be upon the differences in the intellective scores between children whose fathers exclusively farm for their livelihood and those whose fathers follow some other calling even though they may do some farming. For the mothers, a contrast will be made between children whose mothers are employed outside of the home and those whose mothers are not so engaged.

Fathers

Only a few fathers in Millfield are totally unemployed, although much work is seasonal and some is only part-time. There are many different kinds of work, but by far the most frequent full-time occupation is farming. The only subclassification that could yield stable statistical data to relate type of father's work to various intellective measures of the children, therefore, was one in which children whose fathers were full-time farmers were compared to children whose fathers were not full-time farmers. The children were grouped on this basis, and both their ability and achievement scores were analyzed. Mean S-B IQ scores earned by the various groups have been plotted in Figure 5.6.

Among the white children, mean IQ scores are higher for those with fathers who work at some nonfarming job. This is especially true for the boys; at the older age levels it is also true for both boys and girls. Among the Negro children, however, there is essentially no difference in the mean IQ's of the two groups of children. Also, when the S-B Vocabulary scores are plotted, there are only very slight differences between the two groups; this is true for both races and both sexes.

The same pattern depicted in Figure 5.6 for the white children was even more pronounced in the plots of PMA Total Quotient scores. Moreover, there was also some separation in the scores of the Negro children, particularly the Negro girls, with the children of nonfarming fathers earning the higher mean scores. The subtest scores, too, tended to favor the children of nonfarming fathers; again, the differences were more marked among the white than among the Negro children.

The patterns for the several SAT scores were highly similar to those for the PMA scores. Among the achievement data for the white children, however, there was one exception to this conclusion. At ages seven and eight, the average achievement scores of the children from farm families were consistently higher than those of children from nonfarm families; this was true for both boys and girls. It is especially interesting that this achievement differential appeared among the white boys, since, as indicated in Figure 5.6, there were no differences in measured ability at

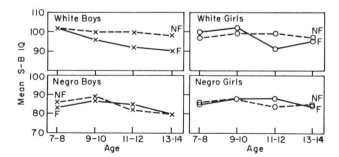

Fig. 5.6: Mean S-B IQ scores for children of each sex of each race at four age levels whose fathers were either full-time farmers (F) or had some nonfarm income (NF).

these ages. More intensive studies are needed to discover both why such an ability-achievement differential occurred and why it did not hold up at the older age levels.

In general, the evidence suggests that the type of employment of the father is related to his child's intellective proficiency. This relationship is more clear-cut among the white children than among the Negro children; it is also sharper for the white boys than for the white girls. (White boys whose fathers farm full-time are especially likely to do poorly on intellective tasks.) Finally, this relationship between a father's work and his child's intellective performance is one which, among the white children at least, tends to grow stronger with advancing age of the children.

Mothers

For this analysis, groups of children were formed on the basis of whether their mothers were currently working outside the home, either part-time or full-time.[4] (Unfortunately, more complete work histories for the mothers were not obtained; hence, the possible impact of the mother's working during the early preschool years could not be evaluated.) The relevant mean IQ scores of the various groups have been plotted in Figure 5.7.

The IQ scores plotted in Figure 5.7 show a slight superiority among the white children for those whose mothers are employed. The difference

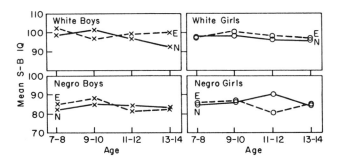

Fig. 5.7: Mean S-B IQ scores for children of each sex of each race at four age levels whose mothers were either employed outside of the home (E) or were not so employed (N).

[4] It should be recalled that the percentages of Negro and white mothers in Millfield who work outside the home are about equal (see Chapter 1). However, proportionately more white than Negro mothers work full-time. There is also a major difference in their types of work: Negro mothers are employed almost exclusively in domestic service, while white mothers most commonly find employment in mills or factories.

is small, however, and cannot be regarded as very meaningful. Among the Negro children, there is no consistent difference between the two groups, either for boys or for girls. And, when the S-B Vocabulary plots, PMA plots, and SAT plots were inspected, the differences were found to be no greater than those depicted in Figure 5.7.

As a predictive variable, therefore, knowledge of a mother's current employment status appears to have little value as far as the child's on-going intellective performance is concerned. Clearly, however, there is little reason to believe that a child's intellective development is adversely affected in this rural area by having a mother who works outside the home.

POSSESSIONS AND SERVICES

As reported in Chapter 1, Millfield's families differ appreciably in the possessions they own: real estate, cars, TV sets, telephones, and so on. To some extent, at least, the availability of these resources is indicative of the general economic well-being of the home. Is the economic level of a family, measured in such terms, related to the intellective performance of its children?

Families were classified with respect to the presence or absence of each of the above four possessions.[5] The mean scores of the children on the several intellective tests were, in turn, plotted with reference to the presence or absence of these items (or services) in their homes. The breakdown on car ownership and possession of TV sets yielded only small, unstable samples in several of these subgroups; consequently, these data are not reported. The data for home ownership and possession of telephone service provided statistical breakdowns that were stable; relevant findings are discussed below.

Home Ownership

Although white families in Millfield own or are buying their homes more frequently than are Negro families (see Chapter 1), home ownership is also reasonably common among the Negro parents. Mean IQ scores earned by the various groups of children who come from families who own or are buying their homes are plotted in Figure 5.8, as are the mean scores of children who come from families who rent their homes, either by monthly cash payments or by sharing the crops raised on the land.

[5] In the total study, the availability in the homes of many other physical and cultural resources was studied. Many of these additional data must be left unreported.

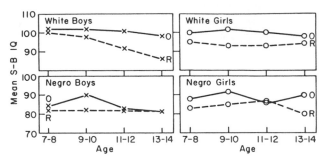

Fig. 5.8: Mean S-B IQ scores for children of each sex of each race at four age levels whose families either own their homes (O) or rent (R).

The separation in IQ scores is more clear-cut among the white children than among the Negro children. In both races, however, children from families owning their own homes perform higher on this ability test than do children from families who rent. This differential is found at both the younger and the older age levels and for both sexes. When the S-B Vocabulary plots were studied, furthermore, similar results were observed.

The PMA plots also revealed consistently superior scores for the white children whose families own their homes. Thus, for the plots of the Total Quotient scores as well as those for the various subtests there was only a single instance in which a mean score for children from home-owning families was lower than that for children of the same age level from families who rent. Among the Negro children such crossovers were more frequent, and the gap between the children from the two types of families was less than that found among the white children. In general, though, the same advantage fell to the Negro children from families who own their homes.

The SAT scores were more sensitive than the PMA scores in reflecting the advantage of the children from home-owning families. This conclusion holds for both races, although again the gap was larger among the white children. There were no crossovers in the plots of the white children, either for Battery Median scores or for subtest scores; moreover, there was only one small reversal in the several plots for the Negro children. Another trend in these data should also be noted—namely, that the differential between the two groups tended to grow larger with advancing age. This trend was evident in the data for boys and girls of both races.

It is clear, then, that home ownership can function as a predictive variable with reference to the children's intellective performance; this is especially true among the white children. For the Negro children, home ownership was more consistently related to performance on achievement tests than on ability tests.

Telephone Service

When the children are grouped on the basis of whether their families subscribe to telephone service, the separations are larger and more stable than those described above for home ownership. Of the indices studied, subscribing to telephone service appeared to be the single best index of economic status.

Mean IQ scores for the several groups of children, separated with respect to the availability of telephone service in their homes, are shown in Figure 5.9. Examination of these plots reveals considerable consistency across racial, sex, and age groups. Clearly, those families who subscribe to telephone service have children who perform, on the average, at higher levels than children from homes without this service. The magnitudes of the differences are greater within the white than within the Negro samples.

The plots for the S-B Vocabulary scores, PMA scores, and SAT scores were very similar to those shown in Figure 5.9. In all the graphs for the white children, there were no crossovers; children from families with telephone service always earned higher mean test scores than their age-mates from families without this resource. Among the Negro children, there were only three crossovers in these 22 plots, two on PMA subtests and one on the plots of S-B Vocabulary scores. Except for these three crossovers, Negro children with telephone service in their homes always earned higher mean scores than children of the same age without telephones in their homes.

The finding that having a telephone in the home is related to high intellective proficiency may seem puzzling to many parents (especially

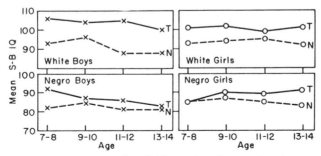

Fig. 5.9: Mean S-B IQ scores for children of each sex of each race at four age levels whose families either have telephone service (T) or do not (N).

those of early adolescents) who probably would swear that hours on the telephone cut into study time seriously. Obviously, however, no causal relationship either way can be inferred from this type of data. (For example, the differences in intellective performance show up at the younger as well as at the older age levels, suggesting that actual telephone usage is probably not at issue.) Rather, the presence of a telephone is better interpreted as an indication of the general socioeconomic position of the family.

SOME CHARACTERISTICS OF FAMILY STRUCTURE

The factors reported above reflect the general status of each family unit in this community, a set of circumstances which may be expected to affect most members of the family. The experiences that any one child may have within a family are more difficult to assess; probably they are determined in part by factors like the size of his family, the presence or absence of siblings, the child's ordinal position, relatives living in the home, and so on. Data showing the significance of several such variables will be examined below.

Father Absence

In recent studies and critiques, investigators have emphasized the importance of father absence as a factor contributing to the poor school performance of Negro children, especially boys. Although father-substitutes are fairly common among both the Negro and white families of Millfield, there are relatively few families without someone serving as a father-figure. Because of this limitation, no stable trends reflecting the significance of a fatherless home can be determined from the Millfield intellective data. The limited data available were inspected, though, to see if any tentative trends could be identified; they did not suggest any relationship between intellective performance and family dislocations of this sort. For example, the single brightest Negro boy in the entire study (as determined by the S-B) was from a fatherless home, while eight of the nine dullest boys were from intact homes; the other boy had a father-substitute in his home. There was a similar lack of support for this relationship in the data for the Negro girls and for both sexes among the white children.

Family Type

Each child's family was scrutinized to determine whether individuals who were not members of the basic family were living in his home; if

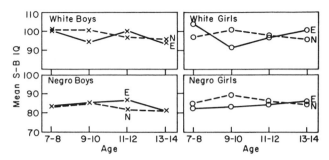

Fig. 5.10: Mean S-B IQ scores for children of each sex of each race at four age levels from either extended (E) or nonextended (N) families.

they were, the family was classified as an extended family (see Chapter 1). The intellective performances of children from extended and non-extended families were tabulated separately, and mean values computed. The results of these analyses for IQ scores are plotted in Figure 5.10.

As Figure 5.10 suggests, IQ scores for the white boys tend to be higher when the boys are members of nonextended families. The overall differences are small, however, and do not appear at every age level. Differences on the S-B Vocabulary were more consistent, favoring the white boys from nonextended families. The several PMA plots, in contrast, showed the same rather inconsistent pattern evident in the plot of the IQ scores. It was striking, then, to discover that on the SAT there were clear and stable differences: on each subtest, as well as for the Battery Median scores, white boys from nonextended homes achieved more adequately at each age level than boys from extended families. Thus, it is their academic achievements rather than their measured ability levels which appear to be most meaningfully related to this dimension of family life.

Negro girls from nonextended families also tended to score higher mean IQ's than girls from extended families; indeed, as Figure 5.10 indicates, this differential was slightly more stable among the Negro girls than among the white boys. On the remaining intellective measures (S-B Vocabulary, PMA, and SAT), the differences also tended to favor the Negro girls from nonextended families. In general, however, the gap was smaller than that present in the plot of the IQ scores, and there was only moderate consistency in the data from the four age levels. (The differences in the SAT data were much less sharply marked than they were in the comparable data for the white boys.)

Among the white girls, the difference between the two groups was very small on each intellective measure and quite unstable from one

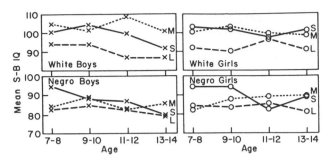

Fig. 5.11: Mean S-B IQ scores for children of each sex of each race at four age levels from families with either one or two children (S = small), three or four children (M = medium), or five or more children (L = large) in the home.

age level to another. The data for the Negro boys also showed small differences between the two groups; however, when a trend appeared for any score, the difference *favored* the boys from the extended families.

The indication, then, is that an extended family setting may be especially unfavorable as far as the intellectual proficiency of the white boys is concerned. This factor also tends to have negative implications for the Negro girls, although perhaps not as strongly as for the white boys. Its implication for the white girls appears to be negligible, while for the Negro boys it actually seems to be slightly positive.

Size of Sibship

Another index of family composition which provides some indication of the nature of the child's home environment is the size of the sibship in which he is being raised. We considered several different ways of assessing this characteristic: (1) the total number of their own children reported by the parents; (2) the total number of their own children now in the home; (3) the number of children in the home, regardless of their relationships to the child's parents or their ages; and (4) the number of children in the household under the age of 18, whether related or not to the child in question. Use was made of this last index, since it promised to reflect the extent to which current parental attention may be diluted by the functional sibship now in the home. Thus, if older children were reported who were not living at home, or who had passed their eighteenth birthday, they were not included in the count of sibship size. Nor was account taken in this index of other adults, related or not, currently living in the home. The child himself, however, was included in the count. For tabulating and analyzing the data, the sibships were divided into three groups: (1) small sibships (one or two children);

(2) medium sibships (three or four children); and (3) large sibships (five or more children in the home).

Mean IQ scores earned by children from these three sizes of sibships have been plotted in Figure 5.11. Another way of demonstrating these relationships has been used in Figure 5.12. Here the data from the several age levels have been collapsed and the *median* values of each subgroup determined. Also, four sizes of sibships have been used (data from singletons have been plotted separately).

Inspection of Figures 5.11 and 5.12 reveals that children from large sibships perform much more poorly on this IQ measure than do children who are from small or medium sibships. This is true for children of both races and both sexes, although it is more marked among the white children, especially the white boys. Furthermore, essentially the same patterns were observed in the plots of the S-B Vocabulary, PMA, and SAT scores. It should be noted, however, that in the Negro samples there were relatively few children represented in the small sibships; consequently, the averages for these groups cannot be regarded as very stable.

In general, there is little difference among sibships that number between one and four in size. Children from larger sibships, however, are likely to perform less well on both ability and achievement tests than are their age-mates from smaller families. And, as a dimension of family structure, the implication of this variable for intellective proficiency appears to be greater for the white children than for the Negro children. For example, white children from sibships numbering between five and eight have a median IQ about 12 points below that of children from sibships numbering between two and four. The corresponding difference among the Negro children is only about four IQ points. More-

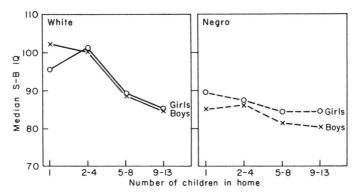

Fig. 5.12: Median S-B IQ scores for children of each sex of each race from families with various numbers of children at home.

over, when even larger sibships (between nine and thirteen) are examined, the median IQ score of the white children is even lower, whereas there is essentially no difference between the comparable scores for the Negro children (see Figure 5.12).

Ordinal Position

Since the children in the study come from a wide range of sibship sizes, there are many different birth-order positions among them. When they are separated into groups of white and Negro boys and girls, however, the numbers in some of these positions are not sufficiently large to provide stable measures of average intellective performance. In the analyses presented below, therefore, the children have been classified simply as being the youngest, the oldest, or in an intermediate position in their sibships.[6]

The mean IQ scores earned by the various groups are shown in Figure 5.13. These plots for the white boys are, in general, representative of those found for them on the other intellective measures (S-B Vocabulary, PMA, and SAT). Thus, for these boys, ordinal position is more clearly related to performance at the older age levels than at the younger age levels. At each age level, however, the lowest mean scores tend to be earned by the white boys who occupy intermediate positions in their sibships. Also, especially at the upper age levels, the first-born boys consistently earn the highest averages.

The patterns on the several tests for the white girls are similar to those just reported for the white boys, yet there are some differences. For one thing, ordinal position has a more pronounced relationship to ability over the entire age range than is true for the white boys. Particularly

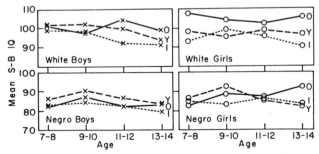

Fig. 5.13: Mean S-B IQ scores for children of each sex of each race at four age levels who occupy the oldest (O), youngest (Y), or an intermediate (I) position in their sibships.

[6] Singleton children, few in number, were arbitrarily assigned to the category of oldest children.

striking is the fact that first-born girls earn the highest averages at each age level on each of the measures. White girls in intermediate positions tend to score lower than last-born girls, but this difference is both small and somewhat inconsistent.

For the Negro boys, the prevailing pattern departs sharply from those just described for the white children. Thus, the Negro boys occupying the youngest position almost always earn the highest averages on these intellective scales. This superiority is more evident, however, on the ability than on the achievement tests. Consistent with the data for the white children is the finding that, on both types of intellective measures, Negro boys in intermediate positions tend to earn the lowest scores.

The pattern appearing in the Negro girls' data appears to be a composite of those described for the white children and the one just reported for the Negro boys. Thus, at the two lower age levels Negro girls in the youngest position tend to exhibit the strongest performances, while at the two upper age levels girls in the oldest position tend to do best. Overall, Negro girls in intermediate positions lag behind their age-mates in the other two positions, but the data are somewhat inconsistent in this regard.

It is clear, then, that a child's ordinal position is related to his intellective performance. It is also apparent that the precise nature of this relationship varies with race, sex, and even age of the child. In general, however, the intermediate position appears to have especially unfavorable implications. Among the white girls, the older white boys, and the older Negro girls, the advantage clearly appears to be with children born first into the family. In contrast, among the Negro boys and the younger Negro girls, the advantage rests with children who are the last ones born to their parents.

CONCLUDING COMMENTS

The general expectation that family variables would be significantly related to the intellective proficiency of the children has been, we believe, amply confirmed by the data which have been presented and discussed. Since the significance of certain variables is sometimes dependent upon the race, sex, and age of the child, however, the overall pattern is a complex one. The implications of the findings are even more impressive in light of the relative homogeneity among Millfield's families. This is particularly true, for instance, with respect to a variable like father's education. If the fathers represented a wider range of educational attainment, the relationship between this variable and the children's intellective characteristics might be stronger than it is. Nevertheless, as we have seen, the relationship between these two variables is a substantial one.

Another aspect of this interfamily homogeneity may relate to the finding that the strength of the relationships between family variables and the children's intellective performance are higher among the white pupils than among the Negro pupils. The fact that the Negro families are more homogeneous than the white families on a number of the variables studied means that the relationships are more difficult to assess for the Negro sample with the present instruments and methods. There are also some additional considerations that may influence some of these relationships. For example, a particular value on a variable like mother's education may not have equivalent meaning among the Negro and white populations as far as actual educational achievement is concerned. Thus, a Negro mother who completed the tenth grade *may* be closer in actual educational achievement to a Negro mother who completed the seventh grade than would be true for two white mothers with similar educational histories. If such a difference in schooling were present, then it is likely that the relationship between mother's education and children's intellective proficiency would show up more strongly in data from the white group.

The analyses suggest that the following family variables are particularly important with respect to children's intellective performance: father's education, mother's education, father's work, home ownership, telephone service, size of sibship, and ordinal position in the family.[7] Less contributory, apparently, are the geographical origins of either parent, whether or not the mother is employed outside the home, father absence, and the presence of other adults in the family. On some of these latter variables, the lack of significance in the findings may be in part attributable to restrictions in the kind of data available. Thus, information about mother's employment during the earlier, formative years of the child's development was not obtained. Also, the incidence of fathers being absent from the home without some surrogate figure being present was found to be too low to generate stable findings.

While each of the variables studied clearly is of interest in its own right, it is also legitimate to consider whether the findings may not be subsumed under some more encompassing concept. Thus we would suggest that most of these findings correspond quite well with the hypothesis that the intellective proficiency of the children is positively correlated with the socioeconomic status of the family from which they come.

---

[7] Several of these variables are more markedly related to intellective performance among the white children than among the Negro children.

Pupils whose parents are better educated, whose fathers have obtained some position outside of farming, whose parents are able to buy their own homes and subscribe to services such as telephones, and whose parents have had relatively few children do better on tests of ability and achievement than do less favored children.

We should also note briefly several findings highlighted in this investigation which need a great deal of more intensive study. First, the stability of each finding should be verified by means of similar studies of other samples. In addition, the data indicated that the family variables are more closely related to the intellective characteristics of the white boys and Negro girls than to the other two groups. We are not certain, however, why this sex difference—opposite in direction within the two racial groups—should appear; consequently, additional studies of the phenomenon would seem to be indicated.

Overall, there is a great deal of consistency between the ability and the achievement tests in the sense of how scores on them relate to family variables. On occasion, however, the achievement measures are more highly and consistently related to family variables than the ability measures. Such findings suggest, of course, that, despite high inter-correlations among ability and achievement scores, it would be incorrect to view these two types of tests as tapping precisely the same intellective domains. These findings also suggest the need for deeper and more comprehensive study into the problem of how and why particular family variables differentially affect behaviors of the sort that are evaluated by these tests.

Another provocative finding is that white children from farm families show better academic achievement than do children from nonfarm families during their initial one or two years in school, after which this relationship is reversed. It may be speculated that farm families tend, in general, to develop greater readiness in their children as they approach the school years and to insist upon the children applying themselves to their studies more intensively than is true in nonfarm families. Very soon, however, the many restrictions present in farm life may begin to have detrimental effects on the children's achievements. Again, more extensive studies of this finding need to be made.

It has been pointed out in several places that the family variables are more highly correlated with intellective proficiency among the white children than among the Negro children. It was also suggested that, at least in part, this fact may be traceable to greater homogeneity among the Negro people. Other possible explanations should certainly be considered, however. It may be, for example, that there are significant differences between Negro and white families with respect to how

parents interact with their children and the ways that they thus affect
or influence them. One of the important needs now is intensive study of
the informal processes used by such families to teach their children.
Also, we need to learn much more about dynamic, emotional factors
within the family, as these factors influence the intellective development
of the children.

Part III

INTELLECTIVE CHANGE

Chapter 6

CHANGES IN IQ AMONG YOUNG NEGRO CHILDREN

The purposes of this chapter are threefold: (1) to describe and evaluate the changes in the functioning intelligence of the Negro children over a three-year span during their early elementary school years; (2) to identify behavioral characteristics of the children related or unrelated to these changes; and (3) to examine family and school factors which may be correlated with changes in measured ability.

In Chapter 3, mean values were reported on the Stanford-Binet Intelligence Scale (S-B; 1960 Revision) for Negro boys and girls (see Figure 3.2). In these two curves summarizing the children's performances, it was not clear whether there was a significant IQ change between the ages of seven and ten. Judging by these cross-sectional data from the Negro children during this age period, there seems to be a tendency for the mean scores to be higher at the older age levels. Moreover, this tendency appears to be stronger among the Negro boys than among the Negro girls. Both of these trends were in marked contrast to findings by other investigators reported in the recent literature. A short-term longitudinal study covering this age period would be helpful, then, in defining the form of intellective growth that may be validly ascribed to the Negro children during this developmental period.

PROCEDURE

This study began in the fall of 1964 with the identification of all Group 1 (i.e., age seven) children from the 1961–62 S-B testing program

109

who were still attending the two Negro schools. These children had been in the first grade in 1961–62; most of them were now in the fourth grade. Of the original 78 children (39 boys), there were 57 (29 boys) who were still in the schools *and* who had been tested on the S-B in 1961–62.[1] All 57 of these children were retested on the S-B in 1964–65 and constitute the sample for this short-term longitudinal study of ability change.

The children were originally tested by two female Negro examiners. One of these women was still on the staff; therefore, it was possible to have her retest the same children (28 in number) whom she had tested in 1961–62.[2] Since the remaining children had been tested initially by a second female Negro examiner who was no longer on the staff, they were assigned to another female Negro examiner who had since joined the project.

After the S-B retesting had been completed, several kinds of data pertaining to the personal and family characteristics of each child were compiled from our files. These data had been collected earlier and, of course, were not influenced by knowledge of the subsequent course of intellective development taken by any child. These data permitted assessment of the extent to which certain personal and family characteristics of a child were correlated with his change in measured ability during this age period.

AGES AND INITIAL S-B IQ'S

As summarized in Table 6.1, the children ranged from age six to slightly more than seven years at the time of the first S-B testing; their mean age was about six and one-half years. At the second testing, the ages ranged from approximately nine to slightly beyond ten years; their mean age was now a bit more than nine and one-half years. Except for three children (all boys), at least three years elapsed between the two assessments; the intervals for these three boys were within three months of this same time span.

In average ability level at the time of the first test, these children are closely comparable to the total sample of Negro children (see Chapter 3). Thus, as shown in Table 6.1, the initial mean S-B IQ scores for both boys and girls are within 1.5 points of 85. Moreover, the initial mean scores of the boys and girls are separated by only one-half point.

---

[1] There were five first-grade children (three boys) in 1961–62 who, for a variety of reasons, were not tested during that year on the S-B.

[2] This retesting was done without the examiner reviewing her earlier test protocols.

TABLE 6.1

Age and S-B IQ Data for the Negro Retest Children

| | | School year | | | | Differences | |
| | | 1961–62 | | 1964–65 | | | |
	N	Mean	Range	Mean	Range	Mean	Range
Age at S-B							
Testing							
(in months)							
Boys	29	78.5	72–89	115.8	110–123	37.3	33–40
Girls	28	80.4	73–85	118.2	109–124	37.8	36–40
Boys*	7	78.0	75–81				
Girls*	9	78.2	72–84				
S-B IQ's							
Boys	29	83.5	68–100	81.6	64–108	−1.9	−26 to +15
Girls	28	84.0	67–103	84.8	66–113	+0.8	−11 to +13
Boys*	7	79.7	66–96				
Girls*	9	85.2	75–100				

* Children who were given the S-B in 1961–62 but who were unavailable for retesting in 1964–65.

Table 6.1 also contains data on the seven boys and nine girls in Group 1 who were tested on the S-B in 1961–62 but who were unavailable for retesting in 1964–65. The data do not suggest that these children, most of whom had moved elsewhere, differ in any meaningful way in either age or ability level from the children who constitute the sample being studied.

STABILITY OF THE IQ

Table 6.1 also gives the mean IQ scores earned by both boys and girls on retesting, as well as the mean differences in the scores for the two occasions. A separate tabulation of the frequencies of various IQ changes is presented in Table 6.2, separately for boys and girls.

Neither the boys nor the girls changed very much during this three-year period in average intellective performance.[3] The boys lost about two IQ points, while the girls gained approximately one point. Thus, the sex difference widened over the period by almost three IQ points. Furthermore, these longitudinal data suggest that the slope of the curve in Figure 3.2 is essentially correct for the girls during this age period,

[3] A chi-square analysis indicated that sex is not significantly related to IQ change.

TABLE 6.2

Frequencies of S-B IQ Changes for Negro Children, 1961–62 to 1964–65

Change in IQ	Boys	Girls
15–19	1	
10–14	2	6
5–9	4	4
1–4	5	3
0	2	2
(−1)–(−4)	5	3
(−5)–(−9)	6	7
(−10)–(−14)	0	3
(−15)–(−19)	2	
(−20)–(−24)	1	
(−25)–(−29)	1	
N	29	28
Mean	−1.9	+0.8

but that the slope for the boys should reflect a slight decrement rather than an increment.

Examination of Table 6.2 reveals a sizable number of children who shift meaningfully in IQ, while other children hold steady. The increments about balance the decrements, though, so that the overall group mean is changed only slightly. If a change of five or more IQ points is regarded as a significant shift (any such cutting point is to some extent arbitrary), then approximately 30% of the children show a meaningful gain, 35% hold even, and 35% reflect a loss. Both boys and girls are found about equally often in the gain and loss columns, yet it is of interest to note that the largest changes, both positive and negative, are found among the boys. No girl's IQ changed by more than 13 points, but five boys changed 15 or more points.

To assess IQ stability, separate product-moment correlation coefficients between the 1961–62 and the 1964–65 scores were computed for the boys and girls. The value of this correlation coefficient for the boys is .62; for the girls it is .77. This sex difference is not statistically significant. Although both coefficients are highly significant, they do *not* justify the conclusion that no meaningful changes in the ordering of the children have occurred.

Significance of Initial IQ

It is of interest to determine whether change in IQ is related significantly to the ability level of the child, as the latter was originally measured in 1961–62. To study this question, the boys and girls were separately partitioned into three ability levels based upon their initial

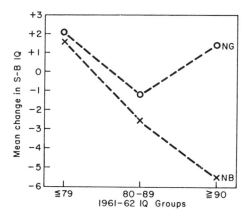

Fig. 6.1: Mean change in S-B IQ from 1961–62 to 1964–65 for Negro boys (NB) and Negro girls (NG) at three initial ability levels.

S-B IQ's. Children in the lowest two groups had initial IQ's of 79 or below; those in the two middle groups had IQ's between 80 and 89; and those in the highest two groups had IQ's of 90 or above. There were between seven and eleven children in each of these six subgroups. The mean IQ change score for each of these six groups is plotted in Figure 6.1. Product-moment correlation coefficients were also computed between the 1961–62 IQ scores and the change scores, again separately for the two sexes. These values were: for the boys —.26, and for the girls —.01. Neither coefficient is significantly different from zero.

The plots in Figure 6.1 are difficult to interpret. The trend for the boys' data suggests statistical regression toward the mean. That is, boys, whether high or low on first testing, shift toward the group mean on the second testing. The plot for the girls, however, does not follow that pattern; girls who were high originally were even higher when they were retested. Actually, the variability among the change scores within each group was so great that little in the way of accurate prediction of IQ change for individual children is possible simply from knowledge of their original IQ scores.

BEHAVIORAL CORRELATES OF IQ CHANGE

Attention was also directed to the problem of whether certain behavioral characteristics relate significantly to the growth or decline of the children's intellective powers during their early school years. Is it possible to differentiate first-grade Negro children with respect to their social and motivational behaviors and, in so doing, define a basis for predicting the subsequent course of their intellective development, as measured by the S-B?

This inquiry had two components. The first study made use of teachers' perceptions—how teachers view their pupils after working with them for one academic year. Do such impressions, recorded in the form of ratings, correlate with IQ change? The second study was concerned with the achievement motivation of the children as inferred from stories that the children told to a series of pictures. Is achievement motivation, so measured, related to IQ change?

Teachers' Ratings

In May of 1962, at the end of the school year, each child was rated by his teacher on a series of 22 behavior rating scales.[4] In May of 1964, the children were rated again on the same scales, but, of course, by different teachers. Three teachers rated approximately equal thirds of 56 of the first-grade children in 1962; a fourth teacher rated the 57th child. Again in 1964, three teachers had most of the third-grade children divided about equally among them. By this time, however, nine children in the original first-grade groups had been separated from the three main groups; among them, they were rated by three other teachers.[5]

Inspection of the teachers' ratings revealed that they sometimes used the graphic scales in different ways; that is, on occasion teachers used different portions of a scale when evaluating the same behavior trait. It was decided, therefore, to compute biserial correlation coefficients (r_{bis}) between IQ change, treated as a continuous distribution, and each of the 22 behavior ratings, treated as dichotomies. For the latter, each teacher's distribution of ratings was formed for each of the 22 traits; medians of these distributions were then determined. Next, each child was classified as being either high or low on each scale, depending upon whether he fell above or below the median score assigned by his

---

[4] These rating data are analyzed more fully in Chapter 10. The behavior rating scales, as they were presented to the teachers, are shown in Appendix E.

[5] The focus of the discussion will be upon the 1962, or first-grade, ratings, since we are interested in the early identification of behavior traits which may be precursors of intellective change. However, analyses involving the 1964 ratings are also presented, primarily for comparative purposes. The reader should recognize, though, that analyses using the 1964 ratings represent more an exercise in *post*diction than in *pre*diction. That is, these ratings related current behavior at the end of the 1963–64 school year to IQ change, most of which may already have taken place during the preceding two years. The 1962 ratings, in contrast, are related to IQ change that takes place in the following two to three years and, hence, are within a predictive framework. For a cleaner effort at postdiction, it would have been desirable to have had teachers' ratings made at the end of the 1964–65 academic year.

teacher on that trait. Since the numbers of boys and girls were almost identical, and since their patterns of IQ change were reasonably similar, biserial r's were computed for the total sample rather than for each sex separately. Biserial r's were computed separately for the 1962 and the 1964 ratings, however; both sets are reported in Table 6.3.

In addition, each of the 57 children was classified as either an Accelerator, a Constant, or a Decelerator with respect to his IQ change.[6] Accelerators were those children who showed an increment of five or more IQ points; Constants remained within four points of their original IQ scores; and Decelerators dropped on reexamination by five or more points. In all, there were 17 Accelerators (10 girls), 20 Constants (8 girls), and 20 Decelerators (10 girls). Mean scores for each of these

TABLE 6.3

Biserial Correlation Coefficients between Teachers' Behavior Ratings
and IQ Change for Young Negro Children

| | Rating date | | | |
| | May, 1962 | | May, 1964 | |
Trait	r_{bis}	p	r_{bis}	p
1. Activity level	.06	N.S.	.31	.10
2. Emotional expressiveness	− .08	N.S.	− .04	N.S.
3. Self-sufficiency	.47	.05	.03	N.S.
4. Need for encouragement	− .44	.01	− .25	.20
5. Sociability	.26	.20	− .06	N.S.
6. Concern for excellence	.32	.10	.52	.01
7. Social poise	.13	N.S.	.48	.01
8. Reaction to failure	.19	N.S.	.17	N.S.
9. Emotional warmth	.42	.05	− .13	N.S.
10. Cooperativeness	.46	.01	.40	.05
11. Effort on schoolwork	.54	.01	.37	.05
12. Emotional stability	.08	N.S.	.10	N.S.
13. Assertiveness	− .24	.20	− .14	N.S.
14. Trustfulness	.49	.01	− .06	N.S.
15. Tenacity	.38	.05	.40	.05
16. Tension level	− .39	.05	− .38	.05
17. Reaction to success	.38	.05	.28	.20
18. Mood	.17	N.S.	.15	N.S.
19. Aggressiveness	− .05	N.S.	− .14	N.S.
20. Absorption in schoolwork	.29	.10	.21	N.S.
21. Consistency	.59	.001	.16	N.S.
22. Teacher's affectionate regard	.45	.01	.50	.01

[6] Mean IQ's for Accelerators, Constants, and Decelerators in 1961-62 were 84.5, 80.3, and 86.6, respectively.

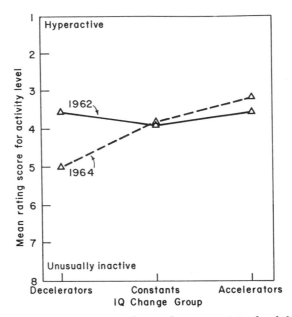

Fig. 6.2: Mean rating scores given by teachers on activity level for three Negro IQ change groups; separately for 1962 and 1964.

three groups were computed then on each of the 22 rating scales, using the *actual* numerical ratings assigned by the teachers. Computations were made separately for the 1962 and the 1964 ratings; some of the results are summarized graphically in Figures 6.2 through 6.12.

Because this is exploratory work, brief mention will be made of the findings with respect to each of the behavior ratings, even though statistically significant relationships were not found for some of the variables. The traits will be considered in the order in which they were rated by the teachers.

1. *Activity level.* A child's characteristic activity level during his first year in school is not significantly related to his subsequent change in IQ. Two years later, however, this attribute shows a stronger relationship to ability change (see Figure 6.2). This difference in the two sets of ratings is due largely to the discrepancy between the Decelerators on the two occasions. In 1962, among the three IQ change groups, they had the highest mean score on activity level, whereas in 1964 their mean score is the lowest. This *may* mean that in 1964 they are more passive and participate less in school activities than was true in 1962.

2. *Emotional expressiveness.* The insignificant correlations between emotional expressiveness and IQ change based on both the 1962 and the 1964 ratings make it clear that this attribute of a child's behavior

provides no reliable basis for estimating growth or decline in his intellective powers. The belief that emotional expression somehow facilitates intellective growth is not bolstered by these findings, nor is its counterpart, which argues that emotional inhibition somehow cripples intellective development.

3. *Self-sufficiency.* The Accelerators, as first-graders, are viewed by their teachers as being relatively self-sufficient. The Constants, in turn, are rated as more self-sufficient than the Decelerators, but less so than the Accelerators. Thus, as shown in Figure 6.3, there is a positive linear relationship between self-sufficiency, as judged in the first grade, and IQ change. There is no such relationship, however, when the third-grade ratings are analyzed.

4. *Need for encouragement.* The need for encouragement is inversely correlated with IQ change, a finding which is consistent with the results just discussed for ratings of self-sufficiency. Again, the relationship is more pronounced in grade one than in grade three. In the first grade, the mean score of the Constants falls about midway between those for the Accelerators and the Decelerators, but in the third grade the mean scores of the Constants and Decelerators are almost identical. For both years, Accelerators stand out in terms of mean scores that indicate rela-

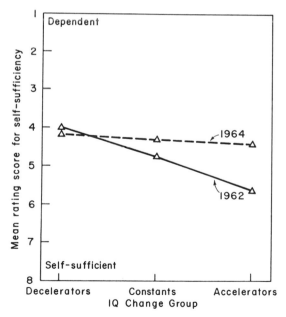

Fig. 6.3: Mean rating scores given by teachers on self-sufficiency for three Negro IQ change groups; separately for 1962 and 1964.

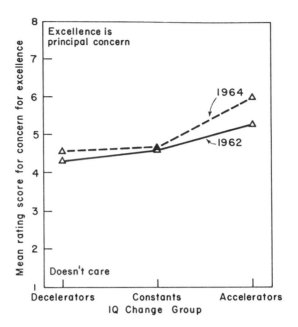

Fig. 6.4: Mean rating scores given by teachers on concern for excellence for three Negro IQ change groups; separately for 1962 and 1964.

tively little need for encouragement in comparison with the other two IQ change groups.

5. *Sociability.* Social participation, like emotional expressiveness, appears to be a poor predictor of intellective change. The relationship between sociability and IQ change is stronger, however, when the first-grade rather than the third-grade ratings are analyzed. The largest difference in mean scores between the 1962 and 1964 ratings occurs for the Accelerators; they are rated as being less sociable in grade three than in grade one.

6. *Concern for excellence.* This rating scale was included in an attempt to measure what McClelland (1953) calls achievement motivation. The mean scores for the six groups on the scale have been plotted in Figure 6.4.

There is a modest but positive correlation between this trait, as rated in 1962, and IQ change. The 1964 data, however, reveal a considerably more substantial relationship. Furthermore, as is apparent from inspection of Figure 6.4, it is the Accelerators in whom this trait is especially salient; this is true for both sets of ratings. On each occasion, in contrast, the mean scores of the Decelerators and Constants do not differ appreciably from one another.

7. *Social poise.* Although the 1962 ratings of social poise are insignificantly related to IQ change, the 1964 ratings show a substantial correlation with this index. It may be that a child's increasing success in mastering intellective tasks is reflected in his general demeanor so that he appears more confident, poised, and so on as he progresses in school. And, conversely, decreasing mastery of intellective tasks may lead to increasing manifestations of uncertainty and other behaviors which are commonly referred to as a lack of social poise.

8. *Reaction to failure.* For both sets of ratings, there is a small and statistically insignificant positive correlation between how children react to failure and IQ change. The *tendency* in each set is for the Accelerators to be most bothered by failure and the Decelerators to be least affected.

9. *Emotional warmth.* There is a significant positive correlation between "warmth" in the first-grade children and IQ change. Although the mean raw scores show a similar trend in the third-grade ratings, the biserial *r* is slightly negative. Additional research will be necessary before the stability and possible meaning of this finding can be determined.

10. *Cooperativeness.* There is either a significant or a very significant positive relationship between cooperativeness and IQ change for each set of ratings. When the mean raw scores are plotted (see Figure 6.5),

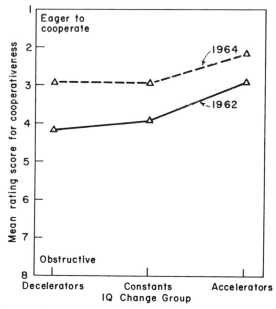

Fig. 6.5: Mean rating scores given by teachers on cooperativeness for three Negro IQ change groups; separately for 1962 and 1964.

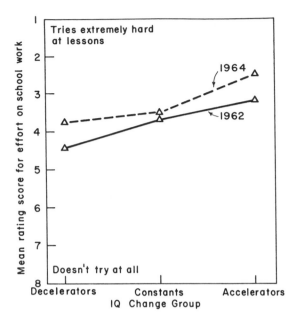

Fig. 6.6: Mean rating scores given by teachers for effort on school work for three Negro IQ change groups; separately for 1962 and 1964.

it is immediately apparent that it is the Accelerators who are set apart as far as cooperativeness is concerned. For each set of ratings, the difference between Constants and Decelerators is slight. Being obstructive, then, is not a good sign as far as intellective growth is concerned.

11. *Effort on schoolwork.* This rating of motivation, or application to the specific tasks of school, is related to IQ change based on both the 1962 and the 1964 data, at the .01 and .05 levels of confidence, respectively. As Figure 6.6 depicts, the relationship is essentially rectilinear; the Accelerators exceed the Constants, who in turn surpass the Decelerators with respect to the amount of effort expended on lessons. The evidence is convincing, then, that a teacher's perception of when a child is trying hard is importantly related to the child's intellective growth.

12. *Emotional stability.* Children who are prone to have emotional upsets are special problems for anyone who is concerned with students in classrooms. Within the range studied here, however, susceptibility to such upsets does not appear to be significantly related to ability change (see Table 6.3).

On the other hand, consideration of the mean raw scores plotted in Figure 6.7 suggests that the biserial coefficients may underestimate the strength of the relationship involved, which appears to be curvilinear. Apparently, the Accelerators are most resistant to emotional upsets, followed by the Decelerators and then the Constants. Different sets of processes may very well be functioning within the Accelerators and Decelerators to give both groups higher scores on freedom from upset than those obtained by the Constants. The unshakable quality of the Accelerators, for instance, may be a manifestation of their general security in the school situation, toward which, as other ratings indicate, they tend to have a positive orientation. The Decelerators, in contrast, may be withdrawing from involvement in the work of the school; as part of this orientation, they may be erecting defenses which tend to control emotional reactions to events occurring therein. Of course, these are, at best, hypotheses which may merit further study.

13. *Assertiveness.* There is a small, statistically insignificant tendency in both sets of ratings for IQ change to be negatively correlated with assertiveness. When the mean raw scores are plotted (not shown here), this relationship is actually more striking for the 1964 ratings than for the 1962 ratings, a fact that is not reflected in the magnitudes of the two correlation coefficients (see Table 6.3).

Ratings on this scale probably reflect in large part the teachers' judgments about the children's readiness to submit to the discipline and orderliness that the classroom situation demands. If so, the Accelerators may be described as relatively submissive in this regard, whereas the Decelerators are relatively resistant. The overlap in the distributions of

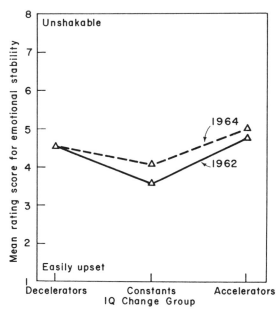

Fig. 6.7: Mean rating scores given by teachers on emotional stability for three Negro IQ change groups; separately for 1962 and 1964.

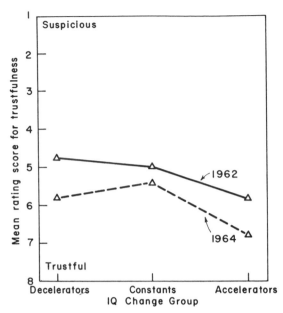

Fig. 6.8: Mean rating scores given by teachers on trustfulness for three Negro IQ change groups; separately for 1962 and 1964.

scores for the two groups is so great, however, that individual prediction of IQ change based upon assertiveness is not promising.

14. *Trustfulness.* It is not uncommon to hear that rural children are especially guarded and suspicious. The absolute level of the mean ratings for this attribute (see Figure 6.8) is not consistent with such a stereotype, although, admittedly, comparative data for town and city groups are not available. The data do indicate, however, that there is considerable variability within the first-grade group with respect to the degree of their trustfulness and that this trait is positively correlated with subsequent intellective growth at a very significant level. Moreover, although the correlation coefficient using the 1964 ratings is not significant, the plot in Figure 6.8 indicates that the Accelerators are again, on the average, more trustful than the other two ability change groups.

The strength of the positive relationship between trustfulness during the first year of school and intellective growth points up the importance of investigating the origin of this trait, especially how it is formed and nurtured within the context of the home. Any child bringing this basic attitude to the school may well differ from other children in his receptivity to what the school and teacher have to offer him. If this is true, then to be effective any preschool work with children probably should try to find how to develop a sense of trust within them.

15. *Tenacity.* A child's tenacity in sticking at a task rather than giving up easily is positively and significantly related to ability change in both sets of ratings. Mean raw scores for tenacity (see Figure 6.9) also reflect the regularity of the differences between Accelerators, Constants, and Decelerators in this attribute. Like trustfulness, the tendency to stick to tasks is another facet of behavior which is poorly understood, yet a teacher's capacity to recognize it along with its relationship to IQ change suggests the importance of additional research. It would seem, for example, that the proper scheduling of reinforcements with pre-school children might enhance the tenacity they manifest when confronted with problems to solve.

16. *Tension level.* The teachers were asked to rate how agitated or composed each child seemed to be, which was our way of getting at the characteristic tension or anxiety levels of the children. Both sets of ratings are consistent in suggesting that tension level is negatively and significantly correlated with ability change; that is, the Accelerators are relatively composed, while the Decelerators are relatively anxious.

17. *Reaction to success.* The tendency to respond positively to experiences of success in the first grade is correlated, at a significant level, with IQ change. The correlation based upon the third-grade ratings falls short of statistical significance, yet the relationship is in the positive

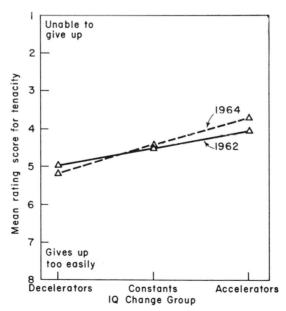

Fig. 6.9: Mean rating scores given by teachers on tenacity for three Negro IQ change groups; separately for 1962 and 1964.

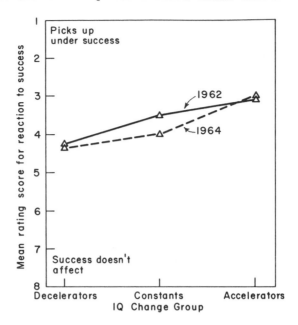

Fig. 6.10: Mean rating scores given by teachers on reaction to success for three Negro IQ change groups; separately for 1962 and 1964.

direction. Furthermore, as Figure 6.10 illustrates, the mean raw scores for both the 1962 and the 1964 ratings show a rectilinear relationship between IQ change and the tendency to "pick up" when success is experienced.

In absolute terms, the correlation coefficients based upon judgments about reactions to failure (see Rating 8 above) and success are modest in size. All four coefficients suggest, however, that children who are unaffected in the face of failure or success are less likely to show positive gains in ability than children who do show definite effects when confronted with such experiences. This relationship between reactivity and intellective change apparently is stronger for reaction to success than for reaction to failure. Obviously, much more needs to be learned about why some children are affected in this way while others are not.

18. *Mood.* In both sets of ratings, the highest average mood score (cheerfulness) is earned by the Accelerators. Overall, however, there is only a small and statistically insignificant correlation between mood and ability change for both the 1962 and the 1964 ratings.

19. *Aggressiveness.* It is possible, of course, to make a distinction between assertive and aggressive behavior. In all likelihood, however, most individuals, including teachers, do not make this differentiation

when describing other people. It is not surprising, therefore, to find
that the ratings of aggresiveness relate to IQ change in essentially the
same way that was found to be true for the ratings of assertiveness (see
Rating 13 above and the data in Table 6.3). The two correlation coefficients again are negative and small.

20. *Absorption in schoolwork.* In both grades one and three, the
tendency of a child to become absorbed in tasks is positively correlated
with ability change. The correlation coefficient based on the 1962 ratings
falls just below the significant level, while the coefficient based on the
1964 ratings is somewhat lower (see Table 6.3). As Figure 6.11 suggests,
the lower coefficient for the third-grade ratings results from the fact
that the mean scores for the Decelerators and Constants are essentially
the same.

As is true for so many behavioral attributes, the origin of this one is
obscure. One suspects, however, that careful planning of a child's preschool experiences might enhance his curiosity about and commitment
to tasks which are presented to him.

21. *Consistency.* The largest correlation coefficient in Table 6.3 involves the 1962 ratings for behavioral consistency. This coefficient is
much lower when the 1964 data are analyzed, yet the mean raw scores

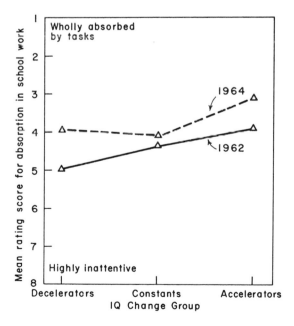

Fig. 6.11: Mean rating scores given by teachers on absorption in school work for
three Negro IQ change groups; separately for 1962 and 1964.

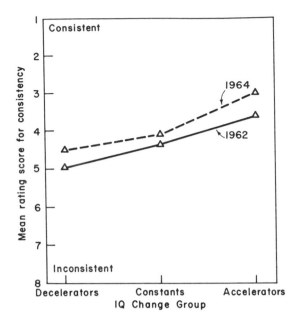

Fig. 6.12: Mean rating scores given by teachers on consistency for three Negro IQ change groups; separately for 1962 and 1964.

for the Accelerators, Constants, and Decelerators follow the same pattern as that obtained with the earlier ratings (see Figure 6.12).

The consistent first-grade student may very well be the child who, by his consistency, is manifesting a relatively well-developed personality structure. Such children are not given to overly erratic, impulsive, or distractible behavior that makes it difficult for the teacher to predict what they are likely to be doing from one moment to the next. In any event, a consistency in the behavior of a first-grade child appears to be a positive sign as far as his growth in ability is concerned.[7]

22. *Teacher's affectionate regard.* In both sets of ratings, there is a very significant positive correlation between how well a teacher likes a child and the intellective growth that he shows. Thus, children gaining in IQ tend to be better liked by their teachers than children showing losses.

One cannot interpret these data in terms of cause-and-effect relationships when the analyses rest on correlation coefficients. It is possible, for instance, that teachers express greater liking for certain pupils in part because they are making more adequate intellective progress. On

---

[7] These ratings do not refer, of course, to the extremely limited and stereotyped behavior characteristic of some retarded children.

the other hand, teachers, because they are more fond of certain children than others, may create a variety of interpersonal relationships within their classrooms which differentially enhance the intellective development of the children in their charge. Indeed, it is quite likely that complex interactions exist in this domain of teacher–pupil relationships so that no single statement which we could formulate now would be adequate for describing these psychological relationships within the classroom. What is apparent, however, is that knowledge of a teacher's regard for a child is useful information if one wishes to anticipate the likely course of his development in ability during this age period.

Summary

Ratings of this type are, admittedly, a rather crude approach to the measurement of behavior; they present a number of technical problems which limit their usefulness. Allowing for these difficulties, it is impressive to find that eleven (50%) of the ratings made by the first-grade teachers correlate significantly with the subsequent IQ changes of the children. Although some of these relationships do not hold up when later ratings are analyzed within a postdictive framework, the general pattern of the postdictive findings leads, we believe, to substantially the same interpretive conclusion as the predictive findings.

The first-grade Negro child who is most likely to accelerate in intellective development tends to have a number of salient characteristics, as he is viewed by his teacher. He is self-sufficient, works hard at his lessons, sticks to the job, doesn't need much encouragement, and is consistent. As a person, he is warm, cooperative, trustful, and relatively free of anxiety. He is somewhat reactive to experiences of success and failure, especially success, and his teacher finds him an easy person to like.

Each of the behavior traits that has been analyzed is, of course, of interest as an individual behavioral domain. It is also of interest, however, to consider whether there is an integrative psychological concept under which the particular findings can be subsumed, just as, in Chapter 5, an integrative concept was sought for the several family variables that had been found to be related to intellective proficiency. In the present instance, the concept of personal maturity would appear to be especially relevant as a construct around which the various empirical findings can be organized. Thus, the traits described above for the Accelerators are similar to those that characterize the child who has, for his age, a well-developed or mature personality structure. The traits typical of the Decelerators, in contrast, are those that are said to be an expression of less adequate or more immature personality development. From a practical point of view, the greatest value of these data is in the clear indication they give that teacher judgments do provide a basis for estimating the growth path that a child's abilities are likely to follow.

Achievement Motivation

The stories a person tells in response to a series of pictures are often used to assess the strength of his achievement motivation. The concern at this point, of course, is with the question of whether achievement motivation, so measured, is related to IQ change. How such scores were derived for these children is described in detail in Chapter 12.

Actually, two such scores were computed for the children. The first score, hereafter called M Ach, is based upon McClelland's (1953) definition of achievement motivation. According to McClelland, achievement imagery is present in a story when the narrative suggests that the teller is concerned with competing against some standard of excellence. Put another way, the imagery suggests that the narrator is not only concerned with a task or performance but has some involvement in doing it well. For example, a story about a boy working routinely in an office would not be scored for achievement imagery by McClelland, but if a boy is trying to do the best job possible, achievement imagery would be scored.

McClelland's criteria for scoring achievement imagery are quite explicit, but they are also very restrictive. On the basis of these severe criteria, achievement imagery is found very infrequently in the stories told by Millfield's children (see Table 6.4; also, refer to Chapter 12). As a consequence, a second achievement score was developed by Baughman, hereafter referred to as B Ach. The basic distinction between M Ach and B Ach is that the latter utilizes a broader range of scoring criteria. To cite a single illustration of this difference, consider a story built around the theme of a boy trying to learn his lessons. This story would probably not be scored for achievement imagery by McClelland, unless the storyteller went on to say that the boy wanted to earn a grade of A, or that he wanted to be the top student in his class, or something similar. The B Ach score, in contrast, accepts any reference to learning activity as a sufficient basis for crediting achievement imagery.

Forty-three of the 57 Negro children who were reevaluated in this study of IQ change had been given the 12 pictures of the Carolina Picture Series in the late spring of 1962. Each of a child's 12 stories was assessed, by different evaluators, for the presence or absence of both M Ach and B Ach imagery. How each of these two scores relates to IQ change will be discussed separately.

1. *McClelland's Achievement Imagery* (*M Ach*). The frequencies of the various M Ach and B Ach scores are recorded in Table 6.4. These

TABLE 6.4

Frequencies of Various M Ach and B Ach Scores for Three Negro IQ Change Groups

	IQ change groups											
	Accelerators				Constants				Decelerators			
	Boys		Girls		Boys		Girls		Boys		Girls	
Score*	M Ach	B Ach	M Ach	B Ach	M Ach	B Ach	M Ach	B Ach	M Ach	B Ach	M Ach	B Ach
0	5	2	3	0	9	5	6	3	5	3	7	4
1	1	1	0	2	1	3	0	1	0	0	0	1
2	0	1	2	1	1	1	0	2	1	0	0	1
3,4	0	1	1	0	0	2	0	0	1	2	0	1
≥ 5	0	1	0	3	0	0	0	0	0	2	0	0
Totals	6	6	6	6	11	11	6	6	7	7	7	7

* A score of 2, for example, means that 2 out of the 12 stories contained achievement imagery.

scores indicate the total number of stories in which a child introduced either one or the other type of achievement imagery. For example, three girls classified as Accelerators told no stories that were evaluated as containing M Ach imagery.[8]

When McClelland's criteria are used, the most striking fact about the results is that 35 of the 43 children have a score of zero; none of their 12 stories contains achievement imagery. Furthermore, of the eight children producing achievement imagery, only two express it in as many as three stories. Three of the eight children with achievement imagery are girls; each showed a subsequent gain of more than five IQ points. Of the five boys with achievement imagery, one gained eleven IQ points, two remained within three points of their initial IQ, and two dropped five points. Overall, the 35 children without achievement imagery dropped, on the average, about one IQ point while the eight children with achievement imagery gained, on the average, approximately three IQ points.

At best, then, there is a hint in these data that M Ach scores *may* be predictive of IQ growth for the girls. When such a large percentage of the children receive the same score, however, it probably means that they are being poorly differentiated from one another with respect to the behavior (or inferred motivation) in question. Certainly the findings

[8] Accelerators, Constants, and Decelerators are defined here in precisely the same way as described above in the discussion of teachers' ratings.

do not suggest that M Ach imagery scores are likely to be very useful indices for describing Negro children at this age level.

2. *Baughman's Achievement Imagery (B Ach)*. As would be expected when the scoring criteria are broadened, more stories are evaluated as containing B Ach achievement imagery than M Ach imagery (see Table 6.4). The distribution of scores is still quite skewed, however, with about 40% of the children continuing to score zero. Of the 26 children with some achievement imagery, 14 are boys and 12 are girls.

Among the trends discernible in the B Ach data, the following appear to be worthy of note:

a. Zero scores are infrequently associated with IQ gain. Thus, 15 of the 17 children with zero scores either remained the same or dropped in IQ.

b. Children with some achievement imagery (B Ach ≥ 1) are about equally divided among the three IQ change groups (10 Accelerators, 9 Constants, and 7 Decelerators).

c. High B Ach scores (B Ach ≥ 3) are more common among the boys than among the girls (8 contrasted to 4, respectively). These high scores, however, tend to be associated with IQ gain more frequently for the girls than for the boys.

It must be emphasized that the above are simply trends in the data; when larger groups of children are studied, these trends may vanish.

Summary

The general conclusion resulting from these analyses is that achievement imagery is both infrequent and unpromising as a predictor of IQ change. The complete absence of such imagery, however, especially when the broader criteria are used to assess it, may be a useful sign pointing to the unlikelihood of a gain in IQ. There is a further suggestion in both the M Ach and B Ach data that relatively high achievement imagery scores *may* have differential significance for the two sexes; high-scoring girls may be more likely to gain in IQ than high-scoring boys.

FAMILY AND SCHOOL CORRELATES OF IQ CHANGE

It was pointed out in Chapter 5 that the Negro families in Millfield are not very heterogeneous with respect to a number of variables which may be used to describe them. This fact, along with the relatively small number of children for whom IQ change data are available, makes it unlikely that, in the statistical sense, many significant relationships can be demonstrated between these family variables and IQ change. Nevertheless, an exploratory study of this domain was undertaken, and the findings will be summarized below. When a relationship is statistically significant (both chi-square and analysis of variance were used), this fact will be noted; otherwise, only tendencies in the data are being described.

Father's education. The fathers of these children had completed, on the average, 6.9 years of formal schooling. This variable did not relate to IQ change.

Mother's education. The mothers had a mean of 8.4 years of schooling. The mothers of the Accelerators actually have the lowest mean (7.8 years), followed by the Decelerators (8.3 years), and the Constants (9.1 years).

Father's occupation. Eighty percent of the children who lost IQ points had fathers who were farmers. For the children who remained the same or accelerated, the comparable percentages were only 47 and 50, respectively. (Chi-square analysis approached a significant level.)

Mother's employment. Fourteen of the mothers were employed, either part- or full-time. Eight of these fourteen were mothers of Accelerators, two were mothers of Constants, and four were mothers of Decelerators. (Chi-square analysis of these data reached significance.)

Possessions and services. A large majority of the families were very much alike as far as possessions and services were concerned. For example, only 15 families either owned or were buying their homes, and an even smaller number (8) had telephone service. None of the analyses involving such variables suggested significant relationships between them and IQ change.

Natural father absence. For the 56 children for whom information pertaining to the father was available, 13 were without their natural fathers. Natural fathers were absent in 35%, 11%, and 24% of the homes of the Decelerators, Constants, and Accelerators, respectively.

Family type. Twenty-one of these children were living in extended families. Only 18% of the Accelerators lived in such families, however, in comparison to 45% of the Constants and 45% of the Decelerators. There is a suggestion, therefore, that intellective growth may be especially difficult for children living in homes where the family has been extended to include individuals other than the parents and their children.

Size of sibship. The finding of an inverse relationship between size of sibship and IQ change is shown graphically in Figure 6.13. The most salient fact is that the Accelerators come from appreciably smaller

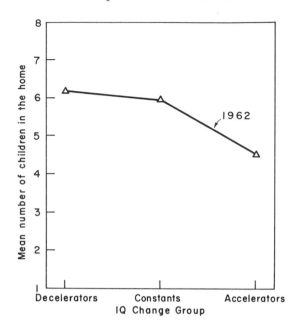

Fig. 6.13: Mean number of children in the homes of three Negro IQ change groups.

families than do the Constants and Decelerators. (Analyses of results were very close to statistical significance.)

Ordinal position. The children were classified as youngest, oldest, or intermediate with reference to the other children in their homes. (Only one child was without siblings, and he was not included in the analysis.) This classification was then related to IQ change, with insignificant results.

Teachers. In addition to the family variables discussed above, the question was asked whether the children's IQ changes are related to the teacher to whom they were assigned for first-grade work. The data indicate no trends in this regard.

Summary

There are some trends in the data which have been briefly outlined above, but it is clear that these relationships need to be studied further with larger and probably more heterogeneous samples. It is also true, however, that homogeneity rather than heterogeneity tends to character-ize Negro families living in these rural areas so that the findings reported cannot be readily discounted on this basis. Mothers who work, fathers who are not full-time farmers, a small number of children in the home, and the lack of other people living with the nuclear family all seem to be factors that are positively related to gains on test scores by children during their first few years in school. On the other hand, not having the natural father in the home may be a negative factor.

CONCLUDING COMMENTS

The mean IQ of these Negro children did not change significantly during an approximately three-year period stretching from grade one to grade four. This stability of mean IQ was characteristic of both boys and girls, yet there was a slight shift in favor of the girls. If this trend continues with advancing age, a statistically significant sex difference in mean IQ scores may develop.

Average scores are, of course, important in both theoretical and practical ways. It is also essential, however, to examine the scores of individual children to achieve a more comprehensive understanding of ongoing change. Thus, we discover that change rather than constancy really typifies these children, because approximately two-thirds of the children showed IQ changes of five or more points over the three-year period.

It would be tempting to explain these IQ changes by invoking the statistical concept of "regression toward the mean" if we had only the boys' data to consider. The data for the girls, however, do not fit into such a formulation. Furthermore, we believe that the data relating teachers' appraisals of children's behavior to their IQ changes offer convincing evidence that factors other than statistical regression are at issue here.

The behavioral ratings indicate that there are social and motivational characteristics of first-grade Negro children that are differentially related to their growth in ability during their early school years. Apparently, teachers are able to make useful judgments about such traits. Judgments of this type proved to be more useful indicators of likely IQ change than measures of achievement motivation using a fantasy technique or information about a number of dimensions of the children's family life.

The findings presented in this chapter point to the importance of further inquiries into the preschool origins of the social and motivational traits which are related to ability change. The findings also suggest that preschool programs might very well concentrate selectively on developing those behavioral traits that do relate to ability growth. Within the school, the data indicate that it is probably feasible to make an early identification of those children whose ability curve is likely to be downward so that preventive programs might be selectively applied. Finally, from a more general theoretical viewpoint, the data are rather compelling in the sense of pointing to the need for studying cognitive development not in isolation but rather in the context of the total social and motivational development of the child.

Chapter 7

CHANGES IN IQ AMONG WHITE ADOLESCENTS[1]

A second short-term longitudinal study of intellective change was conducted, this one among the white adolescent children. The general strategy of this study was similar to that used in the investigation of intellective changes among the young Negro children (see Chapter 6); however, there were some important differences, as will be made clear in the following pages.

PROCEDURE

Children who had been in the sixth grades of the two white schools during the 1961–62 school year were the potential subjects for this study, provided that they had been examined then on the Stanford-Binet Intelligence Scale (S-B). There were 68 such children, 37 of whom were boys. Ten of these children (eight boys), however, had either moved out of the area or had dropped out of sight so completely that it was impossible to include them in the study. There were, then, 58 children, 29 of each sex, who could be reexamined on the S-B.

These 58 children were retested during the 1964–65 academic year to determine the extent of change (if any) in their intellective ability

[1] This chapter is based upon a Ph.D. dissertation completed by Jane Carolyn Church at the University of North Carolina in Chapel Hill in 1965 under the direction of the first author. We are grateful to Miss Church for permitting us to summarize parts of her work here. It should also be noted that we have added certain analyses which were not included in the original dissertation.

135

during the approximately three-year period. Each child was retested by the white female examiner who had tested him originally; none of these three examiners reviewed her previous protocols before giving the second S-B.

Four children (three boys) were retested even though they had dropped out of school. These children—and only these—were paid five dollars each for their cooperation. Three other boys dropped out of school before the 1964–65 academic year was completed, but they had been retested prior to their departure. Although most of the children were in the ninth grade when retested, six boys and one girl had failed one grade and were in the eighth grade. In addition, one boy who was retested had been committed to a training school because of chronic truancy and, on the basis of newly administered achievement tests, had been placed back in the fourth grade.

The two administrations of the S-B provided a basis for computing an IQ change score for each of the 58 children. These change scores then were related to a number of behavioral attributes of the children as well as to various family and school factors. Before these relationships are examined, however, the age and ability characteristics of the sample will be described, and the stability of the S-B IQ at this age period will be summarized.

AGES AND INITIAL S-B IQ'S

As Table 7.1 shows, the mean age of the boys at the time of the initial S-B testing in 1961–62 was slightly above 12 years, while the mean age of the girls was a bit below this figure. All the children, both boys and girls, were at least 11 years old when tested initially. On retesting, the mean age of the boys was just above 15 years; the mean age of the girls was just below 15. Approximately two-thirds of the group were within 10 months of the average figures noted above.

When first tested, the boys averaged a little more than two IQ points below the level that would be expected for a sample drawn from the United States as a whole. For the girls, there was a greater deviation; their average fell more than five IQ points below 100 (see Table 7.1). This sex difference is somewhat greater than the sex difference appearing in the data from the total sample of white 12-year-olds, but it is in the same direction (see Figure 3.2). Moreover, this failure to perform up to national norms is typical for white children of both sexes in Millfield beyond age 11 (again, see Figure 3.2). Note should also be taken of the

TABLE 7.1

Age and S-B IQ Data for the White Retest Children

	Boys (N = 29)		Girls (N = 29)	
	1961–62	1964–65	1961–62	1964–65
Age at S-B Testing (in months)				
Mean	146.5	181.6	142.8	177.8
S.D.	9.8	10.0	7.1	7.6
Range	134–165	170–199	134–171	169–209
IQ Scores				
Mean	97.6	98.2	94.6	95.1
S.D.	17.5	21.6	13.3	15.9
Range	64–128	59–147	64–123	59–133
IQ Change				
Mean	+0.7		+0.5	
S.D.	9.2		7.9	
Range	+28 to −21		+29 to −11	

high variability in the IQ scores of these children, especially among the boys. Thus, as Table 7.1 indicates, the lowest IQ earned by any child in the sample was 59, and the highest was 147; both of these scores were earned by boys.

STABILITY OF THE IQ

The group data in Table 7.1 are supplemented by a tabulation in Table 7.2 of the frequencies of various IQ change scores, separated by sex. It is apparent from these data that the IQ's of the children, as a group, changed very little during the three-year period. For both boys and girls, the mean change score is less than one point. Furthermore, when product-moment correlation coefficients were computed between the scores secured on the two occasions, highly significant values were obtained: .91 for the boys and .87 for the girls. It will be recalled in this regard that there was less stability in the scores of the younger Negro children over a three-year period; comparable correlation coefficients were .62 and .77 for the boys and girls, respectively.

It is very important to note, however, that there were marked individual changes in IQ, ranging from a gain of 29 points to a loss of 21 points. Furthermore, for both sexes, the IQ's of more than 50% of the children changed by five or more points. Thus, although the group

TABLE 7.2

Frequencies of S-B IQ Changes for White Adolescents, 1961–62 to 1964–65

Change in IQ	Boys	Girls
25–29	1	1
20–24		
15–19	2	
10–14	1	1
5–9	4	5
1–4	3	6
0	3	3
(−1)–(−4)	7	4
(−5)–(−9)	5	6
(−10)–(−14)	2	3
(−15)–(−19)		
(−20)–(−24)	1	
N	29	29
Mean	+0.7	+0.5

means are almost identical on the two occasions, appreciable numbers of the children give evidence of change in intellective ability.

Significance of Initial IQ

Does a child's initial IQ provide a basis for predicting his subsequent change in ability? This question was explored first by computing, separately for each sex, a product-moment correlation coefficient between 1961–62 IQ's and IQ change scores. The resulting coefficients were not significantly different from zero: .24 for the boys and .07 for the girls.

The above question was also studied by dividing each sex into High, Middle, and Low groups on the basis of their 1961–62 IQ's. Children in the two High groups had IQ's of 110 or above; those in the two Middle groups had IQ's between 90 and 109; and those in the two Low groups had IQ's of 89 or below. Mean IQ's were then computed for each group from the 1961–62 data and, again, from the 1964–65 data. The resulting means have been plotted in Figure 7.1.

It is clear from these plots that the IQ change cannot be interpreted as a regression toward the mean. Although High girls do show a decrement, High boys, who change the most of any group, show on the average an increment in IQ; that is, they shift away from the mean. Moreover, although neither Low boys nor Low girls show a significant change, both groups do drop slightly during the three years; again, this is a movement away from the mean. Finally, the Middle girls show an increase in mean IQ, but the Middle boys show a decrease.

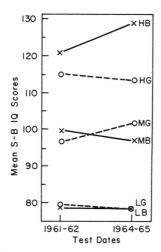

Fig. 7.1: Mean S-B IQ scores at each of two testing dates for white adolescents separated by sex into High, Middle, and Low ability groups on the basis of their IQ scores when tested initially. HB = High boys. HG = High girls. MB = Middle boys. MG = Middle girls. LB = Low boys. LG = Low girls.

The number of children in each of these six groups is small, and it is unlikely that precisely the same pattern of findings would be obtained if the study were replicated. Nevertheless, the data do not readily fit a regression toward the mean interpretation, nor is it easy to interpret the findings as being the result of practice effects. It is clear, however, that the measured IQ of a white child at the beginning of this age period provides little basis for predicting what change, if any, he will manifest in intellective ability during the next several years.

Significance of Academic Achievement

The next question is whether the academic performance of a white child during early adolescence is associated with his subsequent IQ change. Academic performance was measured by the Stanford Achievement Test (SAT) which was administered to 57 of the 58 children (28 boys) in the late spring of 1962. (Detailed findings from the SAT were presented in Chapter 4.)

Although the SAT provides a number of different substantive scores, only the Battery Median score, which is a measure of overall academic achievement, was used in the investigation being reported here. This score was scaled in number of months of age; it indicates the age of the typical child functioning at the level at which the particular child is performing in his general academic work. Thus, if a child's chronological age is 140 months and his score is 140 months, his academic achieve-

TABLE 7.3

Summary of SAT Deviation Scores for White Adolescents (1961–62)

Deviation scores* (in months)	Boys (N = 28)	Girls (N = 29)
Mean	−18.5	−2.7
S.D.	28.0	22.9
Range	+35 to −73	+40 to −55

* Computed by subtracting each child's chronological age (in months) at the time of testing from his Battery Median score (in months).

ments are considered to be directly in line with the norm for his age. For the present analysis, a deviation score was obtained for each child by subtracting his chronological age at the time the SAT was administered from the Battery Median score that he earned on it. Thus, positive deviation scores are indicative of above-average academic achievement, while negative deviation scores reflect below-average achievement.

A summary of the deviation scores earned by both boys and girls is given in Table 7.3. The most striking fact about these data is that the boys fall markedly below the girls in academic performance. Compared with national norms, the boys are on the average more than 18 months behind where they should be, whereas the girls lag behind by less than 3 months. This sex difference in academic achievement occurs even though, as shown in Table 7.1, the boys exceed the girls in mean IQ scores.

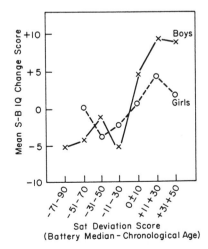

Fig. 7.2: The relationship between SAT deviation scores (computed in months) in 1961–62 and the subsequent IQ changes of white adolescents of each sex.

Product-moment correlation coefficients were computed between these SAT deviation scores and the IQ change scores. A significant positive correlation coefficient was obtained for the boys ($r = .43$), while the positive coefficient for the girls fell just short of significance ($r = .31$). These coefficients are larger than those reported above between initial IQ scores and subsequent IQ change, suggesting that academic performance is a somewhat better predictor of change in intelligence test performance than is the original level of functioning on the ability test. This relationship between academic performance and later IQ change is plotted graphically in Figure 7.2; the regularity of the plots is striking, especially when one recognizes that the 13 points plotted represent data from only 57 children.

BEHAVIORAL CORRELATES OF IQ CHANGE

In the following analyses, the children were divided into three groups on the basis of the stability of their IQ scores. This division was carried out in the same manner as was a similar categorization effected for younger Negro children (see Chapter 6). Accelerators were defined as children whose IQ scores increased by five or more points; Constants as children who remained within four points of their original score; and Decelerators as children whose IQ's decreased five or more points. By these criteria, 8 boys and 7 girls were designated Accelerators (approximately 26% of the sample); 13 boys and 13 girls were classified as Constants (about 45% of the sample); and 8 boys and 9 girls were called Decelerators (approximately 29% of the sample). These percentages, incidentally, agree quite closely with those found for the younger Negro children (compare Table 7.2 with Table 6.2).

Several techniques were used to assess various personal qualities of the children. The question of how these personal attributes relate to change in ability will be reported below. Ideally, all these evaluations would have been made at the time of the first S-B testing, but it was not feasible to carry out each assessment then. Some data come from other parts of the project, carried out separately from this investigation. The details of the timing and administration of each assessment technique will be indicated in the discussions that follow.

Teachers' Ratings A

Each child was rated by his sixth-grade teacher in the late spring of 1962 on the 22-item behavior rating scale which was described in the study of young Negro children (see Chapters 6 and 10; also, Appendix

TABLE 7.4

Biserial Correlation Coefficients between Teachers' Behavior Ratings (1961–62)
and IQ Change for White Adolescents, with Comparative Data
for Younger Negro Children

	White		Negro	
Trait	r_{bis}	p	r_{bis}	p
1. Activity level	$-.30$	.10	.06	N.S.
2. Emotional expressiveness	$-.07$	N.S.	$-.08$	N.S.
3. Self-sufficiency	.09	N.S.	.47	.05
4. Need for encouragement	$-.22$	.20	$-.44$	.01
5. Sociability	$-.05$	N.S.	.26	.20
6. Concern for excellence	.33	.05	.32	.10
7. Social poise	.06	N.S.	.13	N.S.
8. Reaction to failure	$-.02$	N.S.	.19	N.S.
9. Emotional warmth	$-.06$	N.S.	.42	.05
10. Cooperativeness	.15	N.S.	.46	.01
11. Effort on schoolwork	.25	.20	.54	.01
12. Emotional stability	$-.16$	N.S.	.08	N.S.
13. Assertiveness	$-.07$	N.S.	$-.24$	.20
14. Trustfulness	.12	N.S.	.49	.01
15. Tenacity	.15	N.S.	.38	.05
16. Tension level	$-.17$	N.S.	$-.39$	.05
17. Reaction to success	$-.31$	.10	.38	.05
18. Mood	.03	N.S.	.17	N.S.
19. Aggressiveness	.10	N.S.	$-.05$	N.S.
20. Absorption in schoolwork	.21	N.S.	.29	.10
21. Consistency	.32	.10	.59	.001
22. Teacher's affectionate regard	$-.02$	N.S.	.45	.01

E). The bulk of these ratings came about equally often from three teachers, but two additional teachers rated several of the children.

Biserial correlation coefficients were computed between the ratings on each of the 22 behavior scales and IQ change scores. (The procedures followed in making these computations were the same as those described in Chapter 6.) The 22 coefficients are presented in Table 7.4 along with, for comparative purposes, the coefficients previously reported for the Negro children.

Examination of the data in Table 7.4 reveals that the coefficients for white adolescents are appreciably lower than those for the younger Negro children. Disregarding the sign of the coefficient, 18 of the 22 coefficients for the Negro children are larger than the corresponding coefficients for the white children. Also, only one coefficient is significantly different from zero for the white children, whereas eleven are significant for the Negro children. Behavioral ratings by their teachers, then, appear to offer little information that can be used either to predict or understand the ability changes of white children at this age level.

Although the magnitude of each coefficient is low, the pattern for the white children is, in some respects, similar to the one appearing in the data for the Negro children. Thus, IQ change is positive in children rated high in concern for excellence, consistency, effort made on school-work, and tendency to become absorbed in schoolwork, but negative in those rated as showing need for encouragement. Despite some similarity in overall pattern, however, the fact remains that these behavior ratings are much less promising as a means of identifying likely changes in ability level than are the same ratings for younger Negro children. Comparable studies of younger white children are needed, as are similar studies of older Negro children, before firm conclusions can be drawn about the possible developmental or racial significance of these behavioral characteristics.

Peer and Teachers' Ratings B

The white children in Millfield travel by bus to a nearby community to attend the seventh, eighth, and ninth grades with children from other parts of the county. No attempt was made to repeat Teachers' Ratings A in this setting. However, a special rating scale containing eight items (called Ratings B) was developed for use there during the 1963–64 academic year (see Appendix K). Ratings on this scale were obtained for the 45 of the 58 students who were then in the eighth grade of this school; the 10 boys and 3 girls who had either moved elsewhere, dropped out, or been retained in the seventh grade were not rated. Each student was rated independently by both of his teachers and by each of the other students in his room.[2] The question now is whether the data provided by this set of ratings, made closer in time to the S-B retest than Ratings A, relate to the IQ change scores.

In developing the eight items in Ratings B, an effort was made to focus on the student's actual level of performance as well as on the degree of motivation that he characteristically exhibited. Thus, one item asked how hard the child tried to get good grades, while another item focused upon how adequate his grades were. Two additional items referred, respectively, to the child's actual popularity and the effort he made to be popular. The remaining four items centered upon other expressions or areas of achievement striving: (1) the child's desire for further education; (2) his probable efforts to achieve success once out of school; (3)

---

[2] Students were assigned to rooms alphabetically; each room had approximately 30 students. The school's program was arranged so that each group spent one-half day with each of two teachers.

his help-seeking versus independence in school; and (4) his efforts to win in games or contests.

As indicated in Appendix K, each of the stems for the above eight items was placed at the top of a separate page in a booklet. Between four and six numbered statements were listed immediately below each stem; these statements in turn were followed by a list of the names of each child in the class. The children and the teachers were asked to read each stem and its numbered statements, then go down the class roll and place before the name of each child the number of the statement that best described him.

The peer ratings secured in this way were scored by multiplying the numerical value of each rating by the frequency with which a child was given that rating and then summing these products for the item. The resulting sums were rank-ordered for the entire class; then the child's decile standing within the class was determined.[3] Next, chi-square analyses were carried out to determine if children in the three IQ change groups (Accelerators, Constants, and Decelerators) differed with respect to the ratings given them. No significant chi-squares were obtained for either the peer or teachers' ratings. This finding is, of course, consistent with the results reported above for a broader range of ratings obtained in a different fashion in 1961–62 (see Teachers' Ratings A). It tends to confirm the conclusion drawn there that such ratings for white children at this age level are not helpful in either predicting or understanding changes in ability.

Inspection of the data, however, revealed another trend: there is a sharp sex difference with respect to many of these eighth-grade ratings. This sex difference is apparent in both the peer and teachers' data which were analyzed separately. To show this sex difference, chi-square tests were made after each child had been classified as having been rated either favorably (deciles 1–5) or unfavorably (deciles 6–10) on each of the eight items. The frequencies with which boys and girls were given favorable and unfavorable ratings on the eight items, along with the results of the chi-square tests, are given in Table 7.5. Separate entries are provided for the ratings by the peer group (P) and the two teachers (T1 and T2).[4]

Although statistically significant differences are not found for each item in Table 7.5, these data do point up a pronounced difference between the behavior of boys and girls. It is the girls who are described as trying harder, who seem to be more ambitious, and who are most

---

[3] The ratings of the two teachers were analyzed separately; a child's decile standing with each teacher was determined for each item and served as a basis for chi-square analyses as described for the peer ratings.

[4] As can be determined from Table 7.5, ratings were available from T2 for only 41 children.

TABLE 7.5

Numbers of White Adolescent Boys and Girls Rated Favorably and Unfavorably
by Their Peers and Two Teachers in 1963–64

Behavior rated		Boys		Girls			
		F*	U*	F	U	χ^2	p
1. *Tries* to make good grades	Peer	6	13	19	7	7.66	.01
	T1	6	13	21	5	11.07	.001
	T2	6	11	15	9	2.95	.10
2. *Tries* to achieve popular-	Peer	7	12	19	7	5.91	.02
ity	T1	2	17	17	9	13.54	.001
	T2	5	12	15	9	4.36	.05
3. *Wants* to go to college	Peer	8	11	17	9	2.41	N.S.
	T1	7	12	16	10	2.68	N.S.
	T2	8	9	13	11	.20	N.S.
4. Will *try* to achieve "suc-	Peer	8	11	17	9	2.41	N.S.
cess" after school	T1	8	11	14	12	.61	N.S.
	T2	5	12	12	12	1.74	N.S.
5. Works independently in	Peer	11	8	15	11	.00	N.S.
school	T1	15	4	12	14	4.92	.05
	T2	12	5	12	12	1.74	N.S.
6. Has achieved popularity	Peer	8	11	18	8	3.31	.10
in school	T1	8	11	20	6	5.66	.02
	T2	6	11	13	11	1.43	N.S.
7. *Tries* to win in games or	Peer	6	13	16	10	3.94	.05
contests	T1	6	13	17	9	5.02	.03
	T2	3	10	15	5	8.57	.005
8. Makes good grades in	Peer	6	13	18	8	6.25	.02
school	T1	7	12	18	8	4.66	.05
	T2	6	11	16	8	3.94	.05

* F = favorable judgments (deciles 1–5); U = unfavorable judgments (deciles 6–10).

concerned about pursuing advanced schooling. This motivational difference is probably a key reason why the girls do appreciably better
than the boys on academic achievement tests, as noted earlier. Only
when it comes to help-seeking (item 5) does there appear to be a reversal in this pattern. With respect to such behavior, the children themselves see no sex difference, but the teachers perceive the girls as more
often seeking help than the boys. It is quite possible, however, that much
of this greater help-seeking simply reflects the fact that the girls are
making a greater effort than the boys to learn and achieve within the
school setting.

Achievement Motivation (Fantasy)

During the early part of 1965, each of the 58 children was asked to
tell stories in response to a set of six pictures so that the strength of his

achievement motivation could be measured through the fantasy material. The question then was whether achievement motivation, so measured, was related to the IQ changes that had taken place during the preceding three years.

The instructions and general procedures used in this assessment of achievement imagery were similar to those described in Chapter 6 for the younger Negro children, but the pictures were different. This set was the one used by Veroff in a nation-wide interview study; actually, there were separate sets of pictures for boys and girls.[5] Veroff (1960, pp. 3–4) describes these pictures as follows:

Male Set
1. Two men (inventors) in a shop working at a machine.
2. Four men seated at a table with coffee cups. One man is writing on a sheaf of papers.
3. Man (father) and children seated at breakfast table.
4. Man seated at drafting board.
5. Conference group. Seven men variously grouped around a conference table.
6. Woman in foreground with man standing behind and to the left.

Female Set
1. Two women standing by a table. One woman is working with test tubes.
2. Woman (mother) seated by girl reclining in chair.
3. Group of four women. One standing, the others seated facing each other.
4. Woman kneeling and applying a cover to a chair.
5. Two women preparing food in the kitchen.
6. Same as 6 above.

All the children were tested individually by Church, who asked them to tell their stories orally. (The children were not asked to write their stories in order to eliminate the possibility of losing some stories because of poor writing skills.) Many of the stories told by the children were brief, but all were scorable.

The 348 stories (6 from each of the 58 children) were scored independently by two scorers using the method developed by McClelland and his associates (see Atkinson *et al.*, 1958). Interscorer reliabilities (rank-order correlation coefficients) were computed separately for the stories from each of the 12 cards; these values ranged from .74 to 1.00. In addition, 20 protocols (10 boys and 10 girls) were selected randomly

---

[5] We are grateful to Joseph Veroff for making these pictures available to us.

and rescored by one of the scorers. Rank-order correlation coefficients between these sets of scores ranged from .72 to 1.00 for the 12 cards.

The data presented below, however, were derived from a simpler scoring system (see Chapter 12). In this system each story is scored only for the presence or absence of achievement imagery.[6] Therefore, the total score possible for a child ranges from zero to six; zero if none of his six stories contains achievement imagery, and six if each story involves striving for achievement. The criteria used for making the judgment of whether or not achievement imagery was present were those that McClelland and his associates have laid down.

The highest score earned by any child was four; moreover, only 12 children had scores greater than two. The mean score for boys was 1.5; for girls it was 1.6. Clearly, then, achievement imagery does not play a prominent role in the stories created by these children.

The relationship between achievement imagery and IQ change is shown in Figure 7.3. No simple rectilinear relationship exists between these two scores. Children scoring either zero or two on achievement imagery showed, on the average, a drop in IQ, whereas those children scoring one, three, or four showed gains. All 10 children (5 boys) who scored zero on achievement imagery either lost IQ points or secured the same IQ when retested; none gained.

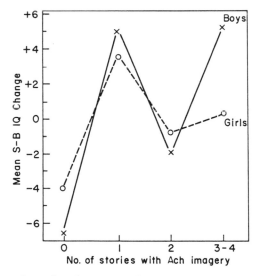

Fig. 7.3: The relationship between achievement imagery in 1964–65 and IQ change for white adolescents of each sex.

[6] The actual ordering of the subjects with respect to the strength of their achievement imagery shifts very little between the two scoring systems.

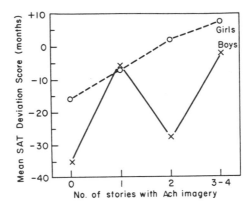

Fig. 7.4: The relationship between achievement imagery in 1964–65 and SAT deviation scores in 1961–62 for white adolescents of each sex.

This absence of a rectilinear relationship between achievement motivation and IQ change has been reported by others (see Kagan and Moss, 1959a, and McClelland *et al.*, 1953). McClelland has suggested that moderate achievement motivation scores may reflect the presence of a fear of failure, rather than sincere motivation for real achievement. Such a fear may lead to behavior that actually interferes with successful achievement rather than facilitating it. The stories given by most of Millfield's children, however, were too limited in detail to be reliably scored for fear-of-failure themes; therefore, McClelland's hypothesis could not be checked by using the present data.

Achievement imagery scores were also plotted against academic achievement test scores (expressed as deviation scores; see Chapter 6). This relationship is shown separately for boys and girls in Figure 7.4. The form of the relationship between achievement imagery and SAT deviation scores is the same for the boys as that between achievement imagery and IQ change (compare Figures 7.3 and 7.4). However, this is not true for the girls. For them, a rectilinear relationship is present: as achievement imagery increases, academic achievement also increases. When biserial correlation coefficients were computed between achievement imagery and SAT deviation scores, a significant coefficient was found for the girls ($r_{bis} = .43$) but not for the boys ($r_{bis} = -.11$). This particular sex difference is rather surprising, since several research studies on school populations in different sections of the country have found more dependable relationships between achievement motivation scores and performance data for boys than for girls. It is not clear to us why Millfield's children show the opposite trend.

Minnesota Multiphasic Personality Inventory (MMPI)

The MMPI had been administered to the eighth-grade students in the spring of 1964 as part of another study connected with the larger project (see Butcher, 1965; also, see Chapter 11 for a description of the test administration). These data were used to determine if dimensions of personality measured by this test are related to IQ change.

MMPI protocols were available for 46 of the 58 children. The remaining 12 children, 11 of whom were boys, either were not in school or were not in the eighth grade when the test was administered. The 46 protocols were scored for each of the validity and clinical scales; also, scores were computed on the supplementary scales for Anxiety, Repression, and Ego Strength.

The data were analyzed separately for the boys and the girls after each sex had been divided into Accelerators, Constants, and Decelerators. Single scale comparisons as well as configural analyses were made, following established procedures (for greater detail, see Church, 1965). No significant relationships were discovered for either sex between MMPI scores, or configurations, and IQ change.

Although the number of children in each IQ change group was small, the results do not suggest that the MMPI will be very useful in predicting or explaining the IQ changes of these children.

Interviews: Aspirations and Friendship Patterns

During the 1963–64 school year, when most of the 58 children were in the eighth grade, 52 of them participated in a comprehensive structured interview designed to explore their family backgrounds, peer relationships, recreational activities, self-attitudes, educational and vocational objectives, and so on (see Appendix B and Chapter 16). These interviews were conducted by the two white female staff members who had administered most of the S-B tests to the children. The remaining six children were interviewed in 1964–65 by Church. Our concern in this section is with how certain information elicited by these interviews is related to IQ change.

It should be recognized that many of Millfield's children are not easy to interview, especially when the interview has a personal orientation. It is, indeed, often easier to administer tests to them, for tests have been a regular part of their school experience, whereas interviews have not. Furthermore, the children are, in many respects, relatively homogeneous as far as their personal backgrounds are concerned. As a result of these two factors, the answers to many of the items in the interview do not provide meaningful discriminations among the children with respect to the variable, or variables, in question.

In all, 54 items in the interview were analyzed to determine if the information they elicited is related to IQ change. Of these items, 31 failed to show either significant or even suggestive relationships.[7] In the paragraphs that follow, attention will be devoted to those items that are indicative of stable relationships with IQ change and that refer to the more subjective components of the children's lives, or to their reports of their social behavior. Those items referring to structural aspects of family or school (for example, mother's education) will be considered in the following section of the chapter.

The results of the analyses of ten items pertaining to the educational and vocational attitudes and ambitions of the children, as well as those

TABLE 7.6

Percentages of White Adolescents in Three IQ Change Groups
Who Answer Certain Interview Questions Affirmatively

Questions	Percentages of Ss (boys and girls) replying in the affirmative			χ^2	p
	Accelerators	Constants	Decelerators		
1. Does mother want S to go as far as college?	67	32	20	7.64	.05
2. Does father want S to go as far as college?	60	32	13	7.26	.05
3. Is mother markedly interested in S's homework?	60	58	47	.61	N.S.
4. Is father markedly interested in S's homework?	40	58	38	2.04	N.S.
5. Does mother want S to enter a profession?	33	27	18	2.28	N.S.
6. Does father want S to enter a profession?	33	12	00	7.46	.05
7. Do S and his parents discuss his eventual occupation?	67	50	29	4.49	N.S.
8. Does S want to be in a profession or highly skilled occupation?	57	27	18	6.02	.05
9. Do girls want husbands who work in a profession?	43	38	22	.89	N.S.
10. If free to do so, would S drop out of school now?	07	20	35	3.96	N.S.

[7] These 31 items, according to their numbers in the interview protocol (see Appendix B) are: 1, 11n, 11o, 39, 43, 52i, 60c, 62, 65, 67, 81, 84, 85, 86, 86a, 89, 90, 90a, 91, 92, 95c, 97a, 100b, 102, 103, 103a, 105, 115, 116, 116a, and 62a.

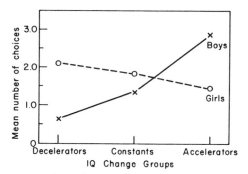

Fig. 7.5: The mean number of times that white adolescents of each sex in three IQ change groups were chosen as best friends by members of their peer group.

of the parents directed toward their children (the latter, it must be emphasized, as reported by the children), are given in Table 7.6. Although statistically significant differences were not found on each item, the pattern is quite clear. The aspirations of both the child and his parents tend to be higher among the Accelerators than among the Constants, and the aspirations of the latter are in turn beyond those of the Decelerators. The goals expressed by the child and those that he believes his parents hold for him do, then, provide meaningful clues as to this past course of his development in ability.[8]

Now attention will be shifted from family to peer relationships, to see what significance IQ change has in this context. One way to do this is to analyze the data with respect to the question, "Who are your best friends?" (item 31). The frequencies with which Accelerators, Constants, and Decelerators were chosen was determined, and means for these three groups were computed separately for boys and girls. The results are shown in Figure 7.5.

It is clear from this figure that there is a sharp, positive relationship between peer popularity for boys and IQ change (the *F* test is significant). Accelerators were selected as "best friends" more often than Constants, and the latter in turn were chosen more often than Decelerators. The reverse pattern is found among the girls, although the *F* test is not significant. In terms of its social implications in the peer group, then, IQ change appears to have a different meaning for the boys than for the girls.

Another way of examining the "best friend" data is to see whether students who are listed as best friends are classified in the same IQ

---

[8] However, there does not appear to be much difference among the three groups with respect to parental involvement in homework.

TABLE 7.7

Numbers of Children in Each of Three IQ Change Groups Who Were Chosen
as "Best Friends" by Members of Three IQ Change Groups

Group membership of S who chooses	Group to which the S mentioned as "best friend" belongs*		
	Accelerators	Constants	Decelerators
Accelerators	5	2	1
Constants	3	7	3
Decelerators	3	5	6

* Only students who were among our subjects could be classified. Many children were mentioned, of course, for whom we had no IQ change scores.

change group as the children who selected them. These data are shown in Table 7.7; they indicate that most of the children report as their best friends students who do fall in the same IQ change group as theirs.

When the children were asked about their friends' plans for further education, 45% of the Accelerators stated that their friends planned to attend college, as opposed to 24% of the Constants and 15% of the Decelerators. On the other hand, 38% of the Decelerators reported that their friends planned to drop out of school as soon as possible, while a similar statement was made by only 19% of the Constants and 9% of the Accelerators.

In summary, while many interview items do not discriminate among the three IQ change groups, it is clear that the groups do differ with respect to how they report aspirational levels—within themselves, as held for them by their parents, and as possessed by their friends. In addition, there is evidence suggesting that friendship patterns are related to the developmental paths that their abilities are following; also, that ability change may have different social implications for boys and girls.

FAMILY AND SCHOOL CORRELATES OF IQ CHANGE

Two sources of information were used to analyze the relationships between the variables discussed in this section and IQ change. The first source was the questionnaire which was sent to the homes of all the children in the spring of 1962 (see Chapter 2 and Appendix C). The second source was the structured interview conducted with the eighth-grade children (see Chapter 16 and Appendix B). In general, the family and school variables are the same as the ones that were studied for the younger Negro children (see Chapter 6).

Father's Education

The questionnaire data revealed the following average number of years of education completed by the fathers of the children in the three IQ change groups: Accelerators = 9.9; Constants = 7.1; and Decelerators = 6.6. (The F value is statistically significant.) These mean values have been plotted in Figure 7.6, along with, for comparative purposes, the values reported for the fathers of the younger Negro children who were discussed in Chapter 6. The sharply positive relationship between father's education and IQ change is, of course, immediately apparent in the plot for the white children. For the Negro children, however, a slightly negative—although not significant—relationship is found. Most salient in the data for the white children is the relatively high educational level of the fathers whose children are Accelerators.

Mother's Education

The questionnaire data show that the average number of years of education completed by the mothers of the Accelerators is 11.4, whereas it is 8.8 for both Constants and Decelerators. (An F test indicates a very significant difference.) Further examination of the data reveals that 50% of the mothers of Accelerators completed high school, compared with 14% and 7% of the Constants and Decelerators, respectively. It is clear, then, that mother's education, like father's education, gives a useful clue as to the likely course of the white child's development in ability during adolescence.

It will be recalled that for the younger Negro children the average number of years of education for the mothers of Accelerators was lower than that of the other two IQ change groups (see Chapter 6), the re-

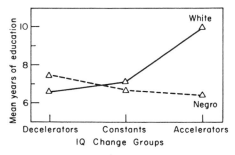

Fig. 7.6: The mean years of education for the fathers of white junior high school children and Negro primary children in three IQ change groups.

verse of what has been reported above for white adolescents. One possible interpretation of the Negro data is that the initial school years have a particularly strong impact on children coming from homes with the most pronounced intellectual deprivation. (There is, clearly, no compelling reason why such a factor as mother's education may not have differential significance at different age levels.) Until additional studies have been made at various age levels for both races, however, we cannot be certain about either the stability or the meaning of these findings.

Father's Occupation

Twelve fathers, out of 56 reported on the questionnaires, were identified as farmers. Approximately 7% of the Accelerators, 28% of the Constants, and 25% of the Decelerators had fathers whose primary occupation was farming. (Only one of these had a child who was classified as an Accelerator.) A chi-square analysis is not significant; nevertheless, there is a tendency which is consistent with one reported in Chapter 6 for the younger Negro children: the children of farming families tend *not* to show gains in ability.

Mother's Employment

Questionnaire data were available for 55 of the mothers. Of these, 24 were reported as being employed, 21 full-time. Employment percentages for the three IQ change groups were as follows: Accelerators = 53; Constants = 44; and Decelerators = 33. Although a chi-square analysis does not indicate statistically significant differences among the three groups, there is a tendency for maternal employment to be positively associated with IQ change. This tendency is consistent with the findings among the younger Negro children (see Chapter 6).

Possessions and Services

The questionnaire data were evaluated with respect to home ownership and the availability of telephone service within the home. Home ownership (usually meaning "in the process of buying") was reported by 85% of the families of Accelerators; by 74% of the families of Constants; and by 69% of the families of Decelerators. Comparable percentages for telephone service in the home were 77, 60, and 54, respectively. Although the chi-square values computed for these two items are not statistically significant, the consistency of the data suggests that there may be a meaningful and positive relationship between the economic well-being of the families and the changes in ability that are occurring among their children.

Absence of Natural Father

On the questionnaire, only four children were reported to be without their fathers or as having father-substitutes in their homes. Therefore, it is not possible to evaluate the impact of the father's absence upon the development of ability.

Family Type

Extended families were also uncommon among these children. Thus, questionnaire data for 52 of the families showed that only nine of them could be so classified (six questionnaires were unclear on this matter). Of this group, two had children who were Accelerators; four had children who were Constants; and three had children who were Decelerators. These differences are so slight that it would be unsafe to infer even a trend.

Size of Sibship

When the data from the questionnaire were analyzed with respect to the mean number of children living in the homes, no significant differences were found among the three groups. Inspection of the data, however, revealed that large sibships were infrequent among the Accelerators. The data were tabulated, therefore, to determine the frequency of families with five or more children in each of the three IQ change groups. Overall, there were 15 families with five or more children; 10 of these had children who were classified as Constants while four had children classified as Decelerators. In other words, only one Accelerator came from a family that had five or more children. This finding is suggestive, yet it must be regarded with caution, since the cutting point was based upon an inspection of the data. It is worth recalling, however, that the Accelerators among the younger Negro children also tended to come from families with small numbers of children (see Chapter 6).

Siblings' Education

As part of the eighth-grade interview, children were asked, "How far have your brothers and sisters gone in school?" The children were then classified according to whether or not they had at least one sibling who had dropped out before completing high school.

Although a chi-square analysis revealed no statistically significant differences between the three groups, there was a consistent trend in the data that should be noted. Fifty-seven percent of the Accelerators had at least one sibling who had dropped; for the Constants and Decelerators, this percentage jumped to 70 and 90, respectively. There is at least a suggestion, then, that there may be differential patterns of educational commitment within the sibships of the three groups and from which these children may secure models.

Ordinal Position

The children were classified as Only ($N = 5$), Youngest ($N = 12$), Oldest ($N = 13$), and Intermediate ($N = 22$) with respect to their positions within their sibling groups using the questionnaire data.[9] The one striking feature of the analysis was that Intermediate children *infrequently* showed IQ gains; only 2 out of the 22 Intermediate children were classified as Accelerators. Two of the Accelerators were classified as Only children, 4 as Youngest, and 6 as Oldest. A chi-square analysis, which divided the children into Intermediates and Others in order to develop adequate cell frequency, resulted in a significant chi-square value. Further work will need to be done, of course, before the suggestion can be accepted that an intermediate position has negative implications for ability change. This is particularly so because no similar tendency was found among the younger Negro children (see Chapter 6).

Teachers and Schools

Fifty-two of the children were divided among three teachers while they were in the sixth grade. An analysis of the data indicated that the particular teacher to whom the child was assigned at that time had no bearing upon his IQ change over the next three years. Furthermore, when the data were analyzed simply with respect to which of the two schools the children attended in the sixth grade, insignificant results were also obtained.

SCHOOL DROPOUTS

Seven students dropped out of school upon reaching the age of 16; a few data pertaining to them (separately for boys and girls) are presented in Table 7.8, along with comparative data for the total sample. Six out of the seven dropouts were boys. On the average, they were functioning at a lower ability level, were behind in academic performance, were older, and showed somewhat less achievement imagery than did the children who remained in school. *None of these seven dropouts showed an increase (even of a single point) in IQ over the three-year period.*

---

[9] This information for six of the children was either ambiguous or absent.

TABLE 7.8

School Dropouts Contrasted with the Total Sample on Several Measures

Groups	1961–62		1964–65		1965 Ach scores (Veroff pictures)	1962 Stanford Achievement Deviation scores
	CA	S-B IQ	CA	S-B IQ		
Boys						
Means for dropouts (N = 6)	160	79	196	72	1.3	−50
Means for all boys (N = 29)	146	98	182	98	1.5	−18
Girls						
Scores for dropout (N = 1)	171	64	209	64	0	−55
Means for all girls (N = 29)	143	95	178	95	1.6	−3

CONCLUDING COMMENTS

On the average, white adolescents—both boys and girls—changed very little over a three-year period in their functioning ability levels. This lack of group change, however, conceals considerable individual change. Actually, more than one-half of each sex group changed by five or more IQ points during the three years. This pattern in the findings is remarkably similar to that which was found to characterize the younger Negro children. Product-moment correlation coefficients between initial and retest S-B scores were higher for the white adolescents, however, than for the younger Negro children.

As was true for the Negro data, the findings are not consistent with statistical regression toward the mean. The original level of IQ offers no very useful basis for anticipating subsequent IQ change. More helpful is a measure of a child's competence in academic work.

One of the most striking differences between the findings of this study and those for the younger Negro children is to be found in the relationship between teachers' behavioral ratings and IQ change: the predictive potential of such ratings appears to be much greater for the Negro children. It could be argued that the basis for this difference might be found in the particular teachers who made the ratings; perhaps the Negro teachers were more observant, or exercised more care and were more accurate in their judgments. Such an interpretation might be more plausible if it were not for the fact that additional teachers *and* the peer group rated the eighth-grade children on different behavior scales, also with negative results. That these latter raters did in fact discern significant differences among the children in the group with respect to the behaviors being judged is suggested by the systematic sex differences that are present in their ratings.

It is possible that intellective growth has become more autonomous by adolescence than is true during the early primary years so that other behavior of the child no longer provides clues about his intellective path in the same way that it once did. Moreover, many adolescents may feel that it is necessary to cover up intellective commitments so that others, be they teachers or peers, do in fact have difficulty making valid judgments about their motivations. It is clear, we believe, that we need to make comparable studies of younger white children and Negro adolescents so that we may discover how accurate such speculations are.

Some of the findings with respect to the significance of family factors reinforce the idea that we must think developmentally; that is, the predictive power of a factor, or set of factors, may change according to the child's age level. For example, parental education for the Negro children was negatively related to IQ change, whereas the reverse condition prevailed among the white children. In this regard, it is possible that the school context may have a strong compensatory impact on many children during their early school years, but this effect may wash out as the children move along so that, by adolescence, there are internalized in the child processes that are more strongly related to certain critical conditions existing within his family.

Although none of the family factors taken singly provides a powerful basis for predicting or explaining IQ change, the pattern of the findings suggests that the socioeconomic status of the family may be meaningfully related to the intellective paths that the children are following at this age. The significance of father's education, mother's education, home ownership, telephone service, and number of children in the home is consistent with such an hypothesis. Moreover, both the educational and vocational aspirations articulated by the children pattern themselves in such a way as to be consistent with the interpretation that there may be socioeconomic differences between Accelerators, Constants, and Decelerators. Finally, the friendship patterns, which are known to be powerfully affected by class factors, would seem to fit in with such a general interpretation of the results. The fact that the relationship between each of these factors, taken singly, and IQ change is not stronger than it is may be due to the fact that this population, in contrast with many reported in the literature, is relatively homogeneous with respect to such factors. Also, of course, this sample is small in number.

Of special importance, we believe, is the fact that so many sex differences emerged. Thus, it is clear that the boys are seen as being more alienated from school than are the girls with respect to both motivation and performance. This judgment by both peers and teachers is, of course, consistent with the comparative performance of the two sexes on the achievement battery but, interestingly enough, it does not fit in with their comparative performance on the S-B. It is also of interest to note that IQ change and peer popularity are not related in the same way for the two sexes, and that, in contrast with other populations, achievement imagery is more systematically related to academic performance among the girls than among the boys.

Chapter 8

THE EFFECT OF KINDERGARTEN
TRAINING UPON THE INTELLECTIVE
FUNCTIONING OF NEGRO AND WHITE CHILDREN

Kindergarten programs have a long and honored history. For many years, communities, and even whole states, have had a kindergarten year as a regular part of their public school programs. North Carolina, however, has never included kindergarten work in its statewide, centrally financed educational program. Although any local school system has the authority to introduce enrichment programs like kindergartens, no school board has used local resources to initiate kindergartens in its system. A number of privately sponsored kindergartens operate in many communities of moderate size, but most rural families cannot take advantage of these programs. There is a growing statewide interest, however, in the possible benefits for children from a year or more of preparation in kindergarten.

The present chapter summarizes findings coming from three years of study of children in Millfield who attended special kindergarten programs that were set up as a regular part of the public school program in two schools in this area. Data on the impact of this experience upon the children's intellective performance were gathered by means of the same standard intelligence scales that were used in the studies reported in Part II. (Many other kinds of performance data were gathered and will be reported elsewhere; see Long, 1966.) Behavioral and family characteristics of the children were also examined to determine correlates of the intellective changes which they manifested during the kindergarten year.

160

PROCEDURE

Two kindergartens (one Negro, one white) began operating in Mill-field in September, 1962; new groups have been admitted to them each succeeding September.[1] In this report, data from the 1962–63, 1963–64, and 1964–65 classes will be considered. As of September, 1966, kinder-gartens also were established in Millfield's other two schools; these four programs remain the only public school kindergartens in North Carolina.[2]

Admission to the Kindergartens

Enrollment in the free kindergartens during the years that we are considering here was restricted to five-year-old children living in two of the four school districts. By limiting enrollment to the two school dis-tricts, it was possible to seek out the five-year-olds living in the other two school districts (one Negro, one white) to serve as control subjects. To enroll, a child had to be due to reach age six by October 15 of the following year, but be ineligible on the basis of age for the current first-grade class.

Parents were notified about the kindergarten program and invited to enroll their children; however, attendance was not compulsory. The best available data indicate that about 70% of the eligible white children and 95% of the eligible Negro children were enrolled during this three-year period.[3]

Teachers

A young Negro woman who was beginning her first teaching assign-ment taught the 1962–63 and 1963–64 Negro groups. She was succeeded

[1] Token integration began at the Negro kindergarten in September, 1965, when one white boy was enrolled. Data from the 1965–66 school year, however, were not available for the present report.

[2] These kindergartens were established under the impetus of Eugene R. Long, who desired such settings in order to experiment with the development of pro-grammed instructional materials which would be appropriate for children of this age and ability level. Support of the entire enterprise was shared by the United States Office of Education, the National Institute of Mental Health, the University of North Carolina at Chapel Hill, and the Orange County Board of Education.

[3] Eligible white children who had not been enrolled in the 1962–63 and 1963–64 classes were tested in their homes to determine if there was evidence of a sampling bias in the intellective level of those children who had been enrolled. The mean S-B IQ of the nonattenders in 1962–63 was 97.9 on initial testing; in 1963–64 it was 95.6. (See Table 8.3 for comparative figures for the attenders.) The non-attenders in 1962–63 were, then, somewhat higher in mean IQ than the attenders; in 1963–64 the reverse was true.

in September, 1964, by a somewhat older Negro woman who, for health reasons, had to resign after about three months of the school year had passed. She, in turn, was succeeded by a Negro woman of comparable age who had had previous teaching experience at the primary level.

For each of the three years, the white kindergarten groups were taught by a different teacher. These teachers were young and inexperienced. Each one had been trained in primary education, however, and the third one had had some prior experience teaching in a kindergarten in a midwestern state. Finally, it should be noted that each teacher was provided with a full-time classroom assistant. These assistants were married women living in Millfield; they had not had teacher training.

Academic Program

All the children attended kindergarten for a full school day during the entire academic year, except when illness or other personal considerations kept them at home. They rode to school in the morning in the buses along with the older children, ate lunch in the school cafeterias, and rode home in the buses at the end of the school day. Cots were provided so that the children could take naps immediately following lunch.

Each kindergarten was reasonably well equipped with toys, books, games, and other materials judged to be appropriate for five-year-old children. The activities carried out in the classes were planned by the teachers, sometimes in consultation with the principals and other teachers. No attempt was made to impose uniform programs in the two schools, nor from one year to the next in the same school. However, each teacher had the goal of developing programs that promised to improve the readiness of the children for the curriculum that they would encounter in the first grade.

In addition to this classroom work, approximately one-half of the children in each class devoted time to the special programs being developed by Long.[4] The time spent in this activity—which took place in another building—was short, usually averaging no more than one hour per week for any child. The groups in each class chosen to receive this special training were matched with classmates not given it with respect to their S-B IQ's at the beginning of the school year (see below).

Intelligence Testing

The children entering the kindergartens were tested early in the fall using the S-B and the PMA tests (see Chapter 3). Both were administered individually to each child by a regular member of the project

---

[4] Analyses of the impact of the programmed material are reported elsewhere (see Long, 1966).

TABLE 8.1

Numbers of Boys and Girls in Each Kindergarten and Control Group
Who Were Tested in the Fall and Spring on the Stanford-Binet

| | White | | | | Negro | | | |
| | K* | | Non-K* | | K | | Non-K | |
Academic year	Boys	Girls	Boys	Girls	Boys	Girls	Boys	Girls
1962–63	17	10	10	14	9	17	12	14
1963–64	17	14	7	15	7	15	10	13
1964–65	14	11	12	15	16	16	14	11
Totals	48	35	29	44	32	48	36	38

* K = kindergarten group; Non-K = control group.

staff. This meant, of course, that white children were evaluated by white examiners and Negro children by Negro examiners. The children were then reevaluated on both tests in the spring, as close to the end of the academic year as was feasible. The numbers of children tested on each occasion on the S-B and PMA are given in Tables 8.1 and 8.2, respectively.

A similar testing program was conducted during the fall and spring of each year with five-year-old children living in the two school districts in which kindergartens had not been established. This was done to compare changes in intellective test performance of children not attending kindergarten with changes shown by children attending the kindergartens. These nonkindergarten children were tested in their homes by the same examiners who tested the kindergarten children.

TABLE 8.2

Numbers of Boys and Girls in Each Kindergarten and Control Group
Who Were Tested in the Fall and Spring on the PMA

| | White | | | | Negro | | | |
| | K* | | Non-K* | | K | | Non-K | |
Academic year	Boys	Girls	Boys	Girls	Boys	Girls	Boys	Girls
1962–63	18	11	10	14	9	17	12	14
1963–64	16	14	7	14	8	15	10	13
1964–65	14	11	11	14	16	16	13	11
Totals	48	36	28	42	33	48	35	38

* K = kindergarten group; Non-K = control group.

It should be pointed out that the retesting interval was somewhat longer, on the average, for the kindergarten children (hereafter called K children) than for the nonkindergarten children (hereafter called Non-K children). Thus, for the S-B, the mean retest interval for the white K children was 1.4 months longer than it was for the Non-K children. For the Negro children, the retest interval was 1.8 months longer for those attending kindergarten. For the PMA, the comparable figures were 1.6 and 1.4 months, respectively. In general, about seven months elapsed between the two assessments of the K children, contrasted with an interval of approximately five and one-half months for the Non-K children. (The quotient scores used to report the findings from the S-B instrument are not affected by the differences in ages at retest of these groups of children. There may be a slight distortion introduced, however, in the raw score data from the PMA scales.)

Examination of the fall and spring test scores of the K children, in comparison with those for the Non-K groups, can furnish evidence about the impact of kindergarten training upon their intellective functioning.[5] It should be clear, however, that this analysis is limited to intellective functioning; social and motivational effects were not measured in this study. Some observations on these other behavioral areas by parents and teachers will be reported, though, in a later section of the chapter.

Teachers' Behavior Ratings

The children in the 1962–63 and 1963–64 kindergarten classes were rated,[6] at the end of the school year, by their teachers on the 22-item behavior scale discussed in Chapters 6 and 7 and reproduced in Appendix E. These ratings were analyzed to see if they related to the intellective changes shown by the children during their kindergarten year, and the findings also will be reported. Similar ratings could not be secured for the Non-K children, of course, since they had not been under observation during the year.

Family Data

In the fall of 1965, a short questionnaire was sent to the home of each child who had been enrolled in one of the kindergartens during the preceding three years. This questionnaire asked for information

---

[5] The teachers were unaware that performance on intelligence tests was to be used as a criterion measure of the effect that the kindergartens were having. To the best of our knowledge, they did not engage in coaching the children on the types of items and problems ordinarily encountered in intelligence tests.

[6] Unfortunately, owing to an oversight on our part, we failed to request similar ratings for the 1964–65 classes.

about parental education, occupations of the parents during the time the child was in the kindergarten, ages of siblings, and other family information (see Appendix D). In addition, the parents were asked to make a judgment as to whether the kindergarten training had helped their child, and in what way. The relation of some of the information so elicited to the intellective changes shown by the children will be discussed later.

CHANGES IN S-B IQ'S

An IQ change score was computed for each child by subtracting the S-B IQ score he obtained in the fall from the one obtained in the spring. Frequency distributions of these change scores, for white and Negro children separately, are shown in Figures 8.1 and 8.2, respectively. Data for K and Non-K children are separated in each of these two figures.

The mean IQ scores earned by each class on each testing occasion (as well as mean scores for each racial group when the three classes are combined) have been summarized in Table 8.3 (A and B) and are shown graphically in Figures 8.3 and 8.4. The results of t-tests computed to determine whether the mean IQ change secured by the K group differed significantly from that secured by its control group are also listed in Table 8.3. Finally, Table 8.3C contains the results of computations made to determine if the IQ change scores of boys differed significantly from those of girls. (Since there was no significant sex difference within either race, the values plotted in Figures 8.3 and 8.4

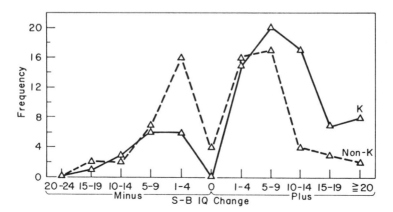

Fig. 8.1: Frequencies of various S-B IQ changes from fall to spring among white kindergarten (K) and nonkindergarten (Non-K) children (three years combined).

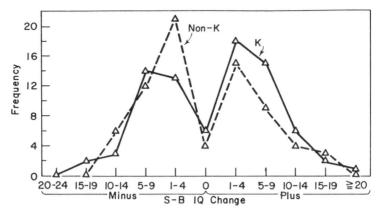

Fig. 8.2: Frequencies of various S-B IQ changes from fall to spring among Negro kindergarten (K) and nonkindergarten (Non-K) children (three years combined).

have been based upon boys and girls combined. Also, the two sexes have been combined for the other analyses of IQ change scores to be considered later.)

The data in the tables and figures just cited show that kindergarten attendance resulted in an increment in the mean IQ of the white children. Each year's K group gained more IQ points, on the average, than its control group; when the groups were combined for the three years, the difference between the K and Non-K children's mean amount of change in IQ was found to be highly significant. Overall, each white K

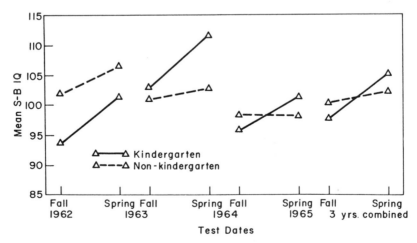

Fig. 8.3: Mean S-B IQ scores of white kindergarten and nonkindergarten children in fall and spring (three years separately and combined).

TABLE 8.3

S-B IQ Scores for Kindergarten (K) and Control (Non-K) Children

Academic year	Group	Mean IQ, fall	Mean IQ, spring	Mean change in IQ	N*	t	df	p
A. White children								
1962–63	K	93.6	101.4	7.8	27(17)	1.56	49	N.S.
	Non-K	102.0	106.5	4.5	24(10)			
1963–64	K	103.0	111.5	8.5	31(17)	2.43	51	.05
	Non-K	100.9	102.8	1.9	22 (7)			
1964–65	K	95.9	101.3	5.4	25(14)	2.71	50	.01
	Non-K	98.3	98.0	−0.2	27(12)			
3 years	K	97.8	105.1	7.3	83(48)	3.91	154	.001
combined	Non-K	100.3	102.2	2.0	73(29)			
B. Negro children								
1962–63	K	89.2	90.7	1.5	26 (9)	.98	50	N.S.
	Non-K	90.7	90.4	−0.2	26(12)			
1963–64	K	97.1	97.0	−0.2	22 (7)	.79	43	N.S.
	Non-K	90.7	88.6	−2.1	23(10)			
1964–65	K	88.6	90.4	1.8	32(16)	.03	55	N.S.
	Non-K	84.8	86.5	1.7	25(14)			
3 years	K	91.2	92.3	1.1	80(32)	1.13	152	N.S.
combined	Non-K	88.7	88.5	−0.2	74(36)			
C. Sex groups								
3 years	W Boys, K	94.9	102.9	8.0	48	.68	81	N.S.
combined	W Girls, K	101.8	108.3	6.5	35			
3 years	W Boys,	98.3	101.0	2.7	29	.72	71	N.S.
combined	Non-K							
	W Girls, Non-K	101.6	103.0	1.5	44			
3 years	N Boys, K	89.8	92.2	2.3	32	1.12	78	N.S.
combined	N Girls, K	92.0	92.4	0.4	48			
3 years	N Boys,	86.5	87.6	1.1	36	1.60	72	N.S.
combined	Non-K							
	N Girls, Non-K	90.7	89.4	−1.4	38			

* Numbers in parentheses refer to the numbers of boys in the groups.

child gained about five more IQ points than each white Non-K child[7] (7.3 vs. 2.0, respectively).

[7] The average increment of two IQ points in the Non-K group probably can be interpreted as evidence of a practice effect. It is, indeed, the best empirical estimate available of how much the IQ may increase on retesting for children like these, over a five- to six-month interval, owing largely to greater familiarity with the test materials and situation.

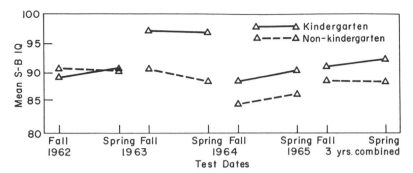

Fig. 8.4: Mean S-B IQ scores of Negro kindergarten and nonkindergarten children in fall and spring (three years separately and combined).

It is equally clear that there was no comparable gain in IQ among the Negro children who attended kindergarten. The K children, for the three years combined, showed a mean gain of 1.1 IQ points compared to a mean loss of 0.2 of an IQ point for the Non-K children. (Thus, as these figures indicate, there was no evidence for any practice effect in the scores of the Negro Non-K children.) This slight difference between Negro K and Non-K children cannot be interpreted as a reliable or meaningful kindergarten effect.

The net result of these findings is to show that, when both Negro and white children have attended kindergarten, the gap between their mean S-B IQ scores is widened. This is true for each year's racial groups, and for the two racial groups when their three classes are combined (see Figure 8.5).

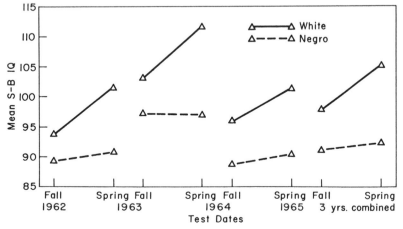

Fig. 8.5: Mean S-B IQ scores of white and Negro kindergarten children in fall and spring (three years separately and combined).

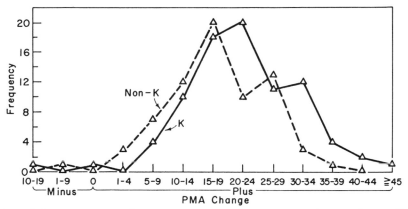

Fig. 8.6: Frequencies of various PMA Total Raw Score changes from fall to spring among white kindergarten (K) and nonkindergarten (Non-K) children (three years combined).

CHANGES IN PMA RAW SCORES

PMA change scores were also computed for the children by subtracting their fall scores from their spring scores. In all, five PMA change scores were secured for each child; findings with respect to each score will be reported below. The first of these, the child's Total Raw Score change, was based upon his performance on the entire test. His remaining four change scores were derived from the subtests described in Chapter 3: Verbal Meaning, Perceptual Speed, Number Facility, and Spatial Relations. Raw scores rather than quotient scores were used in

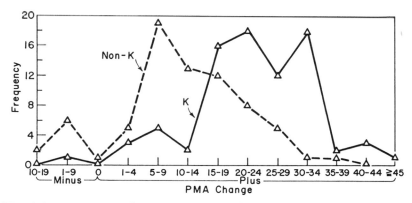

Fig. 8.7: Frequencies of various PMA Total Raw Score changes from fall to spring among Negro kindergarten (K) and nonkindergarten (Non-K) children (three years combined).

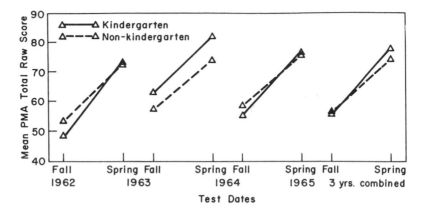

Fig. 8.8: Mean PMA Total Raw Scores of white kindergarten and nonkindergarten children in fall and spring (three years separately and combined).

these computations, since many of the children scored below the norms provided in the quotient tables; consequently, it is impossible to compute exact change scores for them based upon quotient values.[8] Since the primary concern here is with intraindividual changes among children of the same age level, the use of raw scores appears to be quite defensible.

Total Raw Scores

The frequency distributions for the Total Raw Score changes of the white and Negro children are plotted in Figures 8.6 and 8.7, respectively.

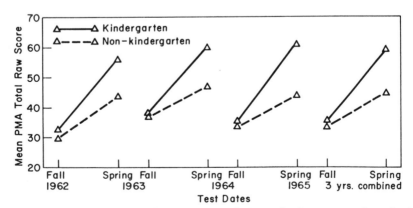

Fig. 8.9: Mean PMA Total Raw Scores of Negro kindergarten and nonkindergarten children in fall and spring (three years separately and combined).

[8] More exactly, 71 children (12 white) earned Total Raw Scores below the norms given in the manual.

TABLE 8.4

PMA Total Raw Scores for Kindergarten (K) and Control (Non-K) Children

Academic year	Group	Mean raw score, fall	Mean raw score, spring	Mean change	$N*$	t	df	p
		A. White children						
1962–63	K	48.3	73.3	25.1	29(18)	2.04	51	.05
	Non-K	53.1	72.2	19.1	24(10)			
1963–64	K	62.9	81.8	18.9	30(16)	.88	49	N.S.
	Non-K	57.2	73.9	16.7	21 (7)			
1964–65	K	55.2	76.8	21.5	25(14)	2.30	48	.05
	Non-K	58.5	75.4	16.9	25(11)			
3 years	K	55.6	77.4	21.8	84(48)	2.89	152	.01
combined	Non-K	56.2	73.8	17.6	70(28)			
		B. Negro children						
1962–63	K	32.5	55.9	23.3	26 (9)	3.15	50	.01
	Non-K	29.7	43.5	13.7	26(12)			
1963–64	K	38.0	59.7	21.6	23 (8)	3.89	44	.001
	Non-K	36.7	46.7	10.0	23(10)			
1964–65	K	35.6	60.6	25.0	32(16)	6.28	54	.001
	Non-K	33.3	43.7	10.4	24(13)			
3 years	K	35.3	58.8	23.5	81(33)	7.39	152	.001
combined	Non-K	33.1	44.6	11.5	73(35)			
		C. Sex groups						
3 years	W Boys, K	52.5	73.6	21.1	48	.76	82	N.S.
combined	W Girls, K	59.6	82.4	22.8	36			
3 years	W Boys, Non-K	54.8	73.7	18.9	28	1.10	68	N.S.
combined	W Girls, Non-K	57.2	74.0	16.8	42			
3 years	N Boys, K	34.0	58.5	24.5	33	.82	79	N.S.
combined	N Girls, K	36.2	59.0	22.8	48			
3 years	N Boys, Non-K	32.7	42.5	9.8	35	1.43	71	N.S.
combined	N Girls, Non-K	33.5	46.5	13.1	38			

* Numbers in parentheses refer to the numbers of boys in the groups.

In each figure, K and Non-K children are reported separately. Mean fall and spring Total Raw Scores for each year's groups, as well as for the three years combined, are listed in Table 8.4 and are plotted in Figures 8.8 and 8.9. The results of t-tests to determine whether the gain in each K group differed significantly from that of its control group are also given in Table 8.4. In addition, the results of t-tests to see if the change scores of the boys differed significantly from those of the girls are given in Section C of the same table. (As was true for the S-B, no significant sex differences were found. Consequently, the sexes were combined for the analyses reported below.)

The data in these tables and figures indicate that the total PMA performance of both Negro and white K children improved more than did that of their Non-K controls. It is also apparent that the gain of the Negro K children, compared to their controls, was much greater than that of the white K children compared to their controls. Thus, for the three years combined, white K children gained an average of 21.8 points, while white Non-K children gained 17.6 points, a difference of 4.2 points. For the Negro children, the comparable figures were 23.5 and 11.5, a difference of 12.0 points. The same conclusion is suggested by the fact that the overlap of the distributions for the two white groups in Figure 8.6 is considerably greater than that for the two Negro groups in Figure 8.7.

Furthermore, the rate of gain for the Negro K students matched that for the white K students, a fact reflected in the similar slopes of the racial plots shown in Figure 8.10. This result stands in sharp contrast to the S-B findings; with that test the racial gap increased as a result of kindergarten training (compare Figures 8.5 and 8.10). It is important to note, too, the relatively small gain made by the Negro Non-K children; the gap between them and the white Non-K children did widen appreciably between the two testings. Thus, the white Non-K children, for the three years combined, showed a mean gain of 17.6 points, compared to a mean gain of only 11.5 points for the Negro Non-K children.[9]

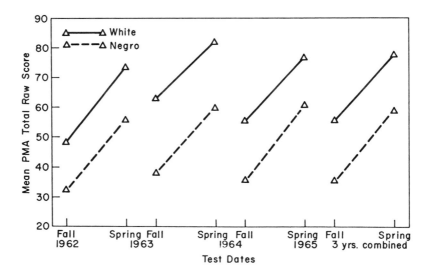

Fig. 8.10: Mean PMA Total Raw Scores of white and Negro kindergarten children in fall and spring (three years separately and combined).

[9] When raw scores are used, the scores earned by children should advance with increasing age, under normal conditions. This would not be true for quotient or IQ scores.

TABLE 8.5

PMA Verbal Meaning Scores for Kindergarten (K) and Control (Non-K) Children

Academic year	Group	Mean raw score, fall	Mean raw score, spring	Mean change	N^*	t	df	p
		A. White children						
1962–63	K	21.7	29.5	7.8	29(18)	1.89	51	N.S.
	Non-K	25.5	30.7	5.2	24(10)			
1963–64	K	28.3	32.0	3.7	30(16)	.35	49	N.S.
	Non-K	25.8	30.1	4.2	20 (7)			
1964–65	K	25.7	32.7	7.0	25(14)	.64	48	N.S.
	Non-K	24.2	30.4	6.2	25(11)			
3 years combined	K	25.2	31.3	6.1	84(48)	.96	152	N.S.
	Non-K	25.1	30.4	5.3	70(28)			
		B. Negro children						
1962–63	K	18.5	25.2	6.7	26 (9)	2.65	50	.05
	Non-K	16.3	19.5	3.2	26(12)			
1963–64	K	19.7	23.9	4.2	23 (8)	1.34	44	N.S.
	Non-K	17.7	20.2	2.5	23(10)			
1964–65	K	19.9	25.9	6.1	32(16)	2.00	54	N.S.
	Non-K	18.5	21.6	3.2	24(13)			
3 years combined	K	19.4	25.1	5.7	81(33)	3.56	152	.001
	Non-K	17.4	20.4	3.0	73(35)			

* Numbers in parentheses refer to the numbers of boys in the groups.

When given kindergarten training, then, the Negro children, as assessed by the PMA, develop intellectively at a rate equal to that of the white children who are receiving similar training, but without such training the Negro children develop more slowly than their white counterparts.

The questions raised by the difference between the findings on the S-B and the PMA will be considered later in the chapter. Before addressing this problem, each of the PMA subtests will be considered briefly to see if there is evidence that kindergarten training has similar effects upon these different components of intellective performance.

Verbal Meaning

On this subtest the child is presented with rows of pictures. For each row, and in response to instructions given by the examiner, the child must mark through the one picture that will indicate that he has correctly understood what the examiner has said. (There is a more detailed description of this subtest in Chapter 3.) Mean Verbal Meaning scores for the 12 groups at each testing time, as well as mean scores for the combined groups, are given in Table 8.5. The results of t-tests to compare K and Non-K groups are also listed in this table.

TABLE 8.6

PMA Perceptual Speed Scores for Kindergarten (K) and Control (Non-K) Children

Academic year	Group	Mean raw score, fall	Mean raw score, spring	Mean change	N*	t	df	p
		A. White children						
1962–63	K	11.6	17.1	5.6	29(18)	.06	51	N.S.
	Non-K	10.5	16.2	5.6	24(10)			
1963–64	K	12.9	18.0	5.1	30(16)	.61	49	N.S.
	Non-K	11.4	17.3	5.9	21 (7)			
1964–65	K	12.8	18.4	5.7	25(14)	.55	48	N.S.
	Non-K	13.2	18.3	5.1	25(11)			
3 years combined	K	12.4	17.8	5.4	84(48)	.10	152	N.S.
	Non-K	11.8	17.3	5.5	70(28)			
		B. Negro children						
1962–63	K	5.3	13.0	7.7	26 (9)	1.54	50	N.S.
	Non-K	5.4	10.6	5.2	26(12)			
1963–64	K	7.6	15.2	7.6	23 (8)	2.02	44	.05
	Non-K	6.7	11.2	4.5	23(10)			
1964–65	K	6.8	16.1	9.3	32(16)	4.45	54	.001
	Non-K	6.0	10.1	4.1	24(13)			
3 years combined	K	6.5	14.9	8.3	81(33)	4.38	152	.001
	Non-K	6.0	10.6	4.6	73(35)			

* Numbers in parentheses refer to the numbers of boys in the groups.

These analyses indicate that kindergarten training had only a slight, statistically insignificant effect on the verbal comprehension of the white children. The gains each year for the Negro K children were very similar to those for the white K children, but the Negro Non-K children failed to keep pace with the white Non-K children. The failure of the Negro Non-K children to keep pace results in a highly significant difference between Negro K and Non-K children when the data from the three years are combined. The conclusion is justified, therefore, that kindergarten training does stimulate the development of the Negro child's verbal capacity in a way that is not apparent among the white children.[10]

[10] Performance on the vocabulary items on the S-B showed no impact of kindergarten training among either the white or Negro children. As indicated in Chapter 3, this scale is more demanding than the PMA Verbal Meaning test in that the child is asked to define words; hence, he must express his thoughts orally. A child may understand the meaning of certain S-B words, yet, from shyness, inexperience in verbalizing, or for other reasons, he may fail to give a response that merits a plus score.

TABLE 8.7

PMA Number Facility Scores for Kindergarten (K)
and Control (Non-K) Children

Academic year	Group	Mean raw score, fall	Mean raw score, spring	Mean change	$N*$	t	df	p
		A. White children						
1962–63	K	5.6	12.6	6.9	29(18)	2.03	51	.05
	Non-K	7.2	12.0	4.8	24(10)			
1963–64	K	9.7	15.0	5.3	30(16)	2.09	49	.05
	Non-K	8.8	12.1	3.2	21 (7)			
1964–65	K	6.8	12.0	5.3	25(14)	1.92	48	N.S.
	Non-K	8.2	11.5	3.4	25(11)			
3 years combined	K	7.4	13.3	5.9	84(48)	3.46	152	.001
	Non-K	8.0	11.8	3.8	70(28)			
		B. Negro children						
1962–63	K	3.7	8.1	4.4	26 (9)	2.18	50	.05
	Non-K	3.9	6.2	2.4	26(12)			
1963–64	K	4.5	9.6	5.1	23 (8)	2.88	44	.01
	Non-K	4.3	6.5	2.2	23(10)			
1964–65	K	3.5	8.5	5.0	32(16)	3.81	54	.001
	Non-K	3.6	5.5	2.0	24(13)			
3 years combined	K	3.8	8.7	4.8	81(33)	5.11	152	.001
	Non-K	3.9	6.1	2.2	73(35)			

* Numbers in parentheses refer to the numbers of boys in the groups.

Perceptual Speed

On this scale, the child is shown 28 rows of pictures and his task is to identify the two pictures in each row that are exactly alike. This is the only PMA subtest at this level which is timed; the child is given three and one-half minutes to complete it (see Chapter 3 for a fuller test description).

The analysis of the Perceptual Speed scores is summarized in Table 8.6, following the same format used in Table 8.5 for the Verbal Meaning scores. The data consistently indicate that the white K children showed no more gain in competence on these items than the white Non-K children. The gain of the Negro K children, however, not only exceeded the gain of the Negro Non-K children (at a highly significant level), but was also markedly above that shown by the white children. Apparently, then, kindergarten training has effected unusually large increments in the competence of the Negro children on this kind of task.

Number Facility

On this subtest, the child is presented 27 rows of pictures which contain different numbers of drawings of the same object. Then, in response to instructions given by the examiner (for example, "Mark three airplanes."), the child marks figures in each row to indicate his understanding of numbers or quantities.

The analysis of the scores for Number Facility is summarized in Table 8.7. For the three years combined, both white K and Negro K children gained more than their controls (both differences are highly significant). The white K children made the greatest absolute gains, but the Negro K children made the greatest relative gains in number facility.

Spatial Relations

This subtest has two parts; there are 12 rows in each part. In Part I, there is a line drawing in a separate box on the left of each row. To the right, in a rectangular box, are four additional line drawings. The child's task is to select the one drawing from among these four which, when placed with the drawing at the far left, will make a perfect square. In Part II, each of the 12 rows contains two pictures. The figure on the right in each instance is an incomplete copy of the figure on the left. The child is told to draw lines on the figures on the right to make them look just like the ones on the left.

The scores on Spatial Relations are summarized in Table 8.8. Each year the white K children gained more, on the average, than the white Non-K children, but the differences were small and not statistically dependable. When the three years were combined, however, the difference in favor of the white K children proved to be very significant. The difference between the Negro K and Non-K children was more substantial; for the three years combined, it was highly significant. It is worthy of note, too, that the Negro Non-K children showed the smallest gain among the four groups of children. (They also performed most poorly on each of the other subtests in the PMA battery.)

Summary of PMA Results

The data presented show that kindergarten training had a positive effect upon the PMA performance of the children of both races. Relatively speaking, *the effect was greater for the Negro children than for the white children*. There was no suggestion of a sex difference for the children of either racial group, when total scores were analyzed.[11]

The analysis of the subtest data (for the three years combined) revealed that Negro K children gained much more than Negro Non-K

---

[11] Subtest scores were not analyzed for sex effects.

TABLE 8.8

PMA Spatial Relations Scores for Kindergarten (K) and Control (Non-K) Children

Academic year	Group	Mean raw score, fall	Mean raw score, spring	Mean change	N*	t	df	p
		A. White children						
1962–63	K	9.1	14.2	5.1	29(18)	1.77	51	N.S.
	Non-K	9.9	13.4	3.5	24(10)			
1963–64	K	11.9	16.5	4.5	30(16)	1.86	49	N.S.
	Non-K	11.1	14.5	3.3	21 (7)			
1964–65	K	10.0	13.6	3.6	25(14)	1.49	48	N.S.
	Non-K	12.9	15.2	2.3	25(11)			
3 years combined	K	10.4	14.9	4.5	84(48)	3.02	152	.01
	Non-K	11.3	14.4	3.0	70(28)			
		B. Negro children						
1962–63	K	5.1	9.5	4.4	26 (9)	1.95	50	N.S.
	Non-K	4.4	7.2	2.8	26(12)			
1963–64	K	6.3	11.0	4.7	23 (8)	3.48	44	.01
	Non-K	8.0	8.9	0.9	23(10)			
1964–65	K	5.5	10.3	4.8	32(16)	3.94	54	.001
	Non-K	5.2	6.7	1.5	24(13)			
3 years combined	K	5.6	10.2	4.6	81(33)	5.36	152	.001
	Non-K	5.8	7.6	1.7	73(35)			

* Numbers in parentheses refer to the numbers of boys in the groups.

children in each of the four ability areas. In contrast, the white K children showed meaningful gains over the white Non-K children on only two subtests, Number Facility and Spatial Relations. Furthermore, when rate of growth was considered, it was apparent that Negro K children kept pace with white K children, but that Negro Non-K children failed to match white Non-K children.

One major implication of these findings is that kindergarten training is more critical for the intellective development of the Negro children than it is for the white children. Thus, the white Non-K child is more likely to learn some of the skills which are ordinarily emphasized in kindergartens than is the Negro Non-K child. This is probably due to the fact that the Negro homes are more lacking in intellectual stimulation and guidance than are the white homes.

COMPARISON OF THE S-B AND PMA CHANGES

It is obvious that the conclusions drawn about the effect of kindergarten training upon intellective functioning are dependent upon the instrument used to assess intellective performance. If only the S-B had been used, for example, no evidence could be cited to show that kindergarten training had influenced the Negro children, but there would be evidence that the white children had been helped. The PMA data, however, show quite clearly that Negro children have benefited from kindergarten training, and that the S-B apparently was insensitive to this effect. Indeed, there are grounds in the PMA data for concluding that the Negro children have benefited more from the kindergarten experience than the white children. Thus, for the three years combined, Negro K children showed a mean gain in Total Raw Score that was larger than that earned by the white K children (23.5 vs. 21.8 points, respectively).

In a number of ways, the PMA tasks appear to resemble more closely the daily learning activities that take place in the kindergarten than do the S-B items. Perhaps this is one reason why the PMA change scores reflect important kindergarten effects for the Negro children, whereas the S-B change scores do not. This interpretation, however, does not explain the significant gain shown by the white K children on the S-B. So far as we can determine, the data do not suggest why this effect should be shown only by the white children. Additional studies will need to be made to clarify this matter.

TEACHERS' BEHAVIOR RATINGS RELATED TO INTELLECTIVE CHANGE

The relationships between teachers' behavior ratings and intellective changes manifested by the kindergarten children will be examined in this section. First, however, the statistical procedures will be described.

Biserial correlation coefficients were computed between each of the 22 ratings and the children's S-B and PMA change scores. Separate coefficients were computed for each of the four classes, two Negro and two white. Distributions were made of these ratings on each of the 22 items for each of the four classes. Each of these distributions, then, was divided as close to its median value as possible in order to differentiate two groups with respect to the trait; that is, children rated high on the trait as distinguished from those rated low on the trait. Change scores for both the S-B and PMA tests were treated as continuous distributions in order to compute biserial correlation coefficients between each of the intellective change scores and the dichotomized teachers' ratings.

S-B Results

Of the 88 biserial correlation coefficients computed between the behavior ratings and IQ change scores, only one was significantly different from zero. It is obvious, then, that these ratings do not enlarge our understanding of the changes in S-B performance which occurred during the year in kindergarten. This conclusion holds for both the Negro and the white children.

PMA Results

Of the 88 biserial correlation coefficients computed by using the PMA change scores (Total Raw Score), one was very significant and two were significant. In general, then, these coefficients were a bit more substantial than those based upon the S B, yet the number of significant relationships is still within chance expectations. Moreover, each of the 22 items that showed a significant relationship with the PMA change scores within one of the four classes failed to show such a relationship in the other three classes. The results based upon the PMA, therefore, are not substantially different from those reported above for the S-B.

Summary

This finding of no relationship between teachers' behavior ratings and intellective change stands in sharp contrast to the results of the study reported in Chapter 6 for Negro children in the primary grades. In that study a number of important relationships between teachers' behavior ratings and intellective change were identified. These kindergarten-age children were, of course, younger than the primary children, and it may be that their behavior patterns were neither as salient nor as fixed as those of the older children, but there is no empirical evidence that this was so. It should also be recognized that the current study deals with intellective change over a much shorter period of time than the one reported in Chapter 6 (about one-half year vs. three years, respectively). There is no way of knowing, however, whether this difference between the two studies accounts in any way for the differences in results.

Another characteristic of the present study must not be overlooked: this is a study of postdiction (see Chapter 6). Thus, it is very likely that the teachers' ratings in the current study were heavily influenced by what the child seemed to be like toward the close of the school year rather than what he was like either at the beginning or even in the middle of the year. If this conjecture is valid, and if many of the children did in fact show appreciable changes in behavior under the socializing impact of the school, then the correlation coefficients obtained may be different from those that would have been obtained by using ratings secured early in the school year. Indeed, it might very well be that the ratings used in this study would correlate more highly with ability changes during the early primary grades than they have with such changes during the kindergarten year that had already been effected when the ratings were made. Again, this is a problem that will need additional research.

FAMILY CHARACTERISTICS RELATED TO INTELLECTIVE CHANGE OF KINDERGARTEN CHILDREN

Of the 83 white children who had been in the three kindergarten classes, 75 were still living in Millfield in the fall of 1965 when a short questionnaire (see Appendix D) was sent to their parents. Completed questionnaires were returned by 69 of these parents—that is, by 92% of them. Of the 80 Negro children who had been in the three kindergarten classes, 75 were living in Millfield when the questionnaire was circulated. Completed questionnaires were returned by 72 of their families—that is, by 96% of them. The data reported below refer only to those children whose families returned completed questionnaires.[12]

Father's Education

The fathers of the white children were reported as having had a wide range of formal education: a low of 3 years and a high of 16 years (mean = 9.8). The range for the Negro fathers was comparably broad, from 2 to 16 years (mean = 8.5). Product-moment correlation coefficients were computed (separately for the two races) between fathers' education, given in years, and the S-B and PMA score changes of their children. None of these coefficients was reliably different from zero. There is, therefore, no basis for concluding that the education of a child's father is related to the intellective change of the child while he is in kindergarten.

Mother's Education

The range of education for the white mothers was from 0 to 16 years (mean = 10.6). For the Negro mothers, the range was also very wide, from 1 to 16 years (mean = 9.5). The product-moment correlation coefficients which were computed between mothers' education and the S-B and PMA change scores of their children were very similar to those obtained for the fathers' data; that is, they were small and statistically insignificant. As was true for father's education, then, mother's educa-

---

[12] Occasionally, of course, an item was not answered on one of the "completed" questionnaires. One white mother returned an unanswered questionnaire with the comment, "These questions infringe upon my privacy."

tion is not related significantly to the intellective change of the child during the kindergarten year.

Father's Employment

The data for the white fathers' employment were so homogeneous that they did not permit a meaningful analysis of their relationship to the intellective changes of the children. However, two analyses were carried out for the Negro sample. In the first analysis, the mean IQ change of the children with working fathers in the home was compared to the mean IQ change of the children without working fathers in the home. The second analysis made a similar comparison of PMA scores (Total Raw Scores). On the S-B, Negro children *without* working fathers gained, on the average, 1.6 IQ points more than did the children *with* working fathers in their homes. On the PMA, the gain was again in favor of the children without working fathers in their homes, this time by an average of 3.5 raw score points. Neither of these differences is statistically significant.

Mother's Employment

Of 69 white mothers, 37 were employed—32 full-time and 5 part-time. Of 71 Negro mothers, 36 were employed—20 full-time and 16 part-time. For the purpose of statistical analysis, working mothers were defined as those who worked outside their own homes, either full-time or part-time.

Children of the white working mothers gained, on the average, 7.6 IQ points on the S-B, whereas the children of white nonworking mothers had a mean gain of 7.2 IQ points. On the PMA, the comparable figures for the two groups were 21.4 and 23.1 raw score points, respectively. These differences between the children of white working and nonworking mothers are small and statistically insignificant.

On the S-B, the children of Negro working mothers gained an average of 3.4 IQ points; in contrast, the children of Negro nonworking mothers showed a mean loss of 0.2 IQ point. This difference between the two groups is statistically significant. (It is also consistent with the findings in the study of Negro children in the primary grades; see Chapter 6.) However, PMA change scores in the present inquiry failed to show a similar relationship to the working status of the Negro mothers. Children of the working mothers gained an average of 23.8 raw score points on the PMA, while children of the nonworking mothers had a mean gain of 24.3 points. Overall, then, the data afford little support for the hypothesis that either a Negro or white mother's working status is meaningfully related to her child's intellective growth during kindergarten.

Natural Father's Absence

Except for one child, both natural parents of the white children were living with their children. In the Negro sample, however, there were 16 children whose natural fathers were separated from them. The mean gain of these 16 children was greater—on both the S-B and the PMA— than the mean gain of those Negro children living with their natural fathers. These mean differences were very small (1.6 points on the S-B, 1.5 points on the PMA), however, and cannot be regarded as meaningful. Therefore, for this age period and in this context, there is no evidence that the absence of a natural father in the Negro homes affects the intellective development of the children.

Telephone Service

It was pointed out in Chapter 5 that the presence or absence of telephone service in the home provides a useful, although admittedly rough, index of a family's socioeconomic status in Millfield. Of the white families in this sample, 48 reported having such service, as compared to 21 Negro families.

White children from families with telephone service did not differ significantly in either their S-B or PMA change scores from children whose families were without this service; a comparable result was found for the Negro children. Within both races, then, this index of a family's material well-being gives no reliable hint of the intellective change its child is likely to show during his kindergarten year. This finding is in close agreement with the results of the analyses reported earlier with respect to the significance of parental education, which is often used as an index of a family's socioeconomic status.

Size of Sibship

The average size of the sibship was 3.8 for the white families and 4.8 for the Negro families. The range for the white families was from 1 to 12, whereas it was from 1 to 10 for the Negro families. There were, however, fewer white than Negro families with 8 or more children.

Product-moment correlation coefficients computed between size of sibship and ability change scores (both S-B and PMA) revealed no significant relationships between these variables for either the white or the Negro children. The intellective changes of these children during their kindergarten year could not have been anticipated from knowledge about the size of the sibship from which they came.

Summary

It is obvious, we believe, that the family variables analyzed show little promise in terms of providing a basis for predicting or explaining the intellective development of these children during a year in kindergarten. There may be other family variables which are more powerful in this regard, but it will be up to future research to identify them.

PARENTS AND TEACHERS JUDGE THE KINDERGARTEN

The questionnaire, distributed in the fall of 1965, asked the parents to describe the value of kindergarten for their children. More specifically, two questions were asked: (1) Do you feel that the kindergarten helped this child?[13] and (2) How did it help or fail to help him?

Sixty-six of the white parents replied that their children had benefited from the kindergarten, two said no, and one said maybe. Seventy-one Negro parents responded affirmatively; the remaining Negro parents failed to answer these two questions. It is clear from this simple tabulation that the parents of both races had an overwhelmingly favorable opinion about the worthwhileness of the kindergarten program. As one parent commented on the form, "Kindergarten has help (sic) my child very much. I wish all of my old children has (sic) went to kindergarten."

In commenting upon how the kindergartens had helped their children, parents mentioned behavioral changes in both the social and intellectual domains. Quite frequently, for example, there were comments that the child had learned how to get along better with other children, or that he had learned letters, numbers, and other intellective skills that he had not had before entering kindergarten. Overall, the Negro parents seemed to be somewhat more impressed with how their children had gained in intellectual competence (as reflected in remarks about learning their ABC's, how to count, and so on) than the white parents were; the latter seemed to give greater emphasis to the development of social skills. In this regard, it must be remembered that the white children were more advanced intellectively when they entered kindergarten than were the Negro children. Also, as has already been shown in the analyses of the S-B and PMA data, the Non-K white children tended to develop their intellective skills more in keeping with the white K children than was true for the two comparable Negro groups. It is likely, therefore, that the intellective gains of the Negro K children were more salient with respect to their Non-K counterparts than was true for the white K children with respect to their controls. In any event, it is clear that

[13] The form of this question is probably somewhat conducive to favorable endorsements; more negative remarks may have been made had the question been slanted for problems rather than benefits.

parents of both races saw intellective and social advances by their children which they attributed to the kindergarten experience.

No formal effort was made to obtain teachers' judgments about the value of kindergarten training. From time to time, however, casual inquiries were addressed to the two first-grade teachers in order to elicit judgments from them about the value of such preparation. The Negro first-grade teacher gave unqualified endorsement to the kindergarten program, emphasizing that when children had attended kindergarten she could begin teaching them reading and arithmetic early in the fall. Without this background, it was late in the school year before she could begin teaching these skills effectively. The white first-grade teacher, however, was more ambivalent about the kindergarten program. Its worth was, as she saw it, very much dependent upon who the kindergarten teacher happened to be. In addition, her endorsement of the program was restrained because she felt that children of kindergarten age were too young to be associating with the older children in the school. (No data in this study bear directly upon this issue raised by this teacher, but no independent evidence in support of this alleged adverse effect of such programs came to light during these three years.)

CONCLUDING COMMENTS

The data presented provide firm support for the conclusion that kindergarten training can elevate the average intellective functioning levels of both Negro and white children. It is apparent, however, that the precise nature of the conclusions to be drawn in this regard depend to a considerable degree upon the instrument used to measure intellective functioning.

The total evidence suggests that kindergarten training is a more critical need for the Negro children in Millfield than it is for the white children. This conclusion is based largely upon the relatively inferior mental growth rates shown by the Negro children who were not enrolled in the kindergarten program when they were compared to the other three groups on the PMA scales. The Negro children who attended kindergarten, on the other hand, matched the white children stride for stride as far as rate of advance in competence on the PMA tests was concerned. The pattern of these findings is consistent with other evidence which suggests that the intellectual stimulation and guidance within the Negro homes is especially impoverished.

In addition to the test data, the responses of the parents support the conclusion that kindergarten training had a beneficial impact upon the development of their children. Indeed, the near unanimity of response in this regard is something of a rarity as far as parental approval of a particular school program is concerned. The emphasis which the Negro parents placed upon the intellective gains of their children suggests, we believe, that many of these parents are acutely aware of the fact that their children need more intellectual stimulation and guidance than they are receiving. With limited backgrounds and resources, however, many of these Negro parents are unable to provide for such needs.

Although the test performance of the children was, on the average, improved as a result of kindergarten training, improvement was not noted for every child. Even among the children who did improve, the rates of improvement were frequently different. Attempts to identify factors either within the families or in the behavioral repertoires of these children which might relate to these individual differences in intellective change were, in the main, unsuccessful. It is clear, therefore, that much more penetrating research will have to be carried out if this problem is to be solved. On the other hand, the results suggest that the factors that were studied do not necessarily restrict a child's potential for positive intellective change.

Chapter 9

A PILOT PROJECT TO ACCELERATE THE INTELLECTIVE DEVELOPMENT OF FOUR-YEAR-OLD NEGRO AND WHITE CHILDREN

Educators and psychologists have devised a number of programs during the last half-century with the objective of enhancing the intellective development of the participants. These programs have been aimed at various target groups and age levels. The successes achieved have varied greatly, depending upon many factors in the children themselves, in the programs and their staffing, and even in the criteria used to evaluate them. These efforts have been given considerable impetus in the last few years by federal antipoverty programs.

As an outgrowth of our work, and the findings that suggested that many children in Millfield were not adequately prepared, intellectively or motivationally, for school, the staff initiated a pilot study to determine the feasibility of a home-visiting program for four-year-old children. This project, labeled Project Acceleration, or, more simply, Project A, will be described in this chapter.

Unlike the other work discussed in this book, *the current report is essentially qualitative in nature.* And, except for the experimental kindergarten program discussed in the previous chapter, Project A represented our only attempt to intervene in the life of Millfield with the objective of producing changes. The remainder and bulk of our work was, of course, directed toward the assessment, evaluation, and better understanding of existing conditions and processes.

186

THE CHILDREN AND THEIR FAMILIES

As noted in Chapter 1, there are some well-to-do and well-educated families in Millfield, families whose adult members make every reasonable effort to see that their children are properly prepared for their school years. Other not-so-fortunate parents also attempt to train and inspire their children so that they will take advantage of learning opportunities which were not in fact available to the parents. In general, however, the children in Millfield are psychologically deprived in the sense that they are taught relatively little in their homes that will prepare them for the various learning experiences of the schoolroom. Consequently, when school age arrives, they enter the schoolrooms intellectually and socially handicapped.

Members of the project staff were convinced that efforts at intervention should be concentrated at the preschool level rather than directed toward the rehabilitation of children who were already in the school system. Moreover, since it was clear that Project A would be able to work with only a small number of children, staff members concluded that their efforts should be concentrated at one age level rather than scattered over several preschool years. A decision was made, therefore, to work with children who, in one more year, would be of kindergarten age. This meant, then, that all the children participating in Project A were more than four years of age but less than five and one-half years when staff members began working with them. Age ranges, as well as other descriptive data pertaining to the children and families who participated in Project A, may be found in Table 9.1.[1]

To locate suitable children, a roster was compiled of all children living in the area who would be of kindergarten age by the following September.[2] This roster included children in the two school districts without kindergarten programs, as well as children from the two school districts with kindergarten programs (see Chapter 8). Twenty-five children (seven Negro boys, six Negro girls, seven white boys, and five white girls) were then selected as being generally representative of the families living in Millfield. The number of children was determined by the practical matter of how much time staff members could free from their other duties for Project A work.

---

[1] The chronological ages given in Table 9.1 are the ages of the children in January, 1965, the month when staff members began working with most of the children.

[2] For a variety of reasons, several children were added to this roster who were slightly older than this criterion suggests.

TABLE 9.1

Subject, Family, and Sibship Data

Child's number	C.A.	PPVT M.A.	Race	Sex	Worker	Number in family*	Number of older sibs	Number of younger sibs	Number of rooms	Condition of house†
1	5–2	4–11	W	F	W1	6	4	0	5	A
2	5–3	3–8	N	F	N2	8	1	1	8	E
3	5–1	4–5	N	F	N3,N1	4	1	0	6	A+
Sibs { 4	4–7	2–6	N	F	N2	5	1	1	5	E
5	5–5	4–8	N	F	N2	5	0	2	5	E
6	5–3	2–9	N	F	N1,N2	9	11	0	4	A
7	4–4	3–6	N	M	N1	5	1	1	5	A+
8	5–0	3–5	N	M	N3,N1	5	2	0	?	A−
9	4–9	5–1	W	M	W3	3	0	0	6	A
10	5–1	4–10	W	M	W2	5	2	0	5	A
11	4–8	3–8	W	M	W2	4	0	1	2	A
12	5–1	5–5	W	M	W1	6	3	0	5	A
13	5–3	4–11	W	F	W3	4	0	1	5	A
14	4–11	6–1	W	F	W2	4	0	1	6	E
15	5–1	6–10	N	M	N1	7	3	1	3	D
16	4–6	3–2	N	M	N1	6	3	0	5	A+
17	5–0	2–8	N	M	N1	6	1	2	4	A
18	4–11	3–5	N	M	N1,N2	6	3	0	10	A+
19	4–8	4–11	W	M	W3	4	0	1	4	A−
20	5–1	3–1	N	M	N3,N1	14	9	2	6	A
21	5–1	6–1	W	F	W3	4	1	0	5	A−
22	4–8	5–5	N	F	N1	11	5	3	4	D
23	4–8	3–1	W	M	W1	8	4	0	2	D
24	4–8	4–8	W	F	W2	6	0	1	6	A−
25	5–1	5–7	W	M	W3	6	3	0	6	A
Means	4–11	4–4				6.0	2.3	0.7	5.0	

* At home during Project A.
† E = excellent, A = adequate, D = dilapidated.

THE VISITING STAFF

Six workers (three Negro, three white) participated in Project A.
Each was a mature woman with a family of her own, and each had been
a member of the main project staff for a period of at least two years.
They had had, then, considerable experience in Millfield before they
initiated Project A.

Each worker was assigned at least three but not more than five children.[3] This small number of children for each staff member was dictated primarily by the limited amount of time which the workers could divert from other duties to Project A. Also, this was a new role for the workers, and they wanted an adequate amount of time to prepare materials and share experiences with one another.

The workers were assigned only children of their own race. It was our impression, though, that most, if not all, of the Negro families would have accepted white workers in this role. It is much less clear how many of the white families would have participated if Negro workers had been assigned to them.

DEVELOPING THE PLAN

The workers were eager to participate in an interventional program. Translating this desire into action, however, proved to be a formidable task. There are, after all, few sources of information available about how to introduce intellectual stimulation into Southern rural homes. The initial efforts of these women were rather tentative and cautious as they confronted this challenge.[4]

The great and unique advantage that these workers possessed, of course, was their personal experience over several years with the families of Millfield, experience which they could articulate and share within the framework of their professional training. The workers were somewhat reluctant about acknowledging their own strengths, however, feeling somehow that there must be others who knew the answers and could say what ought to be done. Because of this reluctance, and also because they were highly motivated to do a thoroughly professional job in a form that would be of value to other workers, it took several months to formulate the plan which ultimately developed for Project A.[5]

The workers recognized that the children would have many individual differences. Therefore, no rigid procedure applied uniformly to all of

[3] One staff member took over extra children when two other workers ran short of time. These cases are identified in Table 9.1 by double entries for the workers.

[4] It should be noted that the field workers assumed major responsibility for the development and implementation of Project A. Also, they prepared a draft of a paper reporting their work which was very helpful to the authors in preparing this chapter.

[5] The workers spent many hours together in small group discussions, exchanging experiences and judgments with one another. They also visited nursery schools and observed experienced teachers working with preschool children. In addition, they reviewed and discussed a great deal of literature on the intellectual and personal development of preschool children.

them would hold much prospect of success. Given this reality, the workers might have decided to proceed "playing it by ear." That is, they might have worked with each child without forming any plans very far in advance about the activities that they would have him engage in. However, the workers felt the need for more structure than such a method of operation would have provided. Also, they believed that if they used such a procedure it would be much more difficult to communicate the substance of their work to others than if they developed more specific plans. Together, therefore, they developed the plan described below. This plan gave the workers the security of having worked out in advance many different activities to use with the children and their families, yet the plan respected individual differences, since it did not insist that each child had to be subjected to each unit of the plan or that its parts had to be taken up in a particular order.

SUBSTANCE OF THE PLAN

Most social action programs are rooted in deep personal convictions of their promoters. Sometimes these beliefs are given explicit articulation, but oftentimes they are not. As the workers shared experiences and worked together on Project A, they reached a point where they felt that the convictions which were directing the development of their plans should be given clear expression. This statement of belief, as the workers drafted it, is reproduced below:

A *Statement of Belief.* From babyhood a child explores the world of things and of people around him. He is constantly confronting new experiences and assimilating and making sense out of the experiences he has already had. Gesell and Ilg, who have made extensive studies of children at various age levels, describe the four-year-old as characterized by high drive and rapid acculturation. He appears to strive for command of language and needs to identify with his environment. He is always asking "Why?" and "How?". While his attention span is short and he tends to go out of bounds, he is capable of considerably more organization in his play activities than he was a short time ago. His small muscle coordination is better, making it possible for him to develop such skills as cutting with a scissors and crayoning with large crayons.

In many of the homes that we have visited in Millfield, we have not found an environment sufficiently stimulating for the optimum development of a child in today's world. These children arrive in the first grade, at age six, already behind the national norms in pre-reading skills and in the perceptual discriminations upon which these skills are based. Many of our children have had little experience of being talked to, read to, answered in all seriousness when they asked about things that puzzled them. Many don't ask "Why?" or "How?".

We hope to stimulate the natural curiosity of the children with whom we will be working at the same time that we demonstrate by our own behavior the reciprocal attitude of being eager to supply any and all information that the children seem to be interested in. We will seek to engage the mother who may be home in our effort to best understand and respond to her child, hoping thereby to involve her in similar efforts on his behalf. We hope to provide a warm interpersonal situation in which the child can develop interests and skills, secure in the sense of his own worthwhileness. We will best convey our philosophy by an unswerving respect for the child as creator and learner as well as individual.

Recognizing that children are different and reflect not only their age and environment but their individual rate of maturation and their unique individuality, we propose to start with each child where he is.

Stages in the Work

In looking ahead to the work with the children and their families, an evolutionary development was foreseen. More particularly, three stages in these working relationships were expected and planned for prior to initiating Project A.

1. Rapport and role definition. The workers anticipated, correctly, that establishing rapport with these families would be reasonably easy. They had had prior contacts with some of the families which they knew that they could draw upon as they approached the families to enlist their participation in Project A. In addition, they had interviewed more than 200 mothers of young children (see Chapter 15) and had tested more than 300 children of kindergarten age (see Chapter 8). Experiences like these had taught the workers a great deal about how to establish effective relationships with these people.

Many individuals in Millfield were in the habit of referring to the workers as teachers, even though the workers had never so identified themselves. In the context of Project A, however, the workers decided to structure their role in teaching terms to capitalize on what seemed to be a natural tendency within the community. In addition, the workers felt that it was important for the families to recognize immediately that it was the four-year-old child in the family who was to be the focus of their teaching efforts. Consequently, during the initial contact with the mother, the worker made certain that she presented some variation of the following statement:

We are interested in helping children learn some of the things that are interesting and helpful at an early age. We believe that what children learn before they go to school is important. Our plan is to bring books and materials that we may use and that you or others in the family may use with the children.

The first stage in a developing relationship was viewed, then, not only as a time for establishing rapport but also as a time for defining the worker's role as a teacher of a particular child.

2. Assessment of child and family. Once the mother (or other family spokesman) had agreed to participate, the worker began to structure for her what was conceptualized as the second stage or phase of the developing relationship. During this period, as she explained it to the mother, she would want to talk with her about the child and the family so that she could come to know the child's present situation. The worker also explained that she would ask the child to do various things so that she could learn about his abilities and how she, the worker, might best assist the child. Phase two was, then, essentially a time of appraisal of both the child and his family.

This initial assessment of the family was divided into two parts. In part one, the worker, using a face-sheet as a guide (see Appendix G), obtained a sketch of the family—its structure, its situation in the community, and its resources (newspaper and magazine subscriptions, books, etc.). In part two, a structured interview (see Appendix H) was conducted with the mother to determine her views of the child's behavior, what training practices were used with the child, and other information that might be helpful in planning the work to be done with the child. (This interview was a shortened version of the one used in the study reported in Chapter 15.)

There was also an early evaluation of the child to determine his capabilities and deficiencies. As part of this assessment, each worker used three devices: (1) the Peabody Picture Vocabulary Test (PPVT); (2) selected items from the Stanford-Binet Intelligence Scale; and (3) a nonstandardized sorting task for shape, color, and size. The last two procedures did not provide standard test scores; rather, they provided the worker with an opportunity to observe the child confronting a variety of problems calling for the utilization of diverse talents. The PPVT, however, provided a measurement of mental age, based upon the child's understanding of words. These mental ages are listed in Table 9.1; they show that the children earned a mean of four years and four months, which was about seven months less than the children's average chronological age at the time of the examination. About one-third of these children scored at or beyond their chronological age level when first evaluated on the PPVT.

These tests and the mother interviews were merely the early, relatively formal probes used to gain a tentative appreciation of the assets and limitations of the child and his family. Actually, discovering what the child's strengths and weaknesses were, and what resources—tangible or otherwise—the family had, was a continuing process that ended only with the termination of Project A.

3. *Development of competence.* In a sense, stages one and two were phases to be moved through as quickly as possible so that the maximum amount of time would be left for the interventional aspect of Project A.

This latter period was identified as stage three, or as the stage in which the focus of concern was directed toward increasing the child's intellective competence.

Actually, while the assessment work of stage two was still in progress, the worker began making plans and setting goals for the child based upon her accumulating notes and observations. In general, the worker wanted to plan activities which promised to accelerate the child's development in one or more of the following three areas: (1) ability to use the materials and tools of learning; (2) ability to use language for effective communication; and (3) ability to generate and use concepts which promote understanding of the world about him.

To move toward these objectives, the staff members organized nine content areas within which they would work: sound, shape, color, number, size, language, the world about us, visual concepts, and weight. They did not anticipate, however, that each of them would have to work with each child in each of these areas. Rather, the worker would select from them in terms of her appraisal of the child and his needs. They also recognized that the selection of work areas should take into account the interests and motivations of the child and that the child should not be confronted with tasks or materials for which he was not ready.

The activities centered in the above content areas made use of a wide range of simple and inexpensive materials: paper, scissors, paste, crayons, puzzles, manipulative toys, records, and so on. To guide their use of these materials, the workers constructed a manual which will now be described briefly. (This manual is reproduced in Appendix I.)

The Manual

The manual served several purposes for the workers. First, its construction served as a means of organizing their preparatory work. When it was completed, they began to feel that they were ready to begin contacts with the children. Second, it was a useful reminder of activities and materials that could be used in the nine content areas. Finally, by spelling out in the manual the objectives and concepts behind specific activities, the workers were prompted to think of their day-to-day efforts in broader terms than otherwise might have been true.

The manual was organized around seven stages, moving toward increased complexity of performance. For each of these stages, activities relevant to most of the nine content areas were listed along with the materials needed to carry out the activities. In one respect, it should be noted, this organizational scheme may be misleading. By listing activities in each of the nine content areas under most of the stages, an evenness in development within the child may be implied which is, in fact, seldom found. For example, a child may be competent at one stage with respect to language but not with regard to numbers. Therefore, in future work, it would probably be helpful to reorganize the manual in terms of the nine content areas, listing under each (in the order of their difficulty) the various tasks that are relevant to it. The workers were thoroughly familiar with the manual, however, and were able to move freely about within it as the individual needs of the child seemed to dictate. It was not used in a rigid, predetermined manner.

The Log

Staff members, from the outset of their planning, recognized the value of recording their observations and activities, as well as the judgments they made during each contact with a child. Only in this way could they guard against lapses in memory and ensure a solid basis for communicating the fruits of their work to others. To organize such record-keeping, a two-page log (see Appendix J) was filled out at the end of each session with a child. In this way the workers were able to develop a cumulative record for each child and his family.

Judgments of Progress

Although this was not a controlled study, staff members decided that there would be value in making judgments about how each child performed in a number of different areas at the beginning and again at the end of Project A. Each child's performance was rated by his worker, therefore, using the first eight of the following nine scales (see Appendix J):

1. Child's ability to concentrate: D–Poor C–Fair B–Good A–Excellent
2. Child's appreciation for stories: C–None B–Some A–Full
3. Child's receptivity to records: D–None C–Slight B–Very A–Full
4. Child's use of questions: D–Never C–Seldom B–Often A–Always
5. Child's participation in conversation: D–Never C–Seldom B–Often A–Always
6. Child's spontaneous continuation of activities: D–Never C–Seldom B–Often A–Always
7. Child's auditory awareness: D–Poor C–Fair B–Good A–Excellent
8. Child's visual awareness: D–Poor C–Fair B–Good A–Excellent
9. Mother's awareness of child's needs: D–Poor C–Fair B–Good A–Excellent

The judgments made by the workers using these scales have been tabulated in Table 9.2; discussion of their implications will be reserved for the concluding section of the chapter.

TABLE 9.2

Frequencies of Ratings Based upon Early and Late Behavior in Project A

Behavior	Rating category	Number of children	
		Early	Late
1. Child's ability to concentrate	Excellent	1	6
	Good	6	11
	Fair	10	7
	Poor	8	1
2. Child's appreciation for stories	Full	4	17
	Some	15	8
	None	6	0
3. Child's receptivity to records*	Full	0	4
	Very	5	12
	Slight	11	4
	None	5	0
4. Child's use of questions	Always	3	6
	Often	6	11
	Seldom	7	5
	Never	9	3
5. Child's participation in conversation	Always	6	11
	Often	5	10
	Seldom	10	4
	Never	4	0
6. Child's spontaneous continuation of activities	Always	3	8
	Often	10	15
	Seldom	7	2
	Never	5	0
7. Child's auditory awareness	Excellent	2	5
	Good	5	6
	Fair	9	12
	Poor	9	2
8. Child's visual awareness†	Excellent	1	4
	Good	11	14
	Fair	8	4
	Poor	5	0
9. Mother's awareness of child's needs	Excellent	1	8
	Good	6	12
	Fair	14	3
	Poor	4	2

* With a few children, records were not used in such a way as to permit this rating to be made.

† Workers failed to make three late ratings.

IMPLEMENTING THE PLAN

When the above plans had been laid and the materials had been prepared, work with the children began. For a few of the children, contacts began in December, 1964, but for most of them it was January, 1965, before they were seen.

Schedule of Home Visits

Efforts were made to see each child twice weekly in his home for approximately one hour each visit. Sometimes, however, factors such as illness or foul weather made it impossible to keep this schedule. Some families lived on unpaved roads and in isolated areas that made access quite difficult in inclement weather. The workers were unsparing of themselves, however, and did not hesitate to push well beyond what might have been expected of them to carry on Project A.

These home visits continued for approximately three months, which meant that each child was visited about twenty times. Toward the end of March the schedule of visits had to be curtailed, since there were other duties associated with the main project which demanded most of the workers' time. Some of the staff members did maintain contact with their families for the remainder of the school year, but these contacts were usually shorter and more intermittent than the earlier ones.

A different kind of communication was initiated with some of the children when illness or weather conditions kept the workers from making home visits. Under these circumstances, staff members sometimes exchanged letters with the children. (The worth of such an activity had been foreseen during the planning phase of the project and had been listed in the manual.) For some children, receiving mail addressed to them was a unique and exciting experience. For the worker, this activity opened an avenue for instruction about communication and the importance of writing. Occasionally, the children were even taken to the post office to show them, step by step, how this communication system was organized. It should also be pointed out that exchanging letters became a way in which the worker could tell the child that she was thinking about him and was concerned for him even though conditions prevented her from being physically present in his home.

Working within the Homes

The homes visited were of many varieties. Some were painted and in good condition, others were unpainted or in poor physical repair. Some were sunny and bright, others were dark and dingy. Some could best be described in terms of dilapidated, dirty, crowded, and disorganized.

Others were "neat as a pin," even though their contents suggested poverty. All the homes had electricity and TV, but some did not have running water or inside plumbing.

In most instances, the family arranged a special place for the worker and child to use during their time together. This usually necessitated some planning by the mother, and often it involved either clearing space in a communal room or starting a fire in an adjoining room. Sometimes these arrangements were difficult for the mother to make and she did not always succeed, yet there was always some evidence that she had tried. In one instance, one room of a two-room house was consistently made available for the session. This room was dimly lit and sparsely furnished, but there was always a fire blazing in it when the worker arrived. With some children there were occasions when circumstances made it necessary to use the home of a neighbor or relative, but no sessions were canceled for lack of space.

The worker planned the activities in advance and brought the materials with her that she would need during the hour. Since, in addition, the overall plan called for leaving materials with the child which might be useful in promoting learning between visits, the worker also had to plan carefully for this part of the program and bring additional materials with her. One of the first items the worker brought to the child was a box that was to be his own. She helped the child print his name on it, and the box was used to store crayons, pencils, and other small items which would be used both during subsequent sessions and between visits. On each trip to the home, the worker took with her a small folding table and chairs to be used during the session. Oftentimes the child would help unload and carry this equipment into the house. Sharing in such tasks helped the worker develop her relationship with the child.

The worker and the child frequently worked alone. One of the worker's objectives, however, was to determine whether other individuals in the home had the potential for becoming allies in accelerating the child's development. This was felt to be especially important, since the workers were acutely aware of the fact that their contacts with the child would be short, infrequent, and limited to a period of a few months at most. Sometimes, then, another adult or older sibling was brought into the activities of the hour. Sometimes, too, other members of the household were given suggestions about the activities they might pursue with the child between sessions. On some occasions it was obvious that other members of the family were listening from neighboring rooms and that they were acting on what they heard even though they had not been asked to do so. For example, in exploring colors with one child it became apparent that he could not identify them correctly. On his worker's next visit, this child began to point proudly to objects, identifying those that were red.

Some of the materials used especially often during the home visits will be listed below. Also, brief mention will be made of some of the objectives being sought through their use.

1. *Peg boards.* These boards were used for color sorting, color naming, and color matching. They were also used to teach number concepts. For instance, number games were played in which the child was asked to represent on the peg board numbers that were presented in another form (spots on dominoes, number of legs on a cow, number of fingers on a hand, etc.).

2. *Form boards.* These boards had circles, squares, and triangles in four gradations of size. They were used in a variety of impromptu games to teach the child to discriminate shapes and sizes.

3. *Color cones.* The color cones were used to give the child a chance to carry out serious tasks easily and successfully. They gave him experience with color, size, and shape. Simple manipulations were especially helpful in getting acquainted with the child.

4. *Colored paper, scissors, paste, and crayons.* Such items were kept in the child's box and were referred to as his school supplies. They were the basis for various creative activities, including the construction of several little books (animal, food, farm, growing up, shape, color, and textures). Collages and posters were also made, as were original drawings on large sheets of paper. In learning to use these items, the manipulative skills of many children seemed to be increased. On occasion, the worker also found the child's product to be valuable as a means for teaching parents to accept their child's creation as valuable even though it could not be recognized as an object.

5. *Puzzles.* The workers brought a variety of puzzles, ranging from the very simple to the complex. In using them, it was hoped that a child's mastery of spatial relations might be advanced. More certainly, however, the puzzles provided a useful bridge for conversation and cooperative work.

6. *Flannel board picture series.* This picture series included farm objects and animals, vehicles, and family members. Their use, with the flannel board, gave the child opportunities to illustrate and characterize stories and records. For example, several children made a complete train, learning and talking about it in the process. This is another instance where the activity seemed to encourage the child to express himself verbally.

7. *Lego blocks.* These blocks were used to develop fine muscle con-

trol and to stimulate concepts of construction. They were often left with the child between sessions, and apparently many other members of the family enjoyed using them during these periods.

8. *Junior builder and plastic kit.* This kit contained nuts and bolts which were used both to develop manipulative skills and to stimulate creative play.

9. *Large dominoes.* The dominoes provided a means for teaching number concepts by using a variety of grouping and matching procedures.

10. *Books.* A small library of children's books was assembled. The workers read to the children, but they also talked to them about the pictures and ideas in the books. Books were left in the homes between sessions so that other members of the family might read to the children, which they frequently did.

11. *Records and record players.* Each worker had a small, portable, inexpensive record player. In addition, a number of children's records were purchased for their use. It was difficult, however, to find records that could readily be linked to the experiences of these children. Records, then, were of more limited value than the staff members had originally anticipated.

The materials which have been described (and their uses) are only samples of the total array. They should convey, however, a reasonably accurate impression of the activities that went on during the sessions conducted in the children's homes.

Working Outside the Homes

The reader should not conclude from what has been written that all the activities were usual school-like seat work or were conducted within the homes. Several of the activities which extended out of the home will now be described briefly.

1. *Walks.* To encourage the child to share parts of his larger, yet still immediate, environment with the worker, she took him for walks around his neighborhood. During these walks, the worker helped the child observe, talk about, and develop concepts with respect to the objects and situations which they encountered.

2. *Group get-togethers.* After workers had established secure relationships with their children, small group meetings were occasionally arranged for them. For many children, these group experiences helped break down their physical and social isolation and provided them with opportunities for fun and conversation with their peers. These get-togethers also gave the workers a chance to arrange activities and use materials that were more suitable for groups than for individuals. In

addition, the fact that these groups met in various homes encouraged the development of relationships between families; some of these were continued after Project A was terminated.

3. Field trips. The children were taken on several field trips, to such places as a firehouse, a post office, and a children's museum (which was located in a community some distance away). For many of the children, a Project A trip was their first time away from home with anyone other than a family member. The trips were arranged not only because they could offer many new experiences to the child directly, but also because they expressed indirectly to the parents the idea that it was important for even their young children to have opportunities to reach out into the larger world. Also, these trips afforded workers opportunities to observe the children in wider contexts and in relation to peers away from home.

4. Bookmobile. Although a bookmobile made monthly visits to the area, no child was securing books from it when Project A began. Therefore, the workers arranged contacts with the bookmobile, and by the end of Project A many of the children were using it regularly. Moreover, some of the parents began to use the bookmobile to serve their own interests.

These, then, were some of the activities used to expand the children's horizons and to broaden their awareness of the world around them. In a more extensive project, many other activities of a comparable nature could be profitably developed.

SOME GUIDING PRINCIPLES

Although the sessions took many different forms, there were several guiding principles which the workers kept in mind. They tried to follow these guidelines as they prepared for the sessions and as they carried them out. Briefly, these guiding principles were as follows:

1. Use the child's interests. The staff anticipated, correctly, that many of the children would work at tasks primarily to please their workers. They felt, however, that it was of central importance to be sensitive to the child's interests and motivations. As the worker learned about these, therefore, she tried to build upon them in their activities. For example, one boy seemed uninterested in learning color names, but he was strongly attracted to cars and trucks. By bringing miniature cars and trucks of different colors, the worker was able to teach him colors while they played with and talked about these absorbing objects.

2. Vary the activities. There was an expectation that the children would have short attention spans and that, consequently, activities would have to be frequently varied, even during a single session. For some children, this anticipation proved to be correct, but for many it was not. The workers were surprised, in fact, to discover how long many children were able to sit and attend to one activity. Therefore, although most plans called for several activities during a session, it was possible on occasion to carry out sustained work in only one or two areas.

3. Reward the child. The general strategy of a session called for arranging a series of success experiences. In a very loose way, the staff attempted to use some of the things that have been learned from research on programmed instruction. Tasks began at a level that the child had almost certainly mastered, but if he did make an error he was usually given information to this effect immediately and permitted to repeat the task until it was mastered. Moreover, when the child did something well, the worker tried—by words, smiles, and gestures—to communicate her appreciation and approval to the child. The workers quickly learned that most of the children responded very strongly to such reinforcement. They seemed eager to please the workers and often were willing to work at tasks in order to gain approval, even if the tasks were not inherently interesting to them.

4. Encourage verbalization. No matter what the activity was at the moment, the worker made a continuing effort to develop the child's capacity to interact verbally with her. She took pains to establish a common experience with the child, and she directed her efforts toward stimulating him to talk about their activities at some length rather than in monosyllables. For example, she might say, "What did you do in the snow?" instead of "Did you make a snowman?" The latter form of inquiry, of course, tends to elicit from the child no more than a simple yes, no, or shake of the head. The former approach, in contrast, demands a fuller verbal expression from him. In a variety of ways, the worker tried not only to help the child express himself but to realize that someone was interested in what he had to say.

TYPES OF SITUATIONS AND CHILDREN ENCOUNTERED

In work of this sort, communication of impressions and findings is especially difficult. Since Project A was an exploratory effort emphasizing feasibility, and since data from both control and experimental groups are not available, whatever conclusions are reached must be regarded as tentative and subject to bias. Even if such data were available, however, the difficult challenge of sketching with words the characteristics of these children and the conditions of their lives would remain.

Partially to satisfy the needs of the project, case studies were written by the workers for about two-thirds of the children. Space does not permit inclusion of these reports. Instead, brief descriptions of various types of situations and children encountered by the workers will be presented. In this way we hope to give the reader some feeling for Project A at the operational level.

The Harassed Mother

In reporting about Helen, her worker remarked: "Helen seemed bright and capable. We worked, however, against the hardship of a crowded home and a mother much too busy with the cares of a large family, including three children under age five. Moreover, one of these children seemed to be an autistic child. There were days when the mother simply could not get ready for me." The worker partially solved this problem by arranging joint sessions with other children in the latters' homes, whenever possible. The last few sessions were held in the quiet surroundings of an aunt's house, an arrangement worked out by Helen's mother. These special arrangements had the disadvantage, however, of taking Helen out of the family setting for most of the sessions and made it more difficult to involve other members of the family in the work of Project A. Nevertheless, Helen appeared to respond constructively to the program.

Cramped Quarters

Limited physical resources were common, yet moving out, as was done with Helen, usually was not necessary. The extent to which some families would inconvenience themselves in this regard was indeed a good measure of their commitment to the project. Sammy, for instance, lived in a two-room house that had sparse furnishings. One room was always cleared, however, and made comfortably warm for Sammy and his worker.

The Working Mother

Sometimes several different arrangements had to be tried before a suitable one was discovered. Frequently, such trial-and-error procedures helped to illuminate important characteristics of the child. Jack, for example, had a mother who was employed. His worker decided initially, therefore, to see Jack at an aunt's house in the company of another child. However, this situation proved to be too distracting for Jack. He cut up, teased, and generally failed to use the sessions constructively.

The worker concluded, then, that Jack needed individual work and undivided attention. She began working with him in his own home even though his mother was absent. A decided improvement in Jack's use of the sessions ensued.

The Overintrusive Parent

A delicate situation sometimes was created when other members of the family attempted to dominate and control the sessions. On the one hand, the worker wanted their sympathetic involvement so that they would be willing to continue working with the child between sessions and after the project had been terminated. At the same time, if others were too visible and dominant, the child's central role tended to be compromised. Confronted with such a situation, a worker had to use skill and diplomacy to minimize intrusions without alienating anyone. Susan, for instance, seemed capable, but her mother answered all questions for her and attempted to conduct the sessions from the sidelines. She was so anxious to have Susan succeed that the worker had to devise a means of involving her elsewhere before Susan could proceed at her own pace.

Collaborative Parents

Some homes were found to be full of unrealized potential. John's home illustrates this condition. It was well equipped with manipulative toys, and a new record player was shown to the worker on her first visit. John was already interested in copying numbers and letters of the alphabet. Furthermore, his worker found an interested and encouraging mother to work with. Their collaboration provided John with a variety of new experiences, including the companionship of another boy who was less verbal but physically more daring than John. His family also made immediate use of the bookmobile which the worker arranged to have stop at the house. John's mother reported that on the first visit she took out two books, one for herself and one for her husband. Her husband read both books within the first week and, according to his wife, "was looking around for more." John's mother also began to report that John was asking more questions. In the worker's last letter from John, he said, "I got nine books from the bookmobile." The worker, understandably, felt encouraged that this family would continue the activities she had helped start.

Hank provides a second example of a rather fortunate child; his parents were also interested in providing him with expanded experiences and learning opportunities. At many sessions, his worker found herself "performing" before an attentive audience. Uncles, aunts, and even the preacher appeared one morning to observe Hank being taught! It was not surprising, therefore, to find new materials and equipment appearing in the home as a result of the teaching sessions. Staff members recognized, of course, that dangerous overinvolvement or undue pressures could be generated under such circumstances, but it did not seem likely that such negative conditions would develop in Hank's home.

The Adult Child

Most children in Millfield belong to large families, but there are noteworthy exceptions, especially in the white community (see Chapter 1). Mary, for instance, was a lone child in the company of middle-aged adults; it seemed as if she had never quite learned how to be a child. With her, the worker decided, emphasis should be placed on essentially nonintellectual goals if her development was to progress more evenly. Thus, the worker concentrated on communicating to Mary that she really could be a child, that she could relax and stop trying so hard. Also, the worker devoted time to the parents, encouraging them not only to accept but to reinforce such changes in their child's behavior. By the conclusion of Project A, there was evidence that Mary's behavior had become more spontaneous, less formal, and less overly compliant. For Mary, the worker considered this to be a major accomplishment.

The Especially Limited Child

Data in other chapters have shown that the functioning intellective level of many children in Millfield is low (see Chapter 3, for instance). Therefore, these workers, who were examiners in the larger project, were well acquainted with children of limited ability. Coping with such children in an interventional program, however, created new sets of problems for them. Consider, for instance, these words written by one of the workers: "With Bill, I recognized my own impatience and had to work with it. I believe I had overestimated his abilities and maturity initially. When I worked with him on a simpler level and varied the activity in view of his restlessness, the experience became more pleasant for both of us." Such reports point up the importance of having workers who are both sensitive and nondefensive with respect to their own judgments and behavior. They also suggest that such work can be a growth experience for the worker as well as for the child.

The Child with Specific Limitations

Some children are characterized more by severe incapacities in particular intellective areas than by uniformly low ability levels. Tom appeared to be such a child. In her report, Tom's worker emphasized that during her initial assessment of him she began to realize that he needed basic manipulative experiences which would develop fine muscle coordination and a better sense of spatial relations. She went on to say, "In the light of these conclusions, I brought Lego blocks, the Junior Builder kit, and puzzles; and I emphasized manipulation." Later she added this observation: "I was surprised that Tom could not recognize simple pictures of some familiar farm animals." The fact that the worker could be surprised by such a discovery points up, as mentioned earlier, the fact that appraisal of a child is an ever-continuing and developing process. The most helpful attitude for a worker to hold would seem to be that she can never know the total child; yet, by sympathetic and attentive concern, she can get to know him better. Then she can use this increased knowledge to advantage in her efforts to help him.

The Defensive Child

Children can be defensive in a variety of ways and with respect to many different components of their lives. Ann illustrates one pattern in this regard. In contrast to many of the children, she was quite verbal; moreover, she was used to doing things well. Her worker found that she did not want to try tasks in which she would not appear to be an expert. Apparently, although quite capable, Ann was fearful of failure. Her worker had to work through this problem with Ann, therefore, before the two of them could move ahead to problems that would really challenge Ann. She had to learn that failure did not bring catastrophe, that the worker would continue to accept her and hold her in high regard even if she failed on a particular problem.

The Obstructive Child

This type of child is almost guaranteed to try the patience of any worker. Jim, for instance, had the idea that the only way to relate to adults was to thwart them; he devoted little effort to achievement or work. Both of his parents were employed, and his worker gradually realized that behind Jim's negativism was a desperate need for adult attention. Her patient and cheerful efforts to engage him finally began to secure results. His mother also became more involved and responded belatedly to some of her son's needs for recognition and attention. The worker's strategy was to develop awareness of Jim's needs in the mother, with the hope that the mother would increasingly reinforce productive components of her boy's behavior, thereby reducing his need to be obstructive.

The Nonverbal Child

We have saved for last the discussion of perhaps the most common and difficult problem confronting those who attempt to contribute to the intellectual development of children like those in Millfield. Although some of the children are highly verbal, a large number of them are woefully lacking in this skill when they enter school. Normally, the resources of the schools do not permit both rehabilitation programs for the children who are verbally handicapped and a standard curriculum for those children ready to profit from it. A few examples should suffice for suggesting the dimensions of this problem.

Andy's worker reported: "Initially Andy indicated interest in activities, but he exhibited little verbal behavior. He did, however, flash a warm smile and a posture of pride in having me as a teacher. He was especially active in helping transfer equipment from and to the car." The worker capitalized on Andy's ability to concentrate by introducing stories and records. Simple puzzles, basic shapes, cutting, coloring, and pasting were also employed. While these activities were being pursued, *a great deal of emphasis was placed upon conversation as real communication.* Also, since no one had ever read to Andy, his worker began reading very simple stories to him. They talked about these stories, and the worker had Andy act them out with another child in common sessions. She reported that "his alertness and sense of humor became more evident as his verbal participation was elicited during the story sessions."

To continue with Andy, his worker made a deliberate effort not to assume anything about the nature of his experiences. Instead, she conversed simply with him at the beginning of each session with reference to immediate events, situations, or objects. On one occasion, for instance, she mentioned that it had been snowing and asked Andy what he did in the snow. Andy replied glowingly that he had been sliding. Then he took his mother aback by saying, "I almost busted my tail." His worker went on to share with Andy her personal experience of making a snowman with her own children. Andy had never made a snowman but his great interest was evident. In ways like this, Andy's worker moved toward developing language facility in a very nonverbal child.

Earl presented an even more severe problem than Andy; initially, he would not talk at all to his worker. His speech, when it did come, was so babyish that he usually could not be understood. Primarily, he communicated by using gestures. It was only toward the end of his sessions that Earl gained enough security to really try communicating via speech. This was a real and meaningful accomplishment for both Earl and his worker, but, obviously, there was a long road yet to be traveled.

Mike manifested still another type of verbal problem. His initial shyness was so great that his worker had great difficulty establishing a relationship with him, especially since the continuity of the sessions often was interrupted either by Mike's illness or by the sickness of some other member of the family. Furthermore, as his worker reported, "When the initial shyness was overcome, Mike's responses were given in singsong, teasing monosyllables which were very difficult to understand at first. But I did learn to understand, and found that Mike converses with his family in the same way."

This last remark points up the effort that individuals must make if they are going to be successful in this type of work. In this regard, it may be of interest to note that one worker used a tape recorder to marked advantage in coping with difficult speech patterns. By playing back recordings of the child's speech, she was able to develop her ability to understand him.

Finally, to emphasize further the extent of verbal difficulties, brief mention should be made of Bobby. This child seemed shy, yet he had a quiet, friendly manner. His mother was always present during the sessions, yet she was not intrusive. Bobby, however, characteristically turned to her when he was uncertain about something. A comment by his worker, made during the early phases of their relationship, is informative: "Almost all materials except paper and pencil seem unfamiliar to Bobby. It is hard to judge in many cases whether his responsiveness is determined by interest held in restraint or by acquiescence in the person-to-person relationship. His improvement in approach to materials with practice suggests that opportunity to use materials on his own will be beneficial."

Some sessions later, Bobby's worker appeared to have gained additional insight into his deficits and her need to set goals for him accordingly: "Bobby has real limitations which stem from an absence of appropriate labels for his emergent perceptions. His verbal restriction also makes it difficult to either determine easily what his achievements are, or to engage him in exchanges which involve anything except what is immediately in front of him." The verbal problems of many of these children are, clearly, central in importance and challenging in their magnitude.

CONCLUDING COMMENTS

What are some of the major findings growing out of Project A? Also, what are some of the paths which appear most promising for future work of this kind? Our judgments about these matters will be summarized in this final section.

Was Project A a Success?

As was pointed out earlier, Project A was not a controlled study. It did not give rise to objective data relating to its impact on the children and their families, yet there were many observations that can be used to provide at least partial answers to this question.

First, there was a high degree of consensus among workers, children, and parents that Project A had been worthwhile. When the time came to terminate the visits, there was genuine regret on the part of almost everyone involved. Parents and children alike expressed sorrow that the workers would not be returning and, in most instances, the workers had similar feelings. Emotionally, then, Project A seemed to add an important dimension to the lives of its participants.

Another kind of evidence attesting to the success of Project A, although clearly subject to distortions from bias, wishful thinking, and selective recall, was provided by the ratings made by the workers early and late in Project A. These judgments, in eight different areas of the child's performance, are sumarized in Table 9.2. (Included there, also, is a summary of the ratings made of the mother's awareness of her child's needs.) These tabulations reflect the developmental strides taken by the children during this period. Not all these advances can be attributed to the Project A intervention, but they do suggest that Project A may have had a constructive impact.

Some Specific Things Learned

Although the judgments of the participants were resoundingly affirmative, there is little point in belaboring this fact. More important may be the detailing of some of the particular things which the staff members believed that they learned in this exploratory work.

1. Receptivity. In the planning stage, the workers were concerned about parental reaction to such a program. These misgivings were quickly eliminated, however, once the sessions began. Of course, the fact that the workers were already known in the area probably made it easier for them to secure cooperation. Nevertheless, most parents seemed to recognize the importance of education; it was not difficult to persuade them that even preschool learning might benefit their children. In the judgment of the workers, then, most such rural parents, if they are approached sensitively and considerately, will enter into collaborative efforts which promise to give their children increased opportunities.

2. Setting a Process in Motion. Another of the early concerns centered about the question of what a worker could realistically expect to accomplish working with a child for only an hour or two each week. This is obviously such a small fraction of the child's time that the effort might very well prove to be ineffective.

Without question, there were some children who probably would have made better progress if their workers had been able to spend more hours with them each week. Oftentimes, however, the workers were able to initiate activities which were then furthered during their absence by others in the household. Thus, for a meaningful number of children and their families, the workers were able to set processes in motion which gained momentum and did not depend upon the workers' presence for their continuation. Reading to the child, getting him books from the bookmobile, and taking him on trips are examples of such activities.

3. The Worker as a Model. Staff members soon learned that many parents wanted to do the right things for their children, but all they knew how to do was what they and their neighbors had customarily done all their lives. Frequently, this was simply inadequate as far as the children's preschool development was concerned. The workers, in their activities with the children, often gave concrete illustrations of other things that might be done; some parents were able to copy these behaviors, at least in part. This is one of the reasons why it usually proved to be advantageous to have at least one older member of the family at home during a session, even if that person participated only by listening through a wall of the room.

In this regard, it may be worthwhile to point out that there is also a distinct advantage in keeping the focus on the child, from the time of the first contact. Many parents would very likely become quite defensive if one offered to help them directly; in changing parental behavior, it may be the better strategy to proceed subtly and indirectly. Thus, inviting parents to help the child ordinarily is less threatening than offering to help them to be better parents. Their use of the worker as a model may be left, predominantly, to their own initiative.

Numerous examples of how workers served as models could be given; perhaps two will suffice. One mother, for example, exclaimed, "I never know (sic) how to read a book to him until I heard you read." In a similar vein, a father took over at the flannel board to help his child make a paper car for his flannel-backed train. He then explained to the child the function of the brake at the front of the car. This was the kind of activity that the worker herself usually introduced.

4. Family Involvement. In some instances, like those just described, there seemed to be a direct and specific copying of the worker's behavior by a parent or someone else in the family. There was another, perhaps more general way, however, in which the worker seemed to affect family–child relationships. Somehow, as a result of what was being done, many families appeared to generate deeper, more meaningful involvements with their children. Indeed, it was with respect to this matter of family involvement that several of the staff members were most impressed.

It was noted earlier that in most homes special preparations had to be made for the workers' visits: the communal room had to be cleared, a fire had to be built, and so on. Parents considered it important to make these arrangements. Books were left to be read to the child, and usually they were read. Other kinds of "homework" also required the assistance of family members, and the aid ordinarily was given. Siblings, aunts, grandparents, or other relatives took over when a child's parents could not find the opportunity to do these things with him. Often this help was given without a direct request by the worker. For example, if George had difficulty with certain kinds of tasks, his worker simply left the materials with him. Between sessions, George's older siblings joined him in playing with the materials, and in the process taught him how to master them.

We can only speculate about the dynamic properties of Project A which led to a meaningful increase in many families' involvement with their children. In part, the worker, by her very act of coming, said, in effect, "Look, the instruction of this child is so important that I am willing to put myself to considerable trouble in order to come and help." Many members of the families seemed to reply in kind, "Well, if that is true, then perhaps there is something we too can do, so let's give it a try."

Some Thoughts about the Future

The several years of work in Millfield demonstrated the need for an interventional program at the preschool level—if not Project A, then a program of a comparable sort. Despite the limitations within which Project A was carried out, the workers learned some important things. Thus, it became clear that the people welcome such assistance, that constructive processes can be set in motion, and that significant family involvement can be achieved. What, then, is the next step?

It could be argued that Project A has been so successful that programs modeled after it ought to be established in all rural areas where significant numbers of children live under submarginal conditions. We would certainly support such programs if they were proposed, for the social need is compelling and the children have been neglected too long. It is also important, however, to conduct a carefully designed longitudinal study of Project A and its long-term effects. The program should be offered, for example, to a large number of children (perhaps for a two-year period) while it is not made available to a control group. Both groups should be evaluated periodically, then, during their school years to compare their development in the intellective, motivational, and social domains. If this were done, we would know—in unequivocal terms —what effects a project of this kind can achieve.

Some individuals might argue that it would be preferable to establish stimulating nursery schools for children from impoverished homes. We are not convinced, however, that this is the preferred method. For one thing, the cost of the necessary buildings, buses, teachers, and teachers' assistants would necessitate a financial outlay greatly in excess of that needed for the Project A type of program. Aside from money matters, however, the Project A pattern has a basic strength which is not found in the more traditional program. We refer here to the fact that the Project A format seems to lead to an unusually high degree of family involvement, and that processes are set in motion which appear to reach beyond the immediacy of the visit. In a very real sense, the worker becomes a catalyst for constructive family change in a way that does not seem to occur when children are taken from the home, trained, and then returned to the home, which remains basically the same as when the child left it.

Finally, let us turn to a very practical matter. "Suppose," some critics might say, "your workers were able to show that their efforts did enhance the development of these children. What then? After all, aren't your workers exceptional persons, and unusually well-trained? And, if this is true, what chance is there for establishing a multitude of Project A's? Where will you get the personnel?"

We would be the first to offer testimony to the fact that these workers were indeed exceptional persons. Without their talents, loyalty, compassion, sensitivity, and willingness to work for modest material rewards, the study could not have been completed. Nevertheless, we believe that, once a nuclear group of this sort has found the way, the fruits of their learnings can be transmitted to others with lesser amounts of training or education. Mature women with the requisite personal qualities, for example, should be able, with good supervision, to learn the worker's role that has been described in this chapter. In most communities there are probably many women who would respond enthusiastically to an opportunity to engage, either part-time or full-time, in such a worthy undertaking. It is our hope, therefore, that Project A can be expanded and that, simultaneously, a controlled study of its effects can be made.

Part IV

PERSONAL ATTRIBUTES

Chapter 10

MILLFIELD'S TEACHERS VIEW THEIR PUPILS

Each teacher completed a standard set of ratings on each of her pupils late in the school year in both 1962 and 1964. The results of the analyses of these ratings will be reported here in order to describe some of the personality traits of Millfield's children, as these traits were perceived by their teachers.

THE TEACHER'S VANTAGE POINT

A teacher may be in an unusually advantageous position to learn about the personal characteristics of her children. Most of these children, for example, remain with the same teacher for a full academic year; she not only observes them repeatedly as they work and interact with one another in the classroom, but also as they play at recess, as they eat together in the cafeteria, and as they function in other contexts. All along they give expression to various facets of their personalities. By the end of the academic year, when these ratings were made, most teachers should have had a reasonably comprehensive picture of what these children are like.

However, it must be recognized that a teacher, like anyone else, can have various biases which may lead to distorted perceptions.[1] Such

[1] One source of bias, differential use of the graphic scale provided for each rating, is mentioned below under "The Problem of Age." A second powerful bias often found in ratings of this sort, positive or negative halo effects, involves the effect of

judgments, consequently, are likely to be at some variance with other kinds of information about their pupils. Even if distorted, though, teachers' judgments are obviously important and useful. At the very least they represent the teachers' beliefs about what the children are like. And, in varying degrees, these beliefs govern how the teachers approach their teaching tasks and how they respond to the children. These perceptions help set expectations, therefore, and structure the demands the teachers place upon the children. If teachers believe, for example, that girls are more cooperative than boys, this belief itself is important in determining the classroom atmosphere in which both girls and boys are taught, whether the belief has a factual basis or not.

PROCEDURE

The Behavior Rating Scales

The scales used to collect behavioral ratings from the Millfield teachers were described in Chapter 2 and have been cited in several other chapters. The full rating sheet, containing 22 items, is reproduced in Appendix E.

There are at least two major advantages in using such scales to appraise personality. First, each judge or rater must attend to a common set of components of the behavior of each subject. Second, the graphic form in which the judgments are cast permits an easy and direct quantification of the data. There is also a significant limitation—namely, that we must forsake many nuances and subtleties of personality that each judge might provide if she were asked to report in her own words. In the present work, these finer descriptions were passed over to enhance the comparability and uniformity among the reports of dozens of teachers.

Administration of the Scales

As already noted, two sets of ratings were collected, one in May of 1962 and the other in May of 1964. In all, 1064 children were rated on each of the 22 items in 1962, and 1045 children were rated in 1964. The

---

general regard for the child upon the judgments made about his various attributes. Halo effects were examined in these data, but the findings were difficult to explicate. There was no easy way, for instance, to determine when a teacher was rating a child favorably on a number of specific characteristics because she liked him quite well (as indicated by rating No. 22) or was in fact reporting that she liked him because of the number of positive features that she had found in him. In this chapter, the ratings are reported without any special correction for halo effects or other possible biases.

number of boys and girls who were rated at each of eight age levels is given in Table 10.1; separate entries are provided for 1962 and 1964. This table also shows the number of different teachers (again, separately for the two years) who rated one or more children at each of the age levels.[2]

Each teacher in each of the schools was given an individual rating sheet for each child in her room. This legal-size sheet contained the 22 behavior items in graphic form. By placing a check on each line, the teacher recorded her judgment of the child with respect to that particular trait. No effort was made to expand the description of the items, since it was felt that most, if not all, of the items had been cast in terms that would have a reasonably uniform meaning for the teachers. To demonstrate that these ratings were important, and to compensate them in part for their extra work, the teachers were told in advance that each of them would be paid for making the ratings ($10 in 1962, $15 in 1964).

It should be pointed out that each child included in the analyses reported below was rated on each of the 22 items. Occasionally, however, a teacher did fail to rate a child on one or more items. When this occurred, the other data on that child were eliminated from this study.

Analysis of the Data

Separate analyses of variance were made for each item of the 1962 and 1964 data. In all, then, 44 analyses were run, two for each of the 22 behavior items. (Age, sex, and race served as the main effects, with four interactions: Age × Sex, Age × Race, Sex × Race, and Age × Sex × Race.)

In one sense, the 1964 data can be viewed as a replication of the 1962 data. Beyond age eight, the children rated in the 1964 survey were the same as those involved in the 1962 ratings.[3] In 1964, however, they were two years older and they were rated by different teachers from those who had evaluated them in 1962.

In addition to the analyses of variance, trait profiles were drawn for

[2] The reader will note a sharp increase in the number of teachers rating white children at ages 13 and 14 in 1964. These children were then attending a newly established junior high school (see Chapter 2). In this school, the children were scattered among many different teachers. The teacher count recorded in this table may be somewhat misleading, since it shows the number of teachers who rated one or more children at each designated age level. Actually, for both Negro and white children, a large majority of the ratings at each age level were provided by between two and four teachers.

[3] A few children were lost from the 1964 analysis because they had moved out of the area, and a few were added who had moved to Millfield only recently. There was also some turnover in teachers during this interval.

TABLE 10.1

Numbers of Children Rated and Teachers Providing Ratings at Eight Age Levels in 1962 and 1964

| | White | | | | No. of teachers of: | | | | Negro | | | | No. of teachers of: | | | |
| | Boys | | Girls | | Boys | | Girls | | Boys | | Girls | | Boys | | Girls | |
Age	'62	'64	'62	'64	'62	'64	'62	'64	'62	'64	'62	'64	'62	'64	'62	'64
7	26	34	25	28	4	3	2	4	20	27	30	38	3	4	4	5
8	32	34	36	28	5	4	5	5	38	26	36	38	7	4	10	5
9	20	22	22	22	5	6	3	4	33	30	43	27	9	7	8	6
10	27	35	31	33	5	5	4	4	36	46	48	43	6	9	6	7
11	26	23	28	28	7	5	6	6	36	39	37	49	7	10	5	9
12	25	27	30	32	7	6	5	4	44	38	36	45	11	9	7	10
13	36	25	35	24	6	12	8	10	33	44	44	37	9	9	8	9
14	37	20	25	26	7	10	4	10	49	39	40	38	11	7	9	7
Totals	229	220	232	221	46	51	37	47	289	289	314	315	63	59	57	58

white boys, white girls, Negro boys, and Negro girls based upon their mean scores for each of the 22 items; separate profiles were made for the 1962 and 1964 data. Some profiles were also developed using pooled data for the two years. These various profiles were constructed by combining data from all age levels, since, as will be discussed below, there were methodological difficulties related to the age dimension.

The Problem of Age

The way the ratings were made, they cannot be used to plot developmental changes in the behaviors which they describe. Teachers do two things in making their ratings which preclude valid use of the data to assess age changes: (1) they judge a child with reference to other children of his age or grade level, and (2) they vary unpredictably in terms of the point on the scale around which they center their judgments about their pupils. Thus, age effects are confounded with differences in both frame of reference and judges' behavior, a fact that precludes meaningful analyses of the data for age effects.

The above factors, however, did not affect the usefulness of these ratings in studying any sex differences that might be found in the data, since each teacher rated both boys and girls in her room. Also, although there are more difficulties in interpreting racial differences from such data than in interpreting sex differences, the analyses of race effects were examined. In the following section, therefore, both sex and race effects will be considered but age effects will be ignored.

RESULTS

The analyses of the data will be presented in three parts. First, the mean trait profiles for each of the four groups (white boys, white girls, Negro boys, and Negro girls) will be examined. Second, racial differences will be discussed. Finally, attention will be centered upon sex differences.

Trait Profiles

As noted earlier, means were computed for each group on each of the 22 behavioral ratings. These means, for both 1962 and 1964, have been plotted separately for each of the four groups in Figures 10.1 through 10.4. It is obvious from inspection that these profiles are very similar on each occasion for each of the four groups.

The horizontal line in Figure 10.1 (as well as in the remaining figures in this chapter) runs through the midpoint of each rating scale. The

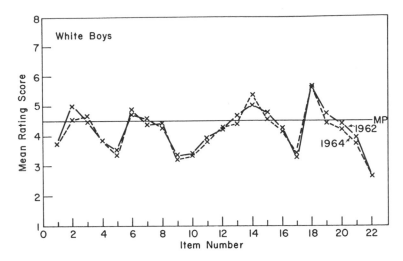

Fig. 10.1: Mean rating scores given by teachers in 1962 and 1964 to white boys on 22 behavior scales. (MP = midpoint of rating scale.)

distance between this line, then, and a given value on the profile shows how far the mean for that item deviates from the midpoint of the rating scale. In this regard, it should be kept in mind that the items were varied so that sometimes the more desirable behavior was to the right, at other times to the left on the graphic scale. (On a few items, middle values probably would be more desirable than either extreme.) This means, in turn, that on some items socially desirable behavior is represented in the figures by peaks on the profile, on other items by valleys.[4]

Each group will be discussed separately in the paragraphs that follow, based on its 1962 and 1964 profiles. Somewhat arbitrarily, attention will be focused upon those points on the profiles that deviate by 1.0 or more points from the midpoint of the rating scale.

1. White boys. There are six items on which the mean rating for the white boys deviates from the midpoint by 1.0 or more points: 22, 18, 9, 10, 5, and 17 (see Figure 10.1). This pattern holds for both the 1962 and the 1964 data, except that in 1962 the mean for item 5 falls short of the stated criterion by a very small amount.

The deviations on these six items suggest that the teachers hold essentially positive views of the boys. They are seen as likable, cheerful,

---

[4] For most of the items, the direction of the socially desirable behavior is readily apparent. On some items, however, this may not be true. We have not tried to determine any consensus in this regard through empirical methods; rather, we leave it to the reader to make his own judgments and then consider our statements in this light.

warm, cooperative, gregarious, and reactive to success; at least these are the qualities that appear to be most salient in the teachers' ratings. Primarily, it is social attributes that are emphasized in this cluster of judgments.

Seven items on the scale (4, 6, 8, 11, 15, 17, and 20) were included because they refer to different components of what has been called the achievement syndrome (see Chapter 12). That is, they reflect different facets of the child's commitment to doing well in school—the motivation that he exhibits, the concern that he has with the excellence of his performance, and so on. Of these seven traits, only one (17, reaction to success) is particularly salient for the white boys.

It is also of interest to note those items on which the mean rating is displaced from the midpoint in a socially undesirable direction, even though the deviation does not meet the 1.0 criterion. These items—4, 15, 8, and 12—indicate that the white boys are seen as needing considerable encouragement, as giving up too easily, as being crushed by failure, and as being easily upset. Three of these items (4, 15, 8) are included in the achievement syndrome noted above. The overall pattern, therefore, is one in which the achievement striving of the white boys is seen as underdeveloped. On the other hand, they are viewed as having a number of positive social qualities.

2. *White girls.* More traits were rated as salient for the white girls than for the white boys—ten versus six, respectively. The salient items for the white girls were 22, 9, 10, 5, 14, 18, 6, 11, 17, and 21 (see Figure

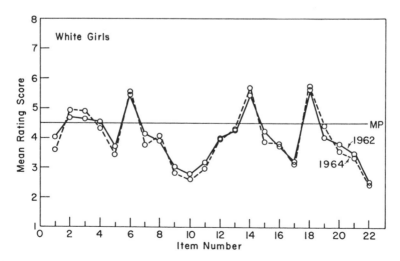

Fig. 10.2: Mean rating scores given by teachers in 1962 and 1964 to white girls on 22 behavior scales. (MP = midpoint of rating scale.)

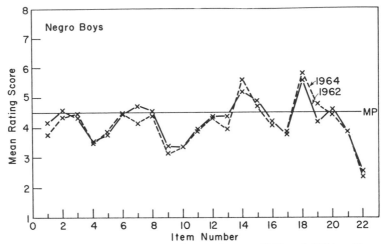

Fig. 10.3: Mean rating scores given by teachers in 1962 and 1964 to Negro boys on 22 behavior scales. (MP = midpoint of rating scale.)

10.2). The pattern was markedly similar for the two years, although for three of the items (5, 6, and 14) the mean rating for one of the two years dropped slightly below our arbitrary 1.0 criterion.

As was true for the white boys, the deviations on the salient items are in what would generally be considered the socially desirable direction. Six of the items (22, 9, 10, 5, 14, and 18) emphasize social and temperamental attributes; thus, the girls are seen as likable, warm, cooperative, gregarious, trustful, and cheerful. Three of the items (6, 11, and 17) are in the achievement syndrome mentioned earlier; that is, the girls are seen as concerned about doing their work well, as expending effort on their lessons, and as responsive to experiences of success. In addition, they are seen as quite consistent (21).

The mean ratings *tend* to deviate in a socially undesirable direction on only two scales (4 and 12). Like the white boys, the white girls are seen as needing to be encouraged and as being easily upset. In general, however, these data reflect a positive view of the white girls. Also, there is a high degree of similarity between the way boys and girls are viewed, although more positive qualities are underscored for the girls. More particularly, the girls are described as being more involved in their work; or, to put it another way, the white girls are seen as having fewer motivational problems than the white boys with respect to schoolwork.

3. *Negro boys.* Six traits were particularly salient among the perceptions of Negro boys by their teachers: 22, 9, 10, 14, 18, and 4 (see Figure 10.3). Moreover, four of these qualities (22, 9, 10, and 18) were ones

that the white teachers had emphasized in rating their boys. The other two traits (4 and 14) reached the criterion in only one of the two years.

The deviations on five of the above six traits are in a socially desirable direction. The Negro boys, according to their teachers, are likable, warm, cooperative, trustful, and cheerful. Again, as was true for the white boys, the emphasis in this description is upon the desirable social and temperamental attributes of the Negro boys. Only one component of the achievement syndrome was selected for emphasis (4), however, and here the rating departs from the mean in a *socially undesirable direction*. That is, Negro boys are reported as needing considerable encouragement. Several other items show slight departures from the midpoint in the socially undesirable direction, but generally these deviations are so small that probably little significance can be attached to them. It should be noted, nevertheless, that the Negro boys are viewed as being somewhat submissive and as tending to give up too easily.

In summary, generally positive social and temperamental traits are attributed to the Negro boys. Passivity also *tends* to be attributed to them, however, and achievement striving certainly is not emphasized as a salient characteristic.

4. *Negro girls*. Eight traits were underscored in the ratings of the Negro girls: 22, 9, 10, 18, 14, 11, 17, and 21 (see Figure 10.4). As was true for the white children, more attributes were emphasized among the Negro girls than among the Negro boys (eight versus six, respectively), and the deviation on each of these eight traits is in a socially desirable

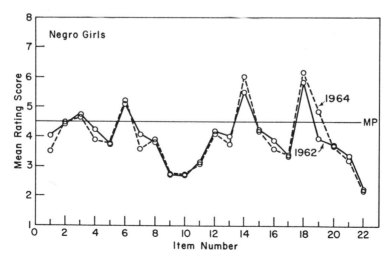

Fig. 10.4: Mean rating scores given by teachers in 1962 and 1964 to Negro girls on 22 behavior scales. (MP = midpoint of rating scale.)

direction. According to these teachers, the Negro girls are likable, warm, cooperative, cheerful, trustful, and consistent; they try hard on their lessons, and are quick to react to experiences of success.

The structure of social and temperamental characteristics, as thus outlined, is almost identical to the one described above for the Negro boys. In addition, however, two facets of the achievement syndrome are included in the description. The Negro girls are seen as expending considerable effort on their lessons and as being responsive to success or achievement experiences.

Only three traits (4, 12, and 13) show means that deviate from the midpoint in the socially undesirable direction, and none of these are marked departures. Apparently, however, there is a tendency for the Negro girls to need encouragement, to be easily upset, and to act somewhat submissively. Overall, though, it is clear that the teachers view the Negro girls quite positively. Not only are they seen as having attractive social and temperamental attributes, they are also regarded as possessing certain motivational strengths, at least insofar as their schoolwork is concerned.

Racial Differences

Some of the discussion that follows has been anticipated in the preceding paragraphs. The objective here will be to examine more closely the question of whether the teachers of the two racial groups attribute substantially similar or different qualities to their students.

As noted earlier, analyses of variance were run for each of the 22 items; the results for race as a main effect have been summarized in Table 10.2.[5] As shown there, significant race effects were found in the data for both years for six items: 2, 6, 13, 17, 19, and 22. For five of these items, the direction of the race difference was the same for both 1962 and 1964. For item 19, however, there was a reversal. Because of this inconsistency, item 19 will be dropped from further consideration.

Racial differences, although not numerous or large compared with sex differences (see the following section), are nevertheless of interest and potentially meaningful. Before discussing them, however, it must be emphasized that there are many more racial similarities than differences in these data. This fact can be readily grasped by inspecting Figure 10.5; the profiles plotted there for the Negro and white children coincide very closely.[6]

[5] There were no significant Sex × Race interactions, and, as suggested earlier, interactions involving age cannot be meaningfully interpreted.

[6] The points in this figure were computed by combining the 1962 and the 1964 data; also, equal numbers of boys and girls were assumed for both races during both years.

TABLE 10.2: Teachers' Ratings Which Showed Significant Race or Sex
Effects for Both 1962 and 1964

| | p level | | | |
| | Race* | | Sex† | |
Item	'62	'64	'62	'64
1. Activity level				
2. Emotional expressiveness	.001	.001		
	W > N	W > N		
3. Self-sufficiency				
4. Need for encouragement			.001	.001
			B > G	B > G
5. Sociability				
6. Concern for excellence	.01	.01	.001	.001
	W > N	W > N	G > B	G > B
7. Social poise			.001	.001
			G > B	G > B
8. Reaction to failure			.001	.001
			G > B	G > B
9. Emotional warmth			.001	.001
			G > B	G > B
10. Cooperativeness			.001	.001
			G > B	G > B
11. Effort on schoolwork			.001	.001
			G > B	G > B
12. Emotional stability			.05	.01
			B > G	B > G
13. Assertiveness	.001	.001		
	W > N	W > N		
14. Trustfulness			.001	.001
			G > B	G > B
15. Tenacity			.001	.001
			G > B	G > B
16. Tension level			.001	.001
			B > G	B > G
17. Reaction to success	.01	.001	.01	.001
	W > N	W > N	G > B	G > B
18. Mood (cheerfulness)				
19. Aggressiveness	.01	.001		
	W > N	N > W		
20. Absorption in schoolwork			.001	.001
			G > B	G > B
21. Consistency			.001	.001
			G > B	G > B
22. Teacher's affectionate regard	.01	.001	.01	.01
	N > W	N > W	G > B	G > B

* W = white, N = Negro. For example, on item 22, Negro children were rated as
being more likable than white children.
† B = boys, G = girls. For example, on item 22, girls were rated as being more likable
than boys.

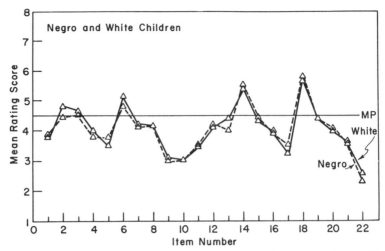

Fig. 10.5: Mean rating scores given by teachers to Negro and white children on 22 behavior scales; both sexes and both years (1962, 1964) combined. (MP = midpoint of rating scale.)

With respect to racial differences, the analyses indicate social and temperamental differences as well as motivational ones. Thus, the white children were rated as being more emotionally expressive, less submissive, and less likable than the Negro children. The white children were also rated higher on their concern about the quality of their work and on their reaction to achievement or success experiences. In short, if

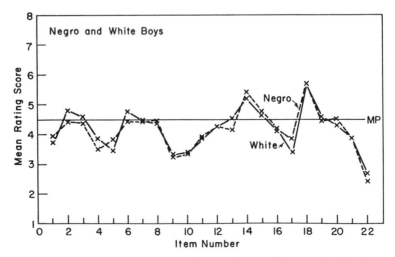

Fig. 10.6: Mean rating scores given by teachers to Negro and white boys on 22 behavior scales; 1962 and 1964 combined. (MP = midpoint of rating scale.)

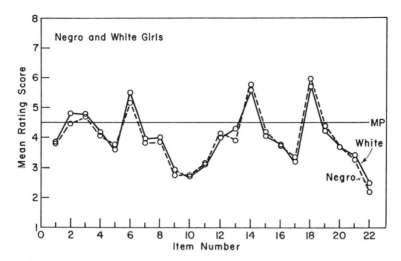

Fig. 10.7: Mean rating scores given by teachers to Negro and white girls on 22 behavior scales; 1962 and 1964 combined. (MP = midpoint of rating scale.)

there is validity in these judgments, the Negro children tend to be more passive and to have less striving for achievement than their white counterparts.

In Figures 10.6 and 10.7, racial comparisons are shown separately for the boys and girls, respectively. Again, for both sexes, the profiles for the two races are very similar. The largest differences between the white boys and the Negro boys suggest that white boys are more emotionally expressive, need less encouragement, are more gregarious, are more concerned with the quality of their work, are more assertive, and are more responsive to success experiences. White girls, compared with Negro girls, are more emotionally expressive, are more concerned with the quality of their work, and are more assertive. In general, the similarity between the girls of the two races is somewhat greater than that between the boys.

These racial comparisons use data that have been provided by different sets of judges. It is possible, therefore, that some of the similarities or differences that have been reported reflect characteristics of the judges rather than actual behavioral features of the children of the two races. If comparable ratings were made by a common set of unbiased judges, some of the findings that have been described might be modified considerably. To obtain such unbiased data is obviously an extremely difficult task; perhaps it is impossible. Until such data are reported, the present ratings can be taken as at least a tentative indication of marked racial similarity in the several behavioral realms which were evaluated.

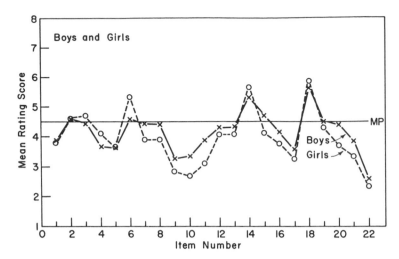

Fig. 10.8: Mean rating scores given by teachers to boys and girls on 22 behavior scales; both races and both years (1962, 1964) combined. (MP = midpoint of rating scale.)

At the same time, the ratings do not show complete equivalence of these groups in the social, temperamental, or motivational spheres.

Sex Differences

The significant sex differences obtained in the analyses of variance have been summarized in Table 10.2. The profiles of mean scores for boys and girls separately (both races combined) have been plotted in Figure 10.8; these plots combine the data for the two years and assume equal numbers of each sex for both years and for both races. Similar plots contrasting white boys with white girls and Negro boys with Negro girls are to be found in Figures 10.9 and 10.10, respectively.

It is immediately apparent from these data and figures that the sex differences are much greater than the racial differences. Thus, for 15 of the 22 traits there is a significant sex difference in each year's data.[7] Furthermore, the direction of the boy–girl difference is the same for each item in each year's data. Finally, the displacements of the two profiles in Figures 10.8 through 10.10 (representing sex comparisons) are more marked than are those for the two profiles in Figures 10.5 through 10.7 (representing racial comparisons).

An examination of the data for the 15 sex-differentiating traits reveals that on 14 of them the girls were rated more favorably than the boys. For instance, the girls are viewed as having more social poise and as

[7] Actually, in most instances the differences are highly significant.

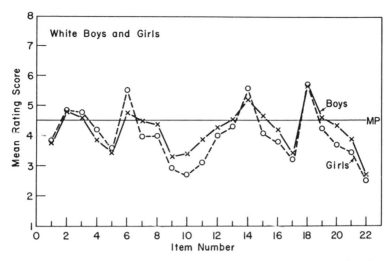

Fig. 10.9: Mean rating scores given by teachers to white boys and girls on 22 behavior scales; 1962 and 1964 combined. (MP = midpoint of rating scale.)

being warmer, more cooperative, more trustful, less agitated, more consistent, and more likable than the boys. Also, girls are seen as needing less encouragement, as being more concerned about the quality of their work, as being more reactive to both success and failure experiences, as expending more effort on their lessons, as being more persistent, and as being more absorbed in the tasks that they undertake than the boys.

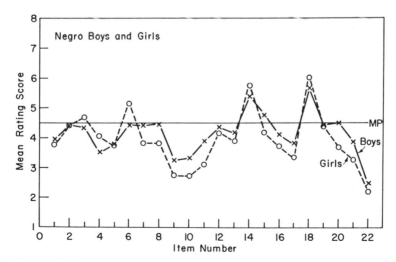

Fig. 10.10: Mean rating scores given by teachers to Negro boys and girls on 22 behavior scales; 1962 and 1964 combined. (MP = midpoint of rating scale.)

With respect to emotional upsets, however, the girls are rated as having a higher degree of susceptibility than the boys. A particularly noteworthy fact is that the sex differences just enumerated occur in almost precisely the same way for each race; that is, the boy–girl differences hold true for both Negro and white children.

The traits showing significant sex differences refer to a wide range of behavior: social, temperamental, and motivational. Especially interesting is the fact that significant sex differences, in favor of the girls, are found for each of the seven components of the achievement syndrome. There can be little doubt, then, that teachers perceive boys in general as differing in many ways from girls in general, but that boys are particularly set off in terms of a lower achievement striving.

It must be recognized, of course, that the vast majority of these ratings were provided by women. Whether or not men, viewing the same behavior, would make comparable judgments cannot be determined here. Nor do we know that the actual behavior of the children would remain unaltered if they confronted men rather than women in their classrooms.

CONCLUDING COMMENTS

As we have attempted to make clear, very real problems arise in using ratings within a developmental framework. Some of these difficulties *might* have been reduced if each teacher had been asked to take all elementary school children as her referent group when she made her ratings, instead of just her class. We do not in fact know, however, that all teachers would be able to use that more comprehensive frame of reference. Studies should be made of the ability of elementary school teachers to use differentially these two frameworks in reporting judgments about children in their classes.

Racial comparisons present a number of difficulties; indeed, some of these may be beyond solution as far as the use of ratings is concerned. A child cannot be observed, for example, without the judge being aware of his skin color. Once that awareness is present, bias, at some level, may be unavoidable. Furthermore, when like-race raters are used—as in the current study—there is a risk that the two sets of raters may be using different standards; hence, identical ratings may not refer to equivalent behavior. The sex of the rater also introduces difficulties in interpreting data. Eventually the significance of this factor should be determined more exactly by careful empirical work. For example, this kind of study could be made in school systems where meaningful numbers of men have joined women in teaching elementary-school children. A comparison of their pupil judgments would be of considerable interest.

There are, then, problems in the interpretation of the data that have been presented in this chapter which cannot be overlooked. Some of these difficulties point to the desirability of conducting a variety of methodological studies before additional inquiries of this type are attempted. On the other hand, we would also argue that it would be quite inappropriate to ignore the data that have been presented just because all methodological problems have not been resolved.

It is apparent, for example, that the teachers of both races perceive important sex differences among the children they teach. The similarities across race in this regard are quite remarkable; that is, the kinds of differences that the white teachers report between boys and girls are almost identical with the sex differences reported by the Negro teachers. Teachers of both races report social, temperamental, and motivational differences between the two sexes, almost always in a direction that can be said to favor the girls. Further research is needed to understand the origins of these differences and the role they play in determining how boys and girls respond to the classroom activities and learning tasks. Perhaps of critical importance in this regard is the lower achievement motivation of the boys.

In contrast to sex differences, reported racial differences are slight. Indeed, when racial comparisons are made it is clear that it is racial similarity rather than difference which must be underscored. Nevertheless, racial differences cannot be ignored completely. Here, too, the factor of achievement striving is important, the difference favoring the white children. Furthermore, there is some evidence that this relative lack of drive may be part of a pattern of greater passivity among the Negro children. In other words, the Negro children in Millfield appear to exhibit less assertiveness in several sectors of their lives than the white children show.

In summary, the findings of the study reported in this chapter are limited, and the conclusions drawn are hedged in by methodological restrictions. Still, the clarity of the findings with respect to sex membership would appear to justify the effort that has been made. Certainly these results focus upon an important area with implications for what needs to be done in school settings like these. Also, the racial differences, while less pronounced than those attributable to sex, may be crucial as far as the differential progress of the two races is concerned.

Chapter 11

EIGHTH-GRADE CHILDREN AS ASSESSED BY THE
MINNESOTA MULTIPHASIC PERSONALITY INVENTORY

To obtain objective and quantitative data on certain personality characteristics of the children in Millfield, the Minnesota Multiphasic Personality Inventory (MMPI) was included in our assessment battery. In addition to the general advantages for research purposes that such a standardized test provides, a growing body of research with this test on the personality characteristics of adolescents provides a meaningful basis for comparison of this research sample with groups differing in ethnic, geographical, social, or economic background. The content and form of the MMPI, however, limited its use to the eighth-grade level, precluding age comparisons in personality development.

THE MMPI

Construction of the Inventory

There are 550 separate statements (16 of them are used twice) in the MMPI to which each subject is asked to answer true or false as they apply to him. The content of these items ranges widely over views of one's self and others, over personal feelings and social attitudes, over physical and mental symptoms, over beliefs, habits, and past experiences. The pool of items was collected with the hope that the major personality dimensions would be covered.

For general use of the MMPI, ten personality scales and three validity scales are scored and plotted in a profile. The original scales were constructed empirically by contrasting the item replies of highly selected groups of psychiatric patients to the way a large group of normal adults answered these items. Only those items that actually separated each criterion group from the normals were retained to make up these scales. In addition, some items were eliminated from these component scales to reduce the biases of age, marital status, and socioeconomic status. Sex differences could not be eliminated from most of the scales, however, and separate norms are used in the profiles for each sex.

Although the original scales were derived from patients showing extreme forms of personality deviation, early research studies indicated that useful and meaningful separations within normal ranges of personality variation were possible. These normative groups were primarily made up of adults and included subjects only as young as the age of 16. More recent work, however, has indicated that the test is appropriate and valid for literate subjects as young as 13 or 14 years of age.

Validity Scales

The MMPI includes some important safeguards against several pervasive difficulties in the use of verbal statements to survey personality status. These safeguards are called validity scales, since they provide information about the acceptability of a particular set of answers from a test subject. The validity scales are scored as a separate group from the clinical, or personality, scales and are evaluated before the rest of the test profile is interpreted.

One common source of difficulty in using these tests is that the subject may not want to cooperate with the examiner or reveal how these various statements may apply to himself. He may prefer to answer them the way he thinks he should to look good, for example, or he may answer the way he thinks the examiner wants him to fill out the answers. The general tendency to distort one's answers in a strongly favorable way is evaluated by the score on the L scale. A score that is high on this scale casts doubt on the dependability of the scores on the rest of the inventory.

In a similar way, the F score reflects the extent to which a subject has marked answers that are very infrequently given to these items either by normal subjects or even by patients of various kinds. Rare answers can reflect valid personality deviations or such kinds of invalidity as unwillingness to cooperate with the test instructions, serious reading difficulties, inattention, confusion, or even a deliberate intention to appear poorly adjusted on the test.

The third validity index, the K score, is a more subtle measure of a subject's tendency to distort his answers to the test in either an unfavorable (low scores) or a favorable direction (high scores). Research has indicated that the influence of these test-taking sets upon the basic personality scales can be offset to a considerable extent by adding parts of the K score to the raw scores of some clinical scales.[1]

A fourth index of test validity, the number of statements that the subject omits, or fails to answer either true or false, is also plotted on the test profile. No subject is forced to answer all the items, of course, since some subjects are bound to find occasional items that do not apply to them among such a heterogeneous collection. All the answer sheets of the subjects in Millfield were checked for omissions; few of the subjects left any of the items unanswered.[2]

Together, these validity indices serve as partial checks on the suitability of the MMPI for the subjects in this study. No scores from any subject who had excessively high values on these scales were included in the analyses of the clinical scales. Perhaps as a result of the variations introduced in the test administration described below, very few invalid protocols were found.[3]

Personality Scales

These scales (also called clinical scales, since they were derived from various clinical groups formed in psychiatric practice and often have provided useful diagnostic information in clinical work) are usually referred to by the number of their position in the regular MMPI profile.[4] The meaning of each scale has been demonstrated to be greater than the specific, and often extreme, features that were true of the patients used as criterion groups. This psychological breadth of interpretive significance dictated abandoning the original diagnostic labels and substituting the numerical system. The personality correlates of the component scales have been collated in several reference works on the

---

[1] Five clinical scales (1, 4, 7, 8, and 9) have been corrected by the customary K-scale weights in the results reported below.

[2] It should be noted, however, that in the 1964 testing program, the white children were not administered the final one hundred items of the test because of time limitations.

[3] Out of 265 tests, six records were eliminated for excessive F scores and one for a high L scale value.

[4] The specific diagnostic groups used to construct the standard MMPI scales were: scale 1 (hypochondriacs); scale 2 (depressives); scale 3 (hysterical conversions); scale 4 (psychopathic personalities); scale 5 (male inverts); scale 6 (paranoids); scale 7 (obsessive-compulsives); scale 8 (schizophrenics); scale 9 (hypomanics); and scale 0 (social introverts).

MMPI, including Welsh and Dahlstrom (1956), Dahlstrom and Welsh (1960), Marks and Seeman (1963), and Gilberstadt and Duker (1965). In addition to the personality implications of particular scales in the test, further interpretive significance has been found for various patterns, or score combinations, appearing in the MMPI profile.

ADMINISTRATION AND SCORING

In the usual form in which the MMPI is now administered, the statements are printed in a booklet and the subject marks his responses to them on a separate answer sheet. This version permits testing large groups of subjects in a single session, if they can read and follow the general test instructions. The validity scale values of each subject (see above) provide checks on the appropriateness of this form of administration for each member of the group tested.

Tape-Recorded Version

Most of the MMPI statements do not demand more than a fifth-grade reading level to understand them, although occasional items require somewhat higher levels of reading comprehension. As shown in Chapter 4, however, some of the eighth-grade students in Millfield are not able to demonstrate even fifth-grade reading mastery. (These achievement test findings on both Word Meaning and Paragraph Meaning were already available when the MMPI test program was planned for these students.) Accordingly, a tape-recorded form of the MMPI was prepared in an attempt to circumvent their serious limitation in reading comprehension.

The tape was specially prepared for this project.[5] After a brief introduction, the tape presents each MMPI statement in the same order as it appears in the standard test booklet. Initially, a pause of ten seconds is made after each item to allow the subject to think over the item and mark his answer to it. After the first ten test items, the pacing of the

[5] We are indebted to James N. Butcher for the preparation and reading of the tape-recorded version of the MMPI used in this study. His West Virginian accent appeared to provide an excellent compromise between the clarity of enunciation needed for full communicative efficiency and the familiarity of accent and emphasis for use with Southern rural subjects. He also carried out the equivalence studies which demonstrated satisfactory stability of the MMPI component scores between examinations by tape and by test booklet on college level subjects (see Butcher and Dahlstrom, 1965).

items is speeded up and five-second intervals are used for the rest of the test.[6]

This tape version of the MMPI was given to each eighth-grade class in their own classroom at the end of the school year in 1963 by our regular field research staff workers. In 1964, however, the white eighth-graders were attending a separate junior high school and had to be examined by a special testing staff in the music room of that school. The subjects, grouped by homerooms, were examined by two women who were not part of our field research staff.[7] The eighth-grade students in the Negro schools were available for testing as usual by the regular research staff in the spring of 1964, as they were in 1963.

The classroom teachers were not present during this examination, but the project staff members were by now quite well-known to these students. The subjects were each given a Hankes answer sheet for the MMPI and told the purpose and nature of the test. The tape recorder was started, and the first MMPI item was played to the group. The research staff made certain that the children understood the instructions and procedures and then resumed the tape. Circumspect proctoring was carried out during the session; the proctors tried to make sure that the subjects continued to be attentive and that they were able to keep up with the tape delivery, but they also tried to avoid any appearance of prying into the specific answers given by any of the test subjects. Routinely, the tape was stopped every half-hour in order to allow the subjects a chance to stand, stretch, and relax before proceeding with the examination. The examiners were successful in maintaining a serious and business-like testing atmosphere. The children's reactions to the items were generally accepting; questions were postponed until completion of the test. The examiners then went back over any items that the children wished to have repeated or failed to understand. Usually there were no more than ten or fifteen such queries, mostly items that some subject wanted to complete after previously skipping them. Some requests for definitions were made, but the examiners provided only occasional synonyms and asked the subjects to make up their own minds

---

[6] Preliminary research indicated that subjects soon accommodate to the task and do not need more than five or six seconds between items to keep up with the tape recording. We are indebted to the Recording Laboratories of the Department of Radio, Television, and Motion Pictures at the University of North Carolina, which provided the equipment and technicians for editing this tape.

[7] The testing was fitted into the regularly scheduled periods of these students, and consequently the last one hundred items on the tape could not be given. This curtailment of the test did not affect any of the regular MMPI scales, but some of the special scales had to be prorated to make them comparable to scores from subjects given the full test.

about the general meaning of the statements. The comments of the children indicated that they had found the test session long, but interesting.

Scoring Methods

The scoring of the MMPI is completely objective and highly reliable. Once the subject has completed his marking of spaces on the answer sheet, the tallying of scores is a simple clerical task: a scoring template for each component scale is placed over the answer sheet, and the number of items showing through the spaces constitutes the score for that scale. Each test protocol was scored twice to assure clerical accuracy; the scores were entered on a standard MMPI profile form appropriate to the sex of the subject. In addition, some research scales were scored for each answer sheet by means of special scoring templates.[8]

METHODS OF ANALYSIS OF THE MMPI DATA

Data obtained from a multivariate instrument like the MMPI can be analyzed in a number of meaningful ways. Each component score can

TABLE 11.1

Raw Score Means and Standard Deviations on the Basic MMPI Scales
for Eighth-Grade Children (1963 and 1964)

MMPI scales	White boys (N = 52)		White girls (N = 66)		Negro boys (N = 59)		Negro girls (N = 81)	
	Mean	S.D.	Mean	S.D.	Mean	S.D.	Mean	S.D.
Validity scales								
L	3.3	2.1	3.6	2.0	3.9	3.0	4.0	2.1
F	10.1	6.7	7.8	5.2	12.5	7.2	10.0	5.7
K	10.2	4.3	11.3	4.2	10.0	4.6	10.7	4.3
Personality scales								
1	6.9	5.3	7.0	4.8	8.1	4.1	8.4	4.7
2	17.9	4.5	19.4	4.4	20.3	5.0	21.9	4.2
3	17.9	4.5	19.1	5.3	16.8	4.8	17.9	4.9
4	19.9	4.8	18.6	4.8	21.3	5.1	20.1	4.5
5	20.3	4.6	32.7	4.4	22.4	3.6	31.6	3.7
6	11.1	3.5	9.9	3.7	12.3	3.5	11.8	4.8
7	18.8	7.0	17.4	7.6	20.4	6.8	20.7	6.6
8	21.8	8.7	19.8	10.1	26.4	9.2	26.1	10.2
9	21.8	5.0	19.2	5.3	23.2	4.2	21.0	3.7
0	28.7	6.9	29.2	6.8	30.9	6.0	30.6	5.5

[8] We are indebted to Stephen Flanagan for scoring and tabulating many of these MMPI data.

be treated independently and analyzed by the usual statistical methods to describe each subgroup—for example, where the group falls on the scale, and how widely it is distributed over the scale range. This scale-by-scale approach was carried out on both the validity and the personality scales of the MMPI, and the results are reported in the next section. These analyses were based on the raw scores obtained from scoring each subject's test record. The means and standard deviations found for each subgroup on the component scales are summarized in Table 11.1 in raw score form.

Since each scale has a different number of items and a different range of variation, it is difficult to compare relative levels on different scales for any one group. In addition, as noted above, there are important sex differences on some of the personality scales which further complicate cross-sex comparisons based on raw score values. Therefore, in addition to the raw score means described above, group mean profiles were prepared based upon standard T-score scales.[9] These profiles for each subgroup are presented in Figure 11.1.

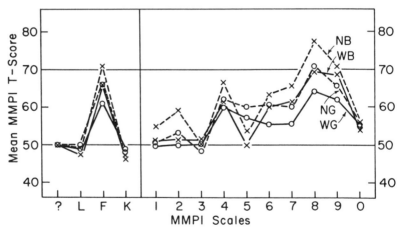

Fig. 11.1: Mean MMPI profiles of eighth-grade white boys (WB), white girls (WG), Negro boys (NB), and Negro girls (NG) from Millfield (1963 and 1964).

[9] On each MMPI scale, a standard reference scale is used, called a T-score scale, to facilitate direct comparisons of a subject's standing on each of the various personality dimensions being evaluated. Arbitrarily, the value of the mean earned by a reference group of Minnesota normal adult men or women is set at the 50 mark for each separate scale. The amount of deviation above or below the mean is scaled by setting the standard deviation of the norm group equal to ten T-score points. Thus, a score of 65 signifies that a subject has scored above the Minnesota group of that sex by one and a half standard deviations, in the direction of the psychiatric criterion group used to develop that scale. A score of 47 indicates that he has scored below the mean by 0.3 of a standard deviation.

If the group that is being summarized in such a mean profile is comprised of individuals who are quite similar to one another, then obviously these composites can be very useful in typifying the group and can facilitate comparisons with other homogeneous groups of subjects. When the subjects that make up a group have widely varying patterns of personality scores, however, a mean profile based upon their records could be quite misleading. Few if any subjects in a heterogeneous group may individually show the pattern of scores in the group profile, and the mean profile would not be accurate if it were used to typify all the subjects in the group. In the same way, the elevation of the mean profile may be misleading. High mean profiles on the MMPI cannot be obtained without many individuals in that group having high values on the scores within their separate profiles, but low mean profiles may result even if many of the subjects have isolated high elevations when they tend to have their high scores on different component scales.

Statistical comparisons based upon mean MMPI profiles of the various groups, such as those reported later in this chapter, should be supplemented by appropriate analyses of the elevations and patterns in the individual profiles obtained from the members of the group. Two simple pattern analytic procedures[10] were carried out on the records from the Millfield children as a precaution to evaluate the dependability of the mean profiles for the separate subgroups and as a basis for gaining additional insights into the personality characteristics of these youngsters.

The profile elevation, as will be made clear below, is important in forming the appropriate inferences of personality characteristics from the component MMPI scales or from the patterns of scores in the profile. Therefore, a tabulation was first made of the number of subjects in each group having one or more scores in their profile exceeding a T-score of 70 and thus obtaining a primed code. (This cutting score lies two standard deviations above the mean of normal adults of that sex and indicates, in general, the level at which a person's scores approach the score elevations of various clinical reference groups.) The results of

---

[10] Pattern analytic work is facilitated by coding each individual's profile in a summary form that preserves both the pattern of score elevations and the absolute elevation of each. There are two methods of coding MMPI records, referred to as Hathaway's method and Welsh's method (see Dahlstrom and Welsh, 1960). Welsh's method was employed in coding for both profile elevation and high points, but the results were identical to those that would have been obtained with Hathaway's method, since the individual profiles were all elevated enough to give a high point code in his approach. In both systems, profiles with some component scale beyond a T-score of 70 are called primed codes. The prime symbol is used to designate this level of absolute deviation from the mean of the Minnesota reference group. Profiles are called nonprimed if no score reaches the level of 70 on the T-scale.

TABLE 11.2

Frequencies of MMPI Profiles with Primed Codes (High Elevations) and
Nonprimed Codes among the Eighth-Grade Samples (1963 and 1964)

Year	White boys			White girls		
	Nonprimed	Primed	Total	Nonprimed	Primed	Total
1963	13	18	31	21	13	34
1964	8	13	21	14	18	32
	—	—	—	—	—	—
Totals*	21	31	52	35	31	66
	Negro boys			Negro girls		
	Nonprimed	Primed	Total	Nonprimed	Primed	Total
1963	9	25	34	17	25	42
1964	8	17	25	11	28	39
	—	—	—	—	—	—
Totals*	17	42	59	28	53	81

* Two profiles from the white children and five profiles from the Negro children were
excluded on the basis of excessively high validity scale values.

these tabulations of the frequencies of primed codes in each of the
subgroups are reported in Table 11.2. These findings, as will be noted
below, were in good agreement with the findings from the mean profiles
for each of these groups of Millfield children, indicating that the composite profiles are suitable for comparisons of relative elevations on the
MMPI.

A second form of pattern analysis carried out on these records was a
tabulation of the frequency with which each personality scale was the
highest score earned by the subject in the profile. These high-point
frequencies, in absolute numbers and percentages, are summarized for
each subgroup in Table 11.3. Since there were some discrepancies noted
in comparing the results of the high-point tabulations with the patterns
reflected in the group mean profiles, special note will be taken of these
differences later in the chapter.

One additional method of data analysis was carried out. Five special
scales were scored on these MMPI records; the means and standard
deviations of the raw scores on each for the Millfield subgroups are
presented in Table 11.4. These scales come from some recent research
of Harrison and Kass (1967) based upon their studies of young
white and Negro women in Boston, Massachusetts, who were tested
when they came to an obstetrical clinic for care during pregnancy. Valid
records were available on 389 white and 383 Negro mothers-to-be, a
large enough sample of each group to permit detailed item analyses in

TABLE 11.3

Frequencies and Relative Percentages of Each High-Point Code
in the MMPI Profiles of Eighth-Grade Children
in Millfield (1963 and 1964)

High-point scale*	White boys		White girls		Negro boys		Negro girls	
	N	%	N	%	N	%	N	%
1	1	2	0	0	0	0	0	0
2	3	6	0	0	2	3	3	4
3	0	0	0	0	0	0	0.5	1
4	7	13	11.5	17	7.5	12	9	11
5	2	4	12	18	0	0	9	11
6	4	7	6.5	10	1	2	7	8
7	4	7	1	2	2.5	4	0.5	1
8	7	13	13.5	20	28	45	36	43
9	23	43	17	26	15	24	14	17
0	1	2	4.5	7	3	5	2	2
Invalid	2	4	0	0	3	5	2	2
Totals	54	101	66	100	62	100	83	100

* Fractions in the frequency columns indicate tied high points in a particular profile.
In these cases the entry was divided between the two high-point scales.

addition to statistical analyses of the standard MMPI scales. Although
213 of the 550 MMPI items showed stable differences in endorsement
patterns between the two groups, only the 150 most discriminating items
were chosen for more elaborate analyses. Using factor analytic procedures on a high-speed electronic computer, these workers were able to
find twenty stable groupings among these selected items which they
used to form special factor scales. Some of these special scales proved

TABLE 11.4

Raw Score Means and Standard Deviations on Harrison and Kass' MMPI Factor
Scales on Eighth-Grade Children (1963 and 1964)

Factor scales	White boys (N = 52)		White girls (N = 66)		Negro boys (N = 59)		Negro girls (N = 81)	
	Mean	S.D.	Mean	S.D.	Mean	S.D.	Mean	S.D.
I. Estrangement	11.9	4.2	10.7	4.1	14.2	3.9	13.3	4.5
II. Intellectual and Cultural Interests	8.5	3.0	10.2	4.5	12.9	3.1	14.3	3.1
III. Denial of Deviant Behavior	6.6	1.9	7.2	1.9	7.2	1.4	7.4	1.6
IV. Cynicism	16.9	4.1	14.6	4.2	19.9	3.1	18.9	3.9
V. Admission of Minor Faults	3.6	1.4	2.8	1.5	2.6	1.5	2.5	1.5

to be quite short and unreliable, but a few seem to be useful in characterizing the differences between these white and Negro women in their self-descriptions on the MMPI. Five of these scales were selected for use in this study; they represent the first five factors to emerge from their analyses and serve to summarize many of the differences that were found. Naming such scales has to be quite arbitrary until further research clarifies the significance each may have for personality interpretations, but the tentative titles suggested by Harrison and Kass appear to be reasonable summaries of the content of the items making up each scale. In the present study they provide us with additional means of examining some of the ways these youngsters are viewing and presenting themselves at this stage of their development.

Factor I is a 26-item scale called, tentatively, Estrangement. It is made up of such items as: The future seems hopeless to me (True); No one seems to understand me (True); I am sure I get a raw deal from life (True); I have a daydream life about which I do not tell other people (True); and These days I find it hard not to give up hope of amounting to something (True). This scale showed higher scores for Negro subjects in Harrison and Kass' study.

Factor II has 21 items and has been labeled Intellectual and Cultural Interests. Some of the items include: I like poetry (True); I like to read about history (True); I like dramatics (True); I read in the Bible several times a week (True); and I think I would like the work of a librarian (True). The Negro subjects in Harrison and Kass' study earned higher scores on this scale, too.

Factor III, called Denial of Deviant Behavior, contains only ten items, among which are: I have never had a fit or convulsion (True); I have never seen a vision (True); and It wouldn't make me nervous if any members of my family got into trouble with the law (False). This scale showed higher scores for the white subjects in the derivational study.

Factor IV is a somewhat longer scale, made up of 26 items, and is labeled Cynicism. Some representative items include: It takes a lot of argument to convince most people of the truth (True); I think most people would lie to get ahead (True); Most people make friends because friends are likely to be useful to them (True); Most people will use somewhat unfair means to gain profit or an advantage rather than lose it (True); and People generally demand more respect for their own rights than they are willing to allow for others (True). On this scale the Negro women earned higher scores than the white women did.

Factor V, Admission of Minor Faults, is a nine-item scale on which the white women earned the higher scores. It contains such items as: I played hookey from school quite often as a youngster (True); I can remember "playing sick" to get out of something (True); At times I feel like swearing (True); and I enjoy gambling for small stakes (True).

MMPI VALIDITY SCALE FINDINGS

The special precautions described above in the administration of this test seem to have paid off in a set of useful and meaningful test records. Almost all the protocols were complete and appropriately filled out. The questions that were raised after the tape was administered to the groups indicated that they had attended well and were able to deal with the content of the items appropriately and comfortably. One Negro boy was absent for part of the tape session and could not be reached to complete the remainder of his test. In all, 265 completed test records were available for study from the 1963 and 1964 administrations.

L scale. One student was found to have answered 13 of the 15 items on this scale in the defensive direction. That test protocol was removed from any further analyses; no other answer sheet had more than nine items answered in the significant direction.

The low scores uniformly found on the L scale (see Table 11.1) indicate that these boys and girls were willing to describe themselves with frankness and candor. The general lack of item omissions supports a similar interpretation. Consistent with this conclusion, also, are the impressions of the research staff while they were administering the test. The students appear to have accepted the task well and complied with the instructions.

F scale. In contrast to the L-scale means, the average performances of all subgroups on this scale deviate from the norms appreciably. Generous limits were allowed on this 64-item scale; only protocols with scores of 26 or more on the F scale were eliminated, since they were highly suggestive of random responding to the scale. Six records were dropped from the analyses.

Both groups of boys scored more deviantly on the F scale than the girls did;[11] the Negro children earned significantly higher scores than the white children. As indicated above, answering statements that are only infrequently endorsed by most people can mean that any one of several possible factors was operating. It is unlikely, however, that certain possibilities were present. Reading difficulties were minimized by the oral presentation. No lack of cooperation or any serious inattention

---

[11] Here and throughout the discussion of results, references to sex differences will make use of the separate norms established for the two sexes rather than raw score differences. These two sets of norms are reflected in the plots of Figure 11.1.

was noted during the test sessions. Therefore, it is likely that the explanations for most of the elevated mean F scores will be found in the personality characteristics of the youngsters themselves. This possibility will be explored in greater detail later in this chapter.

K scale. The average scores on this 30-item scale for all four subgroups fall below the average for the Minnesota normal adults. This deviation is in the direction of lack of defensiveness in describing their feelings and personal reactions. Such a tendency is by no means extreme, yet it is important to recognize that these youngsters appear to be open in their answers to the test, showing no particular sensitivity or defensiveness about stating their attitudes and beliefs.

PERSONALITY SCALE FINDINGS

The personality implications of the mean values earned by the various subgroups under study here are given below. Higher values on these different scales usually mean a greater likelihood of some form of emotional maladjustment.

Scale 1. Extreme values on this scale reflect both a narrow self-centeredness and an over-concern with various bodily symptoms. In its lower ranges, this scale often reflects degrees of lethargy, inactivity, and fatigue. Both white subgroups and the Negro girls seem quite free of any of these features (see Figure 11.1). Only the Negro boys scored high enough to suggest that some of these characteristics may be attributed to them. Generally, these youngsters do not appear to have serious physical preoccupations or overinvolvement with their health and physical well-being.

Scale 2. Both ends of this scale appear to have important personality implications: high values measure unhappiness, poor morale, self-dissatisfaction, and a sober and serious outlook on life (consistent with the depressed individuals used to construct the scale). Low scores are related to buoyancy, self-confidence, and naturalness; cheerfulness, energy, and good spirits can also be inferred from these low scores. Youngsters this age often score below the Minnesota adult norms on this scale, but no subgroup in this study scored below average. In fact, both Negro groups fell significantly above the mean. Negro boys are particularly likely to show evidence of poor morale and a pessimistic outlook on the world.

Scale 3. This scale was constructed to identify individuals who are likely to get ill under stress, as a partial solution to their emotional problems. High scores are related to this tendency to form conversion reactions, and to the basic personality traits associated with that form of hysteria: naiveté, religious idealism, social dependency, and childishness. None of the groups in Millfield showed an appreciable elevation on scale 3. This is particularly noteworthy in the light of claims in the clinical psychiatric literature that there is a high incidence of this personality pattern among people residing in the South.

Scale 4. Individuals high on this scale are generally rebellious, socially aggressive, and selfish, and show a cynical disregard for rules and authority. The scale was constructed to identify people who continually get into one kind of trouble or another because they lack basic character and integrity. All four subgroups earned scale 4 mean scores in the range of moderate elevation, Negro boys earning the highest value. Scores in this middle range are more likely to reflect impulsivity and interpersonal insensitivity than direct expression of hostility, resentment, or defiance of authority, which are implied by the more extreme values. Judging by their scores on scale 4, these youngsters as a group are not yet ready for adult demands and responsibilities.

Scale 5. This scale measures the extent to which a person expresses an interest pattern characteristic of the opposite sex. Thus among boys, higher scores reflect interests in cultural, scholarly, or academic pursuits, gentlemanly behavior, and, at the higher levels, feminine attitudes and values. Neither white nor Negro boys scored appreciably above the mean for men in general on this scale. This finding thus fails to support some contentions in the current literature that Negro males as a group have in some fashion been feminized by their upbringing and experiences in (supposedly) matriarchal families.

The scores of the two groups of girls, however, are elevated moderately on scale 5. They score more like men on this scale than do most adolescent groups or than women in general do, suggesting some systematic rejection of feminine roles and patterns. High-scoring girls on this scale are characterized as rather coarse, striving, and ambitious. In Chapter 16, there is evidence that the girls, particularly Negro girls, are dissatisfied in many ways with both their present lot and future prospects in this community. Perhaps, from the scores they earned on scale 5, it could be added that their future roles as women here may include levels of dominance and self-assertiveness that are not in keeping with the usual concept of femininity.

Scale 6. High scores on this scale reflect such personality features as oversensitivity, stubbornness, irritability, and proneness to misinterpret the actions and intentions of other people. These traits are consistent with the paranoid disorders that made up the group on which this scale was constructed. Moderate elevations on this scale, however, show only the basic emphasis upon rationality, self-dedication, and devotion to others, without the sense of self-importance so characteristic of extreme forms of this personality pattern. If anything, people with only moderately elevated scores on scale 6 are likely to appear more as martyrs than as vain and overbearing egotists. All four subgroups scored within moderate limits on scale 6, the Negro youngsters slightly higher than the white eighth-graders. These children can best be described as sensitive, rather self-effacing and self-conscious, with significant degrees of suspiciousness and guardedness in their relations with others.

Scale 7. Increasing elevations on this scale measure agitation, insecurity, perplexity, and feelings of inferiority. High scorers have many apprehensions, self-doubts, and anxieties. All four subgroups scored at a moderate level on scale 7, in the range that reflects lack of self-confidence, unsureness about personal worth, and worries about social acceptance and popularity. The boys (especially the Negro boys) showed more of these various concerns than the girls did; the white girls were most self-confident and comfortable.

Scale 8. Very high scores on this scale indicate severe personality disorganization or a break with reality. Moderate scores reflect underlying self-doubts, alienation from others, convictions of being inferior or different, and inability to experience the feelings and reactions that normal people do. All the subgroups in this sample had their highest elevations on this scale; the Negro boys and girls were most elevated, exceeding both of the white subgroups. Their scores are consistent with deep crises in personal identity, isolation from others, important doubts about their own capabilities, and lack of a sense of personal worth.

High scores on scale 8 are often accompanied by elevations on the F scale in the validity set. Both scales provide the subject with opportunities to report unusual and atypical experiences, beliefs, attitudes, or feelings. These four groups are ranked in a similar way by both the F scale and scale 8. It is quite likely that these subjects are demonstrating similar personality trends in their answers to both scales, trends which will be explored further by means of the special factor scales from Harrison and Kass. These elevations on scale 8 indicate that the youngsters may be going through important crises in personality organization. Such inferences, however, are at variance with both the reports of their teachers, as summarized in Chapter 10, and the findings from personal interviews with them, as will be reported in Chapter 16. These discrepancies are large; they require considerable additional research to provide adequate explanations for them.

Scale 9. Very high scores on this scale reveal driving energy, over-optimism, ambitiousness, and inability to see one's own limitations or liabilities. The subgroups from Millfield scored in the moderate ranges where nonconformity, excessive energy, lack of control, and poor judgment can more appropriately be inferred. The boys are higher than the girls on this scale, but all four groups are likely to show the impulsiveness, lack of sustained interest, and many short-lived enthusiasms that these scores imply and that are typical of this age range.

Scale 0. This scale was not originally part of the MMPI scale development work at Minnesota. It was devised later to measure differences in social introversion, or the tendency to stay by oneself and avoid wide-ranging social ties and relationships (indicated by high scores). Low scores on scale 0 mean that the person is likely to engage in many different activities, usually seeking out the company of others and actively participating in clubs, socials, and groups. Neither extreme in sociability characterizes the eighth-grade subgroups from Millfield. They are very similar to one another and, as a total group, show only a slight trend toward avoidance of social activities. This level can be best interpreted as lack of assertiveness and social initiative. Once social activities are underway, initiated perhaps by others, Millfield youngsters as a group should be fully participating.

PROFILE PATTERNS

Any behavioral characteristic of a person is expressed in the context of a number of other personality attributes. Often the particular meaning or significance of the behavior is greatly modified or even completely changed by these different contexts. High intelligence may lead to great contributions to humanity in able people with deep social concerns and self-dedication, but it may lead to efficient and devastating bilking of others if high ability is combined with the values of the confidence man. Appropriate personality measures and statistical techniques for preserving and analyzing configural relationships of this sort are still rather primitive. Consequently, a great deal remains to be understood in this area; one important issue revolves about the relative prominence of various personality trends within the individual in contrast to the strength of each attribute relative to its strength of appearance in other individuals. Scaling personality traits one against the other within any one person is one way of dealing with the context for behavioral expression of any one attribute.

In statistical analyses of the MMPI, as noted earlier, pattern analyses are used to preserve the individual patterns that subjects show in their answers to the inventory. The small number of records available from the Millfield eighth-grade students permitted only a few such procedures based upon the highest score in each profile. More refined and meaningful analyses, based upon combinations of the two or three highest scores, or configurations of the highest and lowest scale values in the profile, were not attempted. The methods used, however, served to highlight some of the personality characteristics of these youngsters.

High-Point Codes

In Table 11.3 are presented the results of tabulating the frequency with which each component scale in the MMPI was the highest score earned by a subject. Scales 8 and 9 were the most frequent high scores in all the subgroups. Scale 4 was also well represented among the high points in these profiles. Among the girls, but not the boys, scale 5 appeared as the leading score with a fair frequency. In general, these tabulations are consistent with the results reported in the scale means for these subgroups and demonstrate the dependability of the mean profiles for typifying the personality patterns of these eighth-grade children of Millfield: the prominent scores in the mean profiles for these youngsters appear also as the most frequent highest values of the separate profiles.

There are some inconsistencies, however, which alter the implications of the mean profiles to some degree. Although the means for white and Negro boys are quite similar in their patterns (see Figure 11.1), more of the white boys have peak scores on scale 9 than on scale 8 (43% to 13%), while the reverse is true for the Negro boys (24% to 45%). This reversal holds for the girls as well, although it is less clear-cut in their profiles. The white girls had more peaks on scale 9 than on scale 8 (26% to 20%), but the Negro girls showed the opposite trend (17% to 43%). Thus, although scale 8 scores are typically high in the profiles from both white and Negro children at this age, the score on scale 8 is much more likely to be the most prominent feature of the test record among the Negro subgroups.

This relationship of scales 8 and 9 in the high-point codes of MMPI profiles from adolescents has been analyzed and reported by Hathaway *et al.* (1959), using data obtained from a very large survey of ninth-grade children (almost all white pupils) in schools around the state of Minnesota. Some of their data are summarized in Table 11.5 for comparison with the findings from the Millfield subgroups. The children were grouped by place of residence: urban (Minneapolis, Duluth, and their suburbs), town (up to 30,000 population), and farm. Among their subgroups, they found several shifts in the MMPI high-point frequencies. From urban to small town to farm, scales 4 and 9 decreased as the

TABLE 11.5

Percentages of Each High-Point Code in the MMPI Profiles of Minnesota
Ninth-Grade Samples from Different Locales
(Hathaway, Monachesi, and Young, 1959)

High-point scale	Minnesota boys			Minnesota girls		
	Urban	Town	Farm	Urban	Town	Farm
1	1.9	1.6	2.1	0.3	0.4	0.6
2	4.3	3.8	4.2	1.7	1.3	1.6
3	3.4	2.5	2.5	4.6	4.0	2.8
4	22.1	18.9	12.9	24.0	20.3	14.9
5	5.2	4.9	3.8	9.1	11.5	16.1
6	4.7	5.6	7.1	8.5	8.4	10.1
7	7.1	7.4	8.8	4.3	5.9	4.9
8	17.2	18.0	21.2	9.3	10.4	10.6
9	20.6	22.9	18.1	21.1	18.0	12.7
0	5.4	7.2	10.2	8.0	11.9	16.3
Indeterminant	7.0	5.6	6.9	7.6	6.2	7.9
No high point	1.1	1.6	2.2	1.5	1.7	1.5
Total N	1366	2253	1325	1416	2403	1388

prominent scale in the profile for both boys and girls, while scales 6 and 0 increased in frequency to some extent. Among their ninth-grade girls, scale 5 also was more frequently a high point if the girl came from a farm, while it was less frequently a high point among farm boys than urban or town boys. There was some tendency for scale 8 to increase in frequency from the urban to the farm children, but the relative frequencies of scale 8 and scale 9 high points are more differentiating than either tabulation alone.

The Negro subgroups from Millfield show high-point frequencies that resemble Minnesota farm children in relative high-point proportions more than they do the town or urban samples. The white subgroups in Millfield do not reflect the Minnesota farm pattern in their high-point percentages on scales 8 and 9, but many of the other scale proportions are in keeping with the Minnesota data. In these comparisons, the small numbers of children in the subgroups from North Carolina hamper more detailed analyses. It should also be noted that the Minnesota groups when tested were a year more advanced in school. Rapid changes in personality can be expected to appear in this adolescent period.

In summary, among the personality scales, the Millfield children score closest to the MMPI norms on scales 1, 2, 3, 5, and 0. As a whole, they are relatively free of overconcern with their health or physical well-being, of cross-sex identification and interests, and of insecurities or discomfort in social relationships. They appear generally to be optimistic, socially participating but not socially assertive, and relatively uncomplaining and free of neurotic inhibitions. They also show the typical heterosexual interests, attitudes, and values of normal American adults. In respect to these basic personality characteristics, they do not differ from one another very markedly and do not score much above the normative levels for their age and geographic background.

The eighth-grade students are most deviant from the adult norms on scales 4, 8, and 9. These personality measures characterize the children as showing self-centeredness, lack of effective self-control, and impulsiveness. They also demonstrate some lack of rapport with their families and the adult world, an excess of ready enthusiasms and short-lived interests in any number of projects and endeavors, lack of dependability, and frequent irresponsibility in their duties and assignments, together with a struggle for identity and self-understanding. The levels at which these scales fall do not indicate that these subjects are showing emotional problems quite of the magnitude that medical and psychiatric patients display, but the scores are high enough to suggest important personality trends of the sort indicated.

Comparisons among the four groups indicate that the boys, Negro and white alike, show difficulties more in the areas of emotional control and impulsiveness, while the girls are more likely to have problems of emotional alienation and troubles with parental control and authority. Negro children are more extreme than white children in their deviations, but generally reveal the same patterns. There are two exceptions, however, to this general similarity. One difference is the elevation on scale 2 in the mean profiles of both the Negro boys and girls. Although not a marked rise, this trend reflects lower optimism or less expectation of successful outcomes to their undertakings on the part of the Negro students in Millfield in comparison to their white adolescent counterparts. The second and more important exception is the relative prominence of scale 8 elevations in the profiles from the Negro children. This scale points up many problems with their sense of identity, personal and social alienation, and doubts of their own competencies and personal worth.

Profile Elevation

Another general index of profile patterning is the number of individual profiles showing one or more personality scale values above the primed level (see footnote 10 above). In Table 11.2 are shown the number of profiles in each subgroup which had at least one personality score beyond the level of 70.

Both Negro subgroups had significantly more highly elevated, or primed, profiles than their white counterparts, and the boys had more primed profiles than the girls did. These data serve to document further the appropriateness of the mean profiles shown in Figure 11.1 to summarize the MMPI performances of the subgroups. That is, the mean profiles showed the same relationships among these subgroups in relative deviation from the profile norms as these tabulations of individual records reveal. It is noteworthy that only the white girls, among these subgroups, have more profiles that are nonprimed than are primed. The majority of children in each of the other groups have one or more scale elevations that deviate from the test norms by at least two standard deviations. Two-thirds to three-fourths of the profiles from the Negro children had some score (and often several scores) falling beyond a T-score of 70. The personality characterizations offered above, therefore, would be applicable to a great many of the children in these subgroups, not just to a few, highly deviant youngsters.

COMPARISON WITH OTHER GROUPS

Most published studies using the MMPI to study personality similarities and differences between white and Negro groups have suffered from serious limitations and biases in sampling (see surveys by Dahlstrom and Welsh, 1960; Butcher *et al.*, 1964; and Harrison and Kass, 1967). In the findings of these studies, Negro subjects have been generally reported as scoring higher than white subjects on scales L, F, 1, 8, and 9 and lower on scale 3. It has been impossible to determine, however, to what extent these differences reflect basic personality differences and how much they have been affected by uncontrolled variations in factors like intelligence, education, geographic origin, socioeconomic level, and test-taking attitudes. Nor has it been possible, in the specific studies, to rule out other important selective biases such as differential admission rates into various clinical services, unequal school survival to reach high school or college levels, or different patterns of arrest and sentencing of white and Negro defendants in groups of imprisoned felons.

Obviously, some of these methodological problems also enter into interpretations of the present set of MMPI findings. Intellective differences are present between the two groups, although pains were taken to reduce the importance of these differences and the related difficulties in reading and understanding the test procedures. Socioeconomic differences also exist between the white and Negro children included here,

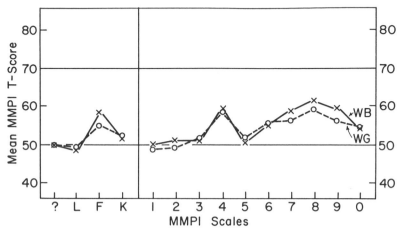

Fig. 11.2: Mean MMPI profiles of state-wide samples of Minnesota ninth-grade white boys (WB) and white girls (WG); from Hathaway and Monachesi (1963).

although the Millfield community is relatively homogeneous in these characteristics in contrast to many urban areas. Stable differences in test-taking attitude were found in the scores on the validity scales, but they were neither large nor pervasive in their effect on the personality measures. By sampling the children in the eighth grade, few school drop-outs were lost; the large losses come typically in the succeeding two or three years for both racial groups. There are no ways to check on other losses from these samples, however, such as the number of families moving out of the community and removing their children from the Millfield area.

The MMPI findings are in fair agreement with the material in the literature. The scales showing higher scores at a stable level for the Negro children were: F, 2, 6, 8, and 9. Scale 1 also showed some trend in the expected direction. Contrary to the expectations from the literature, the L scale and scale 3 failed to provide any dependable separation. The finding in respect to scale 6 is relatively new; only one other study, also based on North Carolina subjects (Panton, 1959), has reported this difference.

Since many of the attributes listed above as characteristic of these children (judging by their MMPI patterns) are frequently given as typical of adolescents generally, and lower socioeconomic adolescent groups in particular, it is useful to compare more closely the MMPI findings on these children with the data from other, similar groups. Figure 11.2 shows the mean profiles from the study mentioned earlier by Hathaway and Monachesi (1963) in which ninth-grade boys and girls were tested throughout the state of Minnesota. Almost all these children were white boys and girls about a year older than the Millfield sample, although a few Negro and Indian youngsters were included. In contrasting the profiles from Figures 11.1 and 11.2, several similarities are obvious: the same sex differences are present, the same general patterns are repeated, and the same elevations are shown deviating from the norms for adult subjects. Although these comparisons show that the children from Millfield score more deviantly on both the validity and the personality scales than their Minnesota counterparts, it may be that *some* of the basic personality characteristics showing up in the mean MMPI profiles from Millfield's eighth-graders are attributable to their slightly younger age level.

The same sort of similarity can be found by comparing both of these sets of data with the profiles presented in Figure 11.3 from some ninth-grade samples from Kentucky. Ball (1962) reported the results of a survey with the MMPI of school children in two moderate-sized communities in the border state of Kentucky. The survey included small samples of white and Negro boys and girls attending the ninth grade in two recently integrated school systems. The mean profiles of each of the four groups are presented here for comparison with the findings from North Carolina and Minnesota.

Although the same patterns appear in the profiles from the Kentucky groups, there does not appear to be the same difference in overall elevations between the boys and girls. The scores from the two racial

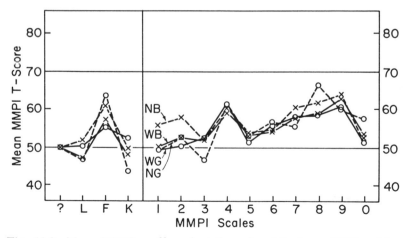

Fig. 11.3: Mean MMPI profiles of ninth-grade white boys (WB), white girls (WG), Negro boys (NB), and Negro girls (NG); from Kentucky urban samples of Ball (1962).

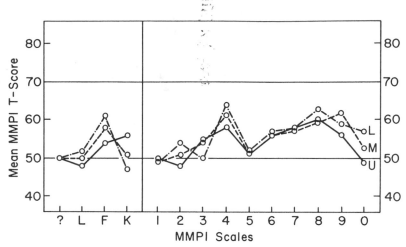

Fig. 11.4: Mean MMPI profiles of ninth-grade white girls grouped by socio-economic level (L = low; M = middle; and U = upper); from Kentucky urban samples of Ball (1962).

groups differ, however, in the ways that they do in the Millfield profiles; within each sex group, the Negro children show more personality deviations than the white children do.

Ball analyzed his data in such a way as to include an evaluation of socioeconomic differences. In Figure 11.4 are plotted the mean profiles from the white girls divided on the basis of the level of their fathers' occupations. Group U is made up of the girls whose fathers were professional men or held semiprofessional and managerial positions; group M, those whose fathers had retail businesses, worked at skilled or semi-skilled trades, or were clerks or farmers; and group L, those whose fathers worked at trades requiring little or no skill or were day laborers. Ball reported statistically stable differences on only two validity scales, F and K, and one personality scale, 0. The trends within the rest of the profile are quite consistent with these stable differences, however; the scores from lower socioeconomic level children indicate greater tendencies to report emotional difficulties and troubles.

The data from the Millfield groups (see Figure 11.1) resemble more the findings from group L in Figure 11.4 than they do the higher socioeconomic samples plotted there. The comparisons are directly relevant, of course, only for the white girls' data; similar but less striking differences were found by Ball among the scores from the white boys when he grouped them in the same way. The groups of Negro boys and girls were too small to permit analyses of this kind between different socioeconomic levels of their families.

The general findings from the MMPI scores obtained on the Millfield eighth-graders suggest that all groups have some personality features in common that are characteristic of their age level and general geographic and socioeconomic backgrounds. The fact that the Negro children in Millfield show more evidence of emotional difficulties is also consistent both with greater socioeconomic deprivation and with their status as minority group members. The greater frequency of high MMPI scores on the personality scales among the boys than among the girls in Millfield cannot be ascribed to age, class, or norm group biases; the explanations must come from other sources.

FACTOR SCALE FINDINGS

By restricting their factor analyses to the items that showed the largest and most dependable differences between their samples of white and Negro women, Harrison and Kass concentrated primarily upon those personality features and behavioral characteristics that most strikingly separate these two groups. This method serves to minimize the many important personality features that people from these different ethnic backgrounds have in common. It must be kept in mind, therefore, in the results that follow that the purpose is to try to characterize the nature of the differences rather than to put into a balanced perspective a complete set of personality descriptions. In addition, only one set of the variables from the Harrison and Kass study were selected for application to the Millfield protocols.[12] Their other scales could have been included, although these additional measures probably would not have been so dependable as the ones that were used.[13]

The means and standard deviations, in raw score form, are reported on each factor scale for the four subgroups in Table 11.4. Even though these scales were devised to represent different and important sources of variance among the MMPI differences found in their samples, the authors were not able to keep these scales independent. They reported one large correlation in this set (.83 between scale I and scale IV) and several moderate values among some of the other scales. Scale III correlated positively with scale V (the two scales that showed higher values for white women than Negro women) but negatively with the other three scores reported here.

[12] We gratefully acknowledge the kindness of Robert D. Harrison in allowing us to make use of these findings prior to their publication.

[13] The MMPI protocols from the white children in 1964 did not include answers to the last 100 items of the test. Three of these scales had to be prorated to allow for the fact that the last few items had been omitted and were unavailable.

In the present study, scales II and IV showed the most dependable differences both between white and Negro subgroups and between the sexes within the racial groupings. All comparisons were highly significant in the statistical evaluations made of these means. On scale I, the contrasts involving the racial subgroups were stable, but the other differences were not. On scale V, the white boys were differentiated from the other groups (significantly higher), but no other differences were stable. The same finding was obtained for scale III, in the opposite direction and at a lower level of significance; the white boys were significantly lower than the other groups on this scale.

Comparing the direction and the magnitude of differences obtained on the original derivational samples and on the Millfield subgroups for these scales, an impressive degree of consistency was found. On four of the five scales the differences between the white and Negro children were in the same direction as those reported by Harrison and Kass; on one (scale III), there was a slight reversal. These separations were obtained in spite of differences in age, geographic locale, marital status, and, for some comparisons, differences in sex as well between the Massachusetts and North Carolina samples.

Equally striking in these findings is the absolute level of the mean scores on these scales earned by the Millfield groups. For example, there are only 26 items on scale IV, but the means for these groups ranged between 15 and 20 items endorsed in the significant direction. The elevations on scales I and II, although less dramatic, also indicate that the Millfield children agreed with the original groups on a majority of the items scored on these scales.

These findings mean that by the time these children have reached the eighth grade, at the age of 13 or 14, many of the attitudes, beliefs, and self-perceptions that differentiate white and Negro adults have already appeared in the self-reports of these Southern rural children. The Negro children describe themselves, and the world as they know it, in terms of estrangement and cynicism. Yet the data from these scales, and from the regular MMPI scales as well, indicate that they are not just reflecting strong and pervasive negative feelings about themselves. On scales III and V, in describing various personal faults and peccadillos, they are likely to place themselves in a moderately favorable light. On scale II, these same youngsters describe themselves as possessing interests and values in general cultural pursuits that are strongly endorsed by middle-class and upper-class adults. In the area of emotional ties and interpersonal relationships, however, these children show pervasive mistrust of themselves and others, extreme pessimism about receiving fair treatment or justice, and expectations that people will be self-seeking, dishonest, and double-dealing. Many of these cynical attitudes extend to social institutions and agencies as well.

Within the data summarized in Table 11.4 it can also be seen that the patterns separating white and Negro children are different from the patterns separating boys and girls within each racial group. It is important to determine in future research whether these same differences appear in other groups of white and Negro subjects examined under a variety of other circumstances.

CONCLUDING COMMENTS

Although the special steps taken to circumvent some severe limitations in reading facility and, in some cases, low general intellective level were not invariably successful, the results of this survey of the personality characteristics of Millfield's eighth-grade children appear to be acceptable and reliable by the usual MMPI indices. The findings highlight many personality characteristics that these groups of youngsters have in common with each other and they share with early adolescent groups elsewhere. The results are consistent with MMPI findings from rural and low socioeconomic groups of children, and fit with the facts that are known about the backgrounds of most of these Millfield children.

These data fail to give support to either a sterotype of pandemic hysteroid tendencies (scale 3 elevations) in this region, at least among the rising generation, or a general expectation that Negro boys are feminine and inadequate in their sex role (scale 5 scores). These characteristics may appear in other groups that are older or that have been raised in different circumstances, but neither expectation was borne out in the present study.

The MMPI findings indicated that these children show evidence of poor control, impulsiveness, lack of self-confidence, insecurities, alienation, and crises in personal identity as a group. Some of these traits have been studied by other personality techniques in this project, but many of these attributes are represented only in the data from the MMPI scales. Some of the MMPI characterizations are not in accord with evidence from other methods, as summarized and reported elsewhere in this volume. For example, data from their teachers' perceptions of them and from our staff interviews with these children fail to agree with some of the MMPI descriptions.

The explanation for the different views of these children may lie in one or more of several possibilities that require additional investigation. The MMPI scores obtained from these youngsters may turn out to have different interpretive significance in personality attributes than they do when obtained on other populations. (The consistencies noted above in the findings from this study when compared with other studies in the literature make this possibility less likely, but do not rule out this alternative.) It is possible, on the other hand, that the material which the teachers and interviewers were able to report on these children provided a limited view of the personality and behavior of these children, impressions obtained under the special circumstances of school or office. That is, these children may be very different outside the school building and without adult surveillance; they may be able to cover up particular characteristics during school hours or when giving oral reports of their activities to an interviewer.

The interview data (reported in Chapter 16) indicate generally favorable impressions of these youngsters and their adjustment to this community. Nevertheless, there were indications that they have problems that should not be overlooked. For example, many of these children, particularly among the Negro subgroups, showed marked discrepancies between their current intellective abilities and level of academic mastery, on the one hand, and their stated educational goals and professional objectives, on the other. Does the magnitude of this sort of discrepancy reflect serious distortions in self-perception and self-insight which may be related to some of the personality features highlighted by the MMPI data? There are similar bases for raising some questions about the judgments and ratings obtained from the teachers of these children (see Chapter 10), since the ratings are so favorable but the level of measured (SAT) school achievement is so discrepant with their grade placement and their measured abilities on the S-B and the PMA. Teachers' ratings, grade assignments, and promotional decisions may all indicate a rather systematic bias that serves to minimize some of the observations and reports that would be needed to establish the appropriateness of some of the MMPI interpretations. In still other instances, the project instruments and report forms may be at fault for failing to request the kinds of data needed for some of these comparative purposes.

A third possibility is also worth considering, particularly in light of present-day limitations in our methods of personality study: both of these descriptions may be reasonably accurate, but may be presenting findings from different levels of personality description. Under restrictive environmental controls (such as in schoolrooms), many potential personality features may be suppressed and not displayed in overt behavior. Unless provoked beyond control or released by withdrawal of surveillance and effective adult controls, these characteristics may remain merely potentialities. One test of this possibility, for example, would be to follow some of these teenagers as they move with their families from the farms to the city. Do they then show some of the traits suggested by the MMPI scales when confronted with urban frustrations, when parental or other adult supervision is weakened, and when they are in the company of peers who facilitate acting-out patterns by their own freedom from inhibitions? Many of the expressions of protest, violence, vandalism, and destruction appearing in our headlines today are acts consistent with these personality findings from the MMPI. If this formulation is correct, the pattern of living in this rural area, with its large families containing many adults in addition to their own parents, with its great distances separating these adolescents from their peers during nonschool hours, and with few direct confrontations with personal insults or intense frustrations, may lead to a systematic underexpression of many aberrant personality features. In fact, the personality traits and the suppressive environments may well act in concert to keep these individuals passive, ineffective, and tied closely to underproductive and unsatisfactory styles of living.

Chapter 12

FANTASY BEHAVIOR: Achievement Motivation

The special focus of this chapter is on achievement motivation, a concept that deals with an individual's concern with doing things well. It will be necessary, first, to show how a quantitative estimate of each child's motivational strength for achievement was determined. Then, this motivational variable will be related to other data reflecting both general background and specific achievement characteristics. More particularly, evidence will be presented to show how achievement motivation relates to the race, sex, age, IQ, verbal productivity, other fantasy measures, and selected behavior ratings of the children in Millfield.

Achievement motivation has been given a great deal of attention in the recent psychological literature because of its important role in our competitive society (see McClelland *et al.*, 1953). Obviously, many other motives could also have been singled out for detailed analysis. A number of these other motives will be examined more briefly in Chapter 13.

THE USE OF FANTASY IN MEASURING
ACHIEVEMENT MOTIVATION

A motive is an *inferred* attribute of an individual. That is, direct observations of motives are not possible; behavior is observed which leads to an inference about the operation of a desire or need on the part of the individual to accomplish certain ends. The inference is used in explaining or understanding the sequence of observed behavior. The choice

260

of which behavior to observe, how to record it, what criteria to use to infer the operation of a motive, and how to scale differences in motive strength are some of the major problems confronting anyone who chooses to study motives. It is clearly premature to claim that most of the measurement problems in this difficult domain have been solved.

One reason that motives are difficult to measure is the fact that often they are not expressed in behavior that can be readily observed by others. Not infrequently, the expression of a motive is blocked by the activity of counterforces in the personality—or in the environment—so that even detection of its existence is quite difficult. For example, an individual may have a strong sexual need, yet because of guilt or restrictions imposed by his surroundings this need may not be made known to others or even directly expressed in behavior. Similarly, an individual's achievement motivation may be difficult to detect. He may feel, for instance, that his peer group does not approve of achievement striving, or he may be so afraid of failure that he is unwilling to express his desire to achieve. Others may, consequently, judge him to be passive and nonstriving when in fact his need to achieve is quite strong.

In the face of the many difficulties confronting the investigator who sets out to measure achievement motivation, McClelland has argued—and has backed his argument with empirical research—that a fruitful approach to the assessment of a person's achievement motivation is through an analysis of his fantasy behavior. The value of measuring achievement motivation this way can in fact be determined only by conducting many studies in which a measure, so derived, is related to various criteria in order to establish its meaning. Much research of this sort has been completed and, although not always successful, in totality it does suggest that such a measure can be a meaningful one (see Atkinson et al., 1958; also, Crandall, 1963). Most of these studies, however, were conducted in the Northern and Eastern parts of this country and involved relatively bright, adult or adolescent subjects. So far as we can determine, only Mingione (1960, 1961, 1965) has used the fantasy method to study the achievement motivation of Southern rural children. Her research was carried out in Millfield in 1960–61 under the authors' direction; later in the chapter, some of her findings will be compared with those of the current study.

Before proceeding to describe the present findings, one further point should be made about the terminology that will be used. In referring to achievement motivation, McClelland and his associates commonly refer to the need for achievement or, more simply, to n Ach. For convenience, we shall sometimes use the same terminology. However, certain modifications were made in McClelland's scoring system so that, for greater accuracy, the scores should be referred to as achievement imagery scores. This modified scoring scheme, which is a frequency count showing how often achievement imagery can be detected in stories made up by the children, is described below.

PROCEDURE

To gather these data, a series of pictures was presented, one at a time, to each child. The child was asked to look at each picture and make up a story about it. The examiner attempted to make a verbatim record of the stories as they were told. After the stories had been collected, each one was individually evaluated against a set of explicit criteria to determine whether n Ach was present in it. By summing scores over all the stories told, a total n Ach score was determined for each child.

The Stimuli

The Carolina Picture Series (CPS), developed originally for Mingione's study, was used in the present work. The CPS consists of 12 line drawings divided into two parallel sets of six pictures each, Series A and Series B (see Figures 12.1 and 12.2). These pictures were drawn specifically for use with both Negro and white subjects; line drawings were decided upon, since it was felt that such pictures might lend themselves most readily to a disguise of the racial identities of the people depicted in them.[1]

Each CPS picture measures 8½ by 11 inches in size and is mounted on heavy cardboard. Series A opens with two school scenes, is followed by two relatively neutral contexts, and ends with two work scenes, one an industrial setting and the other a farm. Series B also consists of six pictures, drawn and ordered in the same manner as Series A with respect to their settings. In addition, each picture in Series B has the same number of people—of the same sex and of approximately the same ages— as its counterpart in Series A. Three pictures in each series contain two

---

[1] Actually, specific instructions were given to the artist, Robert Shannan, who was hired to draw the pictures, that the people depicted therein should not be obviously either Negro or white. Minimization of racial characteristics was believed desirable to make it equally easy for the children of both races to identify with the pictured people. Although the children of both races seemed to accept the pictures quite readily, there is no empirical evidence proving that the objective in this regard was achieved. As will be documented later, children of both races assigned a racial identity to one of the characters in their stories very infrequently.

people, while the other three contain only one person.[2] Briefly, the pictures may be described as follows:

Series A

S1. A young boy is at a table or desk in a schoolroom with a woman teacher bending over him. A globe and blackboards are in the background.

S2. An older boy is in a room; books are on shelves in the background, and a globe and books are on a large desk next to the boy. He has one hand in a pocket, the other contains two books.

N3. A boy has one foot on a step or sill in front of an open door or window. One arm is outstretched towards the place where a doorknob might be.

N4. The heads and shoulders of an older and a younger man are shown.

I5. A workman wearing an apron is standing at a machine in a shop. In the foreground is a man dressed in a business suit.

F6. A man wearing overalls is standing in a field close to a horse. In the background there is a barn and the outline of hills.

Series B

S7. A young boy is seated at a desk facing a woman teacher seated behind her desk. Windows or blackboards are in the background.

S8. An older boy with books in one hand is approaching the door of a room lined with shelves of books. Part of what might be a water-cooler is visible to the right.

N9. A boy with hands in his pockets is slouched against a lamppost on a street corner.

N10. A man and a boy are seated together on some steps.

I11. A man and a boy are standing facing one another across a counter. Factory-like buildings are visible through a window in the background.

F12. A man wearing overalls is coming through a gate. To his right is the head of a cow. To his left along a fence are rows of crops.

The Children

In measuring n Ach, subjects usually write their stories in a group setting. The ages and ability levels of many of the Millfield children,

---

[2] Since the original plan was to give only one series of pictures in a given testing session, it was felt that there might be some advantage in test development if the two series were constructed in this parallel manner. The concern in this report, however, will not be with the equivalence of the two series. The analyses that will be reported are based upon total scores from stories told to all twelve pictures in two testing sessions.

Fig. 12.1: Set A of the CPS pictures.

Fig. 12.2: Set B of the CPS pictures.

however, dictated against the use of a group method. Instead, an individual administration was used (see below). Such a procedure is much more time-consuming than the group technique; consequently, the CPS was administered only to a sample of the children.

In all, 480 children participated. This sample was equally divided between the two races, between the two sexes, among four age levels (7, 9, 11, and 13 years), and among the four schools (two Negro, two white). This meant, then, that 15 boys and 15 girls at each of four age levels at each school created stories for the 12 CPS pictures.

Two restrictions were imposed upon the selection of the children. First, each child had to be within six months of one of the age levels given above. Second, only children who had been tested on the Stanford-Binet Intelligence Scale (S-B) were made eligible. At both of the white schools and at one of the Negro schools, all the children (with a few isolated exceptions) had been tested on the S-B. At the larger Negro school, however, only about 60% of almost 500 children had received this test (see Chapter 3); this meant that approximately 200 of its children were ineligible for the CPS study. To the best of our knowledge, however, there had been no bias involved in the original selection of children for the S-B testing.

The Examiners

Two Negro staff members tested Negro children at ages 9, 11, and 13; children were assigned to them randomly. A third Negro staff member tested all Negro children at age 7. Two white staff members examined white children at ages 9, 11, and 13; assignments to them also were made on a random basis. Again, as with the Negro children, a third white staff member tested all white children at age 7.[3]

The decision to use a third examiner with children of both races at age 7 was made because of practical considerations confronting the project at the time the data were collected. From the point of view of research design, this was not a desirable arrangement. Thus, after the stories had been collected, examination of them strongly suggested that the Negro examiner of 7-year-old children had been unusually effective in eliciting verbal behavior from these children; the average length of the stories told by her children was far greater than that of the stories secured by the other Negro examiners.

To test the hunch that this high productivity was influenced by the examiner, the same examiner and one of the other two Negro examiners

---

[3] The two examiners of 7-year-old children were the only examiners who had not participated in the earlier S-B testing of these children.

were asked to test approximately equal numbers (35 and 37, respectively) of 7-year-old children the following year, without either of them knowing the purpose of the additional study. As had been anticipated, the original examiner of the 7-year-old children obtained stories of significantly greater length from her children. Because the length of stories may affect some (but not all) scores derived from them, an effort was made to correct for this productivity factor in the analyses of the data that were made (see below).

Administration

Series A was always administered first, followed two weeks later by Series B. This two-week interval was rigidly adhered to, except on the infrequent occasions when a child was absent from school for some reason.

The examiner told the child that he was to make up stories for pictures that she would show him one at a time. The child was to tell his stories to her and she would write them down. Also, to help him, she would ask him a few questions on each picture. These questions are those commonly used by McClelland and his associates (see Atkinson *et al.*, 1958, p. 48) and are as follows:

1. What is happening? Who are the persons (or person)?
2. What has led up to this situation? That is, what has happened in the past?
3. What is being thought? What is wanted? By whom?
4. What will happen? What will be done?

When necessary, the examiners reworded some of these questions to ensure comprehension. In addition, the children were assured that there were no correct or incorrect answers, that they were only being asked to use their imaginations to create stories.

Although the examiners attempted to make a verbatim record of the stories, they were not always able to do this as precisely as one would have desired. Nevertheless, it seems fair to say that the records do give a reasonably accurate account of what the children said. Of the total group, 215 Negro and 194 white children took the test in the late spring of 1962. The remaining children, 25 Negro and 46 white, were tested during the first half of the following fall term.

Scoring

In all, 5760 stories were told by the 480 children. To score these stories without knowledge of the child's identity (race, sex, or age), each story was typed on a separate sheet and identified by a code number on the reverse side. In scoring n Ach, then, each of a child's 12 stories was evaluated without knowledge of the child's group membership and independently of the other 11 stories he had told. Actually, all stories were scored twice, using two different sets of criteria. Each of these scoring procedures will now be described.

1. McClelland's Achievement Score (M Ach). Typed copies of the 5760 stories were sent to Joseph Veroff at the University of Michigan to be scored for achievement motivation within the framework previously established by McClelland and his associates.[4] In the discussion that follows, this score will be called the M Ach score. It is important to emphasize, however, that McClelland's standard scoring procedure was modified for the purposes of the present investigation.

McClelland, in his usual procedure, uses four pictures. In scoring a story told to one of these pictures, the first and most critical decision is whether achievement imagery is present in the story. If achievement imagery is present, one point is given to the subject, and the story is then further evaluated with respect to several additional carefully specified criteria. In the event that the subject's story meets these supplementary criteria, additional points are awarded to the storyteller. If no achievement imagery is found, however, there is no way in which the storyteller can earn any of these additional points. In short, the additional points are contingent upon the subject's introducing clear-cut evidence of achievement imagery into his story.

Several psychometric weaknesses are present in any procedure that has the type of contingency just described—that is, a procedure in which the bulk of the scores hinge upon one scoring element. The decision was made, therefore, to increase the number of stories told by each subject from four to twelve, and to score each story simply in terms of the presence (a score of one) or absence (a score of zero) of achievement imagery as defined by McClelland; subscores were ignored. This meant, of course, that any child's M Ach score would fall between zero and twelve.

In scoring M Ach, the scorer first assessed the 480 stories told in response to picture S1; she then proceeded to score all the S2 stories, and so on through F12. After all the 5760 stories had been scored, each child's total M Ach score was determined by adding the scores assigned to each of his stories.

2. Baughman's Achievement Score (B Ach). McClelland's scoring criteria are about as precise and explicit as one could reasonably demand for work with fantasy reports, but in applying them to the Mill-

[4] We are very much indebted to Veroff for his kind cooperation in this work; also, to Joyce Wolf who scored the stories under his supervision.

field protocols it was found that the criteria may be excessively restrictive. By this we mean that some imagery appearing in the stories is not scored for M Ach which might well be concerned with achievement. In part, this exlusion may come about because McClelland has attempted to imbed his scoring decisions within an explicit and rigorous theoretical statement about the nature of the motivational process. In addition, it may be influenced by the fact that much of McClelland's basic work used relatively able and mature subjects.

In any event, the decision was made that the present work would be of greater value if these stories were also scored against criteria with a broader base. It was anticipated, for example, that large numbers of Millfield's children would earn scores of zero under McClelland's system and thus would be indistinguishable one from the other. With broader-based criteria, greater separation of these subjects might be achieved, and perhaps a better basis would be available for assessing the effects of such factors as race, sex, and age on achievement motivation, so defined.

The 5760 stories were scored for the presence or absence of achievement imagery using these broader criteria by one of the authors (EEB). In no sense can this scoring effort be regarded as equal to McClelland's elaborate system in terms of theoretical sophistication, detailed specification of criteria, and so on. Primarily, it represents an effort to evaluate each story from the point of view of this Southern rural community. Thus, achievement imagery is judged in terms of what the people of Millfield seem to consider achievement to be, as we had come to understand their standards during the course of our work. Scores derived in this way will be called Baughman's n Ach scores, or, B Ach.

McClelland's system rules out doubtful imagery; to earn a plus score, the storyteller must leave little question in the judge's mind that he is emotionally concerned with achievement, or an outstanding accomplishment. In contrast, it is fair to say that Baughman's approach "leans over backward" to give the subject the benefit of any doubt. In short, Baughman's method includes all that McClelland would label n Ach, but it also includes much that he would exclude. Although no manual for Baughman's scoring system is available, a few excerpts from stories may help to clarify how it differs from McClelland's approach.

Picture S1

Subject 1087. She's thinking he's not doing his best work. . . . He's thinking he'll try to do good work for her. (Scored plus for both M Ach and B Ach.)

Subject 2106. The boy wants to learn how to write and the lady she will be glad to teach him how to write. (Scored plus for B Ach but not for M Ach.)

Picture S2

Subject 1435. . . . he wants to make an A. (Scored plus for both M Ach and B Ach.)

Subject 1514. He wants to read. . . . He wants to learn things. (Scored plus for B Ach but not for M Ach.)

Picture N3

Subject 1233. . . . maybe he wants to learn more about God. Maybe he'll go to college and he'll learn more about God and he'll be a minister. (Scored plus for both M Ach and B Ach.)

Subject 2919. He'll want to play but he'll have to study. He's going to play instead of study, and it will end in his not knowing how to read. (Scored plus for B Ach but not for M Ach.)

Picture N4

Subject 1089. . . . his father's a famous doctor and he'd like to be famous like him. (Scored plus for both M Ach and B Ach.)

Subject 2376. Douglas thinking if he go ahead and study he'll pass his grade. (Scored plus for B Ach but not for M Ach.)

Picture N5

Subject 2158. He thinks that he wants to win the contest. (Scored plus for both M Ach and B Ach.)

Subject 2241. He wants a job so he's watching what he does to see if he could do it. (Scored plus for B Ach but not for M Ach.)

Picture N6

Subject 1528. The boy will plough real good. He tried hard and did real good. (Scored plus for both M Ach and B Ach.)

Subject 2778. He wonders if the food will bring a big income or a small one. (Scored plus for B Ach but not for M Ach.)

Some of the differences between the two scoring systems should be apparent from these few examples. For instance, to most children in Millfield, learning something or getting a job are achievements and are so scored under Baughman's system. According to the McClelland system, however, such imagery would have to include more evidence of competing with a standard of excellence before n Ach could be scored. Learning more rapidly than others, doing A schoolwork, becoming head of a company, or long-term planning for a career would be examples of such a concern with excellence.

3. *Reliability of Scoring.* Veroff was not asked to determine the reliability of Wolf's scoring of M Ach. In a later study, however, Wolf's ability to score M Ach reliably was determined for another set of pictures. In this other study, both inter- and intrascorer reliability co-

efficients were computed for each of 12 pictures using rank-order correlation coefficients. These coefficients ranged from .74 to 1.00 for interscorer
reliability and from .72 to 1.00 for intrascorer reliability.

A more adequate determination of scoring reliability was made for
the B Ach scores. To accomplish this task, one story was drawn at random for each of the 12 pictures for each sex at each of the four age levels
at each of the four schools. There were, then, 384 stories used in the
reliability check of B Ach scores. These stories were scored independently by a second judge, after he had been trained in the procedure.[5] For 344 stories (89%), his scoring was the same as the author's.
After an interval of approximately three months, the author also rescored
the 384 stories. For 358 stories (93%), the scoring was identical on the
two occasions. These findings indicate that the B Ach scores were assigned in a reliable manner.

RESULTS

Frequency Distributions for M Ach and B Ach Scores

The frequency distributions for M Ach scores are plotted in Figure
12.3, separately for the Negro and white children. In each instance, the

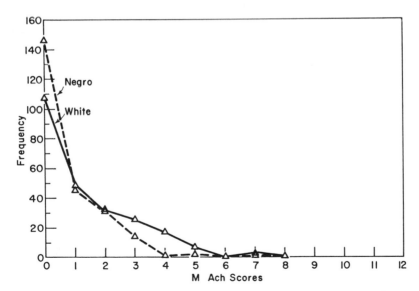

Fig. 12.3: Frequency distributions of M achievement imagery scores for Negro
and white children.

[5] We are indebted to John M. Hatton for his careful assistance in this work.

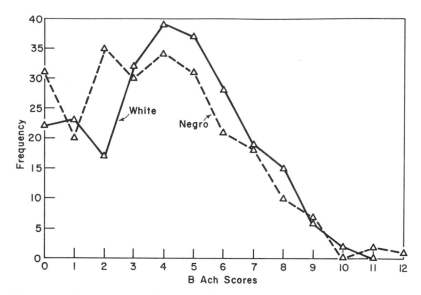

Fig. 12.4: Frequency distributions of B achievement imagery scores for Negro and white children.

distribution has a pronounced positive skewness. More than one-half of the Negro children produced no M Ach imagery in any of their 12 stories; an identical result was obtained for slightly less than one-half of the white children. The mean M Ach score is 1.3 for the white children and 0.7 for the Negro children. Median scores are 0.8 and 0.3, respectively.

Comparable distributions of B Ach scores are shown in Figure 12.4. Again, both distributions are positively skewed, although much less so than the distributions of M Ach scores. The mean B Ach score for the white children is 4.1, while for the Negro children it is 3.8. Median B Ach scores are 4.2 and 3.6 for white and Negro children, respectively.

It is clear, therefore, that the type of achievement imagery which has been at the focal point of McClelland's interest is quite uncommon in these children's stories. As one would expect, however, when broader criteria are applied the incidence of achievement imagery jumps markedly.

Intelligence and Achievement Motivation

It was clear to us that this sample of children would show racial differences in intellective capacity (see Chapter 3). We decided, therefore, to investigate the relationship between intelligence—as measured by the S-B—and both indices of achievement motivation to determine what

TABLE 12.1

Ranges, Means, and Standard Deviations of Eight CPS Groups for Stanford-Binet IQ*

Age	Range			Mean			S.D.	
	White	Negro		White	Negro		White	Negro
7	76–127	66–103		98.6	83.6		12.7	9.3
9	81–130	58–115		103.5	86.6		12.0	11.7
11	69–141	53–111		97.3	86.5		14.0	11.8
13	55–128	60–125		95.3	85.6		15.6	14.3

* N = 60 for each of the eight groups.

effect there might be on the latter scores from intellective differences. Also, there was an interest in the general question of how intelligence and achievement motivation are related.

The ranges, means, and standard deviations of the eight subgroups for S-B IQ scores are given in Table 12.1. (Boys and girls were combined in these groups, since analysis of variance revealed no significant sex differences in IQ scores.) The mean IQ for all 480 children is 92.2; it is 98.7 for the white children, and 85.6 for the Negro children. (The mean IQ scores for both white and Negro children agree quite closely with the means earned by the larger populations from which the present samples were drawn; see Chapter 3.) It is obvious, of course, that there is a highly significant racial difference in IQ scores.

To determine the relationship between intelligence and achievement motivation, product-moment correlation coefficients were computed between, first, M Ach scores and S-B IQ scores, and, second, between B Ach scores and S-B IQ scores.[6] These coefficients, which were computed separately for each of the eight subgroups, are listed in Table 12.2. They show that there is a low, positive relationship between intelligence and achievement motivation. In general, this relationship is somewhat stronger for the B Ach scores than for the M Ach scores; in fact, the only two coefficients that are significantly different from zero involve the B Ach scores. There is no systematic change with age in the strength of the relationship between achievement motivation and IQ scores.

Although there is a weak, positive relationship between IQ and achievement motivation scores, the amount of variance in the achieve-

---

[6] The M Ach scores were subjected to a log $(x + .5)$ transformation before the coefficients were computed. In addition, biserial correlation coefficients were computed between M Ach and S-B IQ scores. Since the conclusions resulting from the two analyses are the same, only the product-moment correlation coefficients are presented here.

TABLE 12.2

Product-Moment Correlation Coefficients between Stanford-Binet
IQ's and M Ach and B Ach Scores for Eight CPS Groups*

	IQ vs. M Ach		IQ vs. B Ach	
Age	White	Negro	White	Negro
7	.22	.17	.30†	.25
9	−.11	.16	.13	.16
11	.11	.21	.17	.20
13	.21	.04	.25	.27†

* $N = 60$ for each of the eight groups.
† $p < .05$.

ment motivation scores that could be attributed to intelligence is actually quite low. For the M Ach scores, this variance ranges between 0% and 5% in the eight groups. For the B Ach scores, the comparable figures are 2% and 9%. It is obvious, then, that knowledge of a child's IQ provides very little basis for predicting his achievement motivation score. Nevertheless, in the analyses of race, sex, and age effects on achievement motivation presented below, the effect of intelligence has been partialed out.

These data, then, support the conclusion that achievement motivation is not just another way of reflecting differences in intellective ability. McClelland and his associates, insofar as we can determine, have not dealt in any comprehensive way with this question of how ability and achievement motivation are related. Thus, in the volume edited by Atkinson (1958), the subject index contains only two references to intelligence. Neither of two studies cited there provides systematic data like those summarized in Table 12.2.

Verbal Productivity and Achievement Motivation

It seems reasonable to expect that, the more a person talks, the greater his chances become of expressing an idea that might be scored for achievement imagery (or, for that matter, for almost any other type of imagery). The relation of achievement motivation to verbal productivity was explored, therefore, in the present inquiry.

Arbitrarily, the verbal productivity of each child was determined by counting the total number of words that he had used in telling his 12 stories.[7] This total was then divided by 12 to determine his mean number of words per story. The ranges, means, and standard deviations computed from these data for each of the eight subgroups are shown in

[7] We want to thank Barbara J. Baughman for conducting this count.

Table 12.3. (The data for the boys and girls were combined, since analysis of variance showed no significant sex differences in verbal productivity.)

The data in Table 12.3 show that the white children differ markedly in verbal productivity between ages 7 and 9; increments after age 9 are comparatively modest. Negro children show a decrement between ages 7 and 9; beyond this age, their means indicate greater verbal output. However, sweeping conclusions cannot be drawn from these data, since there is a distinct possibility that the several examiners were not equally skillful in eliciting verbal behavior. Thus, evidence was presented earlier in the chapter showing that the examiner of 7-year-old Negro children was especially effective in this regard. Moreover, there is no evidence that the two white examiners of 9-, 11-, and 13-year-old children were comparable to the two Negro examiners of 9-, 11-, and 13-year-old children in this respect.

Because of these difficulties, a conservative approach to the interpretation of the data is indicated. More particularly, for the white children there is an indication that verbal output reaches a plateau between ages 9 and 11. For the Negro children, the rather sharp rise between ages 11 and 13 suggests that, for them, if such a plateau is going to come, it is still in the future. Since there were different examiners for both the 7-year-old white and Negro children, the trends for both races between ages 7 and 9 are much less clear than those just described for the older age levels where, for both races, the same examiners tested children in each age group.

The relationship between achievement motivation and verbal productivity will be explored. As in the analysis of intelligence, product-moment correlation coefficients were computed, first, between verbal

TABLE 12.3

Ranges, Means, and Standard Deviations of Eight Groups for
Verbal Productivity (Mean Words per Story) on the CPS*

Age	Range†		Mean		S.D.	
	White	Negro	White	Negro	White	Negro
7	6–143	24–212	48.4	79.9	26.5	47.5
9	28–166	27–149	67.0	53.4	26.8	21.4
11	19–130	1–137	78.0	56.9	22.8	18.7
13	13–136	37–163	72.8	66.6	24.4	28.5

* $N = 60$ for each of the eight groups.

† Among the 480 children, there were only two (one Negro, one white) who gave stories with a mean length less than ten words.

TABLE 12.4

Product-Moment Correlation Coefficients between Verbal Productivity
(Mean Words per Story) and M Ach and B Ach Scores for
Eight CPS Groups*

| | Mean words vs. M Ach | | Mean words vs. B Ach | |
Age	White	Negro	White	Negro
7	.30†	.14	.42§	.24
9	.32†	.25	.45§	.19
11	.33‡	.34‡	.49§	.30†
13	.46§	.24	.43§	.45§

* $N = 60$ in each of the eight groups.
† $p < .05$.
‡ $p < .01$.
§ $p < .001$.

productivity and M Ach scores,[8] then between verbal productivity and
B Ach scores. The resulting coefficients for each of the eight subgroups
are listed in Table 12.4.

If the coefficients in Table 12.4 are compared with those in Table
12.2, it becomes immediately clear that the relationship between verbal
productivity and achievement motivation is stronger than that between
intelligence and achievement motivation. Also, as was true for intelligence, the correlation between verbal output and achievement motivation is higher for the B Ach scores than for the M Ach scores. Furthermore, the correlation coefficients are more substantial for the white
children than for the Negro children. In this regard, it is particularly
important to note the relatively low correlation between verbal productivity and achievement motivation for the 7-year-old Negro children.
This, it will be recalled, is the group with the especially high productivity
level (see Table 12.3).

Overall, then, the data support the expectation that verbal productivity is a factor to consider in evaluating race, sex, and age effects
upon fantasy measures of achievement motivation. Consequently, in the
analyses presented in the following section, covariance techniques have
been used to control for differential productivity levels.

Sex, Age, and Race Effects on Achievement Motivation

To determine the relationships between sex, age, and race on the one
hand, and achievement motivation on the other, M Ach and B Ach scores

[8] The M Ach scores were subjected to a log $(x + .5)$ transformation before these
computations were made.

TABLE 12.5

The Analyses of Variance and Covariance for M Ach Scores

Source	df Var.	df Covar.	MS Var.	MS Covar.	F Var.	F Covar.	p Var.	p Covar.
Sex	1	1	.43	.18	.75	.33	N.S.	N.S.
Age	3	3	13.69	12.66	23.66	23.60	.001	.001
Race	1	1	13.07	5.66	22.58	10.55	.001	.005
Sex × Age	3	3	.92	.96	1.59	1.79	N.S.	N.S.
Sex × Race	1	1	.33	.71	.57	1.32	N.S.	N.S.
Age × Race	3	3	1.17	.42	2.01	.79	N.S.	N.S.
S × A × R	3	3	.42	.18	.72	.34	N.S.	N.S.
Error (within)	464	462	.58	.54				
Total	479	477						

were subjected to both an analysis of variance and an analysis of co-variance. In the analysis of covariance, S-B IQ and verbal productivity were designated as the covariates. This meant, in essence, that sex, age, and race effects were evaluated as if the groups had comparable IQ and verbal productivity levels. To make it clear how the results were in-fluenced by these covariance corrections, Tables 12.5 and 12.6 present both the analysis of variance and the analysis of covariance for M Ach and B Ach scores, respectively. Mean raw scores at each age level for each of four groups (white boys, white girls, Negro boys, Negro girls) are plotted in Figure 12.5 (for M Ach) and Figure 12.6 (for B Ach).

TABLE 12.6

The Analyses of Variance and Covariance for B Ach Scores

Source	df Var.	df Covar.	MS Var.	MS Covar.	F Var.	F Covar.	p Var.	p Covar.
Sex	1	1	2.55	6.98	.53	1.70	N.S.	N.S.
Age	3	3	261.90	244.85	54.48	59.53	.001	.001
Race	1	1	16.50	.61	3.43	.15	N.S.	N.S.
Sex × Age	3	3	1.80	1.55	.37	.38	N.S.	N.S.
Sex × Race	1	1	.00	2.01	.00	.49	N.S.	N.S.
Age × Race	3	3	4.19	9.00	.87	2.19	N.S.	N.S.
S × A × R	3	3	1.95	.12	.40	.03	N.S.	N.S.
Error (within)	464	462	4.81	4.11				
Total	479	477						

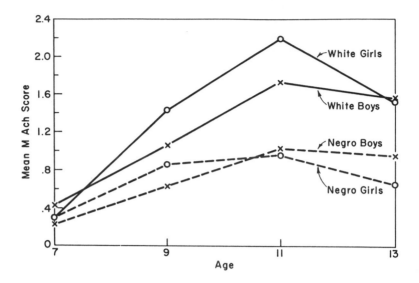

Fig. 12.5: Mean M achievement imagery raw scores for each sex of each race at four age levels.

For the M Ach scores, there are clear-cut age and race differences: older children score higher than the younger children, and white children score higher than the Negro children. These differences remain even when IQ and verbal productivity discrepancies are controlled, al-

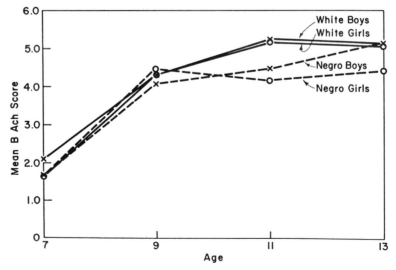

Fig. 12.6: Mean B achievement imagery raw scores for each sex of each race at four age levels.

though the size of the separation related to race is reduced sharply. With respect to age trends, it is apparent from Figure 12.5 that children in each of the four groups increase their M Ach scores from age 7 to age 11, but they either level off or possibly decrease in score between ages 11 and 13. As far as sex effects are concerned, the data in Table 12.5 show that there are no statistically significant sex differences even though the plots in Figure 12.5 are suggestive in this regard.

The B Ach scores also show a significant age effect. However, changes in mean score after age 9 are either quite modest or nonexistent for each of the four groups. Figure 12.6 suggests that there may be a race difference in B Ach scores, but the statistical analyses failed to confirm this suggestion. In addition, none of the interactions are significant, nor is there a statistically significant sex difference in B Ach scores.

In broad terms, these data indicate that the boys and girls of Millfield do not differ very much as far as their achievement motivation is concerned. They also suggest that there is a sharp increase in achievement motivation during the first few years of elementary school, but that increments after the fifth year are negligible. The importance of race as a factor in achievement motivation is more equivocal. Certainly when the severe criteria developed by McClelland are applied, the Negro children score significantly below the white children. When the broader criteria of the Baughman system—which attempts to incorporate local standards and values—are applied, the scores of the two races are appreciably more similar.

The Relationship between M Ach and B Ach Scores

The analyses just reported bring to the fore the question of how M Ach and B Ach scores relate to one another.[9] This question was investigated by computing product-moment correlation coefficients between these two sets of scores (first, the M Ach scores were subjected to a log $[x + .5]$ transformation) for each of the eight subgroups separately. The resulting coefficients are shown in Table 12.7, along with the coefficient which is based upon the entire sample of 480 children.

The correlation coefficients for the four white groups are remarkably consistent in size; those for the four Negro groups show somewhat greater variability. Each of the eight correlation coefficients differs significantly from zero, beyond the .001 level. In general, the two sets of scores share approximately 36% of common variance. It is understand-

---

[9] Because of their overlapping scoring systems, one would, of course, expect significant correlations between the two scores. However, the precise degree of this relationship must be determined empirically.

TABLE 12.7

Product-Moment Correlation Coefficients between M Ach
and B Ach Scores for Eight Race-Age Groups*

Age	Race	
	White†	Negro†
7	.60	.78
9	.58	.67
11	.57	.66
13	.58	.52
All Ss ($N = 480$)	.61	

* $N = 60$ for each of the eight groups.
† Each r is significant beyond the .001 level.

able, therefore, that the analyses of the data that have been presented earlier show both similarities and differences. Clearly, additional research will have to be conducted before it will be known what the differential implications of the two scoring systems are.

The Relationship between Achievement Motivation and Other CPS Scores

In addition to verbal productivity, M Ach, and B Ach, each of the 5760 CPS stories was scored for 31 other variables. As with the achievement motivation scores, a total score for each of these scoring categories was computed for each of the 480 children by summing the scores that he received for each variable on each of his 12 stories. These additional content scores will be discussed in Chapter 13. Now we shall limit ourselves to a brief examination of how both the M Ach and the B Ach scores relate to these other variables.

Scores in each of the 31 content categories were correlated (product-moment) with M Ach scores and again with B Ach scores for each racial group at each of the four age levels. Similar correlation coefficients were also computed with the 480 children treated as a single group. Those coefficients, based upon the total sample which are significant at or beyond the .01 level, are listed in Table 12.8; there are, of course, separate entries for the M Ach and the B Ach scores. (It should also be noted that, whenever the distribution of scores for any variable was badly skewed, the scores were subjected to a log $[x + .5]$ transformation before the correlation coefficients were computed.)

When the data for the eight groups of children were examined (these data are not shown), it was found that there were more than twice as many very significant correlation coefficients (i.e., coefficients at or beyond the .01 level) for the B Ach scores as there were for the M Ach scores (32 vs. 13, respectively). When the total sample is considered, however, there are only 9 very significant correlation coefficients for the B Ach scores but 11 for the M Ach scores (see Table 12.8). Actually, none of the 31 variables shows either a moderate or a large correlation with the achievement motivation scores. Because the sample is large, however, even small correlation coefficients are statistically significant.[10] It seems important, nevertheless, to note that the pattern of the interrelationships is similar for both sets of achievement motivation scores. Brief comments will be made in the paragraphs that follow about those variables that do show very significant correlations with either one or both of the achievement scores.

As noted earlier in the chapter, achievement motivation is associated with verbal productivity. That is, a child with strong achievement moti-

TABLE 12.8

Product-Moment Correlation Coefficients between Achievement
Motivation Scores and Other CPS Variables Which Were
Significant at or beyond the .01 Level*

| CPS Variables | r | |
	With M Ach†	With B Ach†
Mean words per story	.26	.34
Language	.18	.30
Affect	.25	.25
Pleasant affect	.27	.31
Unpleasant affect	.16	.14
Worry, anxiety	.12	.13
Guilt	.12	(.07)
Anger	.12	(.08)
Critical talk	.12	(.09)
Social aggression	.13	.17
Nurturance	.18	.30
Racial imagery	(.05)	.16

* An $r \geq .12$ is significant at or beyond the .01 level ($N = 480$).

† Numbers in parentheses are the r's involving the other scoring system which fail to reach the .01 level of significance.

[10] We decided to report only coefficients that reached the .01 level of significance, ignoring those that reached the .05 level.

vation is likely to tell a longer story than a child with weak achievement motivation. He is also more likely to use language in a precise, differentiated manner rather than in a vague, nonspecific fashion. Of particular interest is the fact that a child with strong achievement motivation is more likely to attribute feelings or affective qualities to the characters in his stories than is the child with low achievement motivation. In other words, he is more likely to say that someone feels good or happy, is worried, is sorry for what he has done, is mad about something, and so on. In this regard, it should be noted that there is a stronger association between pleasant affective words and achievement motivation than between unpleasant affective words and achievement motivation. Put another way, the children are more likely to express achievement imagery in a pleasant affective context than in one that is unpleasant.

Achievement motivation also tends to be associated with the presence of critical talk or conversation and with social aggression. (The latter, incidentally, usually takes the form of competitive sports or athletic endeavors of some type.) In addition, achievement motivation is related to concern about establishing and maintaining friendly relationships with other people, as well as with giving them help or seeking assistance from them. Finally, there is a very small but positive relationship between achievement motivation and the tendency to tell stories that contain some kind of racial imagery—at least when the B Ach scores are analyzed.

Of the relationships just described, the first three plus the one involving nurturance appear to be most clearly defined. That is, most salient is the fact that the child with high achievement motivation tends to be more verbally productive, uses language more precisely, makes more explicit affective references (especially pleasant ones), and is more concerned with either giving or receiving help than is the child with low achievement motivation. These particular findings, moreover, tend to appear under either system for assessing achievement motivation.

Behavioral Correlates of Achievement Motivation Scores

Early in the chapter we made the point that one should not necessarily expect a close relationship between covert and overt behavior in the same domain. Although the general validity of this point has been well documented, we need to determine empirically the actual extent to which achievement motivation in fantasy is related to overt indications of achievement striving. To investigate this question, the achievement motivation scores were correlated with selected behavior ratings that had been assigned to the children by their teachers. These behavior ratings were provided through use of the scale that has been described in previous chapters and is reproduced in Appendix E.

More exactly, items 4, 6, 8, 11, 17, and 22 were selected from the Behavior Rating Scale for analysis. These items focus upon the following components of a child's classroom behavior: his capacity to work independently without needing encouragement (scale 4); his concern with the quality of his work (scale 6); his reaction to failure (scale 8); his effort on lessons (scale 11); his reaction to success (scale 17); and, finally, how well his teacher likes him (scale 22). On each of these items, a child was categorized as either high or low with reference to the other children in his room. This was done by compiling his teacher's distribution of ratings on each of the six rating scales and then making a split as close to the median value as possible. In addition, each child was classified as being either high or low on M Ach imagery (again, by use of a median split) with respect to children of his same age and racial group, and also as either high or low on B Ach imagery (once again, by means of a median split). Chi-square analyses were then made to see if significant relationships existed between either of the two measures of achievement motivation and the six different ratings. (Separate computations were made for the children of each race at each of the four age levels.)

The chi-square values computed in this way do not reflect a meaningful relationship between achievement motivation, as it is expressed in fantasy behavior, and achievement behavior, as it is viewed by teachers in the classrooms. Out of 96 chi-square values, only one was sufficiently large to reach the .05 level of significance.

It may be that fantasy measures of achievement motivation should be regarded more as indicators of potential than as estimates of the strength of a child's current visible striving. It is quite possible, for example, that many children may not show what their teachers consider to be achievement behavior even though they do have a well-developed and internalized achievement drive. Other children, in contrast, may show what the teacher takes to be achievement behavior even though they do not have a strong personal desire of this type. They may, for example, show "achievement behavior" primarily because they want her affection or want to escape the possibility of drawing her wrath, rather than because they are genuinely committed to achievement. These fantasy measures should not be discounted; additional research must be conducted to determine their real significance.

A Comparison with Mingione's Studies

In the introduction to the chapter, we pointed out that Mingione was the first person to study achievement motivation systematically among

Southern rural children. Actually, her inquiry consisted of two parts, both carried out in the Millfield schools. Part one was, in effect, a pilot study which was limited to fifth- and seventh-grade Negro and white children. The larger study, and the one to be examined most closely here, involved 245 children (65 white boys, 62 white girls, 52 Negro boys, and 66 Negro girls) unevenly distributed among grades 3, 5, 7, 9, and 11.

Methodologically, Mingione's investigations differed in several important ways from our study. For instance, she used an individual administration only with the children in grade three (and a few of the children in grade five); the remaining children wrote their stories in a group situation. Also, in scoring the stories, she initially used the more elaborate scoring system developed by McClelland (see Atkinson *et al.*, 1958).[11] Furthermore, she did not control for differences in either intelligence or verbal productivity before evaluating race, sex, and age effects.

In her pilot study, Mingione found significant racial effects (white children higher than Negro children), sex effects (girls higher than boys), and age effects (older children higher than younger children). In her second study, she again found that the scores of white children exceeded those of Negro children and that scores increased with advancing age. There was not an overall sex difference, however, although there was a significant Race × Sex interaction, traceable primarily to the tendency of Negro girls to exceed Negro boys in achievement motivation. Our data, of course, confirm the significant age and racial effects when McClelland's criteria are used; however, they do not show a significant Race × Sex interaction.

Unfortunately, owing to methodological differences in gathering and scoring the stories, the mean scores for Mingione's groups and our groups cannot be plotted on the same scale. Nevertheless, the conclusion that significant racial and age differences appear in achievement motivation—when such motivation is assessed through fantasy behavior—is buttressed by the similarity of the findings of the two studies, despite the methodological differences.

---

[11] Mingione did carry out a second multivariate analysis of variance, however, based upon a simplified scoring system which was similar, although not identical, to the one that we have used. The conclusions based upon this analysis were the same as those obtained using the more detailed scoring system. In arguing the merits of the simplified system, however, Mingione makes one statement which our data fail to support, namely that "The n Ach present or absent scoring also has the advantage of being independent of story length." (1965, p. 111)

CONCLUDING COMMENTS

It is clear that the incidence of achievement motivation is very low in these children's stories, especially when McClelland's criteria are used to evaluate them. There are no significant sex differences in either M Ach or B Ach scores, but there is a significant racial difference (in favor of the white children) in the M Ach scores. Both scores increase sharply during the first few years of elementary school, but somewhere between the ages of 9 and 11 they appear to level off.

The correlations between both achievement motivation scores and intelligence are quite low, but their correlations with verbal productivity are more substantial. They also show significant and similar correlations with several other CPS variables. However, achievement motivation measured through fantasy behavior is not meaningfully related to achievement striving in the classroom, as the latter is rated by teachers.

There are, of course, many questions left unanswered by this effort to contribute to the understanding of achievement motivation among Southern rural children. Is the age plateau in scores, for example, a permanent one, or will there be changes in later adolescence and adulthood? How do the developmental curves compare with those that might be obtained from more privileged children? Why is there so little relationship between achievement motivation in fantasy and achievement striving in the classroom? Undoubtedly, the reader can add to this list.

With respect to the last question, some critics may suggest that the fantasy measure is so unrelated to "real" behavior that we should drop our concern with it. However, we cannot agree with such a judgment. As we shall argue more fully in Chapter 13, we believe that it is important to define, describe, and measure what might be called covert concerns as well as to define, describe, and measure what is overt or observable under ordinary circumstances (and, whatever it is, a fantasy test is not an ordinary circumstance). The interrelationship between these two domains is not unimportant; it is simply an additional problem or question. Achievement motivation in fantasy, for instance, may represent potential, but potential which is not necessarily expressed in behavior under routine conditions as we know them. In other words, the person high in covert achievement motivation but low in overt achievement motivation may have potential—if we stimulate him appropriately —of a different order from that of the individual with low covert achievement motivation, no matter whether the latter appears for the moment to be either achieving or not achieving in his overt behavior. It is obvious, we believe, that there are many additional explorations and studies waiting and needing to be done before we can fully comprehend the many ramifications of achievement motivation.

Chapter 13

FANTASY BEHAVIOR: Other Attributes

The preceding chapter was devoted to an analysis and discussion of the achievement motivation of Southern rural children, as assessed through their fantasy behavior. In the present chapter, the same fantasy behavior will be evaluated again, only within a broader framework. More precisely, the children's stories will be analyzed with respect to 31 additional variables to determine how these other components of fantasy behavior are influenced by race, sex, and age.

WHY STUDY FANTASY BEHAVIOR?

Before proceeding, a few observations must be made. No investigator really can be certain that he is examining the full content of another person's fantasy life. Each individual ordinarily reserves to himself the right to withhold, disguise, or screen in a variety of ways aspects of his inner life which he may be asked to share with others. What he expresses, either in language or in various nonverbal ways, may not bear a one-to-one relationship to what he is thinking or feeling. To remind ourselves of this fact, we prefer to use the term fantasy behavior rather than fantasy life.

Behavioral scientists have been engaged in studies of fantasy behavior for several decades now; achievement motivation has been a central concern, but it certainly has not been the only focus of effort. Much of the work thus far has been devoted to the development of measures which, hopefully, can be used to predict other significant behavior of

287

the individuals who create the fantasy behavior. The fact that accurate prediction of personal behavior has proved to be quite difficult has led to disillusionment in some quarters about the value of studying fantasy behavior for this purpose.

This study departs from the approach just described, in which fantasy behavior serves as an independent variable in the prediction of other, usually overt, behavior. While the prediction of such behavior is obviously of critical importance, the variables affecting fantasy behavior itself must also be studied. Therefore, fantasy behavior here is considered to be an important kind of personal behavior, a dependent variable which *may* be determined, in both content and form, by the group membership of the person producing it. That is, it is hypothesized that a child's group membership (in this instance, specified by his race, sex, and age) will affect his fantasy behavior.

So much attention is focused upon the description and prediction of overt behavior in psychology that the importance of the inner world or private life sometimes is overlooked. Yet, to each of us, the nature of this inner life is of immense importance; it does, in fact, give us our sense of continuity and identity. Depending upon its nature, we feel either relatively fulfilled or incomplete as human beings. We do not, in short, deny its importance to our own selves, even though we may appear to deny its importance in others as we attempt to study them scientifically. Because inner life is extremely important, then, we have chosen to make some inferences about its likely properties among the children of Millfield by studying their fantasy behavior, even though we acknowledge that there probably is not a one-to-one correspondence between fantasy behavior and fantasy life.

PROCEDURE

It is clear that fantasy behavior can be studied in many different ways. For example, reports of dreams and daydreams can be collected, or subjects can be asked to give responses to inkblots. Had resources permitted, we would have used a variety of such data-gathering techniques. Instead, our inquiry has been restricted to a detailed analysis of the stories told in response to the CPS pictures.

The procedures used to gather these stories were described at length in Chapter 12. All told, each of 480 children told 12 stories in two testing sessions separated by a two-week interval. The children were divided equally with respect to race and sex at four age levels (7, 9, 11, and 13). The examiners, all women, were of the same race as the children that they tested. The 12 pictures used to stimulate storytelling were specially drawn line figures which attempted to avoid giving racial identities to the people depicted (see Figures 12.1 and 12.2).

Scoring Scheme and Reliability

The 5760 stories were scored by means of a scheme developed by the first author. This assessment represents his effort to summarize, for quantitative analysis, the important variations which appear in the stories. It does not reflect any one theoretical view of personality.

The scoring categories (in addition to those described in Chapter 12) are listed in Table 13.1.[1] The reader will note that certain entries in this table are indented. These indented scores are subcategories of the more inclusive category under which they are listed. For example, although both anger and worry are scored as unpleasant affective states, they also have been differentiated one from the other. The relationships among the various scores will be further clarified later.

Each variable listed in Table 13.1 will be defined and examples will be given in the section below on Results; then data will be cited to show how the variable relates to race, sex, and age. Before turning to the findings, however, it should be noted that a score of one (present) or zero (absent) was assigned to each story for each variable listed in Table 13.1. Before scoring, all identifying information as to the race, sex, and age of the child had been removed from the 5760 stories (see Chapter 12).

Both intra- and interscorer reliabilities were determined for each variable.[2] To do this, 384 stories were selected randomly, with the following restrictions: There had to be one story for both a boy and a girl at each age level from each of the four schools, and for each of the 12 pictures. These stories were rescored, first by the author, who had done the original scoring about three months earlier, and then by an independent scorer trained by him.[3] The percentages of times when identical scores were assigned to the stories in the various categories are given in Table 13.1, separately for intrascorer and interscorer comparisons. In general, these data show that the scoring system was applied reliably.

Method of Data Analysis

The data were subjected to both an analysis of variance and a multivariate analysis of covariance by using a computer program developed

[1] S-B IQ scores were included as variable 1 and verbal productivity scores as variable 2. The two achievement scores were variables 34 and 35.

[2] With the exception of variables 30 and 33, which were scored at the University of Michigan under the supervision of Joseph Veroff.

[3] We are indebted to John M. Hatton for his assistance in this work.

TABLE 13.1

Intrascorer and Interscorer Agreement on CPS Scores*

	Scored identically	
Scoring variable	Intrascorer (%)	Interscorer (%)
V3. Language	96	96
V4. Sex reversal	99	100
V5. Race	99	97
V6. Religion	100	99
V7. Sex content	100	99
V8. Food and drink	98	97
V9. Money and buying	99	98
V10. Clothing	99	99
V11. Housing	99	98
V12. Affect (total)	99	97
V13. Pleasant affect	99	99
V14. Unpleasant affect	99	98
V15. Pain and hurt	99	99
V16. Worry and anxiety	100	99
V17. Guilt and shame	99	99
V18. Anger	99	100
V19. Sad and unhappy	99	100
V20. Aggression (total)	92	89
V21. Physical punishment	99	100
V22. Nonphysical punishment	95	89
V23. Critical talk	92	90
V24. Physical abuse	97	98
V25. Social aggression	99	99
V26. Antisocial aggression	99	99
V27. Injury	97	98
V28. Conflict	90	89
V29. Other aggression	97	94
V30. M affiliation†	—	—
V31. Nurturance	93	89
V32. Rejection	97	94
V33. M power†	—	—

* Based upon the scoring and rescoring of 384 stories. One story was drawn at random for each of 12 stimuli and for each sex at each of the four age levels at each of the four schools.

† These variables were scored under the supervision of Joseph Veroff; the determination of scoring reliability was not requested of him (see text).

by R. D. Bock[4] (1963). The analysis of variance permits examination of sex, age, and race effects (as well as their several interactions) on each of the scores listed in Table 13.1 before effects attributable to IQ and verbal

[4] We want to thank Darrell Bock for permitting use of this computer program and Steve J. Zyzanski for assisting us in its application.

productivity differences among the groups have been removed. The analysis of covariance shows sex, age, and race effects (together with their interactions) on each of these scores after IQ and verbal productivity differences have been controlled. Before the analyses were run, the following scores were subjected to a log $(x + .5)$ transformation: sex reversal, racial imagery, religion, sex content, clothing, housing, pleasant affect, unpleasant affect, pain–hurt, worry–anxiety, guilt–shame, anger, sad–unhappy, physical punishment, physical abuse, social aggression, antisocial aggression, injury, and other aggression.

RESULTS

Space does not permit presentation of the full analyses for each of the 31 variables listed in Table 13.1. Instead, all the significant effects are listed in Tables 13.2, 13.3, 13.4, and 13.5. Table 13.2, for instance, lists each variable that showed a significant sex effect (at or beyond the .05 level of significance) either in the analysis of variance or in the analysis of covariance. Tables 13.3 and 13.4 list the significant effects for age and race, respectively, and Table 13.5 lists the significant interactions.

A regular format has been adopted for the discussion of each scoring variable. First, the scoring category is defined. Second, one or more excerpts from stories told by the children are presented (in some instances, full stories are given) to illustrate the category and its scoring

TABLE 13.2

CPS Scores Showing Significant Sex Differences in the
Analysis of Variance or in the Analysis of Covariance

	p level		
Scoring variable	Variance	Covariance	Sex comparison*
V8. Food and drink	.005	.005	Boys > girls
V9. Money and buying	N.S.	.05	Boys > girls
V14. Unpleasant affect	.05	.05	Girls > boys
V23. Critical talk	.001	.001	Girls > boys
V25. Social aggression	N.S.	.05	Boys > girls
V28. Conflict	.05	.05	Girls > boys
V30. M affiliation	.005	.005	Girls > boys
V31. Nurturance	.05	.05	Girls > boys
V32. Rejection	.05	.05	Girls > boys

* Boys, for example, produced significantly more imagery than girls which pertained to food and drink.

TABLE 13.3

CPS Scores Showing Significant Age Differences in the Analysis
of Variance or in the Analysis of Covariance

| | p level | | Change with |
Scoring variable	Variance	Covariance	advancing age*
V3. Language	.001	.001	Increases
V4. Sex reversal	.01	.05	Decreases
V5. Racial imagery	.05	.005	Decreases
V6. Religion	.005	.001	Decreases
V7. Sex content	.001	.001	Decreases
V8. Food and drink	.001	.001	Decreases
V9. Money and buying	.05	.01	Decreases
V10. Clothing	.001	.001	Decreases
V11. Housing	.001	.001	Decreases
V12. Affect (total)	.001	.001	Increases
V13. Pleasant affect	.001	.001	Increases
V14. Unpleasant affect	.001	.001	Increases
V15. Pain and hurt	N.S.	.005	Decreases
V17. Guilt and shame	.001	.001	Increases
V18. Anger	.001	.001	Increases
V19. Sad and unhappy	.05	N.S.	Increases
V20. Aggression (total)	.001	.05	Increases
V22. Nonphysical punishment	.001	.001	Increases
V23. Critical talk	.001	.001	Increases
V27. Injury	.001	.001	Decreases
V28. Conflict	.001	.001	Increases
V30. M affiliation	.05	.05	Decreases†
V31. Nurturance	.05	.01	Increases
V32. Rejection	.005	N.S.	Increases
V33. M power	.001	.001	Increases

* These trends are based upon differences between ages 7 and 13. They do not neces-sarily mean that age changes during this interval are rectilinear.

† True only when Negro children at age 7 are included; otherwise, the scores of both Negro and white children show a slight tendency to increase with age.

standards. Third, the most important findings with respect to age, sex, and racial differences are summarized. (In selected instances, graphs showing these effects are included.) Finally, for a few variables, reference is made to the correlations between them and other CPS scores, when such data add to the understanding of the scoring category under consideration.[5]

[5] A correlation matrix was developed for each of the eight race–age groups (N = 60 children in each group); in each instance, the matrix involved all the variables. A similar matrix was also computed for the total group of 480 children.

V3. Language

This category was developed to provide a rough index of the child's specificity or precision in the use of language. More particularly, is the child explicit in his identification of each of the 18 human figures pictured in the stimuli, or does he settle for vague, nonspecific, general references? The child's reference to each of the human figures was scored (one for specific language, zero for nonspecific language); therefore, his total score could vary from zero through 18, with the higher scores representing the more specific use of language.

> *Example 1: Card S2 (S3223).* A man. He's learning language in school./ Cause he wants to learn./ Don't know. Wants books./ Don't know. (Nonspecific "man" and "he," scored 0)
> *Example 2: Card S2 (S1136).* It looks like Howard in his room . . . he's my brother. It looks like he's going to carry a book to his class./ They might study the lessons./ He's thinking it might be a hard book./ He's going to read it. (Specific "Howard" and "brother," scored 1)[6]

Other examples of nonspecific language would be references to a female figure simply as "woman" or "she," whereas a specific response might involve calling her a "mother," a "teacher," or a "nurse." Similarly, to call a male figure a "boss," a "father," or a "farmer," would earn a

TABLE 13.4

CPS Scores Showing Significant Racial Differences in the Analysis of Variance or in the Analysis of Covariance

	p level		
Scoring variable	Variance	Covariance	Race comparison*
V3. Language	.001	.005	White > Negro
V8. Food and drink	.001	.001	Negro > white
V9. Money and buying	.05	.005	Negro > white
V10. Clothing	.005	.05	Negro > white
V11. Housing	.001	.005	Negro > white
V14. Unpleasant affect	.05	.05	Negro > white
V16. Worry and anxiety	.001	.001	Negro > white
V22. Nonphysical punishment	.05	N.S.	White > Negro
V27. Injury	.05	N.S.	Negro > white

*White children, for example, earned significantly higher language scores than Negro children.

[6] The slants (/) in the stories (or excerpts) indicate those points where the examiner asked a question following McClelland's procedure (see Chapter 12).

TABLE 13.5

CPS Scores Showing Significant Interactions in the Analysis of Variance or in the Analysis of Covariance

Interaction	Scoring variable	p level		Comparisons*
		Variance	Covariance	
Sex × Age	None			
Sex × Race	V12. Affect (total)	N.S.	.05	WG > WB, NG = NB
	V13. Pleasant affect	N.S.	.05	WG > WB, NB > NG
	V14. Unpleasant affect	N.S.	.05	WG > WB, NG = NB
	V16. Worry and anxiety	.05	.05	WG > WB, NB > NG
	V17. Guilt and shame	.05	.01	WG > WB, NB > NG
Age × Race	V4. Sex reversal	.05	.005	Age 7: N > W; age 13: W > N
	V7. Sex content	.001	N.S.	Age 7: N > W; ages 9, 11, and 13: W > N
	V8. Food and drink	.001	.001	Age 7: N > W; other ages about equal
	V9. Money and buying	.001	.05	Age 7: N > W; ages 9 and 11: W > N
	V10. Clothing	.001	.005	Age 7: N > W; age 11: W > N
	V11. Housing	.001	N.S.	Age 7: N > W; other ages about equal
	V12. Affect (total)	.001	N.S.	Age 7: N > W; ages 11 and 13: W > N
	V13. Pleasant affect	.001	N.S.	Age 7: N > W; ages 9, 11, and 13: W > N
	V14. Unpleasant affect	.005	N.S.	Ages 7 and 13: N > W; age 11: W > N
	V15. Pain and hurt	.05	N.S.	Ages 7 and 13: N > W; ages 9 and 11: W > N

Variable			
V19. Sad and unhappy	.005	.05	Ages 7, 9, and 13: N > W; age 11: W > N
V20. Aggression (total)	.001	N.S.	Age 7: N > W; ages 9 and 11: W > N
V21. Physical punishment	.05	N.S.	Age 7: N > W; ages 9, 11, and 13: W > N
V22. Nonphysical punishment	.001	N.S.	Ages 7 and 13: about equal; 9 and 11: W > N
V23. Critical talk	.001	.05	Ages 7 and 13: N > W; ages 9 and 11: W > N
V24. Physical abuse	.001	N.S.	Age 7: N > W; ages 9, 11, and 13: W > N
V26. Antisocial aggression	.001	N.S.	Age 7: N > W; ages 11 and 13: W > N
V27. Injury	.001	N.S.	Age 7: N > W; other ages about equal
V28. Conflict	.001	.05	Age 7: N > W; ages 9 and 11: W > N
V29. Other aggression	.01	N.S.	Age 7: N > W; ages 9 and 11: W > N
V30. M affiliation	.001	.05	Age 7: N > W; ages 9, 11, and 13: W > N
V31. Nurturance	.001	.05	Age 7: N > W; ages 9 and 11: W > N
V32. Rejection	.001	.01	Age 7: N > W; ages 9, 11, and 13: W > N
V33. M power	.05	N.S.	Age 7: N > W; ages 9 and 11: W > N

Sex × Age × Race			
V3. Language	N.S.	N.S.	
V27. Injury	N.S.	.05	
V29. Other aggression	.005	.01	
V33. M power	.05	N.S.	

* WG = white girls, WB = white boys, NG = Negro girls, NB = Negro boys, W = white children, and N = Negro children.
For example, on V13, white girls scored higher than white boys, but Negro boys scored higher than Negro girls (Sex × Race summary).
Also, on V4, Negro children scored higher than white children at age 7, but at age 13 white children scored higher than Negro children (Age × Race summary).

score for specific language, in contrast to the more general "man" or "he" as used by Subject 3223 above.

Boys and girls did not differ significantly in this measure of their use of language. As one would expect, however, language scores were higher at the older age levels. Most interesting, perhaps, is the finding of a very significant racial difference (white > Negro) even after IQ and verbal productivity differences have been controlled. On the assumption that higher scores reflect more advanced levels of language development, this finding indicates that the verbal limitations of the Negro child, so often cited, stem from something more than a low level of general intellective functioning.

The age plots for language scores are given separately for Negro and white children in Figure 13.1. Note that white children have higher mean scores at each age level through age 11, but that the scores of 13-year-old white children do not differ from those of 11-year-old white children. In contrast, 13-year-old Negro children have higher mean scores than 11-year-old Negro children. At age 13, the Negro children are about as far behind the white children, relatively speaking, as they were at age 7. (Continuation of the two curves on their present paths, however, would eliminate this difference within a period of approximately two years.)

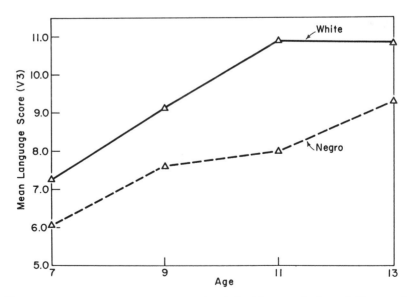

Fig. 13.1: Mean Language raw scores (V3) for Negro and white children at four age levels.

V4. Sex Reversal

The CPS pictures were drawn with the intention of making the sex identity of each of the 18 human beings depicted clear to the child; no ambiguity as to whether a particular figure was male or female was intended. This objective was achieved, as shown by the fact that over 99% of the human beings involved in the stories were given sex identifications in keeping with the intended sex of the person in the picture. In 37 instances, however, either an intended female was given a male identity, or an intended male was given a female identity. When this type of misperception occurred, sex reversal was scored.

> *Example 1: Card N4 (two males) (S2365).* That girl. The man. Getting ready to go to bed./ They getting ready to go to sleep./ About a girl. (Who?) The man. He wants somebody to be with him. The man./ He sleep.

Overall, there were no significant sex or racial differences in this kind of misperception. There was a significant change associated with age, however, and a significant Age $\times$ Race interaction. More than one-third of the sex reversals (13 of 37) were made by seven-year-old Negro children, whereas the remaining 24 reversals were about evenly divided among the other three Negro age groups and the four white age groups. This relatively high incidence of perceptual errors among the youngest Negro children is another indication of their tendency to fall behind the white children in psychological development.[7]

V5. Racial Imagery

This scoring category was used to identify expressions that gave racial identities to the characters in the stories, including characters not actually pictured in the stimuli. An instance of an explicit racial reference in the middle of a story told by a white girl was as follows:

> *Example 1: Card N9 (S1408).* . . . he said that there was a place in Beecher City where she could do her washing. But she said, "Colored people go there."

Such explicit racial references were extremely rare, however; actually, they were made only four times, once each by two Negro girls and once each by two white girls. More common were stories in which characters were identified by name in a way which permitted us to conclude that a racial identity may have been given to them (although not necessarily consciously). Example 2 is such an instance, a story told by a Negro

[7] In some instances, of course, there may be emotional or dynamic reasons behind the reversal rather than, or in addition to, the cognitive factors. It is tempting to infer that important dynamic factors are operating, for example, in the story given above by child number 2365.

boy. (John Glenn, of course, is a white astronaut who was very much in the news at the time.)

> *Example 2: Card S7* (*S2325*). That boy, he's settin' up there and his teacher is asking him questions, about John Glenn./ They're having science./ He's thinking about if John Glenn go around another time will he get killed or will he come back./ Something will go wrong and he won't come back.

Another example of inferred racial identity occurred at the beginning of a story told by a white boy; the Mrs. Griffith referred to in his story below was a white teacher in the school.

> *Example 3: Card S1* (*S1104*). Once upon a time there was a boy and teacher. Mrs. Griffith and he was getting behind with his work.

Such indirect racial references were also infrequent, being given by only 58 children—that is, by about 12% of the total group. There were no significant differences between boys and girls or between Negro and white children, but there was a significant age effect, with the highest scores being earned by the youngest children. More precisely, 15 Negro children and 7 white children at age seven told at least one story which was scored for racial imagery following the guidelines noted above. It is worth noting, too, that indirect references to race by white children always involved their giving white identities to the characters. The large majority of such references by Negro children, in contrast, were to Negro people, but 4 Negro children did give stories in which the characters seen were members of the white race (example 2 above is one such instance).

Not only were racial references infrequent, but this method of scoring undoubtedly inflated their actual incidence. That is, many references scored under this heading were probably made for reasons that had nothing to do with the racial identification of the characters involved. In effect, the boundaries of this category were extended to include all possibilities that might have racial overtones, no matter how remote.

The context of the CPS administration must be considered as providing a reasonable opportunity for expression of preoccupation with racial matters, for the children had been told—by a member of their own race—to use their imaginations, to develop stories around the pictures in any way that they saw fit. Because racial scores—even with stretching of the scoring criteria—were infrequent, and because explicit racial references were very rare, it is probably safe to conclude that racial matters play a minor role in the routine, day-to-day fantasy lives of these children. Unless there is direct racial provocation, their preoccupations appear to be elsewhere. Certainly there is no evidence in these stories that the children are so preoccupied with race that they are ready to give expression to this concern whenever a reasonable opportunity presents itself.

V6. Religion

This category was used to score references to religious topics, church activities, and to persons identified with religious settings—for example, ministers and Sunday School teachers.

> Example 1: Card N3 (S2171). The little boy is looking out the window, he is seeing something./ He seed something funny./ He is thinking about God./ He will close the window back and go set down.
> Example 2: Card F6 (S2139). . . . /He's going to get on his knees and asking God to let it rain. So God lets it rain and it saves his garden.
> Example 3: Card I11 (S1174). Might be a man—the preacher. And after preaching this boy came up to him. It looks like the preacher's telling the boy something./

Fifty-four children told at least one story with religious imagery, a number about equivalent to the number who expressed some racial imagery, broadly defined. Of the 5760 stories, only 77 (less than 2%) contained any type of religious imagery. There were no sex or racial differences, but there was a highly significant age effect. Each of the four groups, in fact, had lower religious scores at the older age levels. (Forty percent of the children who created religious imagery were at age seven.) The data, then, suggest that religious concerns play a very minor role in the fantasy lives of Millfield's children; also, that what concern there is tends to be greater at the younger age levels.

V7. Sex Content

This category was broadly defined to include any imagery having sexual overtones or implications. For example, references to kissing, marriage, dating, boyfriends or girlfriends, having babies, having no clothes on, and so on were scored for sex content.

> Example 1: Card F12 (S2155). . . . /He thinking he will finish this today and do the rest tomorrow./ When he finish he will go back off to see his girlfriend.
> Example 2: Card N10 (S2015). . . . /At school the boy was playing with some girls and his father wanted him to know he was too young to play with little girls./ The boy thinks his father is cruel to him./
> Example 3: Card I5 (S1124). . . . /The man's wife—they just got married and his wife wanted him to find a job./

Sexual imagery was more common than either racial or religious imagery; it was expressed in 143 stories by 98, or approximately 20%, of the children. Again, there were no boy–girl differences nor Negro–white differences, but there was a highly significant age effect and a highly significant Age $\times$ Race interaction (however, the latter appeared only in the analysis of variance). Actually, if it were not for age seven Negro children, no appreciable variation with age would be shown by either white or Negro children. Twenty-six Negro children at age seven produced sexual imagery, in contrast to only 11 children at age 13; comparable counts for white children were 11 and 8.

These data can be interpreted as indicating less suppression by young Negro children than by their white counterparts with respect to what is often considered to be socially taboo material. Inhibitions in this regard appear to be already well established among the white children at age seven, but less so among the Negro children of this age. That the Negro children are rather quickly socialized in this regard after entering school, however, is suggested by their much lower scores for sex content at age nine.

V8. Food and Drink

The CPS stimuli contain no pictures of food, nor of objects used to serve or prepare food and drink, with the exception of part of a water cooler in S8. When children made references to eating or drinking, it meant, therefore, that they were introducing such imagery with little or no provocation from the stimuli provided. Any reference to eating, drinking, or to objects used in these activities (for example, dishes), was scored in the food and drink category. (This is the first of four scoring categories that we refer to as comprising the "basic necessities"; the remaining three—money and buying, clothing, and housing—will be discussed in the succeeding pages.)

> *Example 1: Card S8* (*S2367*). A man. He at home. He open the door and go on in the house. He didn't want to be left—he come home./ He thinking about he want some breakfast./ He ate. He went to bed.
>
> *Example 2: Card F6* (*S2210*). This is a farmer. In the back is the farm—and a horse on one side. He's plowing his field./ It's time to plow./ It's hot, and he's thinking would he get through plowing his field by night./ He'll get through by night, and go home and eat supper and go to bed—or watch television.
>
> *Example 3: Card N3* (*S1324*). Maybe he was going to school and that was a door and he met his buddies in the hall and one of the buddies asked if he could go home with him and he said he didn't know and he might go home for lunch./

Of the 480 children, 413 told at least one story with food and drink imagery. At each age level, mean food and drink scores were higher for boys than for girls (a very significant sex effect), and, overall, the scores for Negro children were higher than those for white children (at a highly significant level). Also, there was a highly significant age effect (decrease with advancing age) and a highly significant Age $\times$ Race interaction. With respect to the latter, it should be noted that mean scores for Negro children markedly exceeded those for white children at age seven, but at the other age levels racial differences were comparatively small.

The racial difference here may very well be related to the relative deprivations that exist among Millfield's children with respect to nourishment. For example, many Negro children were known to come to school without having had breakfast or without provisions for lunch; this situation was much less common among the white children. Therefore, many more Negro than white children may be reflecting a chronic hunger in their CPS stories.[8] In any event, it is clear that thoughts about food and drink must play an important part in the fantasy lives of large numbers of children, both Negro and white.

The age differences are also of interest, especially since the Negro children at age 13 have mean scores that are nearly identical with those of the white children of this age. Perhaps older Negro children fend more adequately for themselves, having learned how to get necessary nourishment from even an impoverished environment. Or perhaps by this age they simply have adjusted to what is a chronic deficiency; it may no longer seem to matter as much. The data, of course, provide only the basis for such speculations but no way of deciding among various possibilities.

The sex differences are also intriguing, but there is no apparent reason why boys should evidence more preoccupation with food and drink than girls.

V9. Money and Buying

Any explicit reference to money, or to an activity that ordinarily involves the use of money (for example, going to the store), was scored in this category.

> *Example 1: Card F6* (S2020). . . . /Since the horse ran away he is thinking about where he will go with nothing to ride on and a little bit of money./
> *Example 2: N10* (S1111). Looks like father and son, setting down on the porch. Father looks like—real worried. Son's looking up at him thinking about what he's worried about./ Maybe he was working in this mill and it closed down and he didn't have no way of making any money./

At least one story involving money or buying was told by 370 of the children. As with food and drink imagery, scores were significantly higher for the boys than for the girls. Also, the scores of the Negro chil-

---

[8] The child in the first example above, for instance, was a seven-year-old Negro boy who created food and drink imagery in 11 of his 12 stories. It is difficult to believe that in so doing he is not telling us something important about his needs.

dren were higher than those of the white children (at a very significant level). In addition, there was a very significant variation attributable to age and a significant Age × Race interaction. With respect to age, mean scores for the white children were higher at age nine than at age seven, whereas scores for the Negro children were lower. After age nine, mean scores showed little variation with age for either race; also, the scores were very similar for the two races at the older age levels.

In general, then, the data suggest that the thoughts of the boys are more likely to involve money and buying than are those of the girls. This sex differential tends to hold after age nine as well as before. In contrast, racial differences are unimportant beginning with age nine.

V10. Clothing

This category was set up to summarize remarks about another one of the basic necessities. Clothing imagery was scored whenever reference was made to the wearing apparel of any individual introduced into the narrative.

> *Example 1: Card N4* (*S2662*). Father, he talking to his son. He told his son is he going to church, with him./ He got all dressed up and his father trying to see why./ He's thinking he like to go to church. He like to sing. He like to hear the preacher too./ He is all dressed so he going on to church with his daddy./
>
> *Example 2: Card I5* (*S1389*). / . . . Boy's thinking if I work I'll have money to buy clothes and a lot of other things I need . . . he wants a lot of money so he can buy some clothes and maybe presents for his mother and daddy./

Although Negro boys tended to score higher than Negro girls, and white boys, on the average, scored higher than white girls, the overall sex difference was not large enough to be statistically significant. There was a significant racial difference, however, with Negro children scoring higher than white children. Also, scores were lower at the older ages (a highly significant age effect), and there was a very significant Age × Race interaction. Again, as with money and buying imagery, the difference in mean raw score between children at ages 9 and 13 was small for each race. Also, the racial differences were slight at these three upper age levels. Seven-year-old Negro children, however, scored very high in comparison with seven-year-old white children. Finally, it is worth noting that references to clothing were much less common than references to either food and drink or money and buying: 143 vs. 413 and 370, respectively.

V11. Housing

This is the final subdivision of the basic necessities category. It was scored if any part of a story included a reference to physical living quarters. Remarks about entering a house or a house burning down, for example, would be scored here. Arbitrarily, however, we decided not to score remarks like "He went home," since it was often impossible to determine if reference was being made to a physical structure.

> *Example 1: Card N4* (*S2124*). / . . . They were playing near a house and the person hit the ball and it accidentally broke out the window./
> *Example 2: Card N9* (*S1408*). Well, uh, it's this house, uh, and he's standin' against this pole and he's waitin' for his mother to pick him up and his mother never did come and it got dark and he started to walk and he came to a house and he thought, "This is my house," but it was somebody else's house./

Housing scores were earned by 215 children, or by almost 45% of the sample. Sex differences were slight, but mean raw scores were greater for the Negro children than for the white children (at a very significant level), and there was a highly significant age effect (the older children earned lower scores). Again, however, the mean raw scores were very similar for both racial groups beginning at age nine, and the age changes after this age were small for both races. Both Negro and white children showed the sharpest age difference between ages seven and nine; it was especially pronounced for the Negro children.

It is apparent from the data pertaining to the four basic necessities that some consistent trends cut across them. Racial differences, for example, were marked at age seven, but the mean raw scores of the two races were almost identical at age 13 for each of the four basic necessities variables. Boys scored higher than the girls on three variables; only on housing was there no sex difference, although the sex difference for clothing scores was not large enough to reach statistical significance. With respect to age, scores on each variable were lower at the older ages, but the differences beyond age nine were small and relatively unimportant when compared with the sharp differences between ages seven and nine. Finally, comparatively speaking, food and drink imagery was most common, followed in turn by money and buying, housing, and clothing.

V12. Affect (Total)

In talking about living organisms, human or animal, a storyteller may attribute feelings or emotions to them. Sometimes affective qualities are only implied, other times they are made explicit. In the scoring scheme followed here, affect was scored for a story *only* when the language of the storyteller was explicit. For affect (total), it made no difference whether the attributed affect was pleasant or unpleasant; however, this distinction will be made in the two subcategories that follow.

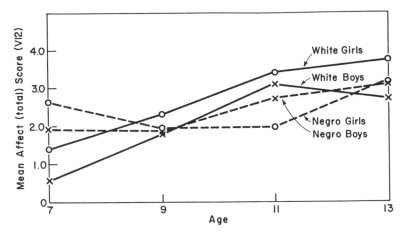

Fig. 13.2: Mean Total Affect raw scores (V12) for Negro and white children of each sex at four age levels.

Example 1: Card S1 (*S1189*). /Maybe he called her. Or maybe she saw that he was in *misery* while he was working, so she came over there to help him./
Example 2: Card S1 (*S2707*). The teacher showing the boy his lesson./ He didn't know how to do it. He couldn't understand it./ He thinking about the way she doing it so he won't forget./ The teacher will go back to doing what she was doing and the boy will start *feeling happy* and do his lesson.

Two findings are particularly worth noting. First, attribution of affect was much more common at the older age levels (a highly significant age effect). Second, there was a significant Sex × Race interaction: the white girls secured higher mean scores at each age level than the white boys, but there was no consistent sex difference among the Negro children. These relationships can be seen in Figure 13.2. Overall, the age curves in this figure appear to be flatter for the Negro children than for the white children; this is true primarily because the data at age seven have not been corrected for marked differences in verbal productivity favoring the Negro children. (At age seven there is a correlation of .59 between verbal productivity and affect [total] scores.)

V13. Pleasant Affect

Whenever an affective expression was included in a story, a judgment was made as to whether it involved essentially a pleasant or an unpleasant state. Words indicating happiness, cheerfulness, contentment, pleasure, liking someone or something, and so on were considered to be varieties of pleasant affective states.

Example 1: Card N9 (*S1385*). / . . . He wants everybody to *like* him.

Example 2: Card 111 (*S2387*). A man telling a boy about his factory./ The boy haven't been there before and seen what is made there./ Boy thinking it's gonna be *wonderful* to go back to school and tell his class what he has seen./ The children will ask him questions when he get back to school.

The pattern of results for pleasant affective scores was very similar to that just described for total affective scores: there was both a highly significant age effect (the scores of the older children were higher) and a significant Sex $\times$ Race interaction. With regard to the latter, the white girls used more pleasant affective words than the white boys, whereas the Negro boys tended to surpass the Negro girls in their usage.

V14. Unpleasant Affect

The use of any word or expression that explicitly indicated an unpleasant or negative affective condition was scored under this heading. Thus, words pointing to unhappiness, fear, anger, shame, and so on were scored here. (Further differentiations of unpleasant affective states will be considered as variables 15 through 19: pain, worry, guilt, anger, and sadness.)

Example 1: Card S7 (*S1172*). /The boy's thinking all them D's, wow! With that certificate that he hadn't missed a day he'll get a paddle with it./ The boy goes home, he has a *bad surprise* and when he gets home his mother and father are going to whip him . . .
Example 2: Card F12 (*S2172*). /The man wants to think and find out who took the cows so he can find them and bring them back to his other cow so his other cow won't be so *lonesome*./

The girls used significantly more expressions with unpleasant feeling qualities than the boys did; also, such expressions were significantly more frequent among the Negro children than among the white children. In addition, there was a highly significant age effect (higher scores at the older age levels) and a significant Sex $\times$ Race interaction. With regard to the latter, the white girls' scores were greater than those of the white boys, whereas Negro boys and girls, overall, had nearly equal scores.

An important implication in these data is the suggestion that the internal lives of the Negro children are more likely to be burdened with unpleasant affective qualities than are the internal lives of the white children. In considering these racial effects, it is particularly important to keep in mind that there was no comparable difference in the amount of pleasant affective imagery: the Negro children and the white children were very similar in this regard. Thus, to be a Negro in Millfield seems to mean that one's expression of unpleasant affect will be increased without a compensating increment in pleasant affective imagery. Such counterbalancing increments in both positive and negative affective imagery, however, do occur among the white girls, when their scores are compared with those of the white boys.

V15. Pain and Hurt

When unpleasant affective imagery was found in a story, an effort was made to classify it under one of five subheadings, the first of which was pain and hurt. (Occasionally, of course, the affect could not be so classified. Sometimes, too, more than one type of unpleasant affect was found in a given story and was scored accordingly; that is, two or more subcategories were scored.) As the words identifying this subcategory suggest, it was scored if the child used language that was explicit in referring to an experience that was painful.

> *Example 1: Card N3 (S2764).* /He had a wreck. His son got *hurt.* He got his car bent up and his children crying. His children didn't want to go to the doctor . . . /
>
> *Example 2: Card N4 (S1446).* /Thinking about the boy so he won't do naughty things that might cause somebody to get *hurt.* They want the boy to learn so he won't be naughty and won't have to be punished too much./

Actually, imagery of this type was infrequent; it was created by only 60 children, or one-eighth of the total sample. There were no significant racial or sex differences, but there was a very significant age variation. Scores were especially high in this category at age seven.

V16. Worry and Anxiety

Expressions indicative of worry, apprehension, fear, and anxiety were scored under this heading. No effort was made to distinguish among these states; for example, fear and anxiety were not differentiated.

> *Example 1: Card I5 (S1032).* Looks like this little boy is working for a man in a factory and sees his boss man and gets *frightened,* but then he gets O.K. . . ./
>
> *Example 2: Card F12 (S2128).* This man is Mr. Tom Farmer. He has a bull. The bull hangs on to him, but he might kill anyone else. So he comes out to feed the bull./ He's *scared* the bull will knock down the fence and go in and eat the corn . . . /

Almost twice as many children told stories with worry and anxiety imagery as told stories with pain and hurt imagery (110 vs. 60). The number of children at each age level who gave worry and anxiety imagery in at least one story has been plotted in Figure 13.3, separately for the four groups.

At each age level, fewer white boys told stories with worry and anxiety imagery than was true for any of the other three groups. At ages 7 and 9, fewer Negro boys gave such stories than Negro girls, but at

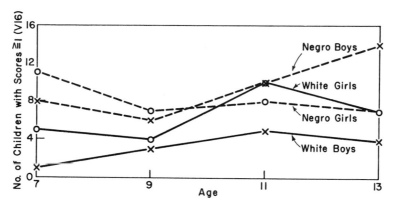

Fig. 13.3: The number of children of each sex of each race who told at least one CPS story with worry or anxiety imagery (V16).

ages 11 and 13 this relationship was reversed. The overall racial difference is highly significant, and there is a significant Sex × Race interaction.

V17. Guilt and shame

Any expression indicating that a character feels guilty, ashamed, or sorry for what he has done or wants to do was scored under this category.

> *Example 1: Card S8 (S1452).* He's a high school student and he's gone to the library to get some books./ He had checked out some books and kept 'em two weeks overdue and so he's bringin' 'em back now./ He *feels ashamed* he left 'em overdue so long./ The librarian isn't gonna let him check out any more books for two weeks.
>
> *Example 2: Card I11 (S2195).* . . . /I think the boy is *feeling sorry* for what he have done and the principal is telling the boy what his punishment will be . . . /

The number of children who expressed guilt and shame in their fantasy behavior was considerably less than the number who expressed worry and anxiety (73 vs. 110), but slightly more than the number who gave pain and hurt imagery (73 vs. 60). There was not a significant racial difference, although more white than Negro children earned guilt and shame scores (40 vs. 33). There was a very significant Sex × Race interaction: white girls exceeded white boys, but Negro boys exceeded Negro girls. Figure 13.4 shows this Sex × Race interaction; it also suggests what indeed is a highly significant age effect. Guilt and shame imagery was quite infrequent at age 7 (only 6 out of 120 children

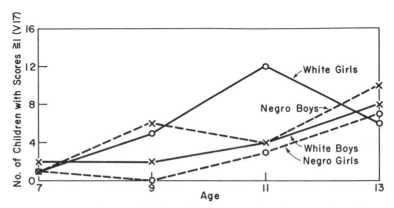

Fig. 13.4: The number of children of each sex of each race who told at least one CPS story with guilt or shame imagery (V17).

earned such scores), but it was appreciably more common at age 13 (31 out of 120 children secured these scores).

V18. Anger

A comment that explicitly referred to a person or animal as mad or angry was scored under this subheading.

> *Example 1: Card S2* (*S2267*). A man is standing in the library with one hand on the shelf and one hand in his pocket. He look sad./ The teacher has made him come to the library to get a book and he's *mad.*/ He thinking about whether to get the book or not./ He will not get the book; he will go back to his room.
> *Example 2: Card 15* (*S3316*). Two mans. One man's painting. (E: The other one?) Comin' to watch him./ Watch him paint./ Something to eat./ Looks like they gonna get in a fight. (E: Why?) Get *mad.*

More children (a total of 159) expressed anger in their stories than expressed any of the other unpleasant affective qualities that have already been discussed. There was neither a significant racial effect nor a significant sex effect, but age was a highly significant factor. About twice as many children at age 13 included anger in their stories as at age 7 (53 vs. 26).

V19. Sad and Unhappy

Expressions that referred explicitly to crying, depression, unhappiness, sadness, or lonesomeness were scored under this subheading.

> *Example 1: Card N10* (*S1233*). /Probably thinking about what he'll say next. Man's probably thinking that he hopes the boy will stay and talk to him—he's very *lonely*. If the man's *lonely*, the boy wants him to have friends and the boy probably wants to get friends, too./

Example 2: Card S7 (S2563). A boy and a woman. He couldn't talk and the woman started *crying*./ 'Cause he broke out his teeth./ He thinking about he wish his teeth would grow back./ And so all his teeth growed back.

The only significant effect with respect to sadness imagery was the Age × Race interaction: the scores of the Negro children were higher than those of the white children at every age level except 11; at age 11, the scores of the white children exceeded those of the Negro children. Since there is no apparent explanation for this inversion at age 11, there must be a question as to whether it would reappear upon replication.

Among the five subcategories of unpleasant affect, the frequency of children giving at least one expression of sadness was second only to the frequency of children producing at least one reference to anger (133 vs. 159). Table 13.6 has been prepared to permit ready comparisons among the several affective categories in this regard.

V20. Aggression (Total)

A story was scored plus (or one) for aggression (total) if one or more of the subcategories of aggression appeared in the story. In other words, any form of aggressive imagery in a story was sufficient to earn for that story a score of one for aggression (total). Nine subcategories of aggression were scored; since these will be defined and examples will be given for them below, illustrations of aggressive imagery will not be presented here.

Aggressive imagery, in one form or another, was quite common; only eight children failed to give at least one story that was so scored. Moreover, the mean number of stories with some type of aggressive imagery was 6.0 for all 480 children. In other words, one out of two stories contained aggressive imagery of some type.

TABLE 13.6

The Number of Children Who Told One or More Stories That
Earned Scores in the Affective Categories

Scoring variable	Number of children with scores ≥ 1	Percent of sample
V12. Affect (total)	373	78
V13. Pleasant affect	229	48
V14. Unpleasant affect	333	69
V15. Pain and hurt	60	13
V16. Worry and anxiety	110	23
V17. Guilt and shame	73	15
V18. Anger	159	33
V19. Sad and unhappy	133	28

There was a tendency for girls to produce more aggressive imagery than boys, but the difference was not statistically significant. Nor was there a significant racial difference; in fact, the overall distributions of scores for the Negro and white children were almost precisely the same. There was a significant age effect, however: aggressive imagery was more common at the older age levels.

V21. Physical Punishment

Any mention of whipping, spanking, or other physical assault (even as a possibility rather than as an actual occurrence) in a context where the recipient had done something wrong was scored in this subcategory.

> *Example 1: Card N10 (S1000).* Boy and his father sitting on the steps./ Boy did something wrong and the father's talking to him about it./ The father's thinking that he needs a *whippin'!* And the boy's thinking can't he ever do anything right? Boy wants him to hurry up and get it over with. (E: Father?) Wants his son to do right, for once./ The father'll tell the boy not to do it again, and he'll let it go at that.
>
> *Example 2: Card N3 (S2764).* / . . . After he went home—he went home to eat. After he eat he sent children to bed. And his children didn't want to go to bed. They wanted to stay up and look at TV. And he got a switch and *whip* 'em and they went to bed. They took their books to bed to read with them.

About one out of three children gave at least one story with this type of imagery (see Table 13.7). There were no significant sex, racial, or age effects.

V22. Nonphysical Punishment

References to punitive actions which did not involve corporal punishment were scored under this heading. As one might expect, there was

TABLE 13.7

The Number of Children Who Told One or More Stories That
Earned Scores in the Aggression Categories

Scoring variable	Number of children with scores ≥ 1	Percent of sample
V20. Aggression (total)	472	98
V21. Physical punishment	164	34
V22. Nonphysical punishment	369	77
V23. Critical talk	409	85
V24. Physical abuse	155	32
V25. Social aggression	96	20
V26. Antisocial aggression	145	30
V27. Injury	287	60
V28. Conflict	438	91
V29. Other aggression	329	69

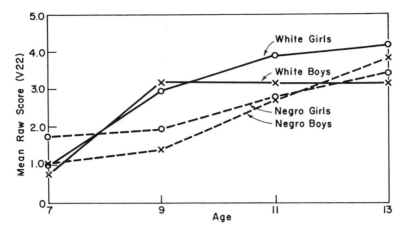

Fig. 13.5: Mean nonphysical punishment raw scores (V22) for each sex of each race at four age levels.

considerable diversity in this regard: being sent to bed, receiving a verbal reprimand, being given a low grade, and so on.

> *Example 1: Card N9 (S1506).* It's a little boy and he's in the night and he's got a light beside him. He's thinking about if he goes to bus stop and gets a bus he'll go home, and he don't want to go. (E: Why?) Because his mother wouldn't let him go to his friend's./ *I think that his mother told him not to go because he didn't get an A on his report./*
> *Example 2: Card S8 (S2080).* / . . . his teacher told him to go to the library and he found an interesting book about geography and he took the book home, but *the teacher told him not to take the book home* . . . / When he brought that book home *the principal expelled him from school* . . . /

Approximately three out of four children created at least one story with nonphysical punishment imagery; this frequency is more than two times as great as that for physical punishment imagery. There is a highly significant age effect (higher scores at the older age levels); however, there is no significant sex or racial effect, when verbal productivity and IQ differences are eliminated. The mean raw scores earned by each of the four groups at each of the four age levels are shown in Figure 13.5.

V23. Critical Talk

Negative remarks or thoughts about someone or something were scored in this subcategory. It is important to emphasize that critical talk was scored even if it remained covert; that is, critical thoughts as well as critical verbalizations of the characters in the stories were scored.

> *Example 1: Card F12 (S1438).* The farmer is openin' the gate so the cow can get out to pasture./ The boy come along and shut the gate when the farmer

opened it./ *The man thought that the boy should be punished some way./* The man opens the gate and the cow gets out and eats grass. (E: Boy punished?) Yes, Ma'am.
Example 2: Card I11 (S2137). Teacher asking—man asking the little boy *how come he didn't get his lessons./*

At each age level, mean raw scores were higher for Negro girls than for Negro boys. The sex difference was less pronounced among the white children; however, at three age levels mean scores were higher for the girls (at age 11, scores for the white boys and girls were almost identical). Overall, there was a highly significant sex effect, with the higher scores being received by the girls.

There was also a highly significant age effect and a significant Age $\times$ Race interaction. For the white children, the mean score at age 9 was markedly higher than that at age 7. However, the differences between the mean scores at ages 9, 11, and 13 were small. In contrast, the mean score of the Negro children was higher at each succeeding age level, and at age 13 the mean score of the Negro children exceeded that of the white children.

V24. Physical Abuse

Any type of physical assault—except that which was used as punishment (see above)—was scored in this category. Fighting, biting, and kicking are typical illustrations of what was scored here. It made no difference, incidentally, whether such behavior was exhibited by human beings or by animals; both were scored.

> *Example 1: Card F12* (S2772). /He going to save the farmer's life. He going to be out there in the pasture with the farmer and the bull going start charging at him. And Bob he going to save his life by *hitting the bull* in between the head . . . /
> *Example 2: Card S2* (S1012). It's a boy—he's in the principal's office./ *For fighting./*

Approximately one out of three children created at least one story containing this type of rather raw, physical aggression. When verbal productivity and IQ differences were eliminated, there were no significant differences that could be attributed to race, sex, age, or the four interactions.

V25. Social Aggression

This category was used to score behavioral expressions which often are said to indicate "subliminations." More particularly, the category was scored for activities that may be aggressive in nature but are either accepted or even encouraged by the social order in which we live. Participation in competitive sports or military activities are examples of what we have in mind here.

> *Example 1: Card N4* (*S2152*). Boy talking to his father and he wants to *play basketball* . . . /
>
> *Example 2: Card 111* (*S1042*). This looks sorta like a teen-age boy and he's coming to this office building and asked if he could *join the Navy.* / . . . He's been wanting to *go in the Navy and be a hero.* He's thinking about his career and hoping he'll pass the test. This man is probably thinking about this young boy and wondering if he'll make the tests. He wants him to pass the tests and join the Navy because he seems like a nice boy./ He'll pass the test and join the Navy.

Scores in this category were heavily dependent upon the presence of themes in the stories that are usually considered masculine. Perhaps it is not surprising, then, that a significant sex effect was found, with the boys securing higher scores than the girls. Race and age, however, did not contribute significantly to the variance. Overall, social aggression was included in at least one story by 20% of the children.

V26. Antisocial Aggression

Any type of aggressive acting-out which usually earns the disapproval of society was scored in this category. Damaging property, stealing, cheating, and killing would be instances of such antisocial behavior.

> *Example 1: Card N9* (*S2670*). The boy is mad about something./ His father wouldn't give him any money./ He's *thinking he'll steal some.*/ He will steal it. Somebody will catch him and he will have to go to jail.
>
> *Example 2: Card N3* (*S1271*). Boy's standing at the window of his bedroom. He's lookin' out and thinkin' about something./ Maybe *something happened* at the drug store when he was there and he didn't like it or something./ Whether to tell somebody what happened or whether to keep quiet about it./ He decides to *tell the authorities* about what happened.

About 50% more children told at least one story with antisocial aggression than told at least one story with social aggression. There were no significant age, sex, or racial effects in antisocial aggression scores.

V27. Injury

A reference to injury, sickness, or death may be a disguised way of expressing aggression; expressions of this type were scored under injury.

> *Example 1: Card 15* (*S1026*). George Washington—the other one's *arm broke.*/ Maybe he had the arm on then./ Thinking maybe his arm will get well./ He'll have to go to the hospital.
>
> *Example 2: Card F12* (*S2348*). There's a man coming out the gate./ He coming from feeding his cow./ Thinking if the cow didn't get anything to eat she might get hungry./ If he didn't feed the cow the cow liable to *get sick.* He fed the cow so she didn't get sick.

Almost 60% of the children told at least one story with this type of imagery. Although there were no significant sex or racial differences, there was a significant age effect: injury scores were lower at the older ages. As one might anticipate, the age pattern for injury scores was similar to the one reported earlier for pain and hurt imagery. Furthermore, there was a highly significant correlation between pain and hurt scores and injury scores ($r = .38$).

V28. Conflict

Any argument, disagreement, or difficulty between individuals (or between human beings and animals) was scored in this category. The conflict did not have to be expressed openly to merit scoring; for example, a boy *thinking* that he did not want to do what the teacher had told him to do was scored for conflict.

> *Example 1: Card S1 (S2301).* Boy and a girl. *The girl is trying to teach the boy* how to read. She's his sister./ *He hasn't tried hard enough./* She's thinking she can help him to learn to read and it's very important when he becomes an adult. *He don't care one way or another . . . /*
>
> *Example 2: Card 15 (S1159).* Two men—they're at the store or something. *They're fussing,* or something./

About one-third of the stories contained some type of conflict imagery. Moreover, more than 90% of the children told at least one story with such imagery. In many stories, both conflict and critical talk were scored, often for the same expression. That is, an expression which was scored for critical talk was also scored for conflict. There is a product-moment correlation of .82 between scores in the two categories.

It is not surprising, then, to find that the results of the analysis of conflict scores are similar to those previously described for critical talk. Girls scored significantly higher than boys, and scores at the upper ages were higher than those at the lower ages (a highly significant age effect). Also, there was a significant Age $\times$ Race interaction: Negro children's scores were comparatively high at ages 7 and 13, whereas white children's scores were comparatively high at ages 9 and 11.

V29. Other Aggression

This category was used to score imagery which might be regarded as a disguised or indirect expression of aggression and which could not be scored in any of the other aggression categories. Very often these remarks took the form of referring to something as being broken, dirty, deformed, and so on, or to an "accidental" event that had unfortunate implications.

Example 1: Card N3 (S1086). This man's fixing a window./ A neighbor might have called and told the man their latch *was broken* . . . /
Example 2: Card F6 (S2250). /He will not get his garden planted before it rains and *he will get very wet.*

Many of the references scored in this category probably are not psychologically equivalent. If this is so, there should be little or no regularity in the results. Actually, there were no significant main effects and only a significant triple interaction, the meaning of which we cannot determine.

V30. M Affiliation[9]

"Affiliation imagery . . . is scored when the story contains some evidence of concern in one or more of the characters over *establishing, maintaining, or restoring a positive affective relationship with another person. This relationship is most adequately described by the word friendship.* The minimum basis for scoring would be that the relationship of one of the characters in the story to someone else is that of friendship." (Heyns, Veroff, and Atkinson, in Atkinson *et al.,* 1958, pp. 205–206.)

Example 1: Card S7 (S2015). This little boy is mad and the little girl is mad./ The teacher went out and left the little girl in charge; the boy doesn't like her but she likes him./ The boy wish the girl wasn't going to the same school he goes to. *The girl is sorry that the boy doesn't like her./* The boy keep on disliking her.
Example 2: Card S2 (S1078). /Thinking about a fight he might have gotten into, and another boy got hurt, and thinking about how wrong he did and how sorry he is. (E: Wants?) *To make up with the other person. Wants the other peson to like him.* He'll never do it again./

More than three-fourths of the children gave at least one story with M Affiliation imagery. There was a very significant sex difference: at each age level for each race, mean scores for girls were higher than those for boys. There was also a significant age effect and a significant Age × Race interaction; actually, the age pattern was somewhat confused. The mean raw scores for the white children were slightly higher at ages 11 and 13 than at ages 7 and 9. For the Negro children, mean scores were higher at ages 7, 11, and 13 than at age 9.

V31. Nurturance

Giving or seeking help (or material objects) is the focus of this scoring category. In general, any reference that indicates a desire to have

[9] M Affiliation scores were assigned at the University of Michigan under the supervision of Joseph Veroff.

needs satisfied, or to satisfy the needs of others, would be scored as nurturance imagery.

> *Example 1: Card S8* (*S2554*). The man walking in the library./ He going to read./ He thinking about so he can go to school and read library books. He wants something—he wants a book for to carry home and read. Make his *mama help him.*/ The boy is smiling. He going to read.
> *Example 2: Card F6* (*S1261*). A boy out on a farm looking at a horse./ His father was planning to buy a horse and *told him he could go out on the farm and pick out any one he wanted to.*/ He's picked out two horses but doesn't know which one to choose./ Since he has had such a hard time choosin', he chooses both of 'em. Wish I had even one!

Only nine children failed to tell at least one story with nurturance imagery. On the average, each child told almost five stories that were so scored.

The girls' scores for nurturance were significantly larger than were those of the boys. There was also a very significant age effect, and a significant Age × Race interaction. The mean raw scores for the white children were markedly higher at ages 9, 11, and 13 than at age 7. In contrast, the mean raw scores of the Negro children were higher at ages 7 and 13 than at ages 9 and 11.

V32. Rejection

Any expression that suggested rejection by either a person or group (including the total society) was scored in this category. Such references were quite varied in nature; they ranged from being expelled or being put in jail to simply being left out or passed over.

> *Example 1: Card S8* (*S1021*). /I think the bell is going to ring and he'll have to go home and *he won't come back tomorrow.* (E: Why?) Because *he was mad* yesterday—because teacher had to spank him.
> *Example 2: Card S7* (*S2680*). . . . /He's thinking now *he can spell those words* because he's been home to study them./ *She will call on another person* to spell the words.

Approximately four out of five children told at least one story with rejection imagery. On the average, each child gave slightly more than two such stories.

The girls' scores were significantly higher than those of the boys. After differences in IQ and verbal productivity were eliminated, age and racial effects proved to be insignificant. However, there was a very significant Age × Race interaction. At age 7 the mean score of the Negro children was higher than that of the white children, but at ages 9, 11, and 13 the mean scores of the white children were higher. These data, then, certainly offer no support for the idea that Negro children, more than their white counterparts, come increasingly to feel a sense of rejection as they move into early adolescence in a Southern rural environment.

V33. M Power[10]

"In order for the overall code of Power Imagery to be scored, there has to be some reference to the thoughts, feelings, and actions of one of the characters in a story which indicates that the character is concerned with the control of the means of influencing a person. Power Imagery can be indicated in the imagery about any character mentioned in the story." (Veroff, in Atkinson *et al.*, 1958, p. 220.)

> *Example 1: Card S2* (*S2344*). Boy been into the library. He got a piece of wood or a glove in his hand./ *He had to go get a book cause his teacher told him to./* He thinking he ought to get another book./ He will go out the door then go back in the classroom.
>
> *Example 2: Card 111* (*S1021*). This boy done something wrong and *he had to go to the principal* but he didn't get no spanking./ I think he must have hurt a boy and had to go to the principal and then *he had to go home and go to the court./* They thinking about the student going to the court./ I think they come back where they have been.

Approximately four out of five children told at least one story with power imagery. On the average, each child told slightly more than three stories of this type. There were no significant sex or racial effects, but there was a highly significant age effect. Roughly speaking, power scores at age 13 were about twice as large as those at age 7.

CONCLUDING COMMENTS

Descriptively, what we have presented in this chapter is an analysis of verbal behavior elicited by a particular type of examining procedure. Although many variables were discussed, it must be kept in mind that many other analyses of this same verbal behavior could be made. There may, indeed, be more meaningful categories and ways of analyzing verbal behavior than those used. Nevertheless, the results indicate that the evaluative scheme was reasonably productive.

It was not an interest in verbal behavior per se that led to this work. Rather, our concern was with eliciting a type of response from the children which would be highly suggestive with respect to their inner, subjective lives. Furthermore, it was anticipated that the nature of this inner world would be influenced by the class membership of the child

[10] M Power scores were assigned at the University of Michigan under the supervision of Joseph Veroff.

as defined by his sex, race, and age. In general, the data that have been presented are consistent with this expectation. In the concluding paragraphs, then, we shall attempt to summarize what seem to us to be some of the major findings with respect to sex, racial, and age effects.

The Significance of Sex Membership

There were three content areas which were more prominent in the fantasy behavior of the boys than in that of the girls: food and drink, money and buying, and social aggression (a category which was heavily loaded with competitive sports activity). In contrast, the fantasy behavior of the girls, more than that of the boys, emphasized unpleasant affective states, critical talk, conflict, and a concern with interpersonal relationships—as reflected in imagery pertaining to friendship patterns, the giving or seeking of help, and being rejected. Girls, then, appear to be more person-oriented than boys, and to be more expressive of dysphoric affect.

The Significance of Race Membership

The white children showed a more precise use of language than the Negro children, even after IQ and verbal productivity differences had been controlled. The fantasy behavior of the Negro children revealed a much greater preoccupation with the basic necessities of living than that of the white children, as well as a higher incidence of unpleasant affect, especially fear and anxiety. It is also worthy of note that it was only with respect to affective imagery that significant Sex × Race interactions were obtained. More particularly, the white girls were more affectively expressive than the white boys, whereas the Negro girls and boys were either more nearly equal in this regard (on each of the affective categories) or the scores of the Negro boys actually exceeded those of the Negro girls.

The Significance of Age

Although sex and race had significant effects upon fantasy behavior, it is apparent that age was an even more potent variable. Broadly speaking, a concern with the basic necessities of living was less evident at the older age levels, whereas affective expression and involvement in the many facets of interpersonal behavior were more pronounced. Also, perceptual errors were less common at the older age levels, while an explicit use of language was more marked.

With respect to many variables, we are impressed with the plateau which seems to develop for the white children somewhere between the ages of 9 and 11. By this we mean that a number of different scores increase sharply up to or through this age period, then either level off or show a slight decline. In contrast, the scores of the Negro children usually continue to climb between ages 11 and 13, narrowing the gap that is ordinarily found at age 11. We very much need additional data now at older age levels in order to answer several questions: Is this plateau permanent or temporary for the white children? Will a similar plateau occur for the Negro children, but at an older age level? How do the two races compare on these variables when full biological and social maturity have been achieved? Also, we need to know if age plots based upon longitudinal data are consistent with those derived from cross-sectional data.

Finally, examination of all the age plots (most of which could not be presented) impresses upon one the fact that the four groups are more alike on most variables at age 13 than at age 7. That is, the mean scores of white and Negro boys and girls are much more widely dispersed at age 7 than at age 13. With respect to fantasy behavior, then, maturation and socialization appear to be operating in the direction of enhancing similarities rather than differences across racial and sex groups.

Chapter 14

CORRELATES OF PEER POPULARITY

When people work or play together, some individuals ordinarily develop greater popularity with the members of their group than others do. Such a process obviously had occurred within Millfield's classrooms; we decided to study it empirically. More particularly, we sought to determine factors in the child's makeup and background which were related to the degree of popularity that he had achieved with his classmates. Popularity is one aspect of the social effectiveness of a person and is, of course, also an important manifestation of his personality.

DETERMINING PEER POPULARITY

In undertaking this inquiry, the first task was to measure the popularity of each child with his classmates. This was done by means of a sociometric device developed by Hereford (1958) for use in a project studying parent–child relationships.[1] Essentially, this technique presents to each classroom a game-like situation in which each child is arbitrarily assigned to one of three teams and then gets to choose a limited number of children not already on his team to join his team. By totaling the number of times each child is chosen by his classmates, the relative popularity (Hereford seems to prefer the term acceptability) of each child in the room can be determined. The goals of the procedure are described by Hereford as follows:

[1] We are indebted to Lloyd J. Borstelmann for calling this technique to our attention and for assisting us in learning to use it.

320

. . . a method of measuring the individual elementary school child's acceptability to his classmates was needed. Standard sociometric techniques were inadequate for our purposes in that the usual distribution of choices is badly skewed. A method was needed that provided:

1. A numerical score for each child.
2. A reasonably normal distribution of scores for each class.
3. Applicability to grades 1 through 6.
4. High motivation on the part of the children.
5. Protection for children not chosen, i.e., results of choices not made known.
6. Feasibility of administration (time and cooperation).

In addition, the method should show adequate reliability. . . .

Hereford (1958, Section 5, page 1)

After summarizing the above objectives, Hereford proceeds to describe the methodology:

The sociometric method devised is based on the child's choice of classmates to be on his "team," each team to share a prize of an unknown nature. The children are first given numbered plaques to wear in order that they may be identified. The class is then divided into three teams, each team wearing a different colored hat. The children are instructed to choose two members of each of the other two teams to be on their team and to indicate their choices by number on a card provided them. After the children have made their choices, the team leaders (project staff members) make a pretense of tallying the cards. Two-thirds of each team is then rotated, one-third to each of the other two teams according to a prearranged schedule. The children, however, think their choices determine these shifts. The process is repeated two more times, making a total of three sets of four choices by each child. The prearranged schedule is such that each child has an opportunity to choose every other child. During this activity, the teacher fills out an identification sheet, giving the name of the child by the number he is wearing. When all choices are completed, each team is given a bag of prizes . . . that contains a prize for each child.

Hereford (1958, Section 5, page 1)

This procedure was used in each classroom of Millfield's four schools during the spring of 1962 to determine each child's peer popularity. The team leaders (see above) were members of the project staff; white staff members worked only with white children, and Negro staff members with Negro children. The same prize, a Yo-Yo, was given to each child in all the grades, one through eight. Because word of the game spread rapidly through the schools, and because every child received the same prize, there is little reason to believe that the choices of the children were greatly influenced by a competitive orientation. That is, there was no reason for a child to make his choices with the idea that he might thereby enhance his chances for winning a better prize.

After a class had played the game, a tally was made of the number of times that each child had been selected by members of his peer group. This raw score, however, was not appropriate to use in the analyses of the data, since the classes varied in size. (A child in a large class had an opportunity to be selected more frequently than an equally popular child in a small class.) Instead, a decile score (from 1 to 10) was computed for each child based upon his relative standing in his own class. Thus, a decile score of 1 indicated that a child was among the lowest 10% in his class in his frequency of being chosen. A decile score of 10, in contrast, indicated that the child fell in the upper 10% of his class. In the analyses below, a child's decile score has been used as the basic datum summarizing his peer popularity.

As Hereford reported, elementary school children of all grade levels readily accept this device and give every evidence of enjoying it. And, despite the fact that it was a rather odd game in which the groups never really got around to any group play activity, the format was not questioned or challenged; the children simply accepted it and seemed to have fun while participating in it. Finally, it should be noted that the reliability of this popularity score was not determined in the context of the present study. Hereford, however, has reported data attesting to its reliability:

> The reliabilities for all classes in the first school with a test-retest interval of two weeks was .75. For the other two schools, with a time interval of two and one-half months, the average reliabilities were .67 and .69.
>
> Hereford (1958, Section 5, page 2)

FAMILY CORRELATES

The first series of inquiries centered upon family attributes. Data pertaining to several such variables—as they relate to peer popularity—will be examined in this section.

Geographical Origin of Parents

In some communities, a child's acceptance by other children is conditioned in part by the depth of his family's "roots" in that community. If his family is established in the community, the readiness of the children to accept him may be different than if his family is relatively new. If such a factor operates in Millfield, it is reasonable to predict that it will be reflected in the relationship between a child's popularity and the place where his parents were born.

The birthplace of each child's mother and father was classified as being either nuclear or nonnuclear (see Chapter 5). If a mother's birthplace was in one of the four counties that almost touch at a common point on the northwest boundary of Millfield, she was called a nuclear mother; a nonnuclear mother was one who had been born outside of this four-county area. Nuclear and nonnuclear fathers were similarly defined.

As Table 14.1 indicates (see variable 1), white children with nuclear mothers tended to show higher mean popularity scores than children with nonnuclear mothers. This difference was statistically significant for the white girls but not for the white boys. White children with nuclear fathers also tended to be chosen more often than their classmates with nonnuclear fathers, but this difference was not statistically significant for either the boys or the girls.

The implication of parental birthplace for the Negro children was the reverse of that just described for the white children, although the differences obtained between the two groups were not statistically significant. A white child in Millfield would be justified, then, in feeling that there is at least a slight advantage in having parents born in the immediate area insofar as his peer popularity is concerned, but a Negro child would have no objective basis for holding a similar belief.[2]

Education of Parents

Mothers and fathers were separately classified into two groups: those who had not obtained more than an elementary school education, and those who had been educated beyond this level. Does parental education, so differentiated, relate significantly to the peer popularity of a child? As the data under variable 2 in Table 14.1 show, parental education is associated with popularity scores, except for the Negro boys. Moreover, the differences in means are substantial for the white boys, the white girls, and the Negro girls. For each of these groups and for either parent, the mean scores of the children with the relatively well-educated parent are much higher than the mean scores for the children of the relatively poorly educated parent (each difference is highly significant). This positive relationship between parental education and peer popularity holds over the entire age span covered (except, of course, for the Negro boys), as is illustrated for the fathers in Figure 14.1.

It must be emphasized again, however, that the general relationship just described does not hold for the Negro boys. The reasons for this departure cannot be ascertained from the data but will have to be determined by additional inquiries.

---

[2] It is possible that the implications of parental birthplace would have been delineated more sharply if the nuclear area had been defined as only that land which lies within one of the four school districts. However, our data did not permit us to use this more restricted definition.

TABLE 14.1

Mean Decile Scores (Reflecting Popularity of the Children) as Related to Several Family and Personal Variables

Variables	Racial and sex groups			
	WB*	WG	NB	NG
1. Origin of parents				
Nuclear mothers	5.6	5.7	5.1	6.0
Nonnuclear mothers	5.3	4.8	5.4	6.4
t and p	.59(N.S.)	2.17(.05)	.41(N.S.)	.62(N.S.)
Nuclear fathers	5.5	5.7	5.1	6.0
Nonnuclear fathers	5.2	4.8	5.0	6.3
t and p	.73(N.S.)	1.86(.10)	.25(N.S.)	.63(N.S.)
2. Education of parents				
Mothers, 0–8 years	4.6	4.0	5.0	5.5
Mothers, ≥ 9 years	6.2	6.4	5.3	6.5
t and p	4.27(.001)	6.55(.001)	.98(N.S.)	2.68(.001)
Fathers, 0–8 years	4.9	4.8	5.3	5.6
Fathers, ≥ 9 years	6.2	6.2	4.8	7.0
t and p	3.38(.001)	3.62(.001)	1.41(N.S.)	3.78(.001)
3. Employment of parents				
Mother employed	6.3	6.1	5.7	6.2
Mother unemployed	5.2	5.0	5.1	5.9
t and p	2.75(.01)	2.96(.01)	1.69(.10)	.85(N.S.)
Father a farmer	4.8	5.7	5.0	5.9
Father nonfarmer	5.9	5.4	5.4	6.0
t and p	2.47(.05)	.74(N.S.)	1.29(N.S.)	.11(N.S.)

	WB	WG	NB	NG
4. Size of sibship				
1–2 sibs	5.9	5.7	5.9	7.2
3–4 sibs	5.9	5.9	5.7	6.5
≥5 sibs	4.7	4.5	4.8	5.4
F and p	3.62(.05)	5.68(.01)	5.73(.01)	9.09(.001)
5. Ordinal position				
Oldest	5.3	6.2	4.8	6.3
In-between	5.5	5.1	5.1	5.7
Youngest	5.7	5.4	6.0	6.5
F and p	.33(N.S.)	2.79(.10)	3.39(.05)	1.96(N.S.)
6. Possessions and services				
Home owners	6.0	5.8	5.5	6.9
Not home owners	4.3	4.6	4.9	5.4
t and p	4.38(.001)	2.64(.01)	1.84(.10)	4.34(.001)
Car owners	5.5	5.5	5.1	6.2
Not car owners	4.2	3.8	5.0	5.6
t and p	2.39(.05)	2.07(.05)	.36(N.S.)	1.54(N.S.)
TV owners	5.5	5.5	5.2	6.1
Not TV owners	4.3	4.4	4.6	5.6
t and p	2.44(.05)	1.24(N.S.)	1.35(N.S.)	1.16(N.S.)
With telephones	3.9	6.1	6.1	7.5
Without telephones	4.8	4.3	4.9	5.5
t and p	2.82(.01)	4.47(.001)	2.81(.01)	5.31(.001)
7. Intelligence				
Upper 25%	6.4	6.8	6.3	7.5
Middle 50%	5.7	5.6	5.5	6.2
Lower 25%	4.5	4.2	4.0	4.1
F and p	6.75(.01)	10.25(.001)	12.72(.001)	19.81(.001)

(*continued*)

* Abbreviations: WB = white boys; WG = white girls; NB = Negro boys; NG = Negro girls.

TABLE 14.1 (*continued*)

Variables	Racial and sex groups			
	WB	WG	NB	NG
8. Motives in fantasy				
Achievement				
High	6.2	5.9	5.7	6.2
Low	5.1	5.6	4.7	6.6
t and *p*	1.96(.10)	.42(N.S.)	1.88(.10)	.60(N.S.)
Affiliation				
High	6.2	5.8	5.7	6.3
Low	4.8	5.6	4.5	6.5
t and *p*	2.62(.02)	.43(N.S.)	2.43(.02)	.46(N.S.)
Power				
High	5.7	5.8	5.5	6.6
Low	5.4	5.7	4.8	6.2
t and *p*	.66(N.S.)	.26(N.S.)	1.32(N.S.)	.67(N.S.)
9. Popularity with teacher				
High	6.4	6.1	5.8	6.5
Low	4.5	4.6	4.6	4.9
t and *p*	5.10(.001)	3.90(.001)	4.16(.001)	4.55(.001)
10. Sex	5.6	5.4	5.2	6.0
t and *p*	.57(N.S.)		3.54(.001)	

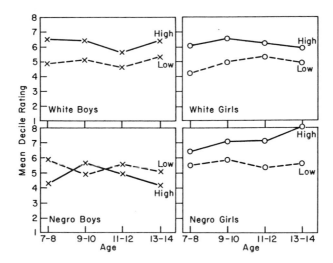

Fig. 14.1: Mean peer popularity scores for children of each sex of each race at four age levels whose fathers' education was either low (⩽8 years) or high (⩾9 years).

Employment of Parents

The mean popularity scores for the white children of both sexes whose mothers were working outside the home are higher (at a very significant level) than those of the children whose mothers were not employed (see variable 3 in Table 14.1). Moreover, this differential is found at each of four age levels, as is shown in Figure 14.2. A similar tendency is found among the Negro children, but the differences are smaller and statistically insignificant for both sexes.

Only a few fathers in Millfield were unemployed (see Chapter 1), so a similar classification was not used for them. Instead, the popularity of children whose fathers were farmers was contrasted with that of children whose fathers had significant earnings from nonfarm work. As the data in Table 14.1 show (see variable 3), this distinction has little relevance as far as the popularity of the girls is concerned, either white or Negro. With respect to the white boys, however, it appears to be a somewhat more relevant consideration. Thus, white boys whose fathers were farmers earned significantly lower popularity scores than boys whose fathers were not full-time farmers. A similar tendency among the Negro boys is so slight that it cannot be regarded as meaningful.

Size of Sibship

The next inquiry focused upon the question of whether the number of children in a child's family is related to his peer popularity. To explore

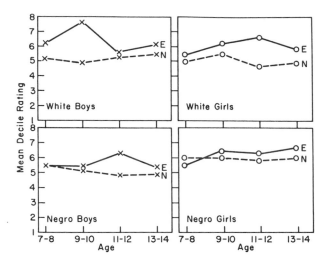

Fig. 14.2: Mean peer popularity scores for children of each sex of each race at four age levels whose mothers were either employed (E) or not employed (N).

this question, children were divided into three groups: those from families with one or two children; those from families with three or four children; and those from families with five or more children. Data bearing on this analysis may be found in Table 14.1 under variable 4.

It is apparent that no consistent distinction can be made between children from families with one or two children and those from families with three or four children, as far as peer popularity is concerned. It is also obvious that a significant difference exists between these two groups and children from larger families—families with five or more children. Thus, for each of the four groups, the children from the largest families get the lowest mean popularity scores. Furthermore, this relationship tends to hold at each of the four age levels in each of the four groups (see Figure 14.3).

It might be argued that being born into a large family enhances opportunities for the learning of multiple social skills, which in turn might be reflected in enhanced popularity among one's peers when school age is reached. But these data make it clear that such a chain of behavioral events does not occur among these children. Instead, children from large families are less popular than children from relatively small families.

Ordinal Position

Is the order of a child's birth related to his peer popularity? To investigate this question, the children were grouped according to three possible positions in their sibships: oldest children, youngest children, or children occupying middle positions.[3] The mean popularity scores earned by the children in these groups are recorded in Table 14.1 under variable 5.

The findings with respect to this factor are not sharply defined, nor are they consistent across the four groups. There are some trends, however, which perhaps should be noted. For example, among the boys, both Negro and white, the youngest children earned the highest mean popularity scores, while the oldest children had the lowest scores. Among the girls, in contrast, in-between children of both races scored the lowest. Among the white girls, it was the oldest children who got the highest mean scores; but among the Negro girls, it was the youngest ones who, like the boys of both races, obtained the highest mean scores. These are only trends, however, and their stability must remain in question until additional studies have been made.

Possessions and Services

Four variables (home ownership, car ownership, television ownership, and telephone service) were analyzed to determine if these indices of the economic status of a child's family are related to his peer popularity. Data summarizing these analyses are listed in Table 14.1.

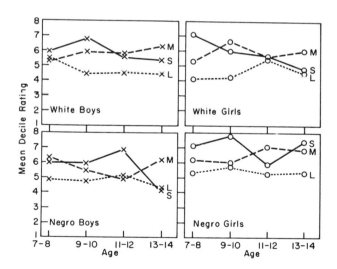

Fig. 14.3: Mean peer popularity scores for children of each sex of each race at four age levels from families with either small (S = 1–2 children), medium (M = 3–4 children), or large (L ⩾ 5 children) sibships.

[3] Children without siblings were not included in this analysis.

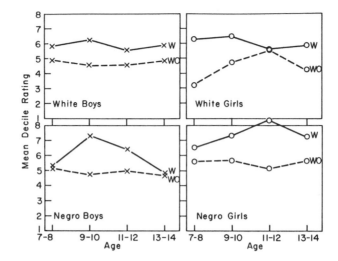

Fig. 14.4: Mean peer popularity scores for children of each sex of each race at four age levels from families either with (W) or without (WO) telephone service.

1. Home ownership. Children from families who owned or were buying their homes obtained higher mean popularity scores than children from families who were renting. This differential was present in all four groups, but it was particularly pronounced among the white boys and Negro girls.

2. Car ownership. Statistically significant differences on this variable were found only among the white groups. Higher mean popularity scores were secured by children whose families owned a car.

3. Television ownership. Although the differences in mean popularity scores consistently favored children from homes with television sets, a statistically significant difference was found only among the white boys.

4. Telephone service. Of the four variables discussed in this section, the availability of telephone service in the home proved to be the consistently best indicator of a child's popularity with his peer group. This is clearly indicated by the very significant (and for some, highly significant) differences tabulated in Table 14.1, as well as by the plots shown in Figure 14.4. In each of the four groups, children with telephone service definitely are favored.

Sixteen comparisons were made between children from homes with and without the advantages represented by these four variables. In each comparison, the mean popularity score for the more privileged group exceeded that of the less privileged. Furthermore, in ten instances, the difference was large enough to be statistically significant. It seems clear, therefore, that a meaningful positive relationship exists between the economic status of a family in Millfield and the peer popularity of its children.

THE CHILD'S INTELLIGENCE

A study was also made of how a child's intellective ability relates to his peer popularity. Intellective ability was determined by administering the Stanford-Binet Intelligence Scale (S-B), Form L-M (see Chapter 3).

Using the separate distributions of S-B IQ scores for each racial group (see curves B and C in Figure 3.1), the children were grouped into three ability levels representing the upper 25%, the middle 50%, and the lower 25% of their racial group with respect to intellective capacity. Mean peer popularity scores for the children of each IQ level at each of four age levels were then computed (separately for each racial and sex group). These mean scores have been plotted in Figure 14.5. In addition, mean popularity scores were computed for the four groups at each of the three ability levels, collapsing the age groupings. These means, along with F-tests, have been recorded in Table 14.1 as variable 7.

The data just noted show that intellective ability is very significantly and positively related to peer popularity; also, that this relationship exists at each of the four age levels. Overall, this positive relationship is

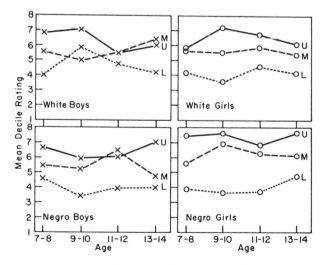

Fig. 14.5: Mean peer popularity scores for children of each sex of each race at four age levels and at three intellective levels (U = upper 25%; M = middle 50%; and L = lower 25%).

somewhat stronger among the girls than among the boys in both racial groups. Thus, it will be noted that in Figure 14.5 there are no crossovers among the three curves for either the white or the Negro girls. There are some crossovers, however, in the curves of the boys, both white and Negro. Even in the boys' data, though, there is nothing approaching a crossover between the curve for the most intelligent group and the curve for the least intelligent group.

THE CHILD'S MOTIVATIONS (FANTASY VARIABLES)

The measurement of motivational strength through the analysis of fantasy behavior has been discussed in Chapters 12 and 13. We shall now consider whether three motives (achievement, affiliation, and power) so measured relate to the peer popularity of a child. Data relevant to this problem were secured from 480 children equally divided as to race and sex; also, there were equal numbers of children at each of four age levels: 7, 9, 11, and 13 years. Each child told 12 stories; these were scored for the motives listed above at the University of Michigan under the direction of Joseph Veroff.

Achievement

Each child was classified as either high or low in the strength of his achievement imagery.[4] This was done by comparing his achievement motivation score with those secured by the other children in his racial, sex, and age group. For example, the distribution of achievement motivation scores obtained by nine-year-old white boys was formed, and their median value was determined. Boys scoring above this median value were classified as high in achievement motivation, while those falling below it were classified as low. A similar procedure was followed to classify each child in each of the other 15 groups.

After the children had been divided into two groups (high, low) at each age level in the manner just described, mean peer popularity scores were computed for each group, based on decile values. These means have been plotted in Figure 14.6.[5] Also, mean scores were computed for

[4] In this discussion, achievement imagery and achievement motivation are used interchangeably and refer to the M Ach scores described in Chapter 12. For a definition of achievement motivation, see Chapter 12.

[5] The reader will note that no mean scores have been plotted for high achievement children at age seven in Figure 14.6. At this age level, few children told any stories that contained achievement imagery (see Chapter 12). It is impossible, therefore, to cut these distributions of scores so that the high achievement group contains a sufficient number of children to provide a stable mean score.

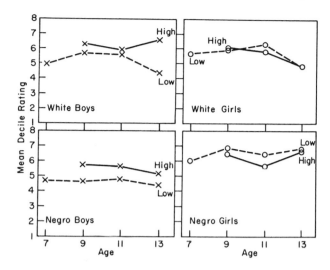

Fig. 14.6: Mean peer popularity scores for children of each sex of each race at several age levels and with either high or low M achievement imagery scores. (Means are not plotted for groups composed of less than 10 children.)

the four racial and sex groups combining the four age levels. These scores have been recorded in Table 14.1 under variable 8, along with *t*-tests computed to determine the significance of the differences between groups high and low in achievement imagery.

Boys (of both races) who produce achievement imagery relatively often in their stories tend to be chosen more often in the sociometric game than are the boys who create achievement imagery less frequently. There is little difference among the white girls, however, while among the Negro girls the relationship described above for boys is reversed at each age level. That is, the high achievement motivation groups among the Negro girls earn lower mean popularity scores than the low achievement motivation groups at each of three age levels (see Figure 14.6). The relationship between achievement motivation and peer popularity, then, appears to be complex; both the sex and race of a child must be considered in evaluating the implications for peer relationships of such imagery in his fantasy behavior.

Affiliation

The analysis of the data pertaining to affiliation imagery[6] was made in a fashion similar to that described above for achievement imagery. Plots of the mean scores so derived are shown in Figure 14.7. The

---

[6] See Chapter 13 for a definition of affiliation imagery.

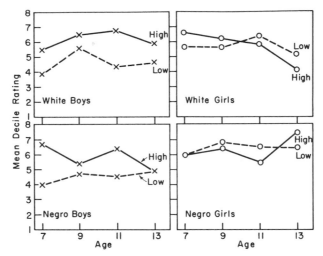

Fig. 14.7: Mean peer popularity scores for children of each sex of each race at four age levels and with either high or low M affiliation imagery scores.

analysis of the data combining the four age levels for each racial and sex group is summarized in Table 14.1 under variable 8.

As was true for achievement imagery, the differences are more pronounced among the boys than among the girls. Boys of both races who were high in affiliation imagery earned significantly higher mean popularity scores than boys who were low in affiliation imagery. For the girls of both races, the overall mean popularity scores of the high and low affiliation groups were very similar; also, the direction of the score difference from one age level to the next was less consistent among the girls than among the boys (see Figure 14.7).

Power

The analysis of the data for power imagery[7] was also made in a manner analogous to the one described above for achievement imagery. Plots of the mean popularity scores for high and low power groups are shown in Figure 14.8, while the additional analysis has been summarized in Table 14.1 under variable 8.

In each of the four groups, children high in power imagery have slightly higher mean popularity scores than children low in power imagery. However, the differences are small and statistically insignificant. Also, there is little consistency between the age levels (see Figure 14.8). Therefore, we must conclude that power motivation is not meaningfully related to peer popularity in any of the four groups.

[7] See Chapter 13 for a definition of power imagery.

In summary, our study of these three motives indicates that they do have some predictive potential with respect to peer popularity among the boys of both races; this is especially true for affiliation and secondarily for achievement motivation. In each instance, the scores have positive implications; that is, the boys whose affiliation and achievement motives are relatively strong are the ones who are likely to enjoy greater popularity with their peers. The data for the girls are much less promising, although there is the interesting possibility that high achievement motivation among Negro girls may have negative rather than positive implications as far as peer popularity is concerned.

POPULARITY WITH PEERS RELATED TO
POPULARITY WITH TEACHERS

Ordinarily, there are two foci for a child in his classroom. On the one hand, there is his peer group; on the other, his teacher. Sometimes a child may seem to curry favor in one of these quarters at the expense of alienating himself in the other. The available data made it possible for us to explore empirically the question of whether children popular with their peer groups are in fact also popular with their teachers. This inquiry was made in the following way.

In the spring of 1962 each teacher in Millfield's four schools completed a behavior rating scale (see Chapters 2 and 10, and Appendix E)

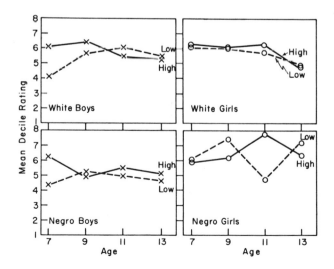

Fig. 14.8: Mean peer popularity scores for children of each sex of each race at four age levels and with either high or low M power imagery scores.

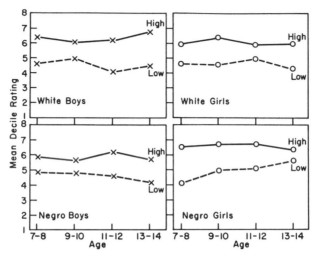

Fig. 14.9: Mean peer popularity scores for children of each sex of each race at four age levels who were either high or low in popularity with their teachers.

for each of her pupils. Item 22, the last item on the scale, asked the teacher to rate the pupil in terms of her personal feelings for the child —that is, to what extent she either liked or disliked him. For the purpose of this analysis, a distribution of ratings on this item was formed separately for each teacher.[8] Each of these distributions, then, was cut as close to the median value as possible. A child who had been placed below this median value was characterized as high in popularity with his teacher, whereas a child who had been placed above this value was characterized as low in popularity with his teacher, forming thereby two groups, highs and lows.

Mean decile scores were computed for each of four age levels of children rated high or low by their teachers. These means, which were computed separately for each of the four racial and sex groups, have been plotted in Figure 14.9. In addition, grand means (combining the four age levels) were computed for each of the four groups. These scores have been recorded in Table 14.1 as variable 9, along with the results of t-tests run to test the significance of these differences.

The plots in Figure 14.9, along with the data in Table 14.1, make it perfectly clear that, in general, the child who is popular with his teachers is also the child who is popular with his peers. Also, the child who is negatively evaluated at one of the two foci in the classroom is

---

[8] The ratings of one fourth-grade teacher were dropped from the study, however, because she assigned the same rating to each of her pupils.

likely to be judged negatively at the other. These conclusions are valid for the children of both races, of both sexes, and at each age level studied.

We suspect, furthermore, that the child who is disliked by both his peer group and his teacher very often senses his unfavored position, at some level within himself. And, since the patterns described above are identifiable in the earliest grades (note, for example, the gap at ages seven and eight between the highs and lows of each group in Figure 14.9), their implications for the child's future course of development within the school context must be considerable. At the very least, we certainly need to learn through empirical studies much more about their possible implications. Do unpopular children, for example, become alienated from school, taking an early opportunity to drop out? Do some fight back, and, if so, how? Is there some way to predict which child will fight and which child will withdraw? We need, in short, to study children longitudinally to better understand the true significance of both popularity and unpopularity in the classroom. In addition, we should undertake more analytical studies of popularity in order to see both what it is based upon and how it may be modified.

SEX DIFFERENCES IN POPULARITY

In most of the presentations thus far, portions of the data have been considered separately for each of the four groups of white and Negro boys and girls. Now, perhaps somewhat belatedly, we shall consider the question of whether consistent sex differences exist in peer popularity.

It should be noted that within each racial group approximately equal numbers of boys and girls participated in the sociometric game. There was some variation in their relative numbers, however, from one age to another. The exact numbers of boys and girls in each of the racial groups at each of the eight age levels are given in Table 14.2. Mean peer popularity scores were computed for each of these 32 groups; these scores are plotted in Figure 14.10. Overall mean scores for the four racial and sex groups are recorded in Table 14.1 as variable 10.

It is apparent from inspection of Figure 14.10 that a consistent sex difference exists among the Negro children but not among the white children. For the former, the mean scores of the girls exceed those of the boys at each age level, whereas for the latter there is no trend in either direction. Also, the sex difference among the Negro children appears to be larger at the upper age levels.

These findings on the preferences of the Negro children are dis-

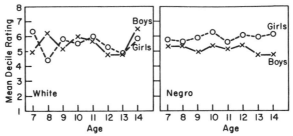

Fig. 14.10: Mean peer popularity scores for each sex of each race at eight age levels.

turbing. A relatively disparaging view of the adult Negro male is, of course, quite commonly held by Negro adults of both sexes (see, for example, Kardiner and Ovesey, 1951). Therefore, perhaps it would not be surprising to see such views reflected in the choice behavior of early teenagers (for example, the two oldest groups). Finding a consistent sex preference during the early school years, however, suggests that such attitudes probably have been well-formed during preschool years. In terms of peer acceptance or rejection, these Negro boys are already at a disadvantage at the very beginning of their school experiences.

CONCLUDING COMMENTS

The data presented in this chapter clearly indicate that peer popularity is a meaningful concept to apply to these children, even at the lowest

TABLE 14.2

The Number of Children Participating in the Sociometric Game at Each of Eight Ages

Age	Racial and sex groups			
	WB*	WG	NB	NG
7	25	23	31	28
8	28	34	44	42
9	19	21	45	41
10	24	29	32	39
11	24	25	42	36
12	23	30	43	33
13	33	35	38	42
14	34	22	44	33
Totals	210	219	319	294

* Abbreviations: WB = white boys; WG = white girls; NB = Negro boys; NG = Negro girls.

age levels studied. Furthermore, the fact that there is a high degree of agreement between the ratings made by teachers and those made by classmates suggests that the qualifying term "peer" might justifiably be dropped from the descriptive term. In other words, it can be argued that the children tend to have a social stimulus value which causes both other children and adults to respond to them similarly.

A number of the variables investigated suggest that the social class level of a child is a factor operating within both the white and Negro groups to affect his popularity. Thus, the more popular children tend to come from families in which the parents have higher educations, have two incomes (one provided by a working mother), have a small number of children, and have more possessions and services than the parents of the children who are less popular. There is no evidence, however, that the above factors operate directly to influence the choices of the children. That is, it cannot be said that Johnny chooses Jimmy because he comes from a well-educated family, or one with money, and so on. It is more likely, we believe, that families rear their children differently when they are better educated, when their aspirations lead both parents to work, and so on, creating behavior patterns in their children which are different from those developed by their less well-educated and less ambitious neighbors. The child's peer group and his teacher respond to these differential behavior patterns, then, rather than directly to components of his social class standing.

It is also important to recognize that a child's intellective ability is strongly correlated with his popularity. Acting "smart" probably works to a child's disadvantage, but, clearly, being smart does not. Again, however, a child's brightness may not operate in a direct way to influence his popularity. Instead, the bright child may simply be quicker and more adept in developing a number of behavior patterns, including social skills, than the dull child. This interpretation of intelligence operating indirectly receives some confirmation from the interviews conducted with eighth-grade children (see Chapter 16). In these interviews, the children, in talking about what makes a child popular in Millfield, almost always mentioned social rather than intellective skills. Another possibility to be considered is that the relationship of popularity to measured IQ is an artifact of the relationship that popularity has to socioeconomic level. Thus, it will be recalled that in Chapter 5 considerable evidence was cited to show the close relationship between ability test performance and socioeconomic level.

The findings with respect to the relevance of motivational variables, insofar as these are validly assessed by the fantasy approach, are more complex than those relating to the socioeconomic and intellective variables. Of the three motives studied, the strongest relationship between motive and popularity emerged for affiliation. Considering the definition of this motive, perhaps this finding is not surprising. It is a meaningful relationship, however, only for the boys (of both races). And, again, it is only for the boys that a positive relationship tends to develop between achievement motivation and popularity. There is no ready explanation for this pattern of findings.

Finally, we must reemphasize that Negro girls received higher popularity scores at each age level than Negro boys, but such a sex difference was not found among the white children. This would appear to be a very important finding, for it indicates that at the age of seven the male in this Negro culture is in a disadvantageous position relative to the female. Already, at this young age, his alleged unattractiveness is being emphasized.

Part V

PERSONAL PERSPECTIVES

Chapter 15

MOTHERS OF KINDERGARTEN-
AGE CHILDREN REPORT ON THEIR
CHILDREN, TRAINING PRACTICES, AND FAMILIES

We turn our attention now to the first of two studies which used the interview as the chief assessment device. More particularly, we shall focus on kindergarten-age children and their worlds, as both are described by the children's mothers. In so doing we hope to expand our appreciation and understanding of the many factors that interact to shape the personal development of children growing up in Millfield.

PROCEDURE

The Children and the Informants

An effort was made to interview the mother of each Negro and each white child who attended kindergarten during the 1962–63 and 1963–64 academic years, as well as the mother of each child in the control groups (see Chapters 2 and 8). These interviews were conducted during the year when the child was actually enrolled in the kindergarten. Since some families had two different children in the kindergarten program (one during each of the two years), for the purpose of this study, data were included only for the first child to attend kindergarten. (If this procedure had not been followed, some mothers would have contributed more than once to the statistical data.)

In all, the data reported in this chapter pertain to 200 children: 51 white boys, 59 white girls, 36 Negro boys, and 54 Negro girls. The mean

343

age of these children when their mothers were first interviewed was approximately five years and nine months; at the time of the second interview, their mean age was just about six years (see Table 15.1). No child was less than five years of age at the time of the first interview nor more than six and one-half years of age at the time of the second interview. Forty-five percent of the white children and 47% of the Negro children were attending kindergarten. The mean S-B IQ of the white children was in the upper 90's; that of the Negro children was in the lower 90's (see Table 15.1).

For 191 of the 200 children, the child's natural mother served as the informant for the interviews. For the remaining nine children, information was provided by a mother-substitute.[1] Forty-eight percent of the white mothers and 55% of the Negro mothers were interviewed during the 1962–63 academic year; the remaining mothers were interviewed during the 1963–64 school year.[2]

The Structured Interview

An interview schedule was developed so that comparable information would be secured by the several interviewers. The items were generally structured to specify what the interviewers would ask and to direct the form of the answers. This mother interview schedule was created with the active cooperation of the staff members who eventually used it; considerable effort was made to keep the format and wording as natural as possible. Before the schedule was used, the interviewers became thoroughly familiar with it by means of role-playing techniques. (The interview schedule has been reproduced in Appendix A.)

The interview schedule was lengthy. Largely because of its length, it was divided into two parts. Also, it was felt that two visits with a mother might be more productive than one. At the end of each of the two sessions, the interviewer used several rating scales to record various judgments about the interview situation and the mother (see Appendix A).

We attempted to make this a comprehensive study. Thus, the mother was asked about her pregnancy with the child, his developmental difficulties, his current motor skills, his temperamental and personality

[1] It could be argued that data for these nine children should have been dropped from the analysis, yet, since they represent less than 5% of the sample, it seems unlikely that their inclusion has led to any marked alteration in the findings. Moreover, there was no apparent difference in the kinds of answers given by the mother-substitutes and the natural mothers.

[2] All informants will be called "mother" throughout this chapter, referring to both natural mothers and mother-substitutes.

attributes, his intellective talents and motivations, his interpersonal skills, and his misbehaviors. At the beginning of the second interviewing session, the items from the Vineland Social Maturity Scale were incorporated into the interview schedule so that the children could be compared in terms of scores secured on this assessment device. The focus was not entirely upon the child, however, for questions were also directed toward the family—its history, its material resources, its role or amount of involvement in community institutions, its behavior toward the child, and so on. In sum, a real effort was made not only to assess the child's behavior but also to evaluate critical components of the family context in which he was being reared. Some understanding of the range of material covered can be gathered by examining the data recorded in Tables 15.1 through 15.12.

Conducting the Interviews

As noted above, two sessions were held with each mother. On the average, approximately three months elapsed between the two sessions. At least one of the sessions was conducted in the child's home. With some mothers, when it was convenient for them, the second of the two sessions was held in a small house which served as headquarters for the project in Millfield.

Uninterrupted interviews were not always possible, especially in the homes. Occasionally, too, the confidentiality of the exchange was compromised either by the intrusion of other people into the interview or by the fact that the structure of the home made it impossible to rule out the possibility that others could be listening through the walls. At the end of each session, the interviewer made judgments about the conduct of the interview and the extent to which confidentiality had been maintained. These judgments have been recorded separately for each session in Table 15.1 (see questions 9 through 12). These data show that less than 10% of the interviews were seriously interrupted and that confidentiality was compromised even less frequently.

Table 15.1 also provides a record of the judgments made by the interviewers about the degree of rapport which they felt they had been able to achieve with the mothers (see questions 13 and 14). These data show that, in the interviewers' judgments, they were very warmly received by a large majority of the mothers. Thus, for 90% of the interviews the mothers were rated as being either "Very hospitable" or "Friendly." In only 10% of the sessions did the interviewers feel that they had received a cool reception.

In summary, while the interviews were sometimes carried out in less

TABLE 15.1
Background Data and Conduct of Interview

Question	Response	Frequencies or means				p values*						
							Race			Sex		
		WB	WG	NB	NG	O	$\frac{N}{W}$	$\frac{NB}{WB}$	$\frac{NG}{WG}$	$\frac{B}{G}$	$\frac{NB}{NG}$	$\frac{WB}{WG}$
1. How many children were in each group?		51	59	36	54							
2. How many children were attending kindergarten?		28	21	14	28							
3. What was the mean age of the children at first interview (months)?		68.6	68.2	68.7	69.0							
4. What was the mean age of the children at second interview (months)?		72.2	71.4	71.8	72.0							
5. What was the children's mean IQ?		95.8	100.5	92.1	91.5	.01	.001		.001			
S.D.?		16.9	15.1	9.9	11.4							
Range?		61–139	73–137	70–113	56–110							
6. For how many children was the natural mother the informant?		49	57	34	51							
7. How many informants were interviewed each academic year?	1962–63	27	26	20	30							
	1963–64	24	33	16	24							

		NB/WB	WB/WG	NG/WG		O
8. No. of mothers interviewed by W1?		24		24		
No. of mothers interviewed by W2?		19		29		
No. of mothers interviewed by W3?		8		6		
No. of mothers interviewed by N1?		7		9		
No. of mothers interviewed by N2?		29		45		
9. Were there serious interruptions during interview 1?	Yes	4	5	1	2	
	No	44	51	34	49	
10. Were there serious interruptions during interview 2?	Yes	6	8	3	2	
	No	44	50	31	51	
11. Was confidentiality easily preserved during interview 1?	Yes	44	51	29	47	
	No	2	3	3	1	
12. Was confidentiality easily preserved during interview 2?	Yes	43	53	31	47	
	No	4	3	1	6	
13. What degree of rapport existed during interview 1?	Very hospitable	10	24	13	19	.10
	Friendly	33	28	21	26	
	Cool	4	3	1	6	
14. What degree of rapport existed during interview 2?	Very hospitable	15	18	14	20	
	Friendly	27	30	20	27	
	Cool	8	8	1	6	

* Based upon chi-square, F-, and t-tests.

O = overall test.

$\dfrac{N}{W}$ = Negro vs. white children; $\dfrac{NB}{WB}$ = Negro boys vs. white boys; $\dfrac{NG}{WG}$ = Negro girls vs. white girls.

$\dfrac{B}{G}$ = boys vs. girls; $\dfrac{NB}{NG}$ = Negro boys vs. Negro girls; $\dfrac{WB}{WG}$ = white boys vs. white girls.

than ideal circumstances, these difficulties ordinarily were offset by the fact that the interviewers were received in a hospitable manner. In almost every instance, the interviewer was able to work cooperatively with the mother so that the interview gave a good picture of the child and his background.

In keeping with our usual procedure, mothers were interviewed by staff members of the same race. Each interviewer was a mature woman; four of the five women who served as interviewers had children of their own. Actually, 87% of the white mothers were interviewed by two white interviewers, while 82% of the Negro mothers were interviewed by one Negro interviewer. The number of interviews conducted by each of the five interviewers has been tabulated in Table 15.1 (see question 8).

Analysis of the Data

Questions in the interview were arranged in a sequence which was intended to promote an easy and natural flow of communication between the two participants. In presenting the data, however, this natural order will not be followed; instead, the data have been organized under twelve headings. Therefore, a particular type of information will be found under its appropriate heading irrespective of where it happened to be elicited within either of the two parts of the total interview. The twelve headings used to organize the data can be examined by referring to the titles of Tables 15.1 through 15.12.

It should be understood that not all the data elicited in the interviews have been summarized in these 12 tables; space does not permit such a full summary. The data included, however, were not selected on the basis of the results of the statistical analysis; that is, the significance or lack of significance of the findings was not a determinant of what data were included or omitted. Rather, we have tried to include findings which, in our judgment, are the most interesting and most relevant to the children's personal development.

Most of the data in the 12 tables are in the form of frequency counts, with separate entries for each of the four groups: white boys, white girls, Negro boys, and Negro girls. In column 1 of these tables, questions are asked for which answers can ordinarily be found in the interview material. In column 2, the response categories (when appropriate) are given which were used to summarize the information provided by the mothers. In columns 3, 4, 5, and 6 the frequency with which each of these response categories was used is given for each of the four sub-groups. Finally, in the remaining columns, the results of the statistical tests are listed which were significant at or beyond the .10 level.

For the frequency data, seven chi-square tests were run for each item in each of the 12 tables:

O — an overall or total chi-square

$\dfrac{N}{W}$ — a racial comparison; all Negro vs. all white children

$\dfrac{NB}{WB}$ — a racial comparison; Negro boys vs. white boys

$\dfrac{NG}{WG}$ — a racial comparison; Negro girls vs. white girls

$\dfrac{B}{G}$ — a sex comparison; all boys vs. all girls

$\dfrac{NB}{NG}$ — a sex comparison; Negro boys vs. Negro girls

$\dfrac{WB}{WG}$ — a sex comparison; white boys vs. white girls

In a few instances, means rather than frequencies have been recorded in columns 3 through 6 of the 12 tables. For these questions, F values were computed to evaluate the significance of the differences among the four subgroups. When a significant F value was obtained, t-tests were run to make each of the last six comparisons noted above in the description of the chi-square analyses. Significant F- and t-tests have been recorded in the last seven columns of the 12 tables following the coding system used for the chi-square tests (significant F's are recorded in column O).

RESULTS

The discussion of the results of this study has been built around the information summarized in Tables 15.2 through 15.12. The first four of these tables contain data about the children's families, their parents, and training practices used by the parents. The last seven tables focus upon the children's developmental histories, skills, abilities, personal traits, and misbehaviors.

Family Structures, Resources, and Activities

The data discussed in this unit have been summarized in Table 15.2.

Most of the children were living with both of their natural parents when these interviews were conducted. However, there was a very sig-

TABLE 15.2
Family Structures, Resources, and Activities

Question	Response	Frequencies or means				p values*						
		WB	WG	NB	NG	O	Race N/W	Race NB/WB	Race NG/WG	Sex B/G	Sex NB/NG	Sex WB/WG
1. Does the child live with both natural parents?	Yes	45	54	28	37	.01	.01		.01			
	No	6	5	8	17							
2. Was the child born out of wedlock?	Yes	2	0	3	10	.01	.01		.01			
	No	49	59	31	41							
3. Does the child live with his natural mother?	Yes	51	59	35	52							
	No	0	0	1	2							
4. Does the child live with his natural father?	Yes	45	54	28	37	.01	.01		.01			
	No	6	5	8	17							
5. Is the child without either a father or father-substitute?	Yes	3	2	1	7							
	No	48	57	35	47							
6. Are more than two adults living in the home?	Yes	13	15	10	17							
	No	38	44	26	36							
7. Are one or more grandparents living in the home?	Yes	9	5	4	12			.10				
	No	42	54	32	42							
8. Mean number of children in the family, including the child?		3.2	4.0	5.7	5.0	.001	.001	.001	.05			.10

		3.1	3.7	5.7	5.4	.001	.001	.001	.01	.01
9. Mean number of children in the home, including the child?		3.1	3.7	5.7	5.4	.001	.001	.001	.01	
10. What is the child's ordinal position, relative to full sibs?	Only	5	6	2	3	.10	.05			.01
	Oldest	11	9	2	7					
	Youngest	20	25	8	19					
	In-between	15	19	24	23					
11. Mean number of people living in the home?		5.4	6.0	8.1	8.0	.001	.001	.001	.001	
12. What was the total family income last year?	<$2500	5	9	19	27	.001	.001	.01	.001	
	$2500–5000	14	7	12	18					
	>$5000	11	16	4	3					
13. How many persons contributed to the family's income last year?	1	28	33	22	24	.10	.01	.05		
	2	21	23	10	18					
	3 or more	1	2	4	9					
14. Do the child's parents own their home (or are buying)?	Yes	37	39	13	23	.001	.001	.001	.05	
	No	13	19	23	31					
15. Does the family pay rent by sharing crops?	Yes	1	7	13	16	.001	.001	.001	.05	.10
	No	50	51	23	38					
16. Does the family have electricity?	Yes	49	57	35	53					
	No	2	0	0	0					
17. Does the family have an inside toilet?	Yes	34	37	5	8	.001	.001	.001	.001	
	No	17	22	31	46					

(continued)

TABLE 15.2 (continued)

Question	Response	Frequencies or means				p values*						
		WB	WG	NB	NG	O	Race			Sex		
							$\frac{N}{W}$	$\frac{NB}{WB}$	$\frac{NG}{WG}$	$\frac{B}{G}$	$\frac{NB}{NG}$	$\frac{WB}{WG}$
18. Does the family have a TV set?	Yes	49	56	33	50							
	No	2	1	2	0							
19. Is visiting mentioned as a source of pleasure?	Yes	17	23	12	26							
	No	34	36	24	28							
20. Are movies mentioned as a source of pleasure?	Yes	12	17	3	3	.01	.001		.01			
	No	38	42	33	51							
21. Are church activities mentioned as a source of pleasure?	Yes	12	12	22	34	.001	.001	.001	.001			
	No	39	47	14	20							
22. Are mother and father of the same religious faith?	Yes	31	41	19	23	.05	.05		.05			
	No	12	11	14	19							
23. How adequate was the family's adjustment judged to be?	Good	26	44	21	27	.01	.05		.01			.05
	Poor	20	10	15	26							

* Based upon chi-square, F-, and t-tests.

O = overall test.

$\frac{N}{W}$ = Negro vs. white children; $\frac{NB}{WB}$ = Negro boys vs. white boys; $\frac{NG}{WG}$ = Negro girls vs. white girls.

$\frac{B}{G}$ = boys vs. girls; $\frac{NB}{NG}$ = Negro boys vs. Negro girls; $\frac{WB}{WG}$ = white boys vs. white girls.

nificant racial difference; 90% of the white children but only 72% of the Negro children were living with both of their natural parents. Of the four groups, the Negro girls were more frequently not living with both of their natural parents. Except for three children (all Negro), each child was living with his natural mother. In contrast, 36 children were living apart from their natural fathers. Again, there was a very significant racial difference, with more Negro children being separated from their natural fathers. In most instances, though, children separated from their natural fathers had father-substitutes in their homes; this was true for the children of both races. Only 5% of the white children and 9% of the Negro children were living without either their natural fathers or father-substitutes. In large part, the greater prevalence of natural-father absence among Negro children may be traced to the fact that more Negro than white children had been born out of wedlock (13 vs. 2, respectively).

As the data discussed in Chapter 1 would lead one to expect, the homes of these children tended to be crowded, especially those of the Negro children. Thus, the mean number of people living in the Negro homes was slightly above eight, while in the white homes it was a bit less than six. About 28% of the homes contained more than two adults; there was no significant racial difference in this regard. Nor was there a significant racial difference with respect to the frequency of grand-parents living in the home; overall, at least one grandparent was living in 15% of the homes. There was, however, a highly significant racial difference with respect both to the number of children in the family and the number of children actually living in the home at the time when the interviews were conducted. On the average, 62% more children were living in the Negro homes than in the white homes.

Given this marked racial difference in the typical number of children in a family, one might very well expect significant differences in the frequencies of various ordinal positions among the white and Negro children. This, indeed, was found to be true. White children are more likely to be classified as "Only," "Oldest," or "Youngest" children than are the Negro children, whereas the latter are more likely to be classi-fied as "In-between." With respect to ordinal position, there is also a very significant sex difference in these samples, owing primarily to the fact that more girls than boys are the youngest children in their families.

Although the families tend to be large, incomes certainly do not. And, as might be expected, the income of the Negro family usually falls markedly behind that of the white family. For example, 55% of the Negro mothers compared to 23% of the white mothers reported yearly family income of less than $2500. In contrast, 44% of the white mothers but only

8% of the Negro mothers reported yearly family incomes in excess of $5000.[3] It is quite common, moreover, for this total family income to be dependent upon the earning power of more than one member of the family. Thus, 44% of the white mothers and 47% of the Negro mothers reported that two or more persons contributed to the family's income during the year just completed.[4] Thirteen Negro mothers and three white mothers indicated that the family's income was dependent upon the earning power of three or more persons.

Consistent with this income differential, it was found that many more white than Negro families either owned or were buying their homes, while appreciably more Negro families were "farming on shares" (the local phrase for sharecropping arrangements). In terms of certain household resources or appliances, there was marked racial comparability; for others, there were pronounced racial differences. Almost all homes, white and Negro, had electricity and television sets, for example, but inside toilets were quite uncommon in the Negro homes compared to the white homes (14% vs. 65%, respectively).

When the interviewers asked about the kinds of activities that the parents shared for pleasure, the range of answers was usually quite limited. The racial patterns did differ, however. White mothers most often mentioned visiting, followed by movies and then church functions. In contrast, Negro mothers mentioned church functions most often, followed by visiting and movies (only six Negro mothers actually mentioned the latter). Watching television was mentioned infrequently, probably because the mothers considered it to be a routine family activity carried on within the home.

At the end of the first interview session, the interviewer rated the adjustment of the family. There was a significant racial difference in this regard in favor of the white families. Although the interviewing teams sought to implement a standard frame of reference for these ratings, it is difficult to determine what weight can be attached to this particular finding, since the several interviewers may have used different criteria.

These data, while not exhaustive, make it clear that family life in Millfield is not the same for the Negro and the white people. While the two races live in close proximity to one another, the structures of their families, their material resources, and their activity patterns tend to differ in many important ways.

[3] These figures are based upon information provided by 92% of the Negro mothers and by 56% of the white mothers. In many instances, the white interviewers did not inquire about family finances (see Chapter 1). In other instances, both Negro and white mothers gave vague answers which could not be classified reliably.

[4] Each mother of both races was asked how many persons contributed to the family's income even if she was not asked to reveal its amount.

Mothers' Histories and Attributes

Data relevant to the mothers' backgrounds and general characteristics have been tabulated in Table 15.3.

Most of the mothers of both races come from North Carolina families; moreover, a large majority of them were born in one of the nuclear counties.[5] There is much more homogeneity in this regard, however, among Negro mothers than among white mothers. Only two Negro mothers are known to have been born outside the nuclear counties, compared to 33 white mothers.

The fact that the families' roots are firmly planted in Millfield is also indicated by the fact that 65% of the white mothers and 75% of the Negro mothers have lived there for at least 10 years. This means, of course, that they were well settled in Millfield before the children who are the focus of this particular study were born. Furthermore, most of the mothers (81% of the white, 89% of the Negro) have relatives living in Millfield who provide them with immediate outlets for the extension of family activities. Another thing that many of the mothers have in common is the fact that their fathers were farmers. This is true more often for the Negro than for the white mothers (72% vs. 50%, respectively).

The mothers' educational backgrounds and aspirations show interesting racial similarities and contrasts. There was, on the average, less than one year's difference between the mean years of education reported by the mothers of the two races (10.4 for white mothers, 9.6 for Negro mothers). On the other hand, there was a marked difference in the quality of their schoolwork, *as the mothers of the two races reported it.* Seventy-seven percent of the Negro mothers but only 42% of the white mothers said that they had done above average work in school. Very similar figures—again in favor of the Negro mothers—were also secured when they were asked if they had wanted to go further in school. It cannot be determined, of course, how accurate these statements are in summarizing actual school achievements. However, they may be indicative of the current value that the mothers are placing upon education. That is, Negro mothers may be especially sensitive to the fact that education provides the primary hope for members of their race (including their children) to escape from a disadvantaged position.

Negro and white mothers also show both similarities and differences in their work histories. Overall, 82% of the mothers reported having worked at one time or another since leaving school; there is no significant racial difference in this regard. Nor is there a significant racial

[5] Four counties which almost touch at a common point on the northwest corner of Millfield.

TABLE 15.3
Mothers' Histories and Attributes

| Question | Response | Frequencies or means | | | | p values* | | | | | | |
		WB	WG	NB	NG	O	Race $\frac{N}{W}$	Race $\frac{NB}{WB}$	Race $\frac{NG}{WG}$	Sex $\frac{B}{G}$	Sex $\frac{NB}{NG}$	Sex $\frac{WB}{WG}$
1. Was the child's mother born in a nuclear county?	Yes	36	41	34	52	.001	.001	.01	.001			
	No	15	18	1	1							
2. How many years has mother lived in Millfield?	0–3	9	6	7	3							
	4–9	11	10	4	5							
	≥10	30	35	23	35							
3. Does mother have relatives living in Millfield?	Yes	36	49	31	48							
	No	12	8	5	5							
4. Was mother's father a farmer?	Yes	23	30	25	33	.05	.01	.05				
	No	26	27	9	14							
5. Mean years of education for mothers?		10.3	10.4	9.4	9.7		.05					
6. Did mother do above average work in school?	Yes	24	21	26	42	.001	.001	.05	.001			
	No	25	37	9	11							
7. Did mother want to go further in school than she did?	Yes	20	20	25	45	.001	.001	.05	.001			
	No	25	36	10	7							
8. Has mother worked since leaving school?	Yes	44	49	30	40							
	No	7	10	5	13							
9. Is mother working now?	Yes	23	21	10	19							
	No	27	30	25	34							
10. Does mother work in a mill or factory?	Yes	12	13	0	0	.001	.001	.01	.001			
	No	39	46	36	54							
11. Is mother a domestic worker?	Yes	0	0	3	14	.001	.001	.001	.001	.05	.05	.10
	No	51	59	33	40							

		Col 1	Col 2	Col 3	Col 4					
12.	What is mother's religion?									.01
	Baptist	24	16	20	27					
	Methodist	11	22	10	21					
	Presbyterian	7	11	0	0					
	Other	7	6	5	5					
13.	Does mother attend church 3 or more times each month?									
	Yes	27	30	11	13	.001	.001	.05	.01	
	No	22	22	25	40					
14.	Does mother often go to revivals?									
	Yes	30	34	31	50	.01	.01	.10	.05	
	No	13	13	4	4					
15.	Has the child's mother been married before?									
	Yes	3	7	2	3		.10			
	No	45	51	33	49					
16.	Does mother have children by a previous marriage or union?									
	Yes	6	6	7	12		.10			
	No	45	53	29	41					
17.	Mean age of mothers when children were born?	26.0	28.2	27.9	27.2					
18.	Was mother pleased to become pregnant with this child?									
	Yes	28	31	8	18	.001	.001	.001	.05	
	No	8	10	18	20					
19.	Did mother think it a bad time to have a baby?									
	Yes	17	14	17	18	.05	.01		.05	
	No	27	39	13	17					
20.	Did mother want the child to be a boy or a girl?									
	Boy	17	16	12	10		.10		.10	
	Girl	12	16	11	24					
	Either	22	24	12	14					
21.	Does mother want to have more children?									
	Yes	5	15	2	5	.05	.10	.10	.10	
	No	31	33	25	33					
22.	Is mother judged to be admiring of her husband?									
	Yes	31	42	15	28	.05	.10	.10	.10	.10
	No	16	16	20	15					
23.	Was mother or father judged to be more dominant?									
	Mother	42	42	23	38	.05	.05	.01	.01	
	Father	4	12	12	16					
24.	Does mother often have to take the child's side against father?									
	Yes	6	6	4	1					
	No	39	49	29	39					

(continued)

TABLE 15.3 (*continued*)

Question	Response	Frequencies or means				p values*						
		WB	WG	NB	NG	O	$\frac{N}{W}$	$\frac{NB}{WB}$	$\frac{NG}{WG}$	$\frac{B}{G}$	$\frac{NB}{NG}$	$\frac{WB}{WG}$
							Race			Sex		
25. Does mother say that she often shows her feelings?	Yes	46	48	35	53	.10	.05		.10			
	No	4	7	1	1							
26. What was mother's basic attitude toward the child judged to be?	Defensive	14	14	6	17							
	Objective	32	41	23	32							
	Critical	4	3	6	4							
27. Does mother seem to know her child well?	Yes	40	44	23	36							
	No	11	13	12	17							
28. Is mother judged to be responsive to her child's needs and interests?	Yes	33	44	20	24	.05	.01		.01			
	No	18	14	14	28							
29. Was mother judged to be responsible about child rearing?	Yes	44	53	28	43	.01	.001	.10	.01			
	No	3	1	8	11							
30. Was mother judged as placing heavy emphasis on child's physical well-being?	Yes	24	33	26	39	.10	.05	.10				
	No	23	22	10	15							
31. How permissive was mother judged to be?	Permissive	20	30	21	39	.05	.05		.10	.10		
	Strict	26	25	15	15							
32. How warm was mother's relationship with the child judged to be?	Warm	41	48	30	46							
	Cool	5	7	6	8							

* Based upon chi-square, F-, and t-tests.

O = overall test.

$\frac{N}{W}$ = Negro vs. white children; $\frac{NB}{WB}$ = Negro boys vs. white boys; $\frac{NG}{WG}$ = Negro girls vs. white girls.

$\frac{B}{G}$ = boys vs. girls; $\frac{NB}{NG}$ = Negro boys vs. Negro girls; $\frac{WB}{WG}$ = white boys vs. white girls.

difference in the percentages of the mothers who were holding jobs at the time of the interviews (overall, 39% of the mothers were). There was a sharp difference, however, with respect to the type of job currently being held by the mothers of the two races. The most common job among the white mothers was mill or factory work, a type of employment that no Negro mother reported. In contrast, only Negro mothers were employed in domestic service.

Racial differences also emerged when the religious affiliations and practices of the mothers were examined. More mothers of both races belong to the Baptist church than to any other denomination, but the proportion of the Negro mothers affiliated with this church exceeds that for the white mothers (53% vs. 38%, respectively). Running second in frequency, again for both races, is the Methodist church. In terms of church attendance, white mothers apparently attend much more often than Negro mothers.[6] Revivals are popular with both races, although attendance at these affairs seems to be more common among Negro mothers.

Only 8% of the mothers reported a prior marriage, but 16% said that they had at least one child either by a previous marriage or union. Previous marriages were more common among the white mothers, whereas more Negro mothers reported that they had had children out of wedlock. Overall, the mean age of these mothers was slightly more than 27 years when the children who are at the focus of these interviews were born. With regard to this age, there was no significant racial difference.

There was a pronounced racial difference, however, in the attitude of the mother toward this particular pregnancy and baby. Thus, 77% of the white mothers said that they had been pleased to become pregnant with this child, but 59% of the Negro mothers said that they had *not* been pleased. Also, more Negro than white mothers said that it had been a bad time to have a baby. It is apparent, therefore, that more Negro than white children in the sample began their lives as unwanted children. As far as the sex of the child was concerned, white mothers indicated that they had had a slight preference for a boy, whereas proportionately more Negro mothers said that they had wanted a girl. Relatively few mothers (overall, only 18%) said that they wanted to have additional children.

The interviewers also attempted to assess certain aspects of the mothers' relationships with their husbands. Most wives expressed admiration for their husbands, but there was a tendency for these positive

[6] Attendance data may be misleading, however, since some Negro churches are able to secure the services of a minister on a biweekly basis only.

attitudes to be expressed more frequently by the white than by the Negro wives. In more than three-fourths of the cases, the interviewer judged the wife to be dominant in the relationship with her husband. Since Negro families are so often described as matriarchal in character, it was a little surprising to find that father dominance was assigned significantly more often to the Negro families than to the white families. Few Negro or white wives felt that they had to intervene very often to take the child's side against his father. As far as her own feelings were concerned, 93% of the mothers said that they did indeed show their feelings often (Negro mothers said yes significantly more often than white mothers).

The last seven items in Table 15.3 summarize data secured from the rating scales which were completed by the interviewer and which pertain to the mother's relationship with her child. Some of these judgments were made at the conclusion of session one, while others were made at the end of session two. The analyses indicate significant racial differences on four of the seven items. White interviewers judged mothers as being more responsive to their child's needs and interests than did Negro interviewers. Negro mothers, however, were more often judged as being permissive. They were also judged as placing greater emphasis upon the child's physical well-being, but at the same time as being more irresponsible about child-rearing. No significant racial differences were recorded with respect to how well the mother seemed to know her child, the objectivity of her attitude toward him, or the degree of warmth that seemed to exist in the mother–child relationship.

In summary, these mothers are essentially country women with firm roots either in Millfield or its immediately surrounding area. While there are a number of similarities in the life patterns of the Negro and white mothers, there are also important differences, some of which probably influence the way in which they rear their young. Perhaps of greatest importance in this regard is the indication that most of the Negro children in this sample were unwanted, whereas most of the white children were wanted by their mothers.

Fathers' Histories and Attributes

Data pertaining to the children's fathers have been summarized in Table 15.4.[7] In the discussion that follows, some comparisons will be made between these data and the data in Table 15.3.

---

[7] The data on the background characteristics of the fathers pertain in all cases to their natural fathers. Some of the data reported later, however, refer to activities of fathers or father-substitutes, whichever was present in the home of the child at the time of the study.

The fathers, like the mothers, come predominantly from North Carolina stock; most of them also were born in one of the nuclear counties. Still consistent, many more Negro than white fathers were born in this locale. A large majority of them (overall, 67%), like their wives, had fathers who were farmers.

The mothers reported that, on the average, the fathers had had less formal education than they. In addition, the gap between the mean educational levels of the Negro and white fathers was larger than that reported between the Negro and white mothers. Indeed, the mean educational level of the Negro fathers falls below a full elementary school education. Many of the women did not know how well their husbands had done at school, but, of those who did offer an answer to this inquiry, 58% of each race said that they had done "above average" work. In this regard, it will be recalled that a majority of the white mothers said that their schoolwork was "average or below," whereas a heavy majority of Negro mothers claimed to have done "above average" work (see Table 15.3, question 6).

The work patterns of the Negro and white fathers clearly differ in their emphases. Thus, 55% of the Negro fathers but only 28% of the white fathers were reported as being full-time farmers. On the other hand, 35% of the white fathers as against only 13% of the Negro fathers were reported as having jobs in mills or factories. These data, of course, suggest that the Negro families are much more closely tied to the land as the source of their livelihoods than the white families.

As for religious preference, the pattern for the fathers is quite similar to that previously described for the mothers. Negro fathers, however, are somewhat more equally divided between the Baptists and Methodists than was true for the Negro mothers.

These fathers were, on the average, about 31 years of age when the children being studied were born. This means that they were, on the average, about four years older than their wives. Many of the women, especially among the Negro respondents, were unable to say how the fathers had felt when they learned about this particular pregnancy. Among the fathers for whom an opinion was reported, however, the prevailing feeling seemed to be more positive than that among the mothers. This was particularly true for the Negro fathers; 78% of those reported on were said to have been pleased, which is in marked contrast to the 41% reported by the mothers for themselves. On the other hand, a number of fathers apparently had thought that it was a poor time to have a baby even though they were pleased that the mother had become pregnant. Finally, fathers, much more often than mothers, wanted the child to be a boy rather than a girl (this was true for both races).

TABLE 15.4: Fathers' Histories and Attributes

		Frequencies or means				p values*						
							Race			Sex		
Question	Response	WB	WG	NB	NG	O	N/W	NB/WB	NG/WG	B/G	NB/NG	WB/WG
1. Was the child's father born in a nuclear county?	Yes	34	42	32	42	.01	.001	.01	.05			
	No	15	16	1	4							
2. Was the father's father a farmer?	Yes	30	36	24	31							
	No	19	21	7	12							
3. Mean years of education for fathers?		9.2	9.0	7.6	7.5	.05	.01	.05	.05			
4. Did father do above average work in school?	Yes	29	23	19	18	.05				.05		.05
	No	10	28	11	16							
5. Is father a farmer?	Yes	12	17	20	21	.01	.001	.01	.10			
	No	36	38	12	21							
6. Does father work in a mill or factory?	Yes	18	18	2	8	.01	.01	.01				
	No	30	38	31	37							
7. What is father's religion?	Baptist	22	16	14	15	.01	.05	.01	.01			.05
	Methodist	11	21	9	17							
	Presbyterian	2	10	0	0							
	Other	6	1	3	1							
8. Mean age of fathers when children were born?		30.4	31.3	32.0	31.3							
9. Was father pleased when mother became pregnant with this child?	Yes	37	37	16	23	.10	.10					
	No	5	2	6	5							
10. Did father think it a bad time to have a baby?	Yes	12	11	12	11							
	No	29	40	14	28							
11. Did father want child to be a boy or a girl?	Boy	17	17	13	10						.10	
	Girl	9	9	4	15							
	Either	18	24	12	15							

		NB	WB	NG	WG	O
12. Does father often show his feelings for the child?	Yes	38	54	29	47	.10
	No	7	4	5	2	
13. Does father enjoy the child?	Yes	39	49	27	39	
	No	1	0	1	0	
14. Does father get much time with the child?	Yes	28	34	21	31	
	No	16	18	11	8	
15. Does father spend too much time with the child?	Yes	0	0	2	2	
	No	48	57	29	36	
16. Does father ignore the child too much?	Yes	2	3	6	5	.05
	No	42	53	27	35	
17. Does father treat the child consistently?	Yes	44	54	31	39	
	No	3	2	0	2	
18. Is father too hard on the child?	Yes	2	2	2	2	
	No	42	52	29	38	
19. Is father too easy-going with the child?	Yes	14	14	12	15	
	No	25	30	16	17	
20. Does father spoil the child?	Yes	11	22	16	17	.10
	No	30	26	16	24	
21. Does father worry about the child too much?	Yes	4	5	3	6	
	No	43	48	30	35	
22. Does father often side with the child against the mother?	Yes	4	7	5	3	
	No	42	47	28	38	

*Based upon chi-square, F-, and t-tests.

O = overall test.

$\frac{N}{W}$ = Negro vs. white children; $\frac{NB}{WB}$ = Negro boys vs. white boys; $\frac{NG}{WG}$ = Negro girls vs. white girls.

$\frac{B}{G}$ = boys vs. girls; $\frac{NB}{NG}$ = Negro boys vs. Negro girls; $\frac{WB}{WG}$ = white boys vs. white girls.

With this background information in hand, a number of inquiries were made to ascertain the nature of the father's attitude toward this particular child, how he interacted with him, and so on. The data that were elicited in this domain have been summarized as questions 12 through 22 in Table 15.4.

The data just referred to suggest a high degree of congruity between the way Negro and white mothers view the relationships of fathers with their children. On only one question (question 16 in Table 15.4) is there a significant racial difference. (More Negro than white fathers were said to ignore their children.) The picture that emerges from the totality of these items is essentially a positive one. For instance, 90% of the fathers were said to be expressive of their feelings toward the child, and all but two were described as enjoying the child. Only a relatively few husbands were described as being too hard on the child, as ignoring the child, as worrying too much about him, or as being inconsistent in their handling of him.

There seem, in fact, to be only two major complaints that the mothers make as far as the father–child relationship is concerned. First, many fathers (32%, overall) are said to have insufficient time to spend with the children. Second, the fathers, in the eyes of the mothers, are too easy-going and tend to spoil the children. In all, about 40% of the women charged that, in effect, the men were too soft or easy as far as discipline was concerned. In contrast, less than 5% of the mothers said that their husbands were too hard on the children.

Like the mothers, then, these fathers are essentially country people with their roots in North Carolina. They tend to be less well-educated than their wives; the racial gap in education is greater among the men than among the women. The occupations they follow are very much dependent upon their racial identities. Most of the fathers are described as having essentially positive relationships with their children; the major criticism offered by the mothers has to do with their belief that the fathers are too easy on the children.

Parental Use of Punishment, Reinforcement, and Models in Training Children

Some of the child-training practices reported by the mothers will now be examined. Relevant data have been tabulated in Table 15.5.

It is clear that the mothers believe that they whip their children more frequently than the fathers. Only three mothers said that they never whipped the child, whereas 35 mothers said that the father never whipped him. On the other hand, most of the mothers denied that whippings were given very often by either parent. More precisely, only 14% of the mothers said that they often whipped the child, while an even smaller 8% reported that their husbands often whipped him. There were no significant racial differences in these reports about the use of whipping.

A very significant racial difference was uncovered, however, when the mothers were asked if they thought that it did the child good to be whipped. Apparently, the Negro mothers are more solidly convinced of the efficacy of whippings than the white mothers are, for 94% of the Negro mothers against 78% of the white mothers answered this question affirmatively.

The mothers were also asked to identify the kinds of occasion on which they whipped the child; their answers were then classified using the categories indicated in questions 4 through 8 in Table 15.5. As the reader can determine by examining these data, disobedience and aggression were mentioned much more often than moral lapses, dependent behavior, or independent behavior as reasons for whipping the child. Only with respect to aggression was a significant racial difference found: Negro mothers mentioned aggressive behavior as a reason for whipping the child more often than white mothers. Actually, most of this racial difference was attributable to the marked difference in the responses of the Negro mothers of girls compared to the white mothers of girls. Mothers of Negro girls mentioned whipping them for aggressive behavior much more often than white mothers mentioned whipping their girls for such behavior.

The following two questions were also asked of the mothers: "Do you ever take away something the child wants as a way of punishing him?" and "Do you do this often?" One-half of the mothers indicated that they had used deprivation as a method of punishing the child, but only 14% reported using it often. Frequent use of deprivation was reported much more often by Negro mothers than by white mothers. Some use of this technique is apparently more common in dealing with boys—especially with white boys—than with girls.

Verbal reprimands are obviously used very often, for 92% of the mothers were able to recall the last time they had scolded the child. Banishment, either to a corner or to another room, appears to be used infrequently, but very significantly more often by white than by Negro mothers (41% vs. 22%, respectively). A majority of the mothers (actually, 68%) acknowledged that they frequently only threaten to punish the child.

Inquiry was made about the reinforcements or rewards used by the mothers when the children exhibited desirable behavior. When asked what they did when the child had been good, 62% of the white mothers but only 38% of the Negro mothers said that they praised the child. When specifically asked if they believed that children should be praised,

TABLE 15.5: Parental Use of Punishment, Reinforcement, and Models in Training Children

Question	Response	Frequencies				p values*						
		WB	WG	NB	NG	O	$\frac{N}{W}$	$\frac{NB}{WB}$	$\frac{NG}{WG}$	$\frac{B}{G}$	$\frac{NB}{NG}$	$\frac{WB}{WG}$
							Race				Sex	
1. Does father whip the child often?	Yes	3	2	5	5							
	No	43	55	30	45							
2. Does mother whip the child often?	Yes	8	3	8	9	.10			.10			
	No	42	56	28	44							
3. Does it do the child good to be whipped?	Yes	36	46	33	50	.01	.01	.05	.10			
	No	13	10	2	3							
4. Does mother mention disobedience as a reason for whipping?	Yes	26	31	17	23							
	No	25	28	19	31							
5. Does mother mention aggression as a reason for whipping?	Yes	23	18	20	35	.01	.01		.001			
	No	28	41	16	19							
6. Does mother mention moral lapses as a reason for whipping?	Yes	2	2	2	4							
	No	49	57	34	50							
7. Does mother mention dependent behavior as a reason for whipping?	Yes	0	1	1	1							
	No	51	58	35	53							
8. Does mother mention independent behavior as a reason for whipping?	Yes	1	2	4	3							
	No	50	57	32	51							
9. Is the child ever punished by depriving him of something?	Yes	31	17	21	28	.01			.05	.05		.01
	No	20	38	14	26							
10. Is material deprivation often used as punishment?	Yes	6	1	9	11	.01	.01		.01			.10
	No	45	54	26	42							
11. Can mother recall her last scolding of the child?	Yes	41	53	33	52	.10	.10					
	No	8	5	2	1							

#	Question	Ans.	NB	WB	NG	WG								
12.	Does mother punish child by banishment?	Yes	23	21	11	8	.01	.01	.05	.10				
		No	27	36	24	45								
13.	Does mother often only threaten punishment?	Yes	32	36	27	38								
		No	19	21	8	16								
14.	Does mother mention praising the child for being good?	Yes	30	34	15	18	.05	.01	.10	.05				
		No	17	22	20	33								
15.	Does mother believe in praising children?	Yes	44	51	30	33	.01	.01		.10	.05	.05		
		No	7	8	6	21								
16.	Does mother sometimes give the child something for being good?	Yes	45	43	33	52	.01	.05	.01	.01				.10
		No	5	14	3	2								
17.	Does mother sometimes hold up parents as models for child?	Yes	26	24	28	39	.001	.001	.05	.01				
		No	25	34	8	15								
18.	Does mother sometimes use siblings as models for child?	Yes	5	9	12	14	.10	.05	.05					
		No	32	37	19	32								
19.	Does mother sometimes use grandparents as models for child?	Yes	6	6	4	12								
		No	43	52	27	42								
20.	Does mother sometimes use other relatives as models for child?	Yes	2	7	4	7								
		No	47	51	26	47								
21.	Does mother sometimes use the child's playmates as models for him?	Yes	2	2	5	1	.05							.05
		No	47	56	26	53								
22.	Does mother sometimes use someone as a negative ("Don't be like him") model for the child?	Yes	15	15	23	25	.001	.001	.01	.05				
		No	35	44	13	29								

* Based upon chi-square tests.

O = overall test.

$\frac{N}{W}$ = Negro vs. white children; $\frac{NB}{WB}$ = Negro boys vs. white boys; $\frac{NG}{WG}$ = Negro girls vs. white girls.

$\frac{B}{G}$ = boys vs. girls; $\frac{NB}{NG}$ = Negro boys vs. Negro girls; $\frac{WB}{WG}$ = white boys vs. white girls.

$\frac{NB}{NG}$ = Negro boys vs. Negro girls; $\frac{NB}{NG}$ = Negro boys vs. white girls.

86% of the white mothers contrasted with 70% of the Negro mothers replied affirmatively, again a very significant racial difference. On the other hand, when asked if they sometimes gave the child something for being good, proportionately more Negro than white mothers said that they did (94% vs. 82%, respectively). These data, then, suggest that Negro mothers may make more of a distinction between verbal and material rewards than white mothers do, and that, comparatively speaking, Negro mothers are more reluctant than white mothers to tell the child that he has been good.[8]

Now we turn to how models are used in training children. Are parents, siblings, relatives, and playmates held up as examples for the child to imitate or copy? Are individuals used as negative models; that is, are they pointed out as examples of how not to act? Data in this area are given in Table 15.5 under questions 17 through 22.

Parents were reported as being used as models more often than other persons, and much more frequently by Negro mothers than by white mothers (74% vs. 46%, respectively). Negro mothers also said that they used siblings as models significantly more often than white mothers did (34% vs. 17%, respectively). Grandparents were identified as models less frequently than siblings, and the same was true for other relatives. (No significant racial differences were reported in the use of either grandparents or other relatives as models.) Playmates of the child were seldom said to be held up as examples (only 5% of the mothers could so remember having used them). Various negative models were commonly reported, however, especially by the Negro mothers.

These data suggest that there may be important differences in the child-training practices of the Negro and the white families. Thus, Negro mothers are more nearly unanimous than white mothers in endorsing the value of whippings. White mothers, in contrast, report a greater use of banishment; they also endorse the value of praise more strongly than Negro mothers do. The latter more frequently report the use of material rewards; also, they more commonly point to the use of models in guiding their children.

Children's Developmental Histories, Including Social Maturity Levels

Attention will now be devoted to what the mothers reported about the developmental histories of their children. Data in this domain have

[8] Such praise is often emphasized as an important factor influencing the self-concept developed by a child. It would be especially interesting in later years to examine the self-concepts of those children who have been reared by mothers expressing belief in praise and to contrast them with the self-concepts of children who have been reared by mothers expressing the opposite opinion.

been listed in Table 15.6. Questions 1 through 10 in this table refer primarily to the motor and verbal behavior of the children. Question 11 provides a mean score on the Vineland Social Maturity Scale (see Doll, 1953) for each of the four groups. Questions 12 through 24 are concerned with special difficulties or traumas that the children may have experienced.

For the behaviors specified in items 1 through 8, the mothers were asked if their children had developed them early, late, or "about right" (that is, average). As one might expect, the most common response was "about right." Departures from this average position were more often toward early rather than late. It is important to note that exceptions in this regard occurred on items 3 and 8; these are the two items that relate to the verbal behavior of the children. On both of these items, more mothers of white boys reported their children as being late than reported them as being early. There was a similar tendency among the mothers of Negro boys, although it was not as pronounced as it was among mothers of white boys. Girls, in contrast, were more likely to be described as early, both in saying their first words and in speaking sentences. (This sex difference was more marked for white children than for Negro children.) There was a significant sex difference on one additional item among the first eight, and this occurred only for the white children. White girls generally were reported as having taken their first steps earlier than white boys (question 4).

As far as racial comparisons are concerned, significant differences were found on three items (5, 6, and 7) among the first eight, and the pattern is similar for each of them. This pattern can best be described as a relative avoidance of the middle category (average) by Negro mothers compared to white mothers and, proportionately, an enhancement of both extremes. Thus, relatively more Negro mothers than white mothers said that their children were toilet-trained early, were weaned early, and learned to use a spoon early, but relatively more Negro than white mothers also said that their children were late in developing each of these behaviors.

When the mean number of reported early developmental appearances was computed for each subgroup, both significant racial and sex differences were obtained. Negro mothers reported early patterns more often than white mothers did, and mothers of girls gave this response more often than mothers of boys (question 9). When the mean number of reported delayed appearances was computed, a significant sex difference was obtained again; also, there was a tendency toward a significant racial difference. Late development was reported significantly more

TABLE 15.6

Children's Developmental Histories, Including Social Maturity Levels

Question	Response	Frequencies or means				p values*						
		WB	WG	NB	NG	O	$\frac{N}{W}$	$\frac{NB}{WB}$	$\frac{NG}{WG}$	$\frac{B}{G}$	$\frac{NB}{NG}$	$\frac{WB}{WG}$
							Race				Sex	
1. When did the child begin sitting up?	Early	10	17	10	21							
	Average	33	39	22	29							
	Late	6	2	2	3							
2. When did the child begin crawling or creeping?	Early	7	13	6	18							
	Average	26	33	24	25					.10		
	Late	7	4	4	5							
3. When did the child say his first real words?	Early	5	21	8	18	.01				.001		.01
	Average	31	33	18	31							
	Late	9	3	9	5							
4. When did the child take his first steps?	Early	13	29	15	20							.05
	Average	26	23	13	24							
	Late	9	4	8	10							
5. When was the child toilet-trained?	Early	10	16	12	26	.05	.05	.10	.10		.10	
	Average	35	34	16	24							
	Late	5	7	8	4							
6. When was the child weaned to the cup?	Early	11	17	15	23	.10	.01	.05	.10			
	Average	31	33	13	20							
	Late	7	7	8	11							

RESULTS **371**

Question	Response					Significance
7. When did the child learn to use a spoon?	Early	9	13	18	18	.05 .01 .01 .01
	Average	37	38	16	30	
	Late	1	5	2	6	
8. When did the child learn to speak sentences?	Early	5	19	8	12	.10 .05 .01 .05 .05 .01
	Average	29	35	16	29	
	Late	12	4	12	12	
9. Mean number of "early" reports? (Based on 1–8)		1.4	2.5	2.6	2.9	.10 .01 .05 .01 .01
10. Mean number of "late" reports? (Based on 1–8)		1.1	0.6	1.5	1.0	.10 .05 .10 .10 .05
11. At interview 2, what are the means and standard deviations on the Vineland Social Maturity Scale?	Mean	103.8	110.2	104.2	106.1	.05 .05 .05 .01
	S.D.	13.2	10.8	11.6	9.5	
12. By interview 2, have special problems developed or increased in intensity?	Yes	8	5	4	1	.10 .10
	No	40	52	32	52	
13. Does mother have special concerns about the child?	Yes	31	38	20	35	
	No	18	20	15	16	
14. Did the child have a difficult birth?	Yes	7	7	2	4	
	No	44	52	33	49	
15. Has the child had a serious illness or injury?	Yes	17	11	11	14	
	No	34	48	25	40	
16. Has a sibling or parent of the child been seriously ill or injured?	Yes	19	21	13	22	
	No	32	36	23	32	
17. Has there been a death in the child's close family?	Yes	25	24	11	24	
	No	26	34	24	30	

(continued)

TABLE 15.6 (continued)

Question	Response	Frequencies or means				p values*						
		WB	WG	NB	NG	O	$\frac{N}{W}$	$\frac{NB}{WB}$	$\frac{NG}{WG}$	$\frac{B}{G}$	$\frac{NB}{NG}$	$\frac{WB}{WG}$
							Race				Sex	
18. Has a parent been absent for a long period of time?	Yes	13	13	11	14							.10
	No	36	45	24	40							
19. Has the child ever been separated from his family?	Yes	7	11	5	1	.05	.10		.01		.10	
	No	44	45	31	51							
20. Has there been a major move of the child's household?	Yes	23	28	23	23						.10	
	No	28	31	13	31							
21. Has there been prolonged unemployment of the main wage earner?	Yes	10	9	11	13							
	No	39	47	25	39							
22. Has the child been in an auto accident, fire, or other catastrophic event?	Yes	13	13	6	4	.10	.05		.10			
	No	37	46	30	49							
23. Has the child had an older sibling leave home?	Yes	2	10	5	8							.10
	No	34	35	28	38							
24. Mean number of special dislocations? (Based on 14–23)		2.7	2.5	2.9	2.5							

* Based upon chi-square, F-, and t-tests.

O = overall test.

$\frac{N}{W}$ = Negro vs. white children; $\frac{NB}{WB}$ = Negro boys vs. white boys; $\frac{NG}{WG}$ = Negro girls vs. white girls.

$\frac{B}{G}$ = boys vs. girls; $\frac{NB}{NG}$ = Negro boys vs. Negro girls; $\frac{WB}{WG}$ = white boys vs. white girls.

often for boys than for girls, and there was a tendency for Negro mothers to report it more often than white mothers (see question 10).

As noted earlier, the Vineland Social Maturity Scale was incorporated into the interview schedule. When these items were scored and analyzed, mean quotients above 100 were secured for each of the subgroups (see question 11). There was no significant racial difference in these quotients, but the variance of the white scores tended to be greater than that of the Negro scores. However, a significant sex difference in favor of the girls was obtained. This difference was attributable almost entirely to the high mean score obtained by the white girls.

During their development, many children confront crises or traumas—serious illness, separation from their families, death in the family, and so on. Questions 12 and 13 in Table 15.6 ask if the child currently has special problems, or if the mother has special concerns about him. The remaining items (14 through 24) focus upon special dislocations that might have occurred during the child's life.

There are few racial or sex differences in these data. The tendency, however, is for white mothers to report more such incidents in the lives of their children than Negro mothers do. White mothers tend to report difficult births more frequently, more deaths in the child's close family, more separations of the child from his family, and more catastrophic events (fires, accidents, etc.). Overall, though, there is no statistically significant difference in the mean number of special dislocations reported for the children of the four subgroups (see question 24). It was noteworthy that almost two-thirds of the mothers (see question 13) said that they currently had special concerns about the child who was being discussed.[9]

These data suggest that, although a majority of the mothers feel that they have special problems with the child in question, they nevertheless do not perceive him as lagging behind in what might be called normal development. In fact, there is a tendency to report the children as being ahead of schedule, especially the girls. This acceleration among the girls is especially pronounced for language usage; also, the social maturity of the white girls is given considerable emphasis. In some training areas (toilet behavior and weaning), Negro mothers report more children who are either relatively early or relatively late in acquiring more advanced forms of behavior. White mothers, on the other hand, tend to report certain disturbing events as having occurred more frequently in the lives of their children than Negro mothers do. In general, however,

[9] The local resources that the mothers can turn to for professional guidance and assistance in handling these problems are, to say the least, meager.

traumas seem to have been rather equally distributed among the racial and sex groups.

Children's Current Motor Skills

Mothers were asked eight questions to get at their judgments of their children's current motor skills. Data summarizing their responses may be found in Table 15.7.

In general, mothers were quite favorable in their evaluations of their children's motor skills. This becomes quite clear when eight forms or expressions of motor skill are rank-ordered in terms of the percentage of mothers who said that their children were "good" at each:

Running	95%	Cutting with scissors	82%
Jumping	90%	Building with blocks	78%
Holding a pencil	**90%**	Coloring pictures	69%
Throwing a ball	86%	Catching a ball	43%

These percentages do not include those children whose mothers said that they had had no opportunity to exhibit the particular skill. Lack of opportunity was reported most often for building with blocks (59 mothers so reported) and for cutting with scissors (18 mothers).

The data reveal two racial differences. First, Negro children received fewer judgments of good for their skill in coloring pictures than white children did. (The Negro boys were judged especially poor in this regard.) Second, when mothers were asked if their children had motor talents in addition to those about which inquiry had been made, white mothers responded affirmatively more often than Negro mothers. In addition, when the mean number of judgments of good was computed for each racial group, it was found that such judgments were made much more often by white mothers.

Sex differences were less definite than racial differences. The girls, however, were judged as being better than the boys at coloring a picture. On the other hand, mothers of white boys mentioned additional motor talents more often than mothers of white girls. Overall, when the mean number of judgments of average or poor was computed, it was found that the mean score for the boys exceeded that for the girls.

These data are not very suggestive. Yet they seem to underscore at least one major point—namely, that a large majority of the mothers are set to report favorably upon the skills of their children. The inquiry also revealed that a sizable number of the homes do not contain items like building blocks which can help a child develop his motor coordination. Moreover, the reported relative inferiority of the Negro children in coloring pictures may reflect, at least in part, a lack of crayons and pictures to color in the Negro homes.

Children's Intellective and Achievement Behavior, with Related Parental Behavior

At various points during the two interview sessions, information was gathered pertaining to the aspirations of the child, his concern with the quality of his schoolwork (if he was attending kindergarten), his interest in learning, and so on. Related information relevant to the views of his parents was also obtained. Data bearing on these issues have been recorded in Table 15.8.

One of our central concerns was the question of whether efforts had been made in the home to teach the child school-related skills (letters, how to use a pencil, etc.). As item 1 in Table 15.8 indicates, such efforts were reported for most of the children (actually, 83%). For both Negro and white children, the mother usually reported that she was the one who did this teaching. However, there is a racial difference: white mothers reported more frequently than Negro mothers that they had worked with the child on school-related skills. The fathers of both races were only infrequently mentioned as having offered such instruction; apparently, they are more likely to teach their daughters than their sons.

The interviewers also endeavored to ascertain what kinds of behavior (motor, social, or intellective) of the child tend to create pleasurable feelings in his mother (questions 4, 5, and 6 in Table 15.8). When asked about this, interesting racial differences (and one sex difference) emerged. White mothers, for example, most commonly mentioned the child's social behavior, followed by his intellective achievements, and then his motor accomplishments. In contrast, Negro mothers most frequently mentioned intellective behavior, then social behavior, and, finally, motor behavior. With respect to intellective behavior, mothers of both races—but especially Negro mothers—mentioned it as a source of pleasure more often for their girls than for their boys.

Several inquiries focused on the achievement striving of the children (questions 7, 8, and 9); no significant racial or sex differences were found. A large majority of the mothers (92%) claimed that their children enjoyed learning school-related skills. A smaller, yet still substantial, majority (69%) went on to say that the child kept at a hard task even if he was not getting it. However, only slightly more than one-half of the mothers (54%) indicated that their children showed a need to do tasks "just right."

It was noted earlier that 91 of these children (see Table 15.1) had already been introduced to formal school instruction through an experimental kindergarten program (see Chapter 8). According to their mothers, these children were responding quite positively to this new

TABLE 15.7

Children's Current Motor Skills

Question	Response	Frequencies or means					p values*					
		WB	WG	NB	NG	O	$\frac{N}{W}$	$\frac{NB}{WB}$	$\frac{NG}{WG}$	$\frac{B}{G}$	$\frac{NB}{NG}$	$\frac{WB}{WG}$
								Race			Sex	
1. Is the child good at throwing a ball?	Yes	43	49	30	46							
	No	8	8	6	6							
2. Is the child good at catching a ball?	Yes	25	28	15	17							
	No	26	29	21	35							
3. Is the child good at running?	Yes	47	56	35	52							
	No	4	3	1	2							
4. Is the child good at jumping?	Yes	42	54	34	49							
	No	9	5	2	5							
5. Is the child good at building with blocks?	Yes	34	34	16	25							
	No	9	6	9	7							

		NB	WB	NG	WG	O	N/W	NB/WB	NG/WG	B/G	NB/NG	WB/WG
6. Is the child good at cutting with scissors?	Yes	34	46	28	38	.001	.05	.05	.10	.01	.05	.10
	No	10	11	5	7							
7. Is the child good at coloring a picture?	Yes	35	49	15	36							
	No	16	9	19	16							
8. Is the child good at holding a pencil?	Yes	43	53	32	51							
	No	8	6	4	3							
9. Does the mother mention other motor talents?	Yes	38	53	22	39	.01	.01	.10		.01		.05
	No	11	4	14	15							
10. Mean number of "good" motor skills? (Based on 1–9)		7.2	7.7	6.5	6.8	.001	.001	.05	.01		.10	
11. Mean number of "average" or "poor" motor skills? (Based on 1–9)		1.3	0.9	1.4	1.2		.05		.05			.05

* Based upon chi-square, F-, and t-tests.

O = overall test.

$\frac{N}{W}$ = Negro vs. white children; $\frac{NB}{WB}$ = Negro boys vs. white boys; $\frac{NG}{WG}$ = Negro girls vs. white girls.

$\frac{B}{G}$ = boys vs. girls; $\frac{NB}{NG}$ = Negro boys vs. Negro girls; $\frac{WB}{WG}$ = white boys vs. white girls.

TABLE 15.8

Children's Intellective and Achievement Behavior, with Related Parental Behavior

Question	Response	Frequencies				p values*						
							Race			Sex		
		WB	WG	NB	NG	O	$\frac{N}{W}$	$\frac{NB}{WB}$	$\frac{NG}{WG}$	$\frac{B}{G}$	$\frac{NB}{NG}$	$\frac{WB}{WG}$
1. Has anyone taught the child school-related skills?	Yes	36	49	32	47							
	No	13	10	4	7							
2. Has mother taught the child school-related skills?	Yes	32	44	18	31	.10	.05		.10			
	No	19	15	18	23							
3. Has father taught the child school-related skills?	Yes	2	10	3	9	.10				.05		.10
	No	48	49	32	41							
4. Is the child's motor behavior mentioned as a source of enjoyment by mother?	Yes	2	4	2	5							
	No	49	55	34	49							
5. Is the child's social behavior mentioned as a source of enjoyment by mother?	Yes	14	14	4	6	.10	.05					
	No	37	45	32	48							
6. Is the child's school-related achievement behavior mentioned as a source of enjoyment by mother?	Yes	6	9	5	24	.001	.01		.01	.01	.01	
	No	45	50	31	30							
7. Does the child like learning school-related skills?	Yes	37	50	30	44							.10
	No	6	1	3	4							
8. Does the child persist at a hard task that he is not getting?	Yes	18	32	24	33							
	No	14	16	9	9							
9. Does the child need to do things just right?	Yes	23	29	23	32		.10					
	No	28	30	13	21							
10. Does the child like kindergarten?	Yes	26	20	13	29							
	No	1	1	0	1							

Question	Response	NB	WB	NG	WG	O	N/W	NB/WB	NG/WG	B/G	NB/NG	WB/WG
11. Does mother have a positive attitude toward kindergarten?	Yes	28	20	14	30							
	No	0	0	0	0							
12. Does mother think the child will do well in school?	Yes	38	51	30	52							
	No	2	1	0	0							
13. How far in school does mother want the child to go?	College	34	33	13	23	.05	.01	.01				
	High school	17	24	23	31							
14. Does mother want the child to be a farmer?	Yes	1	0	2	0							
	No	50	59	34	54							
15. Does mother want the child to enter a profession?	Yes	14	29	20	40	.001	.001	.05		.05	.01	.05
	No	37	30	16	14							
16. Does mother believe the child has a good chance of fulfilling her vocational aspirations for him?	Yes	19	30	14	30	.001	.10	.05	.05	.001	.05	.01
	No	17	3	20	15							
17. Is mother judged as expecting high accomplishments of the child?	Yes	39	46	27	40							
	No	12	12	8	13							
18. Do father and mother agree on plans for the child's education?	Yes	24	49	32	45							
	No	1	3	0	0							
19. Does father expect too much of the child?	Yes	7	6	7	4							
	No	33	46	21	32							
20. Is father satisfied with the way the child is coming along?	Yes	40	53	27	38							
	No	3	2	2	1							
21. Is mother satisfied with the way the child is coming along?	Yes	36	50	24	38							
	No	2	2	1	2							

* Based upon chi-square tests.

O = overall test.

$\frac{N}{W}$ = Negro vs. white children; $\frac{NB}{WB}$ = Negro boys vs. white boys; $\frac{NG}{WG}$ = Negro girls vs. white girls.

$\frac{B}{G}$ = boys vs. girls; $\frac{NB}{NG}$ = Negro boys vs. Negro girls; $\frac{WB}{WG}$ = white boys vs. white girls.

experience. Only three mothers (question 10) said that their children did not like going to kindergarten. These three mothers, however, joined with the others to express a unanimous judgment that the kindergarten was a helpful and desirable program (question 11). In looking ahead to their children's accomplishments in school, the mothers were very much like the managers of baseball teams during spring training: only three mothers expressed the feeling that their children might not do well in school (question 12). Moreover, mothers of both races appeared to hold high educational aspirations for their children. Sixty-two percent of the white mothers and 40% of the Negro mothers (a very significant racial difference) said that they wanted their children to go to college. No mother reported a desire for less than a high school education for her child.

The fact that the mothers have high aspirations for their children is further revealed by their answers to questions about what occupations they would like them to follow. Not surprisingly, very few mothers—in fact, only three—said that they wanted their children to be farmers. In contrast, 39% of the white and 67% of the Negro mothers (a highly significant racial difference) named a profession that they hoped their children would enter. Indication of a professional goal was especially frequent among the mothers of the girls.[10] When asked if she believed that her child had a good chance of fulfilling her vocational aspiration for him, 63% of the mothers who gave a definite answer said yes. Such positive expressions were made much more often by mothers of girls than by mothers of boys. Given these answers, it is not surprising to find that the interviewers rated 77% of the mothers as expecting high accomplishments of their children (question 17).

As far as the interviewers were able to determine, the vast majority of the mothers were unaware of any disagreement between themselves and their husbands with respect to plans for their children's education (question 18). Only 15% said that they felt the father expected too much of the child. Even fewer fathers (5%) were said to be dissatisfied with the development of their children (question 20). A comparably small number of mothers (again, 5%) expressed unhappiness with the overall progress that their children were making.

It is clear, we believe, that many of the mothers express unrealistically high aspirations for their children. There are also meaningful sex differences, with expectations tending to be greater for the girls than for the boys. However, there do not appear to be significant differences between Negro and white mothers in how they evaluate the achievements of

---

[10] For the girls of both races, nursing and teaching were the two professions which their mothers mentioned most frequently.

their children. They do appear to be differentially sensitive to the intellective and social behaviors of their children, though, with the Negro mothers indicating greater sensitivity to intellective behaviors while white mothers are relatively more sensitive to social skills.

Children's Temperamental and Personality Traits

Several temperamental and personality traits will be discussed in the following paragraphs.[11] Aggression, submissiveness, dependency, guilt, and various forms of misbehavior will be treated separately, however, in later sections of the chapter. The data forming the basis for the immediate discussion have been summarized in Table 15.9.

With respect to the behaviors covered by the items in Table 15.9, it is clear that the mothers see few significant differences between their sons and daughters. Thus, boys and girls are seen as being equally happy, solemn, alert, and so on. On two items, however, there is a significant sex difference: girls more frequently are described as being neat than boys are (question 11), while boys—especially Negro boys—more often are described as showing off than girls (question 14). In addition, among the Negro children there is a tendency for girls to be described as fearful more often than boys (question 8).

Whereas sex differences are few in number, racial differences are quite common. In fact, statistically significant racial differences are found on one-half of the items in Table 15.9. While we cannot be certain that there are real behavioral differences of this order of magnitude, it is clear that mothers of the two races emphasize different descriptive terms in referring to their children. What traits are underscored by the mothers of the two races?

More often than white mothers, Negro mothers choose the following traits to describe their children: happy, always in a hurry, and fearful (especially the girls). There is also a stronger tendency to refer to them as affectionate. In addition, Negro mothers see their children—both boys and girls—as preferring their mothers to their fathers (about two to one), while the white mothers, overall, report no particular parental preference among their children.

In contrast, white mothers choose the following traits more often than Negro mothers to describe their children: solemn, cautious, daydreamy, and silly. There is also a greater tendency for white mothers to say that their children are alert and laugh a lot, with the latter (laughing) being particularly common among the girls.

[11] We are not distinguishing here between temperament and personality. However, such a distinction can be made. For a discussion of this conceptual problem, see Baughman and Welsh (1962).

TABLE 15.9

Children's Temperamental and Personality Traits

| Question | Response | Frequencies | | | | p values* | | | | | | |
| | | | | | | Race | | | | Sex | | |
		WB	WG	NB	NG	O	N/W	NB/WB	NG/WG	B/G	NB/NG	WB/WG
1. Does the child laugh a lot?	Yes	46	57	32	43		.10		.05			
	No	5	2	4	9							
2. Is the child usually happy?	Yes	39	46	35	51	.01	.001	.05	.05			
	No	12	12	1	3							
3. Is the child usually silly?	Yes	17	18	0	0	.001	.001	.001	.001			
	No	34	41	36	54							
4. Is the child usually solemn?	Yes	7	9	1	2	.10	.05		.10			
	No	44	50	35	52							
5. Is the child usually sad?	Yes	3	2	0	0							
	No	48	57	36	54							
6. Is the child shy?	Yes	20	19	13	16							
	No	31	40	23	38							
7. Is the child usually cautious?	Yes	41	39	12	23	.001	.001	.001	.05			
	No	10	19	24	31							
8. Is the child fearful?	Yes	8	10	9	24	.01	.01		.01			.10
	No	43	49	27	30							

Question	Response	NB	WB	NG	WG	O	N/W	NB/WB	NG/WG	B/G	NB/NG	WB/WG
9. Is the child alert (wide-awake)?	Yes	49	55	31	47		.01	.01	.10		.05	
	No	2	4	5	6							
10. Is the child daydreamy?	Yes	14	19	4	6		.10			.05		
	No	34	38	32	48							
11. Is the child neat?	Yes	39	49	24	47						.05	.05
	No	12	10	12	7							
12. Is the child careless?	Yes	19	17	12	13							
	No	32	42	24	40							
13. Is the child always in a hurry?	Yes	20	21	22	25		.10	.05	.10		.05	.01
	No	31	38	14	29							
14. Does the child show off?	Yes	33	36	33	32		.01	.01	.10		.05	.01
	No	18	23	3	22							
15. Does the child show affection often?	Yes	47	53	36	50							
	No	4	6	0	3							
16. Which parent does the child seem to prefer?	Mother	12	11	16	19		.01	.01		.05		
	Father	11	12	8	10							
	Equal	19	29	11	13							

* Based upon chi-square tests.

O = overall test.

$\dfrac{N}{W}$ = Negro vs. white children; $\dfrac{NB}{WB}$ = Negro boys vs. white boys; $\dfrac{NG}{WG}$ = Negro girls vs. white girls.

$\dfrac{B}{G}$ = boys vs. girls; $\dfrac{NB}{NG}$ = Negro boys vs. Negro girls; $\dfrac{WB}{WG}$ = white boys vs. white girls.

It is clear, then, that Negro and white mothers differ significantly in how they emphasize a variety of temperamental and personality attributes of their children. At the risk of some oversimplification, it can be said that Negro mothers more often emphasize the extraverted qualities of their children, while white mothers more often underscore introverted qualities. As we mentioned earlier, we cannot be certain that these data reflect anything more than divergent maternal impressions. Nevertheless, there is in fact no basis for discarding the data as being nothing more than this. What we need now are further studies which will clarify the relationship between such maternal reports and evaluations of the same behavioral domains provided by other methods of assessment.

Children's Assertiveness and Submissiveness, with Related Parental Behavior

Reports about the children's social dominance are examined in this section. Data pertinent to this domain have been tabulated in Table 15.10.

The question of parental expectations with respect to the child's compliance behavior will be considered first; that is, do parents expect immediate obedience by the child, or do they tolerate some resistance? As question 1 in Table 15.10 shows, a majority of the mothers (59%) say that they do expect immediate obedience from the child; this is especially true for Negro girls. Moreover, as the data for question 2 suggest, fathers may be more demanding than mothers in this regard (72% of the fathers are said to expect immediate obedience). Also, there is a highly significant racial difference; Negro fathers are described as more demanding of immediate obedience than white fathers (85% vs. 61%, respectively).

Most of the mothers of both races (overall, 84%) acknowledge that there are times when they expect their children—both boys and girls—to fight. Perhaps not surprisingly, mothers of both races tend to see their children more as targets than as initiators of aggressive behavior in their contacts with other children. For example, only 36% of the mothers admitted that their child took things away from other children, but 79% claimed that other children took things away from him (questions 4 and 5).

The mothers' reactions to their children's aggressive or submissive behavior in contacts with other children are also of interest, and there is a tendency toward a racial difference in this regard. Seventy-four percent of the Negro mothers compared to 61% of the white mothers said that they became upset when their child fought with other children (question 6). Also, 78% of the Negro mothers contrasted with 65% of the white mothers admitted to becoming upset when the child fought with siblings (question 7). This tendency toward greater emotional reactivity on the part of the Negro mothers appeared again when inquiry was made about pronounced submissive behavior on the part of the child. Ninety-four percent of the Negro mothers compared with 84% of the white mothers admitted to becoming upset when the child permitted other children to pick on him (question 8).

Inquiries were made to determine if the children act aggressively toward their parents. According to the mothers, 53% of the children sometimes act aggressively toward them (question 9), but only 42% were said to act aggressively at times toward their fathers (question 13). This preference for mother over father as a target for aggression was particularly pronounced among the white girls. Neither parent is inclined to ignore such aggression when it does occur. Thus, only seven mothers said that they sometimes ignored it (question 10); on the other hand, more than two-thirds of both the mothers and the fathers have whipped the child for parental aggression (questions 11 and 15).

At the end of the first interview session (during which there was considerable discussion of the child's aggressive behavior), the interviewers rated the mothers with respect to the value which they seemed to place on aggression. Forty-one percent of the mothers were placed within half a point of the midpoint of the scale in this regard, and no mother was rated at either extreme. Nor was there any significant racial difference in the ratings assigned (question 12).

In summary, these data indicate more racial and sex similarity than dissimilarity as far as aggressive and submissive behavior are concerned. There is an indication, however, that Negro parents—especially fathers —are especially severe or stern in their demands for obedience and in their intolerance of the child's self-assertiveness. There is also a suggestion that Negro mothers may react more strongly than white mothers to both extremely aggressive and extremely submissive behavior. Parents of both racial groups are quite intolerant of aggression directed toward them; apparently, mothers of both races tend to be the recipients of such aggression more frequently than fathers. Both Negro and white mothers commonly see their children as the targets rather than as the initiators of aggressive behavior in their contacts with other children.

Children's Dependency and Guilt, with Related Parental Behavior

The child's tendency to be either dependent or independent in his behavior is the focus of the discussion in this section. A very brief examination is also made of his tendency to violate rules (from which inferences might be made about his experiencing guilt or conscience). Relevant data are summarized in Table 15.11.

TABLE 15.10

Children's Assertiveness and Submissiveness, with Related Parental Behavior

Question	Response	Frequencies					p values*					
							Race				Sex	
		WB	WG	NB	NG	O	$\frac{N}{W}$	$\frac{NB}{WB}$	$\frac{NG}{WG}$	$\frac{B}{G}$	$\frac{NB}{NG}$	$\frac{WB}{WG}$
1. Does mother expect her child to obey immediately?	Yes	29	29	18	39	.05			.01		.05	
	No	21	30	17	13							
2. Does father expect his child to obey immediately?	Yes	28	29	28	41	.01	.001	.05	.05			
	No	17	20	4	8							
3. On occasion, is the child expected to fight by his mother?	Yes	41	51	29	41							
	No	8	6	5	11							
4. Does the child take things away from other children?	Yes	18	22	8	18							
	No	28	34	23	32							
5. Do other children take things away from the child?	Yes	38	42	26	40							
	No	7	14	5	12							
6. Does the child's fighting with other children upset mother?	Yes	29	19	23	33	.05			.05	.10		.05
	No	9	22	8	12							
7. Does the child's fighting with siblings upset mother?	Yes	29	27	24	29	.10						
	No	11	19	4	11							
8. When the child lets others pick on him, is mother upset?	Yes	33	34	32	47	.05	.10		.10			
	No	3	10	1	4							

Question	Response					
9. Is the child sometimes aggressive toward mother?	Yes	29	29	34	18	24
	No	22	22	25	17	30
10. Is the child's parental aggression sometimes ignored by mother?	Yes	2	2	4	0	1
	No	26	26	29	18	23
11. Does the child's parental aggression sometimes lead to whipping by mother?	Yes	16	16	19	14	18
	No	8	8	10	3	5
12. Was mother judged as placing high value on aggressiveness?	Yes	24	24	30	18	34
	No	23	23	25	17	20
13. Is the child sometimes aggressive toward father?	Yes	25	25	22	16	20
	No	26	26	37	19	32
14. Is the child's parental aggression sometimes ignored by father?	Yes	1	1	3	1	0
	No	21	21	18	15	19
15. Does the child's parental aggression sometimes lead to whipping by father?	Yes	13	13	11	12	13
	No	7	7	9	2	5

* Based upon chi-square tests.

O = overall test.

$\frac{N}{W}$ = Negro vs. white children; $\frac{NB}{WB}$ = Negro boys vs. white boys; $\frac{NG}{WG}$ = Negro girls vs. white girls.

$\frac{B}{G}$ = boys vs. girls; $\frac{NB}{NG}$ = Negro boys vs. Negro girls; $\frac{WB}{WG}$ = white boys vs. white girls.

TABLE 15.11

Children's Dependency and Guilt, with Related Parental Behavior

Question	Response	Frequencies				p values*						
		WB	WG	NB	NG	O	$\frac{N}{W}$	$\frac{NB}{WB}$	$\frac{NG}{WG}$	$\frac{B}{G}$	$\frac{NB}{NG}$	$\frac{WB}{WG}$
							Race			Sex		
1. Does the child sometimes report rule violations to mother?	Yes	32	30	16	28	.05		.10				
	No	16	24	20	26							
2. When asked does the child usually admit rule violations?	Yes	45	50	25	39		.01	.10	.10			
	No	4	6	9	13							
3. If rule violations are suspected, does mother punish?	Yes	27	18	27	33	.001	.05		.05	.05		.05
	No	2	10	1	3							
4. Does the child usually try things?	Yes	43	51	32	48							
	No	8	8	4	6							
5. Does the child play well alone?	Yes	43	53	23	40	.05	.01		.05			
	No	8	5	11	13							
6. Does the child need encouragement?	Yes	33	22	24	31	.01			.10	.05		
	No	18	37	12	23							
7. Has the child had a stage of "skirt-hanging"?	Yes	29	29	22	29							.01
	No	21	30	14	25							

#	Question	Response					O	N/W	NB/WB	NG/WG	B/G	NB/NG	WB/WG
8.	When mother is busy, does the child sometimes seek her attention?	Yes	53	37	29	29	.10					.10	.05
		No	17	22	7	25							
9.	When mother is with another child, does the child seek her attention?	Yes	13	9	12	11							
		No	33	44	23	39							
10.	When mother leaves, is the child upset?	Yes	6	9	9	20	.05	.01	.05				
		No	42	43	27	32							
11.	Does the child decide many things for himself?	Yes	29	35	17	27		.10		.10			
		No	11	13	14	18							
12.	Does the child go about the neighborhood unassisted?	Yes	32	31	29	40	.05	.01	.05				
		No	11	17	4	5							
13.	Does mother keep close track of the child's whereabouts?	Yes	25	13	18	32	.01	.01	.001	.01	.05		
		No	25	42	17	21							
14.	Is mother judged as fostering the child's growth and independence?	Yes	34	47	23	30	.10	.05	.05				
		No	17	11	11	21							

* Based upon chi-square tests.

O = overall test.

$\frac{N}{W}$ = Negro vs. white children; $\frac{NB}{WB}$ = Negro boys vs. white boys; $\frac{NG}{WG}$ = Negro girls vs. white girls.

$\frac{B}{G}$ = boys vs. girls; $\frac{NB}{NG}$ = Negro boys vs. Negro girls; $\frac{WB}{WG}$ = white boys vs. white girls.

Only the first three questions in Table 15.11 refer directly to rule be-havior. Question 1 data indicate that a majority (55%) of the mothers reported that their children sometimes spontaneously report rule viola-tions to them. Many more mothers (83%) said that the children usually admit rule violations when asked (question 2). In this regard, more white than Negro mothers said that their children usually make such admissions (90% vs. 74%, respectively). There is also a significant racial difference in the readiness of a mother to punish the child for suspected rule violations, although, indeed, few mothers of either race express much hesitancy to mete out punishment on such occasions. Seventy-nine percent of the white and 94% of the Negro mothers said that they do punish for suspected rule violations (question 3).

A large majority of the mothers (87%) seemed to believe that their children are not too hesitant in trying things (question 4). Eighty-one percent also said that the child plays well alone, although white mothers were more positive about this than Negro mothers (question 5). On the other hand, only a bare majority of the mothers (55%) indicated that the child sometimes needs to be encouraged (question 6). In this regard, there appears to be a significant sex difference—especially among the white children—with the boys more commonly needing encouragement than the girls.

A majority of the children (55%) were reported as having exhibited dependent behavior, or excessive "skirt-clinging," at this age; this was true in the reports for the children of both races and sexes (question 7). An even higher percentage (64%) were said to have sought mother's attention when she was busy; such reports were especially frequent for the Negro boys (question 8). Less common, apparently, is the practice of the child seeking mother's attention when she is busy with another child; only 24% of the children were said to have done this (question 9). A comparable percentage of the children (23%) were described as be-coming upset when mother leaves. Such upsets were more commonly reported for the Negro children, particularly for the girls (question 10).

About two-thirds of the mothers seemed to feel that their children decided many things for themselves, but there was a tendency for white mothers to assert this belief more often than Negro mothers (question 11). In contrast, more Negro than white children were said to go about their neighborhoods unassisted (88% vs. 63%, respectively; see question 12). Negro mothers, however, claimed more often than white mothers that they kept close track of the child's whereabouts (question 13). This assertion was made most often by mothers of Negro girls and least often by mothers of white girls. When the mothers were rated at the end of the second session with respect to whether they fostered the child's growth and independence or were overly protective of him, 69% were rated at the fostering end of the continuum (question 14). This judgment was most frequently made about mothers of white girls and least frequently about mothers of Negro girls.

In summary, there appear to be both sex and racial differences in these data; the latter appear to be more common than the former. Among the sex differences, perhaps the most important finding is that both Negro and white mothers more frequently perceive their sons rather than their daughters as needing encouragement. This sex difference is accentuated among the white children. With respect to racial differences, there is a suggestion that Negro mothers may, in a certain sense, attempt to keep a tighter rein on their children or be more severe with them than white mothers. Thus, there seems to be more certainty that they will punish suspected rule violations; also, that they will keep close track of the child's whereabouts. As to the children themselves, there is an indication that the behavior of white children may be relatively mature compared to that of Negro children. For example, white children in general are described as playing better alone, as being more ready to admit rule violations, and as being less likely to become upset when mother leaves than is true of Negro children. On the other hand, it is also true that Negro children appear to have greater freedom of movement about their neighborhoods than white children do. Why this is so is not clear, however, since Negro mothers also claim to keep closer track of their children than white mothers do.

Children's Misbehavior, with Related Parental Behavior

The interview covered a variety of misbehaviors that children may show. It also explored the question as to what extent these misbehaviors disturb the parents. Data relevant to this domain are summarized in Table 15.12.

The first three items in Table 15.12 focus upon the child's tendency to be messy or dirty. Eighty-one percent of the Negro mothers but only 60% of the white mothers described the child as being messy around the house (question 1). Most of the children were described as getting dirty easily, but again there is a significant Negro–white difference (71% vs. 55%, respectively; see question 3). In contrast, relatively few children of either race were said to spill things while eating; yet, once more there is a significant Negro–white difference (28% vs. 15%, respectively; see question 2).

About one-half of the white mothers reported that their children talk back, but, as question 4 shows, the percentage was appreciably lower for the Negro mothers (30%). There was also a more pronounced

TABLE 15.12

Children's Misbehavior, with Related Parental Behavior

Question	Response	Frequencies or means				p values*						
		WB	WG	NB	NG	O	$\frac{N}{W}$	$\frac{NB}{WB}$	$\frac{NG}{WG}$	$\frac{B}{G}$	$\frac{NB}{NG}$	$\frac{WB}{WG}$
								Race			Sex	
1. Does the child make a mess around the house?	Yes	29	37	31	42	.01	.01	.01				
	No	22	22	5	12							
2. Does the child spill things while eating?	Yes	8	8	12	13	.10	.05	.10				
	No	43	51	24	41							
3. Does the child get dirty?	Yes	30	31	30	34	.05	.05	.05			.10	
	No	21	28	6	20							
4. Does the child talk back?	Yes	25	31	10	17	.05	.01	.05	.05			
	No	26	27	26	37							
5. Does the child not do what he is told?	Yes	34	30	16	29			.10				
	No	16	29	20	25							
6. Does the child fight with other children?	Yes	17	11	16	27	.01	.01		.01			
	No	34	47	20	27							
7. Does the child fail to do his chores around the house?	Yes	8	9	10	8							
	No	42	48	26	43							
8. Is the child rude?	Yes	16	16	9	18							
	No	35	43	27	35							
9. Does the child destroy things?	Yes	10	4	23	18	.001	.001	.001	.001	.01	.01	
	No	41	55	13	36							
10. Does the child get into his siblings' things?	Yes	22	29	25	32		.10	.05				.10
	No	25	25	10	20							

		NB	WB	NG	WG	N/W	NB/WB	NG/WG	B/G	NB/NG	WB/WG
11. Does the child refuse to go to bed on time?	Yes	15	16	19	26	.05	.01	.10	.05		.05
	No	34	41	17	28						
12. Does the child fail to eat everything on his plate?	Yes	16	31	14	30	.05				.01	.05
	No	35	28	22	24						
13. Does the child talk too much?	Yes	20	24	18	36	.05	.01		.01		
	No	31	35	18	18						
14. Does the child wet the bed?	Yes	12	6	9	13				.10		
	No	39	53	27	41						
15. Does the child stutter?	Yes	9	1	5	10	.05					.05
	No	42	58	31	43						
16. Does the child lie?	Yes	12	17	25	39	.001	.001	.001	.01		
	No	39	41	10	15						
17. Is the child noisy around the house?	Yes	34	41	32	36	.10		.05			
	No	17	18	4	18						
18. Does the child play with his sex organs?	Yes	0	5	2	3						.10
	No	50	54	34	51						
19. Mean number of misbehaviors?		6.2	5.9	8.5	8.0	.001	.001	.001	.001		
20. Mean number of misbehavior items that bother mother?		4.1	3.1	5.6	4.9	.001	.001	.05	.01	.10	.10
21. Mean number of misbehavior items that bother father?		3.0	2.5	4.5	3.8	.01	.01	.05	.05		

* Based upon chi-square, F-, and t-tests.

O = overall test.

$\frac{N}{W}$ = Negro vs. white children; $\frac{NB}{WB}$ = Negro boys vs. white boys; $\frac{NG}{WG}$ = Negro girls vs. white girls.

$\frac{B}{G}$ = boys vs. girls; $\frac{NB}{NG}$ = Negro boys vs. Negro girls; $\frac{WB}{WG}$ = white boys vs. white girls.

tendency for white mothers to say that their children do not always do what they are told, but this difference is not statistically significant (question 5). Fighting with other children, however, is apparently much more common among Negro than among white children (48% vs. 26%, respectively; see question 6). The contrast between Negro and white girls is especially marked in this regard.

Work plays a prominent part in the lives of Millfield's children (see Chapter 16). Even these preschool children usually know what chores are. And, according to their mothers, only a small percentage (18%) of them fail to do their chores (question 7). The mothers are less positive, however, about the children's manners. Thus, 30% of the mothers admitted that their children tend to be rude (question 8). With about equal frequency, they also acknowledged that their children are sometimes destructive (question 9). However, there is both a significant sex and racial difference in destructive behavior. Not surprisingly, boys were viewed as being more destructive than girls. And Negro mothers described their children as being destructive much more often than white mothers did.

Difficulties brought about by the child getting into his siblings' possessions were reported frequently, as might be anticipated. Overall, 57% of the mothers said that they have to cope with this problem (question 10). (It was reported most often among Negro boys.) Refusing to go to bed on time was noted somewhat less frequently, yet 39% of the mothers said that they have this problem with their children (question 11). The frequency was even higher among the Negro mothers: 50% of them reported the problem, compared to 29% of the white mothers. Failure to eat everything at the table, on the other hand, appears to be sex-related but not race-related. Thus, 54% of the girls but only 34% of the boys were described as exhibiting this problem (question 12). There was also a greater likelihood of the girls being described as talking too much, but this sex difference is not statistically significant. However, there is a very significant racial difference: 60% of the Negro mothers but only 40% of the white mothers so described their children (question 13). Negro boys were also reported as being noisy around the house significantly more often than white boys, but there was no such difference between the girls of the two races (question 17).

Several behavioral areas will now be touched upon which may be indicative of more severe psychological problems than some of the behaviors discussed so far. For example, 20% of the children were reported as still wetting their beds (question 14). As far as the four groups are concerned, this problem tends to be relatively infrequent among the white girls. Stuttering is even less common; it was reported for only 13%

of the children.[12] Of particular interest is the fact that, for the white children, as expected, stuttering was reported much more frequently for boys than for girls; however, among Negro children the incidence was reported as higher for girls (question 15). On the item pertaining to lying, there is a pronounced racial difference (question 16). Only 27% of the white mothers but 72% of the Negro mothers said that their children tell lies. In contrast, very few mothers of either race (overall, only 5%) said that their children engage in masturbatory activity (question 18). Of these ten affirmative reports, eight were by the mothers of girls.

The total number of behavior problems reported by each mother was tallied to see whether there were differences in the average number of misbehaviors reported for the four subgroups. More misbehaviors were affirmed, on the average, by Negro mothers than by white mothers (question 19). The mothers were also asked, with reference to each misbehavior, whether it bothered them and whether it bothered the child's father. As questions 20 and 21 indicate, the answer was yes much more often for both Negro mothers and fathers than for their white counterparts. Within each racial group, the data indicate that these misbehaviors concern mothers more consistently than they disturb fathers.

In summary, it is clear that there are relatively few sex differences as far as misbehavior is concerned, but there are many racial differences, judging by these reports from the Millfield mothers. However, boys, not surprisingly, are seen as more destructive than girls, while the latter show more eating problems. With respect to racial differences, Negro children are described more unfavorably than white children in these reports. Thus, they are more often seen as messy, as getting into fights, as destructive, as talking too much, as refusing to go to bed, and as telling lies. Such differences suggest that the Negro child tends to be less well socialized at this point than the white child, at least in a variety of behaviors which would affect his readiness to cooperate effectively in group situations, like those found in the schoolroom. It may also be important to note that the white children appear to be more willing to talk back to adults, suggesting that they may be less threatened in face-to-face encounters with authority figures.

CONCLUDING COMMENTS

So much information was generated by these interviews—and only a small fraction of it actually has been presented—that it is difficult to

[12] In the absolute sense, of course, this incidence is high enough to merit concern.

develop generalizations which do justice to the data. However, we shall attempt to summarize here the highlights of each section that has been reported earlier in greater detail.

There are significant differences between Negro and white families with respect to their structures, resources, and activities. Negro families are larger than white ones, they have appreciably less income, and they are more dependent upon the land for a livelihood. Their houses also tend to be in poorer physical repair and less well equipped. Very few children of either race are living apart from their natural mothers, but more Negro than white children are separated from their natural fathers. It is important to note, however, that most children, including Negro children, who are separated from their natural fathers do have father-substitutes.

These families are almost all North Carolina born, usually from the immediately surrounding area; most of them have their roots in the soil. Proportionately more Negro than white parents have been born and reared within a few miles of Millfield. Families of both races tend to have many relatives close at hand. The education of both parents usually has been modest, but, in the families of both races, the mother ordinarily has gone farther in school than the father. In evaluating her educational background, the Negro mother especially is likely to emphasize her positive achievements. Negro and white mothers often work, the former in domestic service and the latter in mills or factories. On Sundays, families of both races typically attend either Baptist or Methodist churches. In talking about their families, two facts seem to stand out and merit special emphasis. First, a majority of the Negro mothers had not wanted to become pregnant with the child who was at the focus of the interview. Second, the father is perceived as being dominant in the Negro homes more often than is true in the white homes. This latter perception, of course, is not in keeping with the commonly accepted picture of the matriarchal organization within Negro families.

The relationship of the father to his children is usually described quite positively; the mother emphasizes that he enjoys them. But the father is criticized, too, primarily for being too easy on the children. The observation is also frequently made that his work does not leave him enough time to spend with his children.

Patterns of child-training appear to be different in a number of ways for the two races. Although most children are whipped, Negro mothers appear to have greater confidence than white mothers in the value of this form of punishment. Negro mothers also report greater emphasis in the use of models in their child-training practices. On the other hand, white mothers are more willing to endorse the usefulness of praise in training. In addition, they describe the use of banishment more often than Negro mothers do.

In recalling the developmental histories of their children, mothers of both races—but particularly Negro mothers—emphasize the relatively early acquisition of many skills. There also tends to be—again, for both races—a belief that the girls acquired certain skills earlier than the boys. Most important, perhaps, is the observation that the boys tended to be slower than the girls in developing verbal behavior. With respect to dislocations or traumas experienced during their preschool years, the incidence appears to have been higher for white than for Negro children.

In discussing motor skills, mothers again underscored the positive. This was especially true for white mothers in regard to school-like skills, such as coloring pictures. In these behavioral areas, the Negro child is likely to be at a special disadvantage due to the relative unavailability in his home of needed tools and supplies. However, Negro and white mothers seem to agree that there is essentially no difference between boys and girls at this age as far as their achievement striving is concerned. Also, overall, Negro and white mothers attribute comparable strengths to their children in this regard. Negro mothers, however, express more sensitivity to the intellectual achievements than to the social achievements of their children, whereas the reverse emphasis is given by white mothers. Mothers in both racial groups seem to expect high accomplishments (occupationally and educationally) from their children; the ambitions of the Negro mothers appear to be particularly unrealistic in this regard. Also, there can be no doubt that it is the rare mother who sees any future in farming for her child.

In describing the temperamental and personality traits of their children, mothers give little emphasis to sex differences. Generally, Negro mothers give comparatively more emphasis to the extraverted qualities of their children, while white mothers more commonly underline introverted qualities. It is also important to remember that Negro mothers more often describe their children as fearful. A marked racial difference was uncovered, too, when inquiry was made about the child's parental preference. White mothers see their children as being equally divided in this regard, but Negro mothers emphasize the child's preference for his mother.

Negro parents particularly seem to expect immediate obedience from their child and to be intolerant of self-assertiveness on his part. Also, Negro mothers seem to become more upset than white mothers when their children are either unduly aggressive or submissive. Parents of neither race, however, appear to be tolerant of parentally directed aggression; the mother appears more often as the target of such aggression than the father. In viewing their children, mothers seem to be more inclined to see them as the victims rather than as the initiators of aggression in their interactions with other children.

With respect to rules, Negro mothers appear to be more ready than white mothers to punish unconfirmed but suspected violations. In terms of ability to play alone, white children are reported as more mature than Negro children, yet the Vineland Social Maturity scores showed little difference between the racial groups. Mothers of both races—but especially white mothers—said that their sons needed encouragement more than their daughters.

As far as misbehavior is concerned, few sex but many racial differences were reported. Negro children more often than white children are described as messy, as getting into fights, as destructive, as talking too much, and as telling lies. The general picture that emerges, therefore, is one in which the Negro child appears to be less socialized than the white child. These differences may assume special importance when the children enter first-grade classrooms.

Chapter 16

EIGHTH-GRADE CHILDREN REPORT ON THEIR WORLDS

Data from a second interview study will be reported in this chapter. This time the interviewees were the children themselves: specifically, those children—Negro and white—who were in the eighth grade when the interviews were scheduled. The main objective was to learn how these children view Millfield, their places within it, and their expectations with regard to the life that lies ahead of them.

PROCEDURE

Staff resources limited the number of children who could be included in this second interview study. A decision was made, therefore, to concentrate upon those children who were the oldest ones regularly included in the various studies which have been reported in previous chapters. It was felt that these children would be best able to respond to a wide range of questions. Also, their responses should provide a good picture—from the child's viewpoint—of how life in Millfield appears to them toward the end of their first important phase of schooling and as they enter adolescence.

The Children

Each child was interviewed who was in the eighth grade during the 1963–64 academic year. In all, 136 children (78 Negro) participated. Each interviewee was at least 13 years of age but less than 17 years of age when he was interviewed. The mean age for all of the children was

399

TABLE 16.1

Age Data (in Months) for Eighth-Grade Interviewees

	White		Negro	
	Boys	Girls	Boys	Girls
N	28	30	32	46
Mean	171.3	166.6	167.8	166.5
S.D.	9.3	5.8	9.5	9.1
Range	160–191	157–180	158–192	157–202

approximately 14 years. Age data for each of the four subgroups are given in Table 16.1.

The Interviewers

The interviews were conducted by five female staff members (two Negro). Each child was, of course, interviewed by a woman of his own race. In addition, the proportions of boys and girls that each interviewer talked with were about equal. Within these two restrictions, assignment of a child to a particular interviewer was made on a random basis.

It should be noted that the interviewers were regular members of the project staff, women who were already well-known to most of the children. It was our hope that the trust previously generated in the children by the women's earlier work in Millfield would enhance the meaningfulness and quality of the responses given by the children.

The Structured Interview

A structured interview was developed to assure that comparable information would be gathered by the several interviewers from children of both races and sexes. The content of the questions and their sequence were determined by several members of the staff working together, including the individuals who ultimately conducted the interviews. Trial interviews were held with a small number of children (children not in the target sample) before the final format of the interview was determined.

The interview questions were arranged in a twenty-page interview booklet. These questions were organized under the following thirteen subheadings (given in the order in which they occurred in the interview): (1) family structure; (2) house; (3) family finances; (4) parent behavior; (5) peers; (6) recreation; (7) television; (8) marriage and family; (9) church; (10) education; (11) work; (12) community; and

(13) self. There was also space on the last page for the interviewer to record special comments about the child and the conduct of the interview. The interview schedule is reproduced in Appendix B.

Conduct of the Interview

Each child was seen individually and privately. The interviews were conducted during school hours; each child was excused from regular classwork to participate. Ordinarily, the interview was carried out in one session that lasted between one and two hours. Sometimes, however, the interview had to be divided into two sessions. The interviewers recognized the importance of rapport and took time to establish a comfortable relationship with the child before starting the sequence of structured questions.

Analysis of the Data and Their Presentation

In the pages that follow, data will be presented and discussed for each of the 13 sections of the interview listed above. For each of these sections, a summary table (see Tables 16.2 through 16.13) was prepared following a regular format. In column 1, specific questions are listed which ordinarily (but not necessarily always) can be answered by analyzing the child's interview data. In column 2, the categories used to classify the answers to the questions—when such classification is appropriate—are given. Then, in columns 3, 4, 5, and 6, the frequencies of each response category are given; column 3 is for white boys, column 4 is for white girls, column 5 is for Negro boys, and column 6 is for Negro girls.[1] Occasionally, however, the question in column 1 required the computation of means rather than tabulating frequencies. When this was true, mean values have been entered in columns 3 through 6 for the various subgroups, and no response categories are listed in column 2.

The last seven columns in Tables 16.2 through 16.13 record the probability levels (p values) determined by applying various statistical tests

[1] In referring to the frequency tabulations in Tables 16.2 through 16.13, note should be made of the fact that the number of children in each of the four groups does not always agree with the numbers given for them in Table 16.1. Sometimes this discrepancy is due to the fact that the question either was not asked or was not answered by all children. In other instances, their responses would not fit into the categorization scheme. Most of the analyses, however, are based upon responses given by all 136 children. The reader should also recognize that the theoretical cell frequencies for some questions are too low to justify utilization of chi-square. Since this is exploratory work, however, the results of the analysis of the data for each question in each table have been included. A quick inspection ordinarily will indicate if the expected frequencies are so low (five or below) that the findings must be considered as extremely tentative.

to the data recorded in these tables; however, probability levels greater than .10 are not entered. The comparisons made are as follows:

O — an overall or total test

$\dfrac{N}{W}$ — a racial comparison; all Negro vs. all white children

$\dfrac{NB}{WB}$ — a racial comparison; Negro boys vs. white boys

$\dfrac{NG}{WG}$ — a racial comparison; Negro girls vs. white girls

$\dfrac{B}{G}$ — a sex comparison; all boys vs. all girls

$\dfrac{NB}{NG}$ — a sex comparison; Negro boys vs. Negro girls

$\dfrac{WB}{WG}$ — a sex comparison; white boys vs. white girls

RESULTS

Family Structure

It is apparent from the data given in Table 16.2 that the families of the Negro and white children are significantly different in a number of important ways. To begin with, there is again the matter of sheer size. The Negro families, on the average, are about 40% larger than the white families, and there are almost 50% more people living in the Negro homes. This greater size does not come about because more adults are living in the Negro homes; instead, it is brought about by a larger child population. In short, the Negro eighth-grade child is likely to be living with both more siblings and more children who are nonsiblings than the white child. The fact that his parents tend to have large families also means that a Negro child in the sample is less likely to be the youngest member of his sibship.

About 86% of the white children and 77% of the Negro children live with both of their natural parents. (For a sample of this size, this racial difference is not statistically significant.) Whenever a child is not living with both of his natural parents, it is almost always the father who is missing. Except in a small number of cases, however, the absent father has been replaced by a substitute—usually either a stepfather, an uncle, or a grandfather. Two important things to recognize are that absence of the father is less common among these Negro families than is reported elsewhere, and, when the natural father is not present, some type of father-substitute is available in the home.[2]

---

[2] In the following discussions, data pertaining to either the natural father or a father-substitute will be reported as descriptive of fathers of these eighth-grade children.

Employment patterns differ markedly across race for both fathers and mothers. All the white children, for example, reported that their fathers were employed full-time, but seven Negro children said that their fathers were either unemployed ($N = 5$) or were able to secure only part-time jobs ($N = 2$). The type of occupation reported for the fathers also differed; many more Negro than white fathers work as farmers (37 vs. 11, respectively), whereas, proportionately, more white than Negro fathers have secured employment in mills or factories (26 vs. 14, respectively). About equal proportions of Negro and white mothers have full-time jobs, but their jobs are markedly different. Most of the employed white mothers (18 out of 24) work in mills, but no Negro mother was reported as holding such a position. In contrast, only Negro mothers were reported to be in domestic service or in farm labor.

These parental employment patterns are important for a number of reasons, but especially because they suggest to the children what line of work they themselves are likely to be following if they remain in Millfield. Paths taken by older siblings may be even more important in this regard, however, and for this reason information was sought about both the migratory patterns and the jobs secured by older brothers and sisters of these subjects. The findings here are quite clear. For example, many more Negro than white siblings had migrated to either the North or West (22 vs. 2, respectively). Twelve out of 45 Negro siblings were reported to be working in factories, but it is important to realize that most of these jobs had been secured in either the North or West rather than in Millfield. In general, these findings pertaining to family patterns in Millfield correspond quite well with the data secured by other methods (see Chapters 1 and 15).

House and Lands

Millfield is made up primarily of small farms and small land holdings which are not farmed, except for gardens. Only six white children and seven Negro children, for instance, reported that their families live on more than 100 acres (see Table 16.3). Moreover, slightly more than one-half of the children indicated that their family's home area contained less than five acres. (The data in Table 16.3 also suggest that boys may be more inclined than girls to exaggerate their families' land holdings!)

About 74% of the white families, but only 36% of the Negro families, either own outright or are buying the land they live on. Overall, approximately 20% of the families pay a cash rent for their property; there is a tendency for this to be more common among the Negro families. A marked racial difference appears when it comes to using a share of the

TABLE 16.2

Children's Responses to Questions about Family Structure

Question	Response	Frequencies or means					p values*					
								Race			Sex	
		WB	WG	NB	NG	O	N/W	NB/WB	NG/WG	B/G	NB/NG	WB/WG
1. What is the mean number of people living in S's home?		5.6	5.7	8.5	8.2	.001	.001	.001	.001			
2. What is the mean number of people in S's family?		6.1	6.1	8.9	8.2	.001	.001	.001	.001			
3. Are there more than two adults in S's home?	Yes	9	16	12	20							
	No	19	14	20	26							
4. Does S live with both of his natural parents?	Yes	23	27	26	34							
	No	5	3	6	12							
5. Do one or more grandparents live in S's home?	Yes	3	8	2	6							
	No	25	22	30	40							
6. Do adult siblings live in S's home? (Age ≥ 18)	Yes	6	10	10	15							
	No	22	20	22	31							
7. What is the mean number of children in S's home, exclusive of S?		2.2	2.0	4.8	4.5	.001	.001	.001	.001			
8. Do children who are nonsiblings live in S's home?	Yes	1	1	3	13	.01	.01		.05	.10	.10	
	No	27	29	29	33							
9. Is S an only child?	Yes	2	2	0	1							
	No	26	28	32	45							
10. Is S the youngest child in his family?	Yes	3	9	1	3	.01	.05		.05			
	No	25	21	31	43							
11. Is S the oldest child in his family?	Yes	10	4	5	12							
	No	18	26	27	34							
12. Has S's father been married previously?	Yes	2	1	2	4							.10
	No	22	25	28	38							

Question	Response					N/W	NB/WB	NG/WG	B/G	NB/NG	WB/WG
13. Is *S*'s father employed full-time?	Yes	27	30	29	35	.05	.05	.05	.10		
	No	0	0	1	6						
14. Is *S*'s father a farmer?	Yes	5	6	15	22	.001	.001	.001	.01		
	No	22	24	14	13						
15. Does *S*'s father work in a mill or factory?	Yes	12	14	9	5	.05	.01		.01		
	No	15	16	20	30						
16. Has *S*'s mother been married previously?	Yes	6	2	2	2	.10					
	No	19	24	28	41						
17. Is *S*'s mother employed full-time?	Yes	10	14	12	20						
	No	18	15	19	25						
18. Does *S*'s mother work (full or part-time) in a mill or factory?	Yes	9	9	0	0	.001	.001	.001	.001		
	No	2	5	16	23						
19. Does *S*'s mother work (full or part-time) in domestic service?	Yes	0	0	7	12	.001	.001	.05	.01		
	No	11	14	9	11						
20. Does *S*'s mother work (full or part-time) in farming?	Yes	0	0	5	6	.05	.01				
	No	11	14	11	17						
21. How many adult siblings live in the places indicated?	Home	7	13	19	25	.10	.01	.10	.10		
	N.C.	12	15	14	25						
	South	2	3	1	1						
	North or West	1	1	11	11						
22. How many adult siblings are employed in the jobs indicated?	Farmers	0	1	12	6	.001	.001	.001	.001	.05	.05
	Mill work	9	6	4	8						
	Domestics	0	0	6	2						
	Unemployed	0	4	1	6						

* Based upon chi-square, F-, and t-tests.

O = overall test.

$\dfrac{N}{W}$ = Negro vs. white children; $\dfrac{NB}{WB}$ = Negro boys vs. white boys; $\dfrac{NG}{WG}$ = Negro girls vs. white girls.

$\dfrac{B}{G}$ = boys vs. girls; $\dfrac{NB}{NG}$ = Negro boys vs. Negro girls; $\dfrac{WB}{WG}$ = white boys vs. white girls.

TABLE 16.3

Children's Responses to Questions about House and Lands

Question	Response	Frequencies or means					p values*						
								Race			Sex		
		WB	WG	NB	NG	O	$\frac{N}{W}$	$\frac{NB}{WB}$	$\frac{NG}{WG}$	$\frac{B}{G}$	$\frac{NB}{NG}$	$\frac{WB}{WG}$
1. What is the mean acreage S reports living on?		39.3	25.6	37.3	15.7					.10	.10	
2. Does S report acreage to be less than 5?	Yes	14	16	13	24							
	No	14	10	19	21							
3. Do S's parents own (or are they buying) their land?	Yes	19	24	14	14	.001	.001		.001			
	No	9	6	18	32							
4. Do S's parents rent the land they live on?	Yes	5	3	3	15	.05			.05		.05	
	No	23	27	29	31							
5. Do S's parents "farm on shares"?	Yes	1	0	11	12	.001	.001	.01	.01			
	No	27	30	21	34							
6. Does S's family have a garden?	Yes	21	22	28	42		.05		.10			
	No	7	8	4	4							
7. Does S's family raise tobacco?	Yes	5	5	21	26	.001	.001	.001	.01			
	No	23	25	11	20							
8. What is the mean number of rooms in S's home?		6.2	6.6	6.0	5.9				.10			
9. Does S say his house is of adequate size?	Yes	23	27	28	41							
	No	5	3	4	5							
10. How does S describe the condition of his home?	Good	22	22	22	21	.05				.01	.05	.10
	Average	4	11	6	21							
	Poor	2	0	4	4							

Question	Response					p					
11. How does S compare the condition of his house to that of others in Millfield?	Better	6	8	8	9						.10
	Average	18	22	22	31						
	Worse	4	0	2	6						
12. Does S's house have electricity?	Yes	28	29	32	46	.001					
	No	0	1	0	0						
13. Does S's house have an inside toilet?	Yes	18	23	3	8	.001	.001	.001			
	No	10	7	26	38						
14. Does S's house have a telephone?	Yes	18	22	10	13	.001	.001	.05	.001		
	No	10	8	22	33						
15. Does S's house have a radio?	Yes	28	28	31	39	.10				.10	
	No	0	2	1	7						
16. Does S's house have TV?	Yes	27	29	31	42						
	No	1	1	1	4						
17. Does S's house have a record player?	Yes	20	29	17	23	.001	.001	.001			.05
	No	8	1	15	23						
18. Does S's house have a washing machine?	Yes	27	28	30	35	.05	.10			.10	.10
	No	1	2	2	11						
19. Does S's house have an electric refrigerator?	Yes	28	29	32	46						
	No	0	1	0	0						
20. Does S's house have an electric freezer?	Yes	15	17	22	28						
	No	13	13	10	18						
21. Does S's family have a car?	Yes	27	30	26	33	.01	.001	.01			
	No	1	0	6	13						
22. Does S's house have an electric water pump?	Yes	24	25	7	8	.001	.001	.001	.001		
	No	3	4	17	31						
23. Does S's house have a wood heating stove?	Yes	10	7	30	39	.001	.001	.001	.001		
	No	18	23	2	7						
24. Does S's house have a wood cooking stove?	Yes	3	4	21	28	.001	.001	.001	.001		
	No	25	26	11	18						

(continued)

TABLE 16.3 (*continued*)

| Question | Response | Frequencies or means | | | | p values* | | | | | | |
		WB	WG	NB	NG	O	N/W	NB/WB	NG/WG	B/G	NB/NG	WB/WG
25. Does S's family get a newspaper?	Yes	18	23	22	30							
	No	10	7	10	16							
26. Does S's family get magazines?	Yes	17	26	23	29				.05			.10
	No	11	4	9	17							
27. What is the mean number of years that S has lived in his present house?		7.2	8.2	8.2	6.5							
28. Does S's family plan to move?	Yes	8	2	11	15	.05	.10		.05		.10	
	No	20	28	21	31							
29. Does S mention a desire for an inside bath and water?†	Yes	4	4	7	13			.05				
	No	6	3	22	25							
30. Does S mention a desire for more rooms, or to fix present ones?	Yes	6	6	4	11							
	No	22	24	28	35							
31. Does S mention a desire for better heating?	Yes	0	3	6	0	.01					.01	
	No	28	27	26	46							
32. Does S mention a desire for more furnishings and appliances?	Yes	6	6	7	11							
	No	22	24	25	35							
33. Does S mention a need for general repairs (paint, clean, remodel, etc.)?	Yes	9	10	10	22							
	No	19	20	22	24							
34. Does S mention at least one home improvement he would like?	Yes	22	22	26	43		.10		.05			
	No	6	8	6	3							

* Based upon chi-square, F-, and t-tests.
† Refers only to children who reported no inside toilet facilities.
For definitions of frequencies or means and p values see pages 401 and 402.

crops to pay for land use; in Millfield this is almost exclusively an arrangement made by Negro families.

Most families raise a personal garden; however, there is a racial difference in favor of the Negro families. Many different crops are grown and dairy farming is on the increase, but tobacco continues to hold on as the major money-crop. Tobacco-growing is becoming more and more a Negro undertaking; only 10 of the 57 families in this sample who were raising tobacco were white.

The average house was reported as having six rooms. Since there is no racial difference in this regard, and since the Negro homes contain about 50% more people than the white homes (see above), it seems clear that the Negro children are living under much more crowded conditions than the white children. Nevertheless, only nine Negro children, as compared with eight white children, said that their houses were inadequate in size. Also, despite the poor condition of many homes by commonly accepted middle-class standards, only ten children (eight Negro) actually described their homes as being in poor condition. In describing the condition of their homes, there is no significant racial difference, but there is a very significant sex difference: boys, both Negro and white, are more positive than girls in their descriptions. When asked to compare the condition of their home with that of others in Millfield, most children settled for the term "average." (Among the four groups, Negro girls were most unfavorable in their comments about their homes.)

Inquiries into the availability of certain major items or resources produced interesting data, highlighting both important similarities and differences between the Negro and white homes. All but one home in the sample, for example, have electricity, and the vast majority have both television and radio sets as well as electric refrigerators. Electric freezers are also surprisingly common, providing many families with the means to preserve foodstuffs grown on their land. Almost 90% of the homes also have electric washing machines. On the other hand, less than 15% of the Negro homes have inside toilets, compared with about 70% of the white homes. Negro homes also have few telephones, and the Negro family is more likely to be without an automobile than the white family. Electric water pumps are quite common in the white homes, but not in the Negro homes. All but 9 of the Negro families still depend on wood-burning stoves to both cook and heat, whereas 41 out of the 58 white families have obtained separate heating systems for these two functions. Most families of both races have access to newspapers and magazines, yet a number of them are without one or sometimes both items. Overall, it is clear that the white homes are much better equipped than the Negro homes.

The typical child in the sample had lived in his present home between six and eight years or, roughly, about one-half of his life at the time he was interviewed. A sizable number ($N = 36$) indicated, however, that their families were planning to move; there was a tendency for such a prospect to be reported more frequently among the Negro children. Moving appears to be particularly common among share-cropping families as they attempt to secure a better financial arrangement with a new landlord.

One of the curious aspects of this part of the interview had to do with the children's responses to the question, "What changes could be made in your house to make it a better place to live in?" In general, their answers were quite limited. For example, only 28 out of 84 children whose houses were without inside toilets mentioned that it would be an improvement to have such a facility. Only nine children mentioned a desire for better heating, although 86 children were from homes with wood-heating stoves. A need for more rooms or to improve existing ones was noted by only 27 children. Indeed, 23 children failed to describe any way in which their houses could be improved. It is obvious that these data should not be interpreted to mean that large numbers of children do not in fact want inside toilets, better heating systems, more rooms, and so on. More likely, many of these children probably do not think about these things, perhaps in part because they have never seemed like real possibilities. When asked a question like the one given above, then, they have difficulty responding to it. On the other hand, if the children had been asked, "Would you like to have an inside toilet?" most, if not all, would probably have answered affirmatively. In a sense, the children's answers to this question may reflect one kind of adjustment to a world where it does not seem likely to them that they will obtain certain items which are more or less taken for granted by middle-class families. Perhaps it is better not to want something other than a wood stove if in fact that is the only type of heating system that one is likely to own.

Family Finances

The children were not asked to report or estimate the yearly income of their families.[3] They were asked, however, if their parents earned enough money to care for the family and if the family had difficulty

---

[3] The mothers of kindergarten-age children provided data on family income; see Chapter 15.

obtaining food, clothing, fuel, and medical care. They were also asked to compare the financial position of their family with that of other Millfield families. Their answers to these questions are given in Table 16.4.

The responses to the first five questions listed in Table 16.4 show that only a few children reported their families as having inadequate funds or as having difficulty in securing any of the basic necessities listed above. By generally accepted middle-class standards, these answers appear at best to be unrealistic, but middle-class standards are not the likely referents for the children. Instead, the controlling standards seem to be those of Millfield and, even more narrowly, the standards of the child's own racial group living in Millfield. Thus, most of the children seem to answer questions like these by comparing their situations with those of the other children with whom they associate on a day-to-day basis.

In regard to the point just made, when the children were asked to make a comparison between their family's financial position and that of other families in Millfield, 85% reported that they saw no difference. While there appears to be more heterogeneity in Millfield than this figure suggests, it is not in fact marked compared to the situation that exists in many communities. These data do not indicate, then, that money is plentiful but rather that most of these children do not perceive any pronounced differences between their circumstances and those of most people in the community. In a sense, many of them have yet to learn that they are poor.

Parental Behavior

The fourth part of the interview focused upon the child's observations about selected components of his parents' behavior. Answers to 23 questions in this domain have been summarized in Table 16.5.

The first point of interest in these data centers about the question of which parent is perceived as being dominant, especially when the control of the child is at issue. In general, both Negro and white children agree that father is the boss. But when the two parents disagree over what the child should do, the white child is more likely than the Negro child to report that the mother prevails. This finding is contrary to what one might anticipate if indeed Negro families are much more matriarchal in character than white families. When Negro fathers are in the home— and it must be remembered that almost all these homes do have a father-figure—maternal dominance does not appear to develop as often as it does in white homes, at least not in the eyes of the children.

Several questions were asked to determine the extent of parental in-

TABLE 16.4

Children's Responses to Questions about Family Finances

| | | Frequencies | | | | p values* | | | | | | |
| | | WB | WG | NB | NG | O | Race | | | Sex | | |
Question	Response						$\frac{N}{W}$	$\frac{NB}{WB}$	$\frac{NG}{WG}$	$\frac{B}{G}$	$\frac{NB}{NG}$	$\frac{WB}{WG}$
1. Does S say parents earn enough money to care for family?	Yes	26	26	28	37							
	No	2	4	4	9							
2. Does S say family has difficulty getting enough food?	Yes	2	0	3	4							
	No	26	30	29	42							
3. Does S say family has difficulty getting adequate clothing?	Yes	2	2	1	8							
	No	26	28	31	38							
4. Does S say family has difficulty getting fuel?	Yes	0	0	1	1							
	No	28	30	31	45							
5. Does S say family has difficulty getting drugs and/or medical care?	Yes	7	1	0	1	.001	.05	.01		.10		.05
	No	21	29	32	45							
6. Financially speaking, how does S compare his family with others in Millfield?	Better	2	1	4	7				.10			
	Average	24	29	26	36							
	Worse	2	0	1	3							

* Based upon chi-square tests.

O = overall test.

$\frac{N}{W}$ = Negro vs. white children; $\frac{NB}{WB}$ = Negro boys vs. white boys; $\frac{NG}{WG}$ = Negro girls vs. white girls.

$\frac{B}{G}$ = boys vs. girls; $\frac{NB}{NG}$ = Negro boys vs. Negro girls; $\frac{WB}{WG}$ = white boys vs. white girls.

volvement in the child's education and to learn what educational goals the child believed his parents had for him. Only a few children seemed to be unaware of parental attitudes in this regard. The vast majority of the parents certainly seem to want their children to finish high school, and many (at least 40%) want their child to obtain a college education. (There is a tendency for more Negro than white children to say that their parents want them to attend college, but this difference is not statistically significant.) With respect to educational aspirations for them, the children report a high degree of agreement between their mothers and fathers. As far as their homework is concerned, both sexes and both races agree that mother rather than father is more likely to be concerned about it.

Almost one-half of the children expressed some idea about the occupation their mothers wanted them to follow, and a comparable number also had an idea about their fathers' preferences in this regard. Thirty-seven children named one of the professions as mother's first choice for them, while thirty children indicated that father wanted them to follow a profession. Of the four groups, Negro girls were especially likely to say that both mother and father wanted them to be in a profession; nursing and teaching were mentioned most frequently.

Next, we attempted to elicit information about patterns of discipline and punishment used by parents. To begin, girls reported more frequent punishment for misbehavior than boys. Whether this is actually true, or whether it simply represents a sex difference in readiness to acknowledge punishment, cannot be ascertained from the data. There was almost unanimous agreement among the children that they could expect to be punished when they disobeyed their parents. It is interesting, though, that punishment seemed a bit more inevitable to them if they disobeyed mother rather than father; 15 children said that father did not punish for disobedience, but only 5 children said that mother failed to do so. Interesting differences also show up in the use of physical punishment. More white fathers than mothers were reported as using physical punishment (18 vs. 12), but more Negro mothers than fathers were said to punish in this way (36 vs. 23). Furthermore, the data indicate a very significant racial difference between Negro and white mothers with respect to the use of physical punishment (Negro mothers were reported as using it more often), but not between Negro and white fathers. It is also noteworthy that fathers were described as using physical punishment on their daughters less often than on their sons; this sex difference was especially pronounced in the reports about Negro fathers.

Approximately 80% of the children said that their mothers gave them enough freedom; the four groups did not differ significantly in this

TABLE 16.5

Children's Reports about Parental Behavior

Question	Response	Frequencies				p values*						
							Race				Sex	
		WB	WG	NB	NG	O	$\frac{N}{W}$	$\frac{NB}{WB}$	$\frac{NG}{WG}$	$\frac{B}{G}$	$\frac{NB}{NG}$	$\frac{WB}{WG}$
1. How often do parents disagree over what S should do?	Frequently	8	7	9	11	.10	.05					
	Infrequently	20	23	22	30							
2. When parents disagree over what S should do, who prevails?	Mother	12	17	10	18							
	Father	6	6	15	16							
3. Which parent is the boss?	Mother	5	7	4	6							
	Father	17	21	23	31							
4. How far does mother want S to go in school?	High School	15	19	15	20							
	College	10	10	14	24							
5. How far does father want S to go in school?	High School	14	20	14	18				.10			
	College	10	9	13	22							
6. How concerned is mother about S's homework?	Very	15	18	16	24							
	Little	13	12	16	21							
7. How concerned is father about S's homework?	Very	10	17	9	20	.10				.05		
	Little	18	12	22	22							
8. Which parent is most concerned about S's homework?	Mother	9	12	9	13							
	Father	6	4	6	2							
9. Does S know what occupation mother wants him to follow?	Yes	14	14	11	24							
	No	16	16	21	23							
10. When the answer to 9 is yes, does S's mother want a profession?	Yes	8	7	4	18						.10	
	No	6	7	7	6							
11. Does S know what occupation father wants him to follow?	Yes	17	12	13	18							
	No	13	17	18	24							
12. When the answer to 11 is yes, does S's father want a profession?	Yes	6	3	6	15	.01	.01				.01	
	No	11	9	7	3							

Question	Response					Significance (p)*						
						O	N/W	NB/WB	NG/WG	B/G	NB/NG	WB/WG
13. How often do parents punish S for misbehavior?	Frequently	5	11	7	19		.05					
	Infrequently	22	19	25	27							
14. Does mother punish S for disobedience?	Yes	26	29	32	42			.05		.01		
	No	1	1	0	3							
15. Does mother punish S physically?	Yes	7	5	15	21			.05		.01		
	No	20	25	17	24							
16. Does father punish S for disobedience?	Yes	24	25	29	36		.05					
	No	4	3	2	6							
17. Does father punish S physically?	Yes	11	7	15	8		.05				.01	.05
	No	17	21	16	34							
18. Does mother give S sufficient freedom?	Yes	22	26	28	34		.05					
	No	6	4	4	11							
19. Does father give S sufficient freedom?	Yes	23	22	28	24		.05				.05	.01
	No	5	7	3	17							
20. What is mother's reputation in the community?	Good	19	25	27	37							
	Average or less	6	3	5	8							
21. What is father's reputation in the community?	Good	16	22	24	32							
	Average or less	10	6	7	10							
22. Is there some way S would like to be like mother?	Yes	22	25	28	43					.10		
	No	6	5	4	2							
23. Is there some way S would like to be like father?	Yes	24	22	26	25		.05				.05	.05
	No	4	7	5	17							

* Based upon chi-square tests.

O = overall test.

$\frac{N}{W}$ = Negro vs. white children; $\frac{NB}{WB}$ = Negro boys vs. white boys; $\frac{NG}{WG}$ = Negro girls vs. white girls.

$\frac{B}{G}$ = boys vs. girls; $\frac{NB}{NG}$ = Negro boys vs. Negro girls; $\frac{WB}{WG}$ = white boys vs. white girls.

regard. Seventy-five percent of the children indicated satisfaction with father in this sense, but it is clear that there is considerable tension in this area between Negro girls and their fathers. Over 40% of the Negro girls said that father was too restrictive.

When asked to evaluate parental reputations in the community, a large majority of the children gave favorable evaluations (good or above average) to both mother and father. Each of the four groups, however, made either average or below average judgments about father more often than about mother. Also, when asked to describe some way in which he or she would want to be like each parent, twice as many children failed to describe some attribute of father which they would like to have as failed to find some characteristic of mother which they would like to make their own. The difference in this regard was particularly pronounced among Negro girls; only 2 Negro girls were unable to mention at least one characteristic of mother that they would like to have, but 17 said that they did not want to be like father in any way.

Peer Relationships

Many questions were asked of each child about his relationships with his peer group. Much of the information elicited, however, did not lend itself to quantitative analysis. Most of the questions that could be so analyzed are listed in Table 16.6 and form the primary basis for the discussion that follows.

All but 12 of the children seemed to feel that they had established stable friendship patterns; that is, they said that they changed friends infrequently. Negro girls reported the greatest instability in this regard. Most of the children also said that they had close friends of both sexes, but there was a significant racial difference: proportionately more white than Negro children said that their friends were of both sexes rather than being limited to children of their own sex. Almost 70% of the children said that they belonged to a group. In only 19 instances, however, was this group identified as one containing children of both sexes; 16 of the respondents who so replied were girls. The predominant tendency, then, seems to be for the children to have close friends of both sexes but to cluster in like-sex groups; girls are more willing than boys to acknowledge participation in mixed-sex groups.

Dating, in the formal sense, has not yet emerged as a common activity for children in this grade; only eight children said that they dated. On the other hand, 45% of the boys and 43% of the girls said that they had either a girlfriend or a boyfriend, respectively. Such an opposite-sex friend was reported significantly more often by white children than by Negro children. Especially pronounced was the relative infrequency of boyfriends reported by Negro girls. It was also the Negro girl who was most likely to say that her parents felt that she was too young to either date or have a boyfriend. White girls made similar comments more often than white boys, but the disparity between the two sexes was not as great as it was among the Negro children.

Two questions attempted to get at the child's perception of what contributed to a girl's or a boy's popularity. Answers to these questions were analyzed to see how often (1) physical appearance and, (2) dress or attire were mentioned by the children in the four groups. With respect to a girl's popularity, appearance was mentioned much more often by boys than by girls of both races. Overall, appearance was also emphasized more by white than by Negro children. A boy's appearance was emphasized as a factor in his popularity more often by white than by Negro children; girls tended to mention this factor more often than boys. In contrast, how a girl dressed was mentioned more frequently by Negro than by white children; the same was even more true of a boy's manner of dress. There were no significant sex differences within either racial group, however, as far as the importance of clothes was concerned. Thus, physical appearance looms relatively large among the white children, and clothes among the Negro children.[4]

Very few of the children (in fact, only 10) declared themselves to be the usual leader of their group. At the same time, only a small number ($N = 19$) went so far as to say that they never served as the leader of their group in any of its activities; most of the children who did say this were Negro girls (12 out of the 19). When asked to estimate how well they liked by the other children in the school, only 5 children (all Negro) said that they probably were not very well liked. But many more Negro than white children described themselves as being popular (45 vs. 17). This last finding is of particular interest inasmuch as reference is commonly made in the literature to the pervasively poor self-concept of the Negro child. Perhaps these Negro children are being especially defensive, or perhaps negative self-views are to be seen only when there is a direct Negro–white confrontation. Their remarks during the interview, however, suggest that many of these Negro children have a healthy self-esteem.

Finally, the interview brought out the fact that about seven out of ten of the children belonged to at least one club or organization. Also, more

[4] Almost all the children emphasized personality in some way as an important determinant of an individual's popularity ("If she's nice"; "If he knows how to talk with you," etc.). Data summarizing such comments have not been included in Table 16.6.

TABLE 16.6

Children's Responses to Questions about Peers

		Frequencies				p values*						
							Race			Sex		
Question	Response	WB	WG	NB	NG	O	$\frac{N}{W}$	$\frac{NB}{WB}$	$\frac{NG}{WG}$	$\frac{B}{G}$	$\frac{NB}{NG}$	$\frac{WB}{WG}$
1. How often does S change friends?	Frequently	3	0	1	8	.05			.05			.05
	Infrequently	25	30	31	38							
2. Of what sex are S's close friends?	Male	9	0	14	0	.001	.05			.001	.001	.001
	Female	0	6	0	21							
	Both	19	23	18	25							
3. Does S "run around" in a group?	Yes	19	22	21	30							
	No	7	8	11	16							
4. If S "runs" with a group, is it of mixed sex?	Yes	1	8	2	8	.05				.01		.05
	No	17	10	19	22							
5. Does S date?	Yes	3	3	0	2							
	No	25	27	32	44							
6. Does S have a boyfriend (if a girl) or girlfriend (if a boy)?	Yes	11	20	15	13	.05	.05		.01			
	No	15	10	17	33							
7. Do parents feel that S is too young to date or have a girl (boy) friend?	Yes	3	14	6	31	.001	.10			.001	.001	.01
	No	25	16	26	15							
8. Are a girl's "looks" important to her popularity?	Yes	15	6	10	2	.001	.01		.10	.001	.01	.05
	No	13	24	22	44							

		NB	WB	NG	WG	O	N/W	NB/WB	NG/WG	B/G	NB/NG	WB/WG
9. Is a girl's dress important to her popularity?	Yes	5	6	13	19	.10				.10	.05	.05
	No	23	24	19	27							
10. Are a boy's "looks" important to his popularity?	Yes	6	16	2	5	.001	.001	.001		.10	.05	.10
	No	22	14	30	41							
11. Is a boy's attire important to his popularity?	Yes	3	3	17	22	.001	.001	.01	.01			.01
	No	25	27	15	24							
12. Does S feel well-liked by other children?	Popular	6	11	20	25	.01	.01	.01	.01			.01
	Average or less	20	15	11	17							
13. Is S the leader of his group?	Usually	0	4	4	2	.10						
	Sometimes	20	19	22	30							
	Never	2	2	3	12							
14. Does S belong to clubs or organizations?	Yes	16	21	24	36							
	No	11	9	8	10							
15. Do S's friends get about the same grades as S?	Yes	24	23	24	40							
	No	4	6	8	6							

* Based upon chi-square tests.

O = overall test.

$\frac{N}{W}$ = Negro vs. white children; $\frac{NB}{WB}$ = Negro boys vs. white boys; $\frac{NG}{WG}$ = Negro girls vs. white girls.

$\frac{B}{G}$ = boys vs. girls; $\frac{NB}{NG}$ = Negro boys vs. Negro girls; $\frac{WB}{WG}$ = white boys vs. white girls.

than eight out of ten children said that they tended to have friends whose academic grades, on the average, were about the same as theirs.

Recreation

The leisure-time activities of the children of both races in Millfield focus upon visiting with friends, watching television, listening to the radio, and playing records.[5] Data regarding their use of other recreational resources are shown in Table 16.7; these data will be discussed in the paragraphs that follow.

There are both racial and sex differences in recreational patterns. Some of the racial differences are traceable to the fact that certain facilities have not been equally available to Negro and white children in the area. Motion picture theatres, skating rinks, and bowling lanes in adjacent towns, for example, have not welcomed Negro customers. To enjoy these recreational activities has meant a longer, more inconvenient, and more expensive trip for the Negro than for the white person. The relative unavailability of these popular pastimes may be a major reason why Negro children, more than white children, reported dances as a source of pleasure. It is also probably a contributing reason for their frequenting what they called "beer joints" more often than white children, even though all children but one claimed that they did not drink beer in these places. For similar reasons, one might expect card-playing to be more popular among Negro children, but the children's responses indicated the reverse to be true.

The sex differences in these data do not appear to be surprising. Thus, more boys than girls said that they drive a car alone, play cards, and gamble. More girls than boys, in contrast, said that they danced and read for pleasure. Except among the white girls, several children in each group reported that they smoked. In contrast to the small number of children who indicated that they dated (11 in this section, compared with 8 in the previous section of the interview), a larger number ($N = 32$) acknowledged that they engaged in petting.

A great deal of information gathered by staff members during their years in Millfield indicated that the large majority of the children have little money to use for recreational purposes. Their feeling of deprivation in this regard, however, is probably muted by at least two factors: (1) There are not many places readily at hand where sizable amounts of money are required for entertainment, and (2) most of a child's friends ordinarily do not have appreciably more money than he does. With

[5] Television habits of the children are examined in detail in the following section of this chapter.

regard to the first factor, there are two large university communities within reasonable driving distance of Millfield that offer athletic, musical, and theatre programs, but very few of the children visit these communities regularly. Indeed, 64% of the white children and 63% of the Negro children said that they had *never* been to one of the two university communities even to look around. With respect to the second factor, 88% of the children said that they did obtain enough money each week to enable them to do the things that their friends did.

We wondered if many of the children had gotten into difficulties with the police through any of their activities, recreational or otherwise. Only two children (both white boys) acknowledged that this had happened to them, but seven children said that their friends had gotten into such difficulties.

Finally, at the close of this section of the interview, each child was asked, "What would you like to see done so that you and your friends could have a better time?" Fifteen white children and 15 Negro children said that a recreation center was needed, while 10 white and 11 Negro children were unable to think of anything at all that could be done. Eight Negro children, but no white children, said that it would help if someone saw to it that there was less fighting and drinking in Millfield.

Television

Answers to a number of questions about the children's television viewing habits and attitudes have been summarized in Table 16.8. These data lead to the following conclusions:

1. Over 90% of the children watch television each day.

2. Almost 50% of the children spend at least three hours of each school day in front of the screen.

3. About 55% of the children devote more than four hours on Saturdays to watching programs, and about 50% give three or more of their Sunday hours to television.

4. Parents—or other adults—make very little effort to control what type of program the child watches; only four children reported restrictions in this regard.

5. Approximately 20% of the children said that they were permitted to stay up as late as they wanted on school nights to watch television; about 50% said that they had such unrestricted privileges on weekends.

6. Roughly four out of five children said that they never watched the one educational channel available on the dial; no child indicated frequent use of this channel. Approximately 30% of the children were unable even to identify the location of this channel.

7. About 94% of the children indicated at least satisfaction with the

TABLE 16.7

Children's Responses to Questions about Recreation

| | | Frequencies | | | | p values* | | | | | | |
| | | | | | | | Race | | | Sex | | |
Question	Response	WB	WG	NB	NG	O	$\frac{N}{W}$	$\frac{NB}{WB}$	$\frac{NG}{WG}$	$\frac{B}{G}$	$\frac{NB}{NG}$	$\frac{WB}{WG}$
1. Does S go to movies?	Yes	25	24	15	25	.001	.001	.01	.05			
	No	3	6	17	21							
2. Does S go to dances?	Yes	12	16	25	40	.001	.001	.05	.01			
	No	16	14	7	6							
3. Does S bowl?	Yes	10	11	1	7	.01	.001	.01	.10			
	No	18	19	31	39							
4. Does S roller skate?	Yes	19	22	1	1	.001	.001	.001	.001			
	No	9	8	31	45							
5. Does S go to parties?	Yes	20	28	28	41	.10						.10
	No	8	2	4	5							
6. Does S go to sports events?	Yes	20	20	23	31							
	No	8	10	9	15							
7. Does S go to beer places?	Yes	1	2	8	6	.10	.05	.10				
	No	27	28	24	40							
8. Does S date?	Yes	3	4	1	3							
	No	25	26	31	43							
9. Does S smoke?	Yes	7	0	5	6	.05	.10			.10		
	No	21	30	27	40							
10. Does S drive a car alone?	Yes	10	5	8	1	.01	.10		.10	.001	.01	.05
	No	18	25	24	45							

Question	Response	NB	WB	NG	WG	O	WB/WG	NB/NG	N/W	B/G
11. Does S drink?	Yes	0	0	1	0					
	No	28	30	31	46					
12. Does S pet?	Yes	5	10	12	5	.05			.05	.05
	No	23	20	20	41					
13. Does S play cards?	Yes	19	17	17	14	.05	.05	.05	.05	.10
	No	9	13	15	32					
14. Does S gamble?	Yes	2	0	4	0	.05		.05	.05	.10
	No	26	30	28	46					
15. Does S dance?	Yes	16	27	23	44	.001		.001	.01	.05
	No	12	3	9	2					
16. Does S read for pleasure?	Yes	21	30	27	43	.05		.01	.01	.05
	No	7	0	5	3					
17. Does S have as much money as his friends?	Yes	24	29	29	38					
	No	4	1	3	8					
18. Has S been in trouble with the police?	Yes	2	0	0	0	.05				
	No	26	30	32	46					
19. Have S's friends been in trouble with the police?	Yes	3	0	2	2					
	No	25	30	30	44					

* Based upon chi-square tests.

O = overall test.

$\dfrac{\text{N}}{\text{W}}$ = Negro vs. white children; $\dfrac{\text{NB}}{\text{WB}}$ = Negro boys vs. white boys; $\dfrac{\text{NG}}{\text{WG}}$ = Negro girls vs. white girls.

$\dfrac{\text{B}}{\text{G}}$ = boys vs. girls; $\dfrac{\text{NB}}{\text{NG}}$ = Negro boys vs. Negro girls; $\dfrac{\text{WB}}{\text{WG}}$ = white boys vs. white girls.

TABLE 16.8

Children's Responses to Questions about Television

Question	Response	Frequencies					p values*					
		WB	WG	NB	NG	O	Race $\frac{N}{W}$	$\frac{NB}{WB}$	$\frac{NG}{WG}$	Sex $\frac{B}{G}$	$\frac{NB}{NG}$	$\frac{WB}{WG}$
1. Does S watch TV every day?	Yes	22	29	29	39	.10						.10
	No	5	0	2	6							
2. Does S spend 3 or more hours each school day watching TV?	Yes	14	15	16	19							
	No	13	14	15	26							
3. Does S spend more than 4 hours watching TV on Saturdays?	Yes	12	15	13	32	.10				.05	.05	
	No	14	14	18	13							
4. Does S spend 3 or more hours watching TV on Sundays?	Yes	14	12	16	24							
	No	13	16	15	21							
5. Is S forbidden to view certain programs or types of programs?	Yes	1	0	2	1							
	No	27	30	30	45							

6. Is S permitted to stay up as late as he wishes to watch TV on school nights?	Yes	6	4	4	14
	No	21	26	27	31
7. Is S permitted to stay up as late as he wishes to watch TV on weekends?	Yes	15	16	13	25
	No	12	14	18	20
8. Does S *ever* watch the educational channel?	Yes	7	4	7	11
	No	21	26	25	35
9. Does S correctly identify the town in which the educational channel is located?	Yes	18	19	26	34
	No	10	11	6	12
10. Is S satisfied with the programs on TV?	Yes	26	27	32	43
	No	2	3	0	3

* Based upon chi-square tests.

O = overall test.

$\frac{N}{W}$ = Negro vs. white children; $\frac{NB}{WB}$ = Negro boys vs. white boys; $\frac{NG}{WG}$ = Negro girls vs. white girls.

$\frac{B}{G}$ = boys vs. girls; $\frac{NB}{NG}$ = Negro boys vs. Negro girls; $\frac{WB}{WG}$ = white boys vs. white girls.

TABLE 16.9

Children's Responses to Questions about Marriage and Family

Question	Response	Frequencies				p values*						
		WB	WG	NB	NG	O	Race $\frac{N}{W}$	$\frac{NB}{WB}$	$\frac{NG}{WG}$	Sex $\frac{B}{G}$	$\frac{NB}{NG}$	$\frac{WB}{WG}$
1. Does S think girls should marry before age 20?	Yes	11	7	10	7	.10				.05		
	No	16	23	22	39							
2. Does S think boys should marry before age 20?	Yes	8	3	1	4	.05	.05	.05				
	No	19	27	31	42							
3. Does S think he (she) will marry?	Yes	15	28	24	28	.01	.10		.01			.01
	No	8	1	8	18							
4. How many children would S like to have?	Two or less	17	18	22	34							
	Three or more	9	12	10	12							
5. How does S's desired family size compare with present family size?	Smaller	17	18	26	40	.10	.05		.05			
	Equal	6	6	5	3							
	Larger	3	6	1	3							
6. Does S have a preference as to the sex of his children?	Yes	19	19	29	37	.05	.01	.05				
	No	7	8	1	5							
7. Would S like his children to grow up in Millfield area?	Yes	23	19	25	25	.01				.01	.05	.10
	No	2	9	5	18							
8. How far in school would S like his mate to go?	College	13	18	13	26	.						
	High school	13	12	19	20							
9. Do boys want their wives to work?	Yes	6		16				.05				
	No	16		9								

* Based upon chi-square tests.

O = overall test.

$\frac{N}{W}$ = Negro vs. white children; $\frac{NB}{WB}$ = Negro boys vs. white boys; $\frac{NG}{WG}$ = Negro girls vs. white girls.

$\frac{B}{G}$ = boys vs. girls; $\frac{NB}{NG}$ = Negro boys vs. Negro girls; $\frac{WB}{WG}$ = white boys vs. white girls.

available programs. Forty-seven percent used even stronger language to express their pleasure with the fare. When asked to name their favorite program, both Negro and white children mentioned the "Beverly Hillbillies" more often than any other program. Also mentioned frequently were "Tarzan," "Outer Limits," "Edge of Night," "Patty Duke," and "Combat."

These findings confirm a number of beliefs that many people hold about children's television viewing behavior. It does occupy a great deal of their time and, for the children of Millfield, it is clearly their chief source of entertainment. Very little use is made of the medium for educational purposes; rather, it is the immediate enjoyment that matters. Adults make almost no effort to direct the viewing habits of their children, who in turn show little critical judgment about what they are watching. Finally, as far as this inquiry was concerned, there was little indication of significant variations among the four subgroups as far as their television viewing behavior and attitudes were concerned.

Marriage and Family

The children were asked several questions to determine how they felt about marriage and what thoughts they had about establishing families of their own. Answers to some of these questions have been tabulated in Table 16.9.

A large majority of the children seemed to feel that it is best for both boys and girls to marry between ages 20 and 25; 66% of all the children chose this as the preferred marriage age for girls, and 78% selected it for boys. As would be expected, more children said that girls should marry before age 20 than said that boys should marry before this age (35 vs. 16, respectively). It is also of interest to note that significantly more boys than girls thought that girls should marry before age 20. With respect to boys, more white than Negro children thought they should marry before age 20. The difference between white and Negro boys was especially pronounced in this regard.

About three-fourths of the children expressed the belief that they would marry. White girls were almost unanimous in this feeling (28 out of 29), but Negro girls had many reservations; in fact, 18 of the 46 Negro girls said they did not plan to marry. Children who said they wanted to remain single were asked why; most of them were unable to give very definite reasons to account for their feelings.

When the children think about having families of their own, it is clear that many of them react to the size of the family in which they live. Sixty-eight percent of the total group said they wanted no more than two children of their own, and less than 4% wanted as many as

TABLE 16.10

Children's Responses to Questions about Church

Question	Response	Frequencies				p values*						
							Race			Sex		
		WB	WG	NB	NG	O	N/W	NB/WB	NG/WG	B/G	NB/NG	WB/WG
1. Does S go to Sunday school regularly?	Yes	16	21	17	31							
	No	12	9	15	15							
2. Does S go to revivals?	Yes	17	24	18	30							
	No	11	6	14	16							
3. Does S's mother go to church regularly?	Yes	14	16	15	21							
	No	14	14	17	23							
4. Does S's father go to church regularly?	Yes	8	11	10	15							
	No	20	19	20	27							
5. What church does S attend?	Baptist	11	6	21	31	.01	.001		.001			
	Methodist	10	13	7	9							
	Other	7	11	4	5							
6. What church do important people go to?	Baptist	3	2	16	21	.001	.001	.10	.001	.01	.05	
	Methodist	7	19	8	22							
	Other	6	5	6	1							
7. Does S mention learning about God or Jesus as a reason for attending church?	Yes	11	16	16	25							
	No	17	14	16	21							
8. Do parents make S go to church and/or Sunday school?	Yes	4	4	4	1							
	No	22	26	28	45							
9. Is there something S dislikes about church?	Yes	8	1	7	16	.05			.01			.05
	No	18	24	24	26							

* Based upon chi-square tests.

O = overall test.

N/W = Negro vs. white children; NB/WB = Negro boys vs. white boys; NG/WG = Negro girls vs. white girls.

NB/NG = Negro boys vs. Negro girls. WB/WG = white boys vs. white girls.

five children. Furthermore, only 10% of the children expressed a desire for a family larger than the one in which they were currently a member. In this regard, there was a greater tendency for the Negro children than for the white children to emphasize their desire for a small family.

Most children (about 77%) expressed a preference about the sex of their children; approximately two-thirds of them said they wanted equal numbers of boys and girls. Thirteen children, however, said they wanted all boys, and 14 children said they wanted all girls. In general, Negro children were more willing than white children to express a sex preference.

While talking with the child about his thoughts regarding marriage, the interviewers asked him if he would like to have his children grow up in Millfield. (The staff felt that such a question would be one way to tap the child's attitude toward his community.) More than 70% of the children replied in the affirmative. They then gave a variety of reasons for feeling this way, the most common ones being variations of the following: "It's a good place;" "I grew up here;" "The people are nice;" and "It's country living." For the children who responded negatively, their reasons most often centered upon the fact that they either did not like farming or that the area was too isolated and underdeveloped. The girls of both races were much more negative than the boys about Millfield as a prospective home for their children.

When asked how much education they would like their mates to have had, 52% of the children said they would like for them to have gone to college. Although two children said, "I don't know," no child suggested less than a high school education.

In the last part of this section, girls were asked what kind of work they would like their husbands to do. Nine Negro and seven white girls answered either medicine or law, while nine Negro but only one white girl indicated teaching. Boys were only asked if they would like their wives to work. Overall, there was close to a 50–50 split in their answers, but there was a sharp racial difference: Negro boys said yes more often than white boys. This racial difference is striking, especially since Negro and white women in the community work with about equal frequency, even though at different types of work. It probably suggests (in part, at least) the general acceptance in the Negro community of the woman as an income producer; acceptance of this pattern is not yet as fully established in the white community.

Church

The next section of the interview focused upon the child's (and his family's) participation in church activities. A portion of the information elicited about this behavior has been summarized in Table 16.10.

Some reports of the church-affiliated activities of Millfield's residents suggested that almost all the children probably attended Sunday school, regularly, but this expectation was not confirmed by the interviews. While a clear majority of the children (63%) described themselves as regular attenders, a substantial number said they were not. In fact, 20% said they never, or only rarely, attended Sunday school. Attendance at revival meetings was reported as a fairly regular activity by most of the children who said they participated in either Sunday school or other church services. There were no significant differences among the four subgroups with respect to attendance at either Sunday school or revival meetings.

The children's remarks also show that their mothers attend church more regularly than their fathers (49% vs. 34%, respectively). Only 15% of the mothers were described as attending rarely or never; however, this figure was much higher for the fathers (39%). There was no significant racial difference for the reported church attendance of either mothers or fathers.

There was a significant racial difference, however, in denominational affiliation. White children belonging to the Methodist Church outnumbered those belonging to the Baptist Church 23 to 17, but many more Negro children were Baptists than were Methodists (52 vs. 16, respectively). Other denominations mentioned by the white children were Presbyterian ($N = 9$), Church of God ($N = 5$), and Episcopalian ($N = 1$). The Negro children mentioned two other denominations, Holiness ($N = 8$) and Church of God ($N = 1$).

When asked to identify the church which most of the important people in Millfield attended, about 18% of the children said, "I don't know." Among the white children, however, there was a clear consensus: the Methodist Church was mentioned most frequently ($N = 26$), followed by the Presbyterian ($N = 10$) and Baptist churches ($N = 5$). The Negro children's opinions were much more evenly divided between the Baptist ($N = 37$) and Methodist ($N = 30$) churches.

The children were also asked about their reasons for going to Sunday school or church. Many different answers were given, but 50% of the children said that they went to learn about God or Jesus. This reason was given least often by the white boys, but the four subgroups did not differ significantly in this regard. When asked specifically, only 10% of the children said that they went to either Sunday school or church because their parents compelled them to attend.

Apparently, there are many different facets of church activities that appeal to the children, but there are racial differences in the emphases that the children give to them. For example, social activities, preaching, and singing were mentioned by 21, 12, and 8 white children, respectively, as being things they liked about church. In contrast, 44 Negro children mentioned preaching, 25 mentioned singing, and only 14 noted social affairs. The suggestion here, of course, is that preaching and singing are much more dynamic and attractive components of church life in the Negro than in the white community. Clearly, though, this should not be taken to mean that Negro children are not also drawn to the church because of its social activities and opportunities.

Children found it easy to identify church activities that they liked, but it was more difficult for them to specify functions that they did not like. The Negro girls were most critical in this regard; 16 of the girls in this group who responded had some criticism to offer of the church. For the total sample, however, only 32 children made one or more negative comments. There was little consensus in these criticisms, except that nine Negro children agreed that services were too long.

In a general sense, the children's responses created the impression that those of them who do participate in church activities do so voluntarily, not because they are required to take part by their parents. Attendance may very well have been required in the past, but coercion is not something the children particularly feel now. Most of the attenders have found some church activities which they enjoy and which draw them back. Criticisms of the church are limited; the forms of the church are accepted very much as they are. Many of the children show what is commonly called a fundamentalistic orientation to this institution.

Education

Many questions were asked of the child about his educational aspirations, those of his peers, his preferred subjects in school, the educational achievements of his parents, and so on. Relevant data are given in Table 16.11.

These children clearly come from families with limited educational backgrounds, as has already been well documented elsewhere (see Chapters 1 and 15). Although some of them did not know exactly how far their parents had gone in school, most of the children did report definite knowledge about this matter. Of the latter, 25% said that their mothers had finished high school, but only 15% reported that their fathers had completed high school. (Significantly more white than Negro mothers and fathers were reported to be high school graduates.) It was also disclosed that 34% of the white mothers, 46% of the Negro mothers, 50% of the white fathers, and 64% of the Negro fathers had not attended school beyond the eighth grade (a level these children had already matched).

TABLE 16.11

Children's Responses to Questions about Education

Question	Response	Frequencies				p values*						
								Race		Sex		
		WB	WG	NB	NG	O	$\frac{N}{W}$	$\frac{NB}{WB}$	$\frac{NG}{WG}$	$\frac{B}{G}$	$\frac{NB}{NG}$	$\frac{WB}{WG}$
1. Did S's mother finish high school?	Yes	10	9	6	6	.10	.05					
	No	13	21	23	36							
2. Did S's father finish high school?	Yes	5	7	2	3		.05					
	No	16	22	24	35							
3. Does S have a sibling who has gone to college?	Yes	2	3	3	1							
	No	27	26	26	45							
4. Do S and his friends talk about how far they want to go in school?	Yes	17	17	25	41	.01	.01		.01			
	No	11	13	7	5							
5. Do S's friends want to drop out of school as soon as possible?	Yes	11	3	3	2	.001	.01	.05		.01		
	No	16	27	27	44							
6. Do S's friends want to go to college?	Yes	7	14	9	29	.01				.01	.01	
	No	20	16	21	17							
7. If free to do so, would S drop out of school now?	Yes	8	2	1	2	.01	.05	.05				.10
	No	20	27	31	44							
8. Does S say that he wants to go to college?	Yes	8	12	16	31	.01	.01		.05	.10		
	No	20	18	16	15							
9. Does S expect to realize his educational ambitions?	Yes	19	28	30	45	.01				.05		
	No	4	0	2	0							
10. Has someone talked personally to S about going to college?	Yes	10	9	10	17							
	No	17	21	22	29							
11. Has a teacher talked personally to S about going to college?	Yes	1	0	0	3							.10
	No	26	29	32	43							

#	Question	Resp.	(1)	(2)	(3)	(4)	O	N/W	B/G	NB/WB	NG/WG	NB/NG	WB/WG
12.	Does S report his average grade to be B− or better?	Yes	8	21	21	40	.001	.001	.01	.01	.001	.05	.01
		No	20	9	11	6							
13.	With maximum effort, does S believe that his average grade would be A− or better?	Yes	9	17	19	30	.01	.01	.10	.10			
		No	18	13	13	16							
14.	Does S usually do his homework?	Yes	19	30	32	45	.001	.001	.01	.01	.01		.01
		No	9	0	0	1							
15.	Does S's mother ever help him with his homework?	Yes	12	11	15	26							
		No	15	19	17	19							
16.	Does S's father ever help him with his homework?	Yes	14	10	9	21							
		No	14	20	22	21							
17.	Does S mention spelling as his favorite subject?	Yes	4	11	12	23	.05	.05	.10		.05		.10
		No	24	19	20	23							
18.	Does S mention science as his favorite subject?	Yes	11	4	1	0	.001	.001	.01	.05	.05		.10
		No	17	26	31	46							
19.	Does S mention math as the subject he likes least?	Yes	9	9	12	15							
		No	19	21	20	31							
20.	Does S mention science as the subject he likes least?	Yes	2	8	3	18	.01				.001	.01	
		No	26	22	29	28							
21.	Did S mention his teachers as something he likes about school?	Yes	7	16	9	24	.05				.01	.10	.10
		No	21	14	23	22							
22.	Is there something about the school S dislikes?	Yes	22	22	17	20	.001	.001	.05	.01			
		No	3	5	13	26							

* Based upon chi-square tests.

O = overall test.

$\dfrac{N}{W}$ = Negro vs. white children; $\dfrac{NB}{WB}$ = Negro boys vs. white boys; $\dfrac{NG}{WG}$ = Negro girls vs. white girls.

$\dfrac{B}{G}$ = boys vs. girls; $\dfrac{NB}{NG}$ = Negro boys vs. Negro girls; $\dfrac{WB}{WG}$ = white boys vs. white girls.

Few children (more precisely, 7%) reported siblings who have gone to college. Moreover, most of the children's siblings who were no longer in school had dropped out before completing high school; this was true for 73% of the white siblings and for 62% of the Negro siblings. Thus, the children are surrounded in their homes by many examples (both parents and siblings) of inadequate or limited educational achievement.

Does the child talk with his friends about his educational goals? Most interviewees said that they do talk—at least occasionally—with their friends about how far they want to go in school. There was a significant racial difference in this regard, however, in favor of the Negro children. Also, more white than Negro children reported that their friends want to drop out of school as soon as possible. This racial difference is attributable primarily to a relatively high incidence of wanting to drop out among the white boys. On the other hand, almost one-half of the children (44%) said that at least one of their friends wants to go to college. Such aspirations among friends are reported significantly more often by girls than by boys; it is, in fact, highest among Negro girls and lowest among white boys. In general, then, education seems to be a more salient topic among Negro than among white children. White boys and Negro girls anchor the two extremes in educational aspirations.

The conclusions are very similar when the focus of the questions is shifted to the child himself. Thus, 8 of 13 children who said that they would drop out of school if they were free to do so were white boys. A desire to go to college was expressed significantly more often by Negro than by white children; the incidence was particularly high among Negro girls and low among white boys. Forty-six children said that someone had talked to them about attending college, but in only four instances was the person identified as a teacher.[6] In most instances, either a parent or another relative had discussed this matter with the child. When asked why they wanted to continue in school, most children linked education with better jobs. Those who wanted to drop out were inclined to say, simply, "I don't like it." Finally, with a few exceptions (six in number), the children were optimistic about reaching their educational objectives.

With regard to classroom grades, both racial and sex differences were reported. Thus, Negro children reported higher grades, on the average, than white children. For each race, girls reported significantly higher average grades than boys. There was also a tendency for Negro children to have higher expectations than white children about the average grades

---

[6] This last figure does not include ten white children who said that a guidance counselor had talked with them about college.

that they could earn if they expended maximum effort on their studies.

A large majority of the children (93%) claimed that they usually did their homework assignments. White boys were the only exception here; 47% of this group acknowledged their failure to complete assignments. Parental assistance with homework was not described as common, yet 48% of the children said that their mothers provided at least occasional assistance, and 41% also said that their fathers sometimes helped them. The four subgroups did not differ significantly in terms of the parental assistance which they reported for homework.

Two questions attempted to define the children's preferences with respect to the various school subjects; several findings are of interest. First, significantly more Negro than white children mentioned spelling as their favorite subject (45% vs. 26%, respectively). Spelling was also mentioned as their favorite subject significantly more often by girls than by boys (45% vs. 27%, respectively). In contrast, 15 out of 16 students who mentioned science as their favorite subject were white children. Also, 11 of the 15 white children who favored science were boys.

Mathematics was frequently selected as the subject that the child liked least (33% of the sample made this choice); the four subgroups did not differ significantly in this regard. Science was also specified frequently as the least-liked subject (by 23% of the children); however, in this instance there was a significant sex difference. Of the 31 children who selected science as their least-liked subject, 26 were girls.

Finally, in the last part of this section of the interview, children were asked to mention both things they liked and things they did not like about their schools. The answers given show both sex and racial differences. Girls mentioned liking their teachers significantly more often than the boys. When it came to dislikes, the white children made many more criticisms than the Negro children did.

Work

Work plays an important role in the lives of Millfield's children. All but three children, for example, said that they had regular home chores to do during the school year (see Table 16.12). And more than one-half of the total sample said that they devoted in excess of one hour to such work each day. However, there was a significant sex difference: girls reported working more hours per day than boys. (This sex difference was especially marked among the Negro children.) Cutting or carrying in wood and taking care of animals were the two chores that the boys of both racial groups reported most often. Both groups of girls reported

TABLE 16.12

Children's Responses to Questions about Work

Question	Response	Frequencies				p values*						
							Race			Sex		
		WB	WG	NB	NG	O	$\frac{N}{W}$	$\frac{NB}{WB}$	$\frac{NG}{WG}$	$\frac{B}{G}$	$\frac{NB}{NG}$	$\frac{WB}{WG}$
1. During school year, does S have chores to do at home?	Yes	28	28	32	45							
	No	0	2	0	1							
2. Does S spend more than one hour per day on chores?	Yes	13	18	9	33	.01				.001	.001	
	No	15	12	23	13							
3. Does S work during the summer?	Yes	27	24	31	36	.01				.01	.05	.05
	No	0	6	1	10							
4. Does S work more than 7 hours per day during the summer?	Yes	15	14	22	25							
	No	11	15	10	20							
5. Does S work in tobacco during the summer?	Yes	15	14	27	33	.01	.01	.05	.10			
	No	12	16	5	13							
6. Is S ever kept out of school to work?	Yes	11	4	18	23	.01	.05		.01			.05
	No	14	23	14	23							
7. Is S kept out of school to work in tobacco?	Yes	4	2	14	22	.001	.001	.10	.001			
	No	21	25	18	24							
8. Has S ever earned money by working?	Yes	27	28	29	37							
	No	1	2	3	9							
9. Has S earned money by working in tobacco?	Yes	15	13	20	25	.001	.001	.001	.001			
	No	13	17	12	21							
10. Where do most children go to work when they grow up?†	In state	29	40	20	21	.001	.001	.001	.001			
	Out of state	0	0	23	37							
11. Does S mention getting a better job or making more money as a factor affecting work locale?	Yes	7	7	21	27	.001	.001	.01	.01			
	No	19	22	11	17							

#	Question	Response	NB	WB	NG	WG	O*	N/W	NB/WB	B/G	NB/NG	WB/WG	NG/WG
12.	Does S mention Millfield as a place where he would like to work?	Yes	3	5	11	10				.10			
		No	24	25	21	36							
13.	Is central N.C. mentioned more often than other states as the place where S would like to work?†	N.C.	18	33	27	33	.05		.01				.10
		Others	9	4	10	20							
14.	Does S mention farming as his first work choice?	Yes	4	0	3	0	.05	.05					.01
		No	24	30	29	46							
15.	Does S mention farming as his second work choice?	Yes	2	0	1	1							
		No	25	30	31	45							
16.	Does S mention nursing, teaching, or secretarial work as first work choice?	Yes	0	22	1	25	.001	.001	.001				.001
		No	28	8	31	21							
17.	Does S mention nursing, teaching, or secretarial work as second work choice?	Yes	0	12	0	23	.001	.001	.001				.001
		No	27	18	32	23							
18.	Does S expect to get his preferred work?	Yes	18	24	30	45							
		No	2	2	1	1							
19.	Does S think a college education is necessary for the kind of work he wants to do?	Yes	14	19	23	42	.01	.01		.05		.05	
		No	12	9	8	4							
20.	Do S and his parents discuss his occupational plans?	Yes	11	17	18	31							
		No	17	13	14	15							
21.	Would S like to do the same work as the like-sex parent?	Yes	13	14	11	10	.05	.10					.10
		No	15	16	20	33							

* Based upon chi-square tests.

O = overall test.

N/W = Negro vs. white children; NB/WB = Negro boys vs. white boys; NG/WG = Negro girls vs. white girls.

B/G = boys vs. girls; NB/NG = Negro boys vs. Negro girls; WB/WG = white boys vs. white girls.

† Some children mentioned more than one location; each location was tabulated.

that cleaning the house and washing dishes were their most common household assignments.

During the summer months, work plays a particularly prominent role in the children's lives. Only 17 children (16 girls) said that they did not work during this period, except to do chores of the type noted above. Summer work days frequently are long for children of this age. For example, 58% of the sample reported daily work in excess of 7 hours. Moreover, 16 white children and 29 Negro children (overall, 34% of the group) claimed that they worked 10 or more hours per day during the summer. For the boys and girls of both racial groups, working in tobacco was by far the most common summertime work reported. However, there was a significant racial difference: 77% of the Negro children compared to 51% of the white children described working in tobacco as their primary summer job.

Early in the study staff members became aware of the fact that a special problem existed at one of the Negro schools because some children were frequently kept out of school to work in tobacco, both at the time of spring planting and during fall processing. A similar problem, although apparently on a lesser scale, was also found at one of the two white schools. In addition, staff members learned that some children, especially Negro children, sometimes were kept out of school so that they might take care of younger children in the family, while the mother either was working outside the home or was occupied elsewhere. In this sample, 29% of the white children and 53% of the Negro children did in fact report that they were sometimes kept out of school for one of the reasons just noted. For all but three of the white children, the total time each lost from school amounted to less than 10 days; 16 Negro children, however, reported losing at least 10 days or more. For children of all groups, "to work in tobacco" was the reason given most often for their being kept out of school.

Although working in tobacco is often difficult, the children reported that it does have positive features. Foremost among these seems to be the fact that it provides many children with their first or most significant money-earning experience. During the summer many children hire out to neighbors or relatives in addition to working for their own parents. Overall, 89% of the children said that they had earned money through their own work, and 54% specifically said that they had earned money by working in tobacco. (There were no significant racial or sex differences with respect to the latter.) In addition to working in tobacco, girls frequently reported earning money by taking care of children or doing housework. Many boys said that they earned money by mowing yards and doing a variety of farm jobs.

The next questions in this section of the interview attempted to explore the child's thoughts about the work that he would be doing when he became an adult. First, we inquired about his perception of where individuals growing up in Millfield obtained work. It developed that there was a marked racial difference in this regard. The white children, both boys and girls, were unanimous in saying that most individuals remained in North Carolina, usually within a short distance of Millfield. In contrast, 77% of the Negro children mentioned out-of-state locales. Among out-of-state locations, Negro children specified New York and New Jersey most frequently. When asked why individuals chose particular locations, significantly more Negro than white children emphasized that getting a better job and making more money were important considerations in these decisions.

Given these data, it was interesting to discover that more Negro than white children specified Millfield as the place that they would choose to work (27% vs. 14%, respectively). Also, a surprisingly large proportion of the Negro children (two-thirds) mentioned locations in central North Carolina as places where they would like to live and work. Northeastern states were mentioned only 12 times by the Negro children, and not at all by the white children, as desirable places in which to work. Taken together, then, these data suggest that the Negro child feels as close to the Carolina soil as the white child does, but that migration is more frequently considered within the Negro community because its members cannot find adequate opportunities within the state.

The children were also asked what kind of work they would like to do when they begin supporting themselves. Not surprisingly, only seven children (all boys) mentioned farming as their first choice. Moreover, only four additional children (three boys) indicated that farming was their second choice. Among the boys, both Negro and white, there was little consensus as to what was a preferred job or occupation. In contrast, there was considerable agreement among both Negro and white girls that they wanted to be either nurses, teachers, or secretaries. When asked to estimate their chances of obtaining their occupational goals, the children expressed marked optimism. Overall, 95% of the children said that they thought that they would be able to get the work they wanted.

The next phase of the inquiry tried to determine the level of education that the children thought was necessary to prepare themselves for the type of work that they wanted to do. It was surprising to find that 75% of the children expressed the belief that a college degree was necessary. There was both a significant racial and a significant sex difference in these answers: more Negro than white children and more girls than boys gave the college response. For many children, such an answer indicated that they had quite unrealistic ideas about the occupation of their choice and its preparatory requirements.

The final questions in this section of the interview attempted to find out if the children discussed occupational plans with their parents. They were also asked if they would like to do the work currently being done by their parent of the same sex. Fifty-seven percent of the children said that they had talked with either one or both parents about their job futures. Moreover, only six children (three white) said that they had serious disagreements with their parents in this regard. Almost two-thirds of the children said that they did not want to do the work that their like-sex parent was doing. There was a significant racial difference in this regard: 47% of the white children but only 28% of the Negro children indicated that they would like to do their parents' kind of work.

Community

In the twelfth section of the interview, the child was asked a number of questions about how he perceived his community. Is it a good place to live? Does he want to live his adult life there? What are its good and bad points? Who is important in the community? What could be done to improve it? Data relevant to questions like these are given in Table 16.13. Additional related data will be cited in the discussion that follows.

Only the Negro children were asked the first question in this section: "What would you say about the Millfield area as a place to live in?"[7] The majority of these children (56%) were quite positive in their responses; they described Millfield as being at least a "very good" place in which to live. Eight Negro children made negative evaluations; of these, only two went so far as to call the area a poor place in which to live.

On the other hand, only 32% of the Negro children indicated that they wanted to live in Millfield as adults. This percentage was less than the percentage of white children (47%) who gave a similar answer. Basically, the Negro girls were responsible for this significant racial effect; only 23% of their group indicated a desire to live in Millfield. Strongly negative opinions ("definitely not") were given by 27% of the Negro children,

---

[7] The white interviewers eliminated this question after talking with 14 children. It was their impression that the question was repetitive, that no information was elicited by it that had not been given in other parts of the interview. Because some white children reacted to the question as being repetitive, they seemed to be annoyed by it. The white interviewers felt, therefore, that rapport with them might be damaged. So far as we know, this is the only point where the Negro and white interviewers differed in procedure.

but by only 16% of the white children. These negative answers were determined by many factors, of course, but certainly a dominant consideration for the Negro children had to do with limited employment opportunities. To live in Millfield means, as matters currently stand, to take jobs (if any) which the children do not want. They like the area, but desirable job opportunities are not available.

A large majority of the children (93%), when asked to identify things that they liked about Millfield, were able to mention at least one positive feature of the community. In contrast, they had great difficulty identifying something about the community that they disliked; this was true for all four subgroups. Overall, 38% of the children failed to note any specific negative attribute of Millfield.

The aspect of Millfield mentioned most often by both Negro and white children as the reason why they liked the community turned upon the people living there. (In this regard, it is of interest to note that "the people" were mentioned more often by girls than by boys.) Characteristics of the countryside—its roomy lands, woods, and peaceful atmosphere—were also mentioned frequently by white children. Negro children were more likely than white children to mention positively various kinds of physical structures—homes, churches, schools, and roads, and so on. As far as dislikes were concerned, "the people" were mentioned by only 11% of all the children. Mentioned negatively most often by the white children were Millfield's country attributes (too isolated, its undeveloped state) and its lack of certain specific resources such as stores, recreation, or job opportunities. Negro children noted such items with about equal frequency, but they, more often than white children (12 vs. 2), also noted drinking and fighting as undesirable components of life in Millfield.

Inquiries about the children's perception of the social structure in Millfield led to the conclusion that most of them had not developed very many ideas in this regard. The general questioning in this area may not have been adequate, yet there was an overriding impression that the children saw very little social stratification in their community. Eighty-six percent of the children finally identified at least one person in Millfield as being an important person, but many children had considerable difficulty arriving at even a single identification. Some children insisted that there just was not anyone in Millfield who was important; more white than Negro children took this position.

There were some interesting racial differences with respect to the types of jobs held by the individuals whom the children did identify as important. Negro children, for example, named a school teacher or school official more often than white children did. They also named

TABLE 16.13

Children's Responses to Questions about the Community and Self

Question	Response	Frequencies				p values*						
		WB	WG	NB	NG	O	Race N/W	Race NB/WB	Race NG/WG	Sex B/G	Sex NB/NG	Sex WB/WG
1. When grown, does S want to live in Millfield?	Yes	14	13	14	11	.05	.01	.10	.05			
	Uncertain	5	6	1	3							
	No	9	11	17	32							
2. Does S mention something about Millfield that he likes?	Yes	24	29	31	42							
	No	4	1	1	4							
3. Does S mention that he likes the people in Millfield?	Yes	14	25	18	31	.05				.05		.05
	No	14	5	14	15							
4. Does S mention something about Millfield that he dislikes?	Yes	16	16	23	30							
	No	12	14	9	16							
5. Does S mention that he dislikes the people in Millfield?	Yes	4	3	3	5							
	No	24	27	29	41							
6. Does S mention that he dislikes the drinking and fighting that goes on?	Yes	1	1	7	5	.10	.05	.10				
	No	27	29	25	41							
7. Does S mention someone as being an important person in Millfield?	Yes	19	25	29	44	.01	.01	.10				
	No	9	5	3	2							
8. Does S mention a school teacher or official as being the most important person?	Yes	2	4	11	17	.01	.01	.05	.05			
	No	26	26	21	29							
9. Does S mention a business man as being the most important person?	Yes	10	12	3	3	.001	.001	.05	.01			
	No	18	18	29	43							

Question	Response	(1)	(2)	(3)	(4)	N/W	NB/WB	NG/WG	B/G	NB/NG	WB/WG
10. Does S mention a preacher as being the most important person?	Yes	1	1	2	5	.05	.05			.05	.05
	No	27	29	30	41						
11. Does S mention a farmer or farm agent as being the most important person?	Yes	1	2	6	11						
	No	27	28	26	35						
12. Does S see some way in which Millfield could be improved as a place to live?	Yes	19	22	27	39			.10			.10
	No	9	8	5	7						
13. Does S mention need for improved roads, schools, and/or houses?	Yes	10	15	15	33	.05	.05	.10	.10	.05	.05
	No	18	15	17	13						
14. Does S mention need for improved recreation?	Yes	5	10	4	16	.10				.05	.10
	No	23	20	28	30						
15. Does S mention need for less drinking, fewer "joints," and/or better law enforcement?	Yes	0	0	4	5	.10	.05				
	No	28	30	28	41						
16. How happy does S think his home life is when compared with others?	More	1	0	6	5	.05	.05		.10	.10	.10
	Same	25	26	26	34						
	Less	2	4	0	7						
17. How satisfied is S with the kind of person he is?	Very	3	1	8	6						
	"Kind of"	23	26	21	34						
	"So-so," or less	2	3	3	6						

* Based upon chi-square tests.

O = overall test.

$\frac{N}{W}$ = Negro vs. white children; $\frac{NB}{WB}$ = Negro boys vs. white boys; $\frac{NG}{WG}$ = Negro girls vs. white girls.

$\frac{B}{G}$ = boys vs. girls; $\frac{NB}{NG}$ = Negro boys vs. Negro girls; $\frac{WB}{WG}$ = white boys vs. white girls.

either a farmer or the county farm agent with greater frequency. In contrast, white children mentioned businessmen much more often than the Negro children. Ministers were mentioned infrequently by children of either racial group, although Negro children tended to designate them as being important more often than white children.

In identifying people of importance, white children named 40 different individuals; almost all were adult white males. Three men were mentioned 16, 13, and 8 times, respectively (each was a businessman and two of the three were brothers); these men represent the closest thing to a consensus in the data. Negro children also stuck predominantly to adult males of their own racial group, but they occasionally crossed racial lines. Their nominations were even more scattered than those of the white children; they involved 90 different individuals! The two Negro principals were mentioned more often than any other individuals, 11 and 9 times.

The last question in this section asked the children to describe things that could be done to make Millfield a better place in which to live. A considerable number of children ($N = 29$) were unable to suggest any improvements at all. (White children tended to have greater difficulty on this question than Negro children.) Mentioned most often by children of both races was a need for improved physical structures, such as roads, schools, and houses. The girls mentioned these items more often than the boys, and there was a tendency for Negro children to mention them more frequently than white children. Second in frequency was an expressed need for improved recreational facilities. There was no racial difference in this expression, but there was a significant sex difference. Girls, apparently, feel the lack of recreational facilities more acutely than boys.

These data suggest that a large majority of the children do feel an affectionate bond with Millfield. Most of them talk about leaving the area not because they dislike it but because they will have to leave in order to earn a living. Furthermore, one effect of living in a segregated society becomes readily apparent when the children are asked to look at the social structure within which they live. Their orientation is almost exclusively to persons of their own racial group, although nothing the interviewers said suggested such a restriction.

Self

The final section of the interview was devoted to the student's view of himself and his adjustment. It soon became apparent that many of the children were not accustomed to talking this way about themselves.

Therefore, they had considerable difficulty formulating any answer that went beyond a simple yes or no.[8] The limited data elicited have been tabulated as questions 16 and 17 in Table 16.13.

The first question in this final section attempted to assess the child's feelings about his life, especially as he experienced it in his home. More particularly, it asked him to compare his happiness with that of other children of his own age. A heavy majority of the children (82%) said that they were much like other children as far as the happiness of their home life was concerned. Of the 25 children who felt that they did deviate from the norm, almost equal numbers said that they were either more happy or less happy (12 vs. 13, respectively) than others were. Interestingly, almost all the children (11 out of 12) who said that they were happier were in the Negro sample. In contrast, about equal numbers of white and Negro children said that they were relatively unhappy (6 vs. 7, respectively). Moreover, all 7 of the self-described unhappy Negro children were girls. (This finding certainly is in keeping with other portions of the interview data from the Negro girls.)

When asked to estimate the degree of their self-satisfaction, again a large majority of the children took a positive position. That is, they indicated basically a positive self-view, but without going so far as to suggest that they might be without any faults. However, 18 children did indicate somewhat greater self-satisfaction than did the remainder of the sample, and, of these, 14 were Negro children. In contrast, 14 children gave a more negative self-picture than was typical of the group; once more, the Negro girls outnumbered children in the other three groups in their frequency of negative statements.

Obviously, these data are neither comprehensive nor penetrating. Nevertheless, the fact that the data tend to contradict what is so often asserted about the pervasively damaged self-percept of the Negro child must be recognized. If nothing more, these findings suggest that the issue is more complicated than it is usually presented; also, it merits a much more thorough investigation using a variety of techniques with individuals at several age levels who live in various types of settings.

---

[8] It is also true that the approach to this facet of their experience was rather crude and may not have provided the children with an effective channel through which to articulate their convictions about themselves. A more detailed picture of how eighth-grade children in Millfield view themselves can be gleaned from an examination of their responses to the Minnesota Multiphasic Personality Inventory (see Chapter 11). In addition, a doctoral dissertation has been initiated under the first author's direction which will explore much more comprehensively the self-concepts of Southern children, Negro and white, rural and urban (Wendland, 1967).

CONCLUDING COMMENTS

Despite the limitations inherent in the use of interview data, there are several important conclusions which are supported by the data presented in this chapter.

Outsiders, on first encountering Millfield, readily identify numerous ways in which many of these children are deprived. It is apparent, however, that the typical child here does not experience an acute sense of deprivation. His judgments and evaluations of his conditions are not made in terms of the standards of middle-class America; rather, they are made in terms of what he has personally experienced. He describes his life by comparing it with what others in Millfield *of his own race* seem to be experiencing. And, as he looks around, his situation does not seem to be much different from that of other people. Although he watches TV several hours a day and often sees represented there different living standards, these standards somehow do not penetrate deeply into his evaluations of his own life or his own community. The televised pictures of life entertain him, but his judgments about his condition are based primarily upon life as he has directly experienced it in Millfield.

It is also apparent that most of these children, at this age, do not even look at Millfield in a comprehensive way. Obviously they know that both Negro and white people reside in Millfield, but the typical reaction is to look at themselves only in relation to their own racial group. Thus, Negro children answer questions within the context of Negro society and white children within the context of white society. If pushed, no doubt many of the children could make meaningful comments about race relations, but the point is that this does not seem to be their natural or spontaneous orientation when talking with an interviewer, even when she is of the same racial group and is well known to them. The usual referent in these descriptions is only one-half of Millfield, not the whole.

It is important to recognize the indications in these data that the self-concepts of the Negro children appear to be appreciably less negative or derogatory than is customarily represented to be true in the literature. These positive self-concepts are reflected in what appear to be the especially high (and unrealistic) educational aspirations of the Negro children. It must be pointed out, however, that the children have not set these aspirations without some reference to their own experiences. For example, if one contrasts the mean IQ's and achievement test scores of the Negro children who want to go to college with those who want only to finish high school (see Table 16.14), it is obvious that the two groups differ significantly. The children who want to attend college

TABLE 16.14

S-B IQ's and Stanford Achievement Test Scores of Eighth-Grade Children
with Two Different Levels of Educational Aspiration

Group	Educational goal	N	Range	Mean	S.D.	t	p
		A. S-B IQ's					
White boys	High school	15	66–108	89.6	12.1	5.49	.001
	College	8	99–147	122.6	14.6		
White girls	High school	20	59–109	90.7	11.6	3.36	.01
	College	10	91–133	107.4	13.4		
Negro boys	High school	8	62–96	79.0	12.5	2.32	.05
	College	11	74–105	90.9	8.7		
Negro girls	High school	8	57–93	80.1	12.4	1.56	.20
	College	25	69–108	87.6	9.9		
		B. Stanford Achievement Test Scores					
		(Total Group-Grade Equivalent)					
White boys	High school	15	3.5–8.8	6.3	1.5	5.00	.001
	College	9	7.1–11.0	9.0	1.1		
White girls	High school	20	4.1–10.1	7.6	1.6	2.59	.05
	College	10	6.6–11.0	9.2	1.5		
Negro boys	High school	14	3.7–6.1	4.9	0.7	4.73	.001
	College	15	5.3–8.1	6.3	0.9		
Negro girls	High school	14	3.6–7.9	5.5	1.3	2.55	.05
	College	27	4.5–10.4	6.6	1.5		

are the ones who are more able and who have been achieving better academically, *relative to their own group.* The point is that many of these children have had important success experiences competing with their peers within their classrooms, and these successes have generated self-esteem. Thus, an IQ of 95 may not seem to be modest if you are competing against individuals whose average ability level is considerably lower, and, as a result, you may very well generate unrealistic ambitions. What happens when you enter the larger world obviously is another question, but a critical one. For the moment, though, these Negro children seem to have developed both restricted frames of reference and special self-protective devices which make life a reasonably pleasant experience for them. Certainly they do not report being overwhelmed with feelings of their own unworthiness.

These conclusions must be tempered by the fact that, of the four groups, the Negro girls seem to be the most troubled. Many of them feel hemmed in, too restricted by their parents and the general environment in Millfield. A considerable number want to leave, to become self-sufficient by developing careers of their own. For a sizable group, marriage does not appear to be very inviting. Some expressed depreciative views of Negro males, views very much in keeping with attitudes that are known to be common in many Negro subgroups.

Despite dissenters, especially among the Negro girls, it is clear that large numbers of the children feel affectionate ties with Millfield. The fact that so many of them do not anticipate spending their lives there appears to be conditioned primarily by the lack of desirable job opportunities. Given worthwhile employment opportunities, migration to the city probably would be appreciably reduced.

Part VI

INTEGRATION AND RECOMMENDATIONS

Chapter 17

SOME SUMMARY COMMENTS AND OBSERVATIONS

This project was initiated to learn more about a neglected group of American children, those residing in the rural South. In previous chapters we have presented our findings, usually in considerable detail. Now we shall attempt to summarize and interrelate these findings.[1] Then, in the final chapter, we shall address the question of how the Negro–white gap might be narrowed by the initiation of a variety of social action programs.

MILLFIELD

Most of our data describe white and Negro boys and girls of elementary school age who live in a rural area of central North Carolina under a racially segregated pattern of social and educational organization. In various places in this volume, we have provided data which help to characterize this land, the background of the people who inhabit it, and the patterns of living which currently exist there. Although the Negro population outnumbers the white, the majority group does not control the power structure.[2]

[1] This summary is by no means exhaustive, and the reader would be well advised not to let it substitute for a careful consideration of the more detailed presentations in the various chapters.

[2] The classification of a person as Negro or white was based upon the social and educational practices of the community; no genetic, biochemical, or anthropometric procedures were used in the classification.

This area that we have called Millfield is only a short distance from the Piedmont region of Southside Virginia studied by Myrtle Bruce in the late 1930's. At that time, she described the area in these terms:

> This population is almost entirely rural. . . . Approximately 86% of the total population of the county live on farms. Of those engaged in agriculture, 66% cultivate land that does not belong to them. Half of these landless farmers are Negroes. In Virginia as a whole, most of the farm laborers and tenants, and from 25 to 50% of the White landowners and 75% of the Negro landowners belong to the marginal population group (i.e., having a family income of $600 or less in 1929).
>
> (Bruce, 1940, p. 6)

Patterns of living in this part of the Middle South have changed considerably since Bruce did her work; for example, there has been a movement away from so complete a dependence upon the land. People seek jobs in the mills and factories of nearby towns, for they find more security there than in farming small plots of land. Such escape from the uncertainties of the land is particularly difficult for the Negro, however, and, if he is to have a chance for a new way of life, he, more than the white man, must migrate to an urban center.

A typical family's dollar income also has changed since Bruce conducted her study, but so has the cost of goods and services. As a result, many families continue to live under the burden of poverty, even though considerable numbers of the children in our study seemed not to realize that they were poor. And, although poverty is not unknown to many of the white families, it is experienced much more frequently by the Negro families. Thus, we must agree with Elizabeth W. Miller when she comments as follows:

> The rapid urbanization of the Negro during recent years has led to a tendency to overlook the problems of the Negroes who are still a part of the farm population. The statistician announces, "In the South more than half of the Negroes are city dwellers." He is less apt to emphasize that one fifth of the Negroes in the United States are in agriculture, and that nearly half of all Southern Negroes are still engaged in rural occupations, including migrant labor, and that the poverty, the disease, the disabilities of all kinds of which they are the victims are among the most stubborn and intractable problems faced by the Negro people in any region of the country.
>
> (Miller, 1966, p. 56)

On the other hand, we must make it clear that the typical families in Millfield are neither destitute nor in abject poverty. They often have very low cash incomes, but, living on the land and raising produce, they are considerably better nourished for example, than equally large families would be if they were completely dependent upon so small a cash income. While some families live in houses that are dilapidated, primitive, and repellent, many landowners keep even their rental houses in fair repair. Also, few farm families are now dependent upon the traditional transportation by mule and wagon, although the farm truck often must double as passenger and work vehicle for some Millfield families. There is a pervasive change in the countryside that has appeared in the last two or three decades, brought about by rural electrification, by better roads and more cars, and by farm extension efforts. Home freezers and television sets have been adopted far more frequently than running water or indoor plumbing, but the latter should also come to more and more homes in the years ahead.

We have tended to think of Millfield as an isolated area, but are we justified in thinking this way? After all, Millfield is close geographically to communities with major universities, urban and suburban shopping centers, and diverse cultural and business activities. Television sets are just about universal in these homes, receiving broadcasts from nearby communities via several channels. Many of Millfield's teachers live in these same towns and commute daily to teach in the country schools. Are these patterns of access, then, compatible with the designation of the area as isolated?

Our data show that, with occasional exceptions, these families do not reach out for meaningful contacts with the larger and more complex environment that is close at hand. Many, because of their impoverished circumstances, simply cannot afford to take advantage of opportunities for recreation and education that are there. Others, because of social class and family background factors, would not be comfortable participating in the affairs of the urban communities. Still others have no appreciation for the cultural resources available in the surrounding towns and cities. In point of fact, then, the gradually extending suburbs of these larger communities have as yet left Millfield rural in outlook and pattern of life. Certainly in the cultural sense Millfield is isolated, even if modern means of transportation and communication make physical access relatively easy.

With respect to racial matters, Millfield resists change, although not violently. No legal constraints stand today to maintain racial separation in the schools, and some Negro students have recently entered all-white schools. Yet it is also true that this breakdown of complete segregation in the schools has been very slow. Changes in racial relationships have been even less evident in organizations like PTA's, churches, or political parties. The basic pattern of parallel activities rather than interactive relationships between members of the two racial groups continues to exist very much as it has for many decades.

This, then, is the area whose residents provided the data that we have analyzed and reported. Although we cannot prove this to be true in any acceptable scientific sense, we do in fact believe that the area and people that we have described are reasonably typical of much of the rural South in the middle 60's. For this reason, we suggest that our findings should not be viewed as those stemming from a single, unique community.

SOME OF THE MAJOR INTELLECTIVE FINDINGS

In our analyses and presentations of intellective data we found it convenient and meaningful to take the natural groupings—white and Negro boys and girls—and compare and contrast them at various age levels on the several measuring devices employed in the study. What did the data indicate for each of these four groups?

White Girls

Among the four groups, the white girls scored closest to national norms on a variety of intellective measures; this was particularly true at the younger age levels. Especially impressive was their performance on academic achievement tests, at all age levels. At the older age levels, their average performance on achievement tests even went beyond what one might have predicted from their ability test scores. As a group, therefore, the white girls were using their talents very effectively for classroom learning.

White Boys

On overall measures of ability, the white boys were not distinguishable from the white girls. There were sex differences on some of the component scores of the PMA, though, as well as on the vocabulary score of the S-B. At the younger age levels the white boys were also found to be competing effectively with the girls on achievement tests, and to be doing reasonably well on these tests by national standards. Older white boys, however, failed to demonstrate comparable proficiencies on the achievement tests; their performance was significantly below national norms in just about every academic area examined and definitely inferior to the performance of the white girls. (Mean IQ scores of the two sexes were almost identical, however, at the older age levels.) It is not surprising, then, that more white boys than girls were retarded in school-grade placement.

Negro Girls

In ability, the Negro girls, on the average, fell about one standard deviation below the national norms for the S-B; on the PMA, their deviation was somewhat greater. Also, they fell more than 10 S-B IQ points and 15 PMA Total Quotient points below the two white groups in the study. These discrepancies are statistically stable and psychologically meaningful; it is clear that the Negro girls are handicapped when they confront ordinary academic demands.

Consistent with their ability test scores, the Negro girls scored lower overall on the achievement tests than either white subgroup and below national norms at almost all age levels. However, their pattern of achievement was not uniform on the subscales of the SAT; rather, it varied considerably from one substantive area to another. Thus, on two subscales (Arithmetic Computation and Language) the scores of the Negro girls were not dependably different from those of the white boys at most age levels, and on one subtest (Spelling) the Negro girls outperformed the white boys at the upper age levels. Finally, when the scores from the component parts of the S-B, PMA, and SAT were examined, there was evidence of a special deficit in verbal comprehension on the part of the Negro girls.

Negro Boys

Among the four groups, the intellective performance of the Negro boys was clearly the most discouraging. At the lower age levels their ability scores were comparable to those of the Negro girls, but the girls were clearly superior at the older ages. And, at every age level, the Negro boys' achievement test scores were inferior to those of the Negro girls. Moreover, this comparative deficiency held for each of the component scores of the PMA (excepting Spatial Relations) and the SAT. Again, as was characteristic of the Negro girls, verbal deficits were very pronounced among the Negro boys. Given these findings, it is not surprising that, as was true for the white children, more boys than girls were retarded in their school-grade placement.

Does Ability Change with Age?

Our most comprehensive ability data were cross-sectional in nature; consequently, since different children were evaluated at each of the age levels, there is a distinct possibility that sampling biases affected the trends that appeared in the age plots of the obtained scores. We did conduct several short-term longitudinal studies, however, so that we are not completely dependent upon cross-sectional data when we attempt to answer the above question.

It is commonly asserted that the inherent limitations of the Negro child become acutely apparent at or about the time of puberty; supposedly, he is unable to keep pace with his white counterpart after this stage of development, even though he may have been able to hold his own up to this point. Clearly, our cross-sectional data fail to support such assertions. A tendency for S-B IQ scores and PMA Total Quotients to decline after age ten does appear in the plots for three groups—white boys, white girls, and Negro boys; however, the Negro girls show no such decrements at the older age levels. Thus the pattern that emerges for the four groups is quite inconsistent with the hypothesis that race and intellective decline with advancing age are linked.[3]

As noted above, our longitudinal data are not as comprehensive as our cross-sectional data. Two studies, however, each covering a span of about three years, suggest that, *on the average,* both Negro children in the primary grades and white children in early adolescence change very little in measured ability over such time periods.[4] It is important to recognize that both of these studies describe growth patterns under currently existing conditions; that is, they do not tell us what effects might be produced on functioning intellective levels by interventional programs.

That meaningful changes in average functioning intellective levels can be produced within relatively short time periods by interventional programs was indicated in the study of the kindergartens. The complexity of the issues involved, however, is suggested by the fact that the conclusions one draws in this regard are very much dependent upon the measuring instruments used in pre- and post-testing. Furthermore, we know nothing about the persistence of such induced changes; it may very well be that the effects attributable to such interventional efforts will wash out as the children grow older, unless special follow-up efforts are made either to maintain or to enhance them.

In a very real sense, however, group averages derived from longitudinal studies may be misleading with respect to the question of

---

[3] On total achievement test scores, the age plot for the white boys is markedly similar to those for the Negro girls and Negro boys; all three groups fall farther behind national norms as they grow older. The white girls, in contrast, evidence no decline with advancing age.

[4] Our findings in this regard agree very well with those of Kennedy (1965). He and his associates reported a decline in S-B performance over age in their cross-sectional survey, but, in a special study carried out later on a subsample of 316 Negro children after an interval of five years, they found almost identical mean IQ's (78.9 vs. 79.2).

whether ability levels change with age. Thus, examination of our data revealed that even in noninterventional contexts a majority of the children showed meaningful shifts in IQ scores over time spans of three years. Some children gained, however, while others lost, so that, overall, the group means were not very much changed. Constancy of IQ, therefore, appears to be more a manifestation of the group than of the individual.

What Family Factors Relate to Intellective Level and Change?

The study of family variables underscored the validity of our hypothesis that measured ability and academic achievement levels of the children would be found to be significantly related to a number of family factors (parental education, size of sibship, material resources in the family, and so on). The overall pattern in these data suggested, not surprisingly, that the individual findings can be subsumed under the integrating formulation that children from families of relatively high socioeconomic status perform better on intellective tests than children from families of relatively low socioeconomic status.

Isolating family correlates of intellective change turned out to be a more complex problem than identifying correlates of intellective level. Thus, we were essentially unsuccessful in such efforts in our study of kindergarten effects, although Church had modest success in her study of intellective changes among white adolescents. More fruitful, too, was the study of young Negro children; Negro first-graders who showed IQ gains over the following three years were not only more mature and stable and more interested and involved in schoolwork, but came from homes with smaller numbers of children than the first-graders who showed IQ losses over the same period. These findings are encouraging and merit follow-up work, particularly because, as pointed out in Chapters 7 and 8, there were methodological limitations in the studies of kindergarten children and white adolescents.

What Factor Is Central in Accounting for Sex Differences in Intellective Functioning?

It is clear from the data, we believe, that motivation or involvement must be specified as the most likely key factor in this regard. And, in broad outline, the situation is similar within both races, although there are also important racial differences in details that should not be overlooked. For instance, the Negro girls' performance is superior to that of the boys on both ability and achievement tests, whereas the white girls' superiority is clear only on the achievement tests at the older age levels. The teachers' evaluations of their pupils, as well as interview statements and ratings made by the children themselves, indicate that the boys are less interested, involved, or concerned with their classwork than the girls.[5] The pattern in the data, furthermore, suggests that the white boys' noninvolvement begins to become accentuated at about age 10 or 11. For the Negro boys, in contrast, noninvolvement appears to be more characteristic from the very beginning of their school years. Until the motivational level of the boys is increased, it is unrealistic to expect a meaningful improvement in their intellective development.[6]

Do We Need Both Ability and Achievement Tests?

It is common now to hear that an ability test is only another form of an achievement test, and it is true that the results of most tests in these two domains intercorrelate at a highly significant level. Nevertheless, our data, taken as a whole, justify the decision that we made to include both types of instrument in the assessment battery. Using the two types of test in conjunction with one another frequently advanced our understanding of certain processes over what would have been possible if we had limited ourselves to only one type of test. To cite a single example, the deficiency in the academic achievement scores of the older white boys (see above) could not be ascribed to their lesser ability levels, for their S-B IQ scores at the older age levels were essentially the same as those of the white girls. Despite overlap, then, there is justification for both ability and achievement tests in an assessment battery.[7]

SOME OF THE MAJOR NONINTELLECTIVE FINDINGS

Our survey of the nonintellective characteristics of these children was, in general, less systematic than our appraisal of their intellective attributes. We found it advisable to use a variety of techniques in studying their personal attributes, yet some of these devices could not be applied at all age levels, while in other instances our resources did not permit application over as wide an age band as would otherwise have been feasible. The material in this section is organized around the assessment devices that were used; the racial and sex similarities and differences which were found are highlighted.

[5] Our work indicates that fantasy measures of achievement motivation are not very helpful in advancing understanding of questions like the one under discussion (see Chapter 12). In a broader sense, however, as will be discussed later, fantasy measures may be quite valuable.

[6] Additional comments on this matter may be found in the next chapter.

[7] We should also point out that the data reported show the value of using both group and individual ability tests.

How Do Mothers of Kindergarten-Age Children Describe the Children and Their Worlds?

When interviewed, most mothers of kindergarten-age children said that they had one or more special concerns about the child in question (there was no racial difference in this regard). Nevertheless, in general, the mothers spoke positively about their children and, in so doing, tended to express unrealistically high educational and vocational aspirations for them. In these data, one can find both racial and sex similarities and differences. When the mothers described the behavioral traits of their children, however, significant racial differences were much more frequent than significant sex differences. We shall not attempt to catalog these findings again here; rather, we shall underscore a few points which, in the light of other findings, appear to be particularly important.

When talking about the development of verbal behavior, the mothers were more likely to describe it as having been slower than average for boys than for girls; this was especially true among the white mothers. Perhaps of greater consequence is the fact that, for both races, the mothers of boys reported that their children needed encouragement more frequently than did the mothers of girls. (This sex difference in the preschool period may be the precursor of the pervasive motivational differences that are found between the two sexes during their elementary school years.) A sex difference in favor of the girls was also found on the Vineland Social Maturity Scale; the mean score of the white girls was particularly high.

As already noted, racial differences in behavior attributed to the children were much more common than sex differences. To some extent, the pattern in these racial differences suggested that the Negro child was viewed as being more extroverted than the white child. Also, he was reported as being more fearful and as more frequently exhibiting certain forms of misbehavior, such as fighting, destroying things, being messy, and telling lies. The white children, in contrast, were described as playing alone better, as admitting rule violations more readily, and as being less upset when their mothers left than the Negro children. In general, the picture that emerges is one in which the Negro child is depicted as less socialized than his white counterpart.[8]

When the mothers told about family circumstances, many racial differ-

---

[8] This comparative picture provided by the mothers is in substantial agreement with observations made by our staff members in the first-grade classrooms where the children enrolled had not attended kindergarten (see Chapter 2). Many more Negro than white children were reported as being unready to cope with the multiple social and intellective demands present in this group context.

ences emerged which might well provide a basis for the types of racial differences in the behavior of their children that have just been described. For example, the Negro families contain more children, their income is lower, parental education is less adequate, there are more father-substitutes, and the jobs held are less desirable than those held by the white adults. Also, there are a number of differences in the reported child-training practices. For instance, white mothers are less convinced of the value of whipping children but express greater belief in the worthwhileness of praise than Negro mothers. Added to these potentially significant differences in family life is the important fact that many more Negro than white children were unwanted by their mothers. In addition, Negro parents appeared to be less tolerant of a child's self-assertiveness in his contacts with adult authority figures than was true for white parents.

We believe that the evidence emerging from the interviews with mothers of kindergarten-age children is compelling in two important ways. First, it insists that there are important racial differences in the typical behavior patterns of the children as they near school age (sex differences within both races are much less salient). Second, the very significant racial differences in family structure, activity patterns, and commitments to various child-training practices would appear to make it inevitable that such behavioral differences among the children of the two races should be recognizable at this time. We believe, in short, that there are many solid reasons why the mothers of the two races should attribute numerous behavioral differences to their children.

In Interviews, How Do Eighth-Grade Children Describe Themselves and Their Worlds?

The mother interviews provided us with a picture of the children as they were about to begin elementary school. To see how Millfield's children appear during adolescence, we depended in part upon interviews with the children themselves. Data so elicited created an impression of family structure which was in essential agreement with that provided by the mother interviews (see above) and by a family questionnaire (see Chapter 1); these patterns will not be described again here. With regard to other sectors of the children's lives, a great many racial and sex differences were identified which are of considerable interest.

Perhaps of overriding significance is the fact that, in looking at themselves and their worlds, the children have a pervasive within-race orientation, even when such a set has not been given to them by the interviewers. Thus, they look at themselves and their situations not in terms of the full society (not even the limited one that exists in Millfield), but rather with respect to the racial group to which they happen to belong. They do not verbalize this restriction in attitude (indeed, we must doubt that many of the children were aware of it), yet it is apparent throughout their responses to the many-sided interview.

Of paramount importance, too, is the fact that a great many of the children do not seem to recognize many of the limitations present in their life situations; also, large numbers of them express very unrealistic views of their own talents and what they can hope to aspire to, given their actual abilities and the training they are receiving. Many children, for example, who are living in poverty fail to evidence awareness of this reality. Their views about the social structure in which they live are equally limited, and they have great difficulty articulating ideas about how various sectors of their living areas might be improved. Verbal commitments to advanced education are quite common (particularly among the Negro children), but, again, many of these stated aspirations are far removed from the educational achievements that the children have thus far managed in their lives, as well as being out of keeping with their measured abilities.[9]

In looking at their environment, it seems clear that the children of both races have warm feelings for Millfield. They are especially positive about the people who live there. In looking ahead, however, there is a marked racial difference in the way that migration looms up as an essential act in the children's lives. Many of the Negro children *are* sensitive to this component of the area; they know that they will have to go elsewhere if they are to hope for a decent job. And, as our data have shown, this is realistic, for the better jobs in the Millfield area continue to go to the white people. In a very real sense, Negro migration is forced rather than voluntary.

When reporting about their families, the children of both races, in overwhelming proportions, say that father is boss. However, when asked who prevails when the parents disagree over what the child should do, more than two-thirds of the white children designated mother, whereas a majority of the Negro children pointed to father. These data, clearly, are inconsistent with the widely accepted view of the matriarchal Negro family as contrasted with the white patriarchal unit. It is doubtful, however, that these children have either read about or been tutored in this important distinction as it applies to them.

In this context, let us remind the reader that, among the four groups,

---

[9] Among the four groups, a verbal commitment to further education is weakest for the white boys.

the interview statements of the Negro girls suggest the greatest degree of estrangement and alienation. Substantial numbers of the Negro girls want to leave the area, do not want their children to grow up in Millfield, and are critical of various components of the life that exists around them. We suspect that their relationships with their fathers (or father-figures) are critical in generating these feelings of alienation (and, indeed, in causing many of them to, at this time, reject the idea of marriage for themselves). Many of the fathers are controlling and protective of their daughters, but the latter experience their fathers' behavior as being arbitrary, unduly restrictive of their freedom, and insensitive to their needs. As a result, a fair number of the Negro girls are angry and resentful of their fathers; many were unable to identify even one attribute of their fathers which they would like to incorporate within their own selves.

When we turn to the self-concepts of these children, their interview statements about themselves are markedly positive. This is particularly true for the Negro children, a fact that is at variance with the widely accepted belief that the self-esteem of the Negro is inevitably damaged, even at an early age. The Negro children in our sample, for instance, much more frequently reported themselves as being popular with their peers than the white children did.[10] Also, there was a tendency for more Negro than white children to say that they were *very* satisfied being the kind of person they were. In addition, significantly more Negro than white children described their home life as being happier than that of the average child. Clearly, if the self-concepts of these Negro children have been unduly damaged, this fact is not reflected in their interview statements about themselves, nor in the educational and vocational aspirations which they report for themselves (and which they seem to be optimistic about realizing).

What Factors Are Related to Peer Popularity?

Our assessment of peer judgments was much more restricted than we would have liked it to have been; this work centered upon peer popularity. Three findings emerged that merit particular emphasis.

First, the data showed, quite clearly, that peer popularity and teachers' affectionate regard are closely linked, at all age levels studied.

[10] There was no significant difference between Negro boys and girls with respect to how they evaluated their peer popularity. Other data, however, show quite conclusively that the Negro girls are in fact much more popular than the Negro boys. Therefore, we must conclude either that the boys are defensive and do not accurately perceive their status, or that they distort their remarks in the interview in an attempt to hide their unfavored position.

That is, the child who is popular with his peer group is also the child who is likely to be popular with his teachers. This fact suggests, in turn, that each child tends to have what might be called a "likability index" that is established at an early age. If this interpretation is correct, its implications for the child's growth and development would appear to be considerable.

Second, it is clear that a number of attributes of a child and his background are related in a meaningful manner to his peer status (for example, his intelligence, the education of his parents, the size of his family, and the possessions and services available in his home). The composition of this pattern is such as to indicate a positive relationship between the socioeconomic position of a child's family and his standing with his peer group. Again, it seems important to recognize that this relationship is apparent at the younger as well as at the older age levels.

Third, there is a pronounced sex difference within the Negro group which is not suggested by the data for the white group and which, once more, spotlights the unfortunate position of the Negro boys. At each of the eight age levels studied, Negro girls were favored over Negro boys. The fact that this gap appears so early and persists into adolescence (in fact, it tends to grow larger with advancing age) indicates that there is a pervasive devaluation of the Negro male within his own culture, and well before he can be expected to demonstrate attributes of manhood. Without question, this systematic devaluation must make it difficult for him to move toward the mature male position.[11]

While limited, then, the study of peer popularity did nevertheless bring to the fore several properties of these children's behavior that are of considerable importance.

How Do Teachers Rate Their Pupils?

Next to parents and the children themselves, teachers are probably in the best position to appraise the children's attributes. If the teachers were candid when they rated their pupils, then we must conclude that they have, in general, positive feelings about the personal qualities of the children. Given particular emphasis are their desirable social and temperamental attributes; teachers see the children as warm, cooperative, cheerful, likable, and so on.

Quite remarkable, we believe, is the marked racial similarity of the mean trait profiles for the two races which were compiled from the teachers' ratings. Without question, racial similarity rather than racial

[11] As indicated earlier, however, interview data give no indication that Negro boys recognize their unfavored position or, if they do, that they can acknowledge it.

difference must be emphasized when these data are considered (this is particularly true for the girls). The racial differences which were found indicate that Negro children, as viewed by their teachers, are somewhat more passive and less striving than are white children, when the latter are evaluated by their teachers.

Sex differences, in contrast to racial differences, are striking. These differences, moreover, are very similar within both races. And, when a sex difference is found on a trait, the difference is almost always in a direction that must be said to favor the girls. Particularly salient is the fact that the girls' achievement motivation appears to be much stronger than that of the boys.

It is clear, we believe, that the teachers of both races view their pupils in essentially the same way. Also, both groups of teachers perceive similar sex differences in their classrooms, differences that center upon the motivational attributes of the two sexes. In general, this view is in harmony with the sex differences in intellective performance that we have reported earlier (see above). The racial similarity, however, exceeds the degree of correspondence that appears to be present in either the mothers' descriptions of kindergarten-age children or the interview statements made by the eighth-grade children.

How Do Fantasy Measures of Achievement Motivation Contribute to Our Understanding of These Children?

There can be no doubt that, behaviorally, there is a sharp sex difference in achievement motivation within Millfield's classrooms, both Negro and white. When we measure the children's achievement motivation through a widely accepted fantasy technique, however, the data make it mandatory that we exercise caution in drawing final conclusions in this regard. Thus, in their fantasy expressions, boys and girls evidence much greater similarity in their concern with achievement than would be anticipated from either the teachers' ratings or their comparative performances on intellective tests. This may be a very important finding; it suggests, for example, that the boys' relative behavioral deficit may arise more from a failure of the classroom situation to engage or arouse them than from a lack of concern with excellence of performance in the broader sense. That is, the boys may feel that other contexts are more appropriate than the classroom for expressing their achievement strivings.[12]

Overall, the strength of achievement motivation, when evaluated

[12] For example, boys, in a competitive sports context, may manifest more achievement motivation than girls.

through fantasy, appears to be quite low among Millfield's children. This insufficiency, however, may in part be an artifact that can be attributed to the particular pictures used in our study. To determine if this is in fact true, we need to use the same pictures to collect comparable data from bright children living in comparatively privileged homes, or from other groups of children for which there are solid reasons for believing that achievement striving is at a higher level than is characteristically true among Millfield's children.

Developmentally, it is clear that achievement motivation increases rapidly until about grade five, after which any additional gains are very slight (indeed, slight decrements are indicated after grade five for all four groups when McClelland's criteria are applied). Additional studies should certainly be made in an effort to determine why the plot for achievement motivation peaks so early in the child's school career. Also, we are very much in need of repeated measures on the same individuals over a broad age span if we are to comprehend more adequately this component of a person's makeup.

The question of racial differences in achievement motivation cannot be answered definitively. By McClelland's standards, there is a definite racial separation in favor of the white children (a finding that is at least consistent with the tendency of the Negro teachers to see their pupils as more passive and less striving than the white teachers see theirs). When broader scoring criteria are applied, the racial difference is sharply diminished and cannot be regarded as stable. Again, additional studies must be made to clarify these matters.

Finally, it is essential to point out that our study revealed an insignificant relationship between fantasy measures of achievement motivation and achievement motivation as rated by teachers. We would be especially interested in studying in depth those children with high fantasy scores for achievement motivation who are not striving in the classroom. These very well may be children who, if engaged properly, might quickly move to substantially higher levels of performance.

What Additional Conclusions May We Draw from Fantasy Measures?

There were as many significant sex differences as racial differences among the many variables used to appraise the fantasy behavior of the children. Significant age differences, however, were more than twice as common as significant sex or racial effects.

With respect to age effects, we were most impressed by an observation which, unfortunately, we could not document adequately; to do so would have necessitated inclusion of age plots for each of the variables analyzed. We refer here to the fact that, for many variables, there was a tendency for the age plots to telescope between ages 7 and 13. That is, the mean scores for the four groups were much closer together at age 13 than at age 7. This was also true for the mean scores of the Negro children (both sexes combined) compared with those of the white children. In this pattern we see confirmation of a point that we made earlier in talking about the data from the mothers' interviews—namely, that the preschool socialization experiences of the Negro and white children differ rather markedly. The fantasy data, however, suggest in addition that, as the children move through school and as they mature and have wider experiences in their worlds, racial differences tend to diminish. Growth and development enhance racial similarity rather than difference, at least insofar as their induced fantasy life is concerned.

With respect to racial differences, we would point to two findings as being of particular interest. First, the fantasy expressions of the Negro children evidenced a much greater preoccupation with the basic necessities of living than did those of the white children. This, we would suggest, is a direct reflection of the more impoverished circumstances under which the typical Negro child lives. Second, Negro children expressed more unpleasant affect, especially fear, anxiety, and apprehension. Again, we would suggest that this may be in part a direct reflection of a racial difference in actual living circumstances; the Negro child may be more threatened than the white child, living as he does in a white-controlled environment in which he cannot be certain that even his basic physical needs will be met. Also, however, we must remember that his home situation, in contrast to that of the white child, is one in which physical punishment is more likely to be forthcoming, and in which the adults tend to be more demanding of obedience and less accepting of his self-assertion. It may be, therefore, that the Negro child also experiences more threat from within his home than the white child does.

The sex differences in fantasy behavior were, perhaps, what might have been anticipated. Thus, the girls showed more concern with interpersonal relationships, as reflected in imagery pertaining to friendship patterns, rejection, and the giving or seeking of help from others. They were also more expressive of dysphoric affect (this was true for both Negro and white girls) than the boys. In contrast, boys were more likely to express thoughts about food–drink, money–buying, and social aggression (especially participation in sports activities).

In summary, it is clear that there are both racial and sex differences in the personal concerns of these children, at least insofar as these concerns are suggested by their induced fantasy behavior. There are also many similarities, however; it is especially important to recognize that growth and development tend to enhance similarities, not differences, in these personal expressions.

Are the MMPI Data Consistent with the Other Personality Data?

In some respects, the answer to this question is yes; in other respects, the answer is unquestionably no. Certainly the personality picture that emerges from the analysis of the MMPI data is less sanguine than that reflected in some of the other assessment data. Indeed, there are clear indications that large numbers of the Millfield children might manifest severe behavior problems, if they were to move to more complex and stressful settings (see below).

When the four groups are compared, there is an essential consistency between the MMPI data and much of the other data that we have presented in this volume. Thus, the Negro boys, according to this test, appear to be in the deepest psychological "trouble."[13] The white girls, in contrast, show the fewest deviations in a psychopathological direction.[14] The mean test profiles for the Negro girls and white boys, interestingly enough, are almost identical, except for their scores on the masculinity–femininity scale. In regard to this scale, it is noteworthy that girls, both Negro and white, show a stronger tendency to reject the feminine position than the boys, either Negro or white, show with regard to rejection of the masculine position. It is also true that the Negro boys show more of a feminine orientation than the white boys, while the Negro girls show more of a masculine orientation than the white girls.

The scales designed primarily to identify neurotic components of personality structure reveal that such tendencies are not very salient among these children. (Negro boys, however, show a meaningful departure from the remaining three groups in such tendencies.) Instead, these children tend to score high on scales that suggest the likelihood of impulsive acting-out, an inadequate sense of self, alienation from self and society, a deficiency in sustained interests and commitments, and an overall disorganization within the personality. Such trends are most pronounced among the Negro boys, and least so among the white girls. Although to some extent this personality pattern can be regarded as "typically adolescent," the deviations are too pronounced (except among the white girls) to be explained as simply an adolescent phenomenon. In other words, the particular characteristics of life in Millfield appear to be creating additional stresses within the personality structures of the Negro boys, the Negro girls, and the white boys.

[13] On eight out of the ten clinical scales, the mean score for the Negro boys deviated more from the normal position than the scores for the other three groups (see Figure 11.1).

[14] On seven out of the ten clinical scales, the score for the white girls showed the smallest deviation from the normal position (see Figure 11.1).

These personality problems revealed by the MMPI are, in our judgment, more severe than would be suggested by the information elicited
either from the eighth-grade children in interviews or from their
teachers. We believe this to be true even though there were, from time
to time, indications throughout our study of certain psychological realities that are consistent with the inferences drawn from the MMPI data.
Thus, the consistently poor intellective work of the Negro boys along
with their poor peer standing would suggest that this group is in serious
psychological trouble. Also, the relatively high dissatisfaction of the
Negro girls, along with a strong tendency to reject the prospect of
marriage (and with it the mother role) for themselves and their great
difficulty in identifying even one positive attribute of their fathers, suggests at least a highly uncomfortable psychological condition for many
of them. Among the white boys, their relatively weak commitment to
pursuing further education in today's world, along with the poor quality
of their academic work, is probably a strong indication that their inner
resources are not as effectively organized as one would like them to be.
On the other hand, and still consistent with the MMPI findings, is the
fact that the white girls are working effectively in school, they are
embracing the idea of marriage for themselves, and in a variety of other
ways they are manifesting well-integrated behavior.

The point is still valid, however, that the frequency of severe personality problems, as identified by the MMPI, is greater than that suggested by the other investigative techniques and greater than can be
written off as "typically adolescent." It is also apparent from the teachers'
evaluations that these personality problems are not manifested in the
day-to-day behavior of many of the children. Nor did the problems
always show themselves clearly in face-to-face interviews with the children. How can we explain these seeming contradictions?

With regard to the interview data, two factors are probably of critical
importance. First, the structure and content of the interview questions
simply did not probe deeply into many of the behavioral domains that
are comprehensively scrutinized by the large pool of MMPI items. And,
clearly, the MMPI items often refer to feelings and overt behaviors that
the child cannot or will not bring up on his own volition; he is not
accustomed to talking about many of these with anyone, least of all
an adult authority figure. Second, even if the interview items had been
more comparable to the MMPI statements, the face-to-face situation
with a prestigious adult might very well have resulted in a significantly
different pattern of responses. In such interpersonal contexts, most respondents tend to present themselves in a favorable light, whereas the
MMPI format seems to the respondent to be more private or anony-

mous. That is, many individuals may be able to acknowledge problems or tensions on the MMPI answer sheet that they would have great difficulty attributing to themselves in an interpersonal situation.[15]

The seeming discrepancy between the teachers' ratings and the MMPI findings may also in part be attributable to the fact that there were many differences between the behavioral domains covered by the ratings and by the MMPI items. We do not believe, however, that this is a full explanation for the discrepancy, nor do we believe that the teachers were biasing their ratings so as to provide us with more favorable descriptions than the actual behavior of the children warranted. Rather, we believe that the structure of life in Millfield is such that many of the internal psychological problems that it is helping to create are not readily externalized in the children's overt behavior. Thus, the MMPI data are pointing to what, for many (but not all) children, is a latent condition, an inadequacy in personality structure and process that often may go unrecognized (both by the child himself and by others)—as long as the demands made upon him are relatively simple, or as long as he can avoid more taxing confrontations than he is accustomed to meeting in the day-to-day affairs of Millfield.[16]

What we are suggesting is that if many of these children were moved to more complex environments (such as urban locales), or if the demands and confrontations pressed upon them in Millfield were intensified significantly, overt behavior pathology among them would become much more prevalent than it currently is. Such a formulation recognizes that visible behavior is a function not only of the personality processes existent within a person but of the context within which he exists. We believe, therefore, that the teachers are providing reasonably accurate reports of the children's behavior as it is manifested in Millfield, but that their reports would be altered sharply if they observed the children confronting very different situational pressures. The MMPI, on the other

[15] The reader should recall here that, on the validity scales (L and K), the children's scores were such as to indicate that they were being very nondefensive in their responses. It would be interesting to administer the MMPI orally in a two-person context to a comparable group of children to see if the interpretation that we have suggested is reflected in less deviant profiles.

[16] Let the reader recall, for example, that most children tended to view Millfield in very simple terms, as a place where everyone was about like everyone else. And in their classrooms (especially those in the Negro schools) many children are protected from the realities of their poor performance by being given better grades than their performance merits, by being passed instead of failed in the grade, and so on. In these and other ways, many children are shielded from many of the realities of their existence, even including the fact that they are poor and that they are not being adequately prepared to reach the goals which they are being taught to embrace.

hand, is identifying an internal structure which would have quite different implications if the children were functioning in a more complex environment than Millfield.

Having reached the above formulation, we were especially interested in the observation offered by a Negro principal in Millfield during the spring of 1967.[17] In talking with him, he commented on the fact that his school's enrollment had increased appreciably during the on-going academic year, even though the overall trend in enrollment for the past several years had been downward. We asked him why his enrollment had increased, and he pointed to several factors. Among these was the fact that a number of families living in a not-too-distant urban area had sent their children to live with relatives in his school district. The reason for this was the fact that these children had gotten into trouble in their home community. Spontaneously, then, the principal went on to point out that these children were no problem at all in Millfield and that if he had not known of their histories he would have no way of separating them from the other children in his school. To this observation we would add the prediction that if these children, as well as many of Millfield's own, were moved to the street corners of a city's ghetto, problem behavior would not be too difficult to identify.

TWO FINAL COMMENTS

Negro Matriarchal Families

We need, we believe, to address ourselves once again to the concept of the matriarchal family, especially as it may or may not exist in the Negro rural subculture. So far, in our judgment, we have not adequately integrated our findings with respect to this concept. Thus, it is clear that the Negro people themselves perceive paternal rather than maternal dominance within their families (more so than is typical among the white families). At the same time, there is decisive evidence pointing to a systematic devaluation of the Negro male by the Negro population itself beginning at a distressingly early age, along with a very poor performance level by the Negro boys. Clearly, the perceived male dominance within the home is not reflected in prestige, status, or effective performance by the males outside of the home. What does this inconsistency suggest?

---

[17] This was an experienced school administrator, but it was his first year in Millfield. We had not had an opportunity to communicate our observations or interpretations to him.

In the community at large, Negro adult males tend to be held in particularly low regard. Because of this fact, we would suggest that many of them, within the confines of their own family settings, attempt to compensate for the hurts which they experience in the larger community where they are so often denied the right of self-assertion. The result, we suspect, is that they are all too often arbitrary and over-controlling in that one setting where they can afford to exercise self-assertive needs without anticipating punitive reactions by others. Furthermore, the children probably learn at an early age that "father at home" is considerably different from "father in the community." Although this variation in father's behavior is undoubtedly true for many white families as well, the contrast is probably sharper and more common within the Negro families.

Our hypothesis, then, is that these rural Negro families, in comparison with rural white families, are not more matriarchal with respect to their within-family functions. However, the Negro male's position is compromised by the fact that he cannot extend his authority into the larger community. The result is that the Negro male is depreciated even within his own racial group, an attitude that begins to affect his development at a very early age.

Cultural Deprivation and Mediating Processes

Much of our work has emphasized the importance of cultural deprivation, socioeconomic conditions, and related factors. These are abstract concepts, however, and, as we have pointed out at times, they do not act directly to shape children's behavior (see Chapter 14, for example). Kenneth B. Clark, in his provocative *Dark Ghetto*, goes to the heart of this matter:

> The cultural deprivation approach is seductive. It is both reasonable and consistent with contemporary environmentalistic thought, which seems to dominate social science thinking. Indeed, it is presented as a rejection of the inherent racial inferiority theories of the nineteenth and early twentieth centuries. The recent rash of cultural deprivation theories, however, should be subjected to intensive scrutiny to see whether they do, in fact, account for the pervasive academic retardation of Negro children. Specifically, in what way does a low economic status or absence of books in the home or "cognitive deficit," referred to constantly by proponents of this point of view, actually interfere with the ability of a child to learn to read or to do arithmetic in the elementary grades?
>
> (Clark, 1965, p. 130)

Clark's question can (and should) be extended to include the problem of how or in what way cultural deprivation influences the social-personal behavior of the child, as well as his intellective behavior.

There is need, we believe, for what might be termed intensive, microscopic studies that would focus upon the interactive behavior characteristic of the culturally deprived family, as contrasted with similar behavior typical of the nondeprived family. We are reminded here, for example, of the spontaneous comment made by a Negro mother that she did not know how to read to her child until she saw one of our staff members doing this (see Chapter 9). Trained observers, living with both deprived and nondeprived families, might be able to provide us with a clear and meaningful description of how cultural deprivation is translated into behavior that has significance for the intellective, social, and personal development of the child. Other methodological approaches might also be used, but, in any event, it is clear that we need to move beyond concepts like cultural deprivation and into interactive behavioral domains.

Chapter 18

NARROWING THE GAP

In this, the concluding chapter, we shall describe some of our ideas about how disadvantaged children might be assisted. The result, we believe, would be a narrowing of the Negro–white gap described in the preceding chapters.

It may be argued persuasively that some components of Negro culture and behavior are superior to those that characterize the dominant white middle-class society in the United States today. Nevertheless, from a functional point of view, most of the Negro–white behavioral differences described in previous chapters must be said to favor the white children. It is hardly conceivable, for example, that our society, including its Negro members, would devote its energies to the development of social action programs whose goals were to make Millfield's white children more like their Negro peers with respect to most of the behaviors that have been considered. Rather, our social conscience must be stirred by both the form and the extent of the gap that has been described, and we must begin to bring into being far-reaching programs which will enable the Negro child to work and compete more effectively with the white child.

While our society haltingly attempts to make amends for its many failures to meet its responsibilities to all citizens on an equal basis, it cannot in fact ask today's rising generation of white children to settle for less than their optimal rate of development so that children in other groups can catch up. This means, we believe, that whenever social action programs are initiated in the countless Millfields throughout the country, they must be open on an equal basis to *all* children. In point of fact, however, in almost every community the extent of deprivation will be found to be greater among minority members (not only Negro, but Mexican–American, Puerto Rican, etc.) than among the majority white groups. The impact of such programs, therefore, should be greater on the nonwhite groups. If this is true, then the effective implementation of action programs of the type described below should gradually lead to a reduction of the Negro–white gap in many behavioral domains.

Although action programs should be open to all individuals, it is also obvious that communities will have to choose among a variety of programs, many of which will not be of equal value or appeal to its majority and minority groups. To make possible any action, the wise political decision in many of these situations may be to institute, simultaneously, programs which have differential significance for the groups that may be affected. If a choice must be made, however, the decision should turn, we believe, on the question of which option promises to accelerate the development of the Negro child so that his capacities will develop at rates closer to those of the white child. Historically, of course, the reverse order of priority all too often has prevailed in many communities; the dominant group has provided for its own interests, and minority groups have had to take what was left.

Can the behavioral development of disadvantaged children, Negro and white alike, who live in situations comparable to those found in Millfield, be improved? Can the Negro–white gap, which has been mapped in these chapters, be obliterated? With respect to the first question, the answer must be an unqualified yes. The data pertaining to the effects of kindergarten training, for example, leave no doubt in this regard. And, although comparably hard criterion data were not gathered, the staff's experience with Project A was most encouraging. Moreover, a number of additional programs could be developed to provide an improved environment for the children's development; several such possibilities will be described below. As far as the second question is concerned, a definitive answer is impossible to give. After all, if the gain of a Negro child is paralleled by a comparable gain of a white child, the gap will remain; it will simply be at a higher level. On the other hand, it may be that innovative programs will have more widespread effects among Negro than among white children so that, over a period of years, the gap will be reduced significantly, even if it does not disappear. To answer the second question, we need to initiate a massive effort in Millfield—as well as in other target communities—to determine the maximum change that can be secured by social action programs (see below).

In the pages that follow, brief descriptions will be offered of programs which could be initiated that promise to promote a more effective development of the children in communities similar to Millfield. We do not wish to mislead the reader into thinking that each of the recommendations to be described is a direct outgrowth of the data presented; however, these recommendations are based upon our experiences in Millfield, the findings that grew out of the studies that we have reported, and our consideration of many articles and books written about the plight of the Negro minority in our society.

PRESCHOOL EDUCATION

The need to establish comprehensive preschool programs for children from culturally disadvantaged families has been demonstrated beyond question in many studies and in many settings. As matters stand now, great numbers of these children are psychologically handicapped when they enter the first grade; they are prepared neither for normal first-grade work nor for competition with their peers who have come out of more favorable home circumstances. Teachers confronted with mixtures of favored and unfavored children have an impossible task; they cannot simultaneously teach those children who are ready to cope with normal first-grade learning experiences and provide rehabilitation programs for children who are already psychologically handicapped. Furthermore, it is likely that prevention of such handicaps by preschool programs will, in the long run, prove to be more effective than attempts to alleviate them through rehabilitation programs.

Is Head Start Sufficient? [1]

The recognition of the widespread need for preschool training was, of course, a major reason for the initiation of the Head Start program. Testimonials as to the value of this program have come from such prestigious sources that, unlike so many federally initiated efforts, critical evaluations of Head Start have been scattered and generally ineffective. Nevertheless, this program should be examined carefully, especially with regard to the question of what effects we may realistically expect from it.

Comments and discussions in the mass media suggest to us that many individuals may be vastly overestimating the difference that Head Start is likely to make in the lives of the children who are enrolled in it.

---

[1] Our discussion here refers only to the summer Head Start program. Evidence still must be accumulated before judgments can be made about the effectiveness of similar programs distributed over longer time periods.

There is, we are afraid, a great deal of well-intentioned but nevertheless wishful thinking in this regard. The magnitude of the problem is so great and its solution so complex that Head Start can be viewed only as a beginning; unless it is expanded substantially, we cannot be optimistic over the possibility that it will have lasting effects upon the children who participate in it.

We have seen statements that Head Start programs have increased the average IQ's of their participants by eight to ten points. However, we have not seen reports of well-controlled studies which would permit us to have confidence in the validity of such statements. Furthermore, our own experience with a much more comprehensive kindergarten program (see Chapter 8) suggests to us that increasing intellective functioning by the above amount is an extremely formidable undertaking not likely to be achieved by the typical Head Start program.

The reader would be wrong, however, if he concluded from our remarks that we do not support Head Start. To the contrary, we feel that it is a good beginning—but only a beginning. We believe that its primary impact on most children is probably in their social behavior; that is, it very likely increases a child's readiness to function as a member of the type of social group which he will be a part of when he enters the regular school system. Such increments in social skill are indeed important, yet they should not be confused with substantial gains in intellective capacity.

There is in this matter a very difficult situation confronting would-be social engineers. On the one hand, to make any impact at all, popular support and enthusiasm must be generated for their proposed programs. In the process of developing such support, however, there is the very real danger that unrealistically high expectations with regard to outcomes may be established in the minds of many people, especially the parents of the children who are scheduled to be a program's primary beneficiaries. Eventually, if it becomes clear that such programs have not made a substantial difference in the lives of the children, then the disillusionment, anger, and frustration of the disadvantaged may become even deeper—if such a deepening is indeed possible. To raise hopes which then are not confirmed may be less kind than not raising them at all. At the very least, individuals responsible for such programs should be candid in communicating to the people they serve that their expectations with respect to outcomes must be kept within realistic and well-defined bounds.

Should All Elementary Schools Have Kindergartens?

The controlled study described in Chapter 8 shows that kindergarten training can improve the intellective functioning of many children. In any school district, therefore, where substantial numbers of disadvantaged children reside, we believe that a kindergarten year should be established as a regular part of the elementary curriculum.

We do not intend to imply, of course, that kindergarten training may not also be of value to children from more privileged homes. For such children, however, there appears to be much less need for intensive formal intellective training during this year than is true for their less privileged peers. A concentration upon social behavior would seem to be apppropriate for most privileged children during this time, whereas for the disadvantaged children social training should be coordinated with intensive efforts to develop intellective skills and to enhance motivation to learn. Experimental preschool programs, like the one conducted for several years at the George Peabody College (see Gray and Klaus, 1966), suggest ways in which such intellective and motivational training of the disadvantaged child may be accomplished. Also, the work of Long (1966) shows how programmed instructional material may be developed for use with these children. In any event, it is clear that kindergarten training should be made available to all children, but the content of such training will need to vary considerably, depending upon the backgrounds of the particular children enrolled.

Should Project A Programs Be Developed?

Unlike the kindergarten program, the effects of the special Project Acceleration (Project A; see Chapter 9) which was developed for four-year-old children were not subjected to controlled evaluation. Judgments of its value, therefore, must of necessity be offered on a tentative basis.

Despite the demonstrated value of kindergarten training, it must be evident that such training alone will not eliminate the Negro–white gap. There is a need, consequently, to push compensatory efforts into even earlier life experiences of children who are being born into impoverished homes. Our impression of Project A is that it does provide a model which might be used productively in the development of these pre-kindergarten programs.

A contrasting model that needs to be considered involves the establishment of nursery schools that would offer stimulation and training for children from disadvantaged homes. Such programs would, of course, require much heavier financing than Project A programs, since large investments would have to be made in physical structures. Aside from the problems of cost and availability of qualified personnel, however, we see another important advantage in the Project A model over the nursery school model. Specifically, the Project A model promises to reorient many families in their child-training practices and to involve them in efforts to provide better developmental experiences for their children.

Thus, it may bring the family and child closer together in an effort to enhance the latter's development. The nursery school approach, in contrast, typically takes the child from his family, attempts to do something for him, and then returns him to an unmodified family setting. Instead of integrative change, disjunctive change may be introduced into the family, and this may create a whole new set of problems.

In addition, the Project A approach provides an opportunity for the child's home teacher to develop unobtrusively into an effective counselor for other members of the family. As she becomes trusted and valued, she may serve as an important resource person guiding other members of the family into more productive uses of various educational, health, and other institutional resources that may be available to them in the area. As matters stand now, the typical member of these families does not reach out on his own initiative to take advantage of such opportunities. It is our impression, however, that many of them could and would respond to guidance offered by a respected individual who has become sympathetically identified with their situation. Project A, therefore, offers a means for introducing constructive change into many families that would reach beyond the target child.

Although kindergartens should be established more widely as quickly as possible, we recommend a two-stage approach to Project A programs. First, several Project A programs should be established in different settings with provisions for objectively evaluating their effects, much as we did in the study of the kindergarten programs. If the results of such pilot projects are as encouraging as our preliminary efforts suggest that they should be, then a rapid multiplication of such programs should be undertaken.

ELEMENTARY SCHOOL EDUCATION

It may be possible to develop a preschool program so comprehensive and penetrating that children exposed to it will be set upon a path which will enable them to rise above classroom deficiencies encountered later during their elementary and secondary school years. However, we should not like to place a high wager that this will prove to be true for large numbers of disadvantaged children; rather, we suspect that the fruits of various preschool programs may very often be diminished considerably when the children become bogged down in clearly inadequate elementary and secondary school programs. Therefore, the gains to be expected from meaningful preschool programs must be protected and nourished by upgrading the quality of the traditional school program.

We are not educational theorists, nor have we been public school teachers or administrators. As psychologists who have directed the studies reported in this book, however, we feel that we would be remiss with respect to our responsibilities if we did not comment upon some of the shortcomings and needs of our public schools. Since most of our work was confined to elementary schools, our observations and suggestions will be directed specifically at this age range. In some instances, though, we suspect that our comments would be equally valid if they were applied to the junior high and high school levels.

Is Teaching a Profession?

As far as the typical public school teacher is concerned, the answer to this question is, unfortunately, clearly no. Large segments of society say yes—especially when teachers move to form what are essentially trade unions—but they seldom behave as if they mean what they say. Hypocrisy is rampant in this matter. Actually, our data indicate that the Negro teacher in Millfield probably has more status than the white teacher, but if the community contained Negro professionals in law, medicine, and other disciplines (or substantial businessmen), we must doubt that the Negro teacher would be regarded or treated as a professional any more than her white counterpart is.

This matter of professional status is critical, since it is unlikely that many of the school's problems can really be solved until more individuals with initiative and great capacity are attracted and retained in this type of work. There is a need for more and better equipment, for more abundant supplies, for improved physical plants, and so on, but all such improvements will be of limited value to the child unless he is provided with much more talent in the form of teachers. And until teachers are treated as professionals, this vocation is not going to recruit its share of the available talent. In this situation, it is the children— particularly the disadvantaged—who suffer. Well-educated and prosperous families can provide compensations for many of the deficiencies present in the classrooms of their children, but few underprivileged families can do the same.

Women Only?

One consequence of the failure to establish teaching as a profession is the fact that most elementary schools, including those in Millfield, are presented to the children as essentially feminine institutions. And, since this is the setting in which society says that learning is to be of foremost importance, the learning process tends to become a feminine undertaking for many of the children. There is a critical need, we believe, to take immediate steps to attract as many men as women into the elementary classrooms. The very presence of men would help to redefine the nature of the learning enterprise; however, in addition, we suspect that they would rather quickly make some important changes in the content of some of the substantive areas which would result in greater involvement on the part of the boys.

Can Men Be Attracted to Teaching?

The fact that most public school administrators and college teachers are men indicates that the educational setting is not unalterably feminine. Moreover, there are substantial numbers of able men in our society who continue in jobs that bore them and who could be attracted to public school teaching—if they were paid an adequate wage. By keeping salaries low, we bar their entry into a vocation that would, for many of them, prove to be much more satisfying than their current work.

As a first step toward making teaching a true profession, we suggest that teaching contracts should be written on a calendar-year basis (with proportionate increases in salaries, of course) for all teachers who desire such opportunities. During the summer months these teachers would be able to initiate and contribute to a variety of educational efforts, according to the needs of their particular school districts. For example, they might conduct adult educational programs, special classes for preschoolers, or vocational training classes for older children which cannot be incorporated into the regular school year. Or, in communities like Millfield, the teachers might devote their summer months to close liaison work with the families of their students, developing for themselves a guidance role not unlike the one described above for staff members of Project A. In addition, sabbatical summers or summers for advanced study should be made a regular part of teaching contracts.

A step like the one just described would, we believe, be a clear signal to men and women that our society is committed to the development of teaching as a profession. Year-round income, moreover, would enable men to enter the field without the necessity of seeking summer employment to support their families during one-fourth of the year. In addition, such a professional corps would be contributing to the educational needs of the country on a full-time basis. As matters stand now, much of this valuable talent is used for only part of the year, in spite of our great needs.

In addition, of course, there are many changes in the teacher's role which could be made to enhance its attractiveness to individuals of talent from both sex groups. If such changes were made, along with higher salary schedules, our elementary school programs could become the joint products of men and women working together creatively.

Additional Professional Specialists

One way in which many communities reveal their unwillingness to grant professional status to teachers is their refusal to provide them with needed secretarial, clerical, and other forms of nonprofessional assistance. Most professional disciplines are, of course, supported by a relative abundance of such ancillary helpers. In addition to similar assistance, teachers should have a variety of professional services available to them on the premises if they are going to be of maximum assistance to their students. Some of the professional specialists who are needed will be noted briefly.

1. Curriculum specialists. In most elementary schools, the principal has the primary responsibility for the overall curriculum. The many demands placed upon him, however, ordinarily leave him little time to work creatively with this critically important phase of his school's program. Furthermore, principals seldom seem to be selected because of their talent in this regard, so the availability of time is not the only factor to be considered. This is an era, however, when new approaches to the teaching of many traditional content areas are being developed, and most schools rather desperately need leadership in redeveloping their curricula to utilize these innovative ideas in ways that will be most meaningful for their particular communities.

Classroom teachers, burdened with heavy loads, have little time to explore how fundamental changes might be made to advantage in their teaching efforts. Therefore, a resource person in the school with full-time responsibilities in this domain could be used to considerable advantage. Such a person would keep abreast of current developments, visit other schools to observe different methods and techniques being used there, comb the literature for ideas that might be applicable locally, and so on. By establishing such a position, the school would be committing itself to change and to the goal of incorporating into its own program more effective ways of reaching its major goals. Generally, such positions should, we believe, be occupied by teachers who have earned the respect of their colleagues for the excellence of their own work in the classroom.

2. School psychologists. It is clear to many educators that properly trained psychologists can make effective contributions to most school programs. Indeed, the time has passed when a major effort should have been initiated to train such professionals in meaningful numbers. The need for their services is, of course, especially acute in schools with large numbers of disadvantaged children, although this need is by no means restricted to such schools. And it hardly needs to be said that psychological services available once or twice a month are no satisfactory response to the need.

A well-trained psychologist can provide many different services in school settings; these services will vary somewhat depending upon the particular school and its social context. However, we should like to emphasize three contributions that would seem to be particularly important. First, he can conduct a comprehensive assessment program so that the progress of the children, both intellectively and socially, will be charted in a way that will have implications for the school's programs. The teachers of Negro children in Millfield, for example, need to be confronted with hard data showing that their bright children are not achieving up to their capacities; only when this is done is it likely that remedial actions will be instituted. Second, the psychologist can serve as a resource person to guide teachers into more effective ways of coping with various problems that develop in their classrooms. Perhaps equally important, he can serve as a resource person to administrative personnel to assist them in handling many problems (for example, interracial difficulties) which are essentially psychological in nature. Third, on a limited basis, he can undertake psychotherapeutic work with some students who present various types of behavioral problems. And, when he is not able to provide such help personally, he can serve as a bridge to other community facilities where the child might be helped.

These are only a few of the ways, of course, in which psychologists might contribute to the school's reaching of its objectives. As matters stand now, few schools really can take advantage of the gains made in psychological knowledge during recent years. And, we believe, the need to apply such knowledge is particularly acute in schools like those found in Millfield.

3. Guidance specialists. The role of the guidance specialist is not easily differentiated from that of the school psychologist. When properly trained, he can, for example, contribute to each of the functions described above for the school psychologist. If both specialists were available in a school, one would indeed anticipate close collaboration between them on many problems.

There is a special need for a guidance specialist, however, with respect to a particular problem that was not mentioned in the discussion of the school psychologist's role. As we learned in our work in Millfield, very few of the older elementary school children have an opportunity to discuss their future plans—educational, vocational, personal—or current problems with their teachers. Even if the teacher is willing to provide such consultation, the definition of a teacher's role makes it difficult for most children to share their feelings, problems, and plans with her. There is, then, a definite need for a person in the school setting whose training and role make him accessible to the students for such personal consultation. Again, the need for such assistance is particularly acute among the disadvantaged children, since so many of their parents are ill-equipped to provide them with guidance which is appropriate for the modern-day world. In short, the school needs to provide the child with a sympathetic, understanding adult who is interested in his total welfare, and not just with teachers whose primary interest is perceived as being the child's mastery of academic content.

These, then, are some of the specialists who need to become regular members of each school's staff. The traditional concept of the school as a building with classroom teachers and a principal is no longer sufficient to cope with the existing problems.

New Courses

Our experiences in the schools did not indicate to us a need for radical revisions in the content of what was being taught, although we must emphasize that we did not focus on this matter (nor did our training prepare us to do so). There was some evidence suggesting that the development of rote memory skills might be receiving undue emphasis in the Negro schools, but we would not want to be too certain about this without additional investigation. It was apparent, however, that much more could and should be done with respect to organizing the curriculum, introducing new teaching methods, grouping students, and so on. These needs, of course, were the basis of our suggestion that each school should have a curriculum specialist (see above).

One learning area, though, was clearly not receiving the attention which, in our judgment, it deserves. We refer to the fact that even eighth-grade children appeared to be so unaware of the immediately surrounding contemporary society in which they live. The realities of this society obviously have important implications for the children, and we feel that they should learn about them in their schools. The upper elementary grades are not too early to begin this teaching, if it is done properly. For example, the children should be taught how to analyze and discuss the biracial society that exists in Millfield, the resources and limitations available in the area, its power structure, and so on. Furthermore, they should be taken on trips to acquaint them with nearby industries and other job settings available in neighboring areas. They should also be taken for observations and discussions of available college and university campuses so that they might begin to form realistic ideas about what opportunities are available to them. In brief, the schools should begin to teach the children at an early age how to analyze their local culture, how to take advantage of opportunities within it, how to escape some of its limitations, how to initiate action programs for constructive change, and how to win effective results.

Is School Integration Necessary?

In introducing our work (see the Preface), we indicated that racial attitudes as such would not be our concern. Obviously, it is too late in this final chapter to make a contribution in this regard. We want, nevertheless, to make a few remarks with respect to school integration.

In our judgment, all children, no matter what their color or talents, are deprived when they are segregated on the basis of some arbitrary and irrational criterion. All are deprived in the sense that they are cut off from potentially rich and rewarding experiences with individuals whose heritage differs from their own. In addition, many are further deprived because they are given inferior teachers and/or facilities. Until full and honest racial integration is achieved and accepted, children are going to suffer in the sense of not realizing their full potential.

These are our convictions, however, and obviously they are not shared by many individuals in communities like Millfield. Those who do share similar beliefs ordinarily find it advisable not to voice them. Even among the Negro population there is widespread reservation about the desirability of pushing for full integration, especially if the right of the Negro child to attend a white school is established by token integration, and if the visible physical facilities in the Negro schools are kept comparable to those in the white schools. In short, there is no realistic basis for expecting effective local initiative with respect to full school integration no matter how strongly educational specialists and others might argue for it.

It is an interesting paradox that geographical pupil assignment, the basis for de facto segregation in most urban communities, would, if instituted in Millfield, result in much greater integration than now exists; this would also be true in many other rural areas. In fact, extensive bussing is necessary to ensure segregated schools. With geographical assignment, the length of the bus trip would be reduced for many children, and the entire transportation system would be made more simple and less expensive.

EXPANDING THE USE OF AVAILABLE FACILITIES

The largest single expenditure of public money in communities like Millfield is for education. And the only substantial public buildings ordinarily are the schools. With such an investment and with so many unmet community needs, it is discouraging to realize that the school facilities are used for less than one-half of the days during a calendar year. An observer is especially struck by this seeming waste if he comes upon the expensive and deserted buildings during the long summer months. Does not such an investment merit fuller use?

School-Year Programs

There are several ways in which these facilities could be used productively on Saturdays and some evenings during the regular school year. For example, a variety of adult educational offerings, both academic and vocational, could be developed. At present, in community after community, nothing of this sort is available, despite overwhelming needs. Moreover, in most areas talented and trained people are available who would be able to contribute to such programs. The relevance of such offerings to the needs of the people being served would be one critical matter that would have to be kept in mind in the development of such programs. However, initiative to develop them appears to be lacking in most communities.

In addition to adult programs, the school facilities should be used to implement parts of a comprehensive prekindergarten program. For example, as a regular part of Project A, small groups of children could be brought together in the schools each Saturday for several hours of guided socializing. Concurrently, mothers who found it feasible might meet in other parts of the building for demonstrations and discussions centered on how to guide the development of their children more effectively.

The school facilities should also be used for recreational purposes during the late afternoons and evenings. The possibility of regular motion picture programs and dances should be explored, for example, as should the establishment of sports activities, like basketball and volleyball leagues. In brief, people should recognize and act upon the fact that they already have available physical plants that could be used for a variety of broad community programs. Schools can be transformed into comprehensive community centers without interfering with traditional educational programs; by doing this, we would provide for a much richer life in the rural areas than now exists.

Summer School Programs

It seems clear to us that, in areas where educational and recreational needs are so great, school facilities should be used for twelve months rather than nine months. A variety of programs similar to those mentioned above could be developed during the summer months on an even more extensive basis than is possible during the school year. Furthermore, as noted earlier, members of the school staffs could contribute to many of these efforts, thereby giving them calendar-year rather than academic-year employment. Again, the emphasis should be placed upon the development of the schools as full-time community centers offering a variety of programs related to community needs.

Educational Television

Our inquiries left no doubt that television sets in Millfield are used solely for entertainment purposes. And, being realistic, we recognize that entertainment is badly needed and is likely to continue to be the primary reason for turning on the set. At the same time, efforts should be initiated to add more attractive educational offerings to this entertainment diet. There are many possibilities, but we shall limit ourselves to one suggestion.

The experience of the staff with Project A convinced us that many mothers are prepared to cooperate in programs which promise to promote a more effective development of their preschool children. However, they are short on initiative and "know-how," so that stimulation and guidance must be provided from the outside. Home visits by teachers can provide this guidance, at least in part, but such contacts are time-consuming and their frequency cannot be as high as one might like. If such visits were supplemented by a regular series of morning or afternoon television programs developed by the staff especially for mothers with children in specified age brackets, the total impact of the home visiting program might be increased markedly.

It should be recognized, we believe, that the development of cable television and other technological innovations may soon make it possible to bring many more channels to even relatively isolated rural areas. Some of these channels should be used to develop educational programs which are shaped with reference to the particular needs of the area being served. When this relevance to local needs is made clear to the people, there is reason to believe that they will sacrifice some time from the entertainment channels.

INCREASING MOTIVATION

Although our society is not as open as the statements of our democratic principles make it appear to be, nevertheless this is a land full of opportunities—even for the disadvantaged child, including the Negro youngster. The problem is to make these opportunities known to him and to see that he is prepared to take advantage of them. Unless he develops desire to move ahead, however, our efforts in this regard are likely to be largely wasted. Without this internal push he will neither see what we show him nor will he develop those skills which we know that he must have if he is to take advantage of opportunities.

Desire, however, is not something tangible, nor is it something that can, in the abstract sense, be injected into someone. Rather, desire must be created out of experiences, experiences which, in the immediate sense, may have other meanings that are primary for the individual participant. Thus, a child may look forward to a field trip to an industrial setting because he will be freed from the constraints of the classroom; however, while there, he may observe a craftsman working on something which excites an interest in him that was heretofore nonexistent. If nourished, this spark of interest may develop so that it does have real meaning for his life.

Many of the programs discussed in this chapter would, we believe, if implemented, increase the probability that the desire to achieve in many of the children would be heightened. If this did not occur, we would have to be pessimistic about the long-term effects of the programs. In developing such efforts, therefore, it is mandatory that their implementors be constantly alert to the likely impact of the program upon the motivational structure of the child. That is, the program should start where the child is, it should be structured in a way that will seem to the child to be relevant to him, and it should attempt both to excite his interest and to challenge him to extend himself.

In addition to keeping the motivational component constantly in mind as efforts are made to assist disadvantaged children, each school system should be provided with the resources to establish concrete incentive systems. Such systems would keep alive for the children the fact that it is important to do well, that effort and accomplishment are rewarded locally. If nothing more, such incentive systems would have important symbolic meanings for the children touched by them. Let us be more concrete about several possibilities in this regard.

The National Merit Scholarship competition has been set up in order to recognize, encourage, and nourish talent wherever it is found. We have no intimate contact with this program, but its objectives appear very laudable to us. Yet we must also recognize that this type of program has no meaning for the kind of children that we have been concerned about; they simply are not in the running. Contrast this, then, with a program that guarantees scholarship support for advanced education to a specified number of children from the local school system, the awardees to be selected on the basis of achievement, ability, and perhaps even financial need. This type of program could have an impact on the motivation of many children in Millfield, whereas there is not much point in even discussing the National Merit Scholarship program with them.

A second type of incentive program which could be initiated would turn upon employment rather than scholarship awards. For example, nearby businesses and industries might be asked to guarantee summer apprenticeship employment to specified numbers of children from particular schools. Children would be selected for these jobs on the basis of achievement, effort expended on schoolwork, and perhaps need. If necessary, financial subsidies from various sources (including government and foundations) could be made available to cover the costs to industries and businesses which otherwise might be unable to participate in such a program. In addition to on-the-job learning, such a program would be a very direct way of bringing home to the children in each school that there really are rewards awaiting individuals willing to extend themselves.

These are only examples of incentive programs which could be established within local school systems; the point we want to emphasize is that much more attention should be given to the establishment of such programs, especially in schools where the disadvantaged attend in large numbers. The two programs which we have described would in fact seem to have greater applicability to high school than to elementary school children. Their presence, however, would be advantageous to those who are working with elementary school pupils, especially the older ones. Furthermore, elementary school pupils with older siblings who were striving for such rewards would very likely come under their influence prior to becoming eligible for the rewards themselves. In other words, such local incentive systems could make a substantial difference in the psychological climate surrounding many of the children.

INDUSTRIAL DEVELOPMENT

Our central concern up to this point has been with the educational system, for, without doubt, most communities must make very substantial improvements in this system if the gap between the advantaged and disadvantaged is to be narrowed. It would be folly, however, to neglect the problem of work opportunities for people like those in Millfield. Unless they see realistic opportunities to move into the world of work at more rewarding levels than is currently the case, it is unlikely that they will take full advantage of the learning opportunities offered them by their educational system.

A New Basis for Locating Industries

The interviews with the older children impressed upon us the fact that a substantial majority of them feel a real affection for Millfield, that they would look ahead with pleasure to establishing their own families in this locale—if there were adequate job opportunities available. Many of them recognize at an early age, however, that they will have to migrate, unless they are willing to scratch out a living on a small plot of land. Insofar as we could determine, much of the migration that does occur is not a result of the appeal of urban areas; rather it is moving away from a setting that is devoid of opportunity. (Unfortunately, the person who does move often is not prepared to take advantage of the greater opportunities which may exist in his new location.)

We are not opposed to urbanization as such, and, clearly, we must protect the freedom of a person to live in the place of his choice. In point of fact, however, vast numbers of individuals, owing to economic necessity, are being forced away from their preferred locales (rural areas) and into sprawling urban areas which have long since demonstrated their inability to cope with them in such large numbers, especially when so many of them are poorly trained. Yet very little is being done to reduce the need for this migration, and the plight of the cities becomes more and more desperate.

A significant contribution to the solution of this problem is to be found, we believe, in the location of new industrial plants. Currently, the states—and communities within the states—are vying with one another for a share of the 50 to 60 billion dollars worth of new plants being erected in this country annually. The owners of these plants quite naturally tend to select locales which promise to be optimal from the point of view of their earnings; the implications of their decisions for the larger society are not weighted heavily. The massive urban areas, moreover, compete for these new plant facilities, as if securing them will somehow alleviate their problems. In all likelihood, however, by the time a plant is secured and is operating, the needs of that urban area have increased to the point where the problem is even greater than when the plant was being sought.

Further industrial development of large urban areas is, then, analagous to treating a symptom rather than the cause of a disease. It is long past time when such development should be permitted to proceed willy-nilly without any overall consideration for what society needs. Instead, an all-out effort should be made to decentralize further industrial development into the countryside, thus stemming at least part of the flow to the cities. This would give the cities more breathing room, and some hope for solving the many problems which confront them.

We would suggest, for example, that government and industry collaborate on a plan whereby a certain percentage (substantially above current rates) of new plant development each year would be placed in the innumerable Millfields which dot our country. That is, these plants would be located in terms of the social needs of the area rather than as a result of competitive bidding among already established communities. If necessary, temporary governmental subsidies might be used to prevent loss to the industry for making its decision with regard to social need.

Obviously, we have presented only the bare skeleton of a plan. Our purpose, however, is to point up the fact that the present course of industrial development is creating serious imbalance in our country, and in so doing it is in fact depriving many individuals of freedom to live where they choose. With modern forms of transportation, rural areas are not physically isolated as in the days of old, and, with proper development, they can provide settings for satisfying living. Both industry and government have responsibilities in this regard which they are not now meeting.

New Commitments for Industries

The responsibility of an industry to the people should not end when it chooses a location, even if social need has affected that decision. The industries of tomorrow should, we believe, be more sensitive than in the past to the total needs of the community in which they are located. And, so that industries can remain competitive in world markets, the government should help them, at least in the beginning, to carry out expanded programs. Let us be a bit more specific about what we have in mind.

Location of a sizable industrial plant in Millfield would have a great impact upon the area, especially if the management followed nondiscriminatory hiring practices. Large numbers of local people would be locked out of employment opportunities, however, unless management also committed itself to training many potential employees who currently lack either experience or appropriate skills. Industry should make such commitments as part of their concern with the general welfare of the society in which they function.

But an industry's commitment to social needs should go even further. Each rural plant should offer health, educational, and recreational services to the people in its area. An outpatient clinic open to all residents of the community would guarantee, for example, that their minimal health needs were being met. An adult education department, with emphasis upon training for skills needed by modern industry, could be especially helpful. And a recreational department could provide leadership in developing activities which would make the area a more attractive place in which to live.

What we are saying is that not only should many more industries be located in rural areas but their responsibilities for the general welfare of the people in the area should be greatly broadened. They should not only provide jobs, they should also be the center around which programs are organized to meet the critical needs of the people living in the area. To encourage such additional commitments by industry, state and federal governments should provide subsidies which would cover the increased costs. If government can subsidize the development of supersonic planes for the airlines, why can it not subsidize the development of services which would hold real promise for narrowing the gap between the advantaged and disadvantaged?

An Experimental Program

As long as the Viet Nam war—or a similar conflict—severely taxes the economy of the country, it is unrealistic to anticipate that substantial sums of money will become available for programs similar to those described. In the meantime, perhaps all that we can hope for is the continuation of a number of the component parts of the antipoverty program. It is difficult to coordinate these efforts, however, so as to maximize their effectiveness. Also, we must be honest and admit that some of the programs function more as props to morale among the disadvantaged groups than as curative agents for the problems which beset them. For the time when adequate funding becomes a more realistic possibility, and to guard against the disillusionment which will eventually accompany ineffective programs, we need to experiment with total community programs which will strike at the roots of the difficulties in rural areas. To put the matter another way, we should begin now with several experimental programs which, hopefully, will show us how the job can be done on a broad basis when more adequate financing becomes available.

To be more concrete, what we are suggesting is that a number of communities like Millfield be identified in several different states. Each of these areas, then, would be developed by utilizing a combination of the ideas described in these pages, or by others, or that might be formulated as a result of studying the characteristics of each particular area. Hopefully, each of these experimental programs would be financed by a single governmental department or private foundation; also, each should be under the direction of a single administrator. In this way, a coordinated attack could be made on the community's problems without devoting an undue proportion of the staff's time to compromising the various interests of multiple funding groups.

Let us outline now how the development of a typical experimental program might proceed, recognizing of course that local realities in a particular community would require deviations from any so-called model plan. Some of the critical steps in the development of such an experimental program would be the following:

1. Elicit the interest of a governmental agency or private foundation in funding the program.

2. Identify an industrial firm that would be willing to establish a plant in a rural area because of the area's social need, with the understanding that social programs of the sort that have been described would be incorporated as divisions of the plant's structure.

3. Select a director for the experimental phases of the program. This person would work directly under the plant's manager and would be responsible for the various educational, health, and recreational programs developed for the area.

4. Select an area where the need for this type of social development is clear. Consult with the leaders in the given area so that they will have a full understanding of the proposal; proceeding with the program in the chosen area would be contingent upon assurances of their support.

5. While the plant is being built (to include space to house central facilities for educational, health, and recreational programs), survey the area to determine more precisely the educational, health, and recreational needs of the people. This survey should be done with later evaluation in mind. For example, the existing academic achievement and ability levels of the children might be measured in ways similar to those reported in this volume. A control group in a separate but similar geographical area should also be studied. After the total program has been operative for an adequate period of time, similar assessments of the children would provide a firm basis for evaluating the impact of the program upon them.

6. The research program outlined in point 5 indicates, of course, that early in the development of the program a research staff should be established to study the significance of this type of program for the lives of the people affected. This staff should be composed of individuals from several disciplines; for instance, education, psychology, sociology, and medicine.

7. While the plant is being constructed, plans for the community-oriented programs should be developed. For example, Project A programs as well as adult educational programs could be planned as part of the plant's educational division. This division should also have money

to use in underwriting the additional costs to the schools for the types of specialists described earlier; it should work cooperatively with the schools to help them upgrade the quality of their programs.

8. The staffing of the plant would be a critical item in the development of the program, and a policy with regard to hiring local individuals would have to be formulated. In general, we would expect that local hiring would be given preference and that only the necessary skeleton staff would be brought in from the outside. Ordinarily the question would not be "Does this individual have the needed skill?" but rather "Can he be trained for a job that needs to be done?"

9. Recruit the personnel necessary to make the educational, health, and recreational programs functional. To the extent possible, local sources of manpower should be tapped.

These, then, are a few of the steps that would have to be taken to implement the type of program that we have in mind. By locating this effort in a job-producing plant, the plant would become a very different kind of place from those that we are accustomed to finding in most areas of our country. If this type of program did indeed narrow the gap appreciably between the advantaged and disadvantaged, then it would merit the support of both government and business in seeing that it was made available to the many Millfields that are to be found in our country. If we can provide 75 billion dollars annually for defense needs, surely the time is near when we can make equal opportunities available to all, regardless of the circumstances under which they begin life. We must find out how this objective can be achieved within the social and economic structure that we have built.

REFERENCES

A large number of articles and books were reviewed and abstracted during the course of this study; most of these pertained to the Negro American. Although this literature conditioned our thought and work, it is not listed here in detail. Rather, we have listed below only those works actually cited in the text. An excellent bibliography, topically arranged, covering the Negro American has been published recently by Elizabeth W. Miller (see below). Another comprehensive reference list is available in Thomas F. Pettigrew's *A Profile of the Negro American* (also, see below).

Atkinson, J. W. (Ed.) *Motives in fantasy, action, and society: A method of assessment and study.* Princeton, N. J.: Van Nostrand, 1958.

Ball, J. C. *Social deviancy and adolescent personality: An analytical study with the MMPI.* Lexington: University of Kentucky Press, 1962.

Baughman, E. E., and Welsh, G. S. *Personality: A behavioral science.* Englewood Cliffs, N. J.: Prentice-Hall, 1962.

Bock, R. D. A computer program for univariate and multivariate analysis of variance. Mimeographed materials, 1963.

Bruce, Myrtle. Factors affecting intelligence test performance of whites and Negroes in the rural South. *Archives of Psychology,* 1940, **36**, No. 252.

Butcher, J. N. Manifest aggression: MMPI correlates in normal boys. *Journal of Consulting Psychology,* 1965, **29**, 446–454.

Butcher, J. N., and Dahlstrom, W. G. Equivalence of the booklet and taped forms of the MMPI for use with college normals. Unpublished materials, 1965.

Butcher, J. N., Ball, Brenda, and Ray, Eva. Effects of socio-economic levels on MMPI differences in Negro-white college students. *Journal of Counseling Psychology,* 1964, **11**, 83–87.

Church, Jane C. A short-term longitudinal study of factors related to IQ change in white Southern rural adolescents. Ph.D. dissertation, University of North Carolina at Chapel Hill, 1965.

Clark, K. B. *Dark ghetto: Dilemmas of social power.* New York: Harper and Row, 1965.

Crandall, V. J. Achievement. In H. W. Stevenson (Ed.). *Child psychology: The sixty-second yearbook of the National Society for the Study of Education.* Chicago: University of Chicago Press, 1963.

Dahlstrom, W. G., and Welsh, G. S. *An MMPI handbook: A guide to use in clinical practice and research.* Minneapolis: University of Minnesota Press, 1960.

Doll, E. A. *The measurement of social competence: A manual for the Vineland Social Maturity Scale.* Minneapolis: Educational Publishers, 1953.

494

Gilberstadt, H., and Duker, Jan. *A handbook for clinical and actuarial MMPI interpretation.* Philadelphia: Saunders, 1965.

Gray, Susan W., and Klaus, R. A. Deprivation, development, and diffusion. Presidential Address, Division of School Psychologists, American Psychological Association, September 4, 1966.

Harrison, R. H., and Kass, E. H. Differences between Negro and white pregnant women on the MMPI. *Journal of Consulting Psychology,* 1967, **31**, 454–463.

Hathaway, S. R., and Monachesi, E. D. *Adolescent personality and behavior: MMPI patterns of normal, delinquent, dropout, and other outcomes.* Minneapolis: University of Minnesota Press, 1963.

Hathaway, S. R., Monachesi, E. D., and Young, L. A. Rural-urban adolescent personality. *Rural Sociology,* 1959, **24**, 331–346.

Hereford, C. F. *A community education project in parent-child relationships: Progress reports and exhibits.* Austin, Texas: Austin Community Guidance Center, 1958. (Mimeographed)

Jones, L. V. A factor analysis of the Stanford-Binet at four age levels. *Psychometrika,* 1949, **14**, 299–331.

Kagan, J., and Moss, H. A. Stability and validity of achievement fantasy. *Journal of Abnormal and Social Psychology,* 1959, **58**, 357–364. (a)

Kagan, J., and Moss, H. A. Parental correlates of child's IQ and height: A cross-validation of the Berkeley growth study results. *Child Development,* 1959, **30**, 325–332. (b)

Kardiner, A., and Ovesey, L. *The mark of oppression: Explorations in the personality of the American Negro.* New York: Norton, 1951.

Kelley, T. L., Madden, R., Gardner, E. F., Terman, L. M., and Ruch, G. M. *Stanford Achievement Test: Manual.* Yonkers-on-Hudson, N. Y.: World Book, 1953.

Kennedy, W. A. A follow-up normative study of Negro intelligence and achievement. Tallahassee: Florida State University, 1965. (Mimeographed)

Kennedy, W. A., Van de Riet, V., and White, J. C. *The standardization of the 1960 revision of the Stanford-Binet Intelligence Scale on Negro elementary-school children in the southeastern United States.* Tallahassee: Florida State University, 1961.

Kennedy, W. A., Van de Riet, V., and White, J. C. A normative sample of intelligence and achievement of Negro elementary school children in the southeastern United States. *Monographs of the Society for Research in Child Development,* 1963, **28**, No. 90.

Korchin, S. J., Mitchell, H. E., and Meltzoff, J. A critical evaluation of the Thompson Thematic Apperception Test. *Journal of Projective Techniques,* 1950, **14**, 445–452.

LaCrosse, Jean Eder. Examiner reliability on the Stanford-Binet Intelligence Scale (Form L-M) in a design employing white and Negro examiners and subjects. M.A. thesis, University of North Carolina at Chapel Hill, 1964.

Long, E. R. The effect of programmed instruction in special skills during the preschool period on later ability patterns and academic achievement. University of North Carolina at Chapel Hill, 1966. (Mimeographed)

Marks, P. A., and Seeman, W. *Actuarial description of abnormal personality.* Baltimore: Williams & Wilkins, 1963.

McClelland, D. C., Atkinson, J. W., Clark, R. A., and Lowell, E. L. *The achievement motive.* New York: Appleton-Century-Crofts, 1953.

Miller, Elizabeth W. (Compiler). *The Negro in America: A bibliography*. Cambridge: Harvard University Press, 1966.

Mingione, Ann Dissinger. Need for achievement in Negro children. M.A. thesis, University of North Carolina at Chapel Hill, 1960.

Mingione, Ann Dissinger. Need for achievement in Negro and white children. Ph.D. dissertation, University of North Carolina at Chapel Hill, 1961.

Mingione, Ann Dissinger. Need for achievement in Negro and white children. *Journal of Consulting Psychology*, 1965, **29**, 108–111.

Morgan, Christiana D., and Murray, H. A. A method for investigating phantasies: The Thematic Apperception Test. *Archives of Neurology and Psychiatry*, 1935, **34**, 289–306.

Panton, J. H. Inmate personality differences related to recidivism, age and race as measured by the MMPI. *Journal of Correctional Psychology*, 1959, **4**, 28–35.

Pettigrew, T. F. *A profile of the Negro American*. Princeton, N. J.: Van Nostrand, 1964. (a)

Pettigrew, T. F. Negro American personality: Why isn't more known? *Journal of Social Issues*, 1964, **20**, 4–23. (b)

Schaefer, E. S. Does the sampling method produce the negative correlation of mean IQ with age reported by Kennedy, Van de Riet, and White? *Child Development*, 1965, **36**, 257–259.

Terman, L. M., and Merrill, Maud A. *Measuring intelligence: A guide to the administration of the new revised Stanford-Binet tests of intelligence*. Boston: Houghton-Mifflin, 1937.

Terman, L. M., and Merrill, Maud A. *Stanford-Binet Intelligence Scale: Manual for the third revision, Form L-M*. Boston: Houghton-Mifflin, 1960.

Thompson, C. E. The Thompson modification of the Thematic Apperception Test. *Journal of Projective Techniques*, 1949, **13**, 469–478.

Thurstone, L. L., and Thurstone, Thelma G. *PMA Primary mental abilities: Examiner's manual*. Chicago: Science Research Associates, 1962.

Thurstone, L. L., and Thurstone, Thelma G. *Primary mental abilities, revised 1962: Technical report*. Chicago: Science Research Associates, 1965.

Veroff, J., Atkinson, J. W., Feld, Sheila C., and Gurin, G. The use of thematic apperception to assess motivation in a nationwide interview study. *Psychological Monographs*, 1960, **74** (12), Whole No. 499.

Welsh, G. S., and Dahlstrom, W. G. (Eds.) *Basic readings on the MMPI in psychology and medicine*. Minneapolis: University of Minnesota Press, 1956.

Wendland, Marilyn M. Self-concept development in the Negro adolescent and its relationship to area of residence. Ph.D. dissertation, University of North Carolina at Chapel Hill, 1967.

Yates, Louise G. Comparative intelligence of Negro and white children from a rural-southern culture. Ph.D. dissertation, University of North Carolina at Chapel Hill, 1967.

APPENDIX A

PARENT INTERVIEW SCHEDULE

CODE NO._____

Part I

CHILD'S NAME_____   INTERVIEWER_____   DATE_____

Interview With Mother

As you know, we are very interested in children about the age of your (X) , and today I would like to ask you to tell me something about him (her). I will be asking you what he (she) was like when he (she) was little, what sorts of things you did with him (her) and what sort of child he (she) is now. We know how hard it can be to try to remember sometimes just what happened way back with some child. (*Where relevant, add:* especially if you have several children to keep track of.) Please, just do the best you can and I will understand if it is hard to remember. I want you to know that these questions are just for our records, *not* for the school or anyone else. They will help us understand children in this age group.

1. Could you tell me, what is X usually like?

    Happy_____ Solemn_____ Sad_____ Silly_____ Other:_____

2. Would you describe him (her) as:

    a. Neat?_____   c. Needing to do things just right?
    b. Shy?_____   _____

497

d. Alert (wide awake)?_____

e. Careless?_____

f. Usually minds?_____

g. Daydreamy (studies things)?_____

h. Cautious?_____

i. Tries things?_____

j. Needs encouragement?_____

k. Always in a hurry?_____

l. Fearful?_____

m. Laughs a lot?_____

n. Shows off?_____

o. Plays well alone?_____

3. Is X good at doing these things?

Indicate degree: ++ = very good; + = good; 0 = uncertain; − = poor; −− = very poor. (*If parent uncertain, try to establish reason:* No opportunity; Parent doesn't know; Physical handicap; Other)

a. Throwing a ball?_____

b. Catching a ball?_____

c. Holding a pencil?_____

d. Running?_____

e. Coloring a picture?_____

f. Jumping?_____

g. Cutting with a scissors?

h. Building with blocks?_____

i. Other talents: 1. _____

2. _____

4. Do you have any special concerns?

a. _____

b. _____

5. Now could you tell me about the times when X misbehaves? When he (she) does some of these things. For each, ask: Does this bother you? Does this bother X's father (surrogate)?

Indicate degree: ++ = very much; + = yes; 0 = uncertain; − = no; −− = not at all.

Item	True for Child	Bothers Mother	Bothers Father
a. Making a mess around the house			
b. Spilling things while eating			
c. Talking back			
d. Not doing what he (she) is told			
e. Talking too much			
f. Wetting the bed			
g. Stuttering			
h. Lying			
i. Yelling around the house; being noisy			
j. Playing with sex organs			
k. Fighting with other children			
l. Not doing chores around the house			
m. Being rude			
n. Destroying things			
o. Getting dirty			

Item	True for Child	Bothers Mother	Bothers Father
p. Getting into sibling's things			
q. Refusing to go to bed on time			
r. Not eating everything on his (her) plate			

6. Do you find you have to whip X often?_____

    6a. How about X's father (surrogate), does he whip X often?_____

    6b. What sort of things do you have to whip him (her) for?

        1. _____

        2. _____

        3. _____

    6c. Does it do X good to be whipped?_____

    6d. How does X act when you whip him (her)?_____

7. Do you ever take away something X wants as a way of punishing him (her)?_____

    7a. Do you do this often?_____

8. Can you think of the last time you had to scold X for something, what did you say to him (her)?_____

    8a. Did you later think of something more you could have said?

_____

9. Do you ever put him (her) in the corner or in another room for punishment?_____

10. What other sorts of punishment have you used?

    1. _____

    2. _____

    3. _____

11. Do you often tell X that you are going to have to punish him (her) and then for some reason you do not do it?_____

    11a. What kinds of things might keep you from doing it?_____

_____

12. Some parents expect their children to obey immediately when they tell them to be quiet or pick up something and so on; others don't think it is terribly important for a child to obey right away. How do you feel about this?_____

    12a. Do you expect this of X now?_____

    12b. How does X's father (surrogate) feel about strict obedience?

_____

13. Some people feel it is very important for a child to learn not to fight with other children; other people feel there are times when a child has to learn to fight. How do you feel about this?_____

_____

14. When X is with other children, is he (she) the one who takes something away from one of the others, or does he (she) have things taken away?

_____

    14a. Does it upset you when he (she) fights with other children?_____

    14b. With sisters and brothers?_____

    14c. Does it upset you when he (she) lets others pick on him (her)?

_____

15. Sometimes a child will get angry at his parents and hit them or kick them or shout angry things at them. When he (she) does this, what do you do?

_____

    15a. How about X's father (surrogate), what does he do?_____

16. When X has done something he (she) knows you don't allow, when your back is turned, does he (she) ever come and tell you about it without your having to ask?_____

    16a. When you ask about things like that, does he (she) usually admit or deny it?_____

    16b. What do you do about it if he (she) denies something you are pretty sure he (she) has done?_____

17. Do you keep track of exactly where X is and what he (she) is doing most of the time, or can you let him (her) watch out for himself (herself) quite a bit?_____

18. Did X ever go through a stage of hanging onto your skirts and following you around?_____

    18a. At what age?_____

    18b. When you get real busy now, does he (she) sometimes try to get you to pay him (her) some special attention?_____

    18c. If you have to be with another child who is sick or something, does X want special attention then?_____

    18d. When you go out of the house and are leaving X, how does he (she) behave?_____

    18e. How do you feel about it when he (she) does this?_____

19. How much does X decide things for himself (herself) now?_____

    19a. What sorts of things can you trust him (her) to do for himself (herself)?

        1. _____

        2. _____

        3. _____

    19b. Can he (she) choose or decide about these things?

20. What do you do when X has been good?_____

    20a. Do you sometimes give him (her) something for this?_____

    20b. (If some limitation is verbalized): What would you like to be able to do?_____

21. Some parents praise their children quite a bit when they are good; others think that you should take good behavior pretty much for granted and there is no point in praising a child for it. How do you feel about this?

_____

22. In training X, do you ever say: "Your daddy and mother do it this way"?

_____

    22a. Who else do you hold up as an example—older brother or sister, grandparents, relatives, playmates?_____

    22b. Is there anyone you mention as an example of what not to do?

_____

23. What sorts of things do you enjoy in X?_____

    23a. Does he (she) show his (her) affection pretty often?_____

    23b. If yes, how?_____

    23c. How about you, do you show your feelings pretty often?_____

    23d. Does X's father (surrogate) show his feelings for X?_____

24. What do you do with X when you spend time together?

    1. _____

    2. _____

    3. _____

25. What does X's father (surrogate) do when he spends time with X?

    1. _____

    2. _____

    3. _____

26. Before X starts school now, has anyone had (or, before X started kindergarten, did you have) a chance to teach him (her) any letters, writing with a pencil, reading words, drawing, telling time—things like that?

_____

    26a. Who was it who helped him (her)?_____

    26b. Do you think X liked doing these things?_____

27. Do you think X will do well in school?_____

    27a. Why do you expect this?_____

    27b. How do you think you will feel about that?_____

    27c. How far would you like X to go in schooling?_____

    27d. Do you think he (she) will?_____

    27e. Does X's father (surrogate) think this way, too?_____

28. Suppose now that X has grown up (the age of, say, 35), what do you imagine he (she) will be doing?_____

    28a. What sort of work would you like X to be doing then?_____

_____

    28b. What are the chances he (she) will be able to do that?_____

29. How old were you when X was born?_____
    29a. Your birthdate:_____
    29b. Birthplace:_____
            (Town)   *(County)*   *(State)*
    29c. What work did your own father do?_____
    29d. What was his education?_____
    29e. Your mother's education?_____
    29f. How many brothers did you have?_____
    29g. Sisters?_____ 29h. Position?_____
    29i. Are you a twin?_____ 29j. Are there twins in your family?_____
    29k. How far did you go in school?_____
    29l. How well did you do?_____
    29m. Did you want to go further?_____
    29n. Have you worked since leaving school?_____
    29o. (*If yes*) What sort of work did you do?_____
    29p. Have you been married before?_____ 29q. Date?_____
    29r. Children?_____
    29s. Outcome?_____

30. How old was X's father when X was born?_____
    30a. His birthdate:_____
    30b. Birthplace:_____
            (Town)   *(County)*   *(State)*
    30c. What work did paternal grandfather do?_____
    30d. Education?_____
    30e. Grandmother's education?_____
    30f. Number of father's brothers?_____ 30g. Sisters?_____
    30h. Position?_____
    30i. History of twinning?_____
    30j. How far did X's father go in school?_____
    30k. How well did he do?_____
    30l. Has he done other work than what he is doing now?_____

31. Was there any time when X was apart from you or his (her) father?_____
    31a. (*If yes*): Mother:_____
    31b. Father:_____
    31c. Who took care of him (her)?_____

32. Have you lived in this place long?_____
    32a. Have you lived in this community long?_____
    32b. Do you have relatives living in this community?_____

33. Do you own your own home?_____
    33a. (*If no*) Rental arrangement:_____
    33b. Physical facilities in home:_____
    33c. Cultural media:_____

34. What do you (and your husband) do for enjoyment?_____

Conduct of Interview

Were there any serious interruptions?_____
Was the confidentiality easily preserved?_____
Degree of rapport: Very hospitable   Friendly   Cool   Remote   Hostile
Areas of refusal_____
Other informant needed_____

Ratings of Mother

A. 1_____2_____3_____4_____5_____6_____7_____8
   Permissiveness   Strictness

B. 1_____2_____3_____4_____5_____6_____7_____8
   Poor family adjustment   Good family adjustment

C. 1_____2_____3_____4_____5_____6_____7_____8
   Warm relationship to child   Cold

D. 1_____2_____3_____4_____5_____6_____7_____8
   Responsibly oriented to childrearing   Irresponsible

E. 1_____2_____3_____4_____5_____6_____7_____8
   Values aggressiveness highly   Low on aggressiveness

F. 1_____2_____3_____4_____5_____6_____7_____8
   Father dominates   Mother dominates

G. 1_____2_____3_____4_____5_____6_____7_____8
   Strong emphasis on child's   Low emphasis
   physical well-being

H. 1_____2_____3_____4_____5_____6_____7_____8
   Object-oriented discipline   Love oriented

List of prompts for 33b and 33c

FACILITIES	CULTURAL MEDIA
Well and pump	TV
Indoor plumbing	Record player
Outhouse	Musical instruments
Electricity	Books
Running water	Magazines
Freezer	Newspaper service
	Book mobile service
	Farm extension contacts
	Radio

PARENT INTERVIEW SCHEDULE

CODE NO._____

Part II

CHILD'S NAME_____ INTERVIEWER_____ DATE_____

Interview with Mother

When we last talked to you about (X) , I (or Mrs. Z) said we would like to come back again and get a little more information about him (her). You were very helpful to us last time. This time we would like to ask you a little more about when X was growing up, how he (she) gets along with other children, and how he (she) has been getting along since we last talked to you. Some of my questions will also be about your family here. These things will help us understand your child better, and other children of this age. These questions are just for our records, too, not for school or anyone else.

   a. (+)   successful performance
   b. (+F)   if formerly successful performance has been outgrown or temporarily discontinued
   c. (+0)   no opportunity
   d. (±)   transitional or emergent
   e. (−)   has not succeeded
   f. (−NO) could not if had opportunity
   g. (NI)   no information

  1. In what way do you think X has changed the most since we last talked?_____

2–9. *At this point in the interview, items from the Vineland Social Maturity Scale were administed. The child's behavior in the area covered by each item was summarized by using the a–g descriptions given above. The item numbers from the Vineland, and the order in which they were used, were as follows:* 35, 41, 51, 66, 38, 39, 62, 67, 37, 40, 42, 47, 50, 52, 54, 64, 65, 70, 45, 53, 61, 36, 43, 48, 55, 57, 71, 72, 44, 58, 63, 73, 60, 76, 46, 49, 56, 59, 68, and 69.

*K 10. How does X like his (her) kindergarten?_____
       10a. Why?_____
       10b. What do you think about it?_____

* K questions were asked of mothers whose children were attending kindergarten, whereas NK questions were used with mothers whose children were not attending kindergarten.

K 11. Has X had any special difficulties with Miss (Mrs.) Z?_____
    11a. With Mrs. Y?_____
    11b. (With Mrs. YY?)_____

K 12. How does X feel about the little work tasks in school?_____
_____

✿✿✿

°NK 10. We asked you last time whether anyone had a chance to start him (her) on letters, writing with a pencil, drawing, things like that. Since then, has he (she) started on any of these things?_____
    (*Or*, have you continued with him (her) on these things?_____)

NK 11. How does he (she) like doing these things?_____
    (*Or*, do you think he (she) would enjoy doing things like that? _____)

NK 12. How does X feel about starting school next fall?_____

✿✿✿

13. Compared to your other children, how much does X work on tasks that are hard for him (her)?_____

14. Suppose he (she) is doing something that is hard for him (her), what does he (she) do when he (she) sees he (she) is not getting it?
_____

(The next items pertain to X's siblings or to other children residing in the home.)

15. Which sister or brother (or other) does X spend the most time with?
_____

16. Which one does he (she) like most?_____
    16a. Why?_____
    16b. How does that sib feel about X?_____

17. Which one does he (she) have the most trouble with?_____
    17a. Why?_____

18. Do you think there is one parent that X seems to prefer?_____

There are some things that may happen to children while they are growing up that we would like to know about. As I go through the list, let me know if any of them has happened to X:

19. *Special Dislocations:*   *X's Age and Reaction*
    a. Difficulties at birth_____
    b. Serious illness or injury to X_____
    c. Serious illness or injury to sibling or parent_____
    d. Death in close family_____
    e. Extended absence of parent_____
    f. X separated from family_____

g. Major move of household_____

h. Prolonged unemployment of wage earner_____

i. Auto accident, fire, etc._____

j. Older sib leaving home_____

(k. Other dislocation offered)_____

20. When X was a baby, do you think he (she) started doing things at about the usual time? How about:

Indicate degree: + = early; 0 = about right; − = late.

Probe 1: Was X early, about right, or late?
Probe 2: Did you have to do anything special to get X started on this?

a. _____Sitting up_____

b. _____Crawling (or creeping)_____

c. _____First real words_____

d. _____First steps_____

e. _____Training for toilet (pot)_____

f. _____Weaning to cup_____

g. _____Using a spoon_____

h. _____Speaking sentences_____

21. Think back to the time when you first discovered you were pregnant with X. How did you feel about that?_____
21a. How did X's father feel about it?_____

22. Considering the money you had, the ages of the other children, and so on, do you feel that this was a difficult time to have a baby?
_____
22a. Do you think X's father thought this way?_____

23. Which did you want, a boy or girl?_____
23a. Did you feel strongly about this?_____
23b. How about X's father?_____

24. (*Where appropriate*) Do you expect to have more children?_____
Reasons (or why omitted):_____

25. In what ways would you say you and your husband are alike? That is, in terms of your temperament, the things you think are important in life, and so on?

a. _____

b. _____

c. _____

26. In what ways are you different from each other?

a. _____

b. _____

c. _____

(*With respect to traits in which different*)

27. Would you rather have X be like your husband in this respect?

_____

28. In what ways would you like the child to be like the two of you and in what ways different?

LIKE   DIFFERENT

a. _____   a. _____
b. _____   b. _____
c. _____   c. _____

29. (*Where husband is now in household*) Does your husband enjoy the children?_____
    a. Does he get much time with them?_____
    b. Does he have a pet?_____ c. Do you?_____
    d. Do you think your husband is too hard on X?_____
    e. Too easy going with him (her)?_____
    f. Spends too much time with him (her)?_____
    g. Ignores him (her) too much?_____
    h. Worries about him (her) too much?_____
    i. Spoils him (her)?_____
    j. Does he expect too much of him (her)?_____
    k. Does he treat X pretty much the same, from day to day?
       _____
    l. Do you have to take the child's side against your husband often?_____
    m. Does he side with X against you often?_____
    n. Is he satisfied with the way X is coming along?_____
    o. Are you?_____

30. What is your religion?_____
    a. Denomination?_____
    b. Is your husband's religion the same?_____
    c. How many times a month do you attend church?_____
    d. Do you go to prayer meetings often?_____
    e. Revivals?_____
    f. Do you hold any office in the church?_____
    g. Do you belong to other organizations?_____
    h. PTA?_____
    i. Do you hold office in any of them?_____

31. Family income: (*Use Query Card if appropriate*)

    For all of the work done by members of your family last year, how much was your total income? (*With the card:* Just tell me the letter beside the amount.)

31a. Total family income: Sources and computation:

    A. Less than $500 _____

    B. Between $500 and $1000 _____

    C. Between $1000 and $1500 _____

    D. Between $1500 and $2500 _____

    E. Between $2500 and $5000 _____

    F. More than $5000 _____

31b. Cash income: _____

  A   B   C   D   E   F _____

Conduct of interview:

Were there any serious interruptions?_____

Was confidentiality preserved?_____

Areas of refusal?_____

Degree of rapport: Very hospitable   Friendly   Cool   Remote   Hostile

Other informant needed:_____

Ratings of Mother

A. 1   2   3   4   5   6   7   8
  Defensive about child   Objective and   Overly critical and
                                     realistic   hostile

B. 1   2   3   4   5   6   7   8
  Knows child well   Superficial knowledge only

C. 1   2   3   4   5   6   7   8
  Mother dictates child's activities   Child's needs and interests
                                                determining

D. 1   2   3   4   5   6   7   8
  Fosters growth and independence   Overly protective of child

E. 1   2   3   4   5   6   7   8
  High expectations of   Matter of fact   Little interest or
  accomplishments   concern

F. 1   2   3   4   5   6   7   8
  Admiring of husband   Critical of husband

Elements in ratings:

A. (*High*) (*Hostility*)
Criticism of child
Derogation of skills
Preference for sib

B. Self-explanatory

C. (*Low*) (*Restrictiveness*)
Punishment for deviations
Channeling of activities
Idiosyncrasies not tolerated

D. (*High*) (*Protection*)
Unnecessary nurturance
Requests for help rewarded
Overconcern for illness or danger

E. (*Low*) (*Acceleration*)
Concern over age of talking, walking, etc.
Child's skills shown off
Dissatisfaction with cognitive development
Encouragement of mastery of skills

F. Self-explanatory

APPENDIX B

CHILD INTERVIEW SCHEDULE

NAME_____   INTERVIEWER_____

CODE NUMBER_____ DATE OF INTERVIEW_____

SCHOOL, GRADE_____

BIRTH DATE_____

SEX_____

Family Structure

1. Let's begin, _____, by having you tell me the names of each person living in your home, how they are related to you (if they are), their approximate ages, and what they do—like work or go to school. Let's begin with your father.

   Name   *Relation to S*   *Age*   *Occupation (full-time?)*

1a. Have either of your parents been married before?
2. Now please tell me the same things about any brothers or sisters that you have who are living away from home. Also, tell me where they live.

   Name   *Relation to S*   *Age*   *Location*   *Occupation (full-time?)*

House

3. Let's talk a little now about where you live. About how much land do you have with your house?

510

4. Who owns this property? (Own outright; are buying; rent; farm on shares)

5. How is this land used? (Grow_____acres of tobacco; dairy farm; personal garden; grow other crops: *list*)

6. Do your parents own other property? How is it used?

7. How large is the house that you live in? (Number of rooms—include bath)

8. Is this a good size for the number of people living in it? (Way too small; a bit cramped; about right; a bit too large; way too large)

9. What condition is your house in? (Real run down; rather poor; so-so; rather good; excellent)

10. Compared with other houses in Millfield, what condition is your house in? (Best, better, average, worse, worst)

11. Which of the following do you have in your house? a) Electricity, b) Inside toilet, c) Telephone, d) Radio, e) Television, f) Record player, g) Washing machine, h) Electric refrigerator, i) Freezer, j) Car (number, model, year), k) Water (how obtained), l) Heating (kind), m) cooking stove (kind), n) Newspapers (name), o) Magazines (name), p) Encyclopedia (name), q) Other books (number and kind)

12. How long have you lived in your present house? (Years or months)

13. Are you planning or thinking about moving? a) When? b) Where to? c) Why?

14. What changes could be made in your house to make it a better place to live in?

Family Finances

15. Do your parents earn enough money to take care of your family? (Help is sometimes needed, we get by on our own but not much more, we do ok, we're in pretty good shape, we have plenty)

16. Does your family have difficulty getting enough food? (Never, not often, occasionally, frequently, constantly) a) How about clothing? b) What is the situation for fuel? c) How do you make out for doctors and medicines?

17. Compared with other families in Millfield, how would you describe your family as far as money is concerned? (We're as well off as anyone, better off than most, about average, most are better off, no one is any worse off)

Parent Behavior

18. I want to talk with you a bit now about your parents. How often do your mother and father disagree on what you should or should not do? (*Very* often, quite a bit, sometimes, infrequently, practically never)

19. When your parents do disagree over what you should or should not do, who usually gets his way? (Mother, father, about equal)

20. Who would you say is the boss in your home? (Mother, father, about equal)

21. How far in school do your parents seem to want you to go? a) Mother b) Father

22. What do your parents say or do about your homework? a) Mother b) Father

23. What kind of work do your parents want you to do when you finish school? a) Mother b) Father

24. Do your parents get after you for not acting the way they think you should? (*Very* often, frequently, sometimes, once in a while, never)

25. Do they give you as much freedom as you think you should have? a) Mother b) Father

26. When you disobey your parents, in what way and how often are you punished? (Always, usually, frequently, occasionally, never) a) Mother b) Father

27. How often, on the average, are you actually punished or corrected in some way by your parents? (Several times a day, several times a week, once a week, once a month, less than once a month)

28. In general, what kind of a reputation do you think your parents have in the community? (Very good, above average, average, not too good, rather poor) a) First, your mother b) Father

29. When you grow up, in what ways would you like to be like your parents? a) Mother b) Father

30. When you grow up, in what ways would you like not to be like your parents? a) Mother b) Father

Peers

31. Who are your best friends?

32. Do you change friends often, or do you pretty much stick with the same ones year after year?

33. Are your close friends all boys, all girls, or some of each?

34. Do you have a group that you run around with? (All boys, all girls, mixed)

35. How about dating—do you date? (Steady, a lot—not steady, sometimes, once in a while, never) a) Do you have a boy (girl) friend? b) How do your parents feel about this?

36. What seems to make a girl popular around here?

37. What seems to make a boy popular around here?

38. Tell me about the things you and your friends do together.

39. In general, how do your friends compare with you in the grades they get? (*They*'re better, same, worse)

40. How do you think you're liked by most children in school? (Quite popular, well-liked, average, not too well-liked, unpopular)

41. What do your parents think about your friends? (Like them a lot; mostly like them; mostly dislike them; don't like them at all; don't know them)

42. How would you describe your position in the group you go with? (Usually the leader, sometimes the leader, never the leader)

43. What clubs and organizations do you belong to—at school, church, and other places? (Hold office? Name)

44. What things about a boy make you like him? a) How about a girl?

45. What things about a boy make you dislike him? a) How about a girl?

Recreation

46. What do you do for fun on school days? a) After school (with whom) b) After supper (with whom)

47. What do you do to have fun on weekends? (with whom)

48. What towns do you go to—how often, with whom, and what do you do there?

Town	Frequency	Companions	Activities

a) M*, b) H, c) D, d) B, e) C, f) G, g) Other

49. Which of the following activities do you take part in, and how do your parents feel about it?

Activity	Participate (Yes, No)	Parent Attitude

a) Picture show, b) Dances, c) Bowling, d) Skating, e) Parties, f) Sports events, g) Going to beer places

50. Where do you get your spending money? a) About how much do you have each week? b) Is this enough so that you can do the things that most of your friends do?

51. Have you or any of your friends ever gotten in trouble with the police? (*If yes*, for doing what?)

---

* The capital letters refer to specific towns mentioned by the interviewer.

52. Do most of the other kids in your grade (Yes, No)? Do you?

           S   *Others*

     a) Date, b) Smoke, c) Drive a car (alone, with adults), d) Drink, e) Pet, f) Play cards, g) Gamble, h) Dance, i) Read books for pleasure (kind?)

53. What would you like to see done so that you and your friends could have a better time?

Television

54. How often do you watch television? (About every day, several days a week, only on weekends, occasionally, practically never)

55. How many hours do you spend watching TV each day? a) School days, b) Weekends—Saturday, Sunday.

56. What programs do you watch regularly?

57. What is your favorite program?

58. Are you allowed to watch any program that you want? a) (*If restrictions*) By whom? b) What are the restrictions? c) Can you stay up as long as you want to watch TV? (*If not*, how late?) School days, Weekends.

59. If you don't have a TV in your house, do you go to someone else's house to watch? (Where and how often—About every day, several days a week, only on weekends, occasionally, practically never)

60. Do you watch Channel 4 outside of school? a) How often? (Regularly, occasionally, rarely or never) b) What programs do you watch on Channel 4? c) Where is Channel 4 located?

61. How satisfied are you with the programs on TV? (Great, good, o.k., not so good, poor)

Marriage and Family

62. What age do you think is best for girls to get married? a) What about for boys?

63. Do you think you will marry or stay single? (*If single*, why?) a) (*If marry*) At what age?

64. How many children would you like to have if you do marry? a) Why this number? b) Any preference as to their sex, and why?

65. Would you like for your children to grow up in the Millfield area? a) Why?

66. What kind of person would you like to marry? Tell me what (he, she) would be like.

67. How far would you like your (husband, wife) to go in school, and why?

68. (*For girls*) What kind of work would you like your husband to do, and why?

69. (*For boys*) Would you like your wife to work? a) Why? b) (*If yes*) What kind of work would you like her to do?

Church

70. Do you go to Sunday School? (*If yes,* how often?) a) What about other church services?

71. Does your mother go to church? (*If yes,* how often?) a) What about your father?

72. Do you ever go to revival meetings? a) (*If yes*) How often?

73. What church do you go to?

74. Which church would you say most of the important people go to?

75. What would you say is the main reason that you go to church and/or Sunday School? a) Do your parents make you go, or do you go because you want to?

76. Are there some things you like about church services and activities? (Name)

77. Are there some things you don't like about church services and activities? (Name)

Education

78. How far did your mother go in school? a) Your father?

79. How far have your brothers and sisters gone in school? (Name, grade in or completed, school, and reason for stopping for each sibling)

80. Do you and your friends talk about how far you want to go in school? (Frequently, occasionally, seldom, never)

81. What plans do most of your friends seem to have about school? (Drop out as soon as possible, finish high school, go to college, go to technical school)

82. If you didn't have to go to school, would you drop out? a) Why?

83. How far would you like to go in school? a) Why?

84. Do you think that you will make it? a) (*If no*) Why not?

85. Has anyone ever talked to you *personally* about your going to college? a) Who? b) What did they say?

86. On the average, what grades do you get? A A— B+ B B— C+ C C— D+ D D— F

87. If you really did your very best, what do you think your average would be? A A— B+ B B— C+ C C— D+ D D— F a) (*When appropriate*) What do you think keeps you from doing this well?

88. Do you usually get your homework done? a) (*If not*) Why not?

89. Does your mother help you with your homework? (If yes, how often?) (Very often, often, sometimes, seldom, never) a) What about your father? (Very often, often, sometimes, seldom, never)

90. What is your favorite subject?

91. What subject do you like least?

92. Tell me some things you like about school. a) What don't you like?

93. What changes could be made in the school that would make it better?

Work

94. During the school year, do you have chores that you are expected to do around home? a) (*If yes*) What are they? b) About how much time do you spend doing them each day? c) What happens if you don't get them done?

95. During the summer, do you work? a) (*If yes*) Doing what? b) About how many hours each day? c) (*If no*) What do you do during the summer?

96. Are you ever kept out of school in order to work? a) How often and by whom? b) To do what?

97. Have you ever earned money by working? a) Where and when? b) Doing what? c) What wage? d) How long did you work? e) How did you like the work?

98. When most children grow up around Millfield, where do they go to live and work? a) Why?

99. What sort of work would you like to do when you grow up? a) First choice? b) Second choice?

100. Where would you like to do this (first choice) work? (Here, elsewhere— name location)

101. How much schooling do you think is necessary for the kind of work you want to do?

102. Do you think that you will someday get this kind of work? a) (*If no*) Why not?

103. Do you and your parents talk about what work you might do when you are grown? a) (*If yes*) How do their ideas agree with yours?

104. (*For boys*) Would you like to do the kind of work your father does? a) Why?

105. (*For girls*) Would you like to do the kind of work your mother does? a) Why?

106. Looking at everything, what do you expect to be doing when you are thirty-five?

Community

107. What would you say about the Millfield area as a place to live in? (Tops, very good, so-so, not too good, poor) a) Why?

108. Do you want to live in the Millfield area when you are grown? (Definitely, probably, uncertain, probably not, definitely not) a) Why?

109. Tell me some of the things that you like about the Millfield area.

110. Tell me some of the things that you don't like about it.

111. Who would you say is the most important person in the Millfield area? (name and occupation) a) Why is he (she) important?

112. Name some other important people in the area and tell me why they are important. (name and occupation)

113. What things could be done to make the Millfield area a better place to live in?

Self

114. In summing up, do you feel that your home life is as happy as that of other young people you know? (Much more, some more, average, somewhat less, much less) a) Why?

115. Again, to sum up, are you pretty much satisfied with the sort of person you are? (Very, kind of, so-so, not too much, very dissatisfied) a) Why?

Interviewer's Notes and Comments

APPENDIX C

FAMILY QUESTIONNAIRE

TO: Parents of All Children in the Millfield School

FROM: Child Study Project

As part of our work in your school this year, we need additional information regarding the family background of your child. We very much hope that you will cooperate by filling out the attached form and returning it to your child's teacher immediately. The form is being sent to you with the approval of school officials.

Each child in the school is being given one of these forms to take home. If you have several children in the Millfield School, however, you need to fill it out for only your *oldest* child in the school. Please make certain that the other children return their forms to their teachers and tell her what child in the school will be returning the completed form.

We very much appreciate your cooperation in our work which we believe will be of benefit to the entire school community.

Remember: 1. Fill this form out completely for your oldest child in the Millfield School.

2. Have your other children in the Millfield School return their blank forms to their teachers.

Family Information

1. CHILD'S NAME?_____

2. BOY OR GIRL?_____ 3. BIRTH DATE?_____

518

Child's Father

4. Father's name?_____

5. Where was father born?_____

6. What is father's main job?_____

7. Does father have a second job?_____

8. If he does, what is it?_____

9. How many grades did father finish in school?_____

10. Is father living in the home?_____

11. Is there a stepfather living in the home?_____

Child's Mother

12. Mother's name?_____

13. Where was mother born?_____

14. Does mother have a job in addition to being a housewife?_____

15. If she does, what is it?_____

16. About how many hours does mother work outside the home each week?

_____

17. Who (older sister, aunt, neighbor, and so on) takes care of the children when mother is working away from the home?_____

18. How many grades did mother finish in school?_____

19. Is mother living in the home?_____

20. Is there a stepmother living in the home?_____

Brothers and Sisters

21. List the full names of all the child's brothers and sisters. Also, indicate sex, either age or birth date, and if the child is living in the home. List the oldest child first and work down to the youngest.

Name	Boy or Girl	Birth Date or Age	Living in Home? (Yes or No)
1. _____	_____	_____	_____
2. _____	_____	_____	_____
3. _____	_____	_____	_____
4. _____	_____	_____	_____

Name	Boy or Girl	Birth Date or Age	Living in Home? (Yes or No)
5. _____	_____	_____	_____
6. _____	_____	_____	_____
7. _____	_____	_____	_____
8. _____	_____	_____	_____
9. _____	_____	_____	_____
10. _____	_____	_____	_____

(If more space is needed, write on the back of this sheet.)

22. List the names of other children and adults living in the home and tell how they are related (if at all) to the child.

_____

_____

23. Do you own your home?_____ 24. A car?_____

25. TV?_____ 26. Telephone?_____

APPENDIX D

KINDERGARTEN QUESTIONNAIRE

TO: Parents of children who have attended kindergarten
FROM: Child Study Project

We are in need of information for each child who has been in the kindergarten. Your help in providing us with this information will be appreciated.

The information which we need is indicated on the enclosed page. Please fill in the answers and have your child return it to his teacher on the day after he brings it home to you.

These forms are being sent home with all of the children who were in kindergarten in 1962–63, 1963–64, or 1964–65. It is not being sent to children who have just been enrolled in this year's kindergarten class. If you have had more than one child in the kindergarten, you should receive a form like this from each one. Since your answers to certain questions may be different for different children, we must ask you to fill out each form sent to you.

Thank you for your help.

A *reminder:* Please have your child return his form on the day after he brings it home. Ask him to give it to his teacher.

Kindergarten Questionnaire

1. Child's name_____

2. When this child was in kindergarten, was his mother working?_____

   3. If she was working, was it part-time or full-time work?_____

   4. If she was working, what kind of work was it?_____

5. When this child was in kindergarten, was his father working?_____

521

6. If he was working, was it part-time or full-time work?_____

7. If he was working, what kind of work was it?_____

8. How many grades in school did this child's mother finish?_____

9. How many grades in school did this child's father finish?_____

10. Do you have a telephone?_____

11. How many older brothers and sisters does this child have?_____

12. How many younger brothers and sisters does this child have?_____

13. How many of these younger brothers and sisters have been born since the child was in kindergarten?_____

14. Were the child's mother and father living together when the child was in kindergarten?

15. Do you feel that the kindergarten helped this child?_____

16. How did it help or fail to help him?_____

_____

_____

_____

_____

Thank you for helping in this way.

APPENDIX E

SCHOOL BEHAVIOR RATING SCALE

1962 INSTRUCTIONS

TO: All teachers

FROM: Child Study Project

As you already know, we are engaged in an extensive study of all elementary school children in the northwest quadrant of the county. You have been extremely helpful to us during the year; indeed, without your cooperation we could not have approached our goals. Eventually, of course, we believe that our cooperative efforts will pay off in a strengthened program of child development.

Clearly, there is no single way by means of which either we or anyone else can come to a completely accurate evaluation of a given child or a group of children. It is for this reason that we have been using a variety of methods to appraise the children. A rich source of information that we have not yet tapped, however, are your own impressions and observations of the children that you have been teaching this year. We very much hope that you will be willing to share these impressions with us now.

To facilitate collecting this information, we have constructed a series of rating scales (a sample form is attached). You will be asked to fill out one of these forms for each child who has been a student in your room for any significant period of time during the year. A member of our staff will meet with you in the near future to answer any questions that you might have about the forms and to provide you with a supply of them.

We recognize that this request means extra work on your part, but it is very important to our study and we earnestly solicit your careful cooperation. As partial compensation for the work involved, each teacher will be paid ten dollars to do these evaluations. Please turn the completed ratings into your principal—your check will be available at that time.

Thank you very much.

1964 INSTRUCTIONS

TO: All Teachers of Millfield Schools
FROM: Child Study Project

In May, 1962 we asked all teachers at the Millfield Schools to rate each of their students on a number of traits. Now, two years later, we are back with a similar request. We are hopeful that you will again cooperate in making the ratings; the forms are the same as those we used in 1962.

As was true before, we will once again compensate each teacher for the time that it takes to make the ratings. We recognize that the payment of fifteen dollars is quite modest but at least it is more substantial than we were able to offer before!

These ratings are most important for the success of our project and we will more than appreciate your making them with care. When you have completed filling out the forms, will you kindly return them to your principal?

We are currently analyzing the data that we have been collecting for three years; it is our hope that a written report covering some of our initial findings will be available for your examination and criticism during the next academic year.

One last reminder: Please be certain to record the birth date of each of your pupils at the top of his or her page since this information is very important to us in our analyses.

Thank you.

School Behavior Rating Scale   FILE NO.

PUPIL_____ GRADE_____ DATE_____

SCHOOL_____TEACHER (AND RATER)_____

Absent about   90   75   50   25   10   5   0   percent of the time (Circle one)

Entered school_____, withdrew on_____ (Give dates)

1. Hyperactive   _____ Unusually inactive
                              1   2   3   4   5   6   7   8

2. Limited overt emotional   _____ Marked overt emotional
   expression   1   2   3   4   5   6   7   8   expression

3. Dependent _____ Self-sufficient

     1 2 3 4 5 6 7 8

4. Needs constant _____ Needs no
    encouragement   1 2 3 4 5 6 7 8   encouragement

5. Gregarious _____ Nongregarious

     1 2 3 4 5 6 7 8

6. Doesn't care about _____ Excellence of performance
    the quality of his   1 2 3 4 5 6 7 8   is his principal concern
    performance

7. Unusual social poise _____ Markedly lacking in
    for age   1 2 3 4 5 6 7 8   social poise

8. Crushed by failure _____ Undaunted by failure

     1 2 3 4 5 6 7 8

9. A very warm child _____ Unusually cold

     1 2 3 4 5 6 7 8

10. Eager to cooperate _____ Obstructive

     1 2 3 4 5 6 7 8

11. Tries extremely hard at _____ Doesn't try at all
    lessons   1 2 3 4 5 6 7 8

12. Easily upset _____ Unshakable

     1 2 3 4 5 6 7 8

13. Extremely submissive _____ Extremely assertive

     1 2 3 4 5 6 7 8

14. Suspicious _____ Trustful

     1 2 3 4 5 6 7 8

15. Unable to give up _____ Gives up too easily

     1 2 3 4 5 6 7 8

16. Unusually composed _____ Highly agitated

     1 2 3 4 5 6 7 8

17. Picks up under success _____ Success doesn't affect him

     1 2 3 4 5 6 7 8

18. Depressed _____ Cheerful

     1 2 3 4 5 6 7 8

19. Nonaggressive   _____ Aggressive
    1   2   3   4   5   6   7   8

20. Wholly absorbed by tasks   _____ Highly inattentive
    1   2   3   4   5   6   7   8

21. Consistent   _____ Inconsistent
    1   2   3   4   5   6   7   8

22. I *really* like this child   _____ I don't care for this
    1   2   3   4   5   6   7   8   child *at all*

APPENDIX F

TEST BEHAVIOR RATING SCALE

PROJECT NO.＿＿＿＿＿＿

SUBJECT＿＿＿＿＿＿＿＿＿＿＿＿ TEST＿＿＿＿＿＿＿＿＿＿＿＿＿＿＿

DATE＿＿＿＿＿＿ EXAMINER＿＿＿＿＿＿＿＿＿＿＿＿＿＿＿＿

A. 1　2　3　4　5　6　7　8
Wholly absorbed　Highly inattentive
by tasks

B. 1　2　3　4　5　6　7　8
A very warm child　Unusually cold

C. 1　2　3　4　5　6　7　8
Needs constant　Needs no en-
encouragement　couragement

D. 1　2　3　4　5　6　7　8
Balanced and appro-　Repetitive
priate self-references　self-references

E. 1　2　3　4　5　6　7　8
Hyperactive　Unusually inactive

F. 1　2　3　4　5　6　7　8
Crushed by　Undaunted by
failures　failures

Comments

527

G. 1   2   3   4   5   6   7   8   *Comments*

Urging needed   Quick to respond
                      to instructions

H. 1   2   3   4   5   6   7   8

Extremely   Extremely
submissive   assertive

I. 1   2   3   4   5   6   7   8

Doesn't care about   Excellence of
the quality of his   performance is his
performance   principal concern

J. 1   2   3   4   5   6   7   8

Initiates activity   Waits to be told

K. 1   2   3   4   5   6   7   8

Tries to prolong   Recurrently tries to
relationship   withdraw from
                       relationship

L. 1   2   3   4   5   6   7   8

Unusual social   Markedly lacking in
poise for age   social poise

M. 1   2   3   4   5   6   7   8

Liked taking tests   Disliked tests
very much

N. 1   2   3   4   5   6   7   8

Unable to give up   Gives up too easily

O. 1   2   3   4   5   6   7   8

Unusually   Highly agitated
composed

P. 1   2   3   4   5   6   7   8

Recurrently seeks   Eager to continue
to terminate tests   tests

Q. 1   2   3   4   5   6   7   8

I *really* like   I don't care for this
this child   child *at all*

R. <u>A   B   C   D   F</u>   *Comments*
Probably a ____ student

S. <u>0   5   10   15   20   25   30   35+</u>
An optimal environment could probably increase test performance by ____ IQ points.

APPENDIX G

PROJECT A FACE SHEET

NAME_____ SEX_____ DATE OF BIRTH_____

PLACE OF BIRTH_____

MOTHER_____ DATE OF BIRTH_____

(*name*)

PLACE OF BIRTH_____

How far did you go in school?_____

Did you want to go farther?_____

What kind of work do you do?_____

Have you worked since leaving school?_____

What kind of work did your father do?_____

FATHER_____ DATE OF BIRTH_____

(*name*)

PLACE OF BIRTH_____

How far did he go in school?_____

What kind of work does he do?_____

Has he done other kind of work?_____

What kind of work did his father do?_____

Mailing address_____ Telephone No._____

How long have you lived here?_____

How long have you lived in this community?_____

Do you or your husband have relatives living in this community?_____

Do you own your farm?_____

530

Do you have? (*check from observation where possible*)

Running water_____	Inside toilet_____
Television_____	Radio_____
Electricity_____	Telephone_____
Books_____	Record player_____
Refrigerator_____	Freezer_____
Magazines_____	Daily newspaper_____

Are there any other adults living in the home?

	Name	Age	Relationship	Education	Occupation
1.					
2.					
3.					
4.					
5.					

Starting with the oldest child, give me the names, birth dates, and grades of your children.

	Name	Birth date	Grade or education	Present occupation
1.				
2.				
3.				
4.				
5.				

(*Continue as necessary.*)

APPENDIX H

PROJECT A MOTHER INTERVIEW SCHEDULE

We are interested in spending time with your four-year-old child, __(X)__. We believe there are many things that children can learn when they are young. There are some things you may be able to tell us about __(X)__ that will help us to know him (her) better.

I will be asking you about what __(X)__ is like and some of the things he (she) may or may not like to do.

1. Could you tell me what X is usually like?
   - a. Happy_____
   - b. Serious_____
   - c. Sad_____
   - d. Silly_____
   - e. Other_____

2. Would you describe him (her) as:
   - a. Shy_____
   - b. Active_____
   - c. Careful_____
   - d. Fearful_____
   - e. Tries things_____
   - f. Shows off_____
   - g. Laughs a lot_____
   - h. Needs encouragement_____
   - i. Always in a hurry_____
   - j. Plays well alone_____
   - k. Would rather play by himself_____
   - l. Would rather play with others_____
   - m. Does he have to do things just right (just so)?_____
   - n. Asks a lot of questions_____

532

3. Do you have any special concerns about X?

a. _____

b. _____

4. Has X had a chance to spend time doing some of these things?

_____ a. Marking with crayon_____

_____ b. Marking with a pencil_____

_____ c. Cutting with scissors_____

_____ d. Pasting _____

_____ e. Collecting things_____

_____ f. Working puzzles_____

_____ g. Building with blocks or sticks_____

_____ h. Looking at magazines or catalogs_____

5. Does anyone read story books to him (her)?_____

(If yes) Does he (she) seem to listen?_____

(If no) Does he (she) listen to someone tell stories?_____

Does he (she) seem to enjoy the stories?_____

What kind does he (she) seem to like most?_____

Does he (she) ever tell a story that he (she) has heard?_____

Does he (she) ever make up a story to tell?_____

Does he (she) ever try to tell a story that he (she) has seen on television?

6. Does X get to play with children other than his (her) brothers and sisters?

7. Where does he (she) see other children?_____

8. Does he (she) get to spend much time with his (her) daddy?_____

9. Does he (she) like to:

_____ a. Throw a ball

_____ b. Run

_____ c. Climb

_____ d. Dance

_____ e. Sing

_____ f. Jump

_____ g. Play games

_____ h. Make believe (play house, play grown-up)

_____ i. Other things (*list*)_____

10. Does X try to help around the house or farm?_____

At this point in the interview, items 35-61 from the Vineland Social Maturity Scale were administered. The child's behavior in the area covered by each item was summarized by using the a-g descriptions given below.

    a. (+)   successful performance
    b. (+F)   if formerly successful performance temporarily discontinued
    c. (+O)   no opportunity
    d. (±)   transitional or emergent
    e. (−)   has not succeeded
    f. (−NO) could not if had opportunity
    g. (NI)   no information

APPENDIX I

PROJECT A MANUAL

Stage 1: Getting Acquainted

I. **Purpose:**
To help the child and the teacher get to know each other and to set the stage for activities to be carried out between the two. To find out if there is an adult in the home who would be capable of later continuing activities which the teacher may start.

II. **Concepts:**

A. A relationship must be established between child and teacher that will involve and develop verbal communication. The child must not feel pushed but must be accepted as he is and an atmosphere of trust developed.

B. Provision of successful experiences lets the child know that he is able to do what is expected and facilitates similar experiences with other adults.

C. A capable adult may be included in activities to (1) help with a positive relationship, (2) stimulate interest, and (3) to become aware of what can be done with the child.

III. **Activities:**

A. Make a book from construction paper, leaves, paste or anything available
B. Use color cones
C. Use peg boards
D. Use form boards

535

   E. Use stringing beads
   F. Use nesting boxes
   G. Play simple records

IV. Materials:
   A. Construction paper
   B. Paste
   C. Leaves, etc.
   D. Form boards
   E. Peg boards
   F. Color cones
   G. Stringing beads
   H. Nesting boxes
   I. Record player and records

Stage 2a: Exploratory Contacts

I. Purpose:
To discover what the child knows about (1) sounds, (2) shapes, (3) color discrimination, (4) numbers, (5) size, (6) language, (7) the world about us, (8) visual concepts, and (9) weights.

II. Concept:
It is important to start where the child is, to know where he is.

III. Preparations for Stage:
The teacher will need to present activities which will give her some insight into the child's previous experiences with each of the nine areas in order that an accurate profile may be drawn.
   A. The teacher may find it helpful to list sounds in the home for discussion with the child. (*examples*—washing machine, radio, television, family talking) Also, lists of outdoor sounds and animal sounds may be made for discussion.
   B. Different shapes may be made available to see if the child recognizes any of them.
   C. A variety of colors could be presented to see if the child knows any of them.
   D. Anything which the child could try to count should be used and his number ability should be recorded.
   E. Objects of varying sizes may be presented to note discrimination.
   F. Purposeful exploratory conversations between the teacher and the child. The areas of conversations should be thought out before hand by the teacher and a record kept of what transpired and how the child expressed self.
   G. The teacher may find it helpful to make a list of things for the child to observe. She should record questions.

H. Items which are obviously of different weight may be presented and the child's ability to discriminate noted.
I. Questions concerning the child's immediate environment may be asked.

(Note: On the basis of this exploration, tentative goals may be set.)

IV. Activities:

A. Sounds
  1. Play listening games
  2. Imitate sounds of animals, etc.
  3. Use appropriate records
B. Shapes
  1. Replace forms
  2. Cut out shapes (circle, square)
C. Color
  1. Talk about colors of cones
  2. Talk about colors of beads
  3. Talk about colors of pegs
D. Numbers
  1. Count fingers
  2. Count beads
  3. Count pegs
E. Size
  1. Ask about sizes of available objects
  2. Play size games
F. Language
  1. Ask child to name objects around him
  2. Talk constantly
  3. Ask questions
  4. Ask the child to tell about something that the teacher is sure that he knows about
G. The World About Us
  1. Talk about things in the house
  2. Talk about work on the farm
  3. Talk about parts of the body—finger plays and sings may be used
  4. Talk about what the child does each day
H. Vision
  1. Play guessing and naming games
  2. Look through cellophane
I. Weights
  1. Try lifting different objects to see if the child knows the difference in their weight

V. Materials:
   A. Form boards
   B. Peg boards
   C. Color cones
   D. Scissors
   E. Paper
   F. Stones
   G. Cotton
   H. Books:
      1. *The Important Book*
      2. *The Shadow Book*
   I. Games:
      1. "I am very tall; I am very small."
      2. "Guess what I see."
      3. "How many fingers do you see?"
         (See mimeographed *Finger Plays*)

Stage 2B: Development of Things Discovered

I. Purpose:
To broaden the child's knowledge of the nine areas, or to introduce areas with which he was not familiar.

II. Concepts to Develop:
   A. 1. Sounds differ
      2. We can hear sounds
      3. We can make sounds
   B. 1. Things are recognized by their shapes
      2. Shapes differ
   C. 1. There are three primary colors
      2. We recognize things by their color
      3. Colors often mean something (traffic light)
      4. Things are dyed or painted to give color
   D. 1. Numbers tell how many
      2. Numbers tell age
   E. 1. Sizes differ
      2. Size shows growth
   F. 1. Language is the most commonly used type of communication among people—there are other forms of communication
      2. By talking we can say more and say more exactly
   G. 1. The world about us helps to make us what we are
      2. The role of an individual in his environment determines the kind of person he may be—a father, mother, baby
      3. When roles of persons are identified, people find it easier to live in a particular setting

H. 1. Visual perceptions differ from person to person
   2. Seeing can be deceptive—near and far
   3. Visual perception serves as a basis for numerous kinds of discrimination
I. 1. Something big may be light; something small may be heavy

III. Objectives:

A. To teach the child to listen to and recognize sounds.
B. To teach the child to recognize and identify shapes.
C. To teach the child to recognize colors and their importance.
D. To teach the child to count and use numbers.
E. To teach the child to communicate easily.
F. To help the child become more aware of the things that are going on around him (his role and roles of others involved). To help the child learn about himself.
G. To help the child understand and appreciate things that he sees.
H. To teach the child to realize the differences in weight.

IV. Activities:

A. Sounds
   1. Listen to sounds in and around the house
   2. Have child imitate animal sounds
B. Shapes
   1. Name shapes
   2. Cut out shapes and paste them in book
C. Color
   1. Name colors
   2. Have child find different colors in the room
   3. Play color guessing games
D. Numbers
   1. Write numbers for child
   2. Count beads or other objects and permit child to do the same
E. Size
   1. Use terms pertaining to size and explain what they mean
   2. Have child start to use new words
F. Language
   1. Have long conversations with child
   2. Promote question asking and answering
   3. Play word games
   4. Read books
G. The World About Us
   1. Role play
   2. Play house
   3. Talk about functions of the parts of the body
H. Vision
   1. Read stories

2. Play games
3. Have child describe things

I. Weight
1. Talk about heavy and light people (fat and skinny)
2. Collect things of different weight

V. Materials:
A. Form boards
B. Stringing beads
C. Play house and furniture
D. Paper
E. Color cones
F. Crayons
G. Scissors
H. Paste
I. Games:
1. "I know a new word"
2. "What do I see?"
J. Book:
1. *How Big Are You Baby?*

Stage 2C: Enrichment of Things Discovered and Developed

I. Purpose:
To have the child work with and become aware of the more complex aspects of the areas.

II. Concepts:
A. 1. Sounds are sometimes difficult to imitate
2. It is important to become sensitive to sounds in our environment
3. Soft sounds may be as enjoyable as loud sounds
B. 1. Names of shapes are important
2. Shapes give us messages (stop signs)
C. 1. Colors may be mixed to make new colors
2. The same color may differ by shades
D. 1. Numbers may be added, subtracted, and divided
2. A child must learn to write numbers eventually
3. Learning number concepts may be as important as counting by rote—grouping of things
E. 1. Sizes graduate
2. Sizes show superlatives
F. 1. It is important for the child's vocabulary to be increased
2. Learning new words should become a part of the child's everyday life—naming things, qualities of things, and actions
G. 1. Knowing about his family and friends is important to the child
2. Habits of people and animals differ
3. Different means of locomotion serve different purposes

H. 1. (same as in preceding stage)
 I. 1. People's weights differ
    2. Height may affect weight

III. Objectives:

A. To continue teaching sound recognition and to introduce how sounds are imitated.
B. To continue teaching recognition of shapes and to introduce differences and similarities among shapes.
C. To introduce shades of colors and color mixing.
D. To expand work with numbers.
E. To continue realization of size and introduce graduating sizes.
F. To increase vocabularies and promote spontaneous conversation.
G. Expansion of objective in preceding stage.
H. To continue teaching an appreciation for and understanding of visual concepts.
 I. To expand experiences with different weights.

IV. Activities:

A. Sounds
  1. Read *Bow, Wow, Meow*
  2. Read *The Noisy Book*
  3. Use records
B. Shapes
  1. Name shapes on form board
  2. Draw shapes
C. Color
  1. Play color matching games
D. Numbers
  1. Write numbers and permit child to do so
  2. Read *Millions of Cats*
E. Size
  1. Arrange forms according to size
  2. Question concerning size differences
  3. Read *The Littlest Rabbit*
F. Language
  1. Make up stories
  2. Make a book and tell a story about it
  3. Play pretend (telephone conversation)
G. The World About Us
  1. Talk about the postman, storekeeper, supermarket
  2. Let child make his own face sheet
  3. Appropriate records
H. Vision
  1. Play describing games
  2. Talk about things we see

I. Weight
   1. Make a book of weights

V. **Materials:**
  A. Form boards
  B. Paper
  C. Scissors
  D. Paste
  E. Crayons
  F. Telephones
  G. Stones, feather, toothpicks
  H. Books:
    1. *Bow, Wow, Meow*
    2. *The Noisy Book*
    3. *Muffin in the Country*
    4. *One, One, and One*
    5. *Millions of Cats*
  I. Games:
    1. "The matching game"
  J. Records

Stage 3A: Extension of Competence with Materials

I. **Purpose:**
To give the child an opportunity to work more on his own with materials.

II. **Activities:**
  A. Sounds
    1. Have child make sounds and talk about them
    2. Ask questions to see if the child has developed an awareness of sounds
    3. Make different sounds with objects
    4. See if child can make loud and soft sounds, high and low sounds—whispering, talking, singing
  B. Shapes
    1. Make larger book of shapes and discuss them (three dimensional shapes)
    2. Talk about what shapes tell us
  C. Color
    1. Draw pictures with crayons or paint
    2. Mix colors
    3. Talk about what colors tell us
    4. Cut out pictures from colored paper
  D. Numbers
    1. Count

    2. Write numbers

    3. Divide things—for example, an apple

E. Size

    1. Cut out large and small shapes

    2. Measure things—measure child, doll, etc.

    3. Compare size of different objects

F. Language

    1. Read stories

    2. Have child picture read

    3. Use telephone

    4. Define words

    5. Role play

G. The World about Us

    1. Go to post office

    2. Go to the supermarket

    3. Go to the school

    4. Have child recieve, then write and mail letters

H. Vision

    1. Read stories

    2. Have child talk about anything he sees

 I. Weights

    1. Have child try to lift something too heavy

    2. Have child lift something very light

J. Spatial Concepts

    1. Read *Up High, Down Low*

    2. Work puzzles

    3. Use nesting boxes

K. Textures

    1. Make a book of different textures

III. Materials:

A. Scissors

B. Paste

C. Crayons

D. Pictures to color

E. Ruler

F. Telephone

G. Sand paper

H. Cotton

 I. Wood

J. Leaves

K. Puzzles

L. Nesting boxes

M. Book:

    1. *Up High, Down Low*

Stage 3B: Mastery in Communication

I. Purpose:
To help the child communicate in a manner which would be typical for his age level using verbs, adjectives, expletives, figures of speech and superlatives.

II. Concepts to Keep in Mind:
    A. These children may be deprived of the art of conversation—talk with them.
    B. Children are often "seen and not heard"—listen to them.
    C. A child's intellectual potential may never be properly assessed if he is nonverbal—help him to express himself as accurately as possible.
    D. When a child is able to communicate, his needs may be easier to recognize and meet. There is satisfaction in this for him as well as reinforcement of a sense of mastery.

III. Activities:
    A. Group experiences—gather at central place for:
        1. Listening to records
            a. Story records
            b. Action records
        2. Games
        3. Songs
        4. Story telling
        5. Story acting
    B. Other activities will be determined by the teacher according to child's interest and development.

IV. Materials:
    A. Record player
    B. Records
    C. Story books

Stage 3C: Extension of Conceptual Skills

I. Purpose:
To expand and enrich conceptual skills with which the child and teacher have worked.

II. Activities:
    A. Repeat any activities from preceding stages which the teacher deems necessary.
    B. Work with the child in any or all of the nine areas at the level which he has achieved during the teaching sessions.
    C. Have responsible adult (where there is one) to work with the child while the teacher is present.

III. Materials:
    A. All the materials used in preceding stages. This will, of course, depend upon the areas that the teacher does additional work with.
    B. Books:
       1. *Color Kittens*
       2. *Wings of a Flea*
       3. *Gilberto and the Wind*
       4. *The Snowy Day*

(Note: See Project A resource file for available books from Bookmobile and school libraries.)

PROJECT A BEHAVIOR RATINGS

	Early	Late

1. Ability to concentrate
    poor   good
    fair excellent		

2. Appreciation for stories
    none   full
    some		

3. Receptivity to records
    none   very
    slight full		

4. Questions
    never   often
    seldom always		

5. Participation in conversation
    never   often
    seldom always		

6. Spontaneous continuation
   of activities
    never   often
    seldom always		

7. Auditory awareness
    poor   good
    fair excellent		

8. Visual awareness
    poor   good
    fair excellent		

9. Mother's awareness of
   child's needs
    poor   good
    fair excellent		

Project A Log

1. CHILD'S NAME_____

2. DATE OF VISIT_____

3. General stage of contact

4. Objectives of visit

5. Activities

6. Response of child

7. Comments regarding mother or family situation

8. Specific goals

APPENDIX K

BEHAVIOR RATING SCALE FOR ADOLESCENTS

Instructions

We would like to know more about several areas in which junior high school students are involved. This booklet consists of eight statements on which you are asked to rate the members of your class. Each page includes a description of a topic in which we are interested and a list of about five items below. Each item has a number, and we would like you to write by each of your classmates' names the number of the item which you feel best describes him or her.

First, read the statement and each of the ratings below it. Then, by each student's name, write the number of the rating that you feel describes that student best.*

1. Several things help children to make good grades, of course. Some students seem to make good grades easily, but others have to work hard in order to make their grades. We are interested in knowing how much each child *tries* to do well, even though his grades may or may not be the best.

   (1) Tries very, very hard
   (2) Tries somewhat more than the average student
   (3) Tries about like the average student
   (4) Tries somewhat less than the average student
   (5) Doesn't try at all

2. Some pupils try very hard to be popular with their classmates while others don't seem to care if they are liked or not. How would you rate each of your

---

* Each item was printed at the top of a separate page of the rating booklet, and was followed by the numbered statements and a list of the class roll.

classmates on this point? Remember, a person may *try* to be popular without actually succeeding.

(1) Tries *very* hard to be popular
(2) Seems to try hard
(3) About average
(4) Doesn't seem to try hard
(5) Doesn't try *at all*

3. Junior high school pupils have quite different feelings about school. For example, some students want to go as far as they can, whereas others would quit school today if they could. How do you think each of your classmates feels in this regard? (Remember, you are being asked to judge what each pupil *wants* to do, not what he is likely to be able to do. Thus, the fact that he may not have enough money to go to college or is not making good enough grades to be admitted to college does not necessarily mean that he does not *want* to enter college.)

(1) Definitely *wants* to go to college
(2) Is thinking about college, but is still uncertain
(3) Wants to finish high school, but doesn't want to go to college
(4) Wants to go past the eighth grade, but may not want to go clear through high school
(5) Will want to quit after finishing either the eighth or ninth grade
(6) Would like to quit now

4. Some people are quite determined to be a "success" once they have finished school and are on their own. For example, they may try very hard to make a lot of money, to become famous, or to achieve success in some line of work so that they can be proud of their accomplishments. In this respect, how do you think each of your classmates will try once he or she is out of school?

(1) Will try very, very hard to be a success
(2) Will probably try hard to be a success
(3) Will probably try about like the average person
(4) Probably won't try very hard
(5) Won't try at all

5. Some students seek help from either the teacher or their fellow students in doing their work, while others prefer to work on their own. How would you rate each of your classmates in this respect?

(1) Never seems to ask for help
(2) Occasionally seeks help
(3) Frequently seeks help
(4) Always seems to be asking for help

6. How popular is each of your classmates?

(1) Extremely popular
(2) Above average

(3) About average
(4) Below average
(5) Quite unpopular

7. Some people go "all out" to win games or contests that they are in, while others make little or no effort to come out on top. How does each of your classmates rate in this regard?

(1) Tries his best to win
(2) Makes a good effort
(3) About average
(4) Doesn't try very hard
(5) Makes no effort at all

8. How does each of your classmates do in school as far as grades are concerned?

(1) Makes excellent grades
(2) Makes very good grades
(3) Makes about average grades
(4) Makes rather poor grades
(5) Makes very poor grades

SUBJECT INDEX

A

Ability changes, *see* Intellective development

Ability differences, *see* Individual differences, ability levels

Ability domain, arbitrary separation from personality, 133–134

Ability tests, *see also* PMA; PPVT; S-B Scale
 relation to achievement tests, 458
 scores of, 37–38

Absence of parent, *see* Fathers; Mothers

Absorption in schoolwork, *see* Teachers' ratings

AC, *see* SAT, Arithmetic Computation

Academic achievement
 achievement tests vs. classroom grades, 61
 contribution of extra-school factors, 62
 core areas, 24, 62
 intercorrelations among content areas, 65–67
 role of measured intelligence, 75–78, 105, 458
 school testing survey, 23–24
 tests of, 23–24, 61–82, 105, 458
 traits in rating scales, 220–221

Academic aspirations, of eighth grade students, 432, 434

Academic progress, *see* SAT; School retardation

Acceleration, *see* Intellective development

Accelerators, *see* Intellective development

Achievement of good grades, *see* Academic achievement; Peer ratings; Teachers' ratings

Achievement imagery, *see* CPS, B Ach; CPS, M Ach

Achievement motivation, *see also* CPS; TAT
 achievement retardation and, 148
 definition, 200
 in fantasy material, 25–26, 128, 145–148, 260–286, 464–465
 intellective development and, 148
 IQ change in Negro children and, 128–130
 McClelland TAT procedures, 268
 measured in CPS, 25–26, 128, 145–148, 260–286, 464–465
 overt vs. covert, 285–286
 in preschool children, 375, 378–380
 role of fear of failure, 148

Achievement syndrome, *see* Teachers' ratings

Activity level, *see* Teachers' ratings

Adolescence
 emotional turmoil, 468
 intellective characteristics, 135–159
 personality changes during, 250

551